A Great Disorder

A Great Disorder

NATIONAL MYTH AND THE
BATTLE FOR AMERICA

Richard Slotkin

THE BELKNAP PRESS OF HARVARD UNIVERSITY PRESS

Cambridge, Massachusetts, and London, England

2024

FIRST PRINTING

Library of Congress Cataloging-in-Publication Data

Names: Slotkin, Richard, 1942– author.
Title: A great disorder : national myth and the battle for America /
Richard Slotkin.
Other titles: National myth and the battle for America
Description: Cambridge, Massachusetts ; London, England :
The Belknap Press of Harvard University Press, 2024. |
Includes bibliographical references and index.
Identifiers: LCCN 2023029111 | ISBN 9780674292383 (cloth)
Subjects: LCSH: Myth—Political aspects—United States—History. |
Culture conflict—United States—History. | United States—History.
Classification: LCC E179 .S63 2024 | DDC 973—dc23/eng/20230725
LC record available at https://lccn.loc.gov/2023029111

For Iris, with love and thanks

A. A violent order is disorder; and
B. A great disorder is an order. These
Two things are one.

—Wallace Stevens, "Connoisseur of Chaos" (1942)

Flags are blossoming now where little else is blossoming
and I am bent on fathoming what it means to love my country.
. . . .
A patriot is not a weapon. A patriot is one who wrestles for the
        soul of her country
as she wrestles for her own being. . . .

—Adrienne Rich, "One night on Monterey Bay the death-freeze
of the century" (1991)

Contents

A Great Disorder

Introduction

OUR COUNTRY is in the grip of a prolonged crisis that has profoundly shaken our institutions, our structures of belief, and the solidarities that sustain us as a nation. The past forty years have seen a steadily intensifying culture war, expressed politically in a hyperpartisanship that has crippled the government's ability to deal constructively with the problems endemic to modern society. Major crises, like the financial meltdown of 2008–2009 and the COVID-19 pandemic, which in the past would have inspired a patriotic rallying of public opinion, have instead intensified our divisions and raised the potential for political violence.

It is as if we are living in two different countries: a blue nation, built around large cities in which many races and ethnic groups mingle and blend, prospering on a wave of technological change, sensitive to persistent economic and racial inequality, and willing to support government programs to regulate the economy and increase social justice; and a red nation of beleaguered smaller cities and towns and rural districts, whose people are resistant to the cultural changes attendant on an increasingly multiethnic society and changing sexual mores, aggrieved by the loss of employment and security inflicted by a heartless corporate economy, and disaffected with a government whose regulations harm their economic interests and foster secular values at the expense of religious tradition. The latter has generated a political movement, Make America Great Again (MAGA), whose angry passion and propensity for verbal and physical violence has altered the language and the conduct of American politics. Some of this partisan rancor can be attributed to the propaganda of well-financed special interest groups, to politicized cable news networks and internet feeds that lock consumers into ideological echo chambers, but it would be a mistake to ignore the depth of the passions behind the partisan split.[1]

The differences between red and blue America are rooted in culture: in enduring systems of belief developed over long periods of time, reflecting different experiences of life and understandings of what America is, what it has been, and what it is supposed to be. Each has a different understanding of who counts as American, a different reading of American history, and a different vision of what our future ought to be. For blue America, the election of Barack Obama, the first African American president, symbolized the culmination of the political and cultural transformations that began in the 1960s. For red America, Obama's election was an affront, a confirmation of the fact that the political power and cultural authority of conservative Christians were inexorably shrinking, as non-White people became an ever-larger share of the population and cultural liberalization continued to undermine traditional values. As Michael Gerson, an anti–Donald Trump conservative who served as speechwriter to George W. Bush, observes in his column in the *Washington Post*, "A factual debate can be adjudicated. Policy differences can be compromised. Even an ideological conflict can be bridged or transcended. But if our differences are an expression of our identities—rural vs. urban, religious vs. secular, nationalist vs. cosmopolitan—then political loss threatens a whole way of life."[2]

National security expert Michael Vlahos, writing in *American Conservative*, argues that the effect of this kind of identity-based conflict "is to condition the whole of society to believe that an existential clash is coming, that all must choose, and that there are no realistic alternatives to a final test of wills." Opinion polls taken before the 2020 election showed that 36 percent of Republicans and 33 percent of Democrats believed there would be *some* justification for using violence to achieve their party's goals. As many as 20 percent of Republicans and 19 percent of Democrats thought there would be "'a great deal' of justification" if their party were to lose the election. Given these terms of conflict, it is easy to see why so many political commentators have compared our era to the decade before the Civil War.[3]

Each side in our culture war appeals to American history to explain and justify its beliefs about who we are and the purposes for which our political community exists. They share the same body of historical referents, the stories we have accepted as symbols of our heritage. These constitute our national mythology, an essential element of the culture that sustains the modern nation-state. It defines *nationality*, the system of beliefs that allows a diverse and contentious population, dispersed over a vast and varied country, to think of itself as a community and form a broad political consensus. It provides models of patriotic action that enable the nation's people to imagine ways of responding to crises in the name of a common good. The irony and peril of our situation is that the myths and symbols that have traditionally united Americans have become the slogans and banners of a cultural civil war.

The crisis we face is not an immediate threat, like Southern secession in 1861, the Great Depression in 1930, or the attack on Pearl Harbor in 1941. Rather, it arises from problems endemic to the modern social and economic order: the economic and social disruptions caused by the globalization of the economy, the extreme inequality between the very rich and the middle and working classes, the growing racial and ethnic diversity of our people, the enduring effects of racial injustice, and the profound challenges posed by global warming and climate change. These persistent and interlocking problems cannot be resolved unless we can reestablish a broad consensus on the meaning of American nationality and the purposes of patriotic action. Failing that, disorder and dysfunction will become the normal condition of our politics, and our future as a civil society and a nation-state will be in danger.

A Great Disorder turns to America's foundational myths to expose the deep structures of thought and belief that underlie today's culture wars. The first half of the book describes the historical evolution of the foundational myths that are most central to our national mythology. These are the Myth of the Frontier, which uses the history of colonial settlement and westward expansion to explain our national character and our spectacular economic growth; the Myth of the Founding, which sanctifies the establishment of our national government and its foundational texts, the revolutionary Declaration of Independence, and the countervailing legal structures of the Constitution; the Myths of the Civil War, which offer conflicting versions of the moral and political crisis that nearly destroyed the nation; and the Myth of the Good War, which celebrates the nation's emergence as a multiracial and multiethnic democracy, as well as a world power. The second half of the book shows how these myths have played through the culture war politics and the multiple crises that have shaken American society since the 1990s.

This book is based on more than fifty years of research on the creation and development of American national myths, which began with my study of the colonial origins of the Myth of the Frontier, *Regeneration through Violence* (1973). In *The Fatal Environment: The Myth of the Frontier in the Age of Industrialization, 1800–1890* (1985), I traced the evolution of the original myth into a fable of imperial expansion and "bonanza" capitalism, and described the interaction of the Frontier Myth with mythic responses to the Civil War and Reconstruction. That study culminated with the publication of *Gunfighter Nation:*

The Myth of the Frontier in Twentieth-Century America (1992), which dealt with the transformations of national myth under the pressures of massive immigration, the Depression and World War II, the cultural transformations of the 1960s, and the emergence of mass media, especially movies and television. In *Lost Battalions: The Great War and the Crisis of American Nationality* (2005), I looked beyond the Myth of the Frontier to consider the ways in which military mobilization in the twentieth century compelled Americans to broaden and reframe their national myth, and extend their definition of nationality to include hitherto marginalized racial and ethnic minorities.

Why National Myths Matter

Nation-states are a political innovation that began to replace dynastic and feudal systems of governance in seventeenth-century Europe, organized by elites to co-opt the power of the emerging middle classes and bring diverse ethnic, religious, and linguistic groups to think of themselves as a single "people," under a common legal regime. Although nation-states have taken the form of monarchies, dictatorships, and republics—and everything in between—all depend for legitimacy on cultural mechanisms that maintain broad popular consent. To win that consent, to get culturally diverse people to identify as members of a single polity, the political classes developed national mythologies: semifictional or wholly imaginary histories of the origins of their people and territories, which would enable Provençals, Bretons, and Franks to see themselves as French, or Bavarians, Prussians, and Swabians as German. They created what Benedict Anderson called "imagined communities"—or, as Immanuel Wallerstein has it, "fictive ethnicities."[4]

No modern nation is more indebted to, or dependent on, its myths than the United States of America. The ethnic origins of our people are the most diverse of any nation. Our myths have to work for the descendants of Indigenous Americans and the settlers who dispossessed them; for the heirs of masters and of the enslaved; for those whose ancestors came centuries ago and those who arrived yesterday; for Yiddish-speaking Jews and Sicilian Italians, Germans and Irish, Brahmins and Dalits, Shia and Sunni, Turks and Armenians; for a public divided by differences of class, culture, provincial loyalties, religion, and interest.

The nation is everywhere and nowhere. We are born to our families and the communities to which they belong, but we have to learn to think of ourselves as spiritual descendants of ancestors not related to us by blood—imaginary ancestors, made kindred by our participation in a shared and ongoing history.

The teaching is done through organized public rituals, in schools provided (mostly) by the state, and by mass media organized to address a national public. The result of this cultural work is to establish a public consensus about a common "American" history: the idea that we belong to a single society, continuous in time, that we are heirs to a common past and bear responsibility for a common future. When that consensus breaks down, or splits into warring camps, it limits or frustrates our ability to act as a People for an idea of the common good.

As I use the term, myths are the stories—true, untrue, half-true—that effectively evoke the sense of nationality and provide an otherwise loosely affiliated people with models of patriotic action. Patriotism in this context is the political expression of nationality. It is not simply loyalty to the state, but the acting out of a particular understanding of why that state exists and for what purposes. It entails a distinct set of understandings about the nation's history, which see its past as the necessary prelude to a certain kind of future or destiny.

Nationality is the concept that defines full membership in the "fictive ethnicity" of the nation-state. It is both a set of publicly accepted standards and a subjective state of mind—the sense of belonging to the society and of sharing fully in its culture. Ethnonationalist states restrict full membership (officially or in practice) to those who belong to the dominant ethnic or racial group. This is the case, or tendency, in countries like Japan, Russia, Turkey, and Hungary. Others (France and the United States are prime examples) have adopted a "civic" model of nationality, which allows immigrants to become active citizens when they have met certain basic requirements, such as learning the language and the laws, and taking an oath of allegiance. The strictness and limiting function of civic standards vary from country to country, and within countries from one period to another. US immigration and naturalization policy changed from "open" to highly restricted in the 1920s, to more broadly "open" again in 1965, to restrictive under the Trump administration.

The concept of civic (or civil) religion, developed by Robert Bellah and his associates in the 1960s, is a useful way of describing the core ideological values carried by American national myth. Its principal features are a reverence for the Constitution; a belief in individual rights; a positive attitude toward religion in general and Christianity in particular, coupled with religious toleration; a commitment to "free enterprise"; and a government that interferes as little as possible with civil society.[5] But the principles of civic religion can be stated as propositions to be argued. Recasting those principles as myth puts them beyond argument. Myth does not argue its ideology; it tells a story and equates that story with history, as if it were undeniable fact. Moreover, myths are not only versions of the past—they are symbolic models that are used to interpret and respond to a present crisis. When myth-histories are invoked as analogies to some present question, we immediately understand how the speaker wants us to respond to the situation. "Our political conflicts are like the Civil War." (Radicals on both sides are destroying the nation.) "Space is the new frontier." (Develop it!) "The 9/11 attack is like Pearl Harbor." (Go to war to avenge it.) National myths transform the principles of civil religion into scripts, in which believers see themselves as actors on a historical stage, ful-filling—or failing to achieve—the nation's historical destiny.

Public awareness of the role of national myth, and of its increasingly em-battled state, has been growing. In 2012 the editors of *Daedalus,* the journal of the American Academy of Arts and Sciences, devoted a whole issue to the ques-tion, "Is there an American narrative and what is it?" The responses of scholars in several disciplines expressed a common concern: "Every nation requires a story—or many stories, which taken together form a national narrative—about its origins, a self-defining mythos that says something about the character of the people and how they operate in the larger world and among each other." And "Americans, having no ethnic uniformity, depend on myths, which lend an aura of destiny to our collective aspirations." But there was no agreement among the contributors as to what that "mythos" was or ought to be. The collection, taken as a whole, expressed a troubled sense of slippage and disparity.[6]

That disparity has developed into the intense partisan and cultural divisions that have been characterized as the "culture war." David Brooks, conserva-tive columnist for the *New York Times,* sees the United States as suffering from a "national identity crisis" arising from the fact that "different groups see them-selves living out different national stories" and therefore "feel they are living in different nations." William Smith, writing in *American Conservative* in 2018, saw blue and red America interpreting the "national story through different symbolic mythologies," leading them to embrace "two diametrically opposed civic religions," one libertarian and the other tending toward socialism. There is a "Civil War on America's horizon," he concluded: "All that's required now is a spark."[7]

How National Myths Are Formed

American culture is rich in myths of all sorts. For immigrants and their de-scendants, the coming-to-America story is their origin myth. The South is still marked by its history of slavery, secession, and Civil War; westerners by their history of settlement and the struggle over rights to public lands and natural resources. Black people and Mexican Americans have their own myths of oppression and Exodus-themed escapes, of trickster ploys and *corrido* outlaws who defend the poor. Beyond this, Hollywood is in the business of fabricating mythologies for the commercial market through the creation of story genres and franchises. Two of these, the Western and the Platoon Movie, became the basis of modern national myths; others, like the current wave of superhero franchises, create mythic fables for imaginary worlds.

"The American Dream" is a compendium of many different beliefs about American life, which we invoke in rags-to-riches or log cabin–to–White House fables, or tales of immigrants seeking religious or political freedom and economic opportunity. Some such fables are historical, others present-day; some represent the American Dream as individual, others see it as a collective aspiration. There is no single master story that grounds the Dream in a *particular* history and links it to a *specific* idea about the power and purpose of the state, so it does not function as a national myth.

Any well-remembered event will have its myth: a story and set of symbols whose interpretation becomes standardized through repetition. Rhetorical tags or memes referring to "Valley Forge" or "the Alamo" will remind most Americans of patriotic endurance and sacrifice. "Custer's Last Stand" evokes the possibility of a disastrous reversal of fortune, "Gettysburg" a decisive moment of supreme moral and military crisis. The same is true of more recent episodes like the appeal for a more inclusive community in Martin Luther King Jr.'s "I Have a Dream" speech, or the surge of patriotic unity roused by "9 / 11."

When we speak of national myths, we refer not to single episodes or stories such as these but to broad and consistent patterns in storytelling, which directly address the fundamental character and purposes of the American nation-state. Such myths arise in response to existential crises in the life of the nation, events that test society's ability to react and adapt to the contingencies of history. They deal with ultimate questions about the meaning and purpose of national life. We invoke those myths, and bring them to bear, when our fundamental values are at stake.[8]

No one storyteller, however great their power, can create a myth. Stories told by people become mythic through a process of repetition and accretion. Like the pearl in the oyster, stories gather around areas of persistent irritation and conflict. In nearly every phase of US history, we can observe the recurrent conflict between individual rights and state power, or between egalitarian ideals and persistent racism, or between market freedom and the public interest. The traditions we inherit, for all their seeming coherence, are a registry of old conflicts, rich in internal contradictions and alternative political visions, to which we ourselves continually make additions. The more vital and enduring the problem, the more powerful and enduring the myth.

Because they encapsulate perennial conflicts, myths are always partially open-ended. The struggles they depict are never fully resolved. They invite us, as believers, to complete the *unfinished business* of destiny left to us by our heroes. By leaving the struggle imperfectly resolved, they also ask us to imagine *alternative histories,* what the nation might have been like if Lincoln had lived, or the Confederacy had won, or Native Americans had succeeded in keeping the wilderness wild. Myths thus preserve, in some form, the values of those who were historically defeated, keeping open the possibility of change.

Implicit in every myth is a theory of historical cause and effect: an explanation of the forces that shaped the historical past that, if properly understood, would give us the power to control the present and future. This is what enables myth to function as a script for action, to promote imaginative responses to present crises.[9]

How Myths Function: Mythological Thinking

Once a myth is well established, new crises can be interpreted by recognizing analogies between current events and the scenarios of the myth, and recalling the historical memories the myth embodies—a process I call mythological thinking. Although it involves a poetic leap rather than rational analysis, mythological thinking can help us imagine effective responses to a crisis and to see those responses as acts of patriotism. Leaders may actually think mythologically when developing policies in response to a crisis, and they will typically deploy mythological thinking as a mechanism for producing *consent*. If the public recognizes and accepts the myth scenario as a valid analogy for the present crisis, it will consent to political measures that conform to that scenario.

When the thinking is creative and based on an understanding of both past and present, our use of myth may help us imagine and legitimize effective responses to new crises. However, it is often the case that mythic precedents *constrain* our ability to understand and respond to unprecedented crises, and provide a limited path of action. In times of great fear and anger, the invocation of myth can lock public consciousness into a preset pattern of thought and action, so that we respond to an imagined past rather than a present reality. When the 9/11 terrorist attacks were compared to Pearl Harbor, and Iraq's Saddam Hussein to Adolf Hitler, the analogy to World War II gave Americans a clear understanding of how their leaders perceived the danger and what kind of response would be forthcoming. But the analogy was misconceived, and the resulting invasion of Iraq was a disaster not anticipated by the historical model.

A culture's heritage of myth can also provide instrumentalities through which people can transform their way of thinking and acting. Lincoln at Gettysburg reframed the nation's understanding of the constitutional order when he characterized the Founders' creation as "dedicated to the proposition that all men are created equal." When Martin Luther King Jr. delivered his "I Have a Dream" speech from the steps of the Lincoln Memorial, he was framing the modern civil rights movement not as a disruption but as the continuation of Lincoln's Civil War, when the aspiration to racial equality was seen as intrinsic to the preservation of the national union.

We use our myths to guide us in moments of crisis. But when we do so, we test their validity against existential reality. In a healthy society, each test produces an adaptation or adjustment of the mythic paradigm, to keep its premises in balance with the conditions we actually face. The fabrication and revision of mythology is an ongoing activity, a coping mechanism of organized society. When a mythic paradigm fails, the consequences can be serious. There have been several such episodes of crisis and readjustment in the course of American history. The most notable of these occurred in the 1850s, when the commitment of North and South to antithetical myths tore the nation apart. The best that can happen is represented by the transformation of American myth during and after World War II, when the Good War Myth redefined America as a multiethnic, multiracial democracy united in struggle against the ethnonationalist tyrannies of Nazi Germany and the Japanese Empire.[10]

National myths themselves have a history—that is, they change through time. The longest-lived mythologies are the highly evolved products of numerous crises of belief and revision. That is why a crisis in the state of public myth signals a potential rupture of the web of beliefs and practices that holds nations together.

The Rupture and Repair of National Mythology

America's crisis of national culture is part of a larger phenomenon. In the aftermath of the Cold War, it appeared that nation-states and nationalism were in decline, as the rapid globalization of economic networks reduced the power of national governments to regulate or otherwise set the terms of trade. Francis Fukuyama and other social scientists saw this as the "end of history," since the political, religious, and ideological conflicts that had hitherto shaped world history were now subsumed by a dominant neoliberal capitalist order. For neoliberal purists, the new order would dispense with national sovereignty in favor of a world governed by market operations. With the collapse of Soviet Communism and China's apparent transition to a market economy, there was not much strength in the Old Left vision of a world governed by an international working class, acting for humanity as a whole.[11]

The fallacy of the globalist view became clear in the aftermath of the 2008 banking crisis and the Great Recession that followed. A wave of nationalist movements espousing populist ideologies swept across the industrialized world, reflecting the deep discontent of working- and lower-middle-class people with the long-term decline of wages and economic security, the pace and direction of cultural change, and the effects of increased immigration on both culture and wages. The Brexit campaign that carried the United Kingdom out of the European Union, the rise of France's National Front and of Hindu nationalism in India, the Fidesz takeover in Hungary, and the MAGA movement in the United States are cases in point.

In America, the division of power between states and the federal government has traditionally served to compartmentalize such movements. But the hyperpartisanship and culture-war rhetoric that now dominate American discourse reflect the nationalization of American politics: the absorption of what once were distinctively local political cultures into national movements exclusively identified with one national party or the other, each with its own nationwide media complex.[12]

For better or worse, the nation-state remains the most powerful political structure in the contemporary world. It is the largest form of political community that has proved capable of maintaining civil order, and some form of consensual governance, among populations that are socially complex and ethnically diverse. It is the only political structure with the authority to regulate the domestic operations of capital for its own people and, in concert with like powers, to regulate the forces of globalization in the interests of humanity.

Patriotism is a concept to which some respond skeptically, because it has too frequently been distorted by nationalist chauvinism and exploited for partisan gain. Samuel Johnson's famous definition of patriotism as "the last refuge of a scoundrel" is all too apt. But patriotism is the active principle of consensual government, the sentiment that expresses the consent of the governed, without which republican and democratic government is impossible. It is an essential act of social and political imagination, in which the people of a state see themselves as a community, acting through chosen leaders and united for self-defense and mutual service.

In recent years, scholars, public intellectuals, and serious journalists have produced a spate of studies aimed at explaining the rise of illiberal populist nationalism and exploring ways of reconciling "patriotism," and the defense of nationality, with liberal values. *The Case for Nationalism,* by the conservative Rich Lowry, argues for a return to traditional nationalism, which has made us powerful and free. Liah Greenfeld's *Nationalism: A Short History* and Amitai Etzioni's *Reclaiming Patriotism* try to find paths to a new kind of liberal nationalism through an examination of the history and variety of nation-state organization. Jill Lepore's *This America* is a plea for historians to rethink how they write (or fail to write) national history, arguing that the way we tell our national story shapes both our sense of membership or belonging and our understanding of what patriotic action can and should be. These studies are, in effect, a call for the revision and renewal of national mythology. They are right to see the loss of a common national story as central to the contemporary crisis of politics and culture.[13]

But a new national myth cannot be fabricated on demand or revised at a stroke. We first have to understand the nature and roots of the myths that are actually operative, as well as the processes through which they have evolved. It is certainly true that national myths, here as elsewhere, have contributed to the development of chauvinist and ethnonationalist movements. But there is more to national mythology, and certainly elements of American national myth have made possible a culture that has become increasingly open to diversity of all kinds and newly sensitized to bigotry and injustice.

The Core Myths

From the country's beginnings as a collection of colonies or settler states, the central question shaping the formation of an American nationality has been whether it was possible—or even desirable—to form a single political society out of diverse racial, religious, and ethnic elements. In colonial and early national times, numerous Native American tribes lived side by side with settlements that included Africans and Europeans of several nationalities—English, Welsh, Scots, Irish, Scots-Irish, Dutch, German, Spanish, French Huguenot, Sephardic Jews. Through the nineteenth and twentieth centuries, the list expanded to include every race and ethnicity on planet Earth. So the reconciliation of diversity and nationality has historically been a central problem of our political culture. It has become the most significant line of cleavage in modern politics, between the White ethnonationalism of the Trump-led Right and the racial and ethnic pluralism of the Democratic Center-Left.

The central conflicts in the evolution of American patriotism have concerned the proper role and ultimate goals of the state in shaping the domestic social order and pursuing the national interest in a world of nations. In both spheres, ideas and issues have been shaped by the extraordinary scale and rapidity of the nation's geographical expansion and economic growth, and its rise from colonial outpost to Great Power. In the domestic sphere, the central questions have concerned the balance between state power and private enterprise, and the role of government in the emerging conflicts among economic interests. On a deeper level, these evolved into a conflict between contending concepts of social justice and individual rights, and of the proper role of government in shaping the conditions of social life.

Four myths have historically been the most crucial to Americans' understanding of what their nation is, where it came from, and what it stands for: the Myth of the Frontier; the Myth of the Founding; three different Myths of the Civil War; and the Myth of the Good War. To fully understand the ideological charge that each myth carries, we have to look closely at its historical origins. That will be the focus of the first part of *A Great Disorder*.

The Myth of the Frontier is the oldest and most enduring of these myths, and the only one that did not arise from a singular crisis. The stories that constitute the Frontier Myth are legion, appearing in every medium and many genres—histories, personal narratives, political speeches, popular fiction, movies—and they refer to episodes from colonial times to the heyday of westward expansion and the jungle wars of the twentieth century. The Myth of the Frontier locates our national origin in the experience of settlers establishing settlements in the wilderness of the New World. It enshrines a distinctively American concept of capitalist development: America has enjoyed extraordinary growth and progress, and development as a democracy, thanks to the discovery and exploitation of abundant natural resources, or "bonanzas," beyond the zone of settlement and established order. However, winning the frontier also required "savage wars" to dispossess and subjugate the Indigenous peoples, which made racial distinction and exclusion part of our original concept of nationality. In the Myth of the Frontier, these wars transform individual frontiersmen into heroes, and the American people into members of a heroic nationality, in a process I have called *regeneration through violence*. The Frontier Myth combines bonanza economics with regeneration through violence to explain the origin of America's exceptional character and unparalleled prosperity.

The Myth of the Founding centers on the creation of our political state, which is seen as the work of an extraordinarily intelligent and virtuous set of men of European descent, the Founding Fathers. Certain preeminent heroes stand out—George Washington, Thomas Jefferson, James Madison, Alexander Hamilton, Benjamin Franklin—each with a story that celebrates his personal character and his moral and political principles. The story of the Founding is so much a given of cultural memory that its meaning is most often invoked by reference to the Declaration of Independence and the Constitution, now sanctified as national scripture. Although these texts are symbols of national unity, they are critically different in character and embody the contradictions at the heart of our ideal of free government: one a revolutionary declaration of principles that transcend law; the other the basis of a fixed and stable governmental and legal structure.

The Civil War would put the Myth of the Founding to its most severe test. That conflict—which threatened America's survival as a nation—led to the creation of three conflicting mythic traditions. The first of these is the Liberation Myth, with its focus on emancipation. It sees the Civil War as an ordeal of *regeneration through violence,* which not only preserved Lincoln's "government of the people, by the people, for the people" but produced what, in the Gettysburg Address, Lincoln called a "new birth of freedom" that included formerly enslaved Black people. A related Unionist variant is the "White Reunion," which sees the war as a conflict between brothers who were divided by politics but reunited through respectful recognition of each other's courage and devotion to their cause—a reconciliation that minimizes the importance of slavery and rejects Black claims to civic equality. Opposed to both of these Unionist myths is the Southern Myth of the Lost Cause, which celebrates the virtues of the Old South and justifies the struggle to restore its traditional culture and the structures of White supremacy. The Liberation Myth would shape Reconstruction and ongoing efforts to build a multiracial democracy. The Lost Cause would overthrow Reconstruction and establish the violent and oppressive regime of Jim Crow, an outcome tacitly ratified by Northerners who embraced White Reunion. As the North and West began to experience mass immigration and labor-capital conflicts between 1875 and 1930, Lost Cause ideology would shape the formulation of a new, ethnonationalist concept of American citizenship in which White Protestant identity was fundamental.

In the Frontier Myth, the Myth of the Founding, and the Civil War Myths, American nationality is defined as White, Christian, and largely northern European. That conception of American nationality would be challenged by a series of linked and overlapping crises in the twentieth century: the Great War, the Depression, and World War II. These crises—especially the two wars—compelled the nation's political and cultural elites to broaden the concept of

American nationality and to embrace on terms of equality racial and ethnic minorities that had hitherto been marginalized or excluded from the body politic. The result was the creation of a new national myth, the Myth of the Good War, which used the war-movie convention of the multiethnic "platoon" to celebrate a diverse American nationality and linked the achievement of unity to our success as a world-liberating Great Power and Cold War "leader of the free world." It also created the basis for public acceptance of the civil rights movement and the overthrow of Jim Crow.

The postwar civil rights movement challenged the racialist presumptions that were so fundamental to our national myths. It would cue a series of cultural transformations, including a wave of "liberation" movements affecting race, gender, and sexuality, which coincided with radical changes in popular culture and music, and in "manners" generally. It would also produce a major movement in universities calling for the wholesale revision of our ways of reading and understanding national history. With hindsight, we can see these developments as the formation of what might be called a "Myth of the Movement," in which the nonviolent victory of civil rights provided a script for transformations that blue America has generally seen as progressive, and red America as the cause of national degeneracy. The Myth of the Movement is only a potential addition to the repertoire of national myth, but that potential has made it a battlefield in the culture wars.

Although the chapters in the first half of the book relate the development of myths to political and economic developments in particular periods, they are not thoroughgoing studies of political history. Rather, they are designed to show how events were organized into story patterns, which gained mythic force through their propagation in public media and systems of education. References in the first half of the book are therefore drawn from my own prior research and from the best recent scholarly books on each period, which describe broad patterns of development, while the discussion is focused on the formation of mythic narratives.

The second half of the book analyzes the use of national myths in the culture-war politics of the past fifty years. It draws on both scholarly literature and a range of primary sources, including political speeches and manifestos, contemporary journalism, and the popular arts (especially film and television). These chapters deal with the ways in which the various national myths have shaped (and been reshaped by) responses to a series of political and economic crises.

The discussion of our culture war begins with the advent of "culture war conservatism," announced by Pat Buchanan in his campaign against George H. W.

Bush for the 1992 presidential nomination. The movement was rooted in the combination of populist reaction against the economic strains of the globalized economy and the anxieties of conservative White Christians at their loss of cultural authority and political power. The latter strain would eventually lead to the formation of a Christian nationalist movement calling for the use of government power to establish a purified moral regime. As they merged to form the popular base of MAGA, both strains of the movement would appeal for historical authority to a Christian version of the Myth of the Founding and, above all, to the Lost Cause Myth that finds national salvation in the overthrow of liberalism and restoration of the traditional social and cultural hierarchies.

After the twentieth century, the "savage war" aspect of the Myth of the Frontier would be reinvigorated as an organizing principle of George W. Bush's Global War on Terror, and the related domestic issues of race and immigration, while the emerging conflict over global warming pitted the imperatives of oil-based bonanza economics against the concerns of ecologists. Finally, the Obama presidency saw the gun rights movement become the nexus of several strains of cultural conservatism and national myth: the fetishization of the 2nd Amendment, which first linked unregulated gun rights to libertarian economics, then asserted the insurrectionary right of "2nd Amendment remedies" to block or overturn government action—the principle behind Frontier vigilantism and the antigovernment violence of the Lost Cause.

The concluding chapters will show that the use of myth by MAGA is more than a one-man show. Rather, it arises from deep roots in American culture and ideological traditions woven into our national myths. As such, I will argue that MAGA is a movement akin to Fascism, but with authentically American roots, combining the ethnonationalist racism of the Lost Cause, an insurrectionist version of the Founding, and the peculiar blend of violent vigilantism and libertarian economics associated with the Frontier.

Reading American history through the lens of national myths will highlight certain critical themes that run through our belief systems and the language of our politics, allowing us to see the connections between seemingly different aspects of our political culture—guns, oil, race, nostalgia, nature, capitalism. It may help explain some of the contradictions of our current politics. Why have gun rights become a signature issue for twenty-first-century conservatives? Why do exponents of American nationalism wave the Confederate battle flag? Why does racial animus often outweigh considerations of economic interest in our elections? How does our history of slave owning affect our beliefs about the relations of labor and capital? Why do we keep opening wilderness areas to oil drilling, even though seven in ten Americans believe that global warming is a menace?

Although we'll examine the conduct of several administrations and consider important changes in the nation's economy, this is not a history of policy, or an analysis of the modern capitalist system. Rather, it is an analysis of the belief structures that *underlie* policymaking and shape our understanding of capitalism. My hope is that this study will help explain how and why historical legacies in mythic form have constrained our responses to the problems of global warming, racism, and economic change.

The American nation was born at a time when culture was being reshaped by the rapid growth of print media and literacy. The nation's development went hand in hand with the expansion of mass-circulation media. Journalism is the oldest and in some ways most critical of these forms, and a primary locus of myth development, but popular fiction is also a central feature of mass culture. Certain story types become so popular that they evolve into formulas or genres; and many of these coalesce around operative myths. The Western movie and its antecedent literary forms are the classic case, but we will look at a number of other genres as we follow the development of national mythology.

American mythology is suffused at every level with the problem of race. To some extent, this is true of all national mythologies. When European nation-states took their modern form in the nineteenth century, their national myths invoked folkloric tribal roots, often called "racial stocks," which lent nationality an imaginary genetic basis. But the settlers who formed the American nation-state came from different European nations, and the state grew in power by displacing Indigenous people and enslaving Black Africans. Hence the most enduring line between those who belonged to the nation and those who did not was drawn not by language, history, or religion (as in Europe) but by color. The contested meanings of the color line have been fundamental to the shaping of American nationality, politics, and mythology.[14]

The traditional forms of national myth were developed by and for a society whose power structures were dominated by White men. In consequence, the balance of gender roles in these myths is radically unequal—men are at the center of the narratives, women at the margins. It follows that a shift in that balance—when new invocations of myth give central roles and agency to non-White people and women—significant social and cultural change may be occurring. As we'll see, changes of that kind began to occur across a range of expressive genres in the 1950s and 1960s.

The culture war of our time can be understood as a clash between conflicting versions of the myths that define our national identity. The dysfunction of our politics and our continued coherence as a nation will depend on our ability to reconcile that conflict, and that will require a reform or revision of our lexicon of myths. The myths we live by arose from, and connect us to, the dark and bloody ground of a history in which slavery shares the space with freedom, dispossession with progress, hatred with heritage. No new or revised mythology can unite us if it does not enable us to recognize and begin to deal with the racial and class conflicts that have divided us. But critical analysis of national myth by itself changes nothing. What will be needed are new ways of telling the American story in order to redefine the nation as the common ground of an extraordinarily diverse people. In the Conclusion I will sketch the form such a story might take.

PART I

Myths of the White Republic

1

The Myth of the Frontier

THE HISTORY of "America" really begins with the migration of Asian peoples out of prehistoric Beringia, along the coasts, through the mountains, across the plains, and into the woodlands, until the North American continent was peopled and parceled into the territories of the First Nations. The history of the nation-state named "the United States of America"—and of the people or nationality called "American"—begins with the invasion, conquest, and colonization of the North Atlantic coast by European settlers, mainly from the British Isles, in the seventeenth century. Over the course of four centuries, the clutch of colonial settlements would grow in population, wealth, and political power while continually expanding their settled territory westward, from the coast to the foothills of the Appalachians by 1750. After the War of Independence united the colonies as a nation-state, population, wealth, power, and territory would expand exponentially: reaching across the Appalachians to the east bank of the Mississippi by 1810, tripling the original colonial domain; pushing west to the Rocky Mountains and south to the Gulf of Mexico by 1820, doubling it again; and seizing Texas and the Southwest from Mexico and sweeping to the Pacific Coast by 1849, increasing national territory by another third. From the settlement of Jamestown in 1607 to 1890, when the Census Bureau declared that the country no longer had a distinct "frontier" facing a wilderness of undeveloped land—the history of the United States is a tale of continual expansion, of the discovery, conquest, and settlement of new frontiers.

This powerful and persistent association between the growing wealth and power of the American nation-state and the expansion of its territory into lands that were, from a European perspective, undeveloped is the core of our oldest national myth, the Myth of the Frontier. It defines American nationality by creating a virtual genealogy: we Americans are the descendants (by blood or acculturation) of those heroes who discovered, conquered, and settled the virgin land of the wild frontier. Only a small minority of Americans ever experienced frontier life, but through history texts and the media of mass culture, later generations nonetheless came to see the frontier as a symbol of their collective past, the source of such markedly American characteristics as individualism, informality, pragmatism, and egalitarianism. The Myth of the Frontier also asserts that our capitalist development has been exceptional in its successful combination of economic growth with liberal democracy, and finds the material basis of that unique history in the continual discovery and rapid exploitation of new frontiers in free land, natural resources, or (in modern times) new technologies.[1]

Colonial Origins: Captives and Indian Fighters, 1600–1776

The colonist is the first "American" in our sense of the term: the first of those whose political enterprise would eventually establish the American nation-state. Colonists stand on the border between two very different worlds: the "civilized" world of the European home country or the metropolis, and the "wilderness" of the continent they have come to colonize.

From the first, the promise that drove the settlement enterprise was the expectation or hope of an economic bonanza—an extravagant return on investment, an unprecedented abundance. British expectations were shaped by Spanish narratives of colonization, which described the Edenic islands of the Caribbean floating in an azure sea, and the fantastically wealthy and sophisticated Indigenous empires of Mexico and Peru. The first British colonizers expected to find empires and mines of gold in North America, and the hope of gold persisted even after it became evident that no empires were hidden among the Appalachians. Still, the chartered corporations that financed the original colonies, and the settlers and entrepreneurs who followed them, did so in the expectation of large returns from the cultivation of tobacco, the fur trade, or the culling of ship timber from the vast American forests, and later from products like rice and indigo.

Extravagant expectations were not restricted to commerce. America was a kind of blank screen, onto which all sorts of fantasy could be projected: not just the literary fantasies of Thomas More's *Utopia* or William Shakespeare's *The Tempest* but operationalized fantasies of economic, political, and religious

organization. All colonies were created by corporate charters, granted or ratified by the king. Each created a unique kind of state, and their ocean-wide
distance from Europe gave them unprecedented license for self-government.
Some were commercial franchises granted to royal clients to produce valuable
commodities—Virginia, the Carolinas, and New York were of this type. Others
were established as refuges from the religious warfare that tore England apart
in the seventeenth century. Sects that obtained charters could establish colonies in which church and state conformed to their peculiar notions, and exclude or disenfranchise the competition. The Puritan colonies of New England
imagined themselves a "New Israel," a "city on a hill" whose model of Christian government would ultimately spread throughout the world. But theological differences led dissenters to set up their own colonies in Rhode Island
(Baptists), Connecticut (quasi-Presbyterians), and New Hampshire (Antino-
mians). The small and persecuted Quaker minority got one of the largest and
richest colonies, Pennsylvania. Catholics had a refuge in Maryland. Georgia
was founded by the Christian philanthropist General James Oglethorpe to re-
habilitate convicts.

It seemed that in America, the ambitious colonist could establish and order
a world entirely to his liking. That was, and is, the grandiose vision at the heart
of what we call the American Dream. In that dream, Indigenous peoples played
a complex role. Early explorers reported that the Natives were innocent, "voyde
of guile, and such as live after the manner of the Golden Age," in a setting
that recalled the Garden of Eden. In going to America, the colonist could si-
multaneously better his material condition and restore his connection to a
prelapsarian world.[2]

There was a dark side to this fantasy. For some colonists, the Natives were
not Arcadian innocents but bloodthirsty savages, cannibals who would cut "col-
lops" of living flesh from their victims and devour them before their eyes.
Native culture also posed a more insidious threat: the temptation for colonists
to "go native," abandoning the constraints of civilized law and Christian morality for the promise of greater sexual freedom and the ability to live off the
natural abundance of the land instead of earning a laborious subsistence by
the sweat of their brows. Emblematic of this problem was the conflict in 1622–
1624 between the Puritan settlers of Plymouth and the fur-trading establishment of Thomas Morton, called "Merry Mount" or "Ma-re Mount." Morton
allied with neighboring tribes, encouraged marriage or sexual relations between
his employees and the Natives, and shared pagan ceremonies with them that
blended Native rituals and costumes with pagan elements from English folk

life, like the Maypole celebrations presided over by a "Lord of Misrule." The menace was both economic and spiritual. Plymouth deployed its military force to drive Morton from the country.[3]

It should be said at the start that all these versions of the Indigenous peoples are fantasies, the projection of European fears and wishes. Europeans buried the extremely varied cultures of Indigenous America in the single concept of *Indians:* a name derived from Christopher Columbus's mistaken identification of the New World with Asia. It is a name that reduced cultural diversity to a single, implicitly *racial* identity and licensed the colonists to treat all Natives the same way: as subjects to be exploited at will, obstacles to settlement, or outright enemies. The real culture, spirituality, psychology, and ambition of the Indigenous peoples differed between nations (or tribes, as they are called), and were in any case not at all what the Europeans imagined them to be. At the core of colonial fantasies about Natives is the half-conscious recognition that such reductivist symbolism was inadequate, and that Indigenous peoples were ever capable of exceeding their presumptions and springing terrible surprises. That sense of unknown potential—for good, for ill, for making history *different*—is responsible for the emotional and moral tension at the heart of the Frontier Myth.[4]

It would eventually become a premise of the Frontier Myth that conflict between Natives and settlers was inevitable: that "savage" hunter and "civilized" farmer, pagan and Christian, "redskins" and White people could not peacefully coexist in the same space. The myth would ultimately see conflict as rooted in *racial* difference, a natural blood antipathy. The history of other European colonies, notably the French in Canada (who encouraged intermarriage), gives the lie to that assumption. But the English were settlers rather than traders. They wanted land for an ever-increasing population, and therefore pressed the Natives first into shrinking enclaves and ultimately into distant territories. Native chieftains had to concede sovereignty to colonial governors; Native villages had to welcome Christian missionaries, but their holy men and women could not proselytize among Christians.

Frontier settlers were also often at odds with colonial magistrates and governors, who tried to regulate their seizure or purchase of Indian lands—to keep the peace, to serve their own trading operations, or simply to maintain social control. As early as 1677, the Puritan minister-magistrate Cotton Mather complained that civil order and Christian piety were being undermined by settlers pushing into the woods in search of "land and elbow room." A hundred years later, Daniel Boone would cite the wish for "elbow room" to explain his motives for moving ever westward, and the phrase would become an American folk idiom. To truly have a world at your will, and enjoy its benefits free of interference, you need to keep your fellow man at a distance. To establish that space, you have to clear out the Indians on one side, then fend off the demands of metropolitan government on the other.[5]

And there you have the situation of the first "American," the pioneer settler. He or she has made a home on the frontier between two worlds. On the west is Indian country, beyond law or regulation, a natural wilderness filled with unknown potential for wealth and power, but haunted by "savages" endowed with a native understanding of the wilderness that can and will be used against the settler. On the east is the metropolis, the home culture that sent the settler forth and to which he or she owes allegiance, but a place whose ministers and magistrates seek to control the opportunities of frontier life.

The First Myth: Captivity and Rescue

The literacy rate in colonial New England was high, and in 1638 Harvard College set up the first printing press in British North America. An active print culture was established, publishing official documents, histories, religious texts, and personal narratives of religious experience. It was here that the first stories appeared that sought to explain and justify the actions and sufferings of the New English Israel during the crisis-ridden 1670s. The Puritan government that had ruled England since the Civil Wars of 1649–1654 was overthrown, King Charles II restored to the throne, and the Anglican church reestablished in England. Then, in 1675, the American colony was nearly destroyed by a ruinous Indian war, King Philip's War—named for the Wampanoag sachem Metacom, whose "Christian" name was Philip. Half the towns in New England were burned out or heavily damaged and hundreds of men, women, and children were killed, wounded, or carried into captivity. For a community that thought of itself as the New Israel, such calamities were inevitably seen as signs of God's displeasure. The ministers who were the colony's spiritual and political leaders published histories of the war framed by sermons, which compared New England's travails to those of the Chosen People, seeking analogies to help them understand what God was trying to tell them. In these sermon-histories the Indians figured as both devils and agents of divine displeasure, rebuking those settlers who had ignored their ministers in their quest for "elbow room."[6]

The most influential interpretation of the crisis was composed not by a minister but by the wife of a frontier preacher whose settlement was destroyed in an Indian attack, and who had endured a long captivity. Mary Rowlandson's *Sovereignty and Goodness of God,* first published in 1682, is a vivid personal narrative that distills the Puritans' troubled experience to its essentials. Her captivity takes her on a terrible journey through a wilderness that seems to her a kind of hell, in which she is carried farther and farther from home and husband, from civilization and the community of Christians. But the journey outward in alien space allows her to turn inward, to undergo self-discovery and spiritual regeneration. She realizes that God has chosen Indians as the instruments of her punishment, because the Natives are fit symbols of her own sins. She had become too acclimated to her American settlement, had come to feel "at ease in Zion" instead of remaining ever fretful about her salvation, like a good Puritan. She took too much pleasure in her food (gluttony) and in smoking tobacco—a sinful pleasure learned from the Natives. In short, she had moved too close to the "Indian" side, and God has turned the Indians into devilish persecutors to scare her back into the fold. Then, when she is reduced nearly to a "savage" herself, God redeems her by an act of arbitrary grace.

Rowlandson's captivity is a tale of spiritual rebirth or regeneration through the suffering of violence. She figures as the representative of Puritan colonial society as a whole, modeling the way it too can achieve redemption—by recognizing that without shedding of blood there is no remission of sin. As such it became the model for the first homegrown myth of American identity. Her book was the equivalent of a best seller in the 1680s, and it was never out of print in the colonial period. It was also the template of a new genre of distinctly American literature, the captivity narrative. These narratives (both historical and fictional) were perhaps the most popular and prevalent form of American adventure story for much of the eighteenth century. Through the captivity myth, the structures of Protestant Christian mythology that the settlers had brought from Europe were applied to the secular experiences of colonization. The captive symbolizes the values of Christianity and civilization that are imperiled in the wilderness war.[7]

As the colonies grew in strength, a second type of narrative developed, in which a male hero rescues the captive and defeats the Indians. One of the earliest exemplars was Benjamin Church, a contemporary of Rowlandson, whose knowledge of Indians and skill in adapting their tactics allowed him to defeat and kill King Philip. Church was the kind of settler the Puritan ministers and magistrates criticized. He lived on close and friendly terms with one of the Native nations on the Plymouth–Rhode Island border, and when war broke out, he formed a "ranger" unit that mixed colonists with Indigenous allies. He was often at odds with the government over strategy. While officialdom incompetently waged a war of indiscriminate violence, Church advocated efforts to persuade Philip's allies to abandon him and come over to the colonists. Church's ideas were vindicated when his Indigenous rangers ambushed and killed Philip and captured his leading chiefs. Church's history of the war—which had the most un-Puritan title *Entertaining Passages*—ends with a scene (apparently factual) of powerful symbolism: the war leader of the captured Indians does homage to Church and clothes him in the "royalties" of the dead King Philip, in effect anointing the Indian fighter as the new "king" of the wild frontier.[8]

It is noteworthy that although Church's narrative covers the same time period as Rowlandson's, his was not published until twenty-four years later, in 1716. Its publication signals the growing confidence of the settlers, and a shift in the development of the Frontier Myth, in which human heroism replaces the sense of vulnerability and helplessness expressed by the captivity narratives. This new hero is "the White Man Who Knows Indians," who uses his understanding of Indigenous ways to defeat the Natives. The warfare between British colonials and the French in Canada (and their Native allies) would produce a series of narratives celebrating the heroism of various "Indian-fighters," like Church, Captain John Lovewell, Sir William Johnson, and Major Robert Rogers of Rogers's Rangers.

The National Frontier: Daniel Boone and Thomas Jefferson, 1776–1824

The American Revolution gave the frontier story a new and explicitly nationalist twist, and produced a figure who was, after George Washington, the first hero of American national myth: Daniel Boone, the "Hunter of Kentucky," the "Columbus of the Woods." Boone was a farmer on the North Carolina frontier whose long hunting expeditions made him a leading explorer of trans-Appalachian trails into Kentucky. As an agent for land developer Richard Henderson, Boone led a party of settlers over Cumberland Gap to establish the settlement of Boonesborough, one of several in eastern Kentucky. These enterprises reflected the determination of colonial entrepreneurs (Washington was one) to exploit the wild lands across the mountains. Their ambitions were blocked by British colonial policy that sought to reserve the transmountain west for Native nations, which would supply furs to British factors in Canada—an attempt to freeze westward expansion that would be a motive for the colonists' rebellion.

The treaties that ended the War of Independence ceded to the United States all the British-controlled territory between the Appalachians and the Mississippi, more than doubling the territory controlled by the colonies in 1776, a windfall of rich farmland, timber, and mineral resources. This was a financial

bonanza for the new government, which could now pay its demobilized soldiers with land grants and use the promise of development to attract settlers
and investors to the United States. It was also a symbol of the limitless potential of the new republic, adding the promise of great riches to the vision of the
United States as a model of enlightened government for the whole world to
follow. Thomas Paine had caught the essence of that promise early in the war,
in *Common Sense* (1776). As Americans, he wrote, "we have it in our power to
begin the world over again."

That utopian vision was linked to a story of frontier adventure in *Kentucke*
(1784), a remarkable little book by John Filson, a country schoolmaster turned
surveyor and land speculator. Filson employed Boone as a guide to help him
survey tracts for potential settlements, and Boone told him about his adventurous life as a hunter, explorer, and Indian fighter. Filson retold the tale, pre-
tending the words were Boone's own; and he made it the centerpiece of an
elaborate promotional document, which described in detail the geography of
eastern Kentucky, the state of Indian affairs, and the wealth of good farmland
and mineral resources lying fallow there, waiting for the firstcomers to exploit
and develop it.

Filson's Kentucky is an earthly paradise, combining the sublimity of wilderness landscape with the pastoral charms of a new Arcadia, "trees . . . gay with
blossoms, others rich with fruits." To settle there would be to recover the lost
innocence of Eden and at the same time put yourself on the way to wealth.
More: the rich promise of Kentucky, and its strategic location on the Ohio
River, would make it the jumping-off point for a new American empire—a
republican empire like that of Rome, which (the reader will recall) was des-
tined to conquer the world. "In your country, like the land of promise, flowing
with milk and honey . . . you shall eat bread without scarceness, and not lack
anything in it. . . . Thus your country, favoured by the smile of heaven, will
probably be inhabited by the first people the world ever knew."[9]

By following the tale of Boone's adventures, we imaginatively enter and take
possession of this landscape. It is Boone the hunter who, on his solitary ram-
bles, introduces us to the gorgeous scenery, the freedom of the wilderness, the
life close to Nature. To gain true title to this paradise, Boone must lead his
family and other civilized folk to settle in Kentucky, replicating beyond the
mountains the original act of colonization that planted Europeans in the New
World. Like the Puritans of Rowlandson's time, Boone and his fellow settlers
must come to terms with the Indians, first of all by defending themselves against
Native enmity. Like Rowlandson, Boone's daughters are captured by Indians;
unlike Rowlandson, they are rescued, not by divine grace but by the skill and

bravery of their father, the Indian-fighting hero. Thus Boone's saga unites the two versions of the frontier story, those of Rowlandson and Church, the captive and the Indian fighter. But Boone goes further than Church in identifying himself with the Native American. When Boone is himself captured by the Shawnee, he earns and accepts adoption into the tribe, so that "the Shawanese King took great notice of me, and treated me with profound respect, and entire friendship, often entreating me to hunt at liberty." A later biographer would say of Boone that the Indian way of life was "the way of his heart." Boone would become famous for his unending quest for "elbow room" and his inability to live in a fully settled society.[10]

What makes him unique as a national hero is that doubleness: though he serves the mission of settlement, his character embodies the *attraction* of being Native, of truly belonging to America. That quality makes him the most effective fighter against the Natives, but it alienates him from the settled life his victories make possible. This irresolution makes him the symbol of a national identity in the process of formation, its final terms unsettled and open to imaginative exploration.

Filson's little book had an astonishing influence on ideas about the American frontier, both in the United States and in Europe. His version of Boone's "autobiography" was frequently reprinted and plagiarized in books and magazine articles, published in England, and translated into French and German and circulated among European intellectuals and businesspeople interested in promoting emigration. Boone became a celebrity—European and American tourists would seek him out (some successfully), as if he were an icon of American scenery like Niagara Falls. American writers produced several highly popular biographies, but Boone would reach a kind of apotheosis as the model for Hawkeye in James Fenimore Cooper's Leatherstocking Tales, a series of novels published between 1823 and 1841 that would codify the Frontier Myth in memorable and enduring symbolism.[11]

Boone's appeal as a symbol of American heroism owed as much to real developments in national policy as it did to the literary skill of Boone's admirers. The settlement of Kentucky was inaugurated by freelance settlers and land developers. Then, under the Articles of Confederation and the Constitution, the national government took charge of fostering and regulating westward expansion. Conflicting colonial land claims were resolved by compromise; a government for the unsettled lands north of the Ohio River was established by the Northwest Ordinance of 1787. The government encouraged settlement by granting parcels of land as payment to Revolutionary War veterans, and the purchase of these grants by speculators was also a factor in the development of

American banking. What had been a random popular movement was transformed into a keystone of national policy, broadly affecting economic development, expanding the powers of the central government, and altering its relation with the states, the Indian nations, and foreign powers.

Thomas Jefferson integrated the economics of westward expansion and the politics of savage war into the first systematic ideology of American nationalism. Jefferson believed that the basis of republican government was the citizen-freeholder, a man with sufficient property (typically a farm) to maintain himself and his family without becoming a client or tenant of wealthy or aristocratic superiors. Such men could be relied on to support and defend a state that protected them and their property, as in the classic republics of Greece and Rome, whose citizen armies were fired by patriotic morale. But Rome degenerated into an aristocratic empire when its freeholder base lost its economic independence. If the American republic was to endure, it had to foster freeholding on a broad and permanent basis, and maintain it against the pressures and blandishments of a world economy in which mercantile and banking interests were preeminent. The free or undeveloped lands of the frontier were, for Jefferson, a vast reserve on which generations of freeholders could establish themselves. This reserve would offset the interests and pressures that might otherwise draw surplus population to the cities, where they would become wage-dependent proletarians.

As president, Jefferson would turn theory into stunning fact, through his ordering of the Lewis and Clark Expedition and purchase of the Louisiana Territory from France in 1803. The Louisiana Purchase would effectively redouble the size of the United States, and the expedition would begin the process of pushing the national territory west to the Pacific. Jefferson believed he had won enough land to provide freeholding for "a thousand generations." With its energies turned toward the development of this vast natural reserve, the nation would have less reason to embroil itself in foreign affairs, avoiding the imperial warfare and mercantile competition that absorbed the European powers and thwarted their peoples' aspirations for democracy. As it happened, the territory that was to have absorbed a thousand generations would be settled in five, and westward expansion would embroil the United States in wars with Britain and Mexico. But Jefferson had succeeded in making frontier expansion a keystone of American political ideology, and of a national sense of destiny.[12]

There were two anomalies in Jefferson's vision. For starters, the "free" lands awaiting American development belonged to the Indigenous nations that already inhabited them. In *Notes on Virginia* (1784), his earliest attempt to articulate a vision of American nationality, Jefferson expressed the hope that the Natives could be induced to accept a "civilized" mode of life, by substituting farming for hunting-gathering and forming civil structures like those of the colonists. As president he made some effort to achieve this goal, by fostering trade relations, trying to prevent uncontrolled settler encroachment on Indian lands, and sponsoring various projects for developing Native agriculture. But the fundamental assumption of Jeffersonian Indian policy was that the continued presence of Natives within the United States was only tolerable if they ceased to be "Indians," abandoning their way of life and tribal patriotism. This they refused to do. In the 1790s a loose confederation of tribes in the Northwest Territory twice routed American armies, before being defeated in 1794.

Faced with Native resistance, Jefferson (as president) considered a plan for removing the tribes to a reserve beyond the Mississippi, thus clearing the most productive of the new territories for settlers.[13] Recognizing the inexorability of American settlement policy, Shawnee chief Tecumseh attempted to organize the tribes between the Alleghenies and the Mississippi, combining political confederation with a movement of cultural revival led by his brother "the Prophet." Tecumseh had some success uniting the Northwest tribes and was a powerful ally of the British in the War of 1812. His death in battle, and the defeat of his British allies, doomed this effort at "nationalizing" Indigenous America.[14]

Jefferson's successors oversaw the removal of most of the Northwest Territory tribes, even those that had allied with the Americans against Tecumseh. In the Southeast several large tribes attempted to meet Jefferson's policy halfway by adopting a "civilized" lifestyle. They had a mixed planting-hunting economy and stable pattern of settlement, accepted White schoolmasters and ministers, and even adopted that hallmark of Southern civilization, chattel slavery. The Cherokee developed a written syllabary and a print culture. Nevertheless, these "Five Civilized Tribes" were targeted for removal by the elected officials of Mississippi, Alabama, Tennessee, Georgia, and North Carolina, as well as the administration of President Andrew Jackson. Over the course of the 1830s, some 80,000 were dispossessed by the armed forces of the government and compelled to make the long march to Indian Territory (present-day Oklahoma). Thousands perished on the Trail of Tears—the largest instance of "ethnic cleansing" in US history. It was an act of outrageous violence, yet not a war, since only one side was armed.[15]

The savage-war side of the Frontier Myth provided another kind of antidote to class differentiation and conflict. In the grand enterprise of displacing the Indigenous tribes, Americans of different classes and ethnic origins were united by the combination of economic interest and racial Whiteness. The difference in wealth and breeding between a Jefferson and a Daniel Boone was offset by their mutual dependence in the war to extend White settlement. Whiteness became the broadest and most unifying way of conceiving American nationality. It canceled the cultural differences among South Carolina rice and indigo planters, Virginia tobacco farmers, Kentucky hunters, Pennsylvania Quakers, and Massachusetts Yankees.

Whiteness also enabled the assimilation of European immigrants, whose numbers drove the population increase on which American enterprise depended. This new concept of American nationality was most clearly described by the French immigrant J. Hector St. John de Crèvecoeur in his *Letters from an American Farmer* (1782). "What, then, is the American, this new man?" he asked. He may be a Dutchman or German or "Hebridean" by "race"—that is, by nationality and birth. But he adapts to the "indulgent laws" of his adopted country, becomes a citizen or freeman, and reaps the "ample rewards" for his labor that the laws and the natural environment guarantee. In so doing he becomes a member of a "new race," the "American." Implicit in Crèvecoeur's narrative is the assumption that this process of rebirth is only open to people of European descent. Indians and Black people remain outside the "American" racial brotherhood. America was to be a White republic.[16]

The second and graver anomaly was the fact that at least half of the western territories gained after the Revolution would be developed with slave labor. Like many of the Founders, Jefferson believed that slavery was incompatible with the ideals of republicanism and a society based on independent farmers. That idea shaped the decision, made under the Articles of Confederation in 1787, to exclude slavery from the Northwest Territory. Yet slavery was the basis of Jefferson's personal wealth, and of the economy of his state. After 1795, the development and expansion of cotton cultivation increased the South's—and the nation's—dependence on plantation agriculture and slave labor. The settlement of the West south of the Ohio River would be driven by the desire for new cotton lands, fueled by the bonanza of productivity and profit promised by the rich alluvial soils of Alabama and the Mississippi valley.

Calculations of economic interest were doubly reinforced by considerations of race. Jefferson saw Black people as slaves, not merely by circumstance but by nature: lacking intelligence and enterprise, incapable of self-government, combining a weak moral sense with strong sensual appetites. He believed that White and Black people could not share the same geographical and political space on terms of equality. One must be subservient to the other, or "savage war" would result. In his *Notes on Virginia,* written in 1784, he warned that emancipating the slaves would "divide us into parties, and produce convulsions, which will probably never end but in the extermination of the one or the other race." In fact, as Jefferson well knew, freed Black slaves had been living peacefully and productively in Virginia since the seventeenth century. His prophecy reflects a deep-seated fear of racial integration, which would have profound effects on the development of American nationality.[17]

Thus the Jeffersonian Myth of the Frontier combined a vision of America's perpetual growth through westward expansion into undeveloped lands with a racially exclusive definition of American nationality that historian Alexander Saxton has called "the white republic."[18]

Codifying the Myth: Cooper's Hawkeye and the Role of Literature

The Frontier Myth was developed and propagated through a variety of print productions, from published sermons and political pamphlets, to newspaper articles, to works of history and philosophy. As the American book trade developed, literary fiction by American writers was added to the mix. Its role in the cultural marketplace would expand dramatically through the next century, as literacy and readership expanded and cheaper forms of publication lowered the cost of books.

The Frontier Myth owes much of its enduring force to the work of James Fenimore Cooper and his innumerable imitators. The materials from which Cooper built his novels—his idea of the relation between wilderness and civilization, his concept of "Indian character," his model of the frontier hero, and even his favorite plot device—the captivity and rescue—were all present in the culture long before he began writing. His greatest creation, the frontiersman Hawkeye, derives not only from Daniel Boone but more distantly from Benjamin Church, and the White women Hawkeye is forever rescuing from Indian captivity are the figurative descendants of Mary Rowlandson. Nevertheless, Cooper (and artists like him) made a critical contribution to national culture by using the novelist's craft to systematize the varied themes and characters of the tradition into a coherent, dramatic, compelling, and memorable set of historically resonant narratives.[19]

Cooper's genre was the historical romance, a type of fiction favored by nationalist writers in the early nineteenth century. These novels typically dramatize an episode from the prehistory of the nation, in which the germs of the nation's present qualities (and problems) are displayed and heroically resolved. Sir Walter Scott, Cooper's model and rival, showed how heroes in England's past had paved the way to Britain's glorious present by overcoming such divisions as those between Saxon and Norman (*Ivanhoe*) or English and Scots (*Rob Roy*). Cooper had a more difficult problem, because the nation whose character he sought to affirm had been produced by elimination rather than reconciliation.

Cooper recognizes the racial opposition of Whites and Indians as the origin of American nationality, and savage war as the crucible of national identity. His Leatherstocking novels amplify this basic imagery systematically, using the White-Indian opposition as a key to interpret other fundamental oppositions: the political rivalry of North and South; the class opposition between landed gentry and social-climbing yeomen, or between masters and slaves; and on a deeper level, the difference between men and women, or more precisely between masculine and feminine ways of thinking about and dealing with the politics of race.

Cooper wrote five Leatherstocking novels: *The Pioneers* (1823), *The Last of the Mohicans* (1826), *The Prairie* (1827), *The Pathfinder* (1840), and *The Deerslayer* (1841). The tales are unified by the recurring figure of Natty Bumppo, also known as Hawkeye, Pathfinder, and Deerslayer. His popularity was such that Hawkeye almost displaced Boone as the model for future versions of the frontier hero, not only in fiction but in the writings of antebellum historians, journalists, and politicians concerned with westward expansion.

Through Hawkeye, Cooper explores and defines the limits of cultural adaptation and the ultimately determinative power of race. For the Puritan historians of King Philip's War, settler-Native conflict was defined as Christian versus heathen, for Boone and Jefferson as civilized versus uncivilized. But Hawkeye is neither a settler nor a Christian. He is a White man who has lived with Indians his whole life and is imbued with their values and knowledge. He stands between the opposed worlds of savagery and civilization, acting sometimes as mediator or interpreter between races and cultures, but ultimately as civilization's most effective instrument against savagery. He continually refers to himself as "a man without a cross," which has religious implications: he never identifies as a Christian and is more deeply influenced by Indian spirituality. However, what he is literally asserting is that he is without admixture of Indian blood, so that we can take his word as authoritative when he speaks about the difference between the values and the racial "gifts" of Whites and Indians.

The Last of the Mohicans is the most emotionally powerful novel of the series, and the one that most explicitly dramatizes the Jeffersonian Myth of the Frontier. The novel is ostensibly based on the Fort William Henry massacre of 1757, but it takes off from history into an archetypal captivity-and-rescue plot. Cora and Alice, the daughters of Colonel Munro (commander of the fort),

are captured by the evil and vengeful Huron Magua. Their rescuers are led by
Hawkeye and his Indian comrades, Chingachgook and his son Uncas. These
latter are "the last of the Mohicans," the last pure-blooded descendants of the
oldest and noblest of the Indian races. The frontiersmen are accompanied by
Colonel Munro and by Captain Heyward, Alice's fiancé, a Virginia-born soldier whom Cooper compares to George Washington—the ideal type of American manhood.

Alice is the pure White maiden, Munro's daughter by his second wife. Cora
is Munro's daughter by his first wife, a West Indian woman of high birth but
partly African blood. She also displays "manly" courage and defiance, testing
the boundaries of gender in ways that are admirable but oddly troubling to
the male characters. Cora's female sexuality is lushly described, and Cooper
intends his readers to find her more sensually appealing than Alice. But within
the novel, only non-White men—the evil Magua and the noble Uncas—are
sexually attracted to Cora. Heyward, the best of American White men, loves
the limpid Alice, which may bemuse the modern reader but suits the nationalist allegory Cooper has in mind. Erotic preference defines, in the most fundamental terms, the difference in what Cooper terms the racial "gifts" of Whites
and Indians.

Cora and Uncas represent an alternative America, which is both physically
and morally attractive but will be thwarted by the laws of race and history.
Uncas has a hidden potential, which is not fully revealed until the rescuers confront the Delaware tribesmen who hold Cora and Alice captive. Then the old
chieftain and prophet who leads these people recognizes Uncas as a kind of
Indigenous messiah (another Tecumseh), because he is the last pure-blooded
chieftain of the "ancient race" of the Mohicans. The reader is invited to fanta-
size Uncas and Cora as king and queen of an alternative America. Uncas
represents the best of the Indigenous race, Cora the best of Black and White—
their child would incarnate an American "rainbow" identity in which all the
nation's racial strains fuse into one.

Then Cooper tells us that this is an outcome history will not permit. In the
novel's catastrophe, Magua kills both Cora and Uncas, and is himself killed by
Hawkeye with one remarkable rifle shot. At the funerals of Cora and Uncas,
the dream of their marriage is invoked by the mourning Delaware maidens, and
a broader vision is invoked by the heartbroken Colonel Munro: "Say to these
kind and gentle beings . . . that the Being we all worship, under different names,
will be mindful of their charity; and that the time shall not be distant, when
we may assemble around his throne, without distinction of sex, or rank, or
colour." But Hawkeye, who understands both sides of the racial borderline,

denies even that possibility: "To tell them this . . . would be to tell them that the snows come not in winter." Hawkeye's insistence on the primacy of "blood" dramatizes Cooper's belief in the necessary link of race and nationality. Heyward and Alice, the White-on-White couple, represent the future of an American nationality from which all "color" has been purged. In Jeffersonian America, the Frontier Myth produces a White man's republic, in which Black people are only acceptable as slaves, and from which Indians must either "vanish" or be forcibly removed.[20]

With Cooper's symbolic summing-up of frontier history, the structure of the Myth of the Frontier was complete and available in a readily comprehensible form for poets, preachers, and politicians to invoke. The hero of the myth is "the Man Who Knows Indians," modeled on historical figures like Church and Boone, later by Andrew Jackson, Davy Crockett, Kit Carson, and others. Because the border between savagery and civilization runs through their moral center, the Indian wars are, for these heroes, a spiritual or psychological struggle, which they win by learning to discipline or suppress the savage or "dark" side of their own human nature. Thus they are mediators of a double kind who can teach civilized men how to defeat savagery on its native grounds—the natural wilderness, and the wilderness of the human soul. They symbolize the creation of a new and exceptional American national character through the fighting of "savage wars."

Yet it is the fantasy of an alternate history, a mythic might-have-been, that gives the novel its poignancy. It also captures an essential quality of myth, which is its imaginative retention of possible outcomes *not* realized in actual history: the achievement of an ideal America, unlike the imperfect one we inhabit. Myths develop around issues basic to the culture, which also endure as issues, unsettled matters, "unfinished business," and the perennial creation of action scripts that might point toward resolution.

Bonanza Economics: The Frontier Myth in the Age of Agrarian Expansion

In the world Americans *did* inhabit, the Myth of the Frontier combined two ideological themes into a single powerful fable: the themes of bonanza economics and savage war. The first is an economic myth, rooted in Jefferson's theory of agrarian expansion; the second a political and social myth, which defines the rights, powers, and roles of different classes and races in the making of American society.

Bonanza economics holds that the key to American development is the continual discovery and exploitation of cheap and abundant resources *outside* the metropolitan center of society. Nature, not labor, gives such resources their value; hence they come to us free of the social costs that burden development in metropolitan Europe. In the Old World (so the story goes), people or classes can only better their condition by undergoing the deprivations of primitive accumulation, by exploiting scarcity and need, or by engaging in social warfare against more established classes. In Frontier America, resources are so superabundant that prosperity can be enjoyed by all, without prejudice to the interests of any—except the Natives who, as savages, are outside the limits of civil society and public concern.

The settlement of the Old Northwest and Old Southwest between 1795 and 1830 for the most part fulfilled the agrarian program, since the character of soil and climate and the state of technology made feasible the exploitation of resources by individuals (or small families) of settlers, artisans, and entrepreneurs. As these settlements matured, they drew emigrants from eastern states and from overseas. Population growth increased the value of the land itself, increased agricultural productivity, and generated new businesses, trades, and industries to serve these growing communities. All of these factors contributed to the rapid growth of the national economy, and to speculative booms or bonanzas of one kind or another.

The most significant of these was the rapid expansion of cotton cultivation between 1795 and 1860, driven by rising demand for cotton in the burgeoning textile industries of England and New England and by the invention of the cotton gin, which allowed semiskilled enslaved laborers to cheaply process large amounts of cotton for baling and shipment. A vast new field for plantation agriculture was opened by the spread of settlement westward from Georgia to the Mississippi. The rich soils of this "Black Belt" enabled the formation of large and highly profitable plantations, which required large numbers of enslaved laborers. The cotton frontier vastly expanded the scope and economic power of slavery, and made the institution—which some of the Founders had hoped would wither away—into a permanent aspect of American life.[21]

In the Old World (so the story goes), social violence is directed inward, deployed by one class to subjugate or overthrow another in the struggle for scarce resources, with the result that Europe is unstable and resistant to democracy. But in America, the social costs of development are externalized. Social violence is projected outward against "them that are not a People" (as the Puritans liked to say)—against tribes of alien races and cultures living beyond the geographical borders of civilization (in the case of Indians and Africans) or beyond the margins of civil society (in the case of domestic slaves). Since the two races cannot share the country, one or the other must be destroyed or driven out. The "war of extermination" that Jefferson envisioned as a consequence of emancipation was a projection based on the experience of the Indian wars, in which genocide was often called for and sometimes carried out.[22]

This view of America's national purpose was codified in the concept of Manifest Destiny. First coined by Democratic Party spokesman Timothy O'Sullivan in 1845 to justify the seizure of Mexican land in the Southwest and out to the Pacific Coast, the concept would also come to define an American world mission: by linking the achievement of imperial power with democratic institutions, America would become a beacon to the peoples of the Old World, a model for the political redemption of civilized humankind. It was a view shared by Theodore Parker, an abolitionist at the opposite end of the ideological spectrum, who saw the American branch of the Anglo-Saxon "race" as uniquely suited to conquer the continent and gain the victory of "civilization over savagery," as well as to triumph over lesser White races like the Spanish and French.[23]

The Frontier Myth thus provided Americans with a satisfying picture of the origin, destiny, and character of their nation. But it left unresolved some basic contradictions in the national ideology. How could the racial exclusiveness of the myth be squared with the ideology of republican citizenship, which offered civil rights to anyone swearing loyalty to the state and obedience to the laws? Or with the principle of human equality affirmed as "self-evident" in the Declaration of Independence? And what was the real and proper relation between the *nation* and the *state*—between the people, acting on their own to settle the wilderness, and the government that grants title to the territory and defends it from enemies foreign and domestic? An answer of sorts can be found in the Myth of the Founding, which celebrates and sanctifies the origins of the American state. But the unresolved conflicts in both the Frontier Myth and the Myth of the Founding would combine to provoke the supreme crisis of the Civil War.

2

The Myth of the Founding

CENTRAL TO American nationality is the belief that our nation-state was created by a unique generation of devoted patriots, brilliant and highly principled philosopher-politicians, the Founding Fathers. Every national myth is a blend of heroic narrative and ideological symbolism, but in the Myth of the Founding the ideological is more heavily weighted than the narrative. The travail and struggle of the Revolutionary War era have value for us because they produced a set of principles embodied in the Declaration of Independence and the Constitution—two documents that have acquired a standing akin to sacred scripture. The promulgation of the Constitution is literally the constitutive act of American nation-state formation. The oath sworn by the president at his or her inauguration is to "preserve, protect and defend the Constitution of the United States," as if the document were the nation. During the formative years of the republic, the principles articulated and enacted in these documents also provided the ideological basis of national unity for a "People" of varied ethnic and national origins, as well as a political history reflecting the very different structures and experiences of the several colonies. As our history developed, they remained a basic reference point for political debate; and every major crisis required reaffirmation or reinterpretation of their meanings.

The Declaration of Independence enacts the transformation of the thirteen colonies into a sovereign confederal state. But it goes beyond what Abraham Lincoln called its "merely national" self-assertion, to promulgate a set of "self-evident" principles that define the ideological and moral basis of a new type of government. This would be a republic based on a concept of "inalienable" *personal* rights to "life, liberty, and the pursuit of happiness," which all people possess equally. Government's only purpose is to "secure these rights," and when it fails to do so, "it is the right of the People to alter or abolish" it by revolution. Those rights are rooted in the ultimate authority of "the laws of Nature and of Nature's God," and America's entitlement to national independence rests on those eternal laws. In appealing to a principle beyond the limits of existing civil law, the Declaration is a call to and justification for *revolution,* the overthrow of the state regime.

The Constitution may be the fruit of revolution, but its purpose is to establish a national regime of law and government, and form a unified American nationality out of a confederacy of separate states. The debates that shaped the Constitution were informed by deep and serious considerations of classical and modern political theory, as well as by the calculation of special interests. The concerns of slaveholders, and of smaller colonies, were behind several major compromises. The new frame of government was designed to strike a balance between state power and public liberty by dividing the different aspects of government (state vs. federal, executive vs. legislative vs. judicial) and establishing a system of checks and balances to prevent any single power from controlling the whole government. It was designed, and by later generations considered, "a Machine that would go of itself," a perfectly balanced and self-correcting system of government.[1]

The Constitution's founding principles were in harmony with the Declaration's concept of natural rights, but it makes no reference to those principles. Rather, the Constitution's authority derives from civil law, from "We the People" acting through legally elected representatives. Its language specifies the legal form of government, without explaining or justifying it. It is aspirational only in its preamble, which declares that the purpose of government is to "form a more perfect Union, establish Justice, insure domestic Tranquility, provide for the common defence, promote the general Welfare, and secure the Blessings of Liberty."

Since the Constitution is the basis of our government and legal system, it is routinely referenced whenever the federal judiciary makes a decision, Congress passes a law, or the executive branch takes action. The Declaration has no legal status, but it is so much a part of our political culture that its principles are also routinely invoked in support of policies or in celebration of national exceptionalism. In these everyday applications, the Founding acts as the basis of civil religion rather than myth. That is, it provides the ideological premises for American concepts of legitimacy, nationality, and patriotism. Although that civil religion is nondenominational, it is infused with biblical symbolism, especially the concept of the "covenant" between

God and his Chosen People, which is the root of American exceptionalism. But it is worth noting that the Declaration refers to "Nature's God" rather than the biblical God; that the Constitution makes no mention of God; and that the Bill of Rights, adopted two years after ratification, forbids the establishment of a state religion.[2]

The distinction between national myth and civil religion is an important one. National myths are narratives that provide Americans with action scripts for heroic responses to current crises. They engage the fundamental conflicts of value and belief around which our politics have developed, and for that reason they take wildly varying forms. As we've seen, the Frontier Myth glorifies the conquest of the wilderness, but also regrets its loss. But the narrative elements of the Founding Myth are fixed. George Washington is the exemplar of republican virtue, Benjamin Franklin the wise old sage, Benedict Arnold the incarnation of treason, James Madison the father of the Constitution. There are at least three major versions of the symbolic meaning of the Battle of Gettysburg, so different in their premises that people have been willing to shed blood to defend their interpretation. But there is only one way that Americans understand "Valley Forge," or "Lexington and Concord."

It is only in times of extreme crisis that narratives of the Founding—accounts of how and why the Founders made certain decisions or proclaimed particular principles—are summoned up and deployed as models of right understanding and proper action. Several such crises occurred during the Age of Jackson (1820–1840), which began the process of transforming a pair of political documents into the basis of an American "covenant." That process was completed by the political struggles that produced and carried through the Civil War.[3]

The Constitution: From Political Compromise to Sacred Text

In the beginning the Declaration of Independence and the Constitution were political documents, responses to particular crises produced through compromise among competing interest groups. Over time the Constitution would come to be thought of as the rock on which the American republic was founded. However, at the time of its adoption, serious questions were raised about the kind of government it prescribed, as well as doubts about whether it would hold under the pressure of events and contending interests. The early national period was rife with projects for secession. The most notorious were the western secessions connived at by George Rogers Clark and Aaron Burr; but New Englanders discussed secession after Thomas Jefferson's election, and again during the War of 1812. While the Constitution made no explicit provision for states to leave the compact, to many of the Founders it seemed quite possible that some or all might do so.[4]

The Missouri Crisis of 1820–1821 tested and confirmed the idea that the Constitution had become the ultimate authority for resolving political questions. Northerners opposed the extension of slavery into the new state being formed out of the Missouri Territory. They cited the Constitution in defense of their view that Congress had the right to forbid slavery in new territories and states, and Article IV, Section 4, which requires Congress to guarantee a "republican form of government" in the states, provocatively assuming that slavery was incompatible with republican government. Southerners likewise cited the Constitution's protection of property and its "fugitive slave" clause in defense of slavery in Missouri and elsewhere. The issue was eventually settled by a compromise which left the ultimate issues unresolved. But the conduct of the debate affirmed the Constitution's translation from a political device to the authoritative basis of national government.

In the wake of the Missouri Compromise, the terms of American nationality and the concept of citizenship were transformed by popular movements that broadened the franchise to include virtually all White men. Here the principles of the Declaration of Independence came into play. The Declaration had begun to be celebrated as the founding text of democratic ideology in the 1790s, when Jefferson invoked its egalitarian principles in partisan battle against Alexander Hamilton and the Federalists. During the period when Jefferson's Democratic-Republican Party had almost uncontested control of government, from 1800 to 1832, ceremonial invocations of the Declaration became part of the ritual July 4 celebrations of independence. When the last surviving signers of the Declaration—Thomas Jefferson and his Federalist antagonist John Adams—both died on the day of the Declaration's fiftieth anniversary, it seemed a providential sign ratifying the grandeur of their achievement.[5]

The radical implications of the document did not come to the fore until they were employed on behalf of the populist uprising historians have characterized as "Jacksonian democracy." The Founding was the work of a political and social elite chosen by an electorate that was generally restricted to holders of a certain amount of property, and in all cases restricted by race and gender. The Founders' ideal of republican government did not contemplate direct democracy or universal suffrage. Federalists like Adams and Hamilton opposed majoritarian rule in principle, and even Jefferson feared an expanded franchise would enable a demagogue to achieve tyrannical power by appealing to class resentments.

Andrew Jackson personified Jefferson's fears; but he would become the figurative leader of a democratizing movement and ultimately be paired with Jefferson as the symbolic fathers of the modern Democratic Party. Jackson asserted the virtues and interests of "the common man" against the propertied elites, promoting free trade and the deregulation of banking in the interest of farmers and planters, and opposing commercial and banking interests. Although he was a wealthy planter who owned a large number of enslaved people, he had reached aristocratic status through his own efforts. He was not only a classic self-made man but also a frontier hero who won fame fighting those twin enemies, the "savage" Indians on the southern frontier and the hypercivilized British at the Battle of New Orleans.

The revolutionary principles and the process of nation-making had inspired many in the Founding generation to contemplate the abolition of slavery, citizenship for Native Americans, and women's rights. By 1840 all of those possibilities had been rejected. The Missouri Compromise recognized the relative permanence of Black enslavement. In the 1840s women gained property rights in most states, but female suffrage was nowhere seriously considered. And though the "Five Civilized Tribes" of the Southeast adopted the settled ways of their White neighbors, they were dispossessed and forced to take the deadly Trail of Tears to Indian Territory. The Missouri Compromise set a northern limit to the possible expansion of slavery, but it implicitly ratified the permanence of slavery as a Southern institution.[6]

Jacksonian democracy opened the franchise for White men but *foreclosed* the potential for a broader definition of nationality and political citizenship. Jacksonian nationalism thus defined America as a White man's republic, and democracy as White men's politics.

Slavery, Race, and the Appeal to the Founders

When the Constitution was ratified, slavery existed in all the states. It was not long before slavery was abolished (immediately or gradually) in the North and Northwest, where economic development was driven by family farms, artisanal entrepreneurship, and manufacturing. Slavery was only central to the states south of Pennsylvania and the Ohio River, where large-scale production of staple crops (first tobacco, then cotton) depended on plantations and an enslaved labor force.

The differentiation of sectional economies produced conflicts of interest over tariff policy (which favored industry at the expense of agriculture), public investment in "internal improvements" or infrastructure, and access to the undeveloped land of the frontier. Economic conflicts were heightened by the development of antislavery ideology in England, France, and the Americas. In the United States the movement to abolish slavery grew out of the ideology of natural rights articulated in the Declaration of Independence, the national myth that saw America as the exemplar of liberty, and a revival movement in American Protestantism in the 1820s and 1830s that linked the renewal of piety to a range of social and political reforms. Although only a small minority supported a national abolition program, there was a substantial Free-Soil movement, which opposed the extension of slavery to newly acquired western territories. Finally, the greater growth of the White population outside the South threatened the congressional balance of power between Free and Slave States.

Slavery was both an economic interest and the basis of the South's distinctive way of life. To defend it, Southern political leaders challenged the supremacy of national law enshrined in the Constitution. In 1832–1833 the passage of a tariff law inimical to Southern interests roused a wave of secessionist enthusiasm in the cotton states. To avoid that revolutionary outcome, John C. Calhoun, the leading theoretician of Southern rights, proposed the doctrine of "nullification": the right of a state to "nullify" or refuse to comply with federal legislation or regulations that violated its rights to life, liberty, and property. A similar doctrine had been asserted by two of the most significant Founders, Jefferson and Madison, in the Virginia and Kentucky Resolutions of 1796. But the status of the Constitution had changed since then. It was no longer a mere political arrangement, but a sacred text. When President Jackson asserted his right to use armed force to compel South Carolina's obedience, the Carolinians backed down and Jackson was seen in most of the country as the champion of a nationalist Constitution.

But Calhoun's premise remained central to Southern political theory: that defense of slavery was the South's paramount interest, and if it could not protect that interest by ordinary political means—or the device of nullification—outright secession would become its last resort. That logic would produce a major crisis in 1848–1851, when the Mexican War gave the nation possession of a vast region stretching from Texas to California. Pro- and antislavery interests clashed over whether slavery should be permitted in the new territories. The Frontier Myth came into play, convincing each side that the system (slave or free) that controlled the West would control the nation's future. The crisis paralyzed government for three years. The threat of secession became real, as conventions met to formulate plans of action. The crisis was seemingly resolved by the so-called Compromise of 1850. But the compromise was a political deal, cobbled together by the adroit manipulations of Senator Stephen Douglas—

unstable because the fundamental questions of principle and long-term interest remained unresolved.

The conflict exploded again in 1854, when Douglas's Kansas-Nebraska Bill reopened the territorial question. The bill was intended to facilitate the building of a transcontinental railroad to enable development of the western frontier. To win Southern support, Douglas abrogated the Missouri Compromise, which banned slavery from new states and territories north of 30°30′ latitude. Advocates of "free soil" in both the Whig and Democratic Parties saw Douglas's ploy as a device for making slavery dominant in the new territories. Some called for a congressional ban on slavery in the territories; others followed Douglas's call for "popular sovereignty"—leaving the decision on slavery to the settlers. Southerners saw both responses as threats to their prospects for economic expansion, and as encouraging antislavery sentiment. They therefore pressed for a constitutional interpretation that would forbid Congress and territorial governments from legislating against slavery until the territory achieved statehood.

The controversy split the Democrats into a Douglas wing, centered in the Old Northwest, and a Southern wing, which included Presidents Franklin Pierce and James Buchanan and much of the party's regular organization. The Whig Party fell apart, and its antislavery elements combined with Free-Soil Democrats and others to form a new Republican Party, dedicated to stopping the spread of slavery. The opening of Kansas to settlement led to open warfare between antislavery settlers and proslavery vigilantes from Missouri—Bleeding Kansas.

All sides in this ideological struggle appealed to the Myth of the Founding to seize for themselves the moral and legal authority that would settle the issue on their terms. What had the Founders intended when they prescribed procedures for organizing new territories? What were their intentions with regard to slavery—to guarantee its perpetuation, or prepare for its ultimate extinction? What were their views on the possibility of secession, and were these embodied in the Constitution?

The strongest and most literal appeal to the Founding was made by Supreme Court chief justice Roger Taney, in the *Dred Scott v. Sandford* decision of 1857. Taney hoped to end the conflict by issuing a definitive interpretation of the constitutional issues. He upheld the Southern position, that Congress had no power to bar the carrying of slaves into new territories, and that the decision to become a Free or a Slave State must wait until statehood was granted. But Taney believed that to thoroughly and permanently settle the issue, he had to go beyond the legal status of slavery to address the fundamental concepts of human nature and natural law embodied in the Declaration. He therefore reached past the constitutionality of slavery, to ground its existence in a racial theory of White supremacy; and he rooted that theory in the Myth of the Founding by proposing an authoritative interpretation of the Founders' belief system: "At the time of the Declaration of Independence, and when the Constitution of the United States was framed and adopted," "[negroes] had for more than a century before been regarded as beings of an inferior order . . . and so far inferior, that they had no rights which the white man was bound to respect; and that the negro might justly and lawfully be reduced to slavery for his benefit." Legislation by the Founding generation and its successors showed an intent to erect a "perpetual and impassable barrier . . . between the white race and the one they had reduced to slavery."[7]

The implications were radical. The decision deprived Congress of the power to make the kind of compromises that had saved the Union in the past. It implicitly nullified the laws in some Free States that granted Black people civil rights or the franchise. Moreover, if enslaved people had no rights as humans, but were simply property, then all states were bound to respect the master's right to use, transport, and deploy them at will. Abraham Lincoln spoke for a large segment of Free State opinion when he asserted that Taney's decision looked like part of a plot, by the slaveholding interests and their Democratic sympathizers, to make slavery a national institution.[8]

The Debate on the Declaration: Lincoln versus Douglas versus Douglass versus Stephens

The movement of Taney's thought anticipates the direction that ideological and cultural conflict would take as the nation moved into and through civil war: away from legal and interest-based arguments for and against slavery, and toward a recognition that the fundamental issue was the status of White supremacy. That drift became clear as the territorial issue was debated by a new political configuration: Southern Democrats, Douglas Democrats, the new Republican / Free-Soil coalition, and the abolitionists. They differed on whether *Dred Scott* must be supported and extended, circumvented by "popular sovereignty," or opposed and overturned. But their arguments about the status of slavery relied less on constitutional legalism than on whether the Declaration of Independence's principle of human equality applied to Black people. To understand the Founders' intentions, it was necessary to return to the story of its adoption.

The debates between Abraham Lincoln and Stephen Douglas during the 1858 Illinois senatorial campaign were the most sustained and sophisticated of these discussions. Debate texts were widely distributed, establishing Lincoln as a presidential candidate, and they have long been considered a classic of American political thought. But Lincoln and Douglas represented only two of the contending political forces, Free-Soil and popular sovereignty. For a fuller understanding of the ideological battle, we need to see it as a four-sided debate, including abolitionists and Southern advocates of slavery as a "positive good."

Frederick Douglass made the most ringing and unequivocal assertion that the promise of universal human rights was the core of the Declaration and was—or ought to have been—the defining principle of the nation's political life. His Independence Day oration, "What to the Slave Is the Fourth of July?" (1852), makes its point through a brilliant inversion of his White audience's expectations. He begins by honoring what the day signifies, likening American government to the biblical covenant. "This, to you, is what the Passover was to the emancipated people of God." He honors as well the Founders who fought for their freedom and authored the Declaration—"the ring-bolt to the chain of your nation's destiny."[9]

Then he turns the tables, by speaking as a Black man and former slave:

> What, to the American slave, is your 4th of July? I answer: a day that reveals to him, more than all other days in the year, the gross injustice and cruelty to which he is the constant victim. To him, your celebration is a sham; your boasted liberty, an unholy license; your national greatness, swelling vanity; your sounds of rejoicing are empty and heartless; your denunciations of tyrants, brass fronted impudence; your shouts of liberty and equality, hollow mockery; your prayers and hymns, your sermons and thanksgivings, with all your religious parade, and solemnity, are, to him, mere bombast, fraud, deception, impiety, and hypocrisy.[10]

In Douglass's Myth of the Founding, America's national identity arises from the Declaration's axiom of universal human equality. Given that self-evident truth, to deny Negroes equality, you must deny they are human. But the denial is absurd on its face. And if Black people are human, there can be no argument about the wrong of slavery: "Would you have me argue that man is entitled to liberty? . . . You have already declared it." That Americans nevertheless license the holding of slaves "brands your republicanism as a sham, your humanity as a base pretense, and your Christianity as a lie." But Douglass's insistence on the primacy of the Declaration's principle of equality is linked to his espousal of American nationalism. "It destroys your moral power abroad; it corrupts your politicians at home." It robs the American example of its standing as a progressive alternative to European monarchism—a claim Lincoln would echo in his debate with Stephen Douglas.[11]

But in 1858 Lincoln was still struggling with the question of how to square the Declaration's doctrine of universal human equality with the problem of racial difference. That struggle would inform and complicate his debates with Douglas, and expose the complex play of ideas, beliefs, and interests that shaped Americans' understanding of their nationality.[12]

Lincoln and Douglas were both nationalists, believers in a strong and permanent union, in America as a rising power and the world's lone exemplar of republicanism after the failed European revolutions of 1848. Both believed in the Frontier Myth, which saw the opening of new territories as the promise of future prosperity to individual citizens and the nation as a whole. Douglas's approach was frankly imperialistic. He had supported the Mexican War (which Lincoln opposed) and was open to expansion into northern Mexico and the Caribbean—projects dear to Southerners seeking new frontiers for slavery. Lincoln's expansionism was limited to development of territories already acquired, and the core of his political platform was opposition to opening any new territory to slavery. But like Douglas, he saw the western territories as "an outlet for free *white* people everywhere . . . [to] find new homes and better their conditions in life."[13]

Throughout the Free States, dislike for slavery was typically matched with animus against Black people. This was especially true in Illinois and neighboring Indiana, whose legal codes barred settlement by free Black people and sharply limited the rights of those already in residence. The southern counties of Illinois, Indiana, and Ohio were settled by White farmers from Kentucky and Virginia, who had failed in economic competition with slave-labor plantations. Continued enslavement ensured that Black people could not migrate to the Free States to "degrade" the status and wages of White workers. Thus, while the vast majority of Free State voters disapproved of slavery, only a sliver of opinion favored abolition.

This state of public opinion complicated Douglas's defense of "popular sovereignty." He had to temporize between his constituents' demand for policies favoring White settlement and acknowledgment that settlers had as much right to vote slavery "up" as to vote it "down." It would also complicate Lincoln's rhetorical task. His main contention was that slavery was morally and politically wrong and inimical to the interests of free White farmers, and therefore should be banned from the territories. But he had also to take account of

Illinoisans' desire to keep their own state, and the new territories, "White." Like Taney in *Dred Scott,* both men were forced to look through questions of constitutional legalism to consider the underlying issue: How should racial difference affect the definition of American nationality, the nature of citizenship, and the understanding of human or natural rights? And how did the Founders understand these things?

It was Lincoln's contention that Douglas was, wittingly or not, part of a movement to make slavery national. The *Dred Scott* decision had prepared the way by forbidding Congress to ban slavery in the territories and declaring Black people could never be citizens. If the law considered Black people property, legally indistinguishable from livestock, how could a nation governed by a single constitution permit any state to forbid slavery? It followed that "this government cannot endure, permanently half *slave* and half *free.* . . . Either the *opponents* of slavery, will arrest the further spread of it, and place it where the public mind shall rest in the belief that it is in the course of ultimate extinction; or its *advocates* will push it forward, till it shall become alike lawful in *all* the States, *old* as well as *new—North* as well as *South.*"[14]

Douglas had a strong rejoinder: the nation had not only existed but prospered, half-slave and half-free. The genius of the Founders was reflected in the federal system, which allowed each state to shape its laws to local conditions. It was the abolitionists who wanted to nationalize *anti*slavery, and the Republicans abetted that movement by agitating the slavery question. The proper response was to "not care" about the issue. Let Maine grant voting rights to free Black people, let Illinois deny both the franchise and enslavement, and let Mississippi and South Carolina maintain slavery—without interference by other states or the federal government.

To Lincoln, Douglas's "don't care" was worse than outright advocacy of slavery, because it diminished popular belief in the Founding principles of republican government, embodied in the Declaration. In a democracy, "with public sentiment, nothing can fail; without it nothing can succeed. Consequently he who moulds public opinion goes deeper than he who enacts statutes or pronounces decisions." Douglas was using his "vast influence . . . to *educate* and *mould* public opinion . . . to not *care* whether slavery is voted *down* or voted *up.*" Lincoln was averse to passionate denunciation, but Douglas's words outraged him: "This *declared* indifference, but . . . covert *real* zeal for the spread of slavery, I cannot but hate." The grounds of Lincoln's outrage are close to those invoked by Frederick Douglass. Lincoln explains, "I hate it because of the monstrous injustice of slavery itself," but also because toleration of slavery "deprives our republican example of its just influence in the world—enables the enemies of free institutions . . . to taunt us as hypocrites—causes the real friends of freedom to doubt our sincerity."[15]

He then offers his own version of the Founding, which contradicts Taney's. In the time of the Founders, "our Declaration of Independence was held sacred by all, and thought to include all; but now, to aid in making the bondage of the negro universal and eternal, it is assailed, and sneered at, and construed, and hawked at, and torn, till if its framers could rise from their graves, they would not recognize it."[16] The Declaration was not the manifesto of a "merely national" movement but a revolutionary reconception of government and society. Its foundation was the "self-evident" truth that all humans are created equal in natural rights, including the right to govern themselves. The Founders did not suppose that, in their society, all men were in fact equal; nor would the Constitution make them so. But they offered the Declaration as "a standard maxim for free society which should be familiar to all: constantly looked to, constantly labored for, and even though never perfectly attained, constantly approximated and thereby constantly spreading and deepening its influence and augmenting the happiness and value of life to all people, of all colors, everywhere."[17]

In effect, Lincoln turns the Declaration into the basis of a new Myth of the Founding. Instead of being the merely rhetorical prelude to the establishment of constitutional government, Lincoln's Declaration provides an *action script* for the heirs of the Founders to follow as they develop the nation's vast moral and material potential. As president, Lincoln would make this version of the Myth of the Founding canonical—the Gettysburg Address would define the meaning of the Civil War, and of American history in general, as fulfillment of a Founding "dedicated to the proposition that all men are created equal."

But in 1858 Douglas saw this doctrine as Lincoln's most vulnerable point. Carry his interpretation of the Declaration to its logical conclusion and the document becomes a charter for racial equality. That idea was anathema North as well as South, and Douglas pounced on it. He accused Lincoln of favoring "nigger equality" and deployed the usual tropes of race-baiting: "I do not question Mr. Lincoln's conscientious belief that the negro was made his equal, and hence is his brother, [*laughter*] but . . . I do not regard the negro as my equal, and positively deny that he is my brother, or any kin to me whatever." He tied Lincoln to Frederick Douglass, whom he described driving about in a "magnificent carriage," loafing at his ease with a White woman at his side, while the carriage's White owner acted as driver—suggesting that abolition implied the reversal of social hierarchy and sponsorship of interracial sex. He affirmed Taney's opinion in *Dred Scott* that the Founders' Declaration referred only to "white men, men of European birth and European descent, and had no reference either to the negro, the savage Indians, the Fejee, the Malay, or any other inferior or degraded race, when they spoke of the equality of men." He stated, "I say to you, frankly, that in my opinion this government was made by our fathers on the white basis. It was made by white men for the benefit of white men and their posterity forever, and was intended to be administered by white men in all time to come."[18]

Douglas thus forced Lincoln to reconcile his adherence to White supremacy with his myth of the Declaration. By our standards, Lincoln was certainly a racist. He believed humankind was divided into distinct "types" endowed with particular "gifts." But this was an idea shared by nearly every one of Lincoln's contemporaries, including militant abolitionists like Theodore Parker and Harriet Beecher Stowe, and even African American leaders like Frederick Douglass and Martin Delany. The question to ask of a nineteenth-century American is not whether he or she was, by our standards, a racist, but what he or she made of that belief.

Lincoln was grappling with a fundamental problem in the current theory of liberal nationalism, which held that every "People"—that is, every "race"—was capable of self-government in a political state formed according to its preferences and predilections. In Europe, liberal nationalism envisioned states that united peoples sharing a common language and culture. But the American people already combined several different European races or ethnic strains. If these differences, significant enough to produce separate nations in Europe, could be blended, why should Black people and Indians *not* be assimilable? To argue that they could not or should not required that their human nature be either denied or found different in ways profoundly inimical to the body politic.

Lincoln's strongest antislavery argument was the assertion that, if left to grow, the slave system would someday be applied to poor White men like himself. That was only conceivable because, as he understood it, the differences between the two races were of less real importance than their common humanity. In private he mused, "Wherein lies the supposed right of one man to enslave another? . . . You say A. is white, and B. is black. It is *color* then . . . ? Take care. By this rule, you are to be slave to the first man you meet, with a fairer skin. . . . You mean the whites are *intellectually* the superior of Blacks? Take care again. By this rule you are to be slave to the first man you meet, with an intellect superior to your own." Lincoln treats racial differences as ephemeral: a *mere* difference in skin tone, a distinction in degrees of intelligence that might exist between any two people of any race.[19]

In his debates with Stephen Douglas, he had to pander to the prejudices of his audience. "I have no purpose to introduce political and social equality between the white and black races. There is a physical difference between the two, which in my judgment will probably forever forbid their living together upon the footing of perfect equality." But he does so in ways that call in question the meanings and importance assigned to racial difference. "I agree with Judge Douglas that [the Negro] is not my equal in many respects—certainly not in color, *perhaps* not in moral or intellectual endowment." The one difference he regards as undeniable is arguably the most trivial—the difference of color. The deeper difference, of morals and intelligence, he describes as possible, but not proved.[20]

While he insists on his personal opposition to the establishment of "political and social equality between the white and black races," he treats this as a necessary submission to the state of public opinion. "My own feelings will not admit of [equality]; and if mine would, we well know that those of the great mass of white people will not. Whether this feeling accords with justice and sound judgment, is not the sole question, if indeed it is any part of it. A universal feeling, whether well or ill-founded, cannot be safely disregarded." Moreover, the basis of that feeling, as Lincoln defines it, may boil down to simple self-interest, rather than natural law or moral principle:

Inasmuch as it becomes a necessity that there must be a difference, I, as well as Judge Douglas, am in favor of the race to which I belong, having the superior position.

Lincoln then challenges the prejudices of his audience:

Notwithstanding all this, there is no reason in the world why the negro is not entitled to all the rights enumerated in the Declaration of Independence, the right to life, liberty, and the pursuit of happiness. [*Loud cheers.*] I hold that he is as much entitled to these as the white man. . . . In the right to eat the bread, without leave of anybody else, which his own hand earns, *he is my equal and the equal of Judge Douglas, and the equal of every living man.*[21]

That was a tough line to take in a state that did not permit free Black people to settle.

However, as Douglas was quick to point out, if Black people were entitled to all the rights in the Declaration, they had a right to vote—to give or withhold their consent to be governed. Lincoln struggled with the problem of Black freedom in a White republic. Colonization? Perhaps the best solution, but a practical impossibility. "Free them all, and keep them among us as underlings," to compete with White people without the political rights they would need to protect themselves? "Is it quite certain that this betters their condition?" Gradual emancipation might work, if Southerners agreed—but Lincoln did not feel sure enough of the end or the method to recommend it. "If all earthly power were given me," he admitted, "I should not know what to do."[22]

But he *was* certain that the preservation of the American republic, and of its free institutions, depended on acceptance of the principle that slavery was practically and morally *wrong* and must be put in the way of "ultimate extinction." To deny that slavery is wrong is to nullify the Declaration's assertion of natural rights, the basis of free government. Nor could the freedom of free labor be guaranteed while slavery existed as an alternative organization of labor and capital. The slave owner's privilege was merely an expression of the privilege the wealthy and wellborn had always asserted over the laboring classes. To make his case, Lincoln again reverts to the Myth of the Founding, drawing a parallel between advocates of slavery and the royalist Tories who opposed America's independence. "It is the eternal struggle between these two principles—right and wrong—throughout the world. . . . The one is the common right of humanity and the other the divine right of kings. . . . It is the same spirit that says, 'You work and toil and earn bread, and I'll eat it.' . . . Whether from the mouth of a king . . . or from one race of men as an apology for enslaving another race, it is the same tyrannical principle."[23]

Lincoln's argument in the debates with Douglas brought him national attention and set him on the path to the presidency. His insistence that slavery be considered morally wrong, and put on the road to ultimate extinction, made him so inimical to Southern interests that the mere fact of his election would provoke the states of the Deep South to secede. Southern leaders agreed with Lincoln's insistence that "he who moulds public opinion goes deeper than he who enacts statutes or pronounces decisions." They read Lincoln's election as a sign that public opinion in the Free States was now so hostile to slavery that there was no safety for the South within the Union.

The crises of the 1850s had also driven Southern statesmen and opinion makers to reevaluate the fundamental bases and premises of American government. They increasingly relied on a racial defense of slavery, asserting that the institution was a "positive good" for both races. Some, like South Carolina's Calhoun and James Hammond, went further, to assert that inequality was a fundamental necessity of higher civilization—that the conditions of economic life required the subordination of the free laboring classes of the North to the will and purposes of capital. Their rationale justified Lincoln's belief that preservation of slavery would ultimately lead to the degradation of White labor. In practice, most Southern leaders still paid lip service to the democratic idea of civil equality for White people—a necessity, since their power required the support of the poor White majority. But that ideal of liberty remained an ideological conundrum for Southern political theory.[24]

Alexander Stephens of Georgia, vice president of the Confederacy and one of the chief authors of its constitution, would cut the Gordian knot that so bedeviled Lincoln. In his 1861 Cornerstone Speech, made in response to his state's secession, Stephens admitted that the Declaration had indeed asserted universal human equality, as Lincoln insisted—but Jefferson was simply wrong. The new light of science proved racial difference to be both real and determinative: "Our new Government is founded upon ideas exactly opposite to the Declaration of 1776; its cornerstone rests upon the great truth that the negro is not the equal of the white man; that slavery, subordination to the superior race, is his natural and moral condition. This, our new Government, is the first in the history of the world, based upon this great physical, philosophical, and moral truth."[25]

Thus the Confederacy embraced the logic of Douglas's "white basis," while Lincoln's Union government would continue to wrestle with the problem. In that sense, the Civil War was the Lincoln-Douglas debate carried on by other means.

The Secession Crisis: Constitutional Right or Revolutionary Act?

Southern secession and the Civil War that followed tested the mythic status of the Founding documents. Both sides appealed to the Constitution and the Declaration of Independence to justify their actions—and in the process exposed the contradictions inherent in them.

Southern secession was defended as a constitutionally legitimate exercise of states' rights; and after the war, Southern defenders of the Lost Cause—most notably ex-president Jefferson Davis and ex–vice president Alexander Stephens—would insist that slavery had had little to do with a movement whose main purpose was to vindicate the constitutional standing of states' rights. In fact, no one at the time doubted that the primary motive for the secession of the Deep South states was to protect slavery. That principle was affirmed at every state secession convention, and when the seceded states sent commissioners to ask the other Slave States to join them, their main argument was that only secession could guarantee the safety and permanence of slavery.[26]

But defense of the constitutionality of secession was important to the Southern cause because of the aura of sanctity that had formed around the document since Jefferson's time. Indeed, the Confederate constitution closely followed the original, reinforcing the secessionists' claim to be acting in defense of the Constitution's true principles. So while Southern radicals frankly embraced revolution, moderate and conservative secessionists sought constitutional cover.

The text of the Constitution ought to have deterred "strict constructionists" like Davis and Stephens, because it made no reference to any method by which a state could "constitutionally" leave the compact—though some states had rhetorically reserved that right at the time of ratification. Justice Joseph Story's "palladium theory" saw the 2nd Amendment as authorizing states to raise militias capable of resisting the central government should it become tyrannical. However, even under Story's interpretation, armed resistance would be the exercise of the Declaration's "right of revolution," rather than a constitutional or civil right.[27]

In his inaugural address, delivered in Montgomery on February 8, 1861, Davis justified secession by an appeal to the Declaration's inalienable "right of the people to alter or abolish governments whenever they become destructive of the ends for which they were established." The American government had become destructive when it committed "wanton aggression" against the rights of the Southern states. At the moment of his inauguration, that aggression was nothing more than the election of a moderate antislavery candidate in a free and fair election, so from a Northern perspective the accusation was absurd. But for the South, Lincoln's election marked a decisive antislavery shift in Northern public opinion, which would inevitably undermine or destroy the basic understandings and political balance of power that had protected the slave system. But Davis was unwilling to characterize the South's attempt to abolish its connection to the national government as a "revolution." He was careful to show that the South's appeal to the "right of revolution" was essentially conservative, because it preserved the existing social and legal order rather than overturning it. The right of the people to "resume the authority" delegated to the national government was in accordance with state laws, and within the seceding states "government has remained, the rights of person and property have not been disturbed." Thus "it is by abuse of language that their act has been denominated a revolution." Thus secession was, in historian James McPherson's view, a "pre-emptive counterrevolution" whose leaders must "exaggerate the magnitude and imminence of the revolutionary threat" to justify radical action.[28]

In practice, the Founders of the Confederacy followed the American Revolution's action script. They called "conventions" to decide on secession and form their confederacy, just as the Founders had done. As the war went on, it would become commonplace for Confederate leaders—even Davis and Stephens—to refer to their movement as "our revolution," and to associate their roles with those of Washington and Patrick Henry. This use of the Founding Myth had enduring cultural effects: reinforcing, from an eccentric angle, the sanctifying power of the documents and identifying the South as the defender of the traditions of the Founders' republic. The eccentricity of Confederate ideology was the coupling of its reliance on the Declaration's right of revolution with rejection of the concept of universal human rights as the basis of all just government.

Lincoln was somewhat more consistent. He conceded the South's right of revolution, as he was logically bound to do. The question he had to answer was whether, and on what ground, the government had a right to suppress such a revolution. He could and did appeal to the text of the Constitution: Article I, Section 10, forbade any state from assuming the rights of sovereignty—to "enter into any Treaty, Alliance, or Confederation; grant Letters of Marque and Reprisal; coin Money; emit Bills of Credit"; or the like. The Constitution also granted the executive power to suppress insurrection by force of arms.

But Lincoln rested his defense of the Union on deeper principles. In its careful delineation of electoral procedures, the Constitution implied that the free and fair election of officials was the central pillar of the republic. However, the moral significance of electoral liberty was most clearly asserted in the Declaration, which saw "the consent of the governed" as the basis of all just government. It followed that "when ballots have fairly, and constitutionally, decided [an issue], there can be no . . . appeal, back to bullets." Moreover, in Lincoln's view, an assertion of the right of revolution is subject to a moral judgment. The Southern revolution aimed to perpetuate and extend the scope of human enslavement. For Lincoln, the right of revolution only made moral sense if, as in 1776, it was asserted for "more than merely national" purposes—that is, for the furtherance of human freedom and political liberty.[29]

Lincoln's argument for Unionism thus posited an organic connection between the moral and revolutionary principles of the Declaration and the statutory structures of constitutional government. Its effect was to read the Declaration's assertions of human equality and consensual government into the Constitution. The action script derived from his Myth of the Founding required the transformation of constitutional government, and of American nationality, not merely their preservation. This transformation would culminate in the 13th, 14th, and 15th Amendments, which abolished slavery and made the federal government the guarantor of civil and voting rights for all races and classes of citizen—a transformation so substantial that it has been characterized as the "Second Founding."

But that vision was utterly at odds with the Southern version of American nationality. The bloodiest, costliest war in American history would barely suffice to resolve that difference.

PART II

Civil War Mythologies

3

Lincoln and Liberation

THE FIRST SHOT of the Civil War was fired on April 12, 1861, and the war has been seen as the defining crisis of American history ever since. Unionists and Confederates were in irreconcilable disagreement about slavery and freedom, nationality, and political rights. But they shared a belief most memorably voiced by Abraham Lincoln: that their "fiery trial" would determine the future of the nation, and perhaps of representative government itself; and that their thoughts and actions would be recalled, in pride or shame, down to "the latest generation."[1]

The passage of time has confirmed Lincoln's prophecy. Since 1865, in each generation and in all the genres of cultural production—histories, literature, folklore, music, film—the old, deadly conflicts have been replayed, often with a passion that implies that a better argument or new evidence could undo or somehow modify the verdicts of the battlefield. Each generation of newly born or newly made Americans is invited to engage with the tale of the war as a kind of initiation into the meaning of American history, and to imagine their place in that history and their connection to the unfinished business bequeathed by the heroic past.

But our American Passover (as Frederick Douglass called it) belongs not only to the people of the Exodus—the enslaved redeemed from bondage, the nation forged in struggle—but to the Egyptians, the masters defeated and despoiled. Our culture is rooted in enslavement as well as freedom. Our ancestry includes enslaved people and slave masters, resisters, and collaborators. Our political culture is still riven by disagreement over the purposes for which the national government can be used, and the division of power between the central government, the states, and the people. We have yet to resolve the contradiction between our belief in equality and the racism that slavery made endemic to our culture. The Civil War remains the symbol of these conflicts, so that more than a century and a half after the last shot was fired, conflicts over the meaning of its symbols—statues of its leaders, the Confederate battle flag—have become central to our political culture wars. Like it or not, Americans today are the heirs of the Union *and* the Confederacy.[2]

I was forcibly reminded of this while rewatching Ken Burns's *The Civil War,* first shown on public television in 1990. Forty million viewers followed the series, and it sparked a revival of interest in Civil War history. Burns cast several historians as interpreters of the events. The Southern perspective was voiced in a melodious drawl by novelist and historian Shelby Foote. In his commentary on the Battle of Gettysburg, he offered the following: "For every Southern boy, it's always in his reach to imagine it being one o'clock on an early July day in 1863, the guns are laid, the troops are lined up, the flags are already out of their cases and ready to be unfurled, but it hasn't happened yet. And he can go back in his mind to the time before the war was going to be lost and he can always have that moment for himself." What the "Southern boy" hopes for is the victory of the Confederacy, the breaking of the Union and the preservation of slavery. The sentiment was not Foote's alone: he was paraphrasing a passage from William Faulkner's *Intruder in the Dust* (1948) and echoing sentiments shared by generations of Southern writers.[3]

What is stunning is that Foote—and most of his viewers—seems blind to the fact that "every Southern boy" excludes the Black Southerners who form 30 to 40 percent of Foote's contemporaries. That kind of blindness is perhaps understandable in Faulkner, born and raised in the Jim Crow South. But Foote was speaking thirty-six years after *Brown v. Board of Education,* twenty-seven years after Bull Connor's police assaulted the protest march in Selma, twenty-five years after the Voting Rights Act finally put Jim Crow on what Lincoln would have called "the path to ultimate extinction." Is restoration of the White man's South the "unfinished business" that Foote's version of the myth of the Civil War calls us to complete?

Foote's Confederate nostalgia was offset by the reflections of African American historian Barbara Fields, who saw the Civil War as the start of a struggle for racial justice that remains America's very much unfinished business. "I think what we need to remember, most of all, is that the Civil War is not over until we, today, have done our part in fighting it . . . the Civil War is . . . still to be fought, and regrettably it can still be lost." In 2011, at the start of the Civil

War Sesquicentennial, Ta-Nehisi Coates took his son to Cemetery Ridge to imagine "Pickett's soldiers charging through history, in wild pursuit of their strange birthright—the right to beat, rape, rob, and pillage the black body." Coates sees the war as "the genesis of modern America" but observes that Black people see it as "a story for white people." He believes they need a deliberate act of imaginative engagement, "taking ownership of the Civil War as Our War."[4]

As a descendant of recent immigrants, I don't have the genetic tie to 1860s America that Faulkner and Foote, Coates, and Fields can claim. But when I was growing up I also felt the need to place myself imaginatively in the frame of the Civil War, as a way of affirming my identity as an American. On a family visit to Gettysburg when I was nine, my brother and I stood among the Union guns on Cemetery Ridge and imagined ourselves facing Pickett's Charge, fighting for freedom.

The hallmark of national myth is that we imaginatively enter its narrative and take upon ourselves the unfinished business of its heroes.

Three different mythic traditions contest the war's meaning, and Gettysburg is their point of symbolic intersection. The first of these is the Liberation Myth, which sees the Civil War as an ordeal of *regeneration through violence* that not only preserves "government of the people, by the people, for the people" but produces a "new birth of freedom" that now includes Black people formerly held as slaves. This Myth of Liberation would shape Reconstruction and continue to inform the efforts to build a multiracial democracy that waxed and waned over the next hundred years. The opposing version is the Southern Myth of the Lost Cause, which celebrates the traditional culture of the Old South and justifies violence to restore that culture and its social and racial hierarchy. A third alternative is the Myth of White Reunion, which sees the war as a conflict between kindred branches of the White race that are finally reunited through mutual recognition of each other's courage and devotion to their cause—minimizing the importance of slavery, emancipation, and Black claims to civic equality.

Gettysburg is where Lincoln and Robert E. Lee, the representative heroes of Union and Confederacy, touched the height of their legendary achievements. It is traditionally regarded as the place where the "Lost Cause" was lost, where Lee reached for final victory—and failed. It is where Lincoln's Gettysburg Address defined the Union victory as a triumph for "the proposition that all men are created equal." Finally, it is the place where, in 1913, veterans of blue and gray met in 1913 for ceremonial reconciliations that made literal the Myth of White Reunion.

The divergence of these three traditions reflects persistent and deeply rooted divisions in the culture of American nationality and patriotism. To appreciate their significance, we need to understand that the Civil War was above all a culture war.

Civil War as Culture War

The Civil War was the bloodiest and costliest war in American history—in proportion to population, it was one of the deadliest in world history. Out of a total population of some 34 million, as many as 750,000 people died as a result of military action. That leaves unaccounted the wounded, as well as the death and suffering caused by armies marching, looting, and fighting across half the country. For soldiers, the odds of surviving whole were poor. Most regiments lost one man in five to camp diseases before they ever saw action, and seriously wounded men had about a one-in-three chance of survival (if the wound could be treated by amputation). Infantry marched shoulder to shoulder into the sustained fire of rifle muskets and artillery, through kill zones 500 yards deep. Units that fought stubbornly sustained battle casualties of between 25 and 85 percent.[5]

By the end of the war's first year, these conditions were well understood by the rank and file. Nevertheless, the war was sustained through four terrible years by volunteer armies. The Confederacy adopted conscription during the first year of the war, and the Union some time later. But conscription was easily evaded, and for American soldiers fighting on American ground, desertion was relatively easy. In the third year of the war, the North held an election in which the question of whether to fight on or seek a negotiated peace was explicitly at issue. The North voted 55 to 45 percent for their war president, and the soldier vote—those who would do the fighting and dying—went strongly for Lincoln. The South affirmed its commitment to the struggle by enlisting some 80 percent of its military-age White manpower. Not until the last year of the war did discouraged Confederates desert in large numbers.

So we have to understand the Civil War as a "people's war," a war Americans chose to fight and willingly maintained despite the cost in blood, suffering, and treasure. They did so because the issues and interests at stake were ones they took deeply to heart. They thoroughly understood those issues, because they had been extensively and intensely debated for more than forty years, and especially in the ten years leading to Lincoln's election in 1860.

The crisis began as American nationalism reached a high pitch of enthusiasm. In 1850 the United States completed a seventy-five-year period of unparalleled growth in population, territory, and national power. Thirteen colonies had become twenty-nine states. Population had grown exponentially, from 4 million in 1775, to 23 million by 1850, and 34 million at the end of the decade. The nation had tripled its territory till it stretched from the Atlantic to the Pacific and from the Canadian border to the Rio Grande. The productivity of the agrarian economy—both Southern cotton and western food grains—made the United States a major factor in the world economy. Industrial and technological innovation were also on the rise, fueled by the growth of railroads—by 1860 the United States already led the world in railroad mileage. Pride in such national achievements was augmented by military success, most recently the Mexican War of 1846–1848, by which the nation acquired California and the Southwest. On a higher moral plane, Americans took pride in having created a uniquely successful model of republican democracy, which stood as an inspiration to the oppressed classes of the Old World and a terror to their aristocratic masters.[6]

But there were profound differences between the cultures of North and South, arising from the fact that slavery and the plantation system were the basis of Southern culture, society, and politics. Those differences would turn every element of their common culture into a ground of conflict.[7] Both sections adhered to the Myth of the Founding, but the South would find in it sanction for secession, the North for a war to enforce Union. Both saw the frontier as the key to a prosperous future, but desire to control that future would provoke the conflict.

North and South, White Americans shared the belief that the constitutional government established by the Founders was meant to be an instrument for ensuring justice, political rights, safety of property, and personal dignity. To the South, the election of a Republican antislavery president signaled that the people of the North intended to use the government to undermine and ultimately destroy the slave-based system of plantation agriculture on which their economy, culture, social order, and politics were built. A transformation to which they could not freely consent would be imposed on them. To accept that result, most felt, would be to acquiesce in their own "enslavement." There was a corresponding belief in the North, which saw the "Slave Power conspiracy" using its control of the Democratic Party, the presidency, and the Supreme Court to overrule the Northern voters who had legislated an end to slavery in the Free States. Secession, when it came, was seen by most as the last and most outrageous assault on Northern citizens' political rights—the use of violence to overturn a free and fair election.

These feelings, powerful enough in themselves, were intensified by the fears and antipathies attached to racial difference. In a nation half-slave and half-free, enslavement was more than a metaphor for a hateful condition of life; it was a living fact. To lose one's liberty, to have one's rights traduced *without political remedy*, was to fall into the condition of the Negro, to lose one's social and racial identity—to become less than human. Thus, on both sides, men were willing to kill and be killed to defend the fundamental ground of their identity, their personal and collective dignity—that is, their standing as free men.

By 1860 American nationality was divided into two distinctly different cultural forms, each coherent in itself. The society of the North and Northwest was "liberal" in the sense that it was devoted to individual liberty and an entrepreneurial economy of competition and innovation marked by social mobility and the "creative destruction" of market capitalism. The Free States had also experienced an age of reformist enthusiasm in matters both religious and secular: women's suffrage, bloomerism, vegetarianism, Perfectionism, prison reform, abolitionism. Southern churches rejected such breaks with orthodoxy. Between 1835 and 1845 the conferences of the three largest Protestant churches—Baptists, Methodists, and Presbyterians—split into Northern and Southern conferences over differences in interpreting the biblical approach to slavery. But the split also reflected a basic difference in culture. Southern society was oligarchic, hierarchic, patriarchal, hostile to social mobility. The maintenance of the South's plantation economy required stability and hierarchy, establishing the authority of the master class over both enslaved people and poor White people disadvantaged by the plantation system.

The cultural significance of Southern secession has been obscured by the constitutional and ideological questions raised by its defenders and opponents. In Chapter 4 we'll look more closely at the cultural basis of Southern nationalism. But the first myth to emerge from the Civil War was created by the victors, who saw it as a fiery ordeal through which the nation purged itself of the original sin of slavery, perfected its liberal regime, and emerged incomparably stronger.

The Liberation Myth: Through Violence, a New Birth of Freedom

The Union's military victory, the reestablishment of national government, and the transformative unmaking of the South's slavery-based social order was the work of a broad and varied alliance. Democrats hitherto supportive of Southern interests became "War Democrats" committed to defeating the Confederacy. Conservative and moderate Republicans who had opposed abolition would support the Emancipation Proclamation as a necessary war measure and ultimately embrace the abolition of slavery by the 13th Amendment. Black Americans, free and enslaved, gained political agency, as the federal government came to rely on Black military enlistments and the support of Black leaders like Frederick Douglass, and as the enslaved staged a nonviolent rebellion by deserting plantations en masse and fleeing to Union lines.

But in myth the forces of historical destiny and moral principle are personified by a hero, and Abraham Lincoln is unquestionably the personification of the Union cause in the Civil War. As president and party leader, his decisions produced the strategic combination of war and politics that won the war and transformed the republic. As a personality, Lincoln was also the representative man of free labor ideology. His rise from the "poor White" class to successful lawyer and then to president of the republic was a heroic enactment of the liberal principles of entrepreneurship, equality of opportunity, social mobility, and self-improvement. His career came to be seen as vindication of the democratic idea itself: the belief that in a republican system "an ordinary man of good will"—in Karl Marx's phrase—chosen from the common run of citizens was capable of rising to the demands of an extraordinary crisis.[8]

This view slights what were in fact Lincoln's extraordinary gifts as a thinker, a strategist, and a political leader. But the image of him as an "uncommon common man" is true to the narrative of his life and the sequence in which his character and gifts became visible to the public. When he became president, he had never managed anything larger than a country law office and his military experience was negligible. He was self-educated in history, political and military theory, and mathematics. He was admired among colleagues and rivals for his skill in debate and legal argument, but his debates with Stephen Douglas took those skills to a new level and made him a national figure. As president he would create and successfully manage a government bureaucracy and armed force of immense and unprecedented size, and he understood before most of his generals the strategy that would be needed to win the war. His presidential speeches and messages to Congress would prove effective in transforming public opinion and shaping congressional action, and they would ultimately be recognized as classic statements of American ideology.

"A patriot," Adrienne Rich has written, "is one who wrestles for the soul of her country / . . . as he wrestles for his own being." Lincoln has come to be seen as the hero of this version of Civil War mythology, because his personal struggle mirrors the travail of the nation as a whole: not a dispute over the legalisms of states' rights but a wrestling with the contradiction between American ideals of civic republicanism and human freedom, and its heritage of racial inequality, fear, and bigotry.[9]

Premonitions of his struggle to reconcile racial difference with democratic equality were clear in his debates with Douglas, in which he asserted the entitlement of Black people to all the rights in the Declaration of Independence but balked at the idea of political and social equality. The narrative arc of his struggle as president begins with his early determination to put saving the Union ahead of the slavery question and bow to the universal prejudice against Black citizenship. It moves through acceptance of emancipation as a necessary war measure to his growing recognition that Black people were entitled to citizenship, not only on the Declaration's philosophical grounds but as a right earned by their service to the Union on the battlefield. To be justified, the war would have to produce "a new birth of freedom," realizing more completely the ideals of the Declaration. Though his assassination would leave that project as unfinished business, his successors in Radical Reconstruction would attempt to realize that "new birth of freedom" in the series of constitutional amendments 13–15 that would make the central government guarantor of basic rights throughout the states.[10]

At the start of his administration, Lincoln faced a task of extraordinary difficulty and complexity. To meet the existential threat posed by secession, he had first to convince Northern opinion that the use of military force to restore the Union was necessary, desirable, and justified. He then had to create from scratch a military capable of conquering a politically unified Confederacy, holding territory equal in size to that of the Free States, with a population only slightly smaller.

A faction of the Northern Democrats, later dubbed Copperheads, took the Southern line on secession, and there was a faction of liberal opinion, given voice by abolitionist William Lloyd Garrison and the idealistic newspaperman Horace Greeley, who were glad to escape association with slavery and inclined to "let the erring Sisters go." Border state Democrats, and those who had supported Stephen Douglas's nomination against Southern opposition, were willing to compromise basic elements of the Constitution if that would call the seceders back. Though they chose, in the end, to support a war for the Union, they advocated a political-military strategy that would end the war by conciliating the South, leaving slavery intact. Within the president's own party there were significant divisions between the Radicals, who advocated a direct and immediate attack on slavery, and various groups of moderates and conservatives, whose anger at secessionists and Slave Power oligarchs was matched by their opposition to any form of racial equality.[11]

Lincoln began by defining the purpose of the war as restoration of the Union and vindication of the principles of republican government. On those grounds, his administration would have the broadest possible backing, excluding only outright partisans of the Southern cause and radical abolitionists. In the aftermath of the attack on Fort Sumter, Lincoln could rely on the outrage, felt by most Americans in the North and West, at the South's violent attack on the government. Secession offended their pride at belonging to a grand continental republic, exemplar of democracy to the world at large. It seemed a dictatorial act, in character for a set of people long regarded as "aristocratic," whose spokesmen had derided Northern workingmen as "mudsills" and "greasy mechanics."

Lincoln's first task was to harness these passions and give them a coherent political direction. His first line of argument was legal: that the Constitution made the Union "perpetual" and did not protect a "right of secession." He could also cite the sanctity of free elections, expressing "the consent of the governed," as enshrined in the Constitution, as the basis of free government: "When ballots have fairly, and constitutionally, decided, there can be no successful appeal, back to bullets." If the South was allowed to nullify his election by resorting to arms, elections would become meaningless, democratic government impossible, and the people would be left to choose between dictatorship and "anarchy." To vindicate a free election, and the dignity of the voting public, a republican government was morally entitled to suppress revolution.[12]

But Lincoln did not, in this phase of the war, take the next step and argue that the South's revolution was unjustified because it was undertaken to deprive Black people of life, liberty, and the pursuit of happiness. He needed to retain the loyalty of Unionists in the slave-owning border states of Delaware, Maryland, Kentucky, and Missouri, and to conciliate the racial animus of western Unionists, who wanted to keep freed Black people from living in their states or taking up land in the western territories. That animus was openly expressed by Copperheads, by Democrats in general, and by Republicans like Montgomery Blair—cabinet member and scion of a powerful political family—who wanted to defeat the South, and even abolish slavery, but still "preserve this exclusive right of franchise in the white race." In 1862 a Republican-majority Congress passed the Homestead Act, fulfilling the party's pledge to open the western territory to free farmers, but barring Black people from taking up homestead land.[13]

For the first eighteen months of his administration, Lincoln walked softly on the slavery question. He agreed to the Congressional Confiscation Acts, making it legal for the government to seize the slave property of those in active rebellion, but this was clearly a war measure and not a principled call for abolition. In public he insisted that preservation of the Union was his primary objective. As he stated in his letter to Horace Greeley, editor of the *New-York Tribune,*

> My paramount objective in this struggle *is* to save the Union, and is *not* either to save or to destroy slavery. If I could save the union without freeing *any* slave I would do it; and if I could save it by freeing *all* the slaves I would do it; and if I could save it by freeing some and leaving others alone I would also do that. What I do about slavery and the colored race, I do because I believe it helps to save the Union; and what I forbear, I forbear because I do *not* believe it would help save the Union.

In fact, as he penned this response to Greeley, Lincoln had already decided to take the radical step of issuing the Emancipation Proclamation, freeing the slaves in all territories controlled by rebel governments.[14]

Lincoln held to the conviction he had reached in the mid-1850s—that the solidarity of the Union and the freedom of White labor would always be endangered by the perpetuation of slavery. His abiding impulse was to persuade slaveholders to consent to emancipation. He proposed a plan for gradual, compensated emancipation to officials from the border states, but they refused to consider it. If these friends of the Union, whose investment in slavery was limited, would not consider ending the institution, what hope was there that the Confederate states could be "conciliated" by such a policy?

By the summer of 1862, Lincoln came to see that the Southern people's commitment to secession was far stronger than he had believed. Confederate resistance had strengthened in response to the North's initial wave of military offensives, and in the summer of 1862 Confederate armies staged a set of counteroffensives that threatened to reverse all the Union's gains, capture the border states, and win foreign recognition. Although these initiatives were defeated, they demonstrated the South's powers of resistance. If the South could be neither conciliated nor rapidly defeated, Lincoln concluded, then the Union war effort would have to be reconfigured to sustain a "remorseless revolutionary struggle" with total victory as its objective. The signature of that new strategy would be issuance of the Emancipation Proclamation, freeing all slaves held in Confederate territory and establishing a precedent for general abolition. Its import was marked by the declaration that those liberated by the proclamation were "now, henceforward, and forever free." By embracing the enlistment of Black soldiers, the proclamation gave Blacks a civil right they had hitherto been denied. Frederick Douglass understood the significance of that act: "Once let the black man get upon his person the brass letter, U.S., let him get an eagle on his button, and a musket on his shoulder and bullets in his pocket, there is no power on earth that can deny that he has earned the right to citizenship."[15]

It was a radical move, amounting to the wholesale confiscation of perhaps $4 billion in legal property, about one-quarter of the total national wealth. If adhered to as policy, it would make conciliation and peaceful compromise impossible. It was a decision that would be wrathfully opposed by a large section of Northern and western opinion. More dangerously, it would be opposed by General George McClellan, commander of the Army of the Potomac and symbolic leader of conservative Democratic opposition to Lincoln, who had made his army into something like a Praetorian Guard, the staff of which talked freely of "a change of front on Washington"—in other words, a coup.[16]

Lincoln accepted the risks, because he believed in the absolute necessity of the measure—first as an aid to mobilizing Union morale, but ultimately because it was the first step to guaranteeing the "ultimate extinction" of slavery itself, without which military victory would be meaningless, and the Union permanently unstable. As he would tell Congress, "In *giving* freedom to the *slave,* we *assure* freedom to the *free*—honorable alike in what we give, and what we preserve." He would reframe the war as a national struggle for spiritual regeneration, the success or failure of which would determine not only America's future but the world's hope for free governments. As he said in his 1862 message to Congress: "The fiery trial" would "light us down, in honor or dishonor, to the latest generation. . . . We—even *we here*—hold the power and bear the responsibility. . . . We shall nobly save, or meanly lose, the last, best hope of earth."[17]

Lincoln thus made the war the basis of a new national myth, built on the old structure of *regeneration through violence.* He would give it its most eloquent statement at Gettysburg, when he called on his hearers to affirm "that we here highly resolve that these dead shall not have died in vain—that this nation, under God, shall have a new birth of freedom—and that government of the people, by the people, for the people, shall not perish from the earth."[18] Lincoln's new myth would belong to the Union as a whole. When he praises the nation, he does not exclude Southern White people from its heritage of liberty and history of achievement. In condemning slavery as a moral evil, he

acknowledges the whole nation's complicity in its establishment and maintenance. In his second inaugural address in March 1865, he told his hearers,

> If we shall suppose that American Slavery is one of those offences which,
> in the providence of God, needs must come, but which . . . He now wills
> to remove, and that he gives to both North and South, this terrible war,
> as the woe due to those by whom the offence came, shall we discern
> therein any departure from those divine attributes which the believers in
> a Living God always ascribe to him?

But to realize that transfigured Union, the God of Justice demands a blood
sacrifice:

> If God wills that it continue, until all the wealth piled by the bond-man's
> toil shall be sunk, until every drop of blood drawn with the lash, shall be
> paid by another drawn by the sword . . . so still it must be said, "the judg-
> ments of the Lord are true and righteous altogether."[19]

Although the sacrifice of wealth is chiefly borne by Southerners, the sacrifice
of blood is borne by *both* sides. In Lincoln's myth, as in Hebrews 9:22, "without
shedding of blood there is no remission [of sin]"—although in the end there
may be peace, "with malice toward none, with charity for all."

If service and sacrifice are the actions through which the nation is to be regenerated, then all who make the sacrifice are entitled to an equal place in the
nation. In a letter to James Conkling, a strong Unionist who opposed the
Emancipation Proclamation, Lincoln linked a restatement of his doctrine, that
free elections are the sine qua non of democracy, with a comparison between
the sacrifices of Black troops and the refusal of "conservative" Whites to fight
an emancipation war:

> I hope [peace] will come soon, and come to stay; and so come as to be
> worth the keeping in all future time. It will then have been proved that
> among free men, there can be no successful appeal from the ballot to the
> bullet; and that they who take such appeal [will] . . . pay the cost. And
> then, there will be some black men who can remember that, with silent
> tongue, and clenched teeth, and steady eye, and well-poised bayonet, they
> have helped mankind on to this great consummation; while, I fear, there
> will be some white ones, unable to forget that, with malignant heart, and
> deceitful speech, they have strove to hinder it.[20]

Lincoln was hardly the only public man to articulate this vision of national regeneration, rooted in the rhetoric and practices of Protestant conversion—Frederick Douglass had been advocating it for twenty years—but he was its most eloquent White spokesperson, and the only one at the center of the national stage. Through his rhetoric, which reached a large public thanks to national media, and through the circulation of his image in lithograph and photograph, Lincoln not only authored the myth, he came to personify it: first as its prophet, and finally as the martyr who sealed his prophecy with his own sacrifice of blood.

Instead of bringing closure to the myth, his death leaves us with the greatest "might-have-been" in American history. Had he lived, would he have managed the Reconstruction of the Southern states in such a way that a genuine multiracial democracy would have emerged—or at least that the horrors of Jim Crow would have been avoided, and race relations established on a more equitable basis?

There is no answer to this question. Lincoln had been slow to accept the idea that it was both right and necessary that Negroes should achieve self-government as Americans, rather than as "colonists" in Africa or the Caribbean. We may guess, from his letter to Conkling and other statements, that he wished to see the extension of civil rights and the franchise to Blacks—but whether universally and immediately, or gradually and limited to veterans or the "highly intelligent," is uncertain. From his statements and past practice, we can guess that he hoped to ease the transition to equality by winning the consent of Southern political leaders and their constituents, and that he would employ a mixture of persuasion, guile, and coercion to win that consent. He would certainly have supported the 14th and 15th Amendments, which established a constitutional basis for the extension of civil and voting rights. But how militant, how forceful—how effective—would he have been in enforcing those rights against the opposition of the White South? The questions remain open, the basis for an unending play of imagination as we pursue the unfinished business of our history.

Reconstruction as the Second Founding

Lincoln's assassination removed the one figure whose prestige and commanding intelligence made him capable of managing the complex process of political reunion and social reconstruction. Instead of continuity in the transition from war to peace, the nation experienced a traumatic disruption when power devolved on Vice President Andrew Johnson. The choice of Johnson as running mate was perhaps the worst decision of Lincoln's presidency. As a senator from Tennessee, Johnson was the highest-ranking Southern Democrat to support the Union cause. But he lacked the political acumen he needed as the Democratic president of a Republican administration and Congress. He was also a viciously bigoted White supremacist who found his most natural allies in ex-Confederates, Democratic "conciliators," and Republicans like the Blairs who wanted to preserve White supremacy in the absence of slavery. His efforts to enfranchise ex-Confederates as rapidly as possible, and his opposition to efforts on behalf of the freedpeople, encouraged Southerners to resist the social and political consequences of emancipation. Legislatures run by ex-Confederates enacted "Black Codes" designed to hold Black people on the plantations where they had been slaves. Vigilante posses, successors of the prewar slave patrols, resorted to violence to intimidate Black people when they sought civil rights or tried to bargain for better wages. In 1866 and 1867 there were major outbreaks of mass violence in Memphis and New Orleans, forerunners of the racial massacres that would later be called "race riots."

All of this produced a powerful reaction in a North still angry at the South for imposing a bloody war on the nation. Though they failed to impeach Johnson, Radical Republicans in Congress succeeded in discrediting his policies. When General Ulysses S. Grant was elected president in 1868, they instituted the programs that have come to be called Radical Reconstruction, which they represented as the fulfillment of Abraham Lincoln's vision of "a new birth of freedom."

The most lasting contribution of the Radicals was the passage of three constitutional amendments that transformed the nature of federalism by making the central government the guarantor of civil rights and rejected the principle of racial exclusion. The concept of human rights developed in these amendments proved to be far in advance of what the culture was ready to embrace. It would take a century for such principles as equal access to public facilities, voting rights, and equal treatment under law to be fully recognized and made enforceable. Nevertheless, the changes in government structure, public policy, and ideological values were so fundamental that they can be considered (in Eric Foner's words) a "second founding."[21]

The 13th Amendment, ratified in 1865, abolished slavery or "involuntary servitude" except as punishment for a crime. It made permanent the freedom granted to Confederate-held slaves by the Emancipation Proclamation and extended it to enslaved people held in states or counties that had stayed with the Union or been occupied by its forces in January 1863. The 15th Amendment, ratified in 1870, forbade states or the federal government to deny the right to vote to any citizen on account of race, color, or prior condition of servitude. It was a direct response to attempts by Southern "Redeemers" to suppress the votes of freedpeople or to disenfranchise them.

The 14th Amendment, which became law in 1868, was the most complex and consequential. Its first section contained three clauses. The Citizenship Clause broadened the definition of citizenship to include all people born or naturalized in the United States, without regard to race or national origin. It thus nullified the *Dred Scott* decision, which had declared Negroes ineligible for citizenship. It also established the principle of "birthright citizenship," which remains one of the most liberal standards in the world. The Due Process Clause prohibited state and local governments from depriving anyone of life, liberty, or property without due process of law. This in effect made the federal Bill of Rights applicable to the states. The Equal Protection Clause required the states to protect the legal rights of all people in their jurisdiction, whether citizens of that state or of other states or noncitizens. The two latter clauses were intended to protect freedpeople in states where Southern opponents of Reconstruction sought to create legal barriers to their exercise of civil rights. Their effect was to broaden the scope of civil rights generally, and to empower the federal government as guarantor of those rights should a state fail in that respect. As law professor Garrett Epps has said, the heart of the 14th Amendment "is the idea that citizenship in the United States is *universal*—that we are one nation, with one class of citizens, and that citizenship extends to everyone born here. Citizens have rights that neither the federal government nor any state can revoke at will; even undocumented immigrants—'persons,' in the language of the amendment."[22]

Congress also created the Freedmen's Bureau, which became the first, and one of the largest, social service programs in American history. It began with the limited charter of aiding Black refugees who had fled plantations during the war and were now homeless and jobless, and it was reorganized in 1867 to provide a broad range of social and political services. It ran schools and helped reunite families that had been separated by slave sales or by the disruptions of war. It provided legal aid for Black people in court cases and supported the efforts of Republican politicians to enroll them as voters and eventually office seekers.

Some of the more radical Radicals hoped to transform Southern society by a massive program of land reform that would break up big plantations and distribute the land to poor Black and White people—the proverbial "forty acres and a mule." Its advocates hoped this Southern version of homesteading would turn the South into a biracial version of the free-labor agrarian paradise Lincoln had envisioned for the western territories. The schools developed by the bureau, and by Republican-led state governments, would provide the South with its first system of public education—a lasting benefit to White and Black people alike. Thanks to the war, the North was more than ever a business-oriented society, and plantations producing staple crops for market were too productive, too profitable to be abandoned in favor of small family farms. So in the end the bureau helped planters (prewar magnates as well as new investors from the North) get back in business and encouraged Black people to stay on the land and work for wages. Its officers did try to act as bargaining agents to obtain fair pay for their clients, and Congress also chartered the Freedmen's Bank as a vehicle to encourage savings and provide mortgages, though the dream of owning land was nearly impossible to achieve.

There was simply no precedent in American history, or indeed in world history, for such a massive program of social engineering. Nothing in American political ideology envisioned or justified federal intervention in directing the civil affairs of a state. The legal and institutional structures had to be invented; the only available models were Lincoln's exercise of war powers and the massive military organization developed during the war. High taxes were required to support these activities, and these were resented by Northern businesspeople as well as Southern planters. Inefficiencies and corruption were inevitable, as they had been in Union war procurement. Reconstruction governments would become notorious for political corruption, although in that respect they were no worse than most governments, state or federal, in what would become known as the Gilded Age.[23]

The political basis of Reconstruction had certain inherent weaknesses. It required that Republicans retain control of Southern state governments, and that Congress sustain those governments against the organized, and often violent, opposition of Southerners bent on "Redeeming" the old order. That opposition inevitably grew in strength as the restoration of political rights brought more and more ex-Confederates back into politics. Republican control of Southern state legislatures depended on the leadership of Northern émigrés— ministers, civil servants, entrepreneurs—dubbed "carpetbaggers" by Southerners who resented them as bullying outsiders. These Northerners were seconded by a minority of native Southerners, including Confederate notables like General James Longstreet—some mere opportunists, others convinced that the South needed to modernize, all dubbed "scalawags" by resentful ex-Confederates. Ultimately, the Republican state governments had to rely for protection on military force. They organized militias that enrolled large numbers of Black people, as well as Whites sympathetic to their cause. But faced with extreme and rising tides of violence after 1869, they had to call on federal occupation forces, which were provided by the Regular Army until 1875.

Northern support for military occupation, and for large-scale emergency interventions, was weakened by political divisions, by Northern racism, and by a gradual shift in public concern from reconstructing the South to dealing with the problems of the emerging industrial economy. In contrast, the Southern opponents of Reconstruction, often identified as Redeemers, were single-minded in their drive to vindicate the "Lost Cause" of the Confederacy by restoring the patriarchal "paradise" of antebellum days. They would succeed, at terrible cost to the freedpeople, the South, and the nation as a whole.

4

Confederate Founding

Civil War as Culture War

THE SOUTH's decision to secede was driven by the conviction that only the achievement of national independence could save its distinctive culture and social order from eventual destruction. The strength of Southern resistance through four years of war, and the bitter persistence with which White Southerners fought to restore and maintain their power and authority, testify to the strength of that conviction. They therefore saw secession as a reprise of the Myth of the Founding: the assertion of a distinct nationality, different in cultural, social, and political essentials from the rest of the United States.[1]

The Primacy of Slavery

In the cotton-producing states of the Lower South, slave labor was the bedrock of production, and investment in slaves the lion's share of capital assets. Even in the mixed economies of the Upper South, property in slaves constituted a preponderant share of private wealth. The commissioner sent by South Carolina to persuade Virginia to secede stated the case in the simplest terms: "The South cannot exist without African slavery. . . . None but an equal race can labor at the North; none but a subject race will labor at the South." South Carolina's William Henry Trescot, a distinguished public official, put the case succinctly. Slavery, he said, "informs all our habits of thought, lies at the basis of our political faith and of our social existence. In a word, for all that we are, we believe ourselves, under God, indebted to the institution of slavery—for a national existence, a well ordered liberty, a prosperous agriculture, an exulting commerce, a free people and a firm government."[2]

The fundamental principle of Southern social order was the division of Black and White, slave and free, into different orders of humanity, one of which must be absolutely subservient to the other. That principle was defined by Justice Thomas Ruffin of the North Carolina Supreme Court in a precedent-setting 1829 case, which denied an enslaved woman the right to sue the man who had "rented" and severely abused her. Ruffin found that civil law could not intervene between master and slave without impairing the master's authority, which would endanger public safety. The slave, he wrote, is one doomed

> in his own person, and his posterity, to live without knowledge, and without the capacity to make anything his own, to toil that another may reap the fruits. . . . [He] surrenders his will in implicit obedience to that of another. Such obedience is the consequence only of uncontrolled authority over the body. . . . The power of the master must be absolute, to render the submission of the slave perfect. . . . The slave, to remain a slave, must be made sensible, that there is no appeal from his master; that his power is in no instance, usurped; but is conferred by the laws of man at least, if not by the law of God.[3]

Southern law gave the plantation owner an almost absolute right to exploit the bodies and labor of enslaved people by whatever means he or she thought necessary, to determine how much sustenance the enslaved would receive, under what conditions they would live and labor, how much free time they might enjoy and how they might enjoy it, and whether they would be permitted to marry or conduct religious services. To enforce labor discipline, the master was free to impose punishments including whipping, branding, mutilation, close confinement, chaining, and binding. Since plantations of any considerable size were necessarily far from each other and from towns, and the master's family and White servants were greatly outnumbered by Black people, masters also had to wield the threat of severe punishment and death for defiance or disobedience, which might be inflicted by overseers or by "slave patrols"—militias or posses of poor White people empowered to chastise or kill recalcitrant or errant Black people.

While the entire South had an interest in slavery, that interest was radically different in the Confederacy's various subregions, and rich and poor had very different kinds of stakes in the system. In the cotton states of the Deep South, politics were quasi-oligarchic and the social order was dominated by planters who owned large estates and hundreds of slaves. In the Upper South states of Virginia, Maryland, Kentucky, North Carolina, and Missouri, there was greater economic diversity, and while wealthy planters were powerful, their influence was offset by other interest groups, including small farmers, tradespeople, and manufacturers. The vast majority of Southern White people were small farmers who owned no slaves and competed with planters over land, taxation, and the funding of internal improvements. They consequently resented the economic advantages and political privileges enjoyed by planters. Nevertheless, they had an economic and cultural investment in slavery. Enslaved Black people could never compete with them for farmland and had limited roles in manufacturing, mining, and railroad building; and Whites enjoyed a social status and dignity absolutely denied to Black people.

Southerners had their own version of the Myth of the Frontier. The cotton South was developed by planters who realized a bonanza by driving Native tribes off the rich lands of the Black Belt. The labor through which they exploited that land was, by their lights, also "natural" rather than "human." Black people, like Indians, belonged to the wild rather than the civilized world. Negro slavery thus appeared to enable economic development without the proletarianization of White people. In the early development of the Black Belt, frontier conditions allowed both yeoman farmers and small-scale planters to acquire land and slaves and gain greater wealth and social status. But by the 1840s the dominance of large plantations limited yeoman opportunities in the settled states, and the depletion of the soil by cotton cultivation made Southerners look to expand their economy into the western territories, or to the weak states of northern Mexico and Central America. The frustration of those ambitions would become a motive for secession.

The Plantation Order: Patriarchy and Capitalism

Defense of an order based on racial slavery ultimately required rejection of the premises of democratic government and the cultural liberalism that prevailed outside the South. Free States cultivated individualism, competition, social mobility, and intellectual innovation. Slave State society was hierarchical, and its prime requisite was stability. George Fitzhugh, a Virginia lawyer and pioneering social scientist, provided the most systematic description and defense of its sustaining ideology in a series of books and articles, beginning in 1845 with *Sociology for the South, or the Failure of Free Society*—which introduced "sociology" as the name for a field of study. Fitzhugh idealized the South's social order as familial and patriarchal, in contrast to "free society," which "chills, stunts, and eradicates" human sympathy and promotes social conflict by fostering competition. In free society, those in subordinate positions contend for power; those with wealth and status resist like tyrants. But Southern society is ordered as a family, the most "natural" of human relations, with the plantation master presiding over all as kindly patriarch. "Is not the head of a large family always kind and benevolent?" Fitzhugh asked rhetorically. "And is not the slaveholder the head of the largest family? Nature compels master and slave to be friends; nature makes employers and free laborers enemies." But the "love" that binds patriarch and family is conditioned on subordination: "A man loves his children because they are weak, helpless and dependent. He loves his wife for similar reasons. When his children grow up and assert their independence, he is apt to transfer his affections to his grand-children. He ceases to love his wife when she becomes masculine or rebellious."[4]

Fitzhugh went on to explain that because "slaves are always dependent [they are] never the rivals of their master. Hence, though men are often found at variance with wife or children, we never saw one who did not like his slaves." Actually, there is ample testimony that slave owners did not like their slaves but were in fact repelled, disgusted, or frightened by them. Even when not physically or sexually abusive, planters ignored or neglected their personal hardships. And the enslaved often showed their "ingratitude" by exhibiting recalcitrant behavior, by running away, or by committing acts of vandalism and violence, which transformed the master's racial contempt into active hatred. But Fitzhugh's fiction was vital to his and his people's imagining of a distinctive Southern national character. "We are better husbands, better fathers, better friends," he concluded, "and better neighbors than our Northern brethren."[5]

The belief that the plantation system was an alternative to capitalist economics, based on mutual obligation rather than wage contracts, was central to the South's emerging sense of national distinction. In fact, despite their substitution of slave for wage labor, planters—like Northern bankers, merchants, and industrialists—were engaged in capitalist development: seeking better returns on investment, working to expand resources and markets, manipulating taxes and tariffs to benefit their enterprises. Slavery did oblige them to provide food and shelter for workers who were not yet (or no longer) productive. But it also enabled them to exploit their workers without having to bargain for services or respect regulations imposed by free-labor governments. In the end, a system supposedly designed to preserve and enlarge familial relations reduced those relations to the purely commercial. Slaves were property. Slave families were often broken up by sale, a procedure not subject to legal regulation though sometimes checked by community disapprobation.[6]

In defending slavery, Southern spokesmen like John C. Calhoun and Jefferson Davis appealed not to precapitalist values as Fitzhugh did but to an extreme assertion of the rights of property. In a nation governed by one set of laws, the law of property must be universal. By what principle of law, Davis asked, "does this Government get the right to ask a citizen what he is going to do with his property" or interfere with "the right of possession and transit with such property?" According to this view, "your socialist is the true abolitionist," because to deny any property right is to deny them all.[7]

What Southerners rejected was not capitalism as such, but the freewheeling version practiced elsewhere in America: a capitalism that privileged competition over consolidation, the "creative destruction" of market-driven innovation, and the agitation and overturning of traditional hierarchies by social mobility. The South's imperative was preservation of its established hierarchies and the culture that sustained them. That required the preservation at any cost of traditional forms of production. Southern plantation owners extrapolated from slave-master relations a general model of class relations, in which capital or ownership must always be politically privileged, and labor entirely subordinate to it.

This was the doctrine that led historian Richard Hofstadter to describe Calhoun as "the Marx of the Master Class."[8] Its principles were most famously stated by Senator James Hammond (D-SC) in his famous "mud-sill speech" of 1858: "In all social systems there must be a class to do the menial duties, to perform the drudgery of life . . . requiring but a low order of intellect and but little skill. Its requisites are vigor, docility, fidelity. Such a class you must have, or you would not have that other class which leads progress, civilization, and refinement. It constitutes the very mud-sill of society and of political government." The "mud-sill" is the packed-dirt base on which a simple cabin is built, so to describe a class as a mud-sill denies its pretension to dignity. In the North, the mud-sill class are "white and free." It is a rebuke to Northern men of property that they oppress those who are their equals by civil and natural right. It is also dangerous: they oppress those who "share your racial endowment, and are capable or resenting subjection. . . . If they knew the tremendous secret, that the ballot box is stronger than 'an army with banners,' and could combine, . . . [your] society would be reconstructed, your government overthrown, your property divided." Southern society, he concluded, is both sounder and more just. Southern mud-sills are "Negro and Slave . . . [for] Blacks, slavery is an 'elevation'" rather than grounds for resentment. As for nonslaveholding White people, as Governor Joe Brown of Georgia put it, they belonged to "the only true aristocracy, the aristocracy of white men."[9]

Hammond's ideology anticipates the "plutocratic populism" of the modern Right, assigning the highest value and power to the holders of wealth, which poor or working-class White people will accept so long as their superiority to non-White people is guaranteed. The planter aristocracy's abiding fear was that poor White discontent might lead them to refuse to support the slave system. Planters depended on poor White people for the slave patrols that kept the enslaved under control. The Confederacy would rely on that same class to supply its armies.

Race War: The Nightmare of Southern Nationalism

Far from being peaceable kingdoms, plantations were haunted by fear that resistance to harsh labor conditions and poor food could cripple productivity— or even lead to violence. Planters and overseers were relatively isolated in country houses, surrounded and outnumbered by slaves. There were notorious cases of murder or poisoning (real and suspected) by slaves acting from pure resentment rather than any realistic hope of escaping sale or punishment. Such fears could be used to justify the violence of discipline enforced by masters or slave patrols, as well as the profound break with basic republican ideals of "equal justice under law" signaled by Justice Ruffin's decision.

This fear of local acts of individual violence had a basis in reality, but it masked a deeper fear: that of a mass uprising of the enslaved followed by a "war of races." As early as 1784 Thomas Jefferson had opposed abolition on the ground that hostility between the races—based on remembered grievances and differences in nature—would lead to "convulsions . . . ending in the extermination of one or the other race."[10] The slave regime had grown harsher and more extensive since 1784, and the harsher the regime, the more plausible the fear of racial revenge. The Haitian Revolution, which lasted from 1791 to 1804, was a terrifying example of cataclysmic racial uprising, and its outbreak was attributed to dissemination of the French Revolution's democratic ideology. Egalitarian ideas had played a role in Gabriel's Rebellion in 1802 in Virginia and in Denmark Vesey's Rebellion of 1822 in South Carolina. From the planters' point of view, any movement that questioned the validity of slavery threatened the regime of laws and customs that protected their community. It followed that the free discussion and publication of ideas, which characterized Northern society, must be repressed in the South.

The planters' fear of an uprising by the enslaved was genuine, and would rise to a critical level in response to John Brown's raid on Harpers Ferry in 1859, which was intended as the prelude to such a rising. However, during the 1850s Southern spokesmen also believed that an American race war would follow a course opposite from Haiti's. Although Whites would suffer murder and outrage, it was the Blacks who would be exterminated. Fitzhugh wrote, "[The negro's] lot is cast among the Anglo-saxon race . . . [with its] adventurous, rapacious, exterminating spirit. Can the negro live . . . under the shade of this Upas tree, whose deadly poison spares no other race?" During the Civil War, Jefferson Davis would describe the Emancipation Proclamation as "a measure by which several millions of human beings of an inferior race, peaceful and contented laborers in their sphere, are doomed to extermination." The maintenance of slavery was, in this view, a guarantee against Black genocide.[11]

To carve out an exception to the ethical imperatives of democratic republicanism, Southerners had to see Black people as less than human, unworthy of empathy, let alone respect, a superior but problematic kind of livestock. A pervasive psychology of racial contempt was encapsulated in the word "nigger." That racial contempt, and the social institutions that enforced it, was not the spontaneous product of White-Black interaction but the creation of a cultural order developed over many generations.

In the colonial and early national periods, Black slaves were often manumitted or freed, and some became freeholders and even slave owners themselves. There was a considerable population of free Negroes, especially in Louisiana, in border states like Maryland and Kentucky, and in Upper South states like Virginia, but as the cotton boom of the early nineteenth century expanded the plantation system to the Southwest and increased the demand for slave labor, planters became fearful of the effect free Blacks might have on plantation discipline. This led the Slave States to severely restrict or forbid manumission and require freedpeople to leave the state. Thus the tendency of the Southern regime was to demand homogeneity: all slaves are Black, and all Blacks are slaves.

The cotton bonanza had created a demographic time bomb, by increasing the demand for slaves in the cotton states, with the result that Black majorities either existed or were imminently expected across the Deep South. If slavery were barred from the western territories, and Free-Soil politics prevented the acquisition of new lands apt for plantation agriculture, White people might be overwhelmed by Black supermajorities. The South, according to Florida senator David Yulee's 1850 speech, would have to choose between sending "the black race . . . out as emigrants," at tremendous pecuniary loss, "or the whites must, by an equally sure and progressive process, emigrate," leaving their societies to be replaced by Black ones.[12]

The common belief at the root of these imagined scenarios is that without the racial order imposed by slavery, Southern society would dissolve in genocidal violence, which, if it did not exterminate the master class, would wipe out the labor on which its mastery depended. It is vital to note that the three perils Southern leaders invoked in defense of their institutions remain the staples of the White supremacist imagination, most recently manifest in the rhetoric of the Proud Boys and various MAGA spokespeople and apologists: race war, genocide, and "replacement."

Creating a Southern Nationality

The South's defense of its way of life, through forty years of intensifying political controversy, ceased to be apologetic and became an affirmation of cultural, social, and political distinction—the basic elements of an emergent nationality. That nationality defined itself in opposition to two "Others," Black slaves within the nation and "Yankees" without. Though enslaved Black people were an essential and characteristic part of Southern society, they were not Southern "nationals"—they could not be trusted with citizenship, and contributed nothing to the definition of national character. Yankees were cultural antagonists, as alien and inimical to Southern nationality as the British had been to the American rebels of 1776.

The one potential fault line in Southern nationalism was the difference in status and interest that divided slaveholding from nonslaveholding and poor White people. Hammond's contemptuous reference to Northern "mud-sills" reflected a class bias, conceding a superiority of interests and social authority to planters that was all too evident to poorer White people. The most obvious way to heal that potential breach was to identify Southern nationality with a racial Whiteness that all classes shared.

In shaping their national ideology, Southern leaders tried to distinguish their "Whiteness" from the American standard, which after all counted the North's money-grubbing merchants, greasy mechanics, and Irish paupers as "White." Before his inauguration as president of the Confederacy in 1861, Jefferson Davis greeted his fellow citizens as "brethren of the Confederate States of America . . . men of one flesh, one bone, one interest, one purpose, and of identity of domestic institutions" and stated that "we shall have nothing to fear at home because we shall have homogeneity" of identity as well as interest.[13]

In the North a similar yearning for "homogeneity" was reflected in the anti-immigrant polemics of the American or Know-Nothing Party, and in New England even abolitionists like Theodore Parker and Harriet Beecher Stowe spoke of "Anglo-Saxon" as the dominant form of American ethnicity. The great waves of the post–Civil War period would provoke a powerful ethnonationalist movement in the North, aimed at preserving something like "homogeneity."

But in 1860 Northern political organizations reflected a general acceptance of ethnic diversity as a fact of social life, as Democrats formed Irish political clubs and Republicans mobilized German and Scandinavian voters in the Northwest.

Davis's "homogeneity" was a political fiction, but of a kind that nationalist movements have typically adopted. For thirty years before the war, Southern separatists had imagined a different genealogy for Northern and Southern White people. It was said that Southern colonists had been "Cavaliers," while Northerners were Puritan "Roundheads"; that Northern Whites were merely "Anglo-Saxon," while Southerners were "Anglo-Norman"—descended from the Norman French aristos who conquered Saxon England in 1066. This was nonsense. Southern settlers reflected the same mix of ethnicities as their Northern counterparts—English, Welsh, Scots-Irish, German, Irish, Huguenot. The Lees were of English origin, the Jeffersons Welsh, Calhoun and Stonewall Jackson Scots-Irish, P. G. T. Beauregard Creole. There were plenty of Northern pioneers among the founders of those huge Mississippi valley plantations.[14]

But the chief point, and the operative power, of such exercises is to create the "fictive ethnicity" that is the basis of every nationality. It is important to understand that from a cultural point of view, Southerners were defending a *nationality*, a cultural identity, not simply a set of political and economic interests. The degree of cultural difference distinguishing the South from the rest of the nation amounts to a good deal more than the "narcissism of small differences." Southern society was organized around an economic and racial order that had no counterpart anywhere else. The pervasive illiberalism of Southern culture, its hostility to women's rights, and the conservatism and proslavery commitment of its churches are expressions of that cultural difference. Although secession was not unanimously favored throughout the Southern states, once enacted it received the support of most Southern communities, and that loyalty was affirmed by the support given the Confederacy through four years of war. By these measures, the Confederate claim to nationality is as clear as that of most of the emergent states that have gained United Nations recognition.

Southern leaders framed the danger confronting them in racial terms. As a secession commissioner from Georgia put it, Republicans "have demanded, and now demand, equality between the white and negro races . . . equality in representation, equality in the right of suffrage, equality in the honors and emoluments of office, equality in the social circle, equality in the rights of matrimony . . . freedom to the slave [is] eternal degradation for you and for us." If the South were to stay in the Union, its people would ultimately have to "flee from the land of their birth, and from the slaves their parents have toiled to acquire as an inheritance for them, or to submit to the degradation of being reduced to an equality with them, and all its attendant horrors." The "cornerstone" of Confederate nationality, Alexander Stephens declared, "rests upon the great truth that the negro is not the equal of the white man; that slavery, subordination to the superior race, is his natural and moral condition."[15]

Secessionist convictions were not universal in 1860–1861, nor were White farmers necessarily supportive of the ideology and political privilege of the planter elite. But faced with the threat of invasion and the overthrow of their elected governments by force, Southern civilians rallied to the cause. The years of battle formed serving soldiers into a fraternity of pride and loyalty, and forged in Southern society at large a common bond of suffering, and ultimately of defeat. When modern-day Southern organizations speak of their history as "heritage, not hate," this is what they are referring to. But without slavery—and the hate it engendered—there would have been no Confederacy, no war, no tattered flags, no ruined plantations.

The racial and ethnonational solidarity of the White South was its greatest strength, but also a fatal weakness in its war for national independence. The commitment to slavery hindered the Confederate government's quest for recognition by Britain and France. More pertinently, by excluding Black people from citizenship, the Confederacy drastically reduced its available military manpower. The fundamental weakness of Confederate nationality was that it excluded between 35 and 40 percent of its people from the body politic. After September 1862, the Emancipation Proclamation gave the enslaved a vested interest in Union victory. The approach of Union armies led slaves to flee plantations, even when the alternative was the squalid and abusive life of "contraband" camps. When Abraham Lincoln authorized the recruitment of Black soldiers in 1863, ex-slaves became a bulwark of Union military strength.[16]

Until 1864 this weakness was masked by the South's ability to mobilize most of its White military-age population, while slave labor maintained the productive economy and assisted with the construction of fortifications. However, the need to maintain control of slave labor meant that planters and overseers were exempted from conscription. These liabilities were cited by General Patrick Cleburne in his January 1864 proposal to recruit a quarter of a million Black men as soldiers, promising freedom to them and their families. This would impose serious losses on the planting interest, but "as between the loss of independence and the loss of slavery, we assume every patriot will . . . give up the negro slave rather than be a slave himself."[17]

Davis recognized some of the force of Cleburne's arguments. In February 1864, he went so far as to assert the national government's authority to draft slaves for building fortifications—an invasion of property rights that drew the wrath of states' rights fundamentalists like Alexander Stephens. But further than that he would not go. He feared that the planter class, the dominant force in the secession movement and in Confederate politics, would withdraw support from a state that did not fully protect its property interest. Desertion might increase if the soldiers came to believe that the sacrifices they had made to prevent "Negro equality" were being thrown away by the government. Cleburne's proposal was suppressed and his career ruined.

Less than a year later, Davis would acknowledge the rightness of Cleburne's analysis by supporting a bill for recruiting and freeing Black soldiers. He would go further, sending a diplomat to England and France with an offer to abolish slavery in exchange for recognition of Confederate independence—an offer that, under the Confederate Constitution, he had no power to deliver. Even then, with the Confederacy at the last extremity, Georgia's Howell Cobb told Davis, "The day you make soldiers of them is the beginning of the end of the revolution. If slaves will make good soldiers our whole theory of slavery is wrong." Davis answered that in that case the Confederacy's epitaph would be "died of a Theory." But the theory of White supremacy on which Confederate nationality was based had already doomed the South to fight a ruinous war with less than its full strength.[18]

Nevertheless, Cobb was right in thinking that preservation of White supremacy, in theory as well as practice, was essential to Southern nationality. The war had tested but in the end reaffirmed that principle. Poor White people had been angered by the "Twenty Negro Law," which exempted owners and overseers on large plantations from conscription; by the draft exemptions planters won for their overseers; and by the planters' resistance to taxation, which left the middling and poor classes to bear the brunt of both military service and runaway inflation. A North Carolina private complained that "poor soldiers . . . are fighting for the 'rich man's negro.'" But in the end, most fought because they had a deep social and psychological investment in the racial order. As one nonslaveholder wrote President Davis, "We have but little interest in the value of slaves, but there is one matter in this connection in which we feel a very deep interest. We are opposed to Negro equality. To prevent this we are willing to spare the last man, down to the point where women and children begin to suffer for food and clothing; when these begin to suffer and die, rather than see them equalized with an inferior race we will die with them."[19]

Southern leaders reinforced fears of Black power by adopting extreme measures of retaliation against Black soldiers and the officers who led them. In 1863 the Confederate Congress considered a bill for "raising the *black flag,* asking and giving no quarter" in future battles. General Beauregard was most eager that the bill be enacted: "Has the bill for execution of abolition prisoners after 1st of next January passed? . . . It is high time to proclaim the black flag. . . . Let the execution be with the garrote." Congress did not pass the bill, fearing retaliation against Confederate prisoners of war, but Secretary of War James Seddon ordered commanders in the field to see that Black soldiers or their officers were "dealt with red-handed on the field or immediately thereafter."[20] Their policies spoke to their soldiers' visceral hatred for Black people, and they proved effective in thwarting Southern peace movements and reviving the commitment of war-weary soldiers to the cause. They also led to the massacres of wounded and surrendering Black soldiers at Fort Pillow, Poison Spring, Plymouth (North Carolina), and the Crater. The last of these, on July 30, 1864, was the war's worst racial massacre, as upwards of 200 Black soldiers, many of them wounded, were killed by Confederate troops after having surrendered.[21]

Instead of adapting racial policy to the necessities of national survival, the political and military leadership of the Confederacy used the racial menace of the armed Negro as an instrument of propaganda, to convince its people that they must fight to the death to save themselves and their families from degradation. In war-weary North Carolina, Governor Zebulon Vance defeated a "peace" candidate by warning that if his people voted to return to the Union, "instead of getting your sons back to the plow and the fireside, they would be drafted . . . to fight alongside [Lincoln's] negro troops in exterminating the white men, women, and children of the South." The rapid decline of Southern fortunes in the last year of the war raised to a high pitch the fear that had haunted the prewar South of retaliation, racial murder, and slave uprising. With the actuality of defeat, those fears would drive resistance to the programs of Reconstruction imposed by the victorious Union.[22]

The Legend of General Lee and the Lost Cause

The most drastic consequence of Confederate defeat was the breakup of the social and cultural order based on slavery. Postwar Southern politics would be shaped by the struggle over how to structure race relations in the absence of slavery, but the first problem faced by Southern thought leaders was how to account for their defeat. Had the South, in Davis's words, "died of a Theory"?

Or was its defeat the result of battlefield mischance, human error, or the over-whelming material strength of the North?

The Lost Cause Myth would provide an answer to these questions. Rich-mond editor Edward Pollard coined the term in his book *The Lost Cause: A New Southern History of the War of the Confederates,* published in 1866. Pollard held that the South had been entirely within its rights in seceding, and that slavery had been a benevolent and productive institution. He blamed defeat on the North's material advantages, its ruthless destruction of Southern prop-erty—and mismanagement by the Davis administration and certain Southern generals. Implicit in that last idea is a *might-have-been:* if the war had been better managed, the Confederacy might have won.

That possibility was symbolized by General Robert E. Lee, whose military genius was such that, with better support and a bit more luck, he might have won Southern independence on the field of battle and vindicated the Southern belief in states' rights and slavery—or so the legend goes. It is from such might-have-beens that myths arise. Lee is to Confederate myth what Lincoln is to the Union myth—the representative man of his culture. Had the South succeeded in winning its independence, Lee would have been its George Washington. Instead he became the hero of the Lost Cause Myth, a symbol of Southern exceptionalism and resistance.

Lee had a brilliant career in the prewar army, as a staff officer under Win-field Scott in the Mexican War, commandant of West Point, director of nu-merous engineering projects, and cavalry commander on the frontier. Though only a colonel in the Regulars, he was regarded as the best military mind and the best soldier in the army. Lincoln was prepared to offer him command of the Union forces, but he resigned, unwilling to raise his sword against his native Virginia, and became chief military adviser to Confederate president Jefferson Davis. As commander of the Army of Northern Virginia from 1862 to 1865, he would dominate operations in the critical Virginia theater and give the Confederacy its best chances for victory.[23]

Lee was also the perfect embodiment of the South's idealized self-image. He was an aristocrat, a soldier, a planter in the patriarchal style. His link to the Founders was direct: he was the son of "Light Horse" Henry Lee, Washing-ton's favorite cavalryman, and his marriage to Mary Custis tied him to the family of Washington's wife, Martha. He lived in a Greek Revival mansion on a hill in Arlington, from whose pillared portico he could gaze at the Capitol across the Potomac.

On the most contentious questions of the Civil War, Lee represented the moderate South, which accepted secession reluctantly, as a last and therefore justifiable resort. He owned slaves and bought and sold them, but was not sympathetic to the "Ultra" ideology, which vaunted the moral excellence of slavery and believed secession the only way to protect it. In an 1856 letter to his wife, Lee wrote, "There are few, I believe, in this enlightened age, who will not acknowledge that slavery as an institution is a moral and political evil." But while he would give eventual abolition "the aid of our prayers," he left "the progress as well as the results in the hands of Him who, chooses to work by slow influences, and with whom a thousand years are but as a single day."[24]

That said, he also believed slavery was an institution divinely ordained to Christianize Africans. In an 1856 letter to his wife, Lee wrote that Negroes were an inferior race, for whom slavery was a "painful discipline . . . necessary for their further instruction as a race, [which] will prepare them, I hope, for better things. . . . The blacks are immeasurably better off here than in Africa, morally, physically, and socially." He therefore saw the maintenance of slavery as an exercise of "spiritual liberty," which abolitionists traduced at the risk of producing "civil and servile war" and exciting "angry feelings in the master" that would not benefit the slaves.[25]

His decision to resign from the army and serve the Confederacy was the result of a spiritual struggle, capped by a long night of meditation in his Arlington rose garden. His deepest loyalties were to family and community, both utterly bound up with the history and society of Virginia. The decision reveals the complex character of that sense of "honor" that has always been identified as central to his character. Lee broke his oath of allegiance when he resigned his commission to take up arms against the United States, an act that led his Unionist contemporaries and some modern military men (such as Joint Chiefs of Staff chairman General Mark A. Milley) to consider him a traitor.[26] But honor, as Lee and the South understood it, was a concept whose values are integral to a particular community. Lee's "honor" was bound up with his identity as a son of Virginia.

He spoke of and treated Union commanders and their troops with the cold dignity that accords with the code of honor for relations among gentlemen—hence his reputation as a chivalrous opponent. But the code did not recognize Blacks as people capable of honor or worthy of honorable treatment; and that ban extended to those Whites who aided Black people in resisting or escaping enslavement. He supported the seizure of fugitive slaves and free Blacks by his troops during the invasion of Pennsylvania and accepted the reenslavement and abusive treatment of captured Black Union soldiers. He said nothing about the massacre of surrendered Black soldiers by troops under his command at the Battle of the Crater. He did not object when A. P. Hill, his senior corps commander, staged a parade of prisoners of war designed to humiliate White officers captured while leading Black troops in that battle.[27]

In the end, Lee's preeminent place in Southern myth is based on his military achievements, the victories he won—and perhaps more significantly, those he did not win, the great might-have-beens of Confederate history. Lee had no peer as a battlefield tactician or in the development of strategy for a particular theater of operations. When he took command of the Army of Northern Virginia in July 1862, a huge Federal army was poised for assault at the gates of Richmond. With great daring he stripped his front lines to form a striking force, which he swung wide to hit the flank and rear of the Federal army, forcing it to abandon much of its materiel and retreat. When Lincoln began shifting troops from the Richmond front to form an army closer to Washington, Lee moved with speed and power to smash that force at the Second Battle of Bull Run. In little more than a month, he transferred the theater of action from the suburbs of Richmond to northern Virginia. That strategic coup would determine the location and course of fighting for the next two years. It brought the Confederacy as close to winning the war as it would ever get.

Having achieved so much, Lee overreached by invading Maryland. His outnumbered and overused army was defeated at Antietam, giving Lincoln the victory he needed to issue the Emancipation Proclamation. In 1862–1863 Lee inflicted humiliating defeats on the Union Army of the Potomac at Fredericksburg and Chancellorsville. Believing these victories gave his army moral and material ascendency, and that a decisive battle won on Northern soil was the only way to reverse the tide of Confederate defeat, he led his army to a defeat at Gettysburg that cost him a third of his strength. In the 1864 Overland Campaign, his skilled defense imposed such heavy casualties on the Union army that Northern support for the war wavered. But in the end he could not break the grip of Ulysses S. Grant's army, or defeat the grand strategy that destroyed the South's capacity for waging war.

By war's end Lee had become the personification of the South and the Confederate cause. His men called him "Marse Robert," suggesting their relation to him was figuratively that of idealized slaves to an ideal master. The most extraordinary portrayal of Lee's importance was purportedly offered by one of his aides as the war was reaching its ruinous end: "The country be damned, there is no country, there has been no country, for a year or more. You are the country to these men. They have fought for you. . . . Their devotion to you and faith in you have been the only things which have held this army together. If you demand the sacrifice, there are still left thousands of us who will die for you!" The scene has been repeated in numerous sources, with some variation in language and in the identification of Lee's interlocutor. Something like it may actually have happened. It was certainly the case that loyalty to Lee had held the hard core of the Army of Northern Virginia together. But the *telling* of the story belongs to the period of postwar mythmaking.[28]

Lee became the South's representative man. What Southerners say of him is what they claim for the South: that they had a moral right to independence, and skill and courage enough to deserve victory. If they were defeated, it was because they were overwhelmed by superior force, betrayed by circumstances, or by the failings (or treason) of lesser men. Those propositions were crystallized in the Southern view of Gettysburg, Lee's greatest might-have-been. While Lee blamed himself for that defeat, the Lost Cause legend blames General James Longstreet—and poses him as a kind of Judas figure. It was well known that Longstreet opposed Lee's plan to fight at Gettysburg; that his attack on July 2 was delivered late; that he also opposed ordering Pickett's Charge and was slow to execute it. In postmortems by Lost Cause historians like Pollard and by ex-generals refighting old battles in their memoirs, as well as in twentieth-century Southern historiography, it was said or suggested that his dilatoriness amounted to deliberate obstruction of Lee's master plan and was responsible for its failure.

On balance, scholars have exonerated Longstreet of those charges and suggested that, even if Lee's orders had been executed as given, the assaults on July 2 and 3 would not have succeeded. But tactical reality has nothing to do with the case. What made Longstreet the villain in the legend of Lee was his role in postwar politics: he was alone among leading Confederate generals in accepting Reconstruction and joining the Republican Party. As commander of the Louisiana militia, under a Republican governor, Longstreet led racially mixed commands in futile attempts to punish or suppress the racial massacres in Colfax (1873) and New Orleans (1874) perpetrated by organizations aiming to restore White supremacy.

The deeper agenda of the Lost Cause Myth was not to resolve quarrels among defeated generals but to idealize the social order of the Old South, and to justify a new phase of political violence to restore that order. As Pollard wrote in *The Lost Cause,* the Civil War "did not decide negro equality; it did not decide negro suffrage; it did not decide State Rights. . . . And these things which the war did not decide, the Southern people will still cling to, still claim and still assert them in their rights and views."[29]

Lee's might-have-beens became the unfinished business of a new generation of Southern leaders. Although deprived of the power to form armies, they would resort to arms, not to defend but to restore the social order of the Old South: its idealized self-image of pastoral contentment, its real dependence on the coercion of Black labor, its patriarchal culture and planter-dominated economics and politics, its religious and cultural illiberalism, its rigid hierarchies and race-based regime of social control. Like the Lincoln myth of the "new birth of freedom," the Lost Cause would follow the script of *regeneration through violence,* achieving the "redemption" of the South via the promotion of vigilantism and campaigns marked by political violence.

5

The Lost Cause

Redemption and the White Reunion

SOUTHERNERS FOUGHT the Civil War to defend their unique culture, which was based on racial slavery and a planter-dominated social hierarchy. With their armies defeated and governments displaced, they would continue the culture war by other means: campaigns of vigilante violence to "redeem" the South by disabling the governments established by Reconstruction and restoring the political power of the Democratic Party's Southern wing. The Redeemers' program followed the classic scenario of regeneration through violence, and added the Lost Cause to the lexicon of American national myths. It has proved in many ways the most durable and potent of the Civil War Myths, as its recrudescence in the MAGA movement illustrates.

Through the last thirty years of the nineteenth century, the influence of the Lost Cause Myth would reach far beyond the South, as its racial animus resonated with an emerging reaction in the North and West against the massive waves of immigration that attended industrialization. Its influence is reflected in the emergence of a new Unionist version of the Civil War—the White Reunion Myth, which saw the war as a conflict between "brothers" who were reunited on the ground of an ethnonationalism that would exclude non-Whites and non-Nordic immigrants.[1]

War by Other Means: Reconstruction and Redemption

The first phase of Reconstruction, from 1866 to 1869, was guided by President Andrew Johnson, formerly a Democratic senator from Tennessee, whose policies set easy terms for restoring political rights to ex-Confederates and maintained the plantation system of labor discipline for Black people. Nevertheless, the program faced widespread local violence and a series of "race riots" against Black communities in Memphis and New Orleans in 1866 and Pulaski, Tennessee, and Opelousas, Louisiana, in 1868. When the so-called Radical Reconstruction began under President Ulysses S. Grant in 1869, federal intervention increased significantly. The Freedmen's Bureau was chartered to provide aid for Black people displaced by emancipation and to protect their rights as workers and later as voters. It was also responsible for providing newly freed Black families with education, and in doing so created some of the first public school systems available to White Southerners. Its personnel included teachers, entrepreneurs, engineers, government bureaucrats, and soldiers assigned to provide protection for these endeavors. They represented a Yankee culture Southerners had been taught to despise.

The deepest threat to Southern culture was the demand that Black people be treated equally in work and trade, and given the right to vote. It should be noted that even at the height of Radical Reconstruction, all of those rights were circumscribed. The redevelopment of the Southern economy was governed by Gilded Age rules, which favored owners at the expense of labor. The right to vote was soon co-opted to serve a Republican Party that could only win the support of a small minority of White people. Nevertheless, newly freed Black people were able to vote and hold office, and to enjoy the benefits of public education. They also formed the largest component of militias that were organized by Reconstruction governors in all the ex-Confederate states to protect the rights of freedpeople and Republicans. The militias were supplemented by the Loyal League, an organization of Black and White Republicans that served to mobilize political support and provide communal self-defense.

From the perspective of Southern Whites, "raising" Black people to civil equality meant Whites' effective "degradation" to the level of Negroes. That the Black people were armed and empowered by the state transformed racial subjugation into the menace of attack, or at least of political coercion. These fears were especially powerful in the cotton states of the Deep South, where Black people constituted or approached a majority of the population.

As the prospect of a Republican presidency had precipitated secession in 1860, so Radical Reconstruction provoked a movement for armed resistance. The Ku Klux Klan was organized in Tennessee in 1867 and was soon joined by the Southern Cross and the Knights of the White Camelia. These were the armed auxiliary of a political movement aimed at ending Reconstruction, restoring the power of the planter elite, and reestablishing White supremacy. The

Klan chose as its first president Nathan Bedford Forrest, a renowned Confederate cavalry officer whose troops had perpetrated the notorious massacre of Black troops at Fort Pillow. State-based chapters were typically led by former Confederate officers and officials. The Klan and its counterparts operated as terrorists or vigilantes, specializing in exemplary beatings, mutilations, and killings designed to frighten political and social leaders into inaction or flight. Although accusations of rape, actual or potential, figured prominently in Klan propaganda, between 1866 and 1873 the primary targets of the Klan were White and Black people who were active in Reconstruction governments, the Freedmen's Bureau, the Loyal League, or the Republican Party. Those killed in small-scale operations numbered in the thousands, and the toll was augmented by large-scale massacres like those in Eutaw, Alabama, and Laurens, South Carolina, in 1870 and in Meridian, Mississippi, and the Kirk-Holden "war" in North Carolina in 1871, in which vigilante organizations attacked Black political assemblies or militia musters.[2]

The Civil Rights Act of 1871 empowered President Grant to suspend the writ of habeas corpus in states affected by Klan violence, to send Regular Army units to bolster state militias, and to launch a series of investigations by the newly created Department of Justice to break up the Klan. The respite was brief. By 1872 nearly all ex-Confederates had regained the right to vote and hold office. The states of the Upper and Middle South were declared to have been successfully "Reconstructed," and freed from federal intervention. This led to the election of "conservative" Democratic governments, and to the end of federal military occupation and Freedmen's Bureau operations. While Black people were not legally disenfranchised, their right to vote was subject to economic pressure from White landlords and employers, as well as intimidation by vigilantes.[3]

In the un-Reconstructed states of the Deep South, new forms of vigilantism replaced the defeated Klan. Armed associations and rogue militias, variously dubbed Red Shirts, Rifle Clubs, and White Leagues, committed acts of terrorism against supporters of Republican governors and mounted semi-military assaults on Black or racially mixed state militias. These operations were coordinated with the political campaigns of Democratic Redeemers. In Louisiana in 1874 and Mississippi in 1875, the elections of Republican governors were challenged by Democrats, who "installed" their own nominees and called out members of the White League and Rifle Clubs to seize power. The White League killed between 120 and 150 Black people in Colfax, Louisiana, 50 of whom had surrendered. In the 1874 "Battle of Liberty Place," 5,000 White Leaguers staged an armed coup in New Orleans against the Republican-led government, and in 1876 they were honored with a statue praising them for reestablishing "White Supremacy."

The climactic race wars were fought in the gubernatorial elections of Mississippi in 1875 and South Carolina in 1876. In South Carolina Red Shirts and Rifle Clubs attacked Black militias attempting to guard polling places, an event known as the Hamburg Massacre, and other local attacks killed hundreds of Black people attempting to vote. In Mississippi, Republican governor Adelbert Ames was faced with an armed uprising that threatened civil war in the state. This time President Grant refused to send federal troops, telling Ames that the Northern public was "tired" of dealing with Southern disorders. Although the withdrawal of federal troops would not be formalized until 1877, Grant's decision marked the effective end of Reconstruction and the triumph of the Redeemers. Their campaign of regeneration through violence had made a heroic myth of the Confederacy's Lost Cause.[4]

Prelude to Reunion: Class Conflict and Reaction in the North

By 1875 Northern voters had turned against Radical Reconstruction as part of a general reaction, self-identified as "conservative," against the political and economic disruption that had dominated the preceding twenty years. Since the 1850s, and through the Civil War and Reconstruction, Democrats had identified themselves as the voice of political and economic conservatism. In 1874 the Democratic Party, strengthened by returning Southerners, won a majority in the House of Representatives, and it won the popular vote for president in 1876 although contested electoral votes and a political compromise elected Republican Rutherford Hayes. A majority of Republicans were willing to abandon Reconstruction because they were tired of policing the political violence that attended Southern elections, and disgusted by reports of rampant corruption in states whose Republican governments depended on federal Reconstruction programs for their survival.

What corruption there was was part of a national pattern. It began with the financing and procurement operations supporting the Union war effort, and continued after the war as the government financed Reconstruction in the South and railroad development in the West. There was neither legal authority nor historical precedent to help state or federal governments manage the huge transfers of wealth and credit involved in these projects. The result, as Mark Twain quipped, was that Gilded Age America had "the finest legislatures money could buy."

Reconstruction governments shared in this pattern of corruption but did not generally exceed it. The spectacle of Black legislators and officers "lording" over White people was nearly as offensive to Northerners as it was to Southerners. Sensational journalists reporting for most of the major New York papers—Democratic, independent, and Republican—described governments controlled by "a mass of black barbarism" making a travesty of legislative sessions and insulting the gentlemanly White men who dared oppose them.[5]

Waves of news stories framed Black enfranchisement as equivalent to a "savage war" against civilization. Thus in 1874 the Democratic-aligned *New York World* editorialized, "The Indian savage gave place to the civilized White man, who made these beautiful Southern lands blossom like the rose. The white man has now been pushed aside, and the negro savage is fast reducing the country to desolation and barbarism." The paper asserted that Northern White people must sympathize with the violence of their Southern race fellows, because they faced a choice between a "War of Races" and "enforced amalgamation."[6]

The irony of Southern history is that by embracing war to save slavery, Southern leaders hastened its destruction. The irony of the Union side is that to win its war for "free labor," it created a financial and industrial order in which free-labor values no longer applied. Over the course of the war, a generation of entrepreneurs, financiers, engineers, and corporate managers had learned how to organize and direct large enterprises, skills they applied to an expanding industrial economy. Industrialization required the concentration rather than dispersion of capital, as well as managerial control of the labor force. As scientist and social philosopher John W. Draper suggested, the Civil War had been a "school" in which a society inclined to rampant individualism learned the need for order and "subordination" of the masses to the wisdom of "superior men."[7]

Abraham Lincoln had distinguished the Southern idea of liberty from that espoused by advocates of free labor. "With some the word liberty may mean for each man to do as he pleases with himself, and the product of his labor; while with others the same word may mean for some men to do as they please with other men, and the product of other men's labor." When it came to labor relations, Northern industrialists had more in common with Southern planters than with the exponents of free labor. Redeemers of the gentlemanly sort, like South Carolina's Wade Hampton, were recognized as exemplars of the new order, "men of ability, trained to deal with great questions of public economy, sound financiers and rational statesmen." It did not matter that Hampton had used vigilante violence to win his 1876 election.[8]

An early sign of the decline of free-labor ideology can be found in an article by Charles Francis Adams Jr. on "protection of the ballot," written for the *Journal of Social Science* in 1869. Adams was an important figure in the postwar political and intellectual elite, grandson and great-grandson of former presidents, son of Lincoln's ambassador to England Charles Francis Adams Sr., a Civil War veteran who was prominent in the movement to reform the dubious business practices of railroad corporations. It was, to him, an inescapable necessity of the capitalist order that employers seek the cheapest and most docile labor available. As a result, industrialization was producing three new "proletariats," markedly inferior to Anglo-Saxon White people in racial character: "Celtic" in the Northeast, "African" in the South, and "Oriental" on the Pacific Coast. If enfranchised under the principle of universal suffrage, Adams said, these groups would threaten "free institutions," because their racial disposition was inimical to White American values like self-reliance and respect for property. Adams's caution extended to those native-born White people who would inevitably be "proletarianized" by the industrial system: "As society develops itself . . . [and] the struggle for existence becomes more and more severe, the inherent difficulties of a broadly extended suffrage will make themselves felt. Starving men and women care very little for abstract questions of general good. Political power becomes one means simply of private subsistence." In their ignorance and need, proletarians of any race are susceptible to demagogues and political bosses, who organize the forces of "ignorance and vice to obtain political control." The emerging industrial order thus forces us to choose between political democracy and the industrial progress of civilization.[9]

The supposed expertise of the masters of capital who presided over the railroad-building and railroad-financing boom of 1869–1873 was a form of hubris. The collapse of inflated values in the Northern Pacific and other transcontinental railroads in 1873 led to a bank panic and triggered a severe economic depression that lasted until 1878. Masses of wage-dependent workers were suddenly unemployed, concentrated in cities, unable to pay rent or buy food. There was no precedent in American history for handling such a crisis. Private charities were not organized to handle needs of the kind that now arose on a scale hitherto unimagined. True to Adams's prediction, those immiserated by the depression tried to use the political system for relief, calling on their representatives to use public funds and legal measures like a rent moratorium to relieve their distress. Mainstream newspapers and politicians condemned these demands in dozens of editorials that repeated the same phrase: the free market required these people to "work or starve." As the depression worsened, an attempt by railroad corporations to lay off workers and roll back wages led to a massive, violent, nationwide railroad strike in 1877, which some saw as the prelude to a new civil war of labor against capital.[10]

The result was an ideological revulsion among leading politicians and opinion makers, who condemned relief for economic distress as inimical to good morals and good government, vilifying the protesting workers for a moral inferiority that likened them to Indians and Negroes. The Indian analogy would acquire outsize importance in 1876, when Custer's Last Stand shocked the nation with proof that the balance of power between savagery and civilization could be reversed—a theme we'll examine in Chapter 6.

But the analogy between workers and Black people suggested a commonality of interest between Northern elites and Southern Redeemers. E. L. Godkin, publisher of *The Nation* and a leader of what had been liberal opinion in the North, condemned White proletarians and their "philanthropist" supporters by comparing them to the Reconstruction regimes overthrown by enlightened Southern elites:

> Some of the talk about the laborer and his rights that we have listened to . . . such as the South Carolina field hand, to reason upon and even manage the interests of a great community, has been enough, considering the sort of ears on which it now falls, to . . . put our very civilization in peril.

The growing population of non-Anglo-Saxon immigrants creates a direct parallel with the Southern "race problem":

> Vast additions have been made to our population . . . to whom American political and social ideals appeal but faintly, if at all, and who carry in their very blood traditions which give universal suffrage an air of menace to many of the things which civilized men hold most dear.

Thus Godkin, the Northern liberal, arrives at the political conclusion embraced by Southern Redeemers; he does so by adopting their racial ideology and extending it to the White laboring classes.[11]

At this point in the evolution of Gilded Age culture, there was still animus in the North and West toward the South. Republican candidates would "wave the bloody shirt" of Union dead and wounded when attacking Democratic opponents. Nonetheless, there was also a convergence of views, especially among the cultural and political elite, on a concept of class relations that privileged the masters of capital, their managers and technical experts, and denigrated the humanity of the working classes by likening them to savages and Negroes. This is the beginning of the White Reunion version of Civil War myth, which rejects the liberating aims of the "new birth of freedom" and sees the war as a disagreement between racial "brothers" now reconciled on the common ground of a renewed ethnonationalism.

Before that Reunion Myth gained currency, a second wave of racial reaction in the South would intensify the emotional charge of the Lost Cause Myth and produce the regime of oppression, segregation, and terror known as Jim Crow.

Jim Crow: Cruelty and Social Control

Reconstruction formally ended after the disputed presidential election of 1876, when Southern representatives accepted the election of the Republican Rutherford B. Hayes in exchange for his adoption of a "let alone" policy toward the South. Godkin of *The Nation* rejoiced that, as a result, "the negro will disappear from the field of national politics. . . . Henceforth the nation, as a nation, will have nothing more to do with him." In 1875 a Southern editor wrote that though the 14th and 15th Amendments would remain in the Constitution, "we intend . . . to make them dead letters." The Supreme Court confirmed that prophecy in a series of decisions that nullified the Second Founding. *US v. Cruikshank* (1876) ignored the clear intent of the 14th Amendment by denying the federal government authority to intervene against violations of the Bill of Rights by states or private organizations. The five so-called Civil Rights Cases of 1883 held that Congress had no power (under the 13th or 14th Amendment) to prevent racial discrimination. The right to vote, guaranteed by the 15th Amendment, would be the next target.[12]

The defeat of Reconstruction did not entirely negate the gains made by Black people since Emancipation. The vast majority remained agricultural laborers and sharecroppers, but some prospered as skilled craftspeople and service providers, teachers, merchants, and independent farmers. Although their right to vote was curtailed and they were subject to threats of violence and economic retaliation, Black men did retain the franchise, which gave them some influence in state politics, and a share in government benefits. In Virginia and North Carolina, for example, successful reform movements were based on cross-racial alliances.[13]

Black people strove to maintain these gains at a time when the Southern economy was being reorganized by the increasing concentration of wealth and power. In the 1880s and 1890s the plantation system was expanded and modernized, engorging land hitherto held by independent White farmers and reducing them to tenantry or sharecropping. The development of cotton-milling factories drew some of the dispossessed into industrial wage labor. Poor White people now had to compete with Black people, on terms that, from the White perspective, were "equal" enough to constitute the racial degradation their culture had taught them to fear. Planters and factory owners could play White and Black tenants, sharecroppers, and workers against each other to drive down wages and working conditions.

On plantations and in the coal mines of Appalachia and the Far West, workers were held in a kind of debt peonage. Sharecroppers and tenants could only make a crop by borrowing from the landlord; they could only sell their crop to the landlord, at a price that ensured their debts would remain unpaid. Planters and railroad developers in the South made extensive use of convict labor. New and draconian criminal laws ensured an ample supply of prisoners. The South's post-Reconstruction ruling classes mixed many of the old planter families with newly rich Southerners and Northern investors. Together they created what Eric Foner describes as "a seamless web of oppression, whose interwoven economic, political, and social strands all reinforced one another." The aftermath of Redemption would validate Lincoln's thesis that, if society permitted the degradation of Black labor, it would enable the future degradation of White labor.[14]

The impoverishment of White farmers led to the rise of the Populist movement. In the North and West, Populists focused on debt and the manipulation of freight rates by railroad corporations. In the South the movement hinged on race. One school of Populism saw Black people as tools of the landowners who controlled their votes, and sought to disenfranchise them. The other sought alliances with Black tenants and sharecroppers for collective bargaining and to press for economic reform. But proponents of such alliances (most notably Tom Watson of Georgia) eventually abandoned them, since they could better win the support of poor White people by playing to their fears and prejudices. Turn-of-the-century Southern Populism was typified by Mississippi's James Vardaman, who campaigned on taxing big planters and depriving them of convict labor, while whipping up anti-Black sentiment and encouraging lynching.[15]

Southern Populism was resisted by old-line "Bourbon" planters, many of whom had important connections with Northern financial and political interests. They usually tried to protect their Black labor force from the violence that might drive them to emigrate. However, "their" Black people had to remain subordinate to plantation discipline and refrain from protest. In a crisis the elites could sometimes play the race card against the Populists, to prevent tran-sracial alliances or simply to win votes.[16]

The result was a perfect storm of political, economic, and cultural tendencies all pointing toward the intensification of race hatred and the steady erasure of what civil rights remained from Reconstruction. The political objective of the Jim Crow movement was to rewrite Southern state constitutions to deprive Black people of the voting rights they had exercised since the 1870s, and to enforce racial segregation in every conceivable aspect of Southern life. The methods chosen had the deeper result, and for some leaders the deeper pur-pose, of radically intensifying the passions and beliefs that sustained White supremacy, transforming racial contempt into active and virulent hatred driven by loathing, rage, and fear bordering on hysteria.[17]

Mississippi began the process with its constitutional convention of 1890, and the rest of the former Slave States followed suit over the next twenty-five years. The 15th Amendment made it necessary to achieve disenfranchisement by indirect means. Many states imposed poll taxes and literacy tests that were designed or applied in ways that made it impossible for Black people to pass, while allowing uneducated Whites to get by. Nevertheless, these measures often disenfranchised poor Whites as well as Black people—a price Whites seemed willing to pay.[18]

Racial segregation had always been part of Southern culture: there were "col-ored galleries" in antebellum churches, "colored cars" on trains, and "Negro quarters" in towns and cities. But the two races often lived and worked in close proximity in cities and towns, and even on plantations where White overseers lived near and worked with Black people. The Jim Crow regime went beyond custom to create a stringent and highly detailed system of separation, designed to confront Black people at every turn with shame-inducing evidence of their inferior status: not just segregated churches and schools and transportation, but drinking fountains and building entrances.

It was almost impossible to distinguish what was banned by law from what was banned by custom—and that was the secret of the system's power. Its ef-fect was to inculcate in *both* races the understanding that a zone of extreme peril existed wherever Black lives impinged on those of White people. Any Black assertion of equal dignity must be seen by a White person as an outra-geous offense, a denial of the racial abjection that was the only guarantee of White status and security: refusing to yield the sidewalk, meeting a glance eye to eye, acting sullen when rebuked, refusing an offer in a trade. To teach Black people that *any* departure was beyond tolerance, the punishment for such vio-lations was to be certain—and extreme.

License to Kill: Murder, Lynching, and Racial Massacres

Lynchings were the hallmark of the Jim Crow system. Between 1882 and 1903—the height of the disenfranchisement campaign—there were over 2,000 recorded lynchings of Black people in the Southern states. The real number was certainly larger. It is perhaps a better measure to note that between 1880 and 1915 there were on average two lynchings every week, so that Europeans considered lynching a characteristically American crime. To this total we should add the incalculable number of racial murders condoned by the Jim Crow system, such as killings in workplace altercations, for not giving way on the sidewalk, for "reckless eyeballing," or for other defiant behavior, under circumstances that ensured the killers would not be charged with a crime—or, if charged, speedily acquitted.[19]

Although they took the form of mob or vigilante violence, lynchings were tolerated and often sponsored by local authorities. Many were promoted in advance by regional newspapers and memorialized in postcards sent as ordinary mail, "Greetings from the Sunny South." Large numbers of White people from all social classes participated—women and children as well as men, the "best people" as well as poor Whites. What they asserted was a version of the old rule that granted masters the privilege of exercising absolute and incontestable judgment over the bodies of the enslaved, a privilege that extended to the White community as a whole. These were rituals that engaged the White community in acts of murder, torture, and mutilation whose effect was to inculcate in both races the understanding that the issues between them were rooted in the deepest and most intimate parts of their bodily selves. Hence the obsessive insistence that Black men were congenitally prone to rape White women, and the sadistic punishments inflicted on those accused of the crime, who were tortured, blinded, and sexually mutilated before death or burned alive—sometimes "roasted" over slow fires. Severed body parts were often taken as souvenirs and displayed in shop windows.[20]

In fact, only 19 percent of the 3,000 men lynched between 1889 and 1918 were accused of rape. Some so charged were guilty only of cohabiting or having a consensual relationship with a White woman. Most of those lynched were charged with murder or other acts of violence against White people, but some were killed for such offenses as engaging in "wild talk"; defying White employers, tradespeople, or business competitors; or otherwise violating the code of racial manners. World War I veterans were lynched for wearing their uniforms in public.[21] Anything that suggested that Black people deserved respect comparable to that accorded Whites was seen as a menace to the system. After

President Theodore Roosevelt invited Booker T. Washington to dinner at the White House in 1901, Senator Benjamin Tillman of South Carolina told the press that because Roosevelt had put wild thoughts in Black people's heads, "we shall have to kill a thousand niggers to get them back in their places."[22]

It was essential to the terrorist function of lynching—its goal of imposing social control through widespread fear—that it could be inflicted for reasons that were trivial or arbitrary. Mobs often assaulted people at random, demonstrating their willingness to punish the community for the deeds of individuals. Take one example out of thousands. In Valdosta, Georgia, in May 1918 a White mob hunting for a Black man accused of murder killed a number of Black men it met at random. Mary Turner, the wife of one victim, complained to the sheriff. Although she was heavily pregnant, he had her jailed and turned her over to a mob, which tortured, mutilated, and burned her alive.[23]

Writers and scholars have struggled to understand the inner lives of people who could do such things. Clearly psychosexual mechanisms were at work. But lynching was a social phenomenon, an expression of the culture of Southern communities. These townspeople and villagers imagined themselves in a perpetual state of impending war, which had to be waged without mercy.

Lynching rose to a peak in the 1890s, an era otherwise known for the ascendancy of the Progressive movement, and remained high during the fifteen-year period in which the legal basis of the Jim Crow system was being established. A series of constitutional conventions were called in the Southern states whose express purpose was to end or radically curtail the rights of Black people to vote, serve on juries, and exercise other civil rights. Florida and Tennessee began the process in 1889, followed by Mississippi in 1890, Arkansas in 1891, South Carolina in 1895, Louisiana in 1898, North Carolina in 1900, Alabama and Texas in 1901, and Virginia in 1902. In a speech defending Mississippi's 1890 convention, James K. Vardaman, who would later serve as governor of Mississippi from 1904 to 1908, said the convention "was held for no other purpose than to eliminate the nigger from politics. Not the 'ignorant and vicious,' as some of the apologists would have you believe . . . I am opposed to the nigger's voting, it matters not what his advertised moral and mental qualifications may be." He added, "If it is necessary, every Negro in the state will be lynched."[24]

The widespread practice of lynching established a moral framework that licensed large-scale violence against whole communities. Assaults were organized to drive Black people out of small towns or rural counties in places like Slocum, Texas (1911); Forsyth County, Georgia (1912); and Rosewood, Florida (1923). One scholar has detailed fourteen such expulsions, with death tolls ranging from 8 to 200.[25]

The most systematic bloodbath of the disenfranchising era was the Wilmington insurrection of 1898. Between 1894 and 1898, an interracial "Fusionist" alliance of Republicans and Populists had won the North Carolina governorship and control of the state legislature. Over 1,000 Black people won elective or appointed office. In 1898 Democrats ran statewide on the "White Declaration of Independence," an invocation of the Myth of the Founding that, like Stephen Douglas's "white basis" and Alexander Stephens's 1861 Cornerstone Speech, inverted the Declaration of Independence's doctrine of equality: "Believing that the Constitution of the United States contemplated a government to be carried on by an enlightened people; believing that its framers did not anticipate the enfranchisement of an ignorant population of African origin, . . . We . . . do hereby declare that we will no longer be ruled and will never again be ruled, by men of African origin . . . a fate to which no Anglo-Saxon has ever been forced to submit."[26]

All the usual accusations of criminality and rape, ignorance and corruption were broadcast in the partisan press, led by the state's largest newspaper, the *Raleigh News and Observer.* Its editor was Josephus Daniels, a leader in the Progressive wing of the national Democratic Party, who would later serve as FDR's secretary of the navy. After Fusionists won the Wilmington city council elections in the fall of 1898, the White Government Union staged a coup. A mob of 2,000 men seized weapons from the armory and raged through Black neighborhoods, killing at random as many as 300 people and burning homes and businesses. They forced the elected officials to resign and seated insurgents in their places. The *Charlotte Observer* praised the coup as a victory of "the business men of the State." The Democrats would go on to achieve the total disenfranchisement of Black people and of some poor Whites at a state constitutional convention in 1900.[27]

In the twentieth century, as America became increasingly urbanized, large-scale racial violence became a recurrent feature of urban life, with hundreds of Black people killed and whole neighborhoods laid waste: Atlanta in 1906, East St. Louis in 1917, Tulsa in 1921, and dozens of cities and towns in the "Red Summer" of 1919, including Chicago, Omaha, and Washington, DC. Economic and political competition were typically the root causes, but accusations of rape and rampant criminality were the ex post facto justification. Atlanta was typical. Mobs scoured the downtown and Black neighborhoods, pulling individuals off streetcars and hanging them to lampposts and burning blocks of residences and businesses. Two Whites were killed, and a hundred or more Blacks. Though police and the National Guard were summoned to stop the killing, some joined in. Mayor James Woodward told the *New York Times* that the only way to prevent such outbreaks was "to remove the cause. As long as the black brutes assault our white women, just so long will they be unceremoniously dealt with."[28]

Black leaders struggled to ameliorate the rigors of Jim Crow. Booker T. Washington rose to national prominence on a program that accepted segregation and disenfranchisement, and he labored to make Black people culturally "respectable" and economically more useful as members of Southern society. But Black respectability and economic success were themselves affronts to the Jim Crow code. Successful Black farmers and store owners were prominent among the chosen subjects of lynch mobs in the decades before the Great War.[29]

The violence of Jim Crow politics would be sanitized, and the Lost Cause Myth engraved on the landscape, through the work of heritage organizations, most notably the United Daughters of the Confederacy (UDC). Starting in the 1880s, the UDC campaigned and raised funds for statues honoring the political and military leaders of the Confederacy. It worked with the Ku Klux Klan and similar organizations, and its spokeswomen honored them for their resistance to Yankee and "Negro rule." The creation of these memorials was linked to celebrations of the passage of Jim Crow laws. The Atlanta statue of General John B. Gordon, who founded the state's Klan, was erected in 1907, one year after the 1906 race riot. The colossal Robert E. Lee statue was installed in Richmond in 1890, as the wave of disenfranchising conventions began, and more statues were added as the movement proceeded, so that a pantheon of Confederate leaders lined the street that fronted the state capitol. A study done more than a century later would show that counties with the largest numbers of Confederate statues also had higher-than-average numbers of lynchings.[30]

The UDC also sponsored educational programs designed to indoctrinate Southern children in Lost Cause Mythology. One of the most influential leaders of the organization was Mildred L. Rutherford, a relative of Confederate statesman Howell Cobb, a historian and educator who headed the Lucy Cobb Institute for girls. Rutherford published dozens of books and pamphlets of Confederate apologetics, but her most important contribution was developing a set of guidelines for choosing textbooks. Books criticizing either secession or slavery were banned, in favor of those representing the Old South as socially harmonious, slavery as a means of uplifting Negro race, and Southerners as morally and legally justified in secession. Typical of such efforts is the *Confederate Catechism,* published in 1920 by lawyer and educator Lyon G. Tyler, president of the College of William and Mary. Distributed widely in Southern school systems, it outlines the principles that should shape the history curriculum: that the "War Between the States" was about states' rights, not slavery;

that secession was "a mere civil process," and the war an act of Northern aggression, which Southerners fought to repel. It declared that slavery was better for the Negro than freedom: "The South took the negro as a barbarian and cannibal, civilized him, . . . and turned him out a devout Christian." The *Catechism* functioned as a "teacher's guide" and a template for textbooks, and texts that departed from its tenets were to be blacklisted.[31]

The White Reunion and Ethnonationalism

While the UDC's activities were exclusively Southern, writers and journalists from the region spoke to a national audience as defenders of Jim Crow, and of the racial and cultural "heritage" that made it necessary. The most successful of these were the novelists Thomas Nelson Page and Thomas Dixon Jr. Most of Page's stories were idyllic pictures of the Old South, with happy "darkies" and kindly masters. However, *Red Rock,* published in 1898 (the year of Wilmington), centers on a corrupt Black political leader of repulsive appearance, who attempts to rape a White woman and is lynched by the forces of Redemption. In *The Negro: The Southerner's Problem* (1904), Page justifies lynching as a regrettable but necessary method of social control in a biracial society.[32]

But the masterworks of this genre were produced by Dixon, whose novel *The Clansman* (1902), a vivid and emotionally appealing dramatization of the Lost Cause / Redemption story, is to the Myth of the Lost Cause what James Fenimore Cooper's *Last of the Mohicans* is to the Frontier Myth. *The Clansman* uses that tale of the sanctified past as a template for interpreting the contemporary struggle over disenfranchisement and Jim Crow. Its popularity was phenomenal and national in scope. The novel was adapted for the stage, and most spectacularly in the epoch-making motion picture *Birth of a Nation,* released in 1915. The film earned President Woodrow Wilson's encomium of "history written with lightning" and inspired the organization of a new Ku Klux Klan.

The popularity of *The Clansman* helped make the Lost Cause Myth an integral part of American *national* mythology. The novel pits Northern Radicals against Southern Redeemers, led by the prewar planter aristocracy. But Dixon's ex-rebels are "progressive" exponents of a "New South," patriots reconciled to the Union, rather than dead-end zealots. As such they were sympathetic figures for the middle-class readership of 1902. Through the action of the novel, White people from North and South are reconciled on the basis of their common revulsion against the Reconstruction programs aimed at establishing Black equality. This is the Myth of White Reunion, and it would become foundational to the ethnonationalist concept of American nationality that emerged as the twentieth century began.[33]

That reunion is figured in the romance between the Southern hero, Colonel Cameron, and Elsie Stoneman, the daughter of Austin Stoneman, a Radical carpetbagger. Their marriage represents both the reconciliation of North and South, and the North's "female" subjection to a patriarchal South, which better understands how to manage the racial order. In an earlier work, *The Leopard's Spots* (1902), Dixon had channeled Stephen Douglas's paean to the "white basis" of American government: "This is a White man's government, conceived by White men, and maintained by White men through every year of its history—and by the God of our fathers its shall be ruled by White men until the archangel shall call the end of time." The point is even more strongly stated in *The Clansman*. Dr. Cameron (the hero's father) declares, "There is a moral force at the bottom of every living race of men," and that of the Anglo-Saxon is to rule and command. "Our future depends on the purity of this racial stock. The grant of the ballot to these millions of semi-savages and the riot of debauchery which has followed are crimes against human progress." The only way to guarantee "the purity of this racial stock," and ensure progress, is to establish a form of political despotism. The point is fully articulated in a conversation between Dr. Cameron and Austin Stoneman. Elsie's father asserts the primacy of democracy: "Manhood suffrage is the one eternal thing fixed in the nature of Democracy. . . . The Negro must be protected by the ballot. . . . The real issue is Democracy." Cameron replies, "The issue, sir, is Civilisation! Not whether the Negro shall be protected, but whether society is worth saving from barbarism." Preserving civilization requires the violent suppression of the Negroes' criminal ambitions through Klan terrorism, lynching, and disenfranchisement. On that ground, the ground of Jim Crow, the White men of North and South can reestablish the national brotherhood broken by the Civil War.[34]

The Myth of White Reunion was given performative expression by the battle-field anniversary reunions that brought Union and Confederate veterans together at the scenes of their deadly combat. The largest and most celebrated of these took place at Gettysburg in 1913. The warmth of these meetings was exaggerated—veterans on both sides held the old grievances and rancor. But the reconciliations, whether real or feigned, embodied the idea that the war had been the White man's business from start to finish, and slavery and Black equality were marginal concerns. A political culmination of this development came in the administration of Progressive Democrat Woodrow Wilson, the first man born in a Confederate state to be elected president, who decreed the segregation of the federal civil service and honored the Lost Cause by naming the new military bases established during World War I for Confederate generals.[35]

It should be noted that this White Reunion Myth never replaced the Lost Cause as the defining myth of Southern identity, but it did become dominant in history writing for most of the twentieth century. Ulrich B. Phillips, the foremost Southern historian of the pre–New Deal era, saw slavery as a benign "school" that civilized an inferior race and Reconstruction as a misconceived attempt to give that race political equality. Similar ideas were foundational to the Dunning School of historians, led by Columbia professor William Dunning, which dominated historical writing on the Civil War and Reconstruction for the first half of the twentieth century. Samuel Eliot Morison and Henry Steele Commager, two of the most distinguished historians of the mid-twentieth century, were neither Southerners nor followers of Dunning. Nevertheless, in *The Growth of the American Republic,* a college history textbook widely used until the 1960s, they took the Confederate view of slavery and denigrated Black people: "As for Sambo, whose wrongs moved the abolitionists to tears, there is some reason to believe that he suffered less than any other class in the South from its peculiar institution."[36]

Jim Crow Nationalized: Ethnonationalism in the Progressive Era

The cultural and political forces that shaped Jim Crow reflected the special conditions of Southern life and history. However, the success of the Reunionist mythology, and national enthusiasm for the work of Thomas Dixon, reflected a consonance between Southern White mythologizing and the development of ethnonationalism elsewhere in the country.

Since 1881, millions of immigrants had arrived from eastern and southern Europe, people whose language, religion, and ways of life seemed repellently alien to Americans of predominantly British and German origins. This was a time in Europe and the United States when "race" was used by social scientists to describe groups we now identify as ethnicities or nationalities. In the vocabulary of American culture, the "racial" differences of the new immigrants could only be interpreted by reference to color-based racialism.

The Immigration Restriction League, formed in 1894 by upper-class Bostonians, was the organizational home of resistance to the new immigration. The league's president, A. Lawrence Lowell, who was also president of Harvard University, echoed Dixon's thesis that true American nationality is defined by descent from "a single race, with substantially the same social and political instincts, the same standards of conduct and morals, the same industrial capability." Like Negroes and Indians, the new immigrants "are beaten men from beaten races; representing the worst failures in the struggle for existence. . . . They have none of the ideas and aptitudes . . . such as belong to those who are descended from the tribes that met under the oak-trees of old Germany to make laws and choose chieftains." In Lowell's view, "Indians, Negroes, Chinese, Jews and *Americans* cannot all be free in the same society." Either the un-American races must be prevented from entering the country, or they must be barred from political society—the solution that had been adopted by the Jim Crow states.[37]

Theodore Roosevelt's administration addressed these possibilities through the work of the Commission on Immigration chaired by John R. Commons, a Progressive labor historian and sociologist.[38] Commons's report, *Races and Immigrants in America* (1907), echoes Lowell and Dixon in its insistence that for America to survive as a democratic state, its people must constitute a single ethnoracial identity. Northern European settlers (termed "Nordics" by some racial theorists) formed the original racial basis of American nationality. Immigrants from northern Europe had been able to *amalgamate* with native stocks, blending both socially and biologically in harmonious hybridity. However, the new immigrants were only capable of *assimilation:* they might adapt their behavior to American standards, but could never truly enter into the spirit or collective psychology of American nationality: "Race differences are established in the very blood and physical constitution. . . . Races may change their religions, their forms of government, their mode of industry, and their languages, but underneath all these changes they may continue their physical, mental, and moral capacities and incapacities."[39]

Echoing Dixon's defense of Jim Crow, Commons compares the corruption of urban political machines to the malfeasance and disorder of Black Reconstruction and finds a common cause underlying both: the attempt to base a democratic government on the racially unfit, under the guidance of spoilsmen and impractical "philanthropic" idealists. The South teaches the nation a vital lesson: if we do not radically reduce immigration, we will have no practical choice but to "despotize our institutions in order to control these dissident elements."[40]

Commons's racial theories underlay the Johnson Reed Act of 1924, which barred all future Asian immigration and excluded new European immigrants on an explicitly racial basis. Passage of the act not only cut off most immigration, it signaled official approval of discrimination against Jews and Italians, inviting private individuals and institutions to restrict their access to housing, university admissions, and professional employment. A 1922 article in the *Atlantic*

Monthly, arguing against admitting Jews to colleges, the professions, and other social institutions, declared, "It is not only the individual [Jew] whom we [must] exclude, but . . . his descendants, whose blood may . . . mingle with and deteriorate the best we have." The triumph of Redemption and Jim Crow, and of the Lost Cause Myth that sustained both movements, was not only fatal to the hopes and dignity of Black people. As Lincoln prophesied, the degradation of Black people opened the door to the degradation of the White working classes, and to ethnic immigrants.[41]

Thus, at the turn of the twentieth century, American national mythology had developed a distinctly ethnonationalist character, equating patriotism with the maintenance of White racial or ethnic supremacy and treating "democracy" as a secondary value. The narrative core of that mythology was the blending of the Lost Cause and White Reunion Myths with a new, industrial-era version of the Myth of the Frontier. Chapter 6 deals with the sources, structure, and consequences of that myth.

PART III

The Nation Transformed

From the Civil War to the Good War

6

Industrialization, Vigilantism, and the Imperial Frontier

THE MYTHOLOGY of the Civil War powerfully affected the way Americans thought about their nationality, but it was the frontier that provided the dominant strain in national myth from 1870 to 1929—the period that began with completion of the transcontinental railroad and ended with the Great Depression. Where the Civil War Myths revolved around destructive violence and the intractable question of racial equality, the Frontier Myth celebrated the vast expansion of the American economy that followed the war and placed the nation among the Great Powers. In the last decade of the nineteenth century, Theodore Roosevelt and Frederick Jackson Turner would codify the Frontier Myth as a grand theory of American exceptionalism, making it in effect the "official" national myth. On the way to that status, the Frontier Myth was adapted to address the special conditions of an industrial economy. New types of bonanza replaced the opening of new lands to agriculture as the measure of progress, and the concept of "savage war" was expanded to link Indian wars with labor conflicts.[1]

The Railroad and Bonanza Economics

After the Civil War, the United States experienced a period of explosive economic growth, which has been called the Gilded Age, marked by rapid industrialization and the growth of big business. The new economy was fueled by gigantic manufacturing and transportation corporations, as well as large corporate "trusts," which engulfed small businesses while great banking houses generated, organized, and ultimately controlled the flow of capital (both international and domestic). Neither state nor federal laws were designed to cope with this kind of economic order, and corruption, speculation, price gouging, and exploitation were rampant.

The expansion of wealth fulfilled the Frontier Myth's promise that new bonanzas would fuel America's perpetually rising prosperity. Yet the new frontier was radically different from the original in form and social function. Instead of a natural paradise where pioneering individuals sought their fortunes, the new frontier was urban, dependent on the massing of workers in industrial settings. Instead of expanding the property-owning classes and promising to diminish the gap between rich and poor, the new order concentrated wealth and power at the top and reduced workers to wage dependency.

The transition between these two frontiers was symbolized by the development of the nation's railroad network. The rebuilding and expansion of Southern railroads, the elaboration of existing networks, and the extension of transcontinental lines to the Pacific stimulated mining and heavy industry to feed the railroads' demands for steel, coal, and machinery. The railroads also opened a new phase of agrarian development, bringing settlers and ranchers to the Great Plains and Intermountain West. The combination made railroading the symbolic center of a revised Frontier Myth, which harmonized the old themes with the new industrial order.

Though projects for a transcontinental rail network in the 1850s had been blocked by the political rivalry between North and South, the literature promoting these projects roused extravagant expectations of their potential for increasing national wealth and power. The prophet of the iron horse was William Gilpin, a promoter of railroading and western settlement, later governor of the Colorado Territory. Gilpin looked beyond the railroad's potential for opening access to new farmlands to more spectacular sources of growth, based on the exploitation of western mineral resources and the development of an industrial economy. America would be transformed, revealed to the world as "a new power, *the People* occupied in the wilderness, engaged at once in extracting from its recesses the omnipotent element of *gold coin,* and disbursing it immediately for the industrial conquest of the world."[2]

The precondition for achieving that grand destiny was the building of a transcontinental railroad. Gilpin drew on a mythological reading of nature to envision a route that would follow the natural flow of warm, fertilizing air up the Missouri River Valley to the South Pass of the Rockies, where it penetrated what Gilpin called "the Mother Mountain," and ultimately end at Puget Sound. The banker Jay Cooke, promoter of the Northern Pacific Railroad, plagiarized Gilpin's vision to promote his enterprise. Other promoters also drew on Gilpin's vision of the undeveloped West as a region rich in potential mineral and agricultural resources, whose value could only be created or tapped by railroads linking them to the industrializing East. The various transcontinental and western lines—Central Pacific, Southern Pacific, Northern Pacific, Denver and Rio Grande—became vehicles for rampant speculation and outright fraud, producing an economic boom from 1867 to 1873 and a catastrophic bust that ran from 1873 to 1878.

Nevertheless, transcontinental railroads did enable frontier farmers and miners to connect with eastern markets, and made possible commercial booms (often called bonanzas) in mining and agricultural commodities. After 1865 the discovery of new lodes of gold, silver, and copper produced a succession of mining booms throughout the Intermountain West. There were also highly touted bonanzas in agricultural commodities like range cattle (1870–1885) and Red River wheat (1880s), in irrigated farming (1890–1920), and especially in energy resources (Texas and Oklahoma oil in the early twentieth century).[3]

The new order brought new problems. Class conflicts sharpened as wealth and power were consolidated in the owning and managing classes, the old middling classes of artisans and tradespeople were reduced to wageworkers, and small farmers became tenants and sharecroppers. Conflicts between labor and capital increased in number and intensity as wageworkers and sharecroppers reacted to their "degradation" in the workplace, and managers and landlords defended their interests with escalating levels of force. In the South these national crises merged with battles over ending Reconstruction and the establishment of Jim Crow. Thus the modernization of American society was accompanied by a rising tide of social violence. At the same time, in order to drive the railroad frontier westward, and protect the economic benefits it produced, the United States would have to fight the last and most celebrated of its "savage wars" against the Indians of the Great Plains.[4]

This same period saw a demographic transformation of the White population. Immigration rose from approximately 100,000 per year in 1865–1867 to 800,000 in 1870, and the foreign-born as a percentage of the American population rose from 10 to 15 percent. Although the rate of immigration would diminish somewhat during the hard economic times of the 1890s, it remained high in comparison to pre–Civil War norms; and after 1900 it would grow explosively, raising the share of the population of foreign-born and first-generation immigrants above 34 percent by 1915. Traditional sources of immigration, such as Ireland and Germany, continued to send large numbers overseas. But most of the new immigrants came from countries and ethnic groups not previously represented in the population: Chinese and other Asians (excluded by special legislation after 1882), and eastern and southern Europeans. Thus the class conflicts that marked life in the new industrial districts and growing cities would increasingly have an ethnic or (in nineteenth-century terms) a "racial" cast.[5]

The passions and anxieties that made the period so violence prone were a response to the paradoxical character of the postwar frontier. In a way, the opportunities for economic growth and for personal advancement had never been greater: new lands for farmers, new lodes for miners to exploit, new industries to provide employment. But at the same time, there was a growing awareness that new businesses and small farms were harder to maintain, and there was stiffer competition for new jobs and wages. There was also a growing sense that the Great Plains and Intermountain West were America's "last frontier." When it was gone—and the process of settlement was now vastly accelerated—the nation's "safety valve" would shut down, trapping labor and capital in a zero-sum struggle for finite resources.

Custer's Last Stand and the Crisis of the Railroad Frontier

The event that would come to symbolize this new and last frontier was Custer's Last Stand, the astounding and catastrophic defeat of a modern military force by a horde of "savages" on the Little Bighorn River in Montana on June 25, 1876. It was a shocking challenge to the promise of perpetual progress inherent in the Frontier Myth. The battle's significance was enlarged by the context in which it occurred. The news arrived in the East just as the nation was celebrating the Centennial of American Independence, with a grand world's fair in Philadelphia that proudly displayed the fruits of American industrial productivity. It was framed by the contested Hayes-Tilden presidential election, as well as racial violence by Southern Redeemers in South Carolina and Mississippi. It came at the height of a depression, which began with the Panic of 1873. The immediate precipitant of the crash was the bankruptcy of the Northern Pacific Railroad, whose interests had been promoted by George Armstrong Custer himself during his 1874 expedition to the Black Hills. It was followed within a year by a nationwide railroad strike, which seemed the prelude to a new civil war pitting capital against labor.[6]

As a result, a relatively minor military engagement and a man of marginal historical importance have acquired a disproportionate weight and presence in our culture. "Custer's Last Stand" is an American idiom, a perennial reference for comedians, cartoonists, politicians, poets, and novelists. From 1886 to 1898, Buffalo Bill's Wild West was one of the nation's most popular entertainments.

It celebrated the conquest of the frontier, and its grand finale was a reenactment of Custer's Last Stand featuring Seventh Cavalry veterans and Lakota warriors, some of whom had actually fought Custer. Studies of Last Stand images by Don Russell and Brian Dippie indicate that the Battle of the Little Bighorn may be the most frequently depicted event in American history. Russell cataloged 1,000 different depictions, many of which have been reproduced thousands and hundreds of thousands of times—in paintings, line cuts, lithographs, posters, bumper stickers, bubble-gum cards, T-shirt logos, even cereal boxes and comic book covers. The famous "Budweiser lithograph" became an icon of popular illustration and has been prominently displayed in saloons and diners since 1885. In 1942 the War Department struck off 2,000 copies and distributed them to army camps to inspire the troops with an icon of heroic sacrifice. Then there are the movies—dozens of films in which the Last Stand is the central catastrophe, from Thomas Ince's silent *Custer's Last Fight* of 1912 to *Little Big Man* in 1970—and hundreds of films (war films as well as Westerns) and TV programs in which Custer's Last Stand is a reference point. These range from classics like John Ford's *She Wore a Yellow Ribbon* to an episode of *The Twilight Zone* in which a National Guard tank crew on summer maneuvers gets caught in a time warp and ends up trying to reach the Little Bighorn to rescue Custer. As if it were worth traveling back in time for that purpose alone.[7]

The enduring cultural power of Custer story's arises from its having served, at its moment of origin, as a symbol of the cultural crisis of modernization. It drew on the imagery of the nation's oldest mythology—the Myth of the Frontier—but modified it to serve the ideological needs of a modern, post-frontier, metropolitan society.

The symbolism of the Last Stand was propagated by mass-circulation newspapers and journals, an industrialized form of cultural production. The papers were cheaply printed in large editions, thanks to new technologies of typesetting, illustration, and printing, and distributed to subscribers across the nation by a mail system accelerated by rail transport. Papers like the *New York Herald, New York Times, New York World,* and *Chicago Inter Ocean* were read by subscribers in every state, making them the first true medium of mass communication. They used the Custer story as a symbolic key to interpreting three great crises of 1876–1877: the Indian war, the overthrow of the last Reconstruction regimes, and the labor disorders arising from the depression. These were seen to have a structural kinship. Each was a conflict between the desires of a "lower" human order or class (Indians, Black people, and urban wageworkers) and the imperatives of the new industrial system as defined by its owners and managers. The health of the new corporate order demanded the subordination of worker to manager, and of private ambition to corporate necessity. But this was an ideology logically at odds with the traditional values of self-government and freedom of opportunity, and the political ideology of free labor for whose vindication the Civil War had been fought.[8]

The contradiction was evaded by ideological sleight of hand: the use of race-war symbolism, drawn from the Myth of the Frontier, to interpret the class warfare of workers and managers. Any class that could be likened to the mythic savage as an enemy to civilization and progress could be seen as eligible for treatment according to the savage war scenario. It would become a candidate for subjugation, segregation, or extermination, rather than a fellow citizen of the democratic polity.

Custer's public adventures in the years before his catastrophic defeat had suggested a dramatic and broadly appealing approach to the industrial-era version of the Frontier Myth. In 1874, when the economic depression was at its height—while the Molly Maguires were striking in the coalfields, Black Union Leaguers and White vigilantes battled in the South, and the unemployed "rioted" in New York's Tompkins Square—Custer was leading an exploratory expedition into the Black Hills, a long-anticipated and controversial move to open the Sioux reservation to gold mining. The major papers sent correspondents, and the *World* arranged for Custer himself to notify editor Manton Marble if gold was discovered. The bankrupt Northern Pacific Railroad and its anxious creditors were intensely interested, since opening the hills would raise the value of the land grants that were the company's collateral. The railroad had also engaged Custer as a publicist, and counted on his giving its lands a good write-up.

He gave it its money's worth. On August 16 the *World*'s front-page lead read, "THE BLACK HILLS / General Custer's Official Report / The Reports of Surface Gold . . . Fully Confirmed / A March Amidst Flowers of Exquisite Color and Perfume / The Garden of America Discovered." Custer's enthusiastic report painted the hills as both a new El Dorado and a Garden of Eden, combining the two ideas in a single image: they had found "gold among the roots of the grass." Newspapers greeted Custer's discovery as renewed proof that the resources of the frontier could still rescue America from the scarcity and social warfare of Europe. The *Chicago Inter Ocean* saw the discovery in providential terms:

> There could hardly be a more fortunate event for the country. . . .
> [Opening the hills] would give occupation to thousands who, from the

dull condition of business, are now without work, and stimulate trade and enterprise in every direction. . . . The sequence is obvious. There was a crisis in 1848–9; California was opened and helped us out. There was a crisis in 1857; in 1858 Colorado was opened and helped us out. There is a crisis in 1873, from the effects of which we have not yet recovered; the Black Hills will be opened and pull us through.[9]

But the Cheyenne, Arapaho, and Lakota resisted opening the hills, which were sacred ground and an essential hunting resource. Their claims were supported by advocates of President Ulysses Grant's "Peace Policy," which offered some protection of Indigenous rights and proposed a plan to educate the tribespeople for integration with civilized society. These liberal humanitarians, derided as "philanthropists" by conservative journalists and politicians, were also identified with the policies and ideology of Radical Republicans, including support for enfranchising Southern Black people and for the claims of unemployed workers. This association of Radical philanthropy with recalcitrant Indians, demands for Black political equality, and the angry protests of the unemployed made possible a creative leap of mythological thinking, which used the Myths of the Frontier and the Lost Cause to interpret the economic crisis.

The conservative turn in Northern opinion, which had already rejected Radical Reconstruction, broadened its focus. Black people, Indians, and strikers must learn that to stand in the way of progress is an unpardonable crime. Black people in the South were accused of "savagery," of inaugurating a "War of Races," a phrase also associated with the Indian wars. On the front pages of the *World,* the *New-York Tribune,* and the *Herald,* words initially belonging to Indian war headlines began to migrate to headlines about labor and Reconstruction. "Redskins" or "Reds," meaning Indians, chimed with references to strikers as "Reds," an epithet that originally applied to the socialist revolutionaries who led the Paris Commune uprising in 1871 and that now applied to European socialist parties generally. Indeed, the *Herald* specifically invoked "the Red spectre of the Commune" in describing mass protests by workers. In condemning the philanthropists' sentimental sympathy for the Indians, the New York *Daily Graphic* likened urban workers to savages who must also learn to be civilized:

The Indian is no such creature as he has been represented to our sympathy and imagination. He is a degraded relic of a decayed race, and it is a serious question whether he is worth civilizing. . . . Were the money and effort wasted in trying to civilize the Indian wisely expended in reclaiming and educating the savages in our cities the world would be vastly better off in the end. The globe is none too large for the civilized races to occupy, and all others are doomed by a law that is irrevocable and is folly to resist.[10]

When, against all expectations, the "degraded" Lakota, Cheyenne, and Arapaho wiped out Custer and his command, the mythic substructure of American ideology was called into question. If the Indians could win, progress could be successfully resisted and the nation would not be rescued from its economic follies by a Black Hills bonanza. And if the red savages could defeat Custer, perhaps Black savages could reclaim the South, and White savages revolutionize the great industrial cities. Here is E. L. Godkin of *The Nation:*

[The Custer tragedy has produced] a loud demand for "extermination" [of the Indians]—a course for which there is something to be said, if by extermination is meant their rapid slaughter. But if they are to be exterminated, why any longer pauperize them [i.e., by maintaining them on the reservations] and then arm them? What would be said if the city of New York, after lodging its thousand tramps in comfortable idleness during the winter, were to arm them on leaving the alms house with a good revolver and knife [to allow them to hunt]. But why should it be worse to do this thing to savage whites than to savage Indians?[11]

Godkin's question was prophetic. Custer's Last Stand was followed one year later by the outbreak of the Great Railroad Strike of 1877, which temporarily stopped railroad traffic across the country and produced what seemed like revolutionary insurrections in most major cities of the East and Middle West. Following the logic of the metaphor that equates Indians, strikers, and Black people, Godkin demanded an end to the liberalization of political and economic life, even an end to talk of human rights: "Vast additions have been made to our population . . . to whom American political and social ideals appeal but faintly, if at all, and who carry in their very blood traditions which give universal suffrage an air of menace to many of the things which civilized men hold most dear."[12]

The Last Stand provided a uniquely American figuration of the perils and potentials of modernization. In Custer and his men, the heroic traits of preindustrial pioneers—Daniel Boone, Davy Crockett, John Charles Frémont, Kit Carson—are merged with the virtues of the managerial elite, professional and commanding men at the head of governments and corporations, with disciplined subordinates serving obediently below. Against them stand all the forces that resist modernization: the unredeemable Others, primitive ethnicities, alien races, and the philanthropists who coddle them.

Class War and the Age of Vigilantism

If those who resist the progress of industrial capitalism are "savages," then the agents of progress are justified in using violence to suppress them. More: the violence they are justified in using may go to the extreme of "extermination," with which the Lakota and Cheyenne were to be threatened, or of exemplary terrorism by vigilantes, as was the case in the South. In this calculus, the necessity of suppression overrides the values of civil liberty, justifying measures to disenfranchise the Black and immigrant elements of the new proletariat.

At the highest level, the premises of this new class war were set by the heads of the giant industrial and banking corporations, trusts, and monopolies. Their policies of corporate consolidation, merger, and monopoly were intended to establish control of all commercial activities connected with their operations. To that end they would accept periods of low profit or even loss, if by price wars they could bankrupt their competitors. They took the same approach to labor, accepting serious losses when, by lockdowns and other antiunion measures, they could keep their workers from organizing. The Homestead Steel Strike of 1892 was a prime example, as was the long struggle of Cyrus McCormick to suppress unionism at the factories producing the industry-standard reaper. When all else failed, they would hire "private armies" of "detectives" and strikebreakers to confront or terrorize their workers.[13]

There were two sides to this budding class war. The industrial workers and the small farmers and tenants impoverished by the operations of corporate management or landlords were imbued with the ideas of free labor. As Americans they felt entitled to equal consideration of their interests, equal protection of the laws, and equal dignity in political controversy. In defense of their rights, they were prepared to take active measures, starting with strikes and rising to the formation of self-defense organizations. The Civil War had trained 3 million men in the use of firearms and left large numbers of war-surplus rifles and pistols. New technology boosted the output of arms manufacturers, who used advertising to exploit and expand the demand for repeating pistols and rifles. With federal and professional policing absent or inadequate, individuals and corporations formed armed groups to prosecute their side of racial or class conflict. The result was a sixty-year period of widespread social violence, which lasted from 1870 to 1930. It was characterized by *vigilantism:* the use of deadly force by private individuals and organizations to promote public or political ends.

A vigilante organization or vigilance movement is an unofficial association of citizens, sometimes calling itself a militia or *posse comitatus,* but not authorized by the state. Indeed, vigilantes often worked against governments popularly elected by the classes they opposed. Leadership of vigilante movements was almost always taken by men of property and social standing. Their methods were essentially those of terrorism: they perpetrated acts of exemplary violence, often atrocious in form, to terrorize and subdue a class of people regarded as dangerous to the social system. Their purpose was to establish or restore social control by the organizing elite. Although there were working-class vigilante movements, vigilantism has more typically been an instrument of the privileged and propertied.

Vigilantism took a variety of forms across the United States. Some movements (San Francisco in 1856, Montana in 1866) were organized to break up criminal organizations that operated in partnership with local political bosses, and dissolved when their task was accomplished. In the South, as we've seen, vigilante operations were first mounted by political organizations and movements of Redemption from Reconstruction, later for the establishment and enforcement of Jim Crow. The range wars in Johnson County, Wyoming, in 1889–1893 pitted gunslingers hired by wealthy cattlemen against posses formed by small ranchers. From the Great Railroad Strike of 1877 to the coal-country wars of the 1920s, labor disputes in every part of the country often degenerated into battles between armed strikers and antiunion vigilantes, Pinkerton or Baldwin-Felts operatives, and mercenaries or "goons" hired by employers.[14]

When these battles escalated beyond the control of local law enforcement, they were usually ended in favor of the employers by the intervention of state militia, National Guard, or federal troops. In the Homestead Steel Strike of 1892, strikers armed themselves from the militia armory and fought off an attack by armed strike-breakers and detectives, but were eventually put down by federal troops. When the 1894 Pullman Strike paralyzed rail traffic, the Seventh Cavalry was withdrawn from its role suppressing the Lakota Ghost Dance movement and used to break the strike. Painter Frederic Remington, who covered the strike for *Harper's Weekly,* thought the strikers no better than Indian savages, a "malodorous crowd of anarchistic foreign trash." He hoped for "a monster vigilance committee" to purge Chicago until they "have a fine population left."[15]

Of course, vigilantism (like terrorism) can be used by the oppressed. That was certainly what the strikers did at Homestead, in the mines of Idaho in 1892, and in southern Colorado in 1893 and 1913, as well as the small ranchers of Johnson County, Wyoming, in 1892 or Mussel Slough, California, in 1880. But in general, when strikers or small farmers resorted to armed struggle, they were either outgunned by their corporate opponents or suppressed when government troops intervened to restore peace. At Blair Mountain, during the West Virginia coal war of 1920–1921, 13,000 miners besieged a private army of 2,000 raised by the Logan County Coal Operators Association. But the 2,000 were better armed and held out until federal troops arrived to break the strike and the union.[16]

Whether the actors were vigilantes, detectives, or government forces, the rationale for the extraordinary application of armed force against working-class activism or political dissidence was the same: that the objects of violence were savages, threatening the civil order and, by extension, civilization itself. The choice, as Thomas Dixon Jr. had said, was between "Democracy" and "Civilization."[17]

The racial symbolism endemic to the Lost Cause and the Frontier Myth was thus applied to the definition of class, ethnic, and ideological difference. That combination would drive the increasingly ethnonationalist character of American ideologies at the turn of the century.

American Exceptionalism: The Frontier Hypotheses of Teddy Roosevelt and Frederick Jackson Turner

The closing of the agrarian frontier in the West and the shift to a corporate-industrial and urbanized economy produced an ideological crisis among the nation's cultural and political elites. The inequalities and social disruptions attendant on the new order challenged the premises of democracy and free enterprise on which American political culture was founded. The emergence of a permanent working class or proletariat, and the changing racial and ethnic composition of that class, called into question the concepts of nationality and equal citizenship that had been the core assumptions of American democracy.

Two theories of American history were developed in response to this ideological crisis, both of which used the Frontier Myth as the key to understanding the meaning and exceptional character of America's national development and gave it quasi-official status as the basis of American historical scholarship and teaching. In 1889 Theodore Roosevelt published his *Winning of the West,* a history of the westward movement in the colonial and early national periods. For Roosevelt the pioneering enterprise was an expression of Anglo-Teutonic racial energy, which hardened White Americans into a singular, heroic, and dominant race. In 1893 Frederick Jackson Turner delivered his epoch-making address "The Significance of the Frontier in American History" to a meeting of American historians at the World's Columbian Exposition in Chicago. For Turner it was the economic aspect of the frontier, the free land with its promise of agricultural abundance and broad access to property, that made America exceptional. Both agreed that the frontier had been responsible for making America a democratic state with a free-enterprise economy, and for giving Americans their distinctive and unifying "national character," built around individualism and love of freedom.[18]

Turner saw the frontier as the guarantor of democracy, which he identified with the "free-labor" ideology of antebellum Republicans. By fostering settlement of the virgin land, the government had facilitated the citizen's desire to own property and continually improve his or her condition. The 1890 announcement of the Census Bureau that there was no longer a substantial reserve of undeveloped arable land marked the end of the Frontier Myth. The question then arose whether America's exceptional democracy could be sustained without the material basis of free land on which it had rested. Turner hoped that the new land-grant-based universities of the Midwest would teach the values of agrarian democracy, though he feared that with shrinking opportunities in agriculture, such teaching might prove ephemeral.[19]

Roosevelt saw the frontier as the Darwinian environment that had transformed the settlers into a singular race capable of dominating the continent and creating a new and extraordinarily powerful nationality. The frontiersmen who led the drive across the Alleghenies were "the vanguard of the army of fighting settlers [who] formed the kernel of that distinctive and intensely American stock." The original elements of that race were mostly (in Roosevelt's view) Anglo-Teutonic, with some Celtic admixture. But they represented a variety of ethnic or national types (English, Scots, Scots-Irish, Dutch, German, Huguenot)—each of which, according to the anthropological theory of that time, was a distinct "race." It was through the long strife of "savage war" that these different varieties learned to think and behave as a single, unified folk.[20]

Recovering the Frontier: Regeneration through Imperialism

For Roosevelt the closing of the continental frontier, the loss of the wilderness and of the savage Indian, meant that the American race had lost access to the realm of adventure and struggle that had shaped its singular conquering character. His sponsorship of wilderness parks, like Turner's praise of land-grant colleges, offered educational experience as compensation for the loss of a material reality. But Roosevelt's real solution to the problem was to open a new imperial frontier in Asia and Latin America, where a virile new generation of Americans could engage in the regenerative violence of "savage war" that made their fathers great. Roosevelt would take an active part in that adventure by recruiting a volunteer cavalry regiment nicknamed "the Rough Riders" and leading it in battle during the Spanish-American War of 1898. What was true in Kentucky and Kansas would be as true in Cuba and the Philippines. In his 1899 essay "Expansion and Peace," written before his nomination as vice president, Roosevelt declares that where civilized and savage races meet, war is inevitable, and progress "due solely to the power of the mighty civilized races which have not lost the fighting instinct, and which by their expansion are gradually bringing peace to the red wastes where the barbarian peoples of the world hold sway."[21]

Roosevelt dismisses the critics of imperialism by describing them as (retrospective) enemies of America's own frontier progress, and by asserting the Jim Crow doctrine that civilized order must be preferred to democracy. He makes the point most forcefully in "The Strenuous Life," also written in 1899, which defends American seizure of the Philippines following the Spanish-American War.

> I have scant patience with those who fear to undertake the task of governing the Philippines, . . . [or] shrink from it because of the expense and trouble; but I have even scanter patience with those who . . . cant about "liberty" and "the consent of the governed" in order to excuse themselves from their unwillingness to play the part of men. Their doctrine, if carried out, would make it incumbent upon us to leave the Apaches of Arizona to work out their own salvation, and to decline to interfere on a single Indian reservation. Their doctrines condemn your forefathers and mine for ever having settled in these United States.[22]

The Jim Crow analogy was openly invoked by American soldiers and by journalists covering the fighting in the Philippines, who approvingly quoted their characterization of Filipinos as "niggers" and identified their killing as equivalent to the lynching of recalcitrant Black people in the South. As president, Roosevelt would suppress the Filipino independence movement and condone the use of what were called "reconcentration camps" for peasants in disaffected areas, the torture of guerrilla captives, and the massacre of civilians in the Samar campaign of 1902.[23]

Popular culture shared Roosevelt's vision of overseas empire as the logical extension of the mythic frontier. In 1898 Buffalo Bill's Wild West replaced Custer's Last Stand with a reenactment of Teddy Roosevelt's 1898 charge up

San Juan Hill in Cuba. In 1900 it played scenes from the Philippine Insurrection against the American takeover, and in 1901 a reenactment of American intervention in the Boxer Rebellion. In each of these reenactments, the part of the enemy—whether Spaniard, Filipino, or Chinese—was played by Indian performers.[24]

Ultimately, the Myths of the Frontier and Lost Cause were mutually reinforcing. Their convergence can be seen in the parallels between Theodore Roosevelt and Thomas Dixon, the most effective popularizer of Lost Cause mythology. Like Roosevelt, Dixon posits that Anglo-Saxons are a distinct and superior race whose nature is to conquer and command. In *The Clansman* he proposes, "This Republic is great, not by reason of the amount of dirt we possess, the size of our census roll, or our voting register—we are great because of the genius of the race of pioneer white freemen who settled this continent, dared the might of kings, and made a wilderness the home of Freedom."[25] Dixon agreed with Roosevelt that overseas empire was the logical and necessary next phase of the American Frontier, and both linked the imperial project to the post–Civil War White Reunion. In his legend-making account of the Spanish-American War, *The Rough Riders* (1900), Roosevelt dwelt on the comradeship of Northerners and Southerners in the Cuban campaign. In *The Leopard's Spots,* published the same year, Dixon presented the "revolutionary" triumph of Jim Crow as the prelude to the Cuban triumph: "America, united at last and invincible, waked to the consciousness of her resistless power. And, most marvellous of all, this hundred days of war had re-united the Anglo-Saxon race. This sudden union of the English-speaking people in friendly alliance disturbed the equilibrium of the world, and confirmed the Anglo-Saxon in his title to racial sway."[26] Senator Albert Beveridge saw that transfigured Anglo-Saxon America extending the frontier into a worldwide civilizing mission: "We will not renounce our part in the mission of our race, trustee, under God, of the civilization of the world. And we will move forward . . . with gratitude . . . to Almighty God that He has marked us as His chosen people, henceforth to lead in the regeneration of the world."[27]

Bonanza Economics in an Industrial Economy

Roosevelt may have been more engaged by the racial revitalization of "savage war" than by empire's commercial benefits. But most advocates of imperialism also saw it as the basis of a new economic bonanza, perhaps even a replacement of Turner's lost frontier. Brooks Adams, a leading theoretician of the new global economic order, favored the acquisition of the Philippines and of strategic islands across the Pacific. These could be used as bases for projecting military force, he argued, which would enable America to compete with the European powers and Japan for control of the China market. Trade with China was the ultimate bonanza, a huge market for the surplus production of America's growing industries and agricultural abundance.[28]

The commercial benefits of these imperial projects would prove debatable. The expense of governing and defending the Philippines outweighed the profits from corporate plantation and mining operations. The promise of the China market was illusory during this period, when the great mass of its people were desperately poor and trade was continually disrupted by uprisings, conflicts among regional warlords, and competition between the imperial powers. Nevertheless, the Frontier Myth retained its appeal, expressed in the perennial hope that some new discovery of natural resources or technology would restore something like the old economy of abundance and opportunity.

One new industry that seemed to embody the Frontier promise was the oil business. From the 1870s onward, the spectacular growth of America's industrial production was made possible by the availability of abundant, and therefore cheap, fossil fuels, primarily coal until the early 1900s, and thereafter oil and natural gas. The discovery and exploitation of oil was strongly associated with the imagery and themes of the Frontier Myth.[29]

Although large oil reserves were first found in Pennsylvania in 1859, the real oil boom began in Texas and Oklahoma at the start of the twentieth century. The discovery there of superabundant oil fields was likened to the California and Alaska gold rushes, and the operational style of oil wildcatters and speculators gave the development a distinctly Wild West flavor—until corporate giants, led by Standard Oil, took over the industry. Early promoters of the oil bonanza painted their enterprise as the latest expression of Manifest Destiny: "Who can doubt but that in the wise operations of God's Providence, the immense oil resources of this country have been developed at this particular time, to aid in the solution of the mighty problem of the nation's destiny?" To make the analogy perfect, exploitation of the Oklahoma fields from 1907 to 1930 was enabled by the use of chicanery, government malfeasance, and murderous violence to deprive Native Americans of their rights to the land and its resources.[30]

In 1870 the young entrepreneur John D. Rockefeller formed an oil refining corporation, which he developed into Standard Oil, one of the largest, most efficient, and most profitable companies in the field. Railroads were hungry for the business of shipping his product to market, and he parlayed that hunger into advantageous contracts that allowed him to buy out or bankrupt his competitors. With substantial control of refining and shipping, he reached out laterally to control the oil business from wellhead to retail outlet. At its peak, Standard Oil controlled 90 percent of the American petroleum market, and Rockefeller became the wealthiest man in America. With the vast capital won by his virtual monopoly, Rockefeller moved beyond industrial production to become a major investment banker, on a par with J. P. Morgan.[31]

Rockefeller's success provided a model for other would-be monopolists of the Gilded Age, such as Andrew Carnegie, Henry Clay Frick, and Andrew Mellon in the steel industry, where accelerating demand and new technologies enabled radical increases in productivity and profitability. This was bonanza economics with a vengeance, on a hitherto unimaginable scale. It created an economic order of unprecedented inequality, dominated by huge corporations and corporate combinations called trusts, and a new class of tycoons who used their power to break the nascent labor movement and control the costs and conditions of labor. As a result, this new bonanza did not produce the diffusion of property and wealth associated with the old frontier.

A more Turnerian alternative was envisioned by Charles A. Beard, the preeminent American historian of the pre–World War II period, and his wife, Mary, with whom he coauthored two monumental interpretations of the American past, *The Rise of American Civilization* (1927) and *America at Midpassage* (1939). In these magisterial works, and in shorter books that addressed special issues, he emphasized the primacy of economic interests in shaping US history. Like Turner, but without regret, he recognized the displacement of agriculture by industry as the prime mover of American economics and politics. He saw the extraordinary productivity of the industrial economy as the basis of a new economy of abundance, in which all classes would eventually share—a precursor of the doctrine that would become political orthodoxy after 1960, that "a rising tide lifts all boats."[32]

However, Beard too sees some races as unfit for or inimical to the development of industrial civilization. In *The Idea of National Interest* and *The Open Door at Home* (1934) Beard complained that the original frontier Eden had been undone by the importation of alien masses, which diluted and displaced the native producing classes of farmers and mechanics. Beard describes the "new immigrants" of the late nineteenth century as "less adapted to the national heritage than many races later excluded by law" (a reference to Asians barred by various "exclusion" acts in the 1870s and 1880s). He asserted that national identity, as embodied in figures like George Washington and Thomas Jefferson, was racial as well as cultural, requiring homogeneity of "blood and language" and an inborn capacity for self-government. In this he followed the lead of John

Commons's report *Races and Immigrants* (1907), which asserted that continued immigration by the racially unfit would force us to "despotize our institutions." Beard saw the Johnson Reed Act of 1924 as a turning point in the development of American culture, because it set immigration quotas based on a given race's present share of the population, which would radically limit immigration from sources other than northern Europe. Beard saw this as a salutary cultural "revulsion" against the "Oriental and European invasion" of American civilization, and the beginning of a determination to "build a civilization with characteristics sincerely our own."[33]

Thus, in the opening decades of the twentieth century, the structures of national mythology had hardened around ethnonationalist concepts of nationality and patriotism. The Roosevelt-Turner codification of the Frontier Myth set the terms for an exceptionalist version of American history, which saw perpetual economic growth as the basis of democracy and used the racialist principles of "savage war" to interpret both foreign affairs and domestic social relations. The ethnonationalist ideology of that myth was supported by the triumph of the White Reunion version of the Civil War Myth over the Liberation version; and by the Lost Cause Myth, which continued to shape the South's sense of cultural particularity and perpetual grievance.

Still, this rising tide of ethnonationalism did not have a monopoly on American ideology: there was a persistent liberal strain in American culture committed (with varying degrees of strength) to the ideals of civil and racial equality and cultural pluralism. The assertion of Anglo-Saxon superiority could not change the fact that America was already racially and ethnically diverse, and was becoming more so with each generation. Black people and the descendants of the new immigrants would form voting blocs that enabled them to articulate and pursue their political interests. Their rising demographic strength would translate into transformative social and cultural change as successive presidents grasped for their allegiance in their efforts to cope with the Great War, the Great Depression, World War II, and the Cold War.

7

The Great Exception
The New Deal and National Myth

THE NEW DEAL is, in historian Jefferson Cowie's phrase, "the great exception" of American history, "a sustained deviation . . . from some of the main contours of American political practice, economic structure, and cultural outlook." During the presidency of Franklin Delano Roosevelt, "the central government used its considerable resources in a systematic, if hardly consistent, fashion on behalf of the interests of non-elite Americans in ways that it had not done before or since."[1]

The Roosevelt administration responded to the two most serious crises in American history since the Civil War, the Great Depression and World War II, by creating a political "order" based on enduring political coalition and an ideological consensus that directed public affairs for more than forty years, constraining even conservative presidents like Dwight Eisenhower and Richard Nixon to accept its basic premises. The regulatory regime FDR established moderated the boom-and-bust swings that had marked the history of American capitalism. Through Social Security, his administration created a "safety net" for working-class Americans, and a model for future programs like Medicare and Medicaid. By supporting the labor movement, it helped create a high-wage economy. The "New Deal order," which guided American politics from 1933 to 1973, saw the American economy achieve unprecedented levels of productivity and abundance, the benefits of which were distributed with greater equality between rich and poor than at any time since the 1850s.[2]

And yet the New Deal, as such, did not become the theme of a distinct national myth, a constantly referred-to fable of crisis heroically overcome. With the major national myths, invocation of a single iconic figure or image, or repetition of a mnemonic phrase, evokes both a myriad of legendary stories and the larger narrative structure of the whole myth. Mention Daniel Boone or George Armstrong Custer and the grand structure of the Frontier Myth is suggested; cite Pickett's Charge and everything from Fort Sumter to Ford's Theater comes to mind. What do we remember of the New Deal? FDR is certainly a heroic figure, with his confident grin and cigarette holder jutting up at a jaunty angle. His speeches still resonate, "nothing to fear but fear itself" and "this generation of Americans has a rendezvous with destiny." The "Hundred Days" of rapid action that began his administration has become a staple of political discourse, but the achievement seems something struck at one blow, as if without struggle. The long campaign of the unions to transform the relations of labor and capital was of utmost importance, and marked by dramatic episodes like the Flint Sit-In Strike of 1936–1937 or the Memorial Day Massacre of 1937. But labor organizing did not generate a novelistic or film genre comparable to the Western or the gangster film, or works like Thomas Dixon Jr.'s Lost Cause romances, to inscribe these events in historical memory. The one enduring fiction to come out of the era is *The Grapes of Wrath* (1939), which concerns agricultural workers and says little about the New Deal as such.

It is not that the 1930s lacked events with story potential. Rather, the moral and ideological core of the New Deal, its commitment to using the instruments of democratic government to achieve a measure of social justice, was subsumed by the Myth of the Good War—the fable that formed out of the struggle between New Deal America and world Fascism. This new myth offered a transformed concept of nationality, broadly inclusive of racial and ethnic groups hitherto excluded from the category of "true Americans"; and it saw the patriotic unity of diverse groups as the basis of America's power among the nations. In the end there was no New Deal myth of regeneration through unionization, or regulation, or public works; but rather a myth continuous with the traditional structure of regeneration through violence.[3]

We therefore have two stories to follow in analyzing the New Deal's effect on national myth. One traces the way existing myths were used and partially revised during the political struggles of the period. The other examines the creation of the Good War Myth, and its propagation through the transition from World War II to the Cold War—a history that begins before the New Deal, in the crisis of American participation in the Great War.

The Last Frontier and the Moral Equivalent of War

The nation's traditional approach to political economy mixed libertarian ideology (individualism, bonanza economics) with policies favoring capital: minimizing regulations, discouraging or suppressing unions, protecting the privileges of property and of creditors, and sponsoring corporate use of public lands and resources. The system was supposed to produce abundance while guaranteeing democracy, but by the end of the 1920s it had produced a society in which inequalities of wealth were the greatest in American history.[4]

The Great Depression exposed the weaknesses of those policies and the myths that sustained them. Investment markets, driven by unregulated speculation and dependent on the confidence and resources of a small wealthy class, saw their valuations crash. Bank failures wiped out the savings of workers and the middle classes; home and farm mortgages went into foreclosure on a massive scale. Deprived of capital, factories and businesses fired workers or closed outright, leading to mass unemployment and immiseration. The Hoover administration's policy was only a slight improvement on the conservative response to the 1873–1878 depression, when the unemployed were told to "work or starve."[5]

The New Deal was framed in direct contradiction to the premises of bonanza economics. Franklin D. Roosevelt made that contradiction explicit in his 1932 presidential campaign: "Our last frontier has long since been reached. . . . There is no safety valve in the form of a Western Prairie. . . . Our task is not the discovery or exploitation of natural resources. . . . It is the less dramatic business of administering resources and plants already in hand . . . of distributing wealth and products equitably."[6] FDR's declaration was not unprecedented in the discourse of the Frontier Myth. Frederick Jackson Turner's Frontier Hypothesis took off from that same assumption. But Turner thought American democracy could survive if a moral equivalent of the frontier were found. Charles and Mary Beard had imagined such an equivalent in the extraordinary productivity of the industrial economy, and the discovery of the natural energy resources needed to sustain it. But it was precisely that corporate-industrial economy that imploded in 1929.

Roosevelt's vision departed from the Turner model, and the Beards' corollary, by envisioning an economy no longer capable of rapid growth, with a limited "bank" of natural resources. Without the safety valve of the open range, Americans had to choose between fighting each other for limited resources or cooperating and sharing on some basis of equity. In fact, Roosevelt was mistaken in thinking that the American economy was no longer capable of great expansion—a mistake he would eventually realize. But his focus on social justice and redistribution would have profound and generally beneficial effects. It would create the basis for future prosperity by rebuilding the working and middle classes, and it saved American politics from the fatal polarizations that overtook most of Europe in the 1930s.

FDR promised an active course of innovation and experimentation, a pragmatic search for what would work. He had a precedent in the "New Nationalism" platform put forward by Theodore Roosevelt as a third-party Progressive candidate in 1912, which called for regulation of corporate oligarchs by a government acting for a "patriotic" public good. FDR would follow that model in framing the National Recovery Administration; but its regulatory regime was unwieldy and was rejected by the Supreme Court. The administration responded by developing a series of focused initiatives, which proved more effective.

The Roosevelt administration often stumbled in its efforts to revive the economy. The Depression would only really end when the threat of war required massive expenditures for rearmament. Nevertheless, the New Deal transformed American society in ways that were unprecedented, positive, and enduring. It created broad and effective programs of public relief. It temporarily shut the banking system to stop a panic, then established the Federal Deposit Insurance to guarantee the safety of personal savings, and the Securities and Exchange Commission to control speculation on Wall Street. It undertook a federally financed public works program, expanding infrastructure to create jobs on a scale far beyond the Whig / Republican programs of "internal improvements." It established the National Labor Relations Board, through which the government would weigh in on behalf of organized labor, generating an unprecedented wave of successful unionization. Finally, simply by displaying the willingness of democratic government to engage the crisis and meet the people's needs, it demonstrated the viability of democracy at a time when other societies descended into Fascism or Communism.

The New Deal also departed from the "savage war" aspect of the Frontier Myth. It stepped back from the imperialist role envisioned by Theodore Roosevelt and pursued by Republican and Democratic administrations in the first thirty years of the century. The Tydings-McDuffie Act of 1934 would grant independence to the Philippines in 1946. The Good Neighbor Policy abjured intervention in the affairs of Caribbean and Latin American nations, which from 1915 to 1934 had seen American marines fighting in Mexico, Nicaragua, Haiti, and Panama.

Roosevelt did liken the Depression crisis to "war" as a measure of its threat to national existence. But he framed the struggle against the Depression as the "moral equivalent of war" for which Progressive reformers had yearned. The centerpiece of the First New Deal, the National Recovery Administration, was promoted with the same kind of parades and pageants that had been used during the Great War to mobilize the Doughboys and sell the Liberty Loan.

The Blue Eagle emblem displayed by cooperating companies, stores, and unions was a counterpart of the blue or gold stars hung in the windows of families with men in the service. The regulatory regime of the National Recovery Administration was "enforced" by moral appeals to the public interest and national patriotism, backed by the distant threat of federal intervention.

The New Deal was also shaped by a hidden legacy of the Great War. To recruit an army large enough to contend with the Great Powers, the government had had to appeal for the support of groups that had been denigrated and targeted for exclusion by the ethnonationalist ideology of the Progressive Era. To meet manpower needs, government propagandists redefined American nationality as an ideal "to which every citizen, of whatever race, may rally," and offered Black people and new immigrants acceptance in exchange for military service. That liberalization was foreclosed by a postwar reaction marked by race riots and passage of anti-immigrant legislation. However, White ethnics continued to vote in growing numbers, and the Democratic Party—traditionally strong with immigrant-based political machines—got the lion's share of their support.[7]

The role of African Americans was more problematic. Although the New Deal extended some relief to Black people, it did little or nothing to end discrimination in jobs, benefits, and housing, or to moderate Jim Crow policies in the South. The Social Security Act of 1935 did not cover farmers and domestic workers, occupations in which Black people predominated. The Wagner Labor Relations Act of 1935 allowed unions to exclude Black people. Nevertheless, enough was done to earn FDR increasing support from Northern Black communities, which would otherwise have gone to the party of Abraham Lincoln. Eleanor Roosevelt's public support for civil rights and opposition to Jim Crow undoubtedly helped foster this shift, but it was also clear that whatever hopes of change the Black community had depended on the kind of activist government FDR was creating.[8]

The Culture of Americanism

The New Deal's political power was based on a coalition of left-liberal intellectuals and labor union organizers, of Southern populist segregationists and ethnic and racial minorities. To pull such diverse elements together, the Roosevelt administration needed a new national myth, one that was not racially or ethnically exclusive, and open to labor's demand for a radical reordering of economic power. The National Recovery Administration's patriotic pageants promoted a generalized spirit of nationalism. More systematic efforts were made through an array of cultural programs, most of which were developed through the Works Progress Administration (WPA), the federal agency that oversaw the New Deal's infrastructure and employment programs. In the end these efforts did not produce a single coherent myth, but they developed certain broad themes that would eventually come together in the Good War Myth.

The Federal Writers' Project produced a series of well-written and well-researched guidebooks describing the attractions and resources of each state and giving an account of its history. They were written by scholars, serious journalists, and creative writers, and their histories often criticized injustices like slavery and the mistreatment of Native Americans. The project also sponsored theatrical productions, which dealt with both historical and current events, not only in the big urban centers but in small cities across the country. The WPA supported regionalist painters like Thomas Hart Benton and Grant Wood, whose work created a kind of visual folklore of the American past, linking iconic images of George Washington and Abraham Lincoln to snapshots of common life in farms and cities, saloons and speakeasies. The Fine Arts Section of the Treasury Department sponsored the creation of murals in post offices and public buildings across the country that celebrated local history as well as the national past. Murals often emphasized the pioneering or frontier phase of development, and employed traditional racial stereotypes of Native Americans and Black people. But the prevalent themes were those of work and production in farm and factory—celebrations of the role of working people in creating the nation.

It was essential to the New Deal's ideology to praise the "common man" and show how ordinary folk shape history. So researchers sponsored by the Smithsonian went out to discover, record, and publicize the folk culture of the American people. They transcribed the stories of formerly enslaved people, whose memories reached back to antebellum plantation life. They recorded the stories and music of marginalized peoples, especially rural White people, African Americans, and immigrant ethnic communities. Radio broadcasters and record publishers picked up and marketed some of the new material, making it part of popular culture. The 1930s saw a revival and transformation of American folk music, and a strong crossover movement bringing Black music and musicians into the popular mainstream. Huddie "Lead Belly" Ledbetter, Woody Guthrie, Pete Seeger, and the Almanac Singers sang traditional folk songs, which blended with their own folk-style songs in support of labor unions, the antiwar movement, and New Deal projects like the WPA and Grand Coulee Dam. For the first time, American culture was being systematically represented as a confederacy of different, but equally *American,* racial, linguistic, and ethnic traditions.[9]

These various elements of New Deal culture suggest the rudiments of a new American myth, in which the working classes—now augmented and varied by immigration and emancipation—are heroes of a national success story. The problem was how to root these images of a new America in an appropriate version of the past. Faced with a crisis in which myth has to be revised, people will ransack their existing heritage of myths and symbols for principles that will allow them to frame a productive response. So in the 1930s New Deal supporters looked to the repertoire of traditional myths for ways of modeling and justifying their endeavor.

The Frontier Myth had limited use in this context. It could be invoked, as it was in WPA murals, in celebration of a heroic past. But FDR had begun by framing the Depression as the End of the Frontier, and popular culture ratified this view. The gangster film replaced the Western as a major Hollywood action genre, reflecting a gritty urban America of constricted economic opportunity. The Western would only be revived at the end of the 1930s, as economic conditions improved and the approach of war led to a demand for more positive visions of American history.

Roosevelt's Myth of the Founding and the Lincoln Problem

The Supreme Court's rejection of the National Recovery Administration and other early New Deal programs, and the emergence of the businessmen's Liberty League to organize conservative opposition, led FDR to take a more radical and confrontational approach to reform. He used the Myth of the Founding to frame the more transformational set of programs known as the Second New Deal.

In his speech accepting the presidential renomination in 1936, Roosevelt invoked the Revolutionary War. The US economy had fallen under the control of "economic royalists"—Tories in the symbology of the Revolution—who built "new kingdoms . . . [based] upon concentration of control . . . [leaving] no place among this royalty for our many thousands of small businessmen and merchants who sought to make a worthy use of the American system of initiative and profit. They were no more free than the worker or the farmer. . . . Against economic tyranny such as this, the American citizen could appeal only to the organized power of government." Thus the New Deal was not "socialism" but the defender, not only of the working classes, but of small businessmen and entrepreneurs. Conservative complaints that the New Deal violated the

Constitution were not only technically incorrect; they obscured the true nature of the struggle, which touched principles so vital they justified something like a revolution: "These economic royalists complain that we seek to overthrow the institutions of America. What they really complain of is that we seek to take away their power. Our allegiance to American institutions requires the overthrow of this kind of power. In vain they seek to hide behind the flag and the Constitution. In their blindness they forget what the flag and Constitution stand for. Now, as always, they stand for democracy, not tyranny; for freedom, not subjugation; and against dictatorship by mob rule and the overprivileged alike."[10]

But between the New Deal and the Founders fell the shadow of the Civil War. Roosevelt's theory of the Founding implicitly follows Lincoln's: the Declaration of Independence sets the moral and political ideal toward which constitutional government was intended to grow. For New Dealers, Lincoln became a vital symbol of the power of American democracy to overcome an extreme political and economic crisis. As Nina Silber documents, New Dealers tended to "hammer home the Civil War analogy, and use the precedent of Abraham Lincoln for insisting on strong federal intervention for humanitarian ends." FDR himself appealed to the "spirit" of Lincoln, which would guarantee that "the men and the means will be found to explore and conquer the problems of a new time with no less humanity and no less fortitude than his."[11]

Lincoln was an especially powerful symbol for the New Deal's prolabor policy. His long and eloquent advocacy of "free labor" made him a rich source of rhetorical appeals on behalf of working people. His December 3, 1861, State of the Union address asserted that "labor is prior to, and independent of, capital. Capital is only the fruit of labor, and could never have existed if labor had not first existed. Labor is the superior of capital, and deserves much the higher consideration." That was close enough to Karl Marx's labor theory of value to please the Far Left. Lincoln's new status as a touchstone of the most liberal strain in New Deal politics was signified by the adoption of the name Abraham Lincoln Battalion by the American volunteers who fought against the Fascists in the Spanish Civil War (1936–1939).[12]

Lincoln's cultural standing had been enhanced during the 1920s by the ceremonies dedicating the Lincoln Memorial in 1925, and by the publication of Carl Sandburg's *Abraham Lincoln: The Prairie Years* in 1927, a best seller and the first of three volumes glorifying Lincoln. The mystique of Lincoln as the emblematic Man of the People gained new currency through the work of WPA muralists, John Ford's film *Young Mr. Lincoln* (1939), and the award-winning play (later filmed) by Robert Sherwood, *Abe Lincoln in Illinois*.[13] However, neither Ford nor Sherwood treated Lincoln as the Great Emancipator. The only noteworthy invocation of Lincoln as a racial liberator came from Eleanor Roosevelt. In 1939 the Daughters of the American Revolution refused to allow their hall to be used for a concert by the African American singer Marian Anderson. Roosevelt protested, withdrew from the organization, and staged an outdoor concert for Anderson on the steps of the Lincoln Memorial. The moment stands out sharply against the inattention to race otherwise characteristic of the New Deal.[14]

A fully "progressive" Lincoln would not emerge until World War II and the Good War Myth challenged the traditional limitations of American nationality. In 1944 "The Lonesome Train," a cantata by Earl Robinson and Millard Lampell, would frame Lincoln as the liberator of both enslaved people and working people, the hero of a multiracial, multiethnic democracy, opposed by Southern bigots and an alliance of planters and plutocrats.

Southern responses to the Depression, in marked contrast, were informed by the Lost Cause Myth. In 1930 twelve Southern intellectuals published *I'll Take My Stand*, a manifesto that called for the restoration of the South's traditional order as a check against the corrupting effects of modern industrial culture. The authors identified themselves as Agrarians, an ideological stance rather than an actual lifeway. They were writers, teachers, and academics, most associated with Vanderbilt University, including poets and literary critics of enduring eminence like Allen Tate, Robert Penn Warren, and John Crowe Ransom, as well as neo-Confederate historians Frank Lawrence Owsley and H. C. Nixon. They "took their stand" in support of the Jim Crow order, though they disapproved its violent excesses. Several would write hagiographic biographies of Confederate leaders—Jefferson Davis, Robert E. Lee, Stonewall Jackson, Nathan Bedford Forrest. Like George Fitzhugh in the 1850s, they wanted to protect the South from the contagions of "free society" and preserve its conservative religious tradition, its patriarchal family values, and its defense of historically continuous communities that were culturally homogeneous and racially segregated. For all but one of the writers (Henry Blue Kline), the New Deal was inimical to Southern agrarian life, despite the relief it provided.[15]

Fear and resentment of federal authority, the legacy of the Civil War and Reconstruction, was augmented by Southern Democrats' essentially conservative economic ideology, which favored planters and mill owners and was opposed (often violently) to the organization of tenant cooperatives and labor unions. Yet the South's practical politicians were not at all averse to the New Deal's programs of relief and job creation. The benefits to their constituents were real, and the programs a rich resource of patronage. But desire for these emoluments was balanced by the conviction that White people must be privileged in the distribution of benefits. Southern politicians who supported the New Deal therefore drew on populist elements in the Lost Cause Myth, which saw an analogy between the Depression and the ruin of the Southern economy by Yankee armies and Reconstruction carpetbaggers.[16]

The South's preferred myths still glorified the lost grandeur of antebellum life. Margaret Mitchell's *Gone with the Wind* was a best seller when it was published in 1936 and became an enduring favorite after it was made into one of Hollywood's all-time blockbuster hits in 1939. Novel and film celebrated the plantation South; presented Black people in stereotyped roles as loyal servants, ignorant fools, violent predators, or racial incompetents; and condemned Reconstruction. More interesting and complex in its cultural resonance was the series of "outlaw" Westerns made in 1939–1941, starting with *Jesse James.* In these films ex-Confederates appear as populist heroes, leading agrarian resistance to the economic royalists of Northern-owned banks and railroads. In these genre films, the defense of democracy and the working / farming class is linked to the South and detached from the idea that the Civil War was about ending slavery.

Thus, while the New Deal broke new ideological and cultural ground, the traditional forms of national myth retained their appeal. No single story form emerged as an adequate and positive representation of the new model of government represented by the New Deal. The strikes and organizing drives through which the labor movement empowered the working class were polarizing rather than unifying stories. The only historical precedent for the New Deal was Radical Reconstruction, which, as a mythic reference, was highly problematic. However, it is worth noting that Radical Reconstruction had enjoyed wide support in the North as long as it was perceived as necessary to complete the work of the War for the Union. World War II would provide that kind of sanction for the New Deal.

From Civil War to the Good War

The lack of a broadly unifying national myth was felt more strongly toward the end of the 1930s, when the rise of Fascism and Communism challenged the premises of democracy and raised the threat of war. In a 1938 *Atlantic Monthly* article entitled "Patriotism—but How?," cultural critic Howard Mumford Jones took note of the way Fascist nations and imperial Japan energized popular support through the manipulation of patriotic myths. In contrast, for twenty years America's national myths had been subjected to a searching critique, first by the artists and intellectuals of the post–Great War disillusionment, and more recently by leftist intellectuals. Jones called for the development of a counter-vailing focus on the positive elements in our history. Writers should actively seek out "thrilling anecdotes" and "glamorous" episodes from the past, in which the audience could see the heroic expression of American and democratic virtues without the "chauvinism, economic self-interest, or racial snobbery of the totalitarian states."[17]

Jones recommended the history of the frontier as an obvious source of such stories. Hollywood was in fact moving in that direction, with its revival of "big" Westerns celebrating pioneer heroism (*Drums along the Mohawk*), tech-nological progress (railroads in *Dodge City*), and populist resistance to eco-nomic oppression (*Jesse James*). All of these films were released in 1939. But so too was *Gone with the Wind,* which took us back to the Lost Cause.

The new myth that would answer Jones's demand was already in prepara-tion. Hollywood was aware of the rising threat posed by the Fascist states and Japan. War in Europe began in September 1939, and Japan's war in China had been expanding since 1935. In 1940 FDR would push Congress to adopt the first peacetime conscription, a massive rearmament and shipbuilding program, and Lend-Lease aid to beleaguered Great Britain. Hollywood would also rearm. Since 1918 Hollywood's treatment of modern war had been largely negative. Its most popular war movie was *All Quiet on the Western Front* (1931), an antiwar film that saw World War I from a German soldier's point of view. Even films with a more heroic style, like *Dawn Patrol* (1938), emphasized the grimness and futility of war.

Two films released in 1940 and 1941 altered that pattern. The *Fighting 69th* honored the heroism of an Irish regiment from New York, and *Sergeant York* celebrated the Tennessee mountaineer and marksman (like Boone and Davy Crockett) who almost single-handedly killed or forced the surrender of an en-tire German company. The York story was especially apropos for a nation re-luctant to go to war—York had been a pacifist who was converted to belief in the justness of the Allied cause. Yet the most striking innovation in both films was their emphasis on the role of immigrants in their exemplary military units. In both films, Jewish characters are used to symbolize immigrants: the Fighting 69th includes a Jewish soldier who passes as Irish to serve in the famous regiment, and Sergeant York's buddy is a Brooklyn Jewish subway worker nick-named "Pusher." The choice may have been a response to the fact that anti-Semitism had made Jews the least acceptable of the "new immigrants" who came between 1880 and 1920. But the large presence of Jews in the movie in-dustry may also have influenced the choice.

This concept of the "platoon" as a representative ethnic and racial mixture would become the central trope of a new genre of war films. That genre would, over time and usage, become the basis of a new national myth, which would expand and "integrate" our concept of nationality. It would alter our understanding of patriotism to incorporate New Deal ideals of social justice and government responsibility, separating them from the divisive political associations of those years and making them available for the postwar completion of the liberal agenda—just as the war itself would finally do what the New Deal could not, which was to end the Depression.

8

The Myth of the Good War

Platoon Movies and the Reconception
of American Nationality

WE ARE WATCHING a movie about American soldiers at war. A sergeant calls the roll—the soldiers are a mixture of ethnic, regional, and racial types, reflecting the diversity of our population. The movie might be *Bataan* (1943), *Fixed Bayonets* (1951), *All the Young Men* (1960), *The Dirty Dozen* (1965), *Platoon* (1986), *Saving Private Ryan* (1998), or *Black Hawk Down* (2002). The "melting pot" roll call is the basic trope of the combat-film genre, popularly known as the "platoon movie." And as Gary Gerstle observes in *American Crucible,* "no narrative of nation building is more important" than the platoon movie to the development of American society and politics in the postwar period.[1]

The platoon movie became the basis of a new national myth, the Myth of the Good War, linking the embrace of ethnic and racial diversity to the transformation of America's role as a world-liberating Great Power. Its symbolism has spread well beyond war to characterize all forms of American striving and labor. Here, for example, is the response of a reporter to the explosion of the *Challenger* space shuttle in 1986: "The shuttle crew, spectacularly democratic (male, female, black, white, Japanese-American, Catholic, Jewish, Protestant), was the best of us, Americans thought, doing the best of things Americans do. The mission seemed symbolically immaculate, the farthest reach of a perfectly American ambition to cross frontiers."[2] Virtually all the ethnic and racial types represented in the *Challenger* crew appear in the roll call of the 1943 film *Bataan,* the prototype of the combat-film genre. To its roster *gender* has been added, a reflection of the new status of women in society and an anticipation of the gender-integrated army that would fight the Persian Gulf War of 1991.

The same trope can be found in the wide range of films and TV shows that deal with American workplaces, especially those engaged in public service. "Teams" representing different races, ethnic or regional groups, social classes, and genders formed the casts of police shows like *Hill Street Blues* in the 1980s, *NYPD Blue* in the 1990s, and the *Law and Order* franchise, which has been spinning off new shows since 1990. Similar groups appear in shows set in law firms (*LA Law*) or hospitals (*St. Elsewhere, Scrubs, House*). The specific makeup of these collectives has varied over time. Since 1990 there has been less attention to different White ethnicities (Jews, Irish, Italians) and more to the representation of women, Black people, Asians, Latinos, and (more recently) LGBTQ characters and Muslims. Science fiction films like the *Star Trek* and *Star Wars* franchises developed after 1975 universalize and abstract the theme of pluralism. The good guys are a federation of spectacularly different races—bony-headed people, lizard people, little green Yoda people—united against aliens who claim racial singularity and superiority (like the Klingons or the Borg in *Star Trek*) or evoke Nazi stormtroopers (*Star Wars*). But whatever the mix, the principle remains the same: "we" Americans (and our sci-fi analogues) are a multicultural, multiracial team.

The platoon movie and its attendant myth were developed deliberately, by a film industry eager to satisfy both the public, which had developed a hunger for images of the world-engulfing conflict, and the Office of War Information, which wanted entertainment media to contribute to public morale and the war effort. With the encouragement of the Office of War Information, Hollywood made so many films (1942–1946) using the platoon formula that a new genre was added to the studio-system repertoire. Like all film genres—the Western, the horror film, the gangster film—it developed a set of conventions, a visual shorthand that told audiences what kind of story to expect, what sorts of motives would shape the action, what kinds of disbelief it must suspend. Such conventions are maintained over long periods of time, and by tracing changes in the way they are used, historians can follow the evolution of public attitudes toward race, war, nationality, and patriotism—the elements of national myth. But to use genre in this way, one first has to understand how these conventions operate in the film narrative, and the historical roots from which they developed.[3]

Lost Battalions: Ethnic and Racial "Platoons" in the Great War

The Hollywood platoon movie was more than a propagandistic idealization of America. It was a utopian fiction, a projection of the kind of nation that Hollywood—acting as custodian of public myth—thought we should and could become. But that fiction was not made of whole cloth. It incorporated and transformed symbols and structures of existing national mythology, and offered a resolution to an ideological conflict that had agitated politics for two generations.

As we've seen, the period between 1880 and 1917 saw both a rapid diversification of American demography and a strong political reaction in favor of ethnonationalism. There remained, as always, a countercurrent of ideology that stood for the civic equality of all citizens, but in this period even political Progressives like Theodore Roosevelt adopted a racially exclusive concept of Americanism.

The Great War transformed the debate. It was simply impossible to raise an army of millions without the active cooperation of minority communities. By 1917, immigrants and first-generation children formed a third of the US population; another quarter were non-White (Black, Chicano, Latino, Indigenous, Asian). Faced with the overwhelming demand for manpower, the nation's leadership rediscovered the traditions of egalitarian liberalism. A wave of official publications, put out by President Woodrow Wilson's Committee on Public Information and by the military itself, now described the United States not as a White man's republic but as a "vast, polyglot community," whose patriotism appealed to an ideal "higher than race loyalty, transcend[ing] mere ethnic prejudices, more binding than the call of a common ancestry." A War Department training manual declared, "Soldier after soldier [is to be] turned out fit and eager to fight for liberty under the Stars and Stripes, mindful of the traditions of his race and the land of his nativity and conscious of the principles for which he is fighting." The official ideologists of America's Great War were offering the minorities a new social bargain: full recognition as Americans *with their differences intact* in exchange for loyal service in wartime.[4]

During the war there were some signs that the promise might be kept. Early in the war the army tried to form units based on particular cities or regions, which would have reflected the ethnic mix or lack of it in particular localities. But the need to fill the ranks quickly, and for replacing combat losses, meant that most White units reflected the melting-pot ideal. Black soldiers served in segregated units, and the majority were assigned to labor battalions. However, two Black combat infantry divisions were organized. The Ninety-Third Division served with the French Army, but White divisions also served with the French or British. The Ninety-Second Division was incorporated with the US Army, and though field officers (major and above) were White, Blacks commanded at the company and sometimes battalion level. Whether combat infantry or labor troops, Black soldiers were subject to often vicious discrimination and mistreatment. But in the Black community their service was a source of pride and high expectations.[5]

Those expectations were disappointed. A postwar racial reaction set in, opposed to the economic and political gains made by Black people and immigrants. The years 1919–1921 saw violent race riots and lynchings of Black people and an anti-Communist Red Scare directed mainly against Italian and Jewish immigrants. By 1920 the Ku Klux Klan counted 5 million members, and a quarter million Klansmen paraded in white hoods through Washington. With the Johnson-Reed Act of 1924, Congress adopted an explicitly "racial" quota for immigration, directed mainly against Jews, eastern and southern Europeans, and Asians.[6]

Nevertheless, the wartime social bargain remained an ideal to which liberals and progressives could appeal. Their efforts were supported by the rise of political activism in the minority communities. In the 1930s assimilated immigrants and some Black people became important parts of the New Deal coalition. Jews and other immigrants also achieved important positions in the film industry, the most powerful of the new mass media, as studio heads, screenwriters, actors, and directors. Finally, as a new war approached and the United States confronted the racialist ideologies of Nazi Germany and imperial Japan, the advocates of American pluralism regained their influence; and Hollywood was prepared to back the shift with persuasive imagery. This was the ideological context in which the platoon movie was conceived.

The Platoon Movie: Conventions of the Form

To appreciate what is transformative about the platoon movie, recall that existing national myths imagined America as a White republic. In the Frontier Myth, America defines itself by destroying or subjugating non-White tribes. The three versions of Civil War mythology similarly define the core of national identity as White—even in the Liberation Myth, historical agency belongs to White men. The platoon movie preserves the essential story structure of the Frontier Myth—the American people are spiritually regenerated through a violent struggle against an alien and savage enemy in a wild or chaotic landscape. However, the heroes of the platoon movie represent different races and ethnicities; and it is their very pluralism that makes them fit to liberate a world from the enslavement of Fascism, Nazism, and (later) Communism.

A roll call or similar device near the start of the film introduces a group of infantrymen, which includes representatives of various classes and regions, and of ethnic communities including Latinos, Irish, Jews, Italians, and Poles—and if the film is set in the Pacific, Filipinos or Chinese. In *Bataan* and *Sahara* (1943), the original films of the genre, the units also include a Black soldier—a most extraordinary inclusion, because the American army in World War II, like most of American society, was racially segregated. White and Black enlisted men never served together at the battalion or company level, though Black units might have White officers. The films' premise was that defeat had broken up the regular, segregated units and forced the integration of our platoon. The message is clear and in its way revolutionary: the platoon's heroism argues that integration is a precondition for victory.

These themes of racial and ethnic inclusion were not reflections of popular ideas or official policy. Southerners were more, not less, inclined to enforce Jim Crow when Black soldiers trained in Southern camps—these soldiers wore uniforms off base at peril of their lives. Army policy made it harder for Black people to qualify for combat in World War II than it had been in the Great War. A 1925 army report on Negro soldiers had declared them, as a race, unfit for the normal requirements of military service, and it took protests by Black civil rights leaders, and the intervention of Eleanor Roosevelt, to win authorization of the all-Black Tuskegee Airmen and 761st Tank Battalion. The Black Ninety-Second Division did not get to Europe till late in the war. Jews were also considered suspect—a Great War–era report held they were prone to Bolshevism and malingering. In fact, the 1930s were a period of intense anti-Semitism, as reflected in the anti-Roosevelt and antiwar polemics of Father Charles Coughlin and the America First movement.[7]

Hollywood's emphasis on *racial* as well as ethnic inclusion was deliberate and systematic. Films made late in the war, about victories won by regularly constituted units, could not credibly include Black people. Some filmmakers tried to compensate for this by having an African American sing the theme music (*A Walk in the Sun*) or showing Black sailors with White marines on an invasion ship (*Guadalcanal Diary*). All such inclusions were radical. These films were seen in Southern theaters with separate seating for White and Black audience members. The films' vision of America as a society in which all races and ethnicities were equal and integrated was certainly in advance of public opinion and the political programs of the Roosevelt administration. But the repetition of that image normalized this vision and associated it with patriotism.

The 1943 movie *Bataan* set the pattern for the racially integrated platoon movie. The film's narrative devices would soon become conventions of the genre. The movie is set in the Philippines, then an American colony, where American troops were defeated and forced to surrender in the opening months of the war. At the time the film was made, US troops had already begun to roll back Japanese gains and were planning the ultimate recapture of the Philippines.

The opening images define the mission of the war, which is to liberate the world from oppression: the Japanese bomb a column of Filipino refugees, Americans protect them. Our "platoon" (technically a squad) forms after this raid. Its mission is to delay the Japanese advance by holding a vital bridge. Their heroism will be defensive and sacrificial, symbolizing the idea that the war is a defense against aggression. Our soldiers line up for a *roll call,* the most distinctive visual convention of the form. The lineup pairs Whites with non-Whites, and with ethnic groups traditionally marked as racially different: first an innocent all-American boy, then a Filipino scout who is a Moro or Muslim, a White medic who is a conscientious objector with a Catholic Latino from Los Angeles, a Black soldier with a Polish American, and an Irishman with a Jewish American—it was a standard joke that the Irish and the Jews never got along. In this sequence, strong visual emphasis is placed on the Black soldier and his friendship with the Polish soldier. Again we must imagine this image of easy and equal friendship playing in a movie theater with separate seating for White and Black viewers. *Race* is being interpreted as a form of ethnicity, and ethnicity as a variation on Americanism.

The men's differences are stereotypical. The Irishman is feisty, the Latino is crazy about jazz, the Black soldier sings blues and spirituals. The film invokes *standard* understandings of ethnic and racial difference because its aim is to persuade "normal"—White, middle-class, native-born—Americans to see differences as benign. The nonethnic White men in the platoon are identified by profession and class. Two worth noting are Purckett, the all-American boy, and Sergeant Dane, whose name suggests Nordic origins, and whose knowledge of the enemy makes him our Hawkeye figure, the White Man Who Knows Indians. The *tough sergeant* assumes command when his captain is killed: another conventional device, which emphasizes the democratic nature of the American army, in which common men rise to the challenge of leadership.

Unlike the Americans, the Japanese are a single race, for whom blood and culture are identical. They assert racial and cultural superiority in their propaganda broadcasts and treat all other races (even the Asian Filipinos) as subjects for domination. This justifies Americans in treating them as blood enemies, as Apaches might be treated in a Western movie. Because they are merciless, they can be treated mercilessly and identified by dehumanizing racial epithets. This creates a paradox: How can the movie condemn racialism in principle while at the same time demonizing the enemy as a race cruel and inhuman by nature?

The film resolves the contradiction through a visual device I call the *race-face* convention. When a White character says something bad about a racial Other, he does so in the presence of figures who are akin to that Other by ethnicity, skin color, or both. In *Bataan* the tough sergeant first praises Japanese skill in war, then calls them "no-tail monkeys"—their strength in war is a function of their *subhuman* character. But in the background as the sergeant speaks are images of American racial partnership: the Black soldier shares grave-digging duties with a White man, a Filipino shares a machine-gun nest with a White soldier. The scene ends with a two-shot of the all-American boy Purckett and the Moro Salazar. When Purckett says he'd like to kill some Japs, the Filipino agrees. The message is clear: if *our* Asian shares Purckett's hate, then our hatred of the Japanese must be morally legitimate.

This sequence also introduces what may be the most significant convention of the genre, the *enemy's lesson*. As the sergeant says, the Japanese win *because* they fight dirty. Through the film's action, the Americans learn that, to win the war, they must fight with the same ruthlessness. The enemy aims to destroy the American people—with merciless and indiscriminate slaughter—or to subjugate Americans to rule by an alien race. These purposes not only justify a response in kind, they require it.

Thus the platoon movie also requires a climactic moment of rage and a spectacular display of annihilating firepower—the *final fury* convention. At the end only Sergeant Dane is left. He has made his own grave into a machine-gun nest. The enemy swarms through the jungle, through a fog straight out of a horror movie, accompanied by horror-movie organ music. Dane rouses himself to a berserker madness, yelling and cursing at the charging Japanese while he fires his machine gun—at last firing it right into the camera's eye as the final title declares our intention to return to Bataan.

We never see Dane die—and that open-endedness is a visualization of the final convention of the platoon movie, its *unfinished business.* Implicit in all these films, explicit in *Bataan,* is the idea that the viewer must think of him- or herself as potentially an actor in the war the film portrays. He or she must leave the theater committed to learning the *enemy's lesson,* and completing the platoon's unfinished mission, either by enlisting in the army or by giving full consent that the war be prosecuted with annihilating violence.

The paradox of *Bataan* is that the final heat that blends the racial ingredients of the melting pot is rage against a racially marked enemy, who functions as a scapegoat for American racism. Dismissed through the front door, racism reenters by the window. Thus the Good War is also a "savage war," and therefore merciless—as the war with Japan proved to be.[8]

The *Bataan* formula proved extraordinarily successful. The form was flexible, allowing filmmakers to address a wide range of issues by altering the mix of characters or redefining the mission. *Sahara,* released in 1943, used an international platoon to represent the wartime Grand Alliance as the extension of American racial and ethnic comradeship to all nations. Although after 1943 the United States was on the offensive everywhere, and victory followed victory, most of these films continued to emphasize defensive action. *Guadalcanal Diary* (1943), which recounts the first offensive in the Pacific Theater, devolves into an extended defense of the beachhead. More striking is the scenario of *Objective Burma* (1945), which begins with the annihilation of a Japanese radar base by paratroopers but ends with the raiders fighting a last stand on a hilltop. John Ford's only war film, *They Were Expendable,* was made in the year of victory, 1945—but its subject is the doomed defense of the Philippines three years earlier.

The Good War Myth and Cold War Liberalism

By dominating movie screens during and after the war, the platoon movie shaped Americans' belief that World War II was a good war: inescapable, essentially defensive, righteous in its aims, and entirely successful in its result, one that united the American people as equal partners in a great cause. In retrospect, after the experience of Korea and Vietnam, Americans would come to think of it as *the* Good War—a standard against which all others are to be measured.[9]

The "goodness" of the war was reflected in the prosperity that marked the postwar era. The United States emerged from the conflict as the preeminent world power. As its rivalry with Soviet Communism intensified, the United States cast itself as the leader of the "free world," providing atomic and conventional forces to defend Western Europe and the Pacific Rim, and delivering massive economic aid to rebuild Western Europe and Japan. The domestic economy began a long expansion as American manufacturing filled the void left by the wrecked industries of Europe and Japan. This prosperity was shared more equitably than in the previous boom years of the 1920s. New Deal support of the labor movement gave unions real bargaining power. But the most significant innovation was the GI Bill of Rights, sponsored by New Dealers and veterans' organizations, which used government funds to underwrite loans for veterans to purchase new homes and go to college. These measures led to a boom in home construction, real estate, and lending that helped drive economic growth. By expanding access to higher education, the GI Bill fostered growth in college enrollments, created a larger educated workforce, and (not incidentally) precipitated the ethnic integration of elite colleges and universities from which Jews, Black people, and (to some extent) Italians had been excluded.[10]

African Americans were still denied full access to the benefits of this new order. Restrictive covenants and discriminatory banking practices barred them from the home loan program and limited their admission to most colleges. Jim Crow kept the South segregated, barred Black people from voting, and licensed wide-ranging violence against returning veterans and civil rights advocates. African American leaders reacted as they had after the Great War, citing their military and war-industry service to renew the claim for full civil rights. The work of national organizations like the NAACP, Congress of Racial Equality, and Urban League were augmented by local movements in Southern communities, which would eventually coalesce in the Southern Christian Leadership Conference. They were joined by a large and growing movement among White liberals, who had taken to heart the antiracist ideology of the war against Nazism. At the 1948 Democratic Convention, passage of a civil rights platform plank (addressed to voting rights) drove Southern Dixiecrats to temporary secession from the party. In 1949 President Harry S. Truman ordered the racial integration of the armed forces, for the first time blending Black and White members down to the squad level. These trends were assisted by Cold War imperatives. The contest against Communism was ideological as well as military; Soviet propaganda effectively cited Jim Crow laws and racial discrimination to discredit America's claim to speak for freedom and democracy, weakening our appeal to both Western Europeans and the emerging nations of the postcolonial world.[11]

In this environment, the platoon movie retained its utility as a vehicle for ideological symbolism and mythmaking. Hollywood extended its engagement with the racial theme in *Home of the Brave,* released in 1949 and based on a Broadway play by Arthur Laurents whose original subject was anti-Semitism. In transferring the play to film, producer Stanley Kramer and screenwriter Carl Foreman made a Black man the central character. The implicit equation of anti-Black racism with the form most identified with Nazis emphatically linked the civil rights struggle with the aims of the Good War. There were also efforts to retroactively "integrate" World War II. *Go for Broke* (1951) was about a famed Japanese American regiment in World War II, and *Red-Ball Express* (1952) featured Black truck drivers during the Battle of the Bulge.

Several platoon movies made during this period set race aside and used the genre to question whether Americans were still willing to fight if the Cold War demanded it. One of the most popular of these was *Sands of Iwo Jima* (1949), the film that established John Wayne as the embodiment of the American soldier. The movie follows a marine platoon, comprising the usual ethnic and social types, from its combat initiation at Tarawa to its triumph on Iwo Jima. Wayne plays Sergeant Stryker, who trains his men harshly to prepare them for the cruelty of war and is vindicated by their victory on Iwo Jima. Although the movie ostensibly deals with the past, it implicitly asks whether the younger generation are as ready to meet the demands of war as their elders.

This question is posed more explicitly in *Halls of Montezuma* (1950), a technicolor epic made while Americans were debating how far to go in supporting Western Europe and our Asian allies (China and Japan) against the advance of Communism. It was released the year after the adoption of the Marshall Plan to rebuild Western Europe and the formation of NATO, and just after the outbreak of the Korean War. The hero is Marine Lieutenant Anderson (Richard Widmark), whose will to fight is drained by a growing sense of the cruel futility of war. His situation thus approximates that of a war-weary American public, questioning whether yet another island, yet another mission, yet another war is necessary or meaningful. When Anderson seems at a spiritual nadir, his sense of mission is renewed by Doc, the medic, who reminds the platoon that war came to them "because our country was weak"—unprepared for war and selfishly unwilling to join the good fight. But "now we are part of the world and the world is part of us. If any part suffers, all suffer. If any part loses freedom, all will lose it." He asks the platoon to swear that, if they survive, they will work to see that the country stays "strong, courageous, and wise in spirit," secure in the knowledge that "we are on God's side." To this another soldier adds, now "we have to be strong for everyone, everywhere."

No more ambitious rationale could be offered for an American commitment to take up the struggle against Communist tyranny anywhere on planet Earth. The film's making reflects a drift of thought in Hollywood and in policy circles that began much earlier. One of the most interesting aspects of *Halls of Montezuma* is the choice of Lewis Milestone to direct it. Milestone was a Russian Jewish immigrant who came to America in 1912, served in the Signal Corps in World War I, and began making films in 1918. He had won an Academy Award for *All Quiet on the Western Front* in 1930, a powerful indictment of the futility and horror of World War I, and was identified with the Hollywood Left and the Popular Front against Fascism. But Milestone's wartime work was regarded as unquestionably patriotic. *A Walk in the Sun* (1945) is the quintessential platoon movie, the last one made during the war itself. The transformation in Milestone's view of war from *All Quiet* to *A Walk* to *Halls of*

Montezuma tracks with the shift in left-liberal opinion from reaction against World War I, to embrace of war and patriotism in 1941–1945, to the dream of extending the wartime ideals of inclusiveness and democracy throughout the nation and beyond it to the world at large—or to put it another way, from the political disillusionment of the 1920s to the idealism of the war against Fascism and to the emergence of liberal anti-Communist internationalism after 1947.

Dubious Battle: Korea Tests the Good War Myth

Whereas World War II was a "war of necessity," the Cold War would engage the United States in "wars of choice," undertaken for reasons of policy, to forestall distant or indirect threats. Where the Good War was an all-out effort ending in total victory, the new wars would require the extraordinary expense of lives and resources for goals that were necessarily limited. This mismatch made the Korean War of 1950–1953 not only unpopular but in many ways incomprehensible. Public support was doubtful at the outset. The country had recently come out of a period of immense suffering and sacrifice, and was beginning to enjoy the fruits of peace and prosperity. The early success of the American-led UN forces briefly reawakened the sense of triumph, only to have it dashed by the Chinese Communist intervention in the winter of 1950–1951, leading to the loss of half the territory the UN had gained and, instead of victory, a permanent stalemate.[12]

During the war, filmmakers attempted to use the devices of the platoon movie to suggest that "Korea" was a remake of *Bataan*. The realities of the war confounded their efforts. Films like Sam Fuller's *Steel Helmet* (1951) and *Fixed Bayonets* (1952) show retreating soldiers stumbling in a literal fog of war, looking for someplace to defend. In *One Minute to Zero* (1951) American troops fire on a column of Korean refugees to prevent Communists from using their cover for infiltration—the kind of action usually attributed to the enemy. In the most ambitious film of the period, *Retreat Hell* (1952), the initial mission of the US Marines is symbolized by their paternal care for Korean children, but by the end of the movie, "victory" is defined simply as escaping the Chinese Communist trap at the Chosin Reservoir and "going home." The narrative mirrors the arc of public opinion on the war, from dutiful engagement to puzzled withdrawal.

Although the armed forces began integrating in 1949, Black soldiers are missing or make perfunctory appearances in these films. Only *Steel Helmet* directly engages the problem of race. Its platoon contains the Japanese

American Sergeant Tanaka, played by Richard Loo, and Thompson, a Black medic played by James Edwards. The casting of these roles has some significance. Loo had become an iconic character actor playing Asian villains before the war, and sadistic Japanese soldiers during it. This role "rehabilitates" his screen character, and implicitly the Japanese Americans whose loyalty was traduced by internment as "enemy aliens" in 1942–1945. We're even told that Tanaka was in a wartime "relocation camp." James Edwards had played the lead in *Home of the Brave*, which made him for a while the go-to actor for Black roles in "problem" films. His character Thompson had served in the Ninety-Second Division and learned medicine under the GI Bill. Thompson's loyalty is challenged by a captured Chinese Communist officer, who reminds him (and the audience) of how White Americans have ill-treated his people. Although Thompson remains loyal, he tacitly acknowledges the truth of the criticism, and serves in spite of it.

In the post-Korea period, American political and cultural leaders rethought Cold War strategy and the meaning of the Korean experience. At the same time, the civil rights movement forced them to confront racism as a domestic social and moral issue, and as a liability in Cold War politics. The political result would be seen in the Kennedy-Johnson administrations, when the achievement of civil rights at home was closely linked with a more aggressive foreign policy—a counteroffensive against Third World Communism under liberal auspices. But that turn was *anticipated* by Hollywood as it continued to play with the materials of public myth.

Producers and artists are always interested in the possibility of exploiting public interest in current issues. Many in Hollywood had close personal relations with political and military leaders—they relied on the latter for technical and logistic support in making war films, and their celebration of military heroism benefited the services in their quest for recruits and funding. Leading actors and producers were also engaged in the civil rights movement. At the end of the 1950s these connections led to the making of two large-scale platoon movies that dealt directly with both the Korean War and race relations—films that referred to the past but looked to the future.

In *All the Young Men* (1960) the emerging Black star Sidney Poitier is the lone Black noncom in a melting-pot platoon, who assumes command of the last-stand defense when his officer is killed. As in *Home of the Brave*, he has to deal with the bigotry of fellow soldiers; and as in *Steel Helmet*, with an Asian Communist's critique of American racism. The film's outcome is predictable. What's interesting is the scale on which its liberal view of race is enacted, as well as the use of Hollywood stars and well-known character actors, along with celebrities like the boxer Ingemar Johansen, the Jewish comedian Mort Sahl, and the singer Bobby Daren.

Pork Chop Hill (1959) is a more interesting, complex, and aesthetically sound film, directed by Lewis Milestone, who was soon to be driven out of Hollywood by the blacklist. The movie is the fourth of his war films and closes his exploration of war and democracy. It presumes America's assumption of the world-liberating mission he articulated in *Halls of Montezuma,* explicitly links the problematics of that mission to racism and civil rights, and integrates the exploration of ideological issues with credible portrayals of combat.[13]

The film is built around two parallel stories, both involving racial conflict. K Company has to recapture Pork Chop Hill from the enemy. As their mission proceeds, the film cuts away to the armistice talks between US and Communist negotiators at Panmunjom. Both the American soldiers at the front and the US negotiators at the table believe that the hill itself is unimportant; and since the war is about to end, it seems pointless to make heavy sacrifices to take and hold it. So the soldiers set out reluctantly—why be the last man to die in a war that's ending? Their commanders hesitate to commit the resources that will allow them to smash the enemy and hold the hill. Such soldier conversations, asking whether their sacrifice will have any meaning, are conventions of the genre. But here the question is enlarged: it worries the high command as much as the men in the trenches.

The difference is that in a war against Communism, and especially Chinese Communism, the stakes of victory are defined not by rational cost-benefit calculations but by the irrational appeal of symbols and ideas. As the soldiers advance on Pork Chop Hill, they are bombarded not by shells but by loudspeakers blaring propaganda. The Chinese broadcaster is the first enemy we see; his sinister and insinuating voice confronts the soldiers at every turn of the action, and behind him stand Communist officers, stone-faced and inhuman, holding him to the party line.

The anti-Asian implications of this imagery are offset by use of the *race-face* convention, the appearance of a racially marked character who is on *our* side. Our hero, Captain Joe Clemons, is played by the quintessentially American Gregory Peck, but his second in command is Lieutenant Ohashi, a Japanese American. Since America has befriended this representative of the Asian enemy in World War II, the hateful portrayal of the Chinese in this film must be based on some "good" idea or emotion, not racism. Ohashi's integration is offset by evidence that the status of African Americans remains unresolved. The soldiers on Pork Chop will discover that to defeat an enemy that fights with propaganda, they must confront the racial problems that divide them internally.

It is extremely important to note that the book by army historian S. L. A. Marshall on which the movie was based makes *no reference* to Black soldiers, or to the integration of the army. The racial theme of this movie is *entirely* Hollywood's invention, and its prominence indicates an intention to adapt the old *Bataan* formula to the new political situation.

The racial theme is carried by a series of scenes revolving around a Black soldier named Franklin. As American troops advance up the hill, they are assailed by the blast of Communist propaganda. The White troops pause, but go on. Franklin falls to his knees, as if physically unable to resist the threats of this iron-voiced enemy—but another Black soldier moves up the hill behind him. Later, while the troops are defending the hill, Clemons stops Franklin from trying to desert. Two Black soldiers back him up as he speaks. Clemons turns Franklin over to a "tough sergeant" played by James Edwards, who is identified with strong Black characters in two earlier war movies. Edwards says he will keep his eye on Franklin—if he acts the coward, it will shame other Black people, who are patriotic Americans.

But the film does not allow us to dismiss Franklin as a coward. In a final defiance, Franklin confronts Clemons and explicitly questions why a Black man should fight and die for a country that abuses and oppresses him. Clemons first *acknowledges* the validity of the criticism. Then he insists that in this crisis a choice must be made—and if the Black man picks up his rifle, he will be joining "an exclusive club," the soldierly platoon called America.

The appeal is moving and meant to be decisive, but it makes no sense. Franklin can win acceptance—but only from his comrades—and then only if he dies with them, fighting for an objective that (we've been told) has no value. But as the film finally makes clear, in this new kind of war, with this new kind of enemy, "logic" is of no use to us. For Franklin, acceptance by his comrades solves the problem of oppression, because the platoon symbolizes the America that *would be* worth fighting for—although it is an America that *does not yet exist*.

This idea—that the symbol can be substituted for the reality—turns out to be the key to understanding the nature of the Cold War. The admiral leading the negotiators at Panmunjom has tried to reason with the enemy and failed. They will not stop fighting till they have recaptured Pork Chop, although everyone at the table knows the hill has no real value. The admiral suddenly realizes that that is the point. The enemy has made the hill a symbolic test of American resolve: "Its value is that it *has* no value." The admiral then tells the field commanders to throw everything they have into the fight for Pork Chop, and in a final fury Clemons's defenders are rescued from the Chinese assault.

This is the new "enemy's lesson," and it defines the unfinished business that the audience must help to complete. To fight this new enemy, in this new kind of war, we must devote our total energy, and the murderous fury of war, to the achievement of objectives that have no real meaning in themselves but are crucial as symbols. When one realizes that, in a sense, the Vietnam War will be the sequel to *Pork Chop Hill*, the admiral's lines are quite horrible. One of the shocking revelations about Lyndon Johnson's 1965–1966 escalation of the war in Vietnam was that administration officials recognized that the reasons for fighting were 70 percent symbolic and no important material interests were at stake. Vietnam's value was that it had no value, except as an opportunity to demonstrate "American resolve." To think this way is to think mythologically, not rationally—to operate in a world where symbols are real and realities meaningless.[14]

And yet the people who made the Vietnam War also transformed American race relations through the passage of the Civil Rights, Voting Rights, and Immigration Reform Acts of 1964–1965. That too involved the embrace of a symbolic ideal and rejection of the logic that said the movement for full civil equality was hopeless, because racial prejudice was too deeply entrenched in American law, institutions, culture, and psychology.

With all that said, it is also true that the Good War Myth preserves the idea that war-fighting is a necessary and morally positive attribute of national existence; that we need the supreme difference of an enemy to allow us to see our likeness as Americans; and that the signs by which we mark our enemies are still recognizably *racial*—differences not merely of interest or belief but of "nature." If you imagine your enemy as evil, implacable, and beyond rational appeals, then any skirmish may put you on the slippery slope to all-out war, and that war will have to be fought mercilessly—perhaps even to the point of nuclear annihilation.

The Vietnam War would test the power of the Good War Myth to justify American intervention in the conflicts between nationalists, Communists, and European colonial powers in the Third World. The reaction against that war would temporarily disrupt but ultimately transform the platoon movie genre to provide symbolic support for the George W. Bush administration's Global War on Terror.

PART IV

American Apotheosis

*From Kennedy's New Frontier
to Reagan's Morning in America*

9

The New Frontier

Savage War and Social Justice

POSTWAR AMERICA seemed to have realized the utopian promises of *both* the Frontier Myth and its nominal antithesis, the New Deal: an America in which economic abundance combined with government programs to make for an equitable distribution of benefits, promising that most citizens could enjoy the American Dream. Cheap energy from oil and coal fueled industrial production and demand for automobiles, the driver of the postwar economy. In a world ruined by war, American industrial production rose to bonanza levels of profitability. Thanks to New Deal support of the labor movement, this was also a high-wage economy. Social Security provided a safety net for old age and disability. The GI Bill of Rights underwrote a huge expansion of home owning by middle- and working-class Americans, and an unprecedented expansion of education at every level. The Cold War spurred government investment in research and development, enabling the development of new technologies. Families that postponed having children because of the Depression and war greeted peace and prosperity by generating the baby boom, and boomers would provide a large and relatively well-educated workforce for another generation. The result was an annual increase (from 1950 to 1973) in both the size of the labor force (1.6 percent) and its productivity (2.4 percent), leading to growth rates that averaged 4 percent a year.[1]

The nation's economic preeminence was matched by its enhanced moral authority. America's wartime leadership proved that democracies had the economic and moral strength to defeat powerful tyrannies. When the Soviet Union imposed Communist rule on the nations it had liberated, dropped the Iron

Curtain across Europe, and raised the specter of renewed warfare, the United States organized alliances to define and defend the "free world."

In 1941 Henry Luce, publisher of *Life,* had framed World War II as the inauguration of "the American Century." The phrase and the concept became central to postwar visions of American preeminence. In *The American Mind* (1950) historian Henry Steele Commager wrote, "Nothing in all history had ever succeeded like America, and every American knew it." Commager's was the first of many books by scholars and public intellectuals analyzing and celebrating America's unique success. Max Lerner's *America as a Civilization* (1957) was a best seller. Scholarly works by Ralph Henry Gabriel, Louis Hartz, and Henry Nash Smith set the agenda for the burgeoning field of American studies, which explored the "exceptionalism" of American history, culture, and politics. David Potter's *People of Plenty: Economic Abundance and the American Character* (1954) echoed Frederick Jackson Turner, finding the roots of American individualism and democracy in the abundance of economic resources that fueled our long history of economic and westward expansion.[2]

This triumphant theme was offset by the menace of Communism. The Russians controlled Eastern Europe, and strong Communist parties contended for power in the West. Chinese Communists overthrew the American-allied Nationalists in 1949 and controlled the mainland. The Soviets and Chinese were bidding for control of the new states emerging from the dismantling of Europe's colonial empires. The Soviets had also developed nuclear weapons, aided in part by spies they had planted in the scientific and intelligence communities. The United States now faced the external threat of nuclear annihilation and a supposed internal threat from Communist "subversion." Our sense of vulnerability was on exaggerated display in the Red Scare led by Senator Joseph McCarthy and a host of conservative organizations.

The administration of President Dwight Eisenhower took a conservative approach to the opportunities and dilemmas of the period. Eisenhower accepted an armistice in Korea, refused to intervene to support the French against Communists in Vietnam, and would not do more than protest when (in 1956) the Soviets repressed anti-Communist uprisings in Hungary and East Germany. Yet his administration would use the newly reorganized CIA to overthrow leftist regimes in Guatemala and Iran and create the anti-Communist government of South Vietnam, establishing the basic structures and policy assumptions that would drive American interventionism for the rest of the century.

Eisenhower preserved basic elements of the New Deal, such as Social Security and the minimum wage, and undertook major new infrastructure spending to create the interstate highway system. But he was no Keynesian. He strove for balanced budgets, cutting spending (even for the military) and raising taxes. When combined with "tight money" by the Federal Reserve, these policies led to three recessions. His administration also saw the opening phase of a new civil rights movement with the Montgomery bus boycott (1955–1956) led by Dr. Martin Luther King Jr. and the movement for school desegregation sparked by the Supreme Court's landmark decision in *Brown v. Board of Education* in 1954. Eisenhower disagreed strongly with the *Brown* decision and was reluctant to enforce it, but the threat of civil violence over the integration of Little Rock High School forced his hand.

Democrats of more liberal inclination were impatient with Eisenhower's moderate conservatism. They wanted the government to take a more positive role in promoting economic growth, and a more energetic stance in opposing Communism in the developing nations of Latin America, Asia, and Africa. The party's liberal wing also wanted the federal government to promote civil rights and end Jim Crow—a stance sharply at odds with the views of Southern Democrats who were intrinsic to the party's base of support.

During the 1960s the progressive elements in American national mythology came to the fore, supporting an ideology that has been called "Cold War liberalism" or the "liberal consensus." The interplay between administration policy, liberal ideology, and the mythmaking instruments of popular culture would transform American culture and politics. It began with a wave of enthusiasm for political and economic reform, as well as a series of "liberation" movements in the areas of race, gender, and sexuality, but ended in a political and cultural crack-up and the rise of a new conservative movement.[3]

Kennedy's Myths: Good War Heroism and the New Frontier

John F. Kennedy won the presidency in 1960 by calling for a "heroic" politics. His inaugural address summoned "a new generation" to take up the Cold War's "long, twilight struggle" and to ensure that economic progress and freedom (as Americans understood it) would develop together. He himself would personify that heroism. He could authentically present himself as a war hero, decorated for his actions in command of PT-109 in the Solomon Islands campaign, and therefore as a leader in the platoon movie mode, uniting a diverse people in the struggle against a world-menacing tyranny. But Kennedy's identification of his program as the "New Frontier" indicates a closer identification with the Frontier Myth and the genre that was its modern vehicle, the Western movie. Kennedy's "New Frontiersmen" would appeal to the economic premises of the Frontier Myth and embrace its concomitant "savage war." The economic component was reflected in the use of quasi-Keynesian stimulus policies and the articulation of a grand theory of economic development with which to contest the appeal of Communism in the Third World. The "savage war" aspect would be reflected in the use of Special Forces, covert operations, and finally combat troops to fight Communism in the jungles of Southeast Asia.

Kennedy criticized Eisenhower's reluctance to use government resources to get the economy moving again. Among his most successful policies was a large tax cut, counterintuitive for a Democratic Party known to "tax and spend," a stimulus that ended the recession that marred Eisenhower's last years in office. The Kennedy administration popularized the slogan that a rising tide—a growing economy—lifts all boats. The slogan seemed to be borne out over the next decade by the high level of wages and general prosperity and the phenomenal expansion of the middle class that was making home owners of factory workers and college grads of their children.

The New Frontier also promoted activism in foreign policy, contrasting itself with the Eisenhower years, during which Communism had expanded its influence by sponsoring anticolonial independence movements. Kennedy's administration designed a liberal counteroffensive, combining foreign aid and military action: the peaceful guidance of USAID and the Peace Corps, authorized in 1961, and the counterguerrilla operations of Special Forces, whose advisory mission in South Vietnam would be expanded to meet new strategic purposes.

Vietnam would become the primary theater for Kennedy's counteroffensive: an attempt to halt the advance of Communist-backed nationalism in decolonizing Southeast Asia and provide an alternative "American" model for creating a modernized postcolonial nationality. American engagement in Vietnam would be interpreted through two mythic paradigms. The Good War Myth was invoked by likening Communist advances to Adolf Hitler's prewar aggression in Czechoslovakia, branding Eisenhower's refusal to engage as a form of "appeasement." But operations in Vietnam were also presented as enactments of the Frontier Myth, as if counterinsurgency were a new kind of Indian war. As American engagement expanded, and became controversial, Westerns—not war films—would be the genre through which the unfolding action would be interpreted.

The administration's response to decolonization was shaped by a theory of "modernization" rooted in the premises of Turner's "Frontier Hypothesis" and Theodore Roosevelt's "frontier" rationale for overseas imperialism. The most influential statement of this theory was *The Stages of Economic Growth: A*

Non-Communist Manifesto (1960) by Walt Whitman Rostow, an adviser on national security policy in the Kennedy and Johnson administrations. Like Turner, Rostow sees America's growth-oriented capitalism as the basis of our democracy and social prosperity, and since the United States began as a colonial settlement, our experience should be a viable model for nations emerging from colonial status. Like Turner, Rostow evades discussing the dark side of modernization: the violence of class and ethnic or racial conflict, the displacement of Indigenous peoples by war and of rural populations by the industrialization of agriculture.[4]

The New Frontier administration's approach to the Third World took a Rooseveltian view of the relation of economic development to savage war. This view was shaped by a consensus in contemporary historiography, that premodern cultures must accept transformation into versions of American and Western European culture. Thus Samuel Eliot Morison, the dean of American historians, in his *Oxford History of the American People* (1965) likens the French withdrawal from Algeria in 1958 to a hypothetical case in which Americans *refused* to fight an Indian war: "It was as if the Tecumseh Confederacy of 1811 had succeeded in forcing all white Americans to return to Britain." There is not much space between Morison and Theodore Roosevelt's declaration that those who opposed the seizure of the Philippines "condemn [their] forefathers and mine for ever having settled in these United States." If modernization on the American plan represents the only valid path to progress, resistance is an attempt to reverse the course of history—and must itself be resisted by any and all means. According to this logic, the destruction attendant on war is actually a precondition for nation-building.[5]

The metaphoric association of counterinsurgency with mythic "Indian wars" became more explicit as the level of violence and American involvement in Vietnam increased. In 1966 Maxwell Taylor (then ambassador to South Vietnam) used that analogy explicitly in describing for Congress the need for counterinsurgency warfare: "It is very hard to plant corn outside the stockade when the Indians are still around. We have to get the Indians farther away." Early journalistic treatments of the New Frontier's plans for Special Forces emphasized their status as the shock troops of Kennedy's New Frontier and traced their fighting style as an American tradition that ran "from the French and Indian wars," to the partisan rangers of the American Revolution and Civil War, to the commandos of World War II. This language acquired a potent new spokesman when Kennedy was succeeded by Lyndon Johnson, whose Texan rhetoric was thick with allusions to a frontier past. He urged American troops to "bring the coonskin home" from Vietnam and "nail it to the barn," and he told *Life* reporter Hugh Sidey that "he had gone into Vietnam because, as at the Alamo, somebody had to get behind the log with those threatened people."[6]

Gunfighters and Green Berets:
Western Movies and Counterinsurgency

Invocations of the Frontier Myth resonated with a public that was deeply familiar with its symbolism, and the moral imperatives implicit in it. From 1945 to 1970 Westerns were the most consistently and broadly popular of American movie genres. Between 1948 and 1956 the number of feature productions (eighty-plus minutes) varied between thirty-one and forty-six films a year. After 1955 Hollywood productions were augmented by television. From 1955 to 1957 Westerns rose from 15 percent to more than 24 percent of prime-time series, and for the next decade averaged 15.6 percent. Westerns were consistently among the top-rated TV shows from the end of the Korean War to the Nixon presidency. No other action-adventure show (detective/police, combat, etc.) absorbed so consistently high a share of prime time over so many years.[7]

The "golden age" of the Western was 1946 to 1960, not only because of its popularity but because of the high level of artistry achieved by directors like John Ford, Howard Hawks, Anthony Mann, Fred Zinnemann, George Stevens, and John Sturges. The films they produced during these years—like *High Noon, Shane, The Searchers,* and *Red River*—are now the canon of "classic" Westerns, and indeed of classic Hollywood cinema. The Western developed a symbolic language that was rich in meanings and widely understood by both the producing communities and the general public. As a result, the genre could be used to address a wide range of difficult or taboo subjects like race relations, sexuality, psychoanalysis, and Cold War politics. In the era of McCarthyism and the blacklist, Westerns provided safe vehicles for disguised commentary on the toughest issues of the day. *Broken Arrow* and *Devil's Doorway,* which sympathized with the Indian side of frontier conflict, addressed the two most controversial issues of the time: the Cold War issue of coexistence with the Soviets and the domestic issue of racial segregation. But they were never targets of McCarthyism—the Western was the most patriotic of genres.

Westerns also mirrored the harder face of Cold War politics. Beginning with Ford's famous cavalry trilogy of 1948–1950 (*Fort Apache, Rio Grande,* and *She Wore a Yellow Ribbon*), Westerns addressed the concerns of the war film—choice of enemy, preparedness, whether to attack or defend. *Rio Grande* was released November 15, 1950, at the turning point of the Korean War. On the same screen that showed newsreels of Douglas MacArthur staring through his binoculars across the Yalu River into China, Ford showed John Wayne as Colonel Yorke, glaring across the Rio Grande at Apache sanctuaries that fussy diplomats forbade him to attack.

The Indian wars were a theme to which the genre continually reverted, braiding two distinct threads. One was the traditional view of "savage war" as the inescapable necessity of frontier progress. Rescue of the White woman captured by Indians emphasizes the ultimately racial stakes in the conflict, and the principle that she must be saved by any means necessary. This is the burden of Ford's *Rio Grande* and *The Searchers* (1956), several of Budd Boetticher's Westerns starring Randolph Scott, and the Vietnam-era *Stalking Moon* (1968). But a second strain of Westerns followed the suggestion of *Broken Arrow,* taking a sympathetic view of Indian grievances and dramatizing efforts at peacemaking. Ford's *Fort Apache* and *Yellow Ribbon* fit this pattern, featuring a classic "White Man Who Knows Indians" who can win the tribesmen's confidence because he has fought them honorably *and* effectively—an anticipation of counterinsurgency doctrine.

Perhaps the most significant subtype of Cold War Western was the gunfighter movie, whose hero is a man alone, marked by his supreme speed and accuracy with a gun. The directors and scenarists who established the type, in films like Henry King's *The Gunfighter* (1950) and George Stevens's *Shane* (1953), imagined gunfighters as dark celebrities renowned for their speed and ruthlessness, isolated by that fame and envied by lesser men who are driven to challenge their reputation as the "fastest gun alive." Gunfighter heroes were at once the most powerful and the most vulnerable men in the world, telling symbols for a Cold War America facing the threat of nuclear war.

The regenerative violence that resolves the conflict in every Western is personalized in the gunfighter, whose dark past will be redeemed by the ritual shoot-out. He fights to save a community he cannot join, driven by a particular heroic ethic: that those who have the power to defeat evil have a responsibility to use that power, and that evil can only be defeated by using its own instruments. The supreme example of the gunfighter hero is Will Kane, played by Gary Cooper, in *High Noon* (1951). The mad and murderous Frank Miller is returning from prison to retake the town he once tyrannized. In a democratic town meeting, the people, from a mixture of cowardice and self-interest, decide not to fight for themselves. To save the town, Kane has to override its democracy and the religious objections of his Quaker wife. His heroic ethic is seen to be superior to both democratic procedure and Christian morality. That superiority is ratified by the final gesture of throwing down his badge, expressing his contempt for those he has saved. On its small scale, the gunfighter's principle is the same as that set forth in Good War movies like *Halls of Montezuma:* the man (or nation) who has the power to defeat evil has the responsibility to use that power—with the addendum that, in the direst circumstances, he must do so even if he has to violate the values he is supposed to defend.[8]

The gunfighter Western was prevalent when Hollywood turned its attention to the emerging problem of American engagement in the decolonizing world. Its conventions suggested an alternative to the militarism of films like *Rio Grande.* During the 1950s the idea of using a mix of military assistance and economic aid, delivered by small groups of specialists working closely with native "counterparts," had been explored by government policymakers and intellectuals, and popularized in books like William J. Lederer and Eugene Burdick's best seller, *The Ugly American* (1958). The concept would find its ultimate expression in the development of Special Forces and new doctrines of counterinsurgency warfare, which would be applied after 1961 in Vietnam.

The New Frontiersmen's expectation that American guns and know-how would transform peasants into democratic self-defense forces was reflected in a new subgenre of Western. In films like *Magnificent Seven* (1960) and its numerous sequels, as well as in *The Professionals* (1966) and *100 Rifles* (1968), American gunfighters cross into Mexico to aid that country's peasants against warlords, tyrants, and foreign occupiers. The gunfighters are a killer elite, technologically more proficient than the peasants they save, and their pride in dominance makes them more willing to risk death and take extreme measures. In the end their skill requires and entitles them to take charge of the natives, in order to complete the "Good War" mission of liberation. In this the movies mirror the development of the Vietnam War. When the counterinsurgency campaign failed to reverse deterioration of South Vietnam's government, or check the advance of the Communist-led insurgency, the Johnson administration ordered the massive intervention of US ground and air forces, until half a million Americans were engaged—with the South Vietnamese army relegated to a supporting role.[9]

The earlier movies in the sequence also enact the "tactical fantasy" of counterinsurgency warfare. In *Magnificent Seven,* for example, the village is captured by the enemy because the peasants become too fearful to resist. The gunfighters storm the village at top speed, kicking in doors and blazing away into darkened interiors. Incredibly, they are killing *only* bandits. The "surgical strike" so central to military scenario makers, in which guerrillas can be blasted by bombs and shells without harming the peasants, is here visualized.

What is most remarkable about the Westerns of this period is that they were the *only* movie genre that dealt with Vietnam while the war was going on. In every other twentieth-century war, American filmmakers made movies about Americans in combat. But during the longest American war in the century, with major combat from 1962 to 1973, only one combat film was made—John Wayne's *The Green Berets* (1968), which was not well received. Filmmakers may have been deterred by the growing controversy over American involvement, and the difficulty of turning a complex mission and unfamiliar tactics into a coherent narrative. Whatever the cause, it was the Western that provided mythological sanction for the war and helped win public consent to its conduct.

Questions about American strategy became increasingly sharp after 1964, when counterinsurgency tactics gave way to the big-unit war and American troops took over combat operations from the Vietnamese. Westerns like Sam Peckinpah's *Major Dundee* (1965) registered the public's sense that the costs of the war were out of all proportion to its nominal objectives. In Peckinpah's masterpiece *The Wild Bunch* (1969), a group of American gunmen confronts a military dictator who has imprisoned and tortured their comrade, a Mexican with revolutionary sympathies. But the classic rescue scene, and the traditional final shoot-out between democratic good and evil tyranny, soon degenerates into the *final fury* of a general massacre, escalating from six-guns to heavy machine guns and hand grenades, killing gunfighters and peasants, dictators and civilians—the perfect visualization of the idea, voiced by an American captain in 1968, that came to embody the ultimate absurdity of the war, that we had to destroy a city in order to save it.[10]

Good War Gone Wrong

Historians have analyzed the flawed strategic assumptions and misconceived tactics that led to defeat in Vietnam. What concerns us here is the war's effect on America's sustaining national myths. The war was justified to the American people by linking modernization and democracy to the "savage war" of counterinsurgency; and by invocation of the Good War Myth, reminding Americans of their role as a liberating world power. The choice of whether to resist Communist advances in Southeast Asia was framed through analogy to Munich: if we failed to intervene, we would repeat Neville Chamberlain's error of appeasing Hitler. By framing the intervention in Good War terms, the Kennedy-Johnson administrations created the expectation that the infusion of American arms and men would totally defeat the enemy, "liberate" the South Vietnamese, and demonstrate America's determination to halt the spread of Communism.

Our declared mission was to win the "hearts and minds" of South Vietnam's people, guiding them toward the establishment of a democratic government and thereby demonstrating the superiority of the American model for postcolonial development. But the government of the Republic of Vietnam was corrupt, ruled at first by the dictatorial Ngo Dinh Diem and, after his overthrow, by a series of military cliques. All were tainted by association with colonial rulers, first the French, now the Americans, while the guerrillas—backed by Communist North Vietnam—won the support of the peasantry with a mixture of nationalist appeal, land reform, and ruthless repression.

The political and military ineffectiveness of the South Vietnamese regime led the Johnson administration to Americanize the war and apply massive man- and firepower against guerrilla forces hidden in jungles or deeply enmeshed in the peasantry. To "pacify" a region, the Americans would conduct "search and destroy" operations to isolate and eliminate enemy forces; then they would make the villages defensible by arming them or stationing troops (preferably Vietnamese) nearby. In many regions, support for the Viet Cong was so ingrained that the only way to "pacify" a given area was to "remove the people and destroy the village." The area was then a "free-fire zone": anyone remaining there became, by definition and without regard to age or sex, an enemy combatant and legitimate target of American firepower.[11]

Policies like this were part of the "savage war" repertoire, developed during the Plains Indian wars to drive the tribes onto reservations. Since these could not support their populations, many bands remained on the buffalo plains and were considered hostile and liable to immediate attack. Similar policies were followed in suppressing Filipino resistance in 1898–1902. In Vietnam, the policy failed to pacify the countryside. Peasants driven off the land wound up in refugee camps around the major cities, impoverished, demoralized, and disaffected. The political scientist Samuel P. Huntington, a civilian analyst who studied the refugee problem for the administration, justified this process as a replication of the move from peasant to urban life that had been an essential part of modernization in the West—a particularly bloody-minded application of Rostow's version of the Frontier Myth.[12]

The failure of pacification led Johnson to shift from the counterinsurgency tactics favored by Kennedy to the use of "big units," conventionally armed and trained infantry and armored divisions, which were largely composed of poorly motivated draftees. These would engage the enemy in campaigns of "attrition," with continuous and intense combat, relying on superior weaponry to inflict heavier casualties on the enemy. Since the United States was incomparably richer than North Vietnam and had more than fourteen times the population, it seemed obvious that the enemy would run out of men and money long before we did.[13]

The American calculus did not take into account the political and cultural dimension of the war. Committed as they were to a life-or-death struggle for national independence, the North Vietnamese and Viet Cong were far more willing to bear the hundreds of thousands of casualties they suffered than Americans were to lose their tens of thousands. That was demonstrated in January 1968, at the Lunar New Year, or Tet, when the North Vietnamese and Viet Cong staged a countrywide offensive, striking all the major cities, including the capital, Saigon, and capturing the old imperial capital of Hue, the nation's second-largest city. American and Vietnamese soldiers had to turn their artillery and bombs against the very cities they had been defending, in order to recapture them (at heavy cost) from the enemy. The absurd inversion to which the logic of our policies had brought us was captured by the American officer who explained the army's evacuation and destruction of the town of Ben Tre by saying, "We had to destroy Ben Tre in order to save it."[14]

Although the Viet Cong and North Vietnamese suffered tactical defeat and immense casualties, the Tet Offensive was a strategic victory, because it discredited American leadership and led many Americans, including those in influential positions, to doubt whether the war was winnable. President Johnson's response was to withdraw his bid for reelection in order to pursue a negotiated settlement. That effort would fail, sabotaged by the Republican candidate Richard Nixon, who would prolong and expand the fighting to win a more advantageous (or face-saving) settlement. But public support for the war continued to decline as it grew clearer that blood and treasure were being spent for objectives more symbolic than real—to protect the Nixon administration, or refute the perception that (in Nixon's words) the United States was becoming "a pitiful, helpless giant."[15]

The moral failure of American policy came to be symbolized by the so-called My Lai massacre, when American infantrymen murdered almost everyone in a village of women, children, and elderly noncombatants. Instead of rescuing the natives, we had slaughtered them. It was My Lai that antiwar protesters had in mind when they called returning soldiers "baby-killers." The My Lai symbol contained both truth and a falsehood. A face-to-face massacre of the kind committed there was rare. What *was* typical was the callousness with which military commanders ordered operations bound to produce large numbers of civilian casualties: search-and-destroy sweeps through villages that were presumed to be hostile, heavy bombardments by artillery and aircraft in free-fire zones—and the policy of judging victory by the "body count," which put a premium on indiscriminate killing.

Public support for the war declined throughout the Nixon administration, divided between an increasingly bitter antiwar movement and a public sick of the war but unwilling to repudiate it in principle. In 1973 the United States agreed to a peace plan that called for the withdrawal of American troops, an end to fighting in South Vietnam, and a place for Communists in South Vietnamese politics. Although the agreement called for American forces to intervene if the Communists violated the pact, when that moment came in 1975, Congress refused to authorize air strikes. South Vietnam collapsed, and television showed the hasty evacuation of Americans and some Vietnamese associates from the embassy roof, terrified people chasing American transport planes down airport runways, and helicopters being dumped in the South China Sea after delivering their passengers.

The war had been justified by appeal to the ethic of "rescuing the captive," popularized by the Frontier Myth and the Western movie genre, and by the Good War premise that aggressors must be resisted, not appeased. But by the end of the war, those objectives had been exposed as either mere pretexts or gross miscalculations, and the war's violence, instead of being redemptive, became meaningless or absurd. After 1973 the Western was virtually abandoned as an expressive form. The discrediting of the Good War Myth led to a long period in which public opinion refused to support the use of military force in foreign affairs—a phenomenon known as Vietnam syndrome, which weighed on American policymakers for the rest of the century.

10

Cultural Revolution

The Sixties, the Movement,
and the Great Society

THE YEARS 1963 to 1975 saw America swept by a wave of cultural changes that were perceived as revolutionary. A newly energized movement for civil rights pushed the "race problem" to the center of political discourse for the first time since Reconstruction. By focusing public attention on a major question of social justice, it also enabled the Johnson administration's ambitious Great Society and War on Poverty programs, intended to complete the unfinished business of the New Deal. A new mythology began to emerge, the Myth of the Movement, in which the success of the civil rights movement figured as the model for social movements aiming at the "liberation" of other racial, ethnic, and gender groups; a new environmentalist movement; and a peace movement aimed at ending the Vietnam War and achieving nuclear disarmament.

These movements were augmented by other forms of cultural liberation, led by the large cohort of baby boomers whose values were shaped by the culture of affluence spawned by the postwar economic boom, by consumerism, by new media, and by new forms of popular culture. At the extreme, this youth culture became a "counterculture" that seemed to reject middle-class concepts of morality, economic success, and disciplined labor. Supposedly devoted to "sex, drugs, and rock and roll," the counterculture also embraced new forms of family and communal organization, and championed the causes of peace and environmentalism in the massive Earth Day demonstrations and the antiwar moratorium rally in 1970.[1]

The radical critique of traditional American values and prejudices provoked by these movements fed a broad-based revisionist movement among American historians, which reevaluated the role of race, class, and gender in American society and developed new critiques of American capitalism and imperialism. Standard paradigms of political and intellectual historiography were called into question, and new fields of scholarship developed in social and cultural history. These in turn led to radical revisions in the understanding and use of national myths.

These liberal triumphs also provoked a powerful racial backlash and a renewed appeal to the symbolism of the Lost Cause, not only in the South but in Northern cities, where White people resisted school integration. The GOP would capitalize on this reaction, deploying a "Southern Strategy" of coded appeals to racism, "states' rights," and "crime in the streets." In 1968 the Democratic coalition would implode, breaking the "liberal consensus" that had sustained the New Deal order and opening the way for a conservative renaissance inaugurated by the presidency of Ronald Reagan.

Framing the Myth of the Movement

The civil rights movement of 1954–1970 began as a challenge to Jim Crow laws in the South. By forcing Americans to see the cruelty and violence inherent in racial injustice, it opened the public mind to larger issues of social justice: the persistence of poverty, gender discrimination, and environmental degradation. Its transformational role can be seen in the shift of priorities between the Kennedy and Johnson administrations, from a primary focus on foreign affairs to an ambitious attempt to complete the New Deal with Lyndon Johnson's Great Society and War on Poverty programs. In mythological terms, this was a shift from the symbolic space of the Western and the Frontier Myth to an expanded understanding of the social justice ethic at the heart of the Good War Myth.

Platoon movie symbolism had prepared a broad swath of the American public to see racial bigotry and exclusion as an anomaly that ought to be eliminated. The shift in White liberal opinion was reflected by the passage of a civil rights plank in the Democratic Party's 1948 presidential platform, which sparked a walkout by Southern segregationists and the formation of the Dixiecrat third party in the 1948 election. More radical in its implications was the change in President Harry S. Truman's position, from supporter of segregation to advocate of civil rights, exemplified by his executive order integrating US military units.

Black civil rights leaders were prepared to seize the opportunity. Older leaders remembered the experience of World War I, when the promise of reform in exchange for wartime service had been broken. They had reason to fear a repetition: Black people were practically shut out of the substantial housing and education benefits granted by the GI Bill, as mortgage lenders' used "redlining" to preserve housing segregation, and most colleges and universities limited or barred Black admissions. Their response was to organize for political and social action in every part of the country, from Northern and Midwestern cities where they enjoyed the support of White allies to Southern towns where they had reason to fear both law enforcement and local vigilantes. Much of this work was sponsored by established organizations like the NAACP, the Congress of Racial Equality, and the National Urban League. Among the new organizations that emerged in the 1950s, the church-based Southern Christian Leadership Conference (SCLC) led by Martin Luther King Jr. would become most prominent. But the ground for the movement was also prepared by grassroots organizers with only local affiliations and little or no institutional support.[2]

The fundamental work of organization and agitation was largely invisible to the national media until a series of dramatic events caught public attention. Then the storytelling apparatus of print and television journalism began the process of transforming a chain of episodes into a story with a strong and distinct narrative arc. In that form, the "civil rights movement" entered into dialogue with the ongoing development of national myth.

In April and May 1963 a campaign to desegregate the downtown shopping and government district in Birmingham, Alabama, produced an "iconic event." Nonviolent demonstrators were met with police violence, mass arrests, and terrorist bombings by the Ku Klux Klan and White Citizens' Council. When older people hesitated to continue demonstrating, the SCLC engaged teenagers—a "Children's Crusade" that heightened the contrast between the brutality of the police and the peaceable behavior of Black demonstrators. King and his colleagues had a perfect foil in Sheriff Eugene "Bull" Connor, a big-bellied racist who made no secret of his contempt for Black people and for federal law enforcement. Connor's police beat nonviolent demonstrators with clubs, hit them with water from high-pressure fire hoses, and set police dogs on them—under the eye of television cameras from national news organizations.[3]

These scenes compelled the Kennedy administration to take a more active role. John F. Kennedy had made overtures to the movement during the election, and his reading of *The Other America* by socialist Michael Harrington made him aware of the anomaly of deep and persistent poverty in the world's richest nation. But the central concern of the New Frontier was a vigorous foreign policy to counter Communist advances in the Third World. TV images of the police assault on the Birmingham demonstrators undercut America's claim to leadership of the democratic West by mirroring the Communist

repression of protesters in East Germany, Poland, and Hungary. Although civil
rights had not been high on Kennedy's agenda, it was now inescapable. In his
"Civil Rights Address," delivered via television from the White House on
June 11, 1963, he invoked the Bible and the Myth of the Founding: the problem
of equal rights was "as old as the Scriptures and . . . as clear as the American
Constitution." But his chief appeal was to the Good War Myth, through which
he also justified his activist foreign policy:

> Today, we are committed to a worldwide struggle to promote and protect
> the rights of all who wish to be free. And when Americans are sent to
> Vietnam or West Berlin, we do not ask for whites only. . . . We preach
> freedom around the world, . . . but are we to say to the world, and much
> more importantly, to each other that this is the land of the free except for
> the Negroes; that we have no second-class citizens except Negroes; that
> we have no class or caste system, no ghettoes, no master race except with
> respect to Negroes?[4]

In a crisis over race relations, the most relevant of national myths was the
Civil War. This phase of the civil rights movement coincided with the war's
Centennial, an event marked by ceremonies, battle reenactments, speeches, and
histories. But invoking that mythology was as likely to produce violent contention as national consensus. The Lost Cause was already being invoked by
partisans of segregation.[5] As a Democrat, Kennedy depended on Southern support for his election, his defense policies, and his legislative agenda. He tried
to defuse Southern resentment by admitting that "difficulties over segregation
and discrimination exist in every city, in every State of the Union." Nevertheless, in the language of American myth, there was one inevitable rejoinder to
racial injustice. Kennedy invoked Abraham Lincoln's Emancipation Proclamation as a promise not kept: "One hundred years of delay have passed since
President Lincoln freed the slaves, yet their heirs, their grandsons, are not fully
free . . . from the bonds of injustice. They are not yet freed from social and economic oppression. And this Nation, for all its hopes and all its boasts, will not
be fully free until all its citizens are free."[6]

To the Lincoln Memorial

The Lincoln connection would provide the culminating scene in this first phase
of the Movement narrative, the March on Washington for Jobs and Freedom
in August 1963. The size of the demonstration, the breadth of its support among

religious organizations and parts of the labor movement, and the prominent role played by celebrities like Charlton Heston and Harry Belafonte and folk singers Joan Baez and Peter, Paul and Mary signaled a broad and significant turn in public opinion outside the South. The event would make Martin Luther King Jr. the hero of a new and emerging Myth of the Movement.[7]

From the podium cameras scanned a Mall filled to the brim with demonstrators. From the audience perspective, the enthroned statue of Lincoln loomed above performers and speakers like a presiding spirit. When King spoke, Lincoln was figuratively among his hearers; and this symbolism was critical, because his appeal was made not to the Black community (which was already enlisted in the cause) but to the White people whose conscience he hoped to touch.

King began by aligning the movement with the Liberation Myth of the Civil War, echoing the opening words of the Gettysburg Address:[8]

> Five score years ago, a great American, in whose symbolic shadow we stand today, signed the Emancipation Proclamation. This momentous decree came as a great beacon light of hope to millions of Negro slaves who had been seared in the flames of withering injustice. It came as a joyous day-break to end the long night of their captivity.

The Proclamation was a pledge that had not been fulfilled:

> But one hundred years later, the Negro still is not free. One hundred years later, the life of the Negro is still sadly crippled by the manacles of segregation and the chains of discrimination. One hundred years later, the Negro lives on a lonely island of poverty in the midst of a vast ocean of material prosperity. One hundred years later, the Negro still . . . finds himself an exile in his own land.

King then invoked the Myth of the Founding, and Lincoln's understanding of the Declaration of Independence as a moral agenda, to root his cause in the origins of the American social contract:

> When the architects of our republic wrote the magnificent words of the Constitution and the Declaration of Independence, they were signing a promissory note to which every American was to fall heir . . . that all men, yes, black men as well as white men, would be guaranteed the "unalienable Rights" of "Life, Liberty and the pursuit of Happiness."

King would emphasize the nonviolent principles of his movement. But he cited the threat of social violence, arising from the anger of Black people at their continued oppression and official disdain for their demands:

> We have also come to this hallowed spot to remind America of the fierce urgency of Now. . . . [Those] who hope that the Negro needed to blow off steam and will now be content will have a rude awakening if the nation returns to business as usual. . . . The whirlwinds of revolt will continue to shake the foundations of our nation until the bright day of justice emerges.

This was not only a necessary reminder of the consequences of delay but an assertion of Black agency, of their willingness to take up arms against injustice as the Founders had done.

King then shifted from American national myth to the deeper structures of biblical mythology: "No, no, we are not satisfied, and we will not be satisfied until 'justice rolls down like waters, and righteousness like a mighty stream.'" From the biblical, he moved on to the poetry of sacred music: first the "White" American anthem, "My Country 'Tis of Thee," but ultimately the Negro spiritual "Free at Last":

> And when this happens, and when we allow freedom ring, when we let it ring from every village and every hamlet, from every state and every city, we will be able to speed up that day when *all* of God's children, black men and white men, Jews and Gentiles, Protestants and Catholics, will be able to join hands and sing in the words of the old Negro spiritual:
>
> > *Free at last! Free at last!*
> > *Thank God Almighty, we are free at last!*

The poetry of that peroration is as significant as its message. With it, King put the language of Black preaching and song into dialogue with the dignity, power, and national patriotism symbolized by the Lincoln Memorial. The effect was to blend the two, investing King with the aura of Lincoln, but also connecting the memory of Lincoln to Black people in a way that transcended the legal abstraction of Emancipation.

The speech registered immediately, and has since become canonical in American political and religious rhetoric. It marked the translation of the civil rights movement itself into mythic form: a historical paradigm that would inspire a broad range of social movements for the "liberation" of oppressed groups and minorities.

King drew on the myth of regeneration through violence, in both traditional and unconventional ways. By invoking Lincoln, he associates the movement with the theme of blood sacrifice in the Gettysburg Address and blood atonement in Lincoln's second inaugural address. But it is with Lincoln the Martyr, rather than the war president, that King identifies. King and his followers are nonviolent actors, who submit their bodies to violence in the hope that their martyrdom will arouse the conscience of the nation—the *White* nation—to purge itself of injustice. The movement's "soldiers" form multiracial "platoons." Their battle is not war but its moral equivalent. At the same time, King turns the Frontier Myth of savage war inside out, proposing a new narrative of "regeneration through nonviolence," a moral war in which non-White people represent civilization and Christianity, to which White bigots respond like "savages."

In public memory King's argument prevailed, and his strategy of disciplined, large-scale nonviolent demonstrations was critical to winning public and political support for the civil rights legislation of 1964–1968 that effectively ended the legal regime of Jim Crow. However, in practice, violent and nonviolent versions of the myth were in continual dialogue. Kennedy and Johnson understood that if King's appeal for reform was rejected, Black communities would respond with violence. They had done so in the urban "riots" that had erupted since the 1930s in response to police brutality; and most recently, it had taken all of King's persuasion to stop Birmingham's Black community from resorting to violence after the church bombing that killed three little girls.

Black leaders repeatedly had to choose between the nonviolent strategy of King and his allies and more militant and confrontational approaches. An early debate pitted King against Robert Williams, president of the Monroe, North Carolina, chapter of the NAACP, who advocated—and practiced—armed self-defense. Williams's *Negroes with Guns* (1962) appeals to the Myth of the Frontier and the tradition of Western vigilantism: "It has always been an accepted right of Americans, as the history of our Western states proves, that where the law is unable, or unwilling, to enforce order, the citizens can, and must act in self-defense." But whereas traditional vigilantism perpetuated lynching, Williams wanted vigilante justice to punish lynchers: "[If] it's necessary to stop lynching with lynching, then we must be willing to resort to that method. We must meet violence with violence."[9]

Throughout the Sixties, nonviolent and integrationist movements were paralleled by other movements, some of which called for some form of separatism or violent resistance, and by spontaneous uprisings by Black communities outraged by police brutality and discrimination. In many Southern communities there was a tradition of armed self-defense—Condoleezza Rice's father led one such group in Lowndes County, Alabama. Edwin Berry of the National Urban League warned, "My message from the beer gardens and the barbershops all indicate the fact that the Negro is ready for war." That message was conveyed by groups like the Deacons for Defense in the South and by the Black Panthers in the North and West—the latter combining self-defense with a program of community self-governance. The Black Power movement went further by rejecting cooperation with the integrationists. The Nation of Islam, which became prominent in the postwar period, called for political separatism, and its leading orator, Malcolm X, called for resistance to racism "by any means necessary."[10]

Fear of violence by Black people, whether in organized movements or spontaneous outbreaks of mob violence, was never far from the consciousness of King and the White political leaders with whom he dealt. Medgar Evers, who led nonviolent demonstrations in Mississippi before his assassination, said that "nonviolence without the threat of armed resistance to racist violence amounted to surrender." The possibility of violence strengthened King's position when dealing with President Johnson and other White leaders: by acceding to King's demands for desegregation and voting rights, they validated nonviolence as a means of achieving real progress.[11]

The power and appeal of the Lincoln myth would be reinforced when, with his civil rights bill held up in Congress, Kennedy (like Lincoln) was assassinated. President Johnson exploited the association of two martyred presidents to gather bipartisan support for the passage of the 1964 Civil Rights Act and used the moral energy roused by the movement to build support for the 1965 Voting Rights Act and his Great Society and War on Poverty programs. Together these guarantees of civil liberties, and promises of government support for the enhancement of social justice, have been considered by some historians a "Second Reconstruction," fulfilling the unmet promises of the original.

Completing the New Deal: The Second Reconstruction and the Great Society

Johnson felt compelled to complete the military mission Kennedy had begun in Vietnam, and the war would ultimately devour his administration. But his own priorities had less to do with "New Frontiers" than with the completion of the project of economic and social uplift inaugurated by the New Deal. The New Deal was his personal myth of choice, expressed not only in his policy statements but in his intense personal identification with FDR.[12] As senator from Texas, Johnson had supported segregation, and as majority leader he had neutered the 1957 Civil Rights Act. But at some point he underwent a moral conversion that would lead him to embrace the political liabilities inherent in support for civil rights. The groundwork for federal action had been laid by Attorney General Robert F. Kennedy and his aides before the assassination. As president in 1964, Johnson laid claim to the project, made support of "Kennedy's civil rights bill" a symbolic test for honoring the martyred president, and augmented that appeal by framing it as a test of American morality and democratic values.

He would go further after his landslide election in 1964, forming an implicit partnership with King to use continued movement activism in support of federal policies that would dismantle the legal structures of Jim Crow. Johnson and King also shared a commitment to the larger problem of establishing economic and social justice, which King would pursue through the Poor People's Campaign of demonstrations and organizing, and Johnson through the programs of the Great Society. While their partnership lasted, it symbolized the connection between a developing Myth of the Movement and the emergence of a New Deal myth from the shadow of the Good War.

The first phase of the Movement narrative culminated in the "Kennedy" Civil Rights Act of 1964, which dealt with segregation in schools, public facilities, and interstate commerce. The movement thereafter focused on voting rights and sponsored a multistate voter registration drive in the Freedom Summer of 1964. National organizations including SCLC, the Student Nonviolent Coordinating Committee, the Congress of Racial Equality, and the NAACP sent volunteers, Black and White, to work with local organizations. They faced harassment, arrest and assault by state and local police, and murder by vigilantes organized by the White Citizens' Councils and the Ku Klux Klan. Black residents who aided the drive or attempted to register were evicted or subjected to arson, physical attack, or murder. The most notorious act of violence was the lynching on June 21, 1964, of three civil rights workers—Michael Schwerner, Andrew Goodman, and James Chaney—by Klansmen in Neshoba County, Mississippi, with the cooperation of the county sheriff's office.

The climax of the campaign was the march of demonstrators from Selma to Montgomery, Alabama, from March 7 to 25, 1965, to demand voting rights. Peaceful marchers were attacked by state and local police as they crossed the Edmund Pettus Bridge in what would become infamous as "Bloody Sunday."

Televised images of the violent and unprovoked police attack were broadcast nationally and internationally.

The confrontation on the Edmund Pettus Bridge became the iconic scene of the Movement Myth. It provoked rhetorical protest, national and international, and a wave of demonstrations, some of which threatened violence. As had happened after the Birmingham church bombing in 1963, public revulsion created a climate of opinion favorable to civil rights legislation, which Johnson seized. His address to the Joint Session of Congress on March 15, 1965, in the midst of the Selma standoff, framed his call for passage of the Voting Rights Act as the culmination of the Myth of the Movement's narrative arc and enriched its appeal by rooting that narrative in the myths that defined the moral core of American nationalism: the Founding, the Good War, and (with a soft pedal) the Liberation version of the Civil War. He also emphasized its connection with his own myth of choice, the New Deal.[13]

Johnson began by linking the violence at Selma with iconic combats of the American Revolution and Civil War: "At times history and fate meet at a single time in a single place to shape a turning point in man's unending search for freedom. So it was at Lexington and Concord. So it was a century ago at Appomattox. So it was last week in Selma, Alabama." Like Kennedy and King, Johnson would cite the sacred texts of American democracy, the Declaration of Independence and the Constitution. But his recurrent appeal was to the memory of the Good War. The "great phrases" like "All men are created equal" had real meaning because "in their name Americans have fought and died for two centuries, and tonight around the world they stand there as guardians of our liberty, risking their lives."[14]

Johnson's high hope was to go down in history as the man who completed FDR's work of lifting Americans out of poverty and extending the social safety net to include health care. But he went beyond Roosevelt to make racial justice coordinate with economic justice. He situated the civil rights movement in the pantheon of American causes, by adopting the refrain of its anthem as his own slogan: "These are the enemies: poverty, ignorance, disease. They're our enemies, not our fellow man, not our neighbor. And these enemies too—poverty, disease, and ignorance: we shall overcome." He underlined the significance of that gesture by reminding his hearers that he spoke as a Southerner who understood the South's "heritage" and "agonizing racial feelings."

His ultimate appeal for unity rested on invocation of the memory and myth of the Good War. In making it, he put particular emphasis on the prominent role of Southerners in the nation's wars:

As we meet here in this peaceful, historic chamber tonight, men from the South, some of whom were at Iwo Jima, men from the North who have carried Old Glory to far corners of the world and brought it back without a stain on it, men from the East and from the West, are all fighting together without regard to religion, or color, or region, in Vietnam. Men from every region fought for us across the world twenty years ago.

And now in these common dangers and these common sacrifices, the South made its contribution of honor and gallantry no less than any other region in the Great Republic—and in some instances, a great many of them, more.

Thus the Good War reconciles the scions of the Lost Cause with the liberated people of Lincoln's republic. The appeal of Johnson's polemic, and of his program, depends on the harmonizing of civil rights and the Civil War through the structures of the Good War and platoon movie, which saw diverse peoples united in struggle for the common good, against a common enemy. But in making that appeal, Johnson also puts the Vietnam War on a par with the Good War—an indication that for him, and for mainstream Democratic liberals, the pursuit of social justice is linked with wars of liberation abroad.

Passage of the Voting Rights Act was the climactic victory of the movement. Its effects were far-reaching and enduring. Coupled with the 1964 act, it constituted something like a "Second Reconstruction," although it would take years of grassroots struggle to begin to realize its potential. The two acts negated the legal basis of Jim Crow and put the powers of the federal government behind those working to destroy it. Southern political and social life was transformed, as more Black people won legislative and executive positions than at any time since 1877. These transformative successes were comparable in significance to those of Reconstruction, and like the original they provoked a violent and enduring racial reaction.

But for both King and Johnson, the Second Reconstruction was just the necessary preliminary to a larger project. King had always insisted that legal and procedural rights were merely means to an end, which was the achievement of economic and social justice through programs that would end poverty and class inequality in America. That was Johnson's agenda as well. Johnson's landslide victory in the 1964 election gave him the popular mandate and congressional majorities he needed to realize his ambition of completing the New Deal. Medicare and Medicaid, authorized by the Social Security Act of 1965, covered major holes in the social safety net, benefiting senior citizens and the poor, although they fell short of universal health care. Johnson attempted to repair the New Dealers' failure to include people of color by enacting anti-discrimination statutes in housing and employment and supporting "affirmative action" to bring people of color (and women) into hitherto exclusive jobs, professions, and corporate hierarchies. In a rebuke to institutionalized racism, the Immigration Act of 1965 abolished the racial and nationality quotas that had been enacted to prevent non-Nordics from becoming citizens. Hailed at the time by descendants of the eastern and southern Europeans whose people had been insulted and abused by the quotas, the act would open the United States to new waves of immigration from Asia, Africa, and Latin America.

Johnson also planned a War on Poverty that would finally bring the rural and urban underclass into the great American middle class. He branded his ultimate vision "the Great Society." It would offer welfare and family aid, but also social work projects to deal with the causes of chronic unemployment, school dropouts, and family breakdown. The VISTA program would engage college graduates in social work and educational improvement in impoverished areas. Head Start would substantially improve the preschool education of children in poor and racially affected communities, and was a promising step toward providing child care for working families.[15]

The military metaphor of the "War on Poverty" also connects Johnson's programs to the Good War Myth in its Cold War liberal incarnation, raising his social justice programs to the moral level of the war against Fascism and Communism. However, the metaphor is reversible: it also implies that the "war for freedom" in Vietnam and the War on Poverty at home are twin variants of the same script.

Degeneration through Violence: The Fall of the New Deal Order

The vision of a two-front war for freedom would fail because its promises were too obviously at odds with the emerging realities of the Vietnam War and the persistence of racial conflict at home. By 1967 American troop strength in Vietnam had risen to half a million, but the United States and South Vietnamese allies continued to suffer embarrassing defeats, and the high toll of civilian dead and ruined villages made it difficult to present the American offensive as a war of liberation. The appeal of Johnson's vision of the Great Society suffered a similar decline, in part as feedback from failure in Vietnam, in part from causes intrinsic to the civil rights movement and the existing state of race relations.

King had always had doubts about the Vietnam War. Growing evidence of its moral failure drove him to oppose it, breaking the tenuous alliance between the movement and the administration. Although many of King's colleagues questioned the political wisdom of his position, it was consistent with his larger role as critic and antagonist of a system based on the sanctification of social violence and racial hierarchy. But in breaking with Johnson over Vietnam, King not only separated his movement from its most powerful ally, he also stepped away from the national myth linking social justice to wars of liberation.

There was a fundamental tension between the movement's insistence on the need for swift and radical change to produce social justice, and the government's inevitable commitment to slow and politically compromised procedures. King understood from the start that voting rights and equal access to economic opportunities were a necessary but not sufficient means to achieving social justice. Thus, in the wake of the passage of the Voting Rights Act, King shifted focus to his Poor Peoples' Campaign, intended to unite poor White and Black people in a common fight for economic justice. The potential of that turn toward a broad, class-based social movement was still undefined when he was assassinated.[16]

Even if the War on Poverty had been perfectly designed, it could not have delivered justice at the requisite speed. The urban riots of the Sixties were the most significant expression of the violent potential of the nation's racial divide. The fundamental causes of unrest in the ghettoes remained: bad housing, oppressive landlords, and predominantly White police forces imposing social control through arbitrary arrests and outright brutality. The annual summer riots that had begun in 1964 continued and intensified from 1965 to 1967. The 1967 Detroit riot was the worst of these uprisings. *Life* magazine devoted a lurid picture-story to it titled "Detroit: City at the Blazing Heart of a Nation in Disorder." The article described the riot as an "insurrection," part of a nationwide "Negro revolt." The governor and mayor requested federal troops, and "paratroopers from the 82nd and 101st Airborne Divisions—many of them veterans of Vietnam—rolled into the continuing fray," suppressing the riot with some of the same weapons used against the Viet Cong.[17]

There was bitter irony in the perception that the War on Poverty, intended to save the urban poor, had ended in the destruction of cities and repression by the regular military in inner-city neighborhoods. That irony was doubled by news of the Tet Offensive, which discredited administration claims that it was winning the Vietnam War. The *goodness* of both wars was discredited by the way in which armed force was used, "to destroy the city in order to save it." This was, as Colonel William Corson, a marine counterinsurgency specialist, said, a descent into "the language of madness, a madness which if allowed to continue will destroy not only the people of Vietnam, but also the moral fabric and strength of America."[18]

Madness indeed. The election of 1968 was marked by the assassinations of King and of Robert F. Kennedy, the Democratic candidate supported by both civil rights and antiwar activists. King's murder on April 4, 1968, would lead to multicity uprisings that again required military intervention. The smoke of burning buildings could be seen from the White House and the steps of the Capitol. Robert Kennedy would be assassinated on June 6. The Chicago convention that nominated Johnson's successor would be marred by chaotic demonstrations and a "police riot" in the streets. Taken with the urban riots, this political violence suggested a potential collapse of the constitutional order.

Two reports commissioned by the Johnson administration attempted to make sense of the chaos. The National Advisory Commission on Civil Disorders, headed by Illinois governor Otto Kerner Jr., warned that persistent racism was threatening to divide America into "two nations," one White and rich, the other Black and poor. The National Commission on the Causes and Prevention of Violence, formed after Robert Kennedy's assassination, documented the history of American violence in exhaustive detail. Its findings, released in 1969, contributed to the sense that the disposition to violence was a congenital flaw in American "national character."[19]

That kind of violence would continue after Richard Nixon succeeded Johnson in 1968. The My Lai massacre was revealed in January 1969, around the time of Nixon's inauguration, and some of the bloodiest and least productive battles of the war (Hamburger Hill, the invasion of Laos, the bombing of Cambodia) would occur on Nixon's watch. In 1970 National Guardsmen would gun down demonstrators at Kent State, and state police would kill Black student demonstrators at Jackson State and Orangeburg State. Terrorist groups like the Weathermen and armed resistance groups like the Black Panthers would form on the left.

By 1968 it appeared that the New Deal order had collapsed in an orgy of *unregenerative* violence. Faced with proof that its operative mythology can no longer explain, let alone control, events, a society must abandon, replace, or revise its understanding of the meaning and direction of its history.

Revisionism and the Crisis of "Public Myth"

The "liberal consensus" that had shaped politics since the New Deal fractured in 1968. Opposition to the Vietnam War was the immediate occasion, but deeper cultural factors were at work. The campaign for racial integration of schools and housing, and for affirmative action to redress discrimination, led Southern White people to embrace the Republicans as the new "White Man's Party." But it also met resistance outside the South, among White working- and lower-middle-class families.

There was more to this conservative resurgence than race. The civil rights movement provided the moral energy for a series of movements that together gave the Sixties its legendary character as a time of cultural revolution. The American Indian movement organized on a racial or ethnic-group basis rather than by individual tribes. It used similar tactics of nonviolent demonstration and sit-ins (or occupation of contested land) to press for recognition of Indig- enous and tribal rights and for equal treatment for Indians living off reserva- tion. Similar movements for group recognition and relief from discrimination emerged among Asian Americans of different nationalities—Japanese Ameri- cans in particular sought reparations for internment during World War II. The farm workers' movement in California, led by Cesar Chavez, linked the fight for unionization and workers' rights to the development of "la raza," an un- derstanding of Chicano identity tied to the fight for racial equality.

The women's movement was the largest and arguably most significant of these movements, since it addressed conditions affecting more than half the population. So-called second-wave feminists went beyond demands for political representation and equal rights in business, education, and the workplace, to insist on reproductive rights, and to tackle the culture and psychology of male privilege. Some feminists offered radically revisionist views of sexuality and mar- riage. That challenge was augmented by the emergence of the gay liberation movement after the Stonewall riots of 1969.

By building on the methods and the narrative of the Black civil rights movement, these campaigns were implicitly creating an enlarged Myth of the Movement—a paradigm that could serve to organize a range of political actions. However, in their group specificity and their opposition to normative values and to a power structure controlled by White men—as well as in their opposi- tion to the Vietnam War—these campaigns departed from the themes and interests of national mythology. They took a critical stance toward nationalist ideologies and institutions, and were drawn (in varying degrees) to "identity politics"—a tendency also pioneered by the Black Power strain in the movement, which rejected integrationist goals.

These liberation movements were part of a larger cultural shift among young Americans who were in high school or college during the Sixties. They were the children of the generation that had served in World War II and moved into the middle class thanks to the GI Bill's housing and education benefits.

They were raised in an era of general prosperity and conditioned by an expansive consumer culture built on the premise of self-gratification. Their politics were shaped by the racial liberalism of the movement and the transformational ambitions of the New Frontier. That combination made them willing to consider and embrace a range of alternative lifestyles, and to challenge the presumptions of the capitalist-industrial consumer culture in which they were raised. This led many to embrace a loosely defined "counterculture," which might take the form of "sex, drugs, and rock and roll" or of a new communalism replacing traditional family structures.[20]

Significant new elements in this critique of middle-class values were the peace movement, which called for nuclear disarmament and an end to the Vietnam War, and a new environmentalism, opposed to the exploitation and pollution of the natural world. To symbolize their break with America's Frontier traditions, these movements adopted "Indian" styles of dress and identified their values as "tribal." The most successful environmentalist advertising campaign of the 1970s used a "weeping Indian" to express grief at the pollution of the natural world. "Pro-Indian" Westerns like *Soldier Blue* and *Little Big Man* would become Hollywood's way of symbolizing disgust with the Vietnam War.

One of the most enduring consequences of the Movement Myth was the impetus it gave to a major wave of revisionism in historical scholarship. This was an aspect of change that directly affected the evolution of national myth, because it altered the way in which national history was understood and disseminated. The central theme of this revisionism was a reevaluation of the role played by race, class, and gender in the development of American culture, society, and politics.

The revisionist wave began in the 1950s as a reaction against the "consensus" school of historiography, which argued that American political and social life had always been dominated by a "vital center" that held a set of standard beliefs about the exceptional character of American economic development and reflected a singular "American national character." Consensus historians tended to disregard or marginalize the strains of dissidence (both conservative and radical) in American history, as well as the experience and agency of marginalized or oppressed groups.[21]

Revisionists sought to amplify and reorient the ideology of consensus history. They were responding to the radical changes in racial politics provoked by the civil rights movement, and to changes in the demography of academia produced by the GI Bill (and the end of the quota system), which brought the children of early twentieth-century immigrants and 1930s radicals into the historical profession—outsiders to the WASP ascendancy that had dominated academic life and historical writing. The work of revisionist historians exposed the dark side of the American narrative of progress: the injustice of Native dispossession, slavery, and Jim Crow; the oppression and marginalization of women; the exploitation of labor and the environment; the creation of orders of power and privilege offsetting the drive for democratization.[22]

By searching out hitherto neglected archives and collections reflecting the lives of enslaved people, immigrants, and industrial workers, and using new methods of quantitative analysis, the revisionists recovered the lives and social agency of the so-called invisible classes. They shifted the focus of historiography from the grand national story (where White men dominated) to the histories of particular communities, Native Americans, African Americans, women, immigrants, and industrial workers. This kind of historical research and writing made visible the connection between the abstractions of high politics and the experience of public life. At the same time, it undermined the grand narrative that had defined US historiography, the nation's rise "from colony to world power," as the title of my high school textbook had it. Revisionists also questioned the concept of a unitary "American national character," emphasizing the variety within American culture—a perspective that was both praised and condemned as "multiculturalism."[23]

The WASP ascendancy did not take the critique lightly. In his 1962 inaugural address as president of the American Historical Association, Carl Bridenbaugh criticized the younger generation of "urban-bred" historians, of "lower-middle-class or foreign origins," who lacked an intuitive sense of nationality: "They find themselves, in a very real way, outsiders in our past, and their emotions frequently get in the way of their historical reconstructions." In other words, despite their assimilation to American culture and their deep study of its history, they were still, in effect, foreigners. As the revisionist critique began to question the premises of conventional liberalism, its practitioners would come under attack by old-line liberals as well as conservatives.[24]

The Crisis of Public Myth

Throughout the 1970s Americans would deal with a crisis of national consciousness, marked by the discrediting of the historical myths that had sustained American nationality for most of the twentieth century. The nature of that crisis, and its effect on the health of American political culture, was described by historian William McNeill in "The Care and Repair of Public Myth," published in the fall 1982 issue of *Foreign Affairs*. The magazine was (and is) the public voice of the Council on Foreign Relations, perhaps the most prestigious think tank in its field, and the importance its editors attached to McNeill's thesis is attested by their making it the headline article for that issue.

McNeill's "public myth" is roughly equivalent to what I've called "national myth": a fiction that shapes public understanding of the historical unfolding of the national experience. The public myth McNeill sought to repair was essentially that of the New Deal order and the liberal consensus that controlled national politics from the Depression and World War II to Johnson's Great Society and the Vietnam War. It was inevitable that new events, new crises, and radical economic and social changes would call elements of that myth into question and stimulate healthy revisions. But revisionism had (in McNeill's view) carried critique too far: "Discrediting old myths without finding new ones to replace them erodes the basis for common action that once bound those who believed into a public body, capable of acting together." McNeill urged cultural and political leaders to attend more deliberately to "the care and repair of public myth."[25]

The Myth of the Movement might have offered an alternative. But despite its legislative successes, it remained the myth of a protest movement—or now a constellation of identity-based movements, each devoted to its own cause, sharing only a sharply critical stance toward national government and societal norms, and mourning for lost leaders and unrealized opportunities. A revised formulation of national myth would come from a new conservative movement, which would assume power in 1980, and revive in their traditional forms the myths that had seemingly been overthrown by the events of the past thirty years: the Myth of the Frontier, celebrating unregulated economic exploitation and "savage war"; and the Myth of the Lost Cause, maintaining White predominance in public affairs and private business. Thus the Second Reconstruction would be followed by a "Second Redemption."

11

Back in the Saddle

Reagan, Neoliberalism, and the War against the Sixties

THE 1970s ended with a crisis of national morale. Failure in Vietnam and the collapse of the Great Society discredited the New Deal order and its sustaining myths. The Nixon presidency ended in the Watergate scandals, and the Arab oil embargo exposed our dependence on foreign oil. President Jimmy Carter's administration floundered in an economy wracked by high inflation, wage stagnation, and low growth—Stephen B. Shepard of the *New York Times* believed this was "the end of the cowboy economy." The public mood reflected general pessimism about the possibilities for positive action. William McNeill saw in that malaise the crisis of public myth.[1]

Ronald Reagan would offer a resolution to these crises, by promoting and personifying a restoration of traditional American conceptions of national power, freewheeling economics, and the cultural traditions of the 1940s and 1950s. He would inaugurate a "neoliberal order" that would direct the course of public affairs for forty years. Neoliberal economics would inform an ideological consensus strong enough to constrain the policies of liberal congressional majorities and of a Democratic president. Indeed, as Gary Gerstle has said, although "Ronald Reagan was its ideological architect . . . Bill Clinton was its key facilitator."[2]

That ideological consensus drew its emotional appeal from its revival of the traditional forms of American national myth, especially the Myths of the Frontier and the Lost Cause, and from a reaction against the cultural transformations and "liberations" associated with the Sixties, which would sound the basic themes of what we've come to call the "culture wars."

Ronald Reagan and the Neoliberal Frontier

The theme of Reagan's campaigns, and of his presidencies, was resanctification of the traditional symbols of national myth. His 1980 campaign promised to restore America's moral preeminence as "a shining city on a hill," invoking the Puritan vision of America as a "new Israel," a light unto the nations. His 1984 campaign declared it was "morning again in America," in ads that showed a nation of farms and country churches and suburban lawns bathed in a mellow light.[3]

This pastoral imagery was a visualization of Reagan's cultural program to restore the authority of traditional values and social hierarchies. His vision of American history had no place for the revisionist critique of Indian dispossession, slavery and Jim Crow, and male privilege, and reverted to the standard tropes of American exceptionalism. The "shining city" symbolism embraced the evangelical and patriarchal values of a newly activated Christian Right and at the same time suggested a restoration of the nation's economic predominance and prestige as leader of the free world after a decade of decline.[4]

The Myth of the Frontier had always been at the root of national exceptionalism, and it would inform the Reagan administration's economic ideology. Through its espousal of "supply-side" economic theory, it promised a bonanza of economic growth through lower taxes and maximal deregulation. It imagined new forms of savage war in which a heroic Reagan would defend White America from the Red Menace. In "A Time for Choosing," the speech at the 1964 Republican Convention that marked his arrival as a political force, he framed that struggle as a "last stand": "If we lose freedom here, there's no place to escape to. This is the last stand on earth."[5]

Reagan would also draw heavily on the themes and imagery of the Lost Cause, offering fearful and angry White people a Second Redemption from the racial uprising of the Second Reconstruction. His slogan, that "government is the problem," implied that businesses and religious organizations would be left free to operate—and discriminate—as they saw fit.

Reagan's experience as an actor was ideal preparation for his role as restorer of American symbolism. He was widely (and inaccurately) identified as a "B-Western cowboy actor" by his detractors. His campaign transformed that slur by embracing the gunfighter ethic of the Western. A famous campaign poster, "Bedtime for Brezhnev," shows a cowboy-clad Reagan holding a six-gun on the Soviet leader, turning Reagan's most ridiculously titled film, *Bedtime for Bonzo,* into a display of Cold War bravado. Reagan acquired a more serious heroic aura through images that linked him to the two most prominent

Western movie stars, John Wayne and Clint Eastwood. The most impressive of these displays came at the 1984 convention, when clips of Wayne introduced a film celebrating Reagan's life and the achievements of his first term. It was a virtuosic performance, validating Reagan's heroic character by associating our first Hollywood president with a figure whose own heroism was purely fictional. At the height of his powers, Reagan was able not only to cover his actions with the gloss of patriotic symbolism but to convince his audience that—in life as in movies—symbolic action is a practical equivalent of the real thing.[6]

The public's favorable response to Reagan's symbol play suggests that on some level it shared McNeill's belief that a refurbishing of public myth was the proper antidote to the demoralization of American culture. By the conviction with which he performed his public role, enacted the rituals of his office, and voiced the requisite religious and patriotic pieties, Reagan dramatized or impersonated the condition of mythic belief whose loss McNeill lamented.

The core of conservative economic theory was the free-market fundamentalism or "neoliberalism" espoused by Nobel Prize–winning University of Chicago economist Milton Friedman. Its central tenet was set out in his highly influential *New York Times* piece, "The Social Responsibility of Business Is to Increase Its Profits": that businesses must be free to operate without regard to the social or environmental consequences of their work. Friedman argued that economic growth and political freedom alike depended on businesses having the utmost freedom to pursue their economic interests, free of government regulations on pollution, fair-trade practices, product quality, workplace safety, and affirmative action—and free as well of the interference of the National Labor Relations Board acting on behalf of labor unions. Corporate taxes—taxes in general—should be lowered to free more capital for investment.[7]

But Friedman's prescription for a high-growth economy was couched in the cold technical terms of his profession. Reagan preferred "supply-side economics," the gaudier version of neoliberal theory espoused by Arthur Laffer, whose "Laffer curve" purported to show that economic growth could be generated by the easy and (for the investing class) pleasant means of radical tax cuts. Laffer and his supporters asserted that the increase in business activity would produce enough tax revenue to offset the cuts and, when combined with drastic cuts in entitlement and social welfare expenditures, would enable a balanced budget, a long-term goal of conservatives. Although the poor and middle classes would not benefit directly, some of the newly generated wealth would "trickle down" through the economy.[8]

Most economists shared the view of George H. W. Bush, Reagan's primary opponent and later vice president, that this was "voodoo economics." But Reaganomics promised a return to the "cowboy economy" for which Americans longed, and Reagan carried the day. At the ceremonies attending his signature of the Garn–St. Germain bill deregulating the savings and loan industry in 1982, Reagan hailed the measure as one that cost the taxpayers nothing but would produce limitless benefits for the whole economy, saying, "All in all, I think we've hit the jackpot." (Within five years, unregulated speculation would produce a wave of bank failures that paralyzed the industry.)[9]

Under Reagan, the term "frontier" enjoyed its widest currency since 1960–1963. Writers on economic subjects and promoters of particular businesses publicized a range of new "frontiers" in marketing and development. Proposals for extraterrestrial colonization transformed "outer space" into "the high frontier." The unexploited realm of the oceans was our "last earthly frontier," a potentially inexhaustible source of nutriment, mineral wealth, and energy. On the left, Robert Reich offered a competing version of "the next American frontier," rooted in technology and the development of human resources. The theme was pushed to its absurd limits in the TV program *Lifestyles of the Rich and Famous*. The introductory voice-over by Robin Leach invites viewers to gaze on "fame and fortune—the final frontier!"—an apt characterization of Reagan's frontier, which primarily benefited the rich.[10]

An unanticipated effect of these policies was the "financialization" of the economy, with the excess cash accumulated by the wealthy being invested in stock speculation, mergers, and stock buybacks while investment in manufacturing withered. The experience of the next forty years would show the limits of supply-side economics. Reagan's tax cuts did provide stimulus by a kind of inadvertent (and inadmissible) Keynesianism; but the growth they produced was limited and unstable, and not of much benefit to wageworkers. From the 1940s to 1980, workers' wages and benefits had grown in rough equivalence to the growth of the economy. After 1980 wages stagnated, and the lion's share of value from productivity and profitability went to ownership. When coupled with the large increases in defense spending required by Reagan's foreign policy, and with rising entitlement costs, Reaganomics increased the deficit and national debt to levels that genuinely conservative economists found alarming. The logical counterpart to deregulation and tax cutting was systematic disinvestment in public goods like schools, infrastructure, and nondefense research and development, which undercut the basis for future economic growth. Nevertheless, the core of supply-side doctrine (tax cuts and deregulation) became part of the canon of the Republican Party, and of movement conservatism.[11]

Second Redemption: Reagan and the Lost Cause

Reagan's neoliberal program went beyond advocacy of deregulation to attack the ethical principle at the heart of the New Deal, that government can act as custodian of a "common good." In his 1970 manifesto, Friedman had declared that businessmen who believe "business has a 'social conscience' and takes seriously its responsibilities for providing employment, eliminating discrimination, [and] avoiding pollution . . . [are] preaching pure and unadulterated socialism." It is this principle that ties Reagan's economic policy to the social and cultural project of conservatism, which was to undo the government-sponsored "equal rights revolution." Many of the targets of deregulation were those laws and rules that allowed government to prevent individuals, businesses, private organizations, and public agencies from discriminating against women or racial minorities.[12]

Reagan's conservative reformation was energized by a coalition of conservative Christian organizations, which had come together in the 1970s. This new movement had originally formed to defend racial segregation after the courts (following the *Brown* precedent) barred tax exemption for Christian schools founded as all-White alternatives to integrated public schools. Their focus broadened in reaction to the secularizing tendencies of postwar liberalism, such as the rejection of prayer in public schools and of the teaching of "creationism" rather than evolution, and against the transformations of traditional concepts of spirituality, gender, and sexuality fostered by the various liberation and rights movements of the 1960s. At a 1979 meeting, several organizations agreed to join forces to organize political support at the grass roots for conservative politicians and causes. The most important of these groups were the Moral Majority, led by televangelist Jerry Falwell; James Dobson's Focus on the Family; the Heritage Foundation (a think tank founded by Paul Weyrich); and the Christian Coalition, organized by televangelist Pat Robertson and Ralph Reed. Opposition to the Supreme Court's 1973 *Roe v. Wade* decision would become the chief symbol of their movement, but their agenda is better understood as a broad-gauge defense of the cultural authority traditionally held by White, native-born Christian men.[13]

The electoral bulwark of this conservative reaction was the reemergence of a "Solid South," illiberal and now reliably Republican. Richard Nixon had adopted the "Southern Strategy," developed by Kevin Phillips and Pat Buchanan, which eschewed explicit racism in favor of the vitriolic denunciation of programs identified with Black people—affirmative action, government-mandated school integration, welfare. That approach worked not only in the

South but nationally. The civil rights movement had won wide public support outside the South for its extension of procedural rights, but demands for social integration (schools and housing), for the integration of power structures (universities, corporations, unions) through affirmative action, and for economic redistribution through tax-funded social welfare programs were angrily resented. School and housing integration threatened the integrity of long-established ethnic neighborhoods and raised fears about safety because racial ghettoes were high-crime areas. Fear of crime threatened to lower the value of homes that constituted the wealth, as well as the pride, of people whose hold on middle-class status was recently acquired and tenuous. Looking back on that time, historian Jefferson Cowie notes that working-class White men also "resented the erosion of the patriarchy, the rise of moral permissiveness and affirmative action programs meant to integrate their historically white union shops. To them, the social contract lay in tatters, torn up by liberals, a meddlesome government, and demands from African-Americans and coddled college students." This complex of resentments would be codified and voiced as an appeal to "family values," whose authority the conservative Christian organizations and the Republican Party pledged to restore and defend. Nixon would claim the support of these aggrieved groups by touting them as his "silent majority," and over the ensuing decades they would—with episodic breaks to support Bill Clinton or Barack Obama—migrate to the Republican Party in national elections.[14]

Defense of the traditional and now imperiled cultural order was the general principle at the heart of Reaganism, but it was the disruption of the old racial order that generated the strongest emotions among large sections of the silent majority. Reagan would deploy what would later be called racial "dog whistles," invoking the staples of White backlash—association of Black people with crime in the streets, derision directed at "welfare queens" supposedly buying Cadillacs with their welfare checks—without saying anything explicitly anti-Black. He would also make use of Lost Cause symbolism. Reagan kicked off his 1980 campaign with a speech supporting "states' rights" in Philadelphia, Mississippi, site of the notorious lynching of three civil rights workers in 1964. The invocation of states' rights in that place was recognized in the White South as a sign of his affiliation with the racial contempt that motivated resistance to integration.[15]

Lost Cause mythology had long been an important strain in postwar movement conservatism. The defense of traditional religious and cultural values espoused by Russell Kirk and William F. Buckley, founders of the *National Review* and Young Americans for Freedom, drew on the work of neo-Confederate intellectuals Richard Weaver, James McGill Buchanan, and M. Clifford Harrison. Buchanan, a Nobel laureate in economics, founded an academic center at the University of Virginia devoted to exposing the "perverted liberalism" of the New Deal state. Harrison put the case in terms that echoed George Fitzhugh's attacks on "free society" in the 1850s. For Harrison, "the Southern Confederacy represented the purest Anglo-Saxon idealism," against "the materialistic, the uncouth" culture of the North. "[The] salvation of America rests in the South. For in the South almost exclusively persists the idealism of the Anglo-Saxon, which, with the power of Christianity, safeguards the ultimate hope of the world."[16]

As publisher of *National Review*, Buckley supported Southern resistance to school desegregation and the enfranchisement of Black voters. In a 1957 piece entitled "Why the South Must Prevail," he argued that the White community was morally entitled to take "whatever measures are necessary" to "prevail on any issue where there is corporate disagreement between Black and White . . . because, for the time being, it is the advanced race." He posed the political choice in precisely the same terms as Thomas Dixon had in 1902: "The question, as far as the White community is concerned, is whether the claims of civilization supersede those of universal suffrage." Buckley carried the argument further, to assert that the enlightened elite has the right to set aside the will of democratic majority: "If the majority wills what is socially atavistic, then to thwart the majority may be, though undemocratic, enlightened. It is more important for any community, anywhere in the world, to affirm and live by civilized standards, than to bow to the demands of the numerical majority."[17]

The use of Confederate symbolism had grown as the civil rights movement progressed. Through the 1950s and 1960s, the Confederate battle flag was displayed at meetings of terrorist organizations like the Ku Klux Klan and White Citizens' Councils. Georgia changed its flag to incorporate the Stars and Bars 1956; in 1961 South Carolina ordered the rebel flag be flown at the state capitol. Alabama's segregationist governor George Wallace invoked the Lost Cause at his inauguration in January 1963, using terms similar to those of Harrison and Buckley—an indication of the consonance of cultural values that linked movement conservatism with populist racialism: "From this Cradle of the Confederacy, the very Heart of the Great Anglo-Saxon Southland. . . . Let us rise to the call of freedom-loving blood that is in us and send our answer to the tyranny that clanks its chains upon the South. In the name of the greatest people that have ever trod the earth, I draw this line in the dust . . . segregation now . . . segregation tomorrow . . . segregation forever."[18]

Popular culture was rife with soft-core displays of neo-Confederate iconography and sentiment. *The Andy Griffith Show* (1960–1968) was set in an idealized Southern town populated exclusively by charming down-home White people. In the Reagan era, rebel associations had more bite. *The Dukes of Hazzard* (1979–1985) pitted the moonshiner Duke brothers and their gorgeous cousin Daisy against a corrupt sheriff, "Boss" Jefferson Davis Hogg. Although identifying the Dukes' nemesis with the Confederate president is a counter-Confederate gesture, the show's dominant image is of the Dukes' souped-up sports car, "General Lee," with a huge Confederate flag emblazoned on its hood. As in *The Andy Griffith Show,* Black people are all but nonexistent in this contest between populist outlaws and corrupt authorities. The crossover appeal of Confederate imagery is attested by the success of the Band's 1969 folk-rock hit "The Night They Drove Old Dixie Down," which mourns the Confederacy's defeat. Both the original recording and a later cover by Joan Baez, a leading voice in the antiwar and civil rights movements, became Top 40 hits. The song later became a favorite of neo-Confederate political organizations.

Reagan's rise as a presidential candidate coincided with the institutionalization of neo-Confederate ideology. Thomas Fleming's *Southern Partisan,* which became the semiofficial journal of the neo-Confederate movement, began publishing in 1979. Contributors came not only from heritage organizations like the United Daughters of the Confederacy and Sons of Confederate Veterans but also from the Republican Party and its Christian Right supporters, including congressional leader Dick Armey, Senators Phil Gramm and Jesse Helms, evangelists Jerry Falwell and Pat Robertson, and antifeminist activist Phyllis Schlafly.

The magazine explicitly linked Confederate illiberalism to the agenda of Reaganite conservatism. It opposed racial civil rights initiatives, gay rights, women's rights, immigration, and gun control. Trent Lott, then Republican leader in the Senate, gave a 1984 interview in which he said the values in the Republican platform were those Jefferson Davis would have espoused. John Ashcroft (then a senator, later George H. W. Bush's attorney general) praised *Southern Partisan* as a source of important conservative ideas and values: "Your magazine also helps set the record straight. You've got a heritage of defending Southern patriots like Lee, Jackson, and Davis. Traditionalists must do more. I've got to do more." In 1996 Colorado senatorial candidate Gail Norton (later secretary of the interior under George W. Bush) compared her own defense of states' rights to the Confederacy's struggle for the same principle. "We lost too much" when the South was defeated, she said: "We lost the idea that the states were to stand against the federal government gaining too much power over our lives."[19]

If the civil rights revolution of the Sixties was a Second Reconstruction, Reaganism offered a Second Redemption.

Overcoming "Vietnam Syndrome": From Rambo to the Gulf War

In the Frontier Myth, economic expansion is organically linked to the regenerative violence of "savage war." Reagan's polemics coupled the idea of economic bonanza with a militant approach to foreign affairs. He announced a more vigorous prosecution of the Cold War, declaring Russia (in the language of *Star Wars*) an "evil empire"; dramatically raised defense spending; and pushed the development of advanced weaponry like the so-called Star Wars Space Defense Initiative. When coupled with Reagan's deft and careful diplomacy with reform-minded Soviet premier Mikhail Gorbachev, that policy contributed to the breakup of the Warsaw Pact and Soviet Union, while setting a tone of détente that prevented the fracture from starting a war.

At the same time, the administration resumed an active counterinsurgency role in the Third World. Through covert or special operations and targeted air attacks, Reagan would prosecute savage wars against terror-sponsoring enemies like Muammar al-Qaddafi of Libya, the Hezbollah in Lebanon, and the Sandinistas in Nicaragua and the Marxist regime of Maurice Bishop in Grenada. These policies required a cure for "Vietnam syndrome": the public's unwillingness to support military engagement in the Third World for fear of becoming trapped in another "quagmire." Overcoming that syndrome was the theme of a Reagan-era film genre of great currency and power that might be called "the cult of the POW / MIA." It focused on the government's failure to account for all servicemen missing in action and its alleged failure to ensure that all American prisoners of war had been returned. *The Deer Hunter* (1978) incorporated this theme in its epic treatment of the Vietnam War, but the genre acquired its widest audience through the films of the *Rambo* and *Missing in Action* series. The heroes of these films are military vigilantes, ex–Green Berets who cannot fully return to America until they have completed their failed mission and canceled their debt of honor to comrades left behind. The American who, as part of the world's mightiest army, had been defeated by ragtag and outnumbered Vietnamese guerrillas now gets to play the movie in reverse. This time he is the guerrilla and defeats a rigid totalitarian regular army that has him outnumbered and outgunned. The redemption of national honor in these films also requires the defeat of a domestic opponent: officials of their own government, the politicians and "big shots" who (as the Nazis said of Weimar liberals) "stabbed the army in the back" and prevented it from winning the war. The films' concentration on the captivity formula links them to the most basic story line of the Frontier Myth; and their obsessive repetition of the rescue fantasy makes them rituals for transforming the trauma of defeat into symbolic victory.[20]

When the savage-war trope is put in play, the hero must use all means, even the dark arts of the enemy, in order to prevail. The Reagan administration pressed this approach to the limits of acceptability in the Iran-Contra Affair, when the administration tried to circumvent a congressional prohibition on direct aid to anti-Communist guerrillas in Nicaragua (the "Contras") by making a secret arms deal with Iran—with whom all dealings were also legally sanctioned. The resulting scandal tainted the administration's final years and led to the convictions (later overturned) of Reagan's CIA chief William Casey and several of his assistants. The covert support provided to right-wing forces in Central America encouraged the operations of death squads, worsening the region's political dysfunction. Reagan's largest military initiative—the intervention in Lebanon's civil war—also ended badly, when 241 marines were killed in a terrorist attack and Reagan withdrew US forces. Rationalized as attempts to recover the mantle of world liberator conferred by the Good War Myth, these military operations were almost uniformly disastrous in their effects.[21]

Nevertheless, Reagan's determination to move beyond Vietnam syndrome remained a centerpiece of his foreign policy. Reagan's secretary of state George Schultz hailed the penny-ante invasion of Grenada to overthrow Bishop as "a shot heard round the world. We were back in the game. We were saying to the people in Angola, everywhere where Soviet advisors and Cuban proxies were, that we . . . will help you." Schultz was part of a bipartisan community of policy intellectuals, known as neoconservatives, who were developing a more systematic approach to the reassertion of American power. Working through conservative think tanks like the Heritage Foundation and the policy-oriented Project for a New American Century, founded by journalist William Kristol and historian Robert Kagan, their movement sought to revivify the American war imaginary by developing credible and appealing scenarios for the use of military force. The "neocons" would have their greatest influence in the administrations of Reagan's successor, George H. W. Bush (1989–1992), and of his son George W. Bush (2001–2008).[22]

The first Bush administration saw the collapse of the Warsaw Pact and the overthrow of Communist regimes in the non-Russian satellite states (1989), followed by the breakup of the Soviet Union itself in 1991. With "victory" in the Cold War, the United States stood as the world's lone superpower. The neocons envisioned a foreign policy that would maximize our use of economic and military power to make "liberal democracy" a universal system. But public willingness to exercise that power would not be forthcoming unless they could overcome Vietnam syndrome. The first targets of their policy were "rogue" regimes in Latin America, North Africa, and the Middle East, where operations would be quick and easy. Bush's invasion of Panama, to overthrow the dictator Manuel Noriega, would be justified as part of the War on Drugs, a Reagan-era campaign that evoked the racial imagery of "crime in the streets." Noriega was an ideal savage-war villain, represented as a physically repellent man (with pocked face and "Indian" blood), a sexual deviant, and a drug addict. The immediate pretext for the invasion itself (Operation Just Cause) was the need to "rescue the captives," American civilians seemingly threatened by Noriega's forces, who had assaulted an American officer and his wife.[23]

The major triumph of neocon policy was the Gulf War of 1991, fought to reverse the seizure of oil-rich Kuwait by Saddam Hussein, the dictator of Iraq—and formerly a US proxy against Iran. Bush deployed the largest US military force since Vietnam, formed an impressive international alliance, and after long preparation annihilated Saddam's forces in Kuwait in a stunningly swift campaign.

Bush framed the war as a combination of savage war and Good War. As head of the quasi-Fascist Ba'ath Party and as a "mad" aggressor, Saddam was likened to Adolph Hitler. His brutal occupation of Kuwait also evoked the classic elements of the Indian captivity trope: Saddam is "Brown," not White; his men raped and murdered the Kuwaitis; and he himself made a dramatic TV appearance holding as hostages the families of Westerners who had been unable to flee. His potential dominance of the Gulf oil fields was seen as a danger to America's future, given our dependence on cheap and abundant oil from the Middle East. Asked what the war was for, Secretary of State James Baker answered, "Jobs, jobs, jobs."[24]

Even at the time, Baker's justification of the war seemed crass. The cost of war in human life and suffering requires some more noble purpose. In the Gulf War that higher purpose was the restoration of Americans' military morale, a ritual of regeneration through violence that finally redeemed our failure in Vietnam and restored public faith in the nation's righteous and victorious use of power. "By God," Bush said to his aides, "we've kicked the Vietnam syndrome." In this formulation, the president had authorized the shedding of blood, not as a cruel means to a necessary end, nor as a defense of material interests, but as a cure for an illness of our imagination. In that sense, the Gulf War served the same imaginative function as the movies of the MIA-rescue genre, but with live ammunition.[25]

Bush himself had a relatively temperate view of America's new status. His success in building the multinational coalition against Saddam reinforced his inclination to use power in concert with others, for the most part within the constraints of international law, balance-of-power moderation, and respect for the opinions of allies. He therefore stopped short of occupying Iraq or overthrowing Saddam—a limitation that left in place a dictator with nuclear ambitions and exposed Kurdish and Shiite ethnic groups to violent repression. Leading neoconservatives in his administration saw this as a mistake. For them, the Gulf War demonstrated that America's military and economic power, and its prestige as the champion of a liberal-democratic world order, entitled it to impose its will on world affairs, transforming rogue regimes and failed states like Iraq into "democracies"—and reliable clients. Through their term of exile during the ensuing Clinton administration, they would develop a new and more ambitious strategy to put in place when Republicans returned to power.

From Reaganism to Culture War, 1988–2000

The Reagan and George H. W. Bush administrations refurbished public myth by taking its three strains back to their roots. Their neoliberal version of bonanza economics was a reversion to the Frontier Myth and pre–New Deal economic doctrine. Nostalgia for a pre–civil rights America infused their public appeal, and their social policies, with echoes of Lost Cause symbolism. Their wars on drugs and terrorism revived the savage-war trope in its classic form, while the Gulf War was played as a reprise of the Good War and an exorcism of the ghost of Vietnam. But their achievement was undermined by failure to address long-term symptoms of economic dislocation and distress. Although the economy expanded under Reagan, the benefits were distributed so unequally that, while the richest Americans were acquiring a larger share of the national wealth, the number of people living in poverty actually increased and the real income and assets of most of the population declined. Bush's failure to recognize and address the public's sense of economic hardship would dog his 1992 reelection campaign.

Bush represented traditional conservatism. He had rejected supply-side economics as "voodoo economics" in his 1980 campaign, and as president he reverted to more conventional methods of budget balancing. The government's colossal indebtedness—the result of Reagan's insistence on cutting taxes while accelerating defense spending—threatened its credit rating and its ability to sustain regulatory operations. When Bush responded by accepting the Democratic Congress's insistence on a tax increase (in violation of his campaign pledge), there was a powerful backlash among conservatives.[26]

Cultural conservatives were also angered by the failure of Reagan and Bush to reverse the policies and challenge the value assumptions generated by the civil rights movement and associated "liberation" movements of the 1960s. Reagan had paid lip service to the Christian Coalition's positions on abortion, racial discrimination, and gay rights, but did very little. Bush denied them even lip service. Although his campaign deployed the racist imagery of the Southern Strategy—visually linking his Democratic opponent to the Black rapist and murderer Willie Horton—Bush characterized his program as "a kinder, gentler" conservatism: that is, one less stringent than Reagan's on social welfare and discrimination.[27]

When Bush ran for reelection in 1992, he was challenged by a conservative and populist reaction within his own party, despite the 90 percent approval ratings he had enjoyed immediately after the Gulf War. Indeed, his foreign policy triumphs contributed to that reaction. Bush had identified his goal as the establishment of a "new world order," in which the principles of liberal society—capitalism, free trade, human rights—would enjoy universal hegemony. But to extreme conservatives like the evangelical potentate (and presidential candidate) Pat Robertson, "new world order" implied the surrender of uniquely American and Christian values to liberal secularists—or worse. In his 1991 book, *The New World Order,* Robertson claimed that Bush was the agent (conscious or not) of an "Establishment" controlling American policy from behind the scenes, whose "principal goal is the establishment of a one-world government where the control of money is in the hands of one or more privately owned but government-chartered central banks." The conspiracy was masterminded by the "Illuminati," a secret organization of Freemasons and Jewish bankers working through such respectable think tanks as the Council on Foreign Relations and the Trilateral Commission. Satan himself (according to Robertson) was the guiding intelligence behind it all.[28]

The most direct challenge to Bush came from Pat Buchanan, a former Reagan speechwriter, developer of the Southern Strategy, and founder of the American Cause, a conservative educational foundation. Buchanan accused Bush of betraying the Reagan "revolution." It was not only that he had reneged on his pledge of "no new taxes." His "kinder, gentler" conservatism weakened public resistance to the appeals of 1960s liberations. Buchanan believed Reagan had erred in limiting his application of conservative doctrine to economics. To truly overturn the New Deal order, Republicans would have to "take up the challenge from the Left on its chosen battleground: the politics of class, culture, religion and race." That would be the task of the movement that would be dubbed "the New Right."[29]

Buchanan's understanding of the liberal-conservative conflict reflects the presumptions of the Lost Cause Myth: that the nation must be redeemed through the restoration of a society in which property rights are unlimited, values and practices conform to Christian doctrine, and traditional social hierarchies of class, race, and gender are reinstated. In his speech to the 1992 Republican National Convention, Buchanan proposed "culture war" as the defining theme of the coming campaign against Bill *and* Hillary Clinton—her activism and lack of womanly deference were critical to his argument—as "a religious war . . . for the soul of America": "The agenda Clinton & Clinton would impose on America—abortion on demand, a litmus test for the Supreme Court, homosexual rights, discrimination against religious schools, women in combat units—that's change, all right. But it is not the kind of change America needs. . . . And it is not the kind of change we can abide in a nation we still call God's country." For Buchanan, the god in question was unmistakably Christian.[30]

The heart of Buchanan's animus was his opposition to affirmative action. In his 1990 memoir / polemic, *Right from the Beginning,* he lamented the passing of that pre-1960s culture, when segregation was peacefully and generally accepted as the social norm. "The 'Negroes' of Washington had their public schools, restaurants, bars, movie houses, playgrounds and churches; and we had ours." Liberal agitators disrupted this peaceful world with their demands for affirmative action: "The 'Negroes' of the '50s became the blacks of the '60's; now, the 'African-Americans' of the 90's demand racial quotas and set-asides, as the Democrats eagerly assent and a pandering GOP prepares to go along."[31]

Buchanan's opposition to affirmative action went beyond the polite formulas of "states' rights" and "freedom of association." In *State of Emergency: The Third World Invasion and Conquest of America,* published in 2006, he forthrightly espoused theories of racial difference and White superiority in terms that echo John Commons's 1907 report on immigration: "It is not true that all creeds and cultures are equally assimilable in a First World nation born of England, Christianity, and Western civilization. Race, faith, ethnicity and history leave genetic fingerprints no 'proposition nation' can erase. . . . The sixty million Americans who claim German ancestry are fully assimilated, while millions from Africa and Asia are still not full participants in American society."[32] The fault for that failure rests with these non-White minorities, not those who systematically excluded them.

Buchanan asserted that failure to limit the immigration of lower races would degenerate American society: "Does this First World nation wish to become a Third World country? Because that is our destiny if we do not build a sea wall against the waves of immigration rolling over our shores."[33] His opposition to feminism and women's rights is similarly based on biological fallacy: "Rail as they will against 'discrimination,' women are simply not endowed by nature with the same measures of single-minded ambition and the will to succeed in the fiercely competitive world of Western capitalism. . . . The momma bird builds the nest. So it was, so it ever shall be. Ronald Reagan is not responsible for this; God is."[34]

Buchanan's call to culture war would fail to sway the 1992 Republican Convention, but it marked a shift in the balance between the neoliberal economics of mainstream Republicanism and those groups for whom cultural issues were critical.

The agenda of cultural conservatism for which Buchanan spoke would be taken up by a growing cadre of spokespeople, based in the media of talk radio and (after 1996) Fox News, a news and opinion network created by newspaper magnate Rupert Murdoch and political consultant Roger Ailes, openly dedicated to propagating conservative views. Rush Limbaugh's call-in program was the most popular and influential of the radio programs, Glenn Beck gained a national following through radio and television outlets, and Fox News commentators like Sean Hannity, Laura Ingraham, Bill O'Reilly, and Tucker Carlson would gain a form of political stardom. Their attacks on "political correctness" and Democratic policies were supplemented by the ongoing critique of liberal and secular culture by the Christian radio and television programs associated with the Christian Coalition and Moral Majority.[35]

A less racist version of Buchanan's populism was represented in the 1992 election by Ross Perot, a maverick oilman running as a third-party candidate. Perot opposed the Gulf War of 1991, tax increases, and free-trade agreements on the grounds that they would cost American jobs. Put Robertson's conspiracy theories and Buchanan's "culture war" together with Perot's protectionism and anti-internationalism and you have an anticipatory sketch of Donald Trump's "America First" platform.

With his Reaganite credentials suspect on the right and an economy in recession; with Perot draining conservative support and a pro-business Southern Democrat running to his left, Bush's 90 percent support vanished in a few

months. Bill Clinton won the election with less than a majority of the popular vote.

Bill Clinton and Reagan Lite

The paradox of Clinton's presidency is that a Democrat whose policies were
consonant with some mainstream conservative principles provoked an ideological backlash of astonishing intensity. Clinton was more effective than
Reagan himself in achieving the goals of a balanced budget, shrinking government, and reducing welfare entitlements. But his two terms also saw the emergence of Buchanan's culture-war politics as a dominant strain in Republican
ideology and polemics—a tendency registered in the inflammatory rhetoric of
Newt Gingrich's victorious 1994 midterm "Contract with America" and in the
demonization of Clinton and his wife by a newly expanded network of right-
wing media outlets.

Clinton presented himself as someone who could strike a balance between
the "liberations" of the 1960s and the demands of an economy that depended
on business to produce "the rising tide that lifts all boats." The connection was
conveyed by symbolism. He spoke of being drawn to politics by John F. Kennedy's call to public service, as well as the moral imperatives of the civil
rights and antiwar movements. He also identified with the cultural and sexual
liberation fostered by the age of "sex, drugs, and rock and roll." He played
rhythm-and-blues sax with a late-night talk show band and seemed at ease
with people of color—especially remarkable in someone born and raised in a
poor White family in Arkansas who had been governor of that ur-Southern
state. On the other hand, his criticism of the rap musician Sister Souljah for
her antipolice rhetoric separated him from the radical, Black Power side of
African American political culture.

His policies on health care and affirmative action were distinctly to the
left of Bush. But in important ways the rest of his program was just an *even
kinder, even* gentler conservatism. Clinton's roots were in the New Democrat
movement, which accepted the demise of the New Deal order and "preached
macroeconomic orthodoxy, deregulation in the name of consumer choice,
public-private partnerships, and fiscal restraint." Its adherents eschewed the
"liberal" label, which had been poisoned by Reagan, and turned away from
"the redistributive and labor-oriented politics of the New Deal order" to embrace the "individualist, meritocratic, suburban-centered priorities of liberal,
knowledge-oriented professionals."[36]

Like Reagan, Clinton called for a balanced budget. Unlike Reagan, he achieved it by raising taxes. From the first he advocated reducing the size and cost of government, although he did so to make it more efficient in delivering services, not simply to abrogate its functions. His deregulation of the financial sector, through the repeal of the Glass-Steagall Banking Act and passage of the Commodity Futures Modernization Act, was more radical than anything attempted by Reagan or Bush, and ultimately disastrous in its unleashing of limitless speculation in mortgage instruments and derivatives.[37]

Clinton did more than any predecessor to achieve the long-standing goal of conservatives and business interests in regularizing international commerce on "free-trade" principles. He was instrumental in creating the World Trade Organization, which was more powerful than the General Agreement on Tariffs and Trade it replaced. His support of the North American Free Trade Agreement (NAFTA), largely negotiated by the previous Republican administration, set him in opposition to organized labor. Ross Perot would make opposition to NAFTA, and similar free-trade agreements, the center of his 1996 third-party campaign. His tagline—"That sucking sound you hear is American jobs going to Mexico"—sounded the main theme of a "populist" resistance to free trade that would triumph with Donald Trump.

Like his predecessors, Clinton believed in the Frontier Myth: rapid economic growth was the necessary precondition for preserving and developing American democracy. His labor secretary, the economist Robert Reich, had outlined the promise of a new, tech-heavy economy in *The Next American Frontier* (1983). Government could foster that kind of growth by investing (or subsidizing business investment) in research and development, and minimizing regulation. Though great profits would accrue to business, gains in productivity and increased employment would also benefit the working classes. Reagan's version of this process was "trickle-down economics." Clinton preferred the more egalitarian-seeming "rising tide that lifts all boats." Nevertheless, the stagnation in wages and decline in union membership that began with Reagan's election accelerated under Clinton.[38]

Clinton's identification with the cultural values of the Sixties was strongest where questions of race, gender, and the environment were concerned. However, even in these areas he was willing to bend to conservative preferences. Although he pressed civil rights and affirmative action cases through the Justice Department, he abandoned a campaign pledge to allow gay people to serve in the military, adopting instead the hypocrisy of "don't ask, don't tell." He also came out in opposition to gay marriage rights by supporting the Defense of

Marriage Act in 1996. Most significantly, he worked with Republicans to "end welfare as we know it"—a staple of Reagan's agenda. He even co-opted the GOP's law-and-order agenda by pushing for mandatory sentences on a range of crimes—a policy that would ultimately lead to scandalous levels of mass incarceration, especially of non-White people.[39]

He was stronger on environmental issues. Clinton believed that developing the tech frontier would reconcile the demand for growth with concern over the environment by enabling the development of clean energy resources. The administration's support of the Kyoto agreement to limit greenhouse gases was in stark opposition to the traditional concept of the Frontier, in which prosperity is won through the unregulated exploitation of natural resources. It ran counter to the drive for "energy independence" that had been a consensus political goal since the oil embargo of 1973. But Republicans naturally opposed any strictures on the oil business, and the high-tech frontier envisioned by Clinton was not convincing to a labor movement concerned about the danger to employment posed by automation.

Clinton's most consequential compromise was purely symbolic. It came when he responded to Democratic defeat in the 1994 midterms by declaring, "The era of big government is over." His own administration's efforts (managed by Vice President Al Gore) to make government more cost efficient were compatible with this view. But stating it that way, at that moment, was a declaration that New Democrats accepted the Reagan principle that "government is the problem."[40]

Despite his relative liberalism on race, health care, and ecology, Clinton's policies were conservative enough to enable him to seize the political center. To drive him out of this position, Newt Gingrich in 1994 promulgated the "Contract with America," an ideological covenant for Republicans.

Framing a Culture-War Ideology, 1994–2000

Gingrich's "Contract with America" was the first attempt to weaponize Pat Buchanan's culture-war rhetoric in a political contest. Its central theme and imperative was to characterize Democrats as "liberals," and liberals as culturally "other"—alien and inimical to the fundamental values of real Americans. Gingrich advised candidates to use viciously polarizing rhetoric that characterized liberals as "bizarre," "alien," and "the enemies of normal Americans." Culture-war staples like affirmative action and abortion rights were to be treated as stigmata of liberal "otherness." Tax increases were anathema; the budget was to be balanced by shrinking government. Liberalism was to be identified with the "excesses" of the 1960s and dismissed as inimical to "real Americans" and their values. The demonization of Bill and Hillary Clinton was extravagant—they were accused of murder, dope dealing, and dabbling in the occult. By fomenting a mass revulsion against the Clintons, Gingrich hoped to alienate Americans from the Sixties' culture of liberation in matters of race, gender, sexuality, and faith.[41]

The "Contract with America" led Republicans to victory in the 1994 mid-terms, ending the Democrats' enduring majorities in the House and Senate. Clinton's political skill enabled him to overcome Gingrich in a budget battle and hold his own with a Republican Congress. His personal appeal would also help him win reelection over Senator Robert Dole and Ross Perot in 1996—although he failed again to win an outright majority. But Gingrich had given Buchanan's culture-war ideology a mainstream voice and presence. It would grow in strength throughout Clinton's presidency and become dominant after 2008.

Buchanan framed that ideology in crude and explicit terms, equating Euro-American supremacy with civilization, and with a reactionary form of Christianity. As he expressed them, these ideas seemed merely to echo and exaggerate regional, class, and religious prejudices. But in the two years that followed Gingrich's "Contract with America," a more sophisticated version of that ideology was developed by policy intellectuals and journalists, which linked a racialized theory of geopolitics to concern about the problematic effects of diversity and affirmative action on the coherence and viability of the American nation-state.

Samuel Huntington's "clash of civilizations" theory of geopolitics, first set out in a 1994 article in *Foreign Affairs* and extended to book length in 1996, would become the neoconservative blueprint for understanding post–Cold War competition and conflict. Huntington divides the world into constellations of nation-states, grouped according to dominant and fixed cultural characteristics, which he terms "civilizations." In this world order, "Western civilization," based on classical and Judeo-Christian sources as modified by the Enlightenment, is in competition with the "Orthodox" (Eastern Europe and Russia), Latin American, "Sinic" (Chinese), Hindu, Japanese, African, and Islamic civilizations. Huntington's map of contending civilizations tracks closely with the race-based geopolitics of T. L. Stoddard's *Rising Tide of Color against White World Supremacy* (1922). Although Huntington's distinctions are cultural rather than biological, his theory is consistent with Stoddard's basic premise: civilizational differences are effectively immutable, and extreme differences inevitably lead to conflict.[42]

Just as civilizational differences make it impossible for rival civilizations to share the same geopolitical space on terms of equality, they make it impossible for the United States to assimilate immigrants from beyond its civilizational boundaries. In 1995 Peter Brimelow, editor of *Forbes,* published *Alien Nation* (also a best seller), which urged a ban on non-White immigrants on the grounds that they could never be fully Americanized. Huntington would support that view in *Who Are We? The Challenges to America's National Identity* (2005), urging an end to Latino immigration (numerically the largest), on the grounds that Latino culture is inimical to American civilization. Racial differences *as such* also militate against attempts to establish equality through affirmative action. In 1994 sociologist Charles Murray's *Bell Curve* became a best seller, and the center of a heated national debate, by purporting to prove that differences in White and Black academic performance were biologically based. His thesis was used by opponents of affirmative action to argue that attempting to bring Black students into elite institutions and higher levels of employment would be of no benefit to them, and would make institutions and businesses less effective.[43]

Robert Kaplan's influential article "The Coming Anarchy," published in 1994, also took a dire view of America's cultural diversity. Unlike Huntington and Brimelow, Kaplan doesn't use "culture" as a cover story for "race," but he did see ethnic diversity as a menace to national survival. He observes the role of ethnic secessions in the breakup of Yugoslavia, notes the rise of ethnic secessionism in Canada and Spain, and sees these developments as a new force in geopolitics, which has dire implications for America: "[It] is not clear that the United States will survive the next century in exactly its present form. Because America is a multi-ethnic society, the nation-state has always been more fragile here than it is in more homogeneous societies like Germany and Japan."[44] His belief that diversity makes our state "fragile" has been partly borne out by the ethnonationalist reaction that carried Trump to power in 2016. But the rending of the social fabric has come not from secessionist racial or ethnic minorities but from White people angry at the loss of political and cultural authority.

Buchanan, Huntington, Brimelow, and Murray share the anxiety of White native-born Christian Americans that the growth of racial and ethnic diversity, empowered by affirmative action and large-scale immigration, endangered not only their material interests but their status as definers of American values and identity. That same anxiety was also being expressed by many in the liberal intellectual establishment. Here it took the form of a reaction against the "revisionist" historiography that emerged from the 1960s, and the politics of "political correctness" that was associated with it.

From the 1940s to the 1960s, American historiography had been shaped by a liberal consensus that posited an American "monoculture," a standard to which all marginalized groups could and should assimilate; a culture centered on the values of individualism, progress, and private enterprise, and on the general sense that Judeo-Christian religious belief is a vital basis of community and morality. It also posited a politics designed to guarantee fairness through minimal regulation, equalizing opportunity but not prescribing a form of social justice. Revisionist analysis assailed this monoculture by questioning the moral and factual validity of its assumptions about other cultures, about labor, about sexuality, about race. It brought forward the dark side of the American narrative of progress: the injustice of Native dispossession, slavery, and Jim Crow; the exploitation of labor and the environment; the creation of orders of power and privilege offsetting the drive for democratization. Revisionists also shifted the focus of historiography from the grand national story (where elites dominated the stage) to the histories of oppressed and marginalized groups. Some posited a "multicultural" historiography, though the ideologies and programs associated with this term varied widely in concept and agenda. For some, multiculturalism was an ideological program aimed at denationalizing the study of history. For most, it meant making visible the hidden histories of Black people, women, and workers; looking at national or mainstream history from the perspective of marginalized groups; and integrating their histories with that of the nation. Critics lumped these scholarly movements together with movements against racist speech on college campuses and denounced an emerging ideology of "political correctness."[45]

In 1992 the publisher and editors of *Partisan Review,* an old and distinguished journal of left-liberal thought, invited a broad range of scholars and writers to consider the problem of political correctness, and whether measures should be taken to oppose it. The contributions were collected in 1994 in a book titled *Our Country, Our Culture: The Politics of Political Correctness.* The contributors ranged from conservatives like columnist Charles Krauthammer and historian Ronald Radosh ("A McCarthyism of the Left") to liberal centrist Arthur Schlesinger Jr. The editors' use of the possessive in the title suggests that "the culture" in some sense *belongs* to these representatives of the academic and journalistic elite. It also reflects the contributors' belief that American culture is singular and distinct, a complex but ultimately unified system to which would-be citizens should seek to assimilate. Schlesinger's criticism catches the central point: "The ideologues of multiculturalism . . . would reject the historical purposes of assimilation and integration. They see America not as a nation of individuals making their free choices but as a nation of ethnic groups more or less permanent and ineradicable in their nature. They would have our educational system reinforce, promote and perpetuate separate ethnic communities . . . at the expense of a common culture and a common national identity." Multicultur-alism would become a recurrent complaint in the conservative polemics of the Clinton and George W. Bush administrations. In the Obama presidency and the Trump presidential campaign, denunciations of political correctness would rise to full-throated war cries.[46]

The virulence of the Clinton-era culture wars is suggested by the title of James D. Hunter's 1994 study, *Before the Shooting Begins,* in which Hunter argues, "Cumulatively, the various issues of cultural conflict point to a deeper struggle over the first principles of how we will order our lives together; a struggle to define the purpose of our major institutions, and in all of this, a struggle to shape the identity of the nation as a whole. . . . When cultural impulses this momentous vie against each other to dominate public life, ten-sion, conflict, perhaps even *violence* are inevitable . . . because *culture wars al-ways precede shooting wars.*"[47]

At the end of Clinton's presidency, there was a nearly equal division in the popular strength of the two parties. In 2000 George W. Bush narrowly lost the popular vote but won the Electoral College, and in 2004 he won a bare popular majority of 50.7 percent, but majorities in the House and Senate gave him the power to remake economic and foreign policy. His administration would see the neoconservatives' geopolitics discredited by the very act that re-alized its ambitions, and the neoliberal order reach its economic high point, then end in a spectacular crash. In the wake of that collapse, the culture-war strain of conservative politics would become dominant.

12

Rising Tide

Climate Change and the Fossil Fuel Frontier

IN GEORGE W. Bush, conservatives found a leader well suited to reconciling the contending elements of the Republican coalition and realizing the larger goals of Reaganist policy. His candidacy was promoted by veterans of the Reagan and George H. W. Bush administrations, including former secretary of state George Schultz and former defense secretary Dick Cheney, as well as policy intellectuals Condoleezza Rice and Paul Wolfowitz. They represented a new school of strategic thought called neoconservatism, which was born in reaction against the supposed "timidity" of George H. W. Bush and Bill Clinton in exploiting the military preeminence America enjoyed after the collapse of the Soviet Union. Between 1989 and 1991 they had developed a strategic doctrine that called for the United States to use its military power to reshape the international order along American lines, driving former Communist states and Third World dictatorships toward the development of more or less democratic polities and economies open to capitalist development. Neoconservatives would form the core of George W. Bush's advisers on foreign and military policy.[1]

Bush's ideas and personal style differed from his father's in ways that promised to bridge the divides among Republican neoliberals, neoconservatives, and culture-war populists. Whereas his father was Texan by transplantation, George W. was Texan born and bred. The struggle with alcoholism he experienced in his thirties ended with a spiritual conversion that imbued him with a deep evangelical faith, in contrast to his father's cool Episcopalianism. His genuine religiosity earned him support among Christian conservatives and the Buchanan / culture-wars wing of the party, who believed he would fight abortion, gay rights, gun control, and affirmative action with more energy than

Ronald Reagan or his father. His espousal of "compassionate conservatism" largely avoided the implied criticism of evangelical rigor in his father's "kinder, gentler conservatism." Unlike his father, he was also a true believer in supply-side economics and was committed to radical tax cuts and deregulation. As a former governor of Texas, he could be trusted to protect the fossil fuel industry from environmental regulations.[2]

During his campaign, Bush strongly supported South Carolina's display of the Confederate battle flag on its capitol grounds as a protest against racial liberalism. He opposed "racial quotas," code for affirmative action. But his campaign had no equivalent of the race-baiting "Willie Horton" ads his father had used in 1988. He appointed African Americans to the most prominent posts in his administration: Condoleezza Rice as national security adviser and General Colin Powell as secretary of state. He would also support immigration reform, offering a path to citizenship for the undocumented and their children. He seemed personally free of racial bigotry, and his support among Black voters significantly improved after his first term. However, his record would be marred by the catastrophic failure to provide timely aid to the mostly Black victims of Hurricane Katrina. And a different form of racialism, inherent in some aspects of neoconservative geopolitical theory, would distort the response to the September 11, 2001, terrorist attacks.

In the end the Bush administration would be defined by 9/11 and its misconceived wars in Iraq and Afghanistan—a history we'll examine in Chapter 13. But when he took office, Bush's agenda was primarily economic. "Compassionate conservatism" was a slogan without a program. The hope that he might pursue a more "populist" approach to economic policy would be disappointed. Although he had defeated Al Gore by the narrowest of margins, his administration leveraged its congressional strength to push through a supply-side program of large tax cuts, which almost immediately ballooned the deficits Clinton's tax reforms had brought under control. Although Democrats briefly held a Senate majority at the start of his term, they accepted the tax cut, reflecting Clinton's deference to "small government" and business-friendly "rising tide" economics. The administration also expanded on Clinton's program of deregulation in banking and finance. This would produce the speculative boom in mortgage-based "derivatives," which crashed the banking system and the economy in 2008.[3]

For much of Bush's presidency, the public focus of deregulation was oil and gas exploration, as well as the effects of carbon-based fuels on environmental pollution and climate change. Bush was a Texas oilman by birth and breeding, imbued with the values and beliefs of that peculiar subculture, in which evangelical Christianity blended with the conviction that oil had been, and must always be, the basis of America's energy system. Although he expressed concern about the environmental effects of high fossil fuel use, he was more deeply concerned about the vulnerability of the oil and gas industry to pressure from the Organization of the Petroleum Exporting Countries (OPEC) and the possibility that "peak oil"—a time when all domestic sources of recoverable oil had been tapped and reserves would begin an irreversible decline—might be imminent.

The problem of oil resources was therefore the theme of an ongoing political debate, which would intensify through the course of Bush's presidency and become critical after Barack Obama took office. The terms of that debate were drawn from the Myth of the Frontier, specifically the belief that economic growth and social peace depended on the continual discovery and development of a natural resource bonanza; and that the "end of oil" would be, in effect, another "end of the frontier," entailing an economy of scarcity and redistribution.[4]

Since the 1960s, the United States had increasingly relied on imports from Venezuela and the Middle East, which made our economy vulnerable to conflicts and political machinations in those regions. The dangers of dependence on foreign oil were made traumatically clear in 1973, when Saudi Arabia nationalized its oil production, launched an oil embargo, and formed the OPEC cartel that enabled Arab producers (and their allies) to control production and price worldwide. Dependence on Middle Eastern oil underlay US involvement in the Iran-Iraq War from 1981 to 1988 and the decision to go to war against Iraq in 1991. But while the Gulf War produced a spectacular military victory, all it did was preserve the status quo, in which OPEC controlled pricing and supply. Neoconservatives regretted the lost opportunity to establish a pro-American regime in Iraq, which would have offset the power of the Saudis' vast reserves. They were drawn to the idea of intervention in the region even before the terrorist attacks of 9/11 provided a justification for war.[5]

To understand the intensity with which partisans attack all proposals to limit the development and use of fossil fuels, and the vast expenses oil companies have borne in their effort to discredit climate science and block environmental regulation, it is useful to remember that twice in the past thirty years we have shown our willingness, as a nation, to pay for oil with blood. The assumptions that made such a trade-off plausible were shaped by the terms of the Myth of the Frontier, which had always seen a necessary connection between savage war and the benefits of bonanza economics, and was intrinsic to the politics of oil development.

Bonanza Economics and the Gospel of Crude

The governing principle of American political economy is the belief that the discovery and exploitation of a series of "bonanzas" in extravagantly profitable natural resources have been the basis of the nation's rise to world preeminence, and of its democratic character. The rapid growth of America's industrial production was made possible by the availability of abundant, and therefore cheap, fossil fuels—primarily coal until the early 1900s, and thereafter oil and natural gas.

The spectacular "gushers" of the Texas and Oklahoma oil fields were bonanza economics made visible. The Oklahoma boom was achieved through a program of murder and legal dispossession directed against Native Americans. Between the 1870s and the Great War, the oil and gas business boomed, generating massive corporate structures, chief among them the Standard Oil monopoly. When government antitrust policy forced the breakup of Standard in 1911, its separate components were still among the richest corporations in the world. The fortune John D. Rockefeller made from oil was parlayed into control of a major investment banking franchise, City Bank.[6]

Cheap and abundant oil would sustain manufacturing and military operations in World War II and underwrite the boom in manufacturing and automobiles that made the postwar economy uniquely bountiful. It was the material basis of America's new role as the planet's dominant military and economic power. Henry Luce's famous proclamation that the twentieth century would be "the American Century" was delivered at a 1941 meeting of the American Petroleum Institute. He hailed "oil-men as the vanguard of our American values, praising their 'dynamic spirit of freedom and enterprise.'" Luce's vision was central to what Darren Dochuk has called the "civil religion of crude": a blend of libertarian economics with symbolism drawn from the Myth of the Frontier and evangelical Christianity. It envisioned an American hegemony that linked the acquisition of resources with the promotion of democratic ideals in the postcolonial societies of Latin America, Asia, and Africa. The Rockefeller Foundation, whose financial resources originated in the Standard Oil monopoly, would be a leader in developing the intellectual rationales and policy programs for the American Century, especially in Latin America, where the Rockefellers were heavily invested.[7]

The roots of the "civil religion of crude"—the Gospel of Oil—were planted in the Texas-Oklahoma region, where wildcatting (the unregulated, speculative, and often semilegal preemption of drilling rights) combined with the illiberal "wildcat Christianity" of Southern evangelical churches to make "Texas oilmen" a distinctive ideological community. H. L. Hunt, H. J. Pew, and Clint Murchison were among the richest and most politically engaged of the group in the postwar era. Fred Koch, founder of Koch Enterprises, was also born and bred in the Texas oil patch and made his money in refining. The chief tenet of these oil magnates was virulent anti-Communism, but their concept of Communism included every aspect of the New Deal order: economic regulation, the rights of labor, civil rights, social welfare, taxation, and conservation. Their principles were a modern version of Confederate ideology: all they asked was to be left alone, to exploit land and labor at will, free of government interference and of criticism by liberals and "outside agitators." They supported a constellation of Far Right organizations, including the John Birch Society, of which they were founding members. In 1960 Fred Koch published *A Businessman Looks at Communism,* which asserted that Communists were infiltrating every level of government, working toward the moment when "the President of the U.S. is a Communist."[8]

The evangelical side of their ideology was expressed in strong support for the Reverend Billy Graham's "crusades," which used television and mass meetings to promote a religious revival in the 1950s and 1960s. They saw the spread of evangelical Christianity as an antidote to both Communism and cultural and political liberalism. As movement conservatism gained strength in the Republican Party, they found it a more useful vessel for their ideology than a fringe group like the Birchers. This linkage of conservative values on sexuality and the family to "libertarian" or wildcat economics anticipated the culture-war ideology that would become central to Republican Party politics after 1990.

The 1973 Oil Embargo and "the End of the Cowboy Economy"

The 1973 Arab oil embargo was not only a traumatic shock to the petroleum industry, it challenged the worldview shaped by the Gospel of Oil. The *New York Times* saw it as "the end of the cowboy economy," negating the presumption that perpetual growth would underwrite democracy. The embargo highlighted the centrality of cheap oil to American economic growth, and the fact that the United States had become increasingly dependent on foreign sources. The price of oil was now determined by the OPEC cartel, whose vast output gave it effective control of world markets. Despite the measures taken to increase domestic production and develop alternative fuels, between 1985 and 1989 US dependence on foreign oil rose from 26 percent to 47 percent. In a *Business Week* interview, Secretary of State Henry Kissinger averred that OPEC's control of oil threatened "the actual strangulation of the industrialized world."[9]

The need to preserve access to the oil resources of the Arabian Gulf states would compel the United States to use its military to protect the cartel, whose price manipulations alternately fed and starved, stimulated and restrained, its economic growth. After Iran's Islamic Revolution established a hostile regime north of the Gulf, President Jimmy Carter declared that any threat to block oil shipments would be met with force. The Carter Doctrine was continued by President Reagan, who backed it by building new bases for American air and naval forces and supporting Iraq's war against Iran (1981–1988). The Gulf War of 1991 was justified as necessary to protect access to oil.

But these wars were costly and controversial, and in the end merely preserved the power of the oil states. To recover the vision of the American Century and the promise of the Frontier Myth, we would have to regain energy independence—and to do that, we would have to recommit ourselves to the Gospel of Oil. To that end, oilmen pushed for permission to explore and drill in areas from which they had been excluded, including wilderness areas and other federal lands, as well as offshore sites on the Atlantic, Pacific, and Gulf Coasts. They also sought to roll back environmental regulations that had barred exploration and blocked or imposed onerous costs on drilling, refining, transporting, and burning petroleum products.[10]

They were opposed by an environmentalist movement that had been growing in popular support, political influence, and scientific authority since the late 1960s. The first "Earth Day" demonstrations in 1970 were linked symbolically to the anti–Vietnam War "Moratorium" as part of the "Greening of America" espoused by the Left of the 1960s. To illustrate their critique of environmental degradation, environmentalist ads pointed to Native Americans as symbols of a culture in which human needs and ecological sustainability were well balanced, thus identifying the movement with the "enemy" in the Frontier Myth. The symbolic opposition of petroleum "cowboys" and environmentalist "Indians" would play out in political debates over the next thirty-five years.

Environmentalism first focused on air and water pollution in and around major cities, attributable to car and industrial exhaust, and in the countryside, where it was mostly caused by the runoff of industrial and agricultural chemicals. Toward the end of Reagan's administration, scientists began to raise concerns about the potential for catastrophic climate change, produced by the accumulation of greenhouse gases. The Clinton-Gore administration made environmental protection a central element of policy. Using the regulatory powers of the Environmental Protection Agency, it strengthened measures to reduce air and water pollution, cleaned up toxic waste sites, and vetoed the attempts of a Republican Congress to roll back regulations. Some of Clinton's most significant actions directly affected the oil business. His executive orders created seventeen new national monuments on federal lands, where commercial activities like drilling and mining were prohibited; permanently barred drilling in marine sanctuaries; and extended a moratorium on new leases for offshore drilling.[11]

The administration's signature act was its negotiation of the Kyoto Protocol, under which the world's major industrial powers agreed to reduce the emission of greenhouse gases. The requirements were actually minimal (and unenforceable) and, according to most scientific opinion, inadequate even if they were observed. Clinton was no more willing than Reagan or Bush to abandon the Frontier theory of economic growth. To compensate for the loss of a resource bonanza, he envisioned a technology-based bonanza and put government resources behind the development of alternative and renewable energy resources like solar power, wind power, and new forms of battery storage.

The fossil fuel producers and their political allies were not interested in alternative frontiers. They regarded Kyoto as the first step on a slippery slope to policies that would limit production and require costly antipollution measures. Several of the largest corporations, including Exxon, set their own scientists to work assessing the problem of climate change. Their research confirmed that global warming was real, and attributable to the increased production of greenhouse gases, but Exxon suppressed the findings and mounted a public relations campaign to support the claim that scientific evidence for climate change was dubious. The Koch brothers went further, commissioning studies that "disproved" climate change or questioned the role of human activity in global warming.[12]

The Reagan administration had treated environmentalism as a menace to the American way of life. Secretary of the Interior James Watt likened environmental protesters to Nazis, and Treasury Secretary John Connally warned that environmentalist policies would cause a new depression. The George W. Bush administration would be more moderate in its language, but equally pro-oil in its policy. Bush did express concern about the environmental effects of burning fossil fuels, but rejected the Kyoto agreement. He was willing to promote the development of renewable energy resources like wind and solar power, and new technologies to reduce pollution, but rejected measures to reduce carbon emissions through taxes or regulation. His primary concern was America's dependence on foreign oil, and he believed that this could best be overcome by opening new US regions to development and minimizing the regulations that made domestic oil production costly.

But there was more to conservative energy policy than a simple calculation of profit and loss. Ideas and beliefs about energy were interwoven with other strands of movement conservatism: the libertarian theory of government, as well as traditionalist responses to social issues like abortion and gun rights and racial issues like affirmative action. Intellectuals and publicists, employed by a network of think tanks and institutes, transformed the movement's sometimes esoteric ideology into persuasive narratives invoking the symbolism of American national myth—most obviously the Myth of the Frontier, but also the Myths of the Founding and the Lost Cause.

The Koch Network

The complex relation between oil and movement conservatism can be traced in the careers of David and Charles Koch, who have exerted a powerful influence on the movement and on Republican Party politics for more than thirty years. Their political enterprise grew out of business interests in the drilling, refining, and marketing of oil, but they expanded the Gospel of Oil into an elaborate intellectual rationale for limited government that could be applied to every aspect of politics, then created a network of organizations to turn their ideas into policy. Their philanthropic foundations supported thirty-four political and policy-developing think tanks, three of which they founded and several of which they directed. As Jane Mayer explains in *Dark Money*, by 2016 they had created a "permanent, private political machine" and a network of political groups with "a bigger payroll than the Republican National Committee." By 2008 the range and financial backing of their engagements had made them preeminent among corporate political contributors. During the Bush administration they became the leading source of "dark money"— contributions made through organizations exempt from rules requiring disclosure of membership and financial operations—for conservative politicians and policies at the state as well as the national level.[13]

Their business developed in the Texas oil patch, and though they moved to Wichita, they played by Texas rules. In 1989 Koch Industries was charged with one of the classic Frontier crimes: a "widespread and sophisticated scheme to steal crude oil from Indians and others through fraudulent mis-measuring." They were also charged with numerous violations of rules against environmental pollution and were assessed more than $400 million in penalties. The Kochs responded by diversifying into less regulated industrial sectors including chemicals, equipment and technology, and pulp and paper, and into finance, including commodity trading and derivatives. They also dramatically increased their political activism, so they could attack the problem of government regulation directly.[14]

The Koch brothers' politics predated the regulatory onslaught they suffered in the 1990s. Like most conservative thinkers after 1945, the Kochs adopted F. A. Hayek's fundamental principle that the free market is "key to all human freedom," and government is inherently destructive of freedom because it is, by nature, coercive. Thus the "standard-bearers for liberty" are not political figures like Thomas Jefferson, Abraham Lincoln, and Franklin D. Roosevelt but "glorified capitalists" like the Kochs themselves. To ground this belief in American tradition, the Kochs emphasized the laissez-faire principles inherent in the text of the Constitution and denied the relevance of studies that emphasized the strong-government intentions of the Founders. In general they wanted Washington to "cut the hell out of spending, balance the budget, reduce regulations, and support business." As a friend of Charles Koch explained, "Perhaps [Charles Koch] has confused money-making with freedom."[15]

Charles and David Koch did not share their father's attachment to the John Birch Society's agenda. However, they believed the regimes of regulation and taxation that evolved out of the New Deal amounted to "incipient socialism." In this they were influenced by Milton Friedman's doctrine that businesses had no responsibilities or obligations beyond those imposed by the market. They characterized their position as "libertarian," but in practice their policies followed the neoliberal customs of the petroleum industry: opposing government regulation while demanding government support in the form of favorable royalty rates and subsidies. They began as libertarians on social issues, supporting a woman's right to abortion and birth control, gay rights, and same-sex marriage; rejecting the government's "war on drugs," which they saw as an infringement of free choice; and supporting stem-cell research. But their primary concern was the oil business, and to protect it they would ally with or actively support antiabortion, anti–gay rights Republicans. They also rejected the use of government to protect or advance civil rights through affirmative action and opposed policies aimed at addressing racial and gender inequality and discrimination.

The rejection of affirmative action was consistent with their adherence to Hayek's philosophy, but it was also consistent with the neo-Confederate ideology of James McGill Buchanan, the Nobel Prize–winning economist who opposed the "perverted liberalism" of the New Deal state and believed that social peace depended on the maintenance (or restoration) of a social order to traditional hierarchies of race, class, and gender—an order that (he believed) still pertained in Virginia. Buchanan opposed school desegregation, claiming it disrupted the existing state of racial peace and would provoke a populist uprising against Virginia's ruling class. The Kochs were also disciples of Robert LeFevre, a California businessman and founder of a libertarian think tank called the Freedom School, who thought "government is a disease masquerading as its own cure." Like Buchanan, LeFevre was moved to activism by the *Brown* decision, and his idea of the good society was shaped by the Myth of the Lost Cause. In the 1950s the Freedom School taught that Southerners had had a right to secede, and that Lincoln was wrong to resist because "slavery was a lesser evil than military conscription." Slavery, as LeFevre conceived it, was somehow a free-market institution, in which the slaves willingly contracted for their enslavement—and "human beings should be allowed to sell themselves into slavery if they wished." Although this was nonsense as a description of chattel slavery, it was consistent with LeFevre's concept of labor relations in general. He held that unions imposed a form of "slavery" on their members by barring them from making independent contracts with employers. Like antebellum planters and Gilded Age monopolists, he believed in the absolute right of the master of capital to control both the use of his property and the laborers who work it without regulation or legal constraint.[16]

The Kochs' response to the *Brown* decision was equivocal. They did not advocate segregation or rave about Black racial inferiority like the Jim Crow populists of 1890–1920 or contemporary segregationists like Georgia's Herman Talmadge. Rather, they argued that whether or not segregation was justified, the government had no right to do anything about it. The same doctrine applied to all other issues of social and economic justice: workplace safety, the right to organize, provision of school textbooks and lunches, social security. Although these measures promoted the general welfare and furthered the principle of equal justice under law, they were illegitimate because to enact them, the government had to tax private income and property—and all taxation is "theft." Moreover, the right of private people to discriminate by (for example) excluding Black people from their schools or businesses is a personal freedom and therefore to be defended. In the 1960s Charles Koch supported a "Freedom School" in Colorado, which refused to admit Black students because to do so would offend students who were "principled segregationists." Thus the effect of their libertarian approach to race relations is to tolerate segregation and the whole system of laws, customs, and beliefs that justifies and perpetuates racial inequality.[17]

During the Reagan and George H. W. Bush administrations, the Kochs conceived or funded a range of think tanks and political action organizations designed to shape and direct the course of conservative politics, such as the Cato Institute, the Federalist Society (which vets conservative judges for the federal bench), the American Enterprise Institute, the Institute for Humane Studies, Frontiers of Freedom (to promote oil drilling on federally protected lands), Citizens for a Sound Economy, the Competitive Enterprise Institute, Freedom Partners, and dozens of others.

Among the most important of these organizations is the American Legislative Exchange Council (ALEC), whose mission is to elect conservative state legislatures and provide them with model statutes for realizing conservative goals. Although the Kochs themselves profess indifference to culture-war issues like abortion and gay rights, ALEC built its conservative credentials in the 1980s by focusing on those issues. It urged state legislators to resist laws banning discrimination against LGBTQ people or legalizing same-sex marriage and framed its opposition in extremist terms, accusing liberals of pursuing a "gay agenda" to "homosexualize society." Although the Kochs favored reforming immigration policy, ALEC sponsored Arizona's model immigration law, SB 1070, which was so rigorous in its treatment of undocumented aliens that it was rejected by the Supreme Court. ALEC was also instrumental in promoting the privatization of state prisons, making corrections a for-profit business. It helped ensure an ample supply of prisoners by pushing for harsher sentencing and mandatory minimums. The organization also took the lead in promoting "stand your ground" laws, an expansion of gun rights that would become a central tenet of conservative politics during the Obama years. The David H. Koch Fund for Science supports science programming on public television, but the brothers' network of think tanks produces research designed to discredit scientists whose work showed the dire effects on public health of cigarettes and industrial pollution. In 1986 ALEC supported the tobacco industry's attempt to suppress or deny scientific evidence of tobacco's dire effects on health.[18]

The organization that most directly reflects the Kochs' personal views is Americans for Prosperity, founded in 2004, which supports a range of conservative causes but is especially strong in opposing action to slow or reverse climate change. Americans for Prosperity's most significant victory was compelling the Republican Party to adopt its No Climate Tax Pledge in its 2008 platform, making climate change denial a core principle of Republican orthodoxy. By July 2013 a quarter of US senators and a third of the House of Representatives had signed the pledge.[19]

Koch versus Gore: The Arctic National Wildlife
Refuge and the Drilling Frontier

Public awareness of the threat of climate change was powerfully augmented by the success of Al Gore's documentary, *An Inconvenient Truth,* in 2006. The film graphically displayed the effects of global warming, providing visual evidence (such as glacier melt-back) to reinforce a scientific argument that was well and simply presented. Gore brought to the film his prestige as a former vice president and presidential candidate. His self-presentation was effective: modest, serious, well informed, stern in exposing the actions of the fossil fuel industry. He likened conservatives' deference to these interests to the appeasement of Adolph Hitler at Munich in 1938, associating the environmentalist side of the "climate war" with the Good War. In the flush of public enthusiasm for Gore's documentary, conservatives like Newt Gingrich and Grover Norquist even appeared alongside liberal icons like Nancy Pelosi to emphasize their common desire to "save the planet."[20]

That response was short lived. For fossil fuel magnates and their conservative allies, an international drive to reduce greenhouse gas emissions was an existential threat. For the Kochs and their colleagues, it was also a threat to their vision of America. Instead of accepting the scientific consensus and adapting to the threat posed by global warming, they intensified the ideological battle, waging a "war of disinformation" against climate science. They were seconded by Exxon, which suppressed the research of its own scientists, and by Senator James Inhofe (R-OK), who used his chairmanship of the Senate Committee on Environment and Public Works to declare global warming a "hoax."[21]

The 2004 GOP platform is noteworthy for its emphasis on opening the Arctic National Wildlife Refuge (ANWR) to drilling, which made this issue the symbolic focus of the fight between drillers and conservationists. It cited an estimate by the US Geological Survey that oil reserves in the refuge might amount to 16 billion barrels, "enough to replace oil imports from Saudi Arabia for nearly 20 years." Although the platform paid lip service to environmental concerns, it dismissed them with the false assurance that through use of "the most sophisticated technologies, we can explore and develop oil resources here . . . with minimal environmental impact . . . leaving little trace of human intervention." The opening of ANWR was to be just a first step: "Republicans strongly support removing unnecessary barriers to domestic natural gas production and expanding environmentally sound production in new areas, such as Alaska and the Rocky Mountains. Increasing supply, including the construction of a new natural gas pipeline from Alaska to the lower 48, will bring needed relief to consumers and make America's businesses more competitive in the global marketplace."[22]

The choice between opening ANWR and preserving its wilderness character was used to symbolize the larger conflict between exponents of unlimited corporate growth and advocates of regulation and environmental protection. The drive to open ANWR repeated the classic Frontier pattern, in which the discovery of valuable resources on Indian land leads the government to dispossess the Indigenous people or end their access to traditional hunting grounds. In the 1830s the prospect of gold led to the dispossession of the Cherokee. In 1874 the discovery of gold in the Black Hills led the government to abrogate its treaties with the Lakota and provoke the war that destroyed the Great Sioux Reservation. In the 1920s, legal chicanery and murder were used to dispossess Oklahoma tribespeople of oil rights on their land. What was different with ANWR was the existence of a powerful alternative political network prepared to defend wilderness and Indigenous rights *as such*. In the 1960s the Frontier Myth had been subjected to a critical revision, as environmentalists and critics of capitalism identified with "the Indians" rather than "the settlers." That movement coincided with the political movement for Native or Indian rights, which called for tribal control of economic development on Indian lands, not only as a matter of legal right but as a means to ecological stewardship.

Because the ANWR controversy engaged the language of the Frontier Myth, it brought into play ideas and symbols derived from the concept of "savage war." Opponents of drilling were attacked in terms first used for the "philanthropists" of the 1870s, as sentimental Indian lovers whose policies supported the enemies of progress and civilization. In "Why ANWR Drilling Makes Sense," conservative writer and conspiracy theorist Jerome Corsi declared that "Environmental Extremists" were undermining national security by acting as agents of the OPEC powers: "Perhaps the Sierra Club ought to be forced to register as a foreign lobbyist for Saudi Aramco . . . they don't want even limited exploration of ANWR because they are afraid of how much oil we might find." Corsi revived the classic fear that weakness on the frontier would lead to "captivities": "[Our] dependence upon foreign countries means we are increasingly vulnerable to being held hostage [for] oil. Do we not send back the flood of Mexican illegal immigrants crossing our borders because we import 1.75 million barrels of oil a day from Mexico? Are we forced to tolerate Hugo Chavez's socialism and insults to America because we import 1.3 million barrels of oil a day?" The critical point here is that "environmentalism" poses an existential threat to America.[23]

Objections to opening the refuge were partly practical. Studies done at the time suggested that there wasn't enough untapped oil in ANWR, or anywhere else in the United States, to allow us to "drill our way to energy independence." But practical objections were soon dismissed in favor of mythic symbolism. Resistance to the opening of the refuge was linked to support of Native American tribal rights and Indigenous lifeways: development would disrupt the migration of caribou, on which the Gwich'in people depended for subsistence. The long history of Indian dispossession suggested that, as one environmentalist put it, the move to open ANWR "has nothing to do with energy independence." Rather, as with the Black Hills in 1874, it was another excuse for enriching speculators, "transferring our public estate into corporate hands, so it can be liquidated for a quick buck."[24]

On a deeper level, the controversy displayed the fundamental ideological conflict between the imperative "growth paradigm" of capitalist economic development and the ideology of balance and redistribution for social justice, which, in the ANWR case, was symbolically linked to Native American culture. In *Oil, Globalization, and the War for the Arctic Refuge,* David M. Standlea sees the conflict as pitting the "social Darwinistic attitude of the radical corporate / Republican right—the belief in survival of the richest"—against the rising appeal of an "ecological and environmental consciousness and political activism." He contrasts Americans' "unconscious conviction in one's inexorable right to exploit and dominate nature for economic profit" with the Iroquois belief that, before taking an action, the tribe must consider its effects on the next seven generations.[25]

The "Indian" motif in environmental resistance was repeated and reinforced by the long battle over authorization of the Keystone XL pipeline, which was charged with bringing shale oil from Canada to US ports and refineries. The pipeline had been opposed by environmentalists and some agricultural interests for threatening to pollute rivers and groundwater. In 2011 the leaders of several American and Canadian tribes joined the Lakota in protesting that the pipeline would imperil or destroy sacred cultural and historical sites. The physical and moral interposition of Native Americans reinforced the idea that this was a crisis to be interpreted through the prism of the Frontier Myth. Environmentalism made it possible to side with the Indians, but for oilmen and their political allies this meant environmental "science" had become an existential threat to "civilization."[26]

In 2004, with Bush reelected by a popular majority, the oilmen had reason to think they had won. The 2005 energy bill provided subsidies and tax breaks for coal and oil interests. In 2000, Senator John McCain had expressed concern about climate change, but when he accepted the Republican nomination in 2008 his platform called for opening ANWR. Alaska governor Sarah Palin was picked as his running mate, and party chairman Michael Steele chanted, "Drill, baby! Drill!" More significantly, a survey of popular opinion showed that 50 percent of Americans supported drilling in ANWR, while 42 percent opposed it—a decisive reversal of opinion.[27]

The oilmen's hopes were dashed by the drastic reversal of fortune in Bush's second term. His Global War on Terror and the invasion of Iraq, undertaken in response to the terrorist attacks of September 11, 2001, promised access to the rich oil fields hitherto controlled by the Saddam Hussein regime. But the occupation of Iraq and Afghanistan degenerated into guerrilla warfare and futile nation-building—the combination that had turned Vietnam into a "quagmire." Bush's mishandling of the catastrophic effects of Hurricane Katrina on New Orleans and the Gulf Coast in August 2005 raised questions about the administration's competence, while the storm itself underlined the warning of climate change dramatized in *An Inconvenient Truth*. Finally, the financial meltdown of 2008, and the Great Recession that followed, discredited Bush's economic policies.

The result was a Democratic triumph in 2008, when Barack Obama swept into the presidency with controlling Democratic majorities in the House and Senate. Obama would make climate change a central concern of his legislative and regulatory programs. He would block the Keystone pipeline and the opening of ANWR, and support the international movement to curb greenhouse gas emissions.

In the language of the Frontier Myth, the Indians had won.

13

Cowboys and Aliens

The Global War on Terror

THE GEORGE W. BUSH administration's concern with oil would be given a violent twist by the terrorist attacks of September 11, 2001. Agents of al-Qaeda, an Afghanistan-based terrorist organization led by Saudi billionaire Osama bin Laden, hijacked four jet airliners. Two were crashed into the Twin Towers of New York's World Trade Center in Lower Manhattan, bringing the country's tallest skyscrapers down in ruin. Another smashed into the Pentagon, and a fourth (Flight 93) was crashed in an open field when passengers rushed the cockpit and attacked the hijackers. Damage was catastrophic at Ground Zero, as the Trade Center site came to be called. The immediate loss of life approached 3,000, a casualty count comparable to that suffered at Pearl Harbor, and deaths related to disease from the chemical-infused dust clouds pouring out of the wreckage would balloon that figure over the succeeding decades.

The Pearl Harbor analogy was immediately and broadly invoked, carrying with it the understanding that a good war must follow. The course that war was to take, first in Afghanistan, then in Iraq, and latterly in the Global War on Terror, would become the central engagement of the Bush presidency. September 11 would become a symbol in its own right, which directed the call for vengeance to a new enemy—marked, like the Japanese in 1941, by both racial difference and an extremist ideology, but also by identification with Islam, one of the major world religions. The war against that enemy would resonate domestically with the anxieties of conservative White Christians about their loss of authority in a multicultural America.[1]

Mythological Thinking and the Global War on Terror

The first response to 9/11 was an intuitive call for revenge. When Afghanistan, ruled by the Islamic fundamentalist Taliban, refused to hand over bin Laden and his colleagues, the administration mounted a punitive expedition, led by Special Forces, which used local warlords to overthrow the Taliban and drive al-Qaeda from its bases. The expedition, and the follow-on effort to establish a secular government in Kabul, was supported by an enraged American public, by our NATO allies, and even (somewhat ambivalently) by our enemies in Iran and dubious friends in Pakistan.

The neoconservatives who formed the core of Bush's foreign-policy advisers also saw in 9/11 an opportunity to win popular support for the forward-leaning foreign policy they favored. The fall of the Iron Curtain and collapse of the Soviet Union in 1991 had left the United States as the world's only superpower. The neoconservatives' strategic doctrine, as described in James Mann's *Rise of the Vulcans,* called for a military buildup "so overwhelming that no country would dream of ever becoming a rival. . . . Thus the United States would be the world's lone superpower not just today or ten years from now but permanently." American power would be used not only to maintain international order but to shape it according to American principles, transforming and regenerating the politics and economics of former adversaries like Russia and of failed or "rogue" states in Latin America, Africa, Asia, and the Middle East. The doctrine required policymakers to overcome the political and moral constraints that had limited US military action since Vietnam. The new superpower was free—and must *feel* free—to act unilaterally, outside and even in spite of the United Nations or our formal alliances.[2]

While the Afghan fighting was still in progress, Bush's advisers began planning a shift of focus and force to Iraq. If Iraq could be "liberated" and given a democratic government, the logic went, the United States would have as its client one of the largest, richest, most technologically advanced of the Arab states, in position to confront Iran. With control of Iraqi oil, we would also have a counter to Saudi Arabia's dominance of the international market. Cast in these terms, Bush's foreign policy promised to realize what for Ronald Reagan and George H. W. Bush had merely been a vision: a "new American Century," in which the "city on a hill" would be transformed from idealized example to actual creator of a democratic new world order.[3]

Although the Gulf War had been touted as "the end of Vietnam syndrome," its popularity was due to the fact that it was so utterly unlike Vietnam: brief, low cost, conventional, and concluded with victory parades—no nation-building, no guerrilla warfare. The public's desire to avenge 9/11 did not imply enthusiasm for a long-term commitment to nation-building in Afghanistan, let alone the extension of the war by invasion and occupation of Iraq.

To justify an invasion of Iraq, the administration used dubious intelligence that Saddam was acquiring "weapons of mass destruction," the most threatening of which were nuclear, but also chemical and biological weapons. Despite the report of UN investigators that Iraq had no active nuclear program and that they had not found credible evidence of a biological weapons program, and against the resistance of the UN and most of our NATO allies, Bush moved deliberately toward war. In place of his father's carefully built grand coalition, he asserted America's right and responsibility to act preemptively and unilaterally, although a few nations did join his "coalition of the willing." He rejected the warning of Secretary of State Colin Powell that if he broke the Iraqi state, America would become responsible for a massive program of nation-building. Bush preferred the advice of Vice President Dick Cheney, Secretary of Defense Donald Rumsfeld, and adviser Paul Wolfowitz, who assured him that the war would be a walkover, and that Americans would be welcomed as liberators. They believed that pro-American Iraqis would speedily establish a friendly government, allowing us to withdraw after a brief occupation.[4]

In the summer of 2002, *New York Times* reporter Ron Suskind challenged a "senior official" on the administration's grasp of the political realities that would limit its ability to impose its will on the Middle East. The official's response was "that guys like [Suskind] were 'in what we call the reality-based community,' which he defined as people who 'believe that solutions emerge from your judicious study of discernible reality. . . . That's not the way the world really works anymore. . . . We're an empire now, and when we act, we create our own reality.'"[5] The premise that America was capable of creating its own reality, turning belief into fact, is consistent with a pattern of mythological thinking that was shaping the administration's Iraq policy. In January 2002, Bush and his close advisers attended a special screening of *Black Hawk Down,* the recently released movie that dramatized the disastrous 1993 defeat of US peacekeeping forces in Somalia. It was in many ways a classic platoon movie, with an ethnically varied American military, a monoracial enemy, a very grim *enemy's lesson,* and a pitch for completion of the soldiers' *unfinished business.* As *Newsweek* later reported, "Bush . . . told his aides that America's hasty exit from Somalia after 18 soldiers died in the 1993 raid made famous in the movie 'Black Hawk Down' emboldened America's terrorist enemies" and so led directly to 9/11. Bush later invited twenty members of Congress to a screening. *Black Hawk*

Down became official Washington's "must-see movie." These viewings took place while Bush was working toward his final decision to invade Iraq and announcing a new campaign of militant confrontation with what, in his State of the Union speech that month, he called the "Axis of Evil," the "rogue states" of Iran, Iraq, and North Korea. The administration was laying the groundwork for invasion, and for the new Global War on Terror, which would become the National Security Council's official National Security Strategy in September 2002.[6]

Bush and his advisers were using the symbolism of *Black Hawk Down*, essentially a work of fiction, to interpret a real-world geopolitical problem. To understand the mythic power of this particular fiction, we need to see it as the culmination of a thirty-year evolution in two distinct but related streams of cultural work through which filmmakers and policymakers tried to overcome the effects of Vietnam syndrome.

Rehabilitating War: From *Star Wars* to *Platoon*, 1978–1990

With the exception of John Wayne's *Green Berets,* released in 1968, no movies were made about Vietnam while the fighting went on. In the aftermath, the film industry invested in three films that tried to sum up the war and put it to rest. Two of these were artistically ambitious epics, *The Deer Hunter* (1978) and *Apocalypse Now* (1979), and one an interesting low-budget platoon movie, *The Boys in Company C* (1978). All agreed that American tactics were misconceived, and the war itself futile. However, none dealt with the moral failure symbolized by My Lai. The atrocities shown in these films are committed by the enemy or by our South Vietnamese allies. When Americans do evil or crazy things, they arise either from panic or from a perverse learning of the *enemy's lesson,* a moral contagion that makes Americans "go native." But scapegoating the Vietnamese was not an adequate way of addressing the real problem, which was not only the fact of defeat but the dark side of American intentions and methods.[7]

Instead of grappling with the reality of Vietnam, Hollywood deflected its treatment of war into the realm of fantasy. One symptom of the nation's lingering trauma was an obsession with the idea that American prisoners of war (POWs) were still being held in secret camps, and that our government had knowingly abandoned them. To this day many public buildings, businesses, and private homes fly a black flag memorializing these POWs and personnel missing in action (MIA). In 1983 the movie *Uncommon Valor* turned this obsession into a platoon movie. Ten years after the war, a racially mixed group of former Green Berets rescues POWs from a hidden camp in Laos. Between 1983 and 1988 Hollywood produced a small subgenre of POW rescue films, including the three installments of *Missing in Action,* starring Chuck Norris, and *Rambo: First Blood Part II,* starring Sylvester Stallone. In effect, these rescue fantasies are "do-overs" in which Americans symbolically win the war they had actually lost. The rescue fantasy offered a way of reimagining Vietnam as a good war: instead of saving the Vietnamese, we are rescuing our own people—a mission to which no American could object. In all of these films, the hero voices some version of Rambo's prayer that "this time" the government will "let us win," affirming the view that our soldiers were "stabbed in the back" by political leaders who gave away their victory. This myth of government betrayal would become a core belief in the emergence of the antigovernment movement that began in the 1980s and turned to White identity ideology and paramilitary organization.[8]

A more popular and potent kind of war fantasy was developed in the new and increasingly active genre of science fiction. The pattern was set by the spectacular success of *Star Wars* (1977) and *Star Trek: The Motion Picture* (1979), both of which inaugurated durable franchises, with numerous sequels and imitations. These films typically evaded reference to Vietnam, offering instead a universalized and abstracted Good War. The good guys are always a federation of different races—Sulu (Asian), Uhura (African American), and the Vulcan Spock; Wookies, Ewoks, little green Yoda—united against aliens who assert racial superiority (such as the Klingons, Romulans, or Borg in *Star Trek*) or are figurative Nazis (such as the stormtroopers in *Star Wars*).[9]

This use of the platoon formula had the perverse but inescapable consequence of reviving (in an acceptable form) the idea that racial enmity is a hallmark of the Good War. Racialization of the enemy has always been a prerequisite for mobilizing public opinion in support of war. That is to say, we imagine that war is *necessary* when we recognize in an enemy the stigmata of race difference—a seemingly organic, bred-in-the-bone animosity arising from motives utterly alien to our ways of thinking and incapable of negotiated resolution. *Star Trek* set the pattern in the movies and the revived television spin-offs. Individuals whose races were implacable enemies in earlier stories (Klingons, the Borg) eventually provide members of the crew / platoon, as Japanese Americans did in Korean War films. Interestingly, the *Star Trek* characters are often of "mixed" race, which suggests that "pure" enemy races remain outside the peace of the Federation. *Star Wars* would eventually adopt a similar device (after the franchise was sold to Disney) by having a stormtrooper go over to the "light side." Significantly, the errant trooper is played by a Black actor.

Until *Aliens* in 1986, none of these films directly addressed the trauma of Vietnam. *Aliens* is the sequel to *Alien,* in which a spaceship crew is destroyed, in horror-movie fashion, by a parasitic insectoid monster. *Aliens* adds platoon movie structure to the horror / sci-fi combination. A unit of space marines is sent to rescue colonists on the planet where the original monster was found. With them is Ripley, the female officer who was the sole survivor in the original film. To use the language of the Frontier Myth, instead of the White Man Who Knows Indians, she is the White Woman Who Knows Monsters.

Platoon references begin when the marines rise from their sleeping pods for a *roll call.* The mix is typical of Vietnam-era films. It includes White people (who are *not* ethnically identified), a Black sergeant, and two Latino / as—but also two female marines, most notably Vasquez, who is physically powerful and macho in style. Gender has joined the platoon. The Vietnam connection is emphasized by measuring distances in "clicks"—the standard mileage unit in Vietnam—and by bits of dialogue, like the soldiers' wish for "a stand-up fight" and not another "bug hunt," which recalls the complaint that the Viet Cong avoided open combat for guerrilla warfare. As in the POW / MIA films, the mission is to rescue our own people; the antigovernment theme is represented by a treacherous agent of the colony-building corporation.

The differences between monsters and humans exaggerate racial distinction and make the stakes of war genocidal. As quasi-insects, the aliens are collectivist and totalitarian (like Communists) and primitive like the "savages" of the Frontier Myth. Like these enemies, they have no moral sense and are guilty of extreme cruelty. They reproduce by immobilizing human prey and implanting eggs in their bodies that, when they hatch, destroy the host. The stakes of battle are therefore racial: either they will rape and impregnate our bodies to breed their kind, or we will exterminate the brutes.

The assignment of the hero's role to a woman has double significance. It registers the rise of feminism and the new role of women in the military. But it is also appropriate that both the hero and the Queen monster are female, because the stakes in a race war are reproduction or extermination. This *enemy's lesson* is vividly dramatized when Ripley confronts the Queen in her hatchery. Ripley has rescued a little girl, the last survivor of the colony. She challenges the Queen and, through gestures with her gun, suggests a treaty: if the Queen lets Ripley save the child, Ripley will refrain from killing the Queen's spawn. But then the instinct of race preservation—and hatred—takes over. The monster's eggs viscously swell, provoking an enraged and disgusted Ripley to obliterate them and then blast apart her enemy's womb. Her rage and the way she uses her weapon all strongly recall the *final fury* at the conclusion of *Bataan,* when the rage born of race war gives the hero extravagant powers of destruction.

The year *Aliens* was released also saw the most significant real-war film of the period, Oliver Stone's *Platoon* (1986). Stone's title assimilates Vietnam to the platoon movie and the Good War. He follows classic form in the use of devices like the *roll call,* but the diversity the film displays reflects post-1960s demography. Non-White people are overrepresented and include Black people and Latinos. The White soldiers are divided by social class (redneck, college boy) rather than ethnicity. The symbolism of American diversity has changed and simplified along lines of class and race.[10]

The protagonist is Chris, a young soldier troubled by the conflict between the idealism that led him to enlist and the cruelty of the war. The moral conflict is embodied in two sergeants: Barnes, who is physically deformed, macho, and evil; and Elias, who is handsome, slightly effeminate, and Christlike. Barnes represents the dark side of American intervention. He and his cohorts want to win at any cost and are more than willing to kill women and children. Elias represents the idealism that led America to intervene, chastened by a war gone tragically wrong. The two are framed as representatives of larger cultural divisions in US society. Barnes's supporters are bigots, rednecks, and bootlickers (including one Black man)—they drink whiskey. Elias's people are 1960s counterculture types, racially integrated rebels who wear peace medals and smoke dope. This division is predictive of red-blue symbolism in the Trump era.

Stone speaks to the moral trauma of Vietnam by identifying the evil intrinsic to *our* side of the war. He stages a village invasion that nearly escalates into another My Lai—a brilliant and disturbing sequence that shows how the rage and fear generated by guerrilla war can make American boys (including our hero) capable of committing atrocities. But in the end he essentializes the evil in Barnes, a character marked by conjoined (and repellent) physical and cultural differences. Having personified the dark side of American heroism, Stone purges it by a symbolic exorcism of the "monster." Barnes kills Elias, and Chris kills Barnes in the wake of an apocalyptic napalm firestorm (the *final fury*).

Stone's exorcism enabled Hollywood to overcome *its* version of Vietnam syndrome. The Vietnam subject was taken up in subsequent films, including *Hamburger Hill* and Stanley Kubrick's *Full Metal Jacket* (both 1987). There was also a pair of TV series: *Tour of Duty,* which followed an infantry platoon (1987–1990), and *China Beach* (1988–1991), which portrayed the experiences of a unit of female nurses—another reflection of the changing characterization of women. As in Stone's film, in these works White ethnic differences are no longer emphasized, Black people and Latinos make up much of the unit, and the enemy is still marked by an inhuman ferocity and fanaticism.

Clash of Civilizations: Enemies and Heroes in the Neoconservative War Imaginary, 1980–2000

Hollywood thus made two major contributions to the rehabilitation of an American war imaginary: it confronted the trauma of Vietnam, and reconciled its dark side with a positive view of American servicepeople. The science-fiction films of the 1980s and 1990s had reframed the Good War in terms that anticipated—and prepared the public to recognize and accept—the war imaginary of the neoconservatives, which envisioned the United States deploying unmatchable military and economic power to universalize American-style democracy and neoliberal capitalism. The hubristic spirit of this worldview is perhaps best captured by the science-fiction epic *Independence Day* (1996), in which the United States leads an international military alliance against alien space invaders. Our victory produces a new world order of peace, under American auspices, and the Fourth of July becomes Independence Day for the whole human race.

One of the structuring principles of neoconservative geopolitics was the theory of "civilizational conflict" articulated by the social scientist Samuel P. Huntington in *The Clash of Civilizations and the Remaking of World Order*. Like the science-fiction movies of the period, Huntington translates the classic terms of racial conflict into a quasi-cultural concept of difference. But he retains the core concept of the movie mythology, that between societies marked by the combination of cultural and racial difference, conflict is inescapable. In Huntington's view, Islamic civilization is most inimical to Western civilization. Current events made the idea credible. Terrorism by Arab Palestinians, aimed at turning world attention against Israel's occupation of the West Bank and Gaza, produced numerous acts of violence starting in the 1970s. The Iranian Revolution of 1979, with its chants of "Death to America," added the Shiite regime to the list of Islamist movements sponsoring terror. Libyan terrorists committed several attacks, including the Lockerbie airplane bombing in 1988, and Libya was attacked by American aircraft in retaliation. US forces that intervened in the Lebanese Civil War in 1981 were decimated by a terrorist bombing, organized by the Islamist Hezbollah. Al-Qaeda began striking US forces and our allies in the Horn of Africa in the 1990s. When the 9/11 attacks came, they seemed to fulfill Huntington's prophecy.[11]

Hollywood's representation of war had developed along parallel lines. As Andrew Bacevich's *New American Militarism* shows, after 1985 Hollywood began to glorify the new military, especially the Top Guns of air power, SEALs, and Delta Force, and to pit them against Islamic terrorists, usually identified as Libyans (in response to the Qaddafi regime's sponsorship of airline sabotage between 1986 and 1988) or Iranians (in response to the hostage-taking of 1979–1980). Here was an enemy Hollywood could readily imagine: non-White and "savage" (like the Apaches or the Japanese), as well as ideologically fanatical (like the Communists or Nazis); an implacable enemy who can't be negotiated with, only killed. *The Delta Force* (1986) was the first of several films to depict imaginary commando raids against Muslim terrorists holding US hostages. The third Rambo film, released in 1988, took its hero from rescuing POWs in Vietnam to rescuing Americans in Afghanistan during the Russian occupation of that country. *Navy SEALs* followed the pattern in 1990. These films linked the rescue theme of the MIA movies to the newly identified Muslim enemy. But while they were naturalistic in style, like *Aliens* they depicted fantasy operations—not wars we had fought, but wars we were dreaming of.[12]

The recovery of the war imaginary was reinforced by the revival of the Good War Myth in its most literal form. This development was marked in 1998 by the publication of Tom Brokaw's best seller *The Greatest Generation* and the release of Steven Spielberg's *Saving Private Ryan*. Both tell their story through the experiences of a "platoon" of representative figures.[13] Brokaw's follows a sampling of individuals from the generation that carried out the New Deal, won World War II, created a broad-based middle-class society, and extended civil rights. Spielberg's movie centers on a rescue mission—the kind sanctified by the POW rescue films. It also returns us to the racially segregated but ethnically mixed platoons of the 1940s. And though it deals with an old victory, the movie ends with *unfinished business*—Private Ryan spends his life wondering whether he has been worthy of the sacrifices made for him. That concern is passed on to the audience, represented by Ryan's children and grandchildren, who must match the Greatest Generation by being willing to fight a good war when their country calls. That summons was implicit in the wave of Good War films and TV shows that followed *Saving Private Ryan* over the next decade, including *Windtalkers*, *Flags of Our Fathers*, and the HBO series *Band of Brothers*. *Band of Brothers* has special significance: its release coincided with the September 11 terrorist attacks, and it helped frame the consequent wars in Afghanistan and Iraq as versions of the Good War.

The other new element in 1990s cinema was the treatment of the Gulf War itself. *Courage under Fire* (1996) follows through on the premise of *Aliens*, that after ethnic and racial integration women would join the platoon: a female captain wins the Medal of Honor for leading her male comrades in battle. More interesting is *Three Kings* (1999), in which cynical American commandos develop sympathy for the Iraqi Shiites who were abandoned to Saddam when George H. W. Bush refused to seek total victory in the Gulf War. The commandos' efforts to save a Shiite community suggest that this is the war's unfinished business.

Hollywood storytelling paralleled the thinking of neoconservative strategists, who also saw the Gulf War as a return to the world of the Good War Myth. The enemy was a brutal dictator, described metaphorically as a "Hitler," guilty of aggression. The military deployment was on a scale comparable to that of Vietnam, but with a broader alliance behind it; and the battle was a stand-up fight and *not* a bug hunt. Yet the neoconservatives in the administration regretted George H. W. Bush's refusal to complete the victory by occupying Iraq and overthrowing Saddam. Nevertheless, the administration could declare that with this victory the United States had cured itself of Vietnam syndrome and regained its faith in the regenerative moral and political potential of warfare. With that cure in hand, and George W. Bush in charge, the neoconservatives would complete the unfinished business of the Gulf War.[14]

Thus the development of war mythology between 1975 and 2000, in media and among policymakers, provided the public with a new set of symbols, scenarios, and concepts that audiences would recognize as the hallmarks of a good war; and having recognized them, would be prepared to imaginatively consent that that kind of war be waged, on-screen and in the real world.[15]

Black Hawk Down: The Enemy's Lesson

All of the major tendencies in post–Vietnam War and science-fiction films reach a consummation in *Black Hawk Down*. By invoking the conventions developed in these films, *Black Hawk Down* arouses and satisfies a set of well-established expectations about the nature of our enemies and the necessity of warfare. The film presents itself not as fiction but as the reproduction of actual events, giving its interpretation of war great authority. Viewing it lent emotional conviction to Bush and his advisers, who watched it repeatedly while planning the invasion of Iraq.

The film frames the Somalia mission as a humanitarian effort to rescue starving Black people from a cruel warlord, Mohamed Aidid. In this it follows the ideological premises laid down in *Bataan* back in 1943, in Cold War–era films set in Korea, and in *Aliens* and *Star Trek,* and echoed most recently in *Three Kings:* that the United States acts to protect "natives" from monstrous dictators. In doing this, it elides the actual policy shift (which had occurred earlier) that changed the Somalia mission from humanitarian aid to nation-building.

The action begins with a successful commando raid (as in 1986's *Delta Force* and 1990's *Navy SEALs*). But when a helicopter is shot down, the raiders' mission changes to a last-stand defense, and the film becomes an account of the desperate effort to rescue the besieged Americans. This shift to the defensive had also been used in World War II–era films like *Guadalcanal Diary* (1943) and *Objective, Burma!* (1945), or Korean War films like *Retreat, Hell!* (1952) and *All the Young Men* (1960), to show that even when Americans take the offensive, their war is ultimately defensive. Now, after Vietnam, the shift more strongly references the premise of the POW rescue films—that the most immaculate mission is the rescue of one's *own* people. The corollary is, *and the natives be damned.* To achieve the rescue, the Americans will have to shoot their way through streets crowded with civilians as well as armed enemies.

The film deploys the "Custer's Last Stand" variation of the Frontier Myth, in which the defeat of an elite American force by overwhelming numbers of "savages" symbolizes a threat to the fundamentally benevolent course of American action. In the terms of Huntington's "conflict of civilizations" ideology, this last stand occurs on the terrain of the Islamic civilization, the most implacable foe of our Western civilization.

The menace of the enemy is conveyed by the skillful combination of several conventional elements, all of which indicate that *racial* difference is the basis of the conflict. Like the enemy in the antiterrorist films of the 1980s, Somalis are Muslim. Like the Comanches in a Western, they are seen as hyperviolent primitives. Like the Asian enemies of World War II and the Korean War, and the "bugs" in *Aliens,* they are monoracial and fanatical in attacking—careless of their own losses. Like the enemy in Vietnam films, even their women and children kill Americans. But most strikingly, the enemy are all Black, whereas the American units are almost exclusively White—just as they were in *Saving Private Ryan.* There are only two Black soldiers in all the American units represented in the film, only one in an important role—a ratio far smaller than was attempted in 1943 in *Bataan* when the army was segregated, or in the just-integrated army of *Pork Chop Hill* in 1959.

This casting decision has been justified on the grounds that there were in fact only two African Americans in the units that fought in Mogadishu. But the movie is a historical fiction, like *Bataan* and *Pork Chop Hill,* not a documentary. Decisions about how to represent race in films are ultimately artistic and ideological. *Bataan* offers a strained rationale in order to place a Black soldier among White troops in a segregated army. In *Pork Chop Hill* several Black characters appear, two in major roles, although the book on which the movie was based never mentions the presence of Black soldiers. This reflects the producers' deliberate intention to deal with racial issues.[16]

Director Ridley Scott's decisions reflect different priorities. The stark visual opposition of Black and White people has aesthetic force, but it also carries the emotional charge of racial antipathy. Moreover, *Black Hawk Down* does not use the *race-face* device to *moderate* that racial distinction. On the contrary, late in the film, the lone Black infantryman in the American unit freezes instead of shooting when a Black Somali woman charges his unit's position—despite the evidence, given throughout the film, that she is likely to be attacking. Indeed, the woman *does* pull a rifle from her dress, and a *White* soldier has to shoot her. This scene is one invented for the movie—a fiction, not the reenactment of an actual event. The film is dramatizing the idea that the Black soldier can't be trusted in war against a Black enemy.

The movie also dehumanizes the enemy by visually associating them with the monsters in *Aliens*. (Scott directed the first movie in the *Alien* series.) The Somalis in *Black Hawk Down* swarm in masses through the narrow streets and alleys, just as the monsters swarmed through the tunnels of the space colony in *Aliens*. In both films, the enemy's final attack is first detected by the swarming of blips on a radar screen. So when the moment of berserk killing comes—the *final fury*—the audience accepts the firestorm as an appropriate response to the massed monsters. But the firestorm in Mogadishu does not complete the mission. It only allows the troops to escape. By the conventions of the genre, the film's unfinished business would be to avenge the defeat and destroy the warlord. This idea is reinforced by a scene in which one of the warlord's men articulates the enemy's lesson: "In Somalia, killing is negotiation. Do you really think if you get General Aidid, we will simply put down our weapons and adopt American democracy? That the killing will stop? We know this: without victory there can be no peace. There will always be killing." The enemy's lesson, as always, is that only victory brings peace, and victory can only be achieved through merciless violence.

The violence that might have revived America's commitment to making the world safe for democracy is rendered pointless by the Clinton administration's decision (referenced at the end of the film) to withdraw from Somalia. The expectation of vengeance and reconquest is frustrated. The viewers will leave the theater haunted and angered by another humiliating defeat, so reminiscent of Vietnam, and denied the prospect that defeat will be avenged, the loss made good.

This was certainly the lesson Bush and his advisers took from the film in 2002. A few weeks after their first viewings, Defense Secretary Rumsfeld told Frank Rich of the *New York Times* that US intervention in Afghanistan was not "Black Hawk Down in the snow," because *this* time, "the United States of America did not decide to withdraw and leave the field." The administration went so far as to hire Jerry Bruckheimer—producer of *Black Hawk Down*—to advise it on ways of controlling the Somalia metaphor going forward. Three years later the president, despite all that had gone wrong in Iraq, *still* read the movie as a warning that failure to persist in the use of military force is a sign of weakness and an invitation to enemy attack. Frank Rich concluded that "the historical analogy that is truly burned into Bush's brain . . . is Somalia"—that is, the "Somalia" fiasco as interpreted in *Black Hawk Down*. By the logic of mythological thinking, Bush's wars in Afghanistan and Iraq, and our embrace of what Dick Cheney called the "dark side" (the use of torture and "black" imprisonment sites) in the Global War on Terror, were sequels in which the unfinished business of *Black Hawk Down* would finally be completed.[17]

The Iraq "Fiasco" and the Breakdown of Neoconservative Myth

The official who twitted reporter Ron Suskind for belonging to the "reality-based community" was expressing the administration's belief that it could, through overwhelming military power, create its own reality in Iraq. But American power could not make reality conform to the Good War Myth. Within a year, stunning military success had degenerated into what reporter Thomas Ricks branded a "fiasco." The "liberation" was marked by widespread chaos, looting, and sectarian violence. It proved impossible to establish a stable national government. Corruption and violence abounded. American troops struggled to preserve civil order against sectarian and tribal militias, who fought each other and the Americans. By 2006 Bush's war policy was thoroughly discredited with the public, and most of its architects (Cheney, Rumsfeld, Wolfowitz) had either been shunted aside or pushed out of government. Although the 2006–2007 "surge" in military operations, backed by the recommitment of large American forces, seemed to stabilize the situation, it was clear that neoconservative strategy had failed, leaving America with an intractable task of nation-building in Iraq and Afghanistan—for which the American public had no appetite. The Iraq side of the conflict would persist long after the withdrawal of combat forces, as the United States was drawn into the struggle against the Islamic State and its successors. The Afghanistan project would end in a disastrous withdrawal in August 2021, which mirrored the humiliating flight from Saigon in 1975.[18]

American political leaders and Hollywood culture makers had responded to defeat in Vietnam by focusing on its demoralizing effects on the public. They sought to cure Vietnam syndrome by a course of mythological thinking, imaginatively reenacting the war in search of a new storyline that would end in victory. Their use of myth and symbol succeeded in preparing the public to consent to the wars they initiated. But they made the mistake of believing the myths they purveyed, and as a result were drawn into a repetition of the Vietnam tragedy. The moral standing that the United States had recouped after the breakup of the Soviet Union and Warsaw Pact, and its UN-sponsored liberation of Kuwait in 1991, was lost. When Russia invaded Ukraine in 2022, on the flimsiest of pretexts, its leaders could counter American accusations of aggression by citing the 2002 invasion of Iraq.

The mythmaking of the 1980–2008 period—the development of "clash of civilizations" ideology, the fight against global terrorist networks, and Hollywood fantasies of sci-fi race wars and captive rescues—had enduring effects on American culture. There is always a feedback loop between the dehumanization of foreign enemies and the dehumanization of some classes of fellow citizens. By the end of the second Bush administration, "radical Islamic terrorism" had become a potent meme for identifying America's most implacable enemies. American Muslims were accused of seeking to promote "Sharia law" in American communities. Acts of violence against American Muslims proliferated; and Islamophobia fed a broader shift in the public mood that was hostile to immigration and immigrants in general.[19]

This new blending of xenophobia and racism would become critical to the conservative reaction against the presidency of Bush's Democratic successor, Barack Hussein Obama.

PART V

The Age of Culture War

14

The Obama Presidency

The Myth of the Movement and
the Tea Party Reaction

In 2008 the neoliberal order experienced a breakdown similar to the collapse of the New Deal order and liberal consensus in the 1970s. Public opinion turned against the wars in Iraq and Afghanistan, as well as the interventionist premises of neoconservative foreign policy. The George W. Bush administration was discredited by its incompetent response to Hurricane Katrina, which nearly destroyed the city of New Orleans. The power of the hurricane provided evidence (for those willing to see it) that climate change was a real danger. Finally, Bush's economic program had ended in an epoch-making crash of the banking system (national and international) and the onset of the Great Recession—the worst decline in the US economy since the Great Depression. The losses of jobs, wages, savings, and homes fell on a working class that had suffered forty years of stagnation in real wages and a decline of full-time employment.

The election of Barack Obama, the first African American president of the United States, along with a filibuster-proof Democratic majority in Congress, seemed to signal a liberal revival. Since the 1960s the history of the civil rights movement had provided a template for the struggle of other minority and disadvantaged identity groups for recognition and civil equality. Obama's election seemed to represent the transformation of that narrative into something like a national Myth of the Movement. It suggested that the GOP's Southern Strategy had failed, and that it was now possible to base a governing majority on a coalition of liberal White people and ethnic and racial minorities.

The first two years of the Obama administration also produced a sort of mini–New Deal, combining stimulus and relief measures with a new regulatory regime designed to prevent a repeat of the crash. The obvious failure of whole-sale deregulation now justified efforts to rein in the power of capital, while the necessity for government intervention to save the banking system and auto-mobile industry refuted Ronald Reagan's claim that "government is always the problem." All of these measures were more limited in scope than progressives wanted, as Obama's economic team felt constrained by the pro-business con-servatism of Clintonian New Democrats. Nevertheless, the election appeared to augur a paradigm shift in American politics toward the liberal vision of strong safety nets, "green" economics, and a more complete civil equality for women, LGBTQ people, and racial and ethnic minorities.

In fact, the scale of Obama's electoral majorities concealed the persistence of political and cultural trends that had produced the hyperpartisanship of the Bill Clinton and George W. Bush years. Those divisions were rooted in cul-tural and demographic changes in the way American communities were con-stituted. Bill Bishop and Robert Cushing dubbed this phenomenon "the Big Sort": the increasing tendency of Americans to choose to live in communities that were *ideologically* homogeneous and tended also to be homogeneous in class and ethnicity. That sorting process was observable in the pattern of sub-urban development around urban areas, but it was most starkly displayed in the differences between rural and urban communities. Once the crisis-born re-action against Bush and his party had passed, those divisions would reassert themselves with a vengeance. To those for whom economic issues mattered most, Obama's policies threatened the basic premises of neoliberal economics: low taxation, deregulation, and antipathy to big government. While economic concerns drove a great deal of the anti-Obama rhetoric, for many they took a back seat to concerns over culture and identity. One of the chief factors driving the rightward movement within the Big Sort was conservatives' fear of perma-nent disempowerment by the alliance of liberals with an emerging non-White near majority.[1]

From the first, GOP opposition to Obama was marked by extreme parti-sanship and personal animus, typified by Senator Mitch McConnell's declara-tion (on November 4, 2010) that the whole purpose of his party now was simply to prevent Obama's winning a second term. That project failed, but morphed into a program of total opposition to anything the president or his party un-dertook or advocated. Then, in 2010, the political balance of power was turned on its head. The midterm elections resulted in a "shellacking" for Democrats (in Obama's words) that gave Republicans majorities in the House and Senate and a raft of governorships and state legislatures.[2]

This rapid reversal of fortune was shaped by the complex interaction of several different forces: changing patterns of party affiliation, the rise of new internet-based media, Fox News' systematic conflation of newscasting with ideological messaging, persistent patterns of racial and cultural resentment, and the rapid expansion of billionaire-backed propaganda outlets and political action committees empowered by the Supreme Court's *Citizens United* decision of 2010. Within these forums, national myths were invoked to explain the partisan conflict and project scripts for political action.

Obama's Victory and the Myth of the Movement

As the first elected African American president, Barack Obama unmistakably symbolized the triumph of the Myth of the Movement—the drive for political rights and social equality that had been a central theme of liberal politics since the 1960s. Even Obama's defeated opponent, Senator John McCain, acknowledged this as a significant turn in the nation's history.

Obama embraced this symbolism and enlarged on it. His "Blackness" was a given, but he often reminded audiences that he was the child of an African immigrant and a White American woman, and had received his early schooling in Indonesia before going to live with his maternal grandparents in Hawaii, a distinctively multicultural society. He would describe his grandparents in terms evocative of the Good War Myth: "a white grandfather who survived the depression to serve in Patton's army during World War II" and a White grandmother who (like Rosie the Riveter) "worked on a bomber assembly line while he was overseas." Obama's marriage to Michelle Robinson linked him to "a black American who carries within her the blood of slaves and slave owners, an inheritance we pass on to our two precious daughters." His extended family is a multiracial, multiethnic platoon: "I have brothers, sisters, nieces, nephews, uncles, and cousins of every race and every hue scattered across three continents." They included Christians of different sects, Muslims, and Jews. In an interesting turn of phrase, Obama said that his family story had "seared into [his] genetic makeup" the idea that "this nation is more than the sum of its parts—that out of many, we are truly one." His family history becomes, metaphorically at least, a parable of racial transformation.[3]

Obama's version of the national myth takes off from Abraham Lincoln's theory of the Founding, which saw constitutional government evolving toward the ideal of equality articulated in the Declaration of Independence. Obama embraced the Liberation version of the Civil War Myth and insisted that those principles had been vindicated, after the long night of Jim Crow, by the Good War and the civil rights movement that followed. He gave a succinct version of this narrative in announcing his candidacy: "In the face of tyranny, a band of patriots brought an empire to its knees. In the face of secession, we unified a nation and set the captives free. In the face of Depression, we put people back to work and lifted millions out of poverty. We welcomed immigrants to our shores. We opened railroads to the west. We landed a man on the moon. And we heard a King's call to let 'justice roll down like waters, and righteousness like a mighty stream.'" He announced his candidacy on the steps of the Old State Capitol in Springfield, Illinois—"where Lincoln once called on a house divided to stand together"—and connected that call with the words of Martin Luther King Jr. "The arc of history is long," he said, quoting King, "but it bends towards justice." His policies often reflected the New Deal concern with workers' issues like wages, pensions, and health insurance. But as president he foregrounded the Good War Myth, describing his coalition as a rainbow "platoon": "young and old, rich and poor, Democrat and Republican, black, white, Hispanic, Asian, Native American, gay, straight, disabled and not disabled Americans who sent a message to the world that we have never been just a collection of individuals or a collection of Red States and Blue States: we are, and always will be, the United States of America!"[4]

There was an expectation that he would use the power conferred by the election to follow the New Deal paradigm. The November 24, 2008, cover of *Time* photoshopped Obama into a classic Franklin D. Roosevelt pose, and the caption suggested he "learn from F.D.R." and seek a "New New Deal."[5] Obama promised a swift and energetic response to the banking crisis, which observers compared to FDR's "Hundred Days." The Troubled Assets Relief Program used federal funds and government credit to rescue banks and investment-insurance firms from collapse—a measure analogous to those by which FDR had saved the banking system in 1933. Like FDR, he enacted a regulatory regime (under the Dodd-Frank Act) that tightened the requirements of bank capitalization and established the Consumer Financial Protection Bureau to regulate predatory lending practices. His administration underwrote labor-management partnerships by which automobile producers were saved from bankruptcy. His "stimulus" bill mirrored FDR's make-work programs by financing infrastructure projects. He also embarked on a major effort to reduce carbon emissions through cap-and-trade legislation and more stringent regulation of power-plant emissions. Finally, he pushed through the Affordable Care Act (ACA; "Obamacare"), the long-sought capstone to the New Deal and Great Society social safety net.[6]

All of these measures were resisted by Republicans and conservative Democrats, in varying combinations. The experience of the New Deal, and Keynesian theory, showed that it was critical for stimulus to go directly to workers and consumers, so that increased spending and demand could restart the economic engine. Nevertheless, a bipartisan community of "deficit hawks" warned against the ballooning of the national debt and drastically reduced the size of the stimulus. The pro-employment and safety-net parts of the program were resisted by conservatives, for whom such expenditures amounted to "welfare," creating the "moral hazard" that workers would lounge about on the dole rather than seek work. But it was the rare conservative who (in 2009) condemned the government for creating moral hazard by bailing out the investment banks and reinsurers, who had caused the crisis through irresponsible lending practices and their marketing of "derivatives."

Obama achieved a great deal in the face of this opposition. But he did so at the cost of compromises that substantially limited the amount of stimulus that went to "Main Street." He also made his administration party to the egregious injustice by which irresponsible lenders were bailed out and borrowers who had been sold mortgages they could not afford received inadequate relief.

The ACA would become the signature issue of the opposition to Obama, and the flashpoint of the political reaction against the administration in the 2010 midterm elections. There was more to that reaction than the traditional antipathy of conservatives for social welfare programs, and for the concept of universal government-supported health care, which they saw as socialized medicine. As originally designed, Obamacare required all Americans to either enroll in the health insurance program or pay a penalty for refusing to do so. For conservatives this was at best illegitimate expansion of the government's power to tax, at worst an egregious act of coercion. And as a medical program, the ACA inevitably raised questions about government support of abortion and contraception.

The size of Obama's electoral triumph may have led him to overestimate public support for major reforms. For more than forty years, Americans had chosen conservatives from both parties as presidents. Obama's real task was to persuade a center-right electorate to support a center-left program. The presidential campaign had exposed the deep cultural rifts that had been driving the parties into intransigence on a wide range of social issues, from gay marriage to gun control. It exposed as well the renewed strength of racism and xenophobia that was already marked in the 1990s and exacerbated by the Islamophobia of the Global War on Terror. Obama's personal attractiveness had overridden but not overcome these rifts.

On the campaign trail he seemed to be the leader of a movement. In office he was more of a pragmatist. His economic advisers were Clintonian in their fiscal conservatism and business-centered approach to policy. Like Clinton, Obama chose not to push organized labor's priorities: passing the Employee Free Choice Act, which would have aided union organizing; putting pro-union people on the National Labor Relations Board; and opposing or restructuring free-trade deals like NAFTA, which had shifted manufacturing jobs overseas. His advisers' slogan, that a crisis must not be wasted, was based on their understanding of FDR's response to the Great Depression. However, Obama himself never explicitly invoked the New Deal as precedent. His 2009 address on economic policy at Georgetown University was intended to justify deficit spending as the proper response in a recession, for which the New Deal is the classic proof. But Obama never mentions it, offering instead the pallid academic reference that "economists on both the left and the right agree that the last thing a government should do in the middle of a recession is to cut back on spending." Of course, invoking the New Deal would have been anathema to Republicans, but GOP opposition was a given. The real difficulty was that it was also problematic for Clintonian Democrats.[7]

Nor did Obama fight for his program as FDR fought for his: by throwing the force of his intellect and personality into a systematic work of political persuasion, speaking directly to the American people to explain what he was doing and why, assuring them that, though mistakes would surely be made, his goals were clear and aimed at achieving common goods. Roosevelt went on radio with his "fireside chats." Later presidents had made effective use of the televised address from the Oval Office, which marked their statements as matters of vital national interest. Obama—one of the most compelling speakers ever to hold the office—worked within the ordinary parameters of political discourse: the meeting, the address on the hustings, the press conference. As a result, the public saw the unfolding of Obama's program—especially the ACA and the stimulus package—as a sordid tale of political sausage-making, of squabbling and horse-trading among the usual suspects, rather than a principled fight for the public good.[8]

Don't Tread on Me: The Tea Party Reaction

The result was a counterrevolution in the 2010 midterm elections, with Republicans winning large majorities in the House, near control of the Senate, and a flock of governorships and state legislatures. The last would produce political gerrymanders that would skew representation to the right, at every level, in every election thereafter. Although Obama retained his personal appeal, and won reelection with a substantial majority in 2012, Democrats would not recoup their losses in the House or the states, and enjoyed only a brief period as Senate majority. Mitch McConnell may have failed to keep Obama to a one-term presidency, but he thwarted every initiative that depended on legislation, forced a budget agreement that "sequestered" funding to limit government operations, and blocked or slow-walked every judicial appointment—in the end refusing to even consider Obama's nominee to replace Supreme Court justice Antonin Scalia. Republican intransigence made politics truly a zero-sum game.

The arc of history, having bent toward justice, flat-lined.

The lead in this counterrevolution was assumed by the Tea Party, a seemingly spontaneous conservative movement characterized by many commentators as "populist." Its formation was supposedly sparked by a now-legendary on-camera "rant" by Rick Santelli, a CNBC financial reporter, against Obama's stimulus package and his proposal to provide relief for home owners ruined by the crash in property values. Santelli was outraged by this attempt to "subsidize losers." "This is America!" he cried, where such things were unthinkable. "If you read our Founding Fathers, people like Benjamin Franklin and Jefferson, what we're doing in this country now is making them roll over in their graves." The attribution of the sudden rise of the Tea Party to "Santelli's rant" is probably an exercise in mythmaking. But the targets of his outrage, and his invocation of the Founders as symbols of the America Obama had betrayed, would be echoed in the popular reaction that developed over the succeeding weeks and months.[9]

The rejection of government-funded relief programs was based on longstanding conservative principles that called for reducing the size, activism, and cost of the federal government. That doctrine had found political expression in the antitax movement, whose most important spokesman was Grover Norquist, a follower of the Austrian school of economics, which held all taxation to be a form of theft. In 1985 he had founded Americans for Tax Reform, which lobbied Republican candidates and officeholders to sign a "Taxpayer Protection Pledge," often referred to as the "No-Tax Pledge," refusing to raise taxes for any purpose. The stated purpose of the pledge was to shrink big government by radically reducing its revenues, and by 2010 it had been signed by all but six Republican House members and forty-one of forty-seven senators.[10]

If this was "populism," the label had lost all meaning. From the age of Jackson in the 1830s to that of Tom Watson, James Weaver, and William Jennings Bryan in the 1890s, populists had favored debt relief for farmers and government regulation of finance. Santelli had no problem with the Troubled Assets Relief Program that rescued the major investment banks; it was relief to the "little man" that was un-American. This was classic conservative doctrine. At the start of the Great Depression, banker and Treasury Secretary Andrew Mellon had advised President Herbert Hoover to let the victims of the Depression suffer its consequences: "Purge the rottenness out of the system. . . . Enterprising people will pick up the wrecks from less competent people." As Republican presidential nominee in 2012, Mitt Romney would divide the American people into "makers" and "takers." Romney told the donors at a campaign fundraiser that "47 percent of the people" would vote for Obama "no matter what," because they "believe that they are victims, . . . believe the government has a responsibility to care for them, . . . that they are entitled to health care, to food, to housing, to you-name-it. . . . And the government should give it to them." If he became president, he said, his job would not be "to worry about those people. I'll never convince them they should take personal responsibility and care for their lives."[11]

But Norquist, Santelli, and Romney represented only one of the strains of ideology and emotion that would shape the Tea Party and its successor movement, Make America Great Again. The movement also spoke to the discontent of the White working class over its long experience of wage stagnation and job loss, which it attributed (with some justice) to the globalist economics of corporate and political elites. This constituency, which could more accurately be identified as "populist," was attracted to the Tea Party by its attacks on "big government," the growing deficit, taxes, and regulations, but their opposition to these things was pragmatic rather than theoretical. The national government's regulatory regime had not checked and was partly responsible for the decline in their economic prospects and for the rising cost of food and energy. They especially resented the use of taxes for social welfare programs, which (as they saw it) benefited the racial minorities who were "clients" of the liberal elites. On the other hand, they put a high value on Social Security and Medicare, the so-called entitlement programs that were the perennial targets of conservative deficit hawks. They were also hostile to many of the policies associated with neoliberalism, especially those free-trade pacts that were blamed for the loss of American jobs to Asian and Latin American competitors.

The Tea Party name was an explicit invocation of the Myth of the Founding, a reference to the 1773 dumping of British tea in Boston Harbor that helped to precipitate the American Revolution. The choice of name signified a return to the original principles on which American government was based: a small and frugal republic, deferential to popular and states' rights and to cultural tradition, leaving civil society free to conduct its affairs without needless regulation. But it also signified *insurrection,* an uprising against the power of liberal elites. Its meetings and demonstrations featured participants in Revolutionary War costume, waving the flags of 1776, the Betsy Ross flag and the Gadsden flag with its coiled rattlesnake and "Don't tread on me" motto. Occasionally someone would bring a Confederate battle flag, the banner of America's other great insurrection.

The Tea Party movement brought to a head trends that had been shaping the Republican Party and conservative movement since Pat Buchanan's "culture war" and Newt Gingrich's "Contract with America" in the 1990s. Its core constituency was White, male, middle aged, and religious, with a high proportion of evangelical Christians. Its aim was to overthrow the cultural authority gained by liberals, minorities, women, and exponents of "political correctness" and to restore the moral, social, and political authority of "real Americans" (and free-market capitalists). If the Tea Party had a slogan, it was, "I want my country back." *My* country—not yours. In their interviews with Tea Party voters, the sociologists Theda Skocpol and Vanessa Williamson found that, "when asked, Tea Partiers would justify that rejection in terms of love: they 'feel anguish about losing the nation they love, the country they planned to leave to their children and grandchildren.'"[12]

The battle was joined over the teaching of American history, the basis of all national myth. In 2014 Tea Party conservatives decried the College Board's promulgation of new standards for high school AP history, which emphasized "critical thinking" about slavery, Jim Crow, and American interventions overseas. Stanley Kurtz, writing in *National Review,* called it "an attempt to hijack the teaching of U.S. history on behalf of a leftist political and ideological perspective." Ben Carson, then a candidate for the Republican nomination and later head of Donald Trump's Housing and Urban Development Department, declared that "most people when they finish that course, they'd be ready to go sign up for ISIS," the Islamist terrorist group.[13]

The movement also attracted religious conservatives, whose opposition to Obama's policies was rooted in cultural as well as economic conservatism. They rejected Obamacare because it financed contraception, abortion, and gender reassignment, not simply because it was "socialistic" or a drain on taxpayers. Their Tea Party affiliation was the start of a new and more militant phase of political action, looking toward a broader restoration of the traditional moral and social values that had been traduced by the "liberations" of the 1960s, and even toward a form of Christian nationalism. They included the conservative wings of mainstream Catholic, Orthodox, and Protestant denominations, as well as new Pentecostal and charismatic sects—some of the latter based in store-front churches, others in huge megachurches with congregations of thou-sands. Although these groups formed a consensus in opposition to Obama and his policies, their components differed on racial issues ranging from the ex-plicit White supremacism of Christian Identity, through Southern Baptist churches grappling with a history and de facto condition of segregation, to megachurches with multiracial congregations. They also differed radically on questions of Christian theology and eschatology.[14]

Perhaps for that reason, when representatives of Christian conservatism ad-dressed the political arena, they typically appealed to the Myth of the Founding. Thus Michael Johns of the Heritage Foundation, speaking at a Tea Party meeting in Boston in 2009, rebuked Obama for failing to recognize the Chris-tian character of the nation: "Mr. Obama, . . . every founding document in this nation has cited the creator. That is the basis on which we distinguish our-selves in the world." Sarah Palin, speaking on Bill O'Reilly's Fox News pro-gram in 2010, asserted that America was a "Christian nation" because the "Founding Fathers . . . crafted a Declaration of Independence and a Constitu-tion that allows that Judeo-Christian belief to be the foundation of our lives."[15]

There was also a racial element in the Republican reaction. Obama personi-fied the rising strength of non-White people and immigrants, and linked that strength to the spread of cultural liberalism. Conservatives were familiar with statistical predictions that, by 2040, the United States would become a "majority-minority" country, with native-born White people outnumbered by non-White people and the foreign born. The numerical strength and cultural authority of White Christians was also declining. In 1992 they formed 73 percent of the voting-age population. By 2012 that share had shrunk to 57 percent, and it was predicted to drop below 50 percent by 2024, with a further drop likely, as church affiliation among young adults was in decline. The hierarchies of political, economic, and cultural power had begun to re-flect greater gender, ethnic, racial, religious, and national-origin diversity, and although some conservatives and populists blamed affirmative action for this loss of primacy, the trend also reflected the rise of a new meritocracy in a rela-tively open marketplace—an equally disconcerting trend, since that meritoc-racy had educational and technological advantages older workers and managers could not match.[16]

The Tea Party had begun by asserting the doctrines of fiscal conservatism, but its emotional charge would come from its populist base, whose constitu-ents viewed economic questions through the lens of culture war. Their activism transformed economic and political issues into tests of national identity and religious values, and in the process brought national myths to bear on key political disputes. The most significant of these was their campaign to repeal Obamacare, which would extend well beyond Obama's presidency. Opposition to the program invoked the condemnations of social welfare policy that had been staples of conservatism since the New Deal. But it would go beyond that critique to invoke a Myth of the Founding, which rooted opposition to Obamacare in a version of the 2nd Amendment and justified armed opposition to the program. Of nearly equal political significance, and arguably of greater policy importance, was the issue of Obama's energy policies, which were designed to address the problem of global warming and climate change. Here the Tea Party attack drew on the Myth of the Frontier to buttress an attack on the policies themselves, and on the scientific consensus that supported them.

Freedom Fuel

The struggle over energy policy had concerned American politics for a generation, but it became central to political warfare in the Obama years. This was the issue that tested most explicitly the premises of the Frontier Myth, on which the American Gospel of Growth had always been based. The Obama administration was committed to policies that would balance economic growth with attention to its effects on the environment. Its concerns included the traditional environmental issues of industrial and chemical pollution of air, soil, and water. But climate change through global warming was a new kind of threat: its spatial dimensions were planetary, its time horizon stretched deep into the new century.

Once in office, Obama actively pressed the environmental agenda, at first relying on his congressional majorities and, when he lost control of Congress after 2010, on executive action. In June 2009 the House approved his American Clean Energy and Security Act, which would have established a cap-and-trade or carbon-trading system, modeled on those already in use in Europe. Although the Senate refused to take up the bill, the administration moved to achieve its environmental goals by enacting new regulations on the emission of greenhouse gases by power-generating utilities, refineries, and factories. Obama also vetoed legislation authorizing the Keystone pipeline, ordered a halt in oil exploration in the Arctic, and dramatically increased the number and extent of national monuments, forbidding oil or mineral development in those areas. As the capstone to this policy, he pushed to conclusion the 2015 Paris Agreement negotiations among industrial and developing nations, a worldwide accord to forestall or prevent climate change, and made the United States a formal party to the agreement by executive action (since the Republican Congress was sure to disapprove it).

Fossil fuel producers were the largest contributors to anti-Obama publicity campaigns. Their power was enhanced by the Supreme Court's *Citizens United* decision in 2010, which abolished the regulations that had limited the amounts that could be contributed to political campaigns by so-called dark money organizations—groups whose membership and accounting methods were exempt from federal and state disclosure rules. In the 2006 election, corporate dark money had amounted to 2 percent of expenditures; in 2010 it constituted 40 percent of the money spent on state and congressional elections.

Among the most significant contributors were the group of advocacy organizations and policy think tanks (some thirty-four in number) organized or supported by Charles and David Koch. By 2014 their primary political operation, Americans for Progress, led all corporate groups in its spending for TV advertisements. By 2018 it was one of fifteen groups that together accounted for three-fourths of the dark money supporting political-issue campaigns and individual candidacies. Foundations supported by the Kochs sought to broaden the power of conservatives at every level, energizing them by appealing to culture-war issues with no direct relation to oil—guns, public education, minority voting rights, Obamacare, Medicaid. Americans for Progress coordinated their national campaigns, and the American Legislative Exchange Council became their chief instrument for empowering conservatives in state and local governments. Although they failed to block the adoption of the ACA, their propaganda helped to demonize the act and make it a centerpiece of the successful Republican 2010 midterm campaign. True to the Kochs' belief that labor unions are illegitimate intrusions in the market economy, the American Legislative Exchange Council and Americans for Progress used their influence at the state level to limit collective bargaining rights by the passage of right-to-work laws and the outright banning of collective bargaining by public-sector employees. The same principle was behind their opposition to raising the federal minimum wage.[17]

In developing these campaigns, the Kochs and their house intellectuals expounded a libertarian reading of the Myth of the Founding, at one point framing their movement as the "Sam Adams Alliance." The Founding theme also reflected the emergence of a radical premise in conservative politics, a wish to remake the American social compact by undoing the changes that had occurred since 1933 and going back to the "original" terms of that compact as modern conservatives understood them. This was a tendency already reflected in the dominance of "originalism" in the Supreme Court's interpretation of constitutional law.

In 2009, as scientists and political leaders prepared for an international conference on global warming, the constellation of think tanks and foundations funded by the Koch brothers and the American Petroleum Institute waged a systematic campaign of disinformation to convince the public that climate science was "dubious," or a falsehood promoted by scientist-conspirators. The alternative would of course be problematic for their personal fortunes; but they also believed it would wreck our industrial economy. So their think tanks and advocacy organizations were employed to convince the American people that oil means progress, and progress is more valuable than nature—the heroic choice dramatized by the Frontier Myth.[18]

President Obama's commitment to substantial reduction of carbon emissions was genuine, but he also subscribed to the Gospel of Growth, all the more so as he had to bring the economy back from the depths of the Great Recession. While a majority of the public was concerned about climate change, there was uncertainty and division about the need for a rapid shift from fossil fuels. A seeming escape from this political bind was delivered by a new bonanza: the development of hitherto untappable natural gas resources through the improved technology of hydrofracturing, or "fracking." Experimental programs had been funded by the government and the Gas Research Institute since 1976. In 1997 a new high-pressure slick-water technique was tried in the shale-rock oil fields of Texas. It proved remarkably productive, and once methods for storing and distributing the gas were in place, the industry boomed. Shale gas business grew 45 percent between 2005 and 2010, and its benefits began to be realized during Obama's administration. Increased production lowered energy prices across the board. Since natural gas produces less greenhouse gas than either oil or coal, its partial replacement of those fuels was a net gain for Obama's campaign against global warming. The fracking bonanza was so productive it obviated the need to open the Arctic National Wildlife Refuge (ANWR) to oil drilling. It not only ended American dependence on foreign oil, it enabled the United States to become, once again, a net exporter of energy.[19]

From the environmentalist perspective, this was a mixed blessing. Natural gas still added carbon to the atmosphere, although at a lower rate than other fossil fuels. Moreover, natural gas is methane, which is worse than CO_2 as a greenhouse gas, so pipeline leaks from an expanded system posed a serious danger. Fracking itself could have dire effects on groundwater and geological stability. Some Native American tribes were as concerned about fracking on their lands as they were about the Keystone pipeline or oil drilling, and for the same reasons. To climate scientists, natural gas was best thought of as a transitional fuel, bridging the gap till noncarbon energy sources could be developed. Nevertheless, the Obama administration seized the fracking bonanza as proof that its climate policies were consistent with economic growth, and that it had produced, or at least presided over, the recovery of America's energy independence.[20]

By embracing the gas bonanza, Obama affirmed and perpetuated the Frontier Myth's "rising tide" theory of economics. That myth would be ready to hand for Donald Trump, who would embrace fracking as part of his antienvironmentalist program.[21]

In the event, fracking followed the classic boom-to-bust pattern of earlier bonanzas—gold in the 1850s, range cattle in the 1870s, wheat in the 1880s, dot-coms in the 1990s. Fracking is extremely expensive, requiring special equipment and difficult drilling techniques. Most of the companies that plunged into the business were small, dependent on loans and the high price of their commodity to be profitable. In 2019 the Saudis and Russians—whose oil and gas reserves dwarfed those of the United States—began a trade war. Each pushed production to glut the market, lower prices, and hurt the other's economy, but an ancillary goal was to wreck America's fracking-based gas production, which needed high prices to survive. Their program had already succeeded in weakening the industry when the outbreak of the coronavirus pandemic caused the bottom to drop out of the oil market and bankrupted most of the small producers who ran the fracking industry.[22]

The Koch brothers' campaign against climate science was not affected by the fracking bonanza or its collapse. They and their allies would persist in demands for opening ANWR, completion of the Keystone XL pipeline, and reversal of regulations to reduce greenhouse gas emissions. Their campaign now emphasized ideology and symbolism over calculations of economic interest: it was the *principle* of open frontiers and unregulated development—the "Economic Freedom Frontier," as the Kochs' Frontiers of Freedom foundation called it—that they were fighting for. Founded in 1995 and allowed to lapse in 2010, Frontiers of Freedom was revived in 2014 as the debate over drilling in ANWR heated up. The organization's website asserts an organic connection between the development of economic frontiers and the growth of "freedom." The Myths of the Founding and of the Frontier are mutually reinforcing and organically linked in its vision of libertarian individualism. According to the website, "Constitutional Freedom" is simply protecting people from taxes, especially those that finance social welfare programs like Obamacare. "Economic Freedom" is essentially the same thing. "Defending Freedom" is about ensuring fairness in granting defense contracts. "Automotive" and "Fuel / Energy Freedom" have special importance, because they involve the development and use of fossil fuels. Your "Automotive Freedom" is denied by regulations that favor electric cars and hybrids. "Fuel / Energy Freedom" is denied when "climate science" blocks the development of energy resources. Not only does the bar against drilling in ANWR hurt the prospects for economic growth; it violates all of the enumerated freedoms, marking the government as tyrannically bent on destroying "personal freedom."[23]

Partisan opposition to Obama's environmental and social justice policies was cast in extreme terms: the policies were not merely mistaken, they imperiled "freedom" itself and the American way of life. This rhetoric was not without precedent. Newt Gingrich and his colleagues had gone to extremes of defamation and obstruction to deprive Bill Clinton's presidency of its legitimacy, although Clinton was a relatively conservative, pro-business Democrat. But the opposition to Obama had a sharper, even hysterical edge and often carried an implicit threat of violence. This was partly because Obama was more liberal than Clinton, and because he came to office with far more political strength. But there was also a racial element in the Republican reaction. Obama personified the rising numbers and political strength of non-White people and immigrants, and linked that strength to the spread of cultural liberalism.

Conservatives began developing strategies for opposing the demographic trend early in the new century. The American Legislative Exchange Council developed plans for extreme gerrymandering and suppression of the vote of minorities, the young, college students, and the poor. Following the electoral triumphs of 2010, they developed model statutes and voting-district maps for Republican-controlled legislatures to enact. In this they followed the model set by the Southern Redeemers, who overthrew Reconstruction and established Jim Crow, substituting the modern techniques of statistical analysis for vigilante violence.

Obamacare as Cultural Crisis

That sense of existential threat was most vividly displayed in the response to the ACA. The measure was intended to complete the unfinished business of the New Deal welfare state by providing universal (or near-universal) government-sponsored medical insurance. Given that ideological ambition and the size and cost of the program, it was the perfect symbol of everything the Tea Party opposed. It would be a major addition to the entitlement programs

(Medicare and Social Security) that conservatives had opposed on ideological grounds, make big government bigger by adding a huge new bureaucracy, and increase the strain on the federal budget and national debt. The program required all Americans who did not have medical insurance to register for the program and sign up with one of the plans offered by the government or pay a penalty if they chose not to join. This "individual mandate" was thought necessary to prevent an "insurance death spiral" or "adverse selection process," in which only the sickest people would enroll and premium costs would therefore rise exponentially. The mandate was seen as an egregious act of government coercion that forced people to buy insurance they might not want or need, suggesting that Obamacare was indeed "socialist medicine." The outrage was not lessened by the fact that Social Security was similarly funded by a mandatory tax. According to Grover Norquist's economic theory, even ordinary taxation was a form of theft perpetrated by a coercive state, justifying resistance by a free citizenry—Obamacare was beyond the pale. For the Tea Party's genuinely populist constituency, no such theory was necessary. They reacted against the imposition of a tax and the high cost of the policies offered in the ACA-sponsored marketplace. Christian conservatives shared all of these grievances and were outraged by having to support or participate in a medical program that would pay for abortions, contraception, and end-of-life care. The last of these became a hot-button issue when opponents of the ACA accused the system of creating "death panels" to reduce costs by rationing care to the ailing elderly, and even to sponsor euthanasia.[24]

In the ACA's promise of medical insurance to the poor, the Tea Party also saw a revival of the welfare state, supposedly ended by Clinton in the 1990s. Despite the fact that the vast majority of those benefiting from the ACA would inevitably be White, resentment of the program had a distinctly racial tinge. Obamacare was the president's gift to *his* people. Like welfare, it would foster a "plantation mentality" in Black people, who were already weak in self-reliance. By treating the ACA as a form of racial welfare, its opponents were able to win support among the poor and working-class White people who would benefit from the program.[25]

In the post–civil rights era, it was no longer permissible for mainstream politicians or media opinion makers to use explicit racial slurs. But the War on Terror had made xenophobia permissible and viable as a cover for racism. The claim that Obama was a Muslim was drawn from the War on Terror lexicon, as was the goofy assertion that Obama and his wife had exchanged a "terrorist fist-bump" after one of his speeches. Rudy Giuliani and conservative commentator Dinesh D'Souza characterized Obama as a "Kenyan socialist" whose "anti-colonialism" was implicitly anti-White or anti-Western. The "birther" movement made a similar substitution of xenophobia for racism, asserting that Obama was born Kenyan and was therefore not a legitimate president. Donald Trump was the birther movement's most prominent spokesman, but his nonsensical claims were given credence and circulation by conservative commentators on Fox News. Adherents of the birther movement filed lawsuits arguing that Obama's presidency was illegitimate; and White "grand juries" authorized themselves to indict Obama for fraud and treason. Fox News condemned the refusal of Obama and other Democrats to denounce "radical Islamic terrorism" by name as a sign of sympathy with the devil. John Bolton, a former diplomat and an influential figure among defense policymakers (later Trump's national security adviser), labeled Obama "our first post-American president."[26]

Obama's electoral victories offered proof that the growing strength of a liberal coalition of well-educated White people and non-White minorities was capable of gaining and holding power at the national level. When Obama defeated Romney in 2012, the Republican National Committee, led by Reince Priebus, conducted an "autopsy," which concluded that, to win elections in a "minority-majority" America, the party needed to be more racially inclusive, more open to immigrants and immigration, and less strident on sexuality and gender issues. It posited a conservatism couched in the "kinder, gentler," and "compassionate" terms espoused by the two presidents Bush.

Although establishment Republicans expected the autopsy to define the terms of future candidacies, there was a powerful culture-war reaction among the grass roots of the party. Tea Party populism was one expression. It was complemented by a new racialist ideology originating in the White nationalist movement but echoed in the increasingly mainstream media of the so-called alt-right: the assertion that liberal elites were working to replace "real Americans" and Christians with non-White people and militant secularists.[27]

This ideological convergence was reflected in the important partnership formed when Virginia Thomas, wife of Supreme Court justice Clarence Thomas and a leader in the Council for National Policy, an established conservative think tank, reached out to Steve Bannon, then chairman of Breitbart News and a powerful figure in Far Right media. Bannon's politics were ethnonationalist but also "populist," critical of corporations and government, and isolationist. The Council for National Policy had a more traditional basis. It was founded in 1981 to restore "righteousness, justice and truth" to America, and its members were drawn from the gun rights movement, the Federalist Society, and the Family Research Council, a religion-based organization opposed to abortion and "gay rights." Its ideology was informed by the principles and predilections of Christian nationalism—the belief that the moral structure of the nation, essentially Christian, had been undermined by the secular liberal elite, which presented an existential threat to "liberty" and national identity.

According to reporting by the *New York Times,* Bannon and Thomas envisioned a "hard-right round table" as an alternative to Priebus's Republican National Committee and Grover Norquist's "No Taxes" organization. Though Norquist's ideology was explicitly antigovernment, his focus on taxes was too narrow and (from Bannon's point of view) insufficiently populist. Bannon dismissed Priebus's autopsy as a surrender to liberalism: "If we were all gay illegal aliens, the party likes us. He is preparing the way for a change on social issues by giving a warning, *'don't go Old Testament.'*" Thomas responded that defense of traditional culture *had* to be "Old Testament." With Bannon's support she founded Groundswell, which took the culture-war metaphor to heart, adopting military-style names for its operations and treating the stakes of conflict as truly existential. In a 2019 address to the group, she described "conservatives and Republicans" as an "oppressed minority . . . falsely vilified, slandered and defamed as extremists and bigots and haters" by a secular Left that wants "to fight us, to hurt us, to kill us even."[28]

The ideas espoused by Bannon and Thomas carried the premises of the Tea Party to a logical extreme. The ordinary workings of politics were insufficient to defeat the cultural forces of secular liberalism. Resistance had to take the form of an insurgency, which implied a willingness to push the limits of legal action to circumscribe the power of the emerging liberal minority-majority. In their 2012 study of political polarization, *It's Even Worse Than It Looks,* political scientists Thomas Mann of the liberal Brookings Institution and Norman Ornstein of the conservative American Enterprise Institute described the triumph of the Tea Party as a sign that the Republican Party was becoming "an insurgent outlier in American politics . . . ideologically extreme; scornful of compromise; unmoved by conventional understanding of facts, evidence and science; and dismissive of the legitimacy of its political opposition."[29]

The adoption of an insurgent mystique implied openness to the possibility of violence in some last extremity, and a distinct inclination to violence was evident in the opposition to Obama and his policies. Opponents of Obamacare threatened to seek "2nd Amendment remedies" if the law went into effect, and some brought weapons to meetings between elected officials and their constituents. Gun purchases skyrocketed after Obama's election and reelection, driven by fear that Democrats and their Black president were "coming for your guns." Paramilitary "militias" multiplied in number or expanded in size, especially among White supremacists and ethnonationalists.[30]

During Obama's presidency, the gun rights movement became the symbolic nexus where the ideological strains of a radicalized conservatism crossed, the common ground on which Bannon and Norquist would meet. Its spirit would inform the emerging ideology of the Make America Great Again (MAGA) movement that would carry Donald Trump to the presidency. Its symbolism and rhetoric invoked three of our national myths in their most traditional forms: the Myth of the Frontier, with its ideology of nonregulation and the mystique of vigilante law; the Myth of the Founding, in the form of a "fundamentalist" understanding of the 2nd Amendment; and the Myth of the Lost Cause, in which merciless vigilante violence is required to save civilization from liberal reformers and their racial clients.

To understand how this nexus developed, we need first to examine the history of American gun culture, and then the ideas and conditions that shaped the emergence of a radical gun rights movement in the 1990s and its political empowerment during the Obama and Trump presidencies.

15

Equalizers

The Gun Rights Movement and
Culture-War Conservatism

FIREARMS HAVE always played a prominent role in American life. The prevalence of a militia system for providing public defense required male citizens to own and become proficient in the use of muskets and rifles. Long guns were a necessity in the early phases of settlement in the colonies and later on the frontier, when hunting provided food for subsistence and peltry for clothing and trade, and hunting for all these purposes remains a feature of rural life to this day. But the idea that America has a unique "gun culture" has always been linked to the prevalence of violence in our civil life. The term was coined by historian Richard Hofstadter in a 1970 article in *American Heritage* magazine, "America as a Gun Culture," which linked the nation's permissive gun laws with a history of civil violence and a modern era marked by high murder rates.[1]

It is easy to see why this association is persuasive. The United States has long had the highest level of firearms ownership of any industrialized nation. Approximately 400 million firearms are currently in circulation, more than one for every American. Gunfire now typically causes more than 40,000 deaths per year, combining homicides, suicides, and accidents. Nonfatal gun injuries typically run to more than twice that number. Although the homicide rate has declined since 1980, it remains the highest among advanced industrial nations. In 2020 gunfire replaced automobile accidents as the largest single cause of death in children (age seventeen and under). This is a measure of the ordinary violence of American society.[2]

To this must be added the cost of "extraordinary violence." Mass shootings, in which four or more people die, have increased dramatically in recent decades. A database compiled by the *Washington Post* lists more than 200 such shootings since 1966, and more than half have occurred since 2005. The comprehensive statistics compiled by the Gun Violence Archive show that mass shootings rose from 383 in 2014 to 647 in 2022, an increase of nearly 70 percent, with an annual average of 490 per year. Among the largest mass shootings are those committed by psychologically deranged individuals, such as the 2012 Sandy Hook Elementary School shooting and the Sutherland Springs church shooting in 2017, with twenty-six killed in each incident; the 2017 Las Vegas Strip massacre, in which fifty-eight were killed; and the 2018 Parkland High School shooting, in which seventeen died, as well as hate crimes like the Tree of Life synagogue shooting in 2018 and the El Paso Walmart shooting in 2019, in each of which eleven people were killed, and the Buffalo supermarket shooting in 2022, in which twenty-three people died.[3]

Widespread gun ownership certainly contributes to this mayhem. But other industrial societies (such as Switzerland and Israel) have very high rates of gun possession without a commensurate experience of interpersonal violence. In Serbia, which has experienced decades of civil war and intercommunal violence, rates of gun ownership and violence are high by European standards at 39 guns and 1.4 murders per 100,000 people. In the United States, 150 years after the Civil War, the ownership rate is 120 guns and the murder rate 5.35 per 100,000.[4]

The difference is cultural. Unlike other industrialized nations, America has a culture that grants broad sanctions for individuals to use violence for private ends. Americans therefore have greater reason to fear violence, and they feel a greater need for weapons of self-defense. But firearms are also instruments of power, and demand for them is driven by desire as well as fear. For Americans who feel an especially intense grievance, the mythic action script of "taking up the gun" is readily available, celebrated in mass media and folklore—and guns themselves are often ready to hand.[5]

The Roots of American Gun Culture

America's gun culture is rooted in our origin as an expanding settler state. Our oldest national myth, the Myth of the Frontier, sees the country as a borderland where White civilization violently advances against the wilderness and its "savage" Indigenous peoples. Our first national heroes were frontier riflemen— Daniel Boone and Davy Crockett—who fought Native Americans for possession of a wilderness rich in natural resources.[6]

Settler-state conditions decreed dependence on citizen militias for defense. The colonies lacked the resources to maintain regular armies. After independence,

Americans were leery of forming a large national army, partly because of its expense, partly out of a belief, rooted in English history, that standing armies are a danger to the liberty of the people. Until the end of the nineteenth century, militias were the basis of the nation's military force and were used in civil disturbances as well as wars. In the absence of official police, communities formed posses, militia-like civilian forces, to deal with crime and local disorders. The slave patrols that maintained social control in plantation districts were a semi-permanent form of posse. In extreme cases, where law enforcement was either absent or politically corrupt, frontier communities resorted to vigilantism—a quasi-revolutionary use of violence to restore order. The tradition of vigilantism survived long after frontier conditions had passed, and would become the basis for widespread social violence after the Civil War.[7]

Away from the frontier, militia service was often avoided or neglected. Even so, the right to serve had cultural significance. It was denied to the enslaved and to free Black people, and (in the colonial period) to suspect classes of White people, such as Catholics and Irish or Spanish immigrants. Thus the right to bear arms became a hallmark of citizenship, manhood, status, and racial identity. The westward movement of the frontier throughout the nineteenth century, and the existence of plantation slavery, produced a culture in which White men generally had broad license to use violence to maintain social control along racial borderlines—to dispossess Indians and Mexicans in the West, and to ensure the subservience of Black people in the South.[8]

Settler-state conditions fostered a legal tradition that took a highly permissive view of self-defense. In English common law, "your home is your castle," which you may forcibly defend, but if you are menaced outside the home, you must retreat (if you can) rather than stand your ground. Between 1820 and 1900, most states revised the "castle doctrine" to declare that a "true man"—a person going about lawful business—has "no duty to retreat" and may even strike first when there is reasonable fear of deadly attack. In 1921 in *Brown v. United States*, the Supreme Court affirmed the principle in an opinion written by Justice Oliver Wendell Holmes Jr.[9]

This legal tradition developed without reference to the 2nd Amendment. The individual right to self-defense rested on English common law, state statutes, and the 9th Amendment, which states that "the enumeration in the Constitution, of certain rights, shall not be construed to deny or disparage others retained by the people." Until the *Heller* decision of 2008, the 2nd Amendment was held to refer only to the establishment of state militias, but it was also seen as the legal expression of a revolutionary principle. In his authoritative *Commentaries on the Constitution* of 1833, Supreme Court justice

Joseph Story declared that the 2nd Amendment was "the palladium of the liberties of a republic." By guaranteeing states their own military forces, "it offers a strong moral check against the usurpations and arbitrary power of rulers." James Madison, in *Federalist Papers* No. 46, had argued that state militias would constitute a force sufficient to resist a central government that tried to "extend its power beyond due limits." This "palladium doctrine," as it became known, would become the ideological basis of the modern gun rights movement, which asserts an individual right to bear arms for the purpose of resisting an arbitrary government. Story and Madison believed that the right of resistance was vested exclusively in state governments, and that if a state were *actually* to resist "usurpations and arbitrary powers," it would not be exercising a constitutional or civil right but rather the natural "right of revolution" asserted in the Declaration of Independence. When the Southern Confederacy seceded in 1860–1861, it appealed to that right of revolution, though it also found in the palladium doctrine an implied constitutional basis for state resistance to the national government.[10]

But the government's right to suppress revolution is explicit in the Constitution (Article I, Section 8), which empowers Congress to "execute the Laws of the Union, suppress Insurrections, and repel Invasions." Behind that statute is a principle of *civil* rather than *natural* law: that a constitutional democracy has the right to defend its institutions. This was the principle on which President Abraham Lincoln raised an army to suppress the Confederate rebellion. As he phrased it, "When ballots have fairly, and constitutionally, decided, there can be no . . . appeal, back to bullets." It took a civil war, and three-quarters of a million dead, to decide the conflict between the states' rights version of the palladium doctrine and civil or constitutional law.[11]

After the war, rapid industrialization and urbanization disrupted the fundamental structures of class, family, and community. A demographic revolution saw White dominance in the South threatened by the emancipation and empowerment of Black people, while the social and cultural structures of communities outside the South were challenged by massive waves of immigration and the conflict between labor and capital. But the traditions and laws that gave broad license for personal self-defense retained their cultural authority. With federal and local policing absent or inadequate, individuals formed armed groups to fight crime or prosecute their side of racial or class conflict.[12]

The result was the period of widespread social violence, which lasted from 1866 to 1930, that I've referred to as the Age of Vigilantism. In the Jim Crow South, it took the form of lynching and racial pogroms. In the Far West, smallholding ranchers and corporate cattlemen fought range wars. Mining towns and industrial cities experienced violence between armed strikers and "detectives" or hired goons, with major fighting at Homestead Steel, the Pullman yards in Chicago, and the coalmines in Colorado, West Virginia, and "Bloody Harlan," Kentucky. In these battles the financial and political power of ruling elites usually gave the victory to "corporate gunslingers" rather than armed populists.[13]

The Age of Vigilantism established the precedents and mythologies that still shape American gun culture. Among its legacies is the special mystique that identifies the modern repeating firearm, in private hands, as the guarantor of personal "freedom" and social order.

The Cult of the Colt

Each stage of America's national development has had its totemic weapon. Daniel Boone's long rifle was the icon of frontier expansion in the early national period. The Minuteman's flintlock won our independence from Britain. Statues of Civil War soldiers on town greens North and South carry rifle muskets. The vigilante era was best symbolized by the Colt revolving pistol. As National Rifle Association (NRA) board member Jeff Cooper eloquently opined, "Just to hold one in your hand produces a feeling of kinship with our Western heritage—an appreciation of things like courage and honor and chivalry and the sanctity of a man's word." A popular slogan asserted what might be called the "Cowboy Corollary" to the Declaration of Independence: "God may have made men, but Samuel Colt made them equal." The slogan suggests a gunfight scenario, in which the affordable and efficient Colt gives every man an equal chance.[14]

Colt himself did not envision a duel between equals as the most marketable use of his invention. His early marketing was directed toward Indian-fighting outfits like the Texas Rangers and Southern planters. In one of the company's earliest promotional statements, published in 1838, Colt described the genesis of his invention this way:

> Mr. Colt happened to be near the scene of a sanguinary insurrection of negro slaves, in the Southern district of Virginia. He was startled to think against what fearful odds the white planter must ever contend, thus surrounded by a swarming population of slaves. What defense could there be in one shot, when opposed to multitudes, even though multitudes of the unarmed? The master and his family were certain to be massacred.

Was there no way, thought Mr. Colt, of enabling the planter to repose in peace? . . . The boy's ingenuity was from that moment on the alert.[15]

This was fiction, not history. The "negro insurrection" to which the passage refers is the Nat Turner rebellion of 1832, which occurred two years *after* Colt created his first repeating firearm. Colt was constructing an ideological paradigm that gave political meaning (and marketing appeal) to his invention: not as an equalizer between matched competitors but as an instrument through which a small number of men could dominate a discontented mass, or as one of Colt's admirers put it, an instrument that allowed "civilized nations" to bring peoples "low in the scale . . . under pupilary subjection."[16]

Through their use in the Plains Indian wars of 1865–1890, the Colt and its repeating-rifle analogues like the Winchester acquired symbolic significance as "the guns that won the West." But the imperial struggle between civilized nations and those "low in the scale" had its counterpart in the social conflicts between what the nineteenth century called "the enlightened classes" and the lower orders: the new and increasingly immigrant industrial proletariat and the sharecroppers or tenant farmers. These were the people who, in the words of E. L. Godkin of *The Nation,* "carry in their very blood, traditions which give universal suffrage an air of menace to many of the things which civilized men hold most dear."[17]

When such savages rise up against order, the ideological paradigm of frontier warfare suggests they be treated as Indians, as objects of coercion, not consenting citizens. And since they are numerous, coercion requires enhanced firepower for the forces of order. The newly invented machine gun eventually took the Colt revolver's principle, the "serial production of fire," to a level that would allow a small professional force to outgun a conventionally armed "mob," even if that mob was wielding Colt "equalizers." In the Colorado coal wars of 1913, National Guardsmen deployed machine guns against strikers; at Blair Mountain in 1925 it was machine guns and airplanes. But the machine gun, like the Colt revolver, was an industrial product that could be made relatively cheaply and in quantity. Thus in the 1920s the Thompson submachine gun, or "tommy gun," became the weapon of choice in the Prohibition-era warfare among rival racketeers.[18]

Put the Saint Valentine's Day Massacre together with the West Virginia coal wars, the Red Summer race riots of 1919, and two to four lynchings a week, and you have some measure of the threat to social peace posed by unregulated armaments and the culture of vigilante violence on the eve of the Great Depression.

Regulation and Reaction, 1933–1980

The New Deal's mix of responsive government and systematic regulation substantially reduced the levels of social violence. The National Firearms Acts of 1934 and 1938 required arms sellers to have a federal license, mandated the registration of machine guns and sawed-off shotguns, and prohibited gun sales to convicted felons. After 1934, regulations were enforced by the first effective national police forces, the FBI and Treasury's revenue agents. In the 1930s the NRA supported regulations limiting gangsters' access to automatic weapons. This regulatory regime limited the scope and scale of social violence through the war years and into the 1960s.[19]

After the war a newly militant civil rights movement increased friction along America's racial fault line, leading to a twenty-five-year crescendo of social violence. That would lead in turn to an escalating demand for weapons of self-defense. The violence began with mob and vigilante attacks by a revived Ku Klux Klan and White Citizens' Councils in response to demonstrations in Birmingham and Atlanta, and crested in response to the voter registration drive of 1964. Although the civil rights movement succeeded in enacting its legislative agenda at the national level, outside the South the rising expectations it engendered were frustrated by the slow pace of reform, the persistence of discrimination, poverty, and police misconduct. Starting in 1964, every summer saw that discontent produce large-scale uprisings in the urban ghettoes of the North and West, and following the 1968 assassination of Martin Luther King Jr., riots broke out in many large cities, including Washington, DC. The threat of "revolutionary" civil violence emanating from the Black community was raised by the Black Panthers, the Deacons for Defense, and other local organizations that espoused armed self-defense.[20]

The social violence of the 1960s at first increased demand for self-defense weapons and for enhanced gun control legislation, to limit the firepower available to criminals and would-be revolutionaries. Americans still accepted the presumption of the New Deal order, that government regulation was a sensible and trustworthy response to social problems. But that presumption changed in the 1970s, when fear of racial violence emanating from Black communities took a new form as Black Panther rallies and urban riots gave way to the endemic street violence of drug-trade gang wars.

The "Reagan Revolution" linked "crime in the streets" with liberal social programs. Politicians and some social scientists defined a new class of savage, the "superpredators," young people so desocialized by ghetto life that they were capable of the most monstrous acts of violence. With *Death Wish* (1974), starring Charles Bronson, Hollywood turned that fear into a new genre of crime film featuring an urban vigilante. In 1984 Bernard Goetz earned brief fame as a "subway vigilante" when he shot four Black teenagers who (he said) had threatened him. He became a hero of the Right and a poster child for advocates of armed self-defense.

In 1968, with fear of the Black Panthers top of mind, the NRA and then-governor Ronald Reagan had *supported* legislation aimed at regulating gun sales. Now, exploiting fear of crime and appealing to a new antigovernment ideology, the NRA advocated deregulation of the firearms market. By appealing to the symbolism of the American Frontier, the NRA associated itself and its products with the defense of White masculinity against the claims and critiques of 1960s racial and feminist liberals. Among the new kinds of weapons promoted by the NRA were what became known as assault rifles: weapons based on the design of the military's M16 (and successor models), adapted for civilian use. These were usable by hunters, but readily imagined as weapons of self-defense in an urban race riot.

Gun Rights and the New Right, 1985–2008

The critical link between gun rights and conservative doctrine was forged not in the Reagan administration but under Bill Clinton. Clinton's policies had combined select liberal programs like universal health care with basic elements of Reaganism: deregulation, ending "welfare as we know it," and a balanced budget (achieved through tax increases). He even co-opted Republican law-and-order rhetoric by adopting the concept of the superpredator and pushing mandatory sentencing. To counter Clinton's centrist appeal, Newt Gingrich promulgated the 1994 "Contract with America," a conservative covenant that called for demonizing "liberals" as "alien" to American cultural values and promised to end affirmative action and abortion rights, and ban tax increases of any kind.[21]

Neither the 2nd Amendment nor "gun rights" are mentioned in Gingrich's original contract. But the ideological groundwork for integrating gun rights with the conservative covenant was being laid by Grover Norquist, who characterized his economic ideas as "libertarian," though they were in effect an extreme version of Milton Friedman's neoliberal doctrine, holding that the very idea of "social responsibility" was the essence of socialism. As founder (in 1985) of Americans for Tax Reform, Norquist had helped prepare the way for the contract's "No Taxes" pledge. Now his Leave Us Alone Coalition was formed to support Gingrich's "Contract." All taxation, in Norquist's view, is essentially socialist; the government "steals money from the strong and corrupts the weak with handouts." The purpose of the "No Taxes" pledge was to radically reduce government by starving it of revenue. Norquist once quipped that he wanted a government "small enough to drown in a bathtub."[22]

But if government is to be emasculated in the name of freedom, then individuals must be empowered to defend themselves against crime and the usurpations of the state. For both purposes, individuals must be able to own and use firearms. Norquist had had little experience with or practical use for guns— he embraced them as ideological symbols. For Norquist as for Justice Joseph Story, gun rights are the "palladium of our liberties," enabling resistance to government coercion. However, whereas Story vested that right in well-regulated state militias, Norquist asserts it as an individual right, and whereas Story saw armed resistance as revolutionary opposition to a tyrannical "usurpation" of constitutional power, Norquist frames the ordinary constitutional activity of taxation as reason to reach for a gun. "If only the government and the criminals have guns," he wrote, "then you're completely at the mercy of the police and the criminals." Police and criminals are morally and politically equivalent, because police incarnate the government's coercive power to seize private property through taxation. Resistance to that power rests on the right to own and use guns. As Norquist said, "Once they get our guns, they don't have to argue with you about taxes anymore."[23]

Gun rights were not Norquist's main concern. By attaching their symbolism to his movement, he added a strong emotional charge and an air of antigovernment radicalism to the otherwise dry matter of tax policy. That antigovernment take on gun rights would become a central tenet of the New Right after passage of two major gun control laws was followed by two cases of government overkill.[24]

The attempted assassination of President Reagan in 1981 produced a movement for stricter regulations on gun sales, formulated in the Brady Bill, named for Reagan's press secretary James Brady, who was wounded in the attack. The movement was reinforced by a pair of 1989 mass shootings, in a Cleveland workplace and a Stockton, California, elementary school, in which military-style assault rifles were used. The 1980s had also seen the proliferation of a new constellation of violent White supremacist groups, including White Aryan Resistance, Christian Identity, and the Order, and antigovernment cults like Sovereign Citizens and Posse Comitatus that offered armed resistance to the collection of taxes. Veterans of the Vietnam War, traumatized and deeply disillusioned by their country's abandonment of the war and neglect of their health and economic conditions, were prominent in these movements. Their terrorist acts included murders of police officers and Treasury agents, bombings and murders at abortion clinics, and shootings of Jews, Black people, Asians, and Hispanic immigrants. Their activities became a focus of federal law enforcement under George H. W. Bush and were of great concern in Clinton's administration, consistent with its "tough on crime" policy. The Brady Bill finally passed in 1993 and established the limited background checks for gun buyers in force today. In 1994 Clinton won passage of the assault weapons ban, which barred the public sale of military-style semiautomatic rifles.[25]

Reagan and Bush supported both measures, but the NRA, Gun Owners of America, and the Second Amendment Foundation strongly opposed them. In 1991 Wayne LaPierre assumed the NRA presidency and promoted the idea that the 2nd Amendment protected the right of Americans to arm themselves to resist the government. NRA spokesman Fred Romero stated the principle quite bluntly: "The Second Amendment is there as a balance of power. It is literally a loaded gun in the hands of the people held to the heads of government."[26]

Ruby Ridge and Waco seemed to prove their contention that gun control was a form of government overreach. In August 1992 US Marshals tried to arrest antigovernment survivalist Randy Weaver for "failure to appear" on a firearms possession charge. Weaver resisted. In the siege of his Ruby Ridge homestead in Idaho, gunfire killed one marshal, Weaver's wife and fourteen-year-old son, and a friend of Weaver's. Then, in February 1993 (one month into Clinton's presidency), FBI and Bureau of Alcohol, Tobacco, and Firearms (ATF) agents raided the compound of the Branch Davidian cult outside Waco, Texas, to enforce a firearms search warrant. The Davidians killed four ATF agents and were besieged by federal officers for fifty-one days. Newly appointed attorney general Janet Reno lost patience with negotiations and ordered an attack. But cult leader David Koresh had prepared the compound for self-immolation. It exploded in flame and seventy-six men, women, and children were killed. Justice Department and congressional reviews of both incidents concluded that the government's aggressive approach had caused needless loss of life and may have been unconstitutional.

Ruby Ridge and Waco seemingly confirmed the belief that government, especially liberal government, was inherently aggressive and intrusive, and therefore that (as Norquist had suggested) the police *were* as dangerous to American freedoms as criminals. NRA advertisements showed Koresh's compound burning with the caption, "Your rights and home next?" When coupled with the revelations of the Senate Select Committee to Study Governmental Operations with Respect to Intelligence Activities in 1975 regarding secret surveillance and covert actions against American citizens by the FBI, CIA, and

NSA, Ruby Ridge and Waco lent credibility to a growing belief among Far Right conservatives that the government was really run by a shadow cadre of permanent bureaucrats acting in concert with various nefarious elements (some leftist, some Jewish or Chinese) to control the US government.[27]

According to the palladium principle, this state of affairs could be seen as justifying armed resistance to the government. Neither Norquist nor the NRA went that far, but there *were* extremists prepared to act on those principles. Sovereign Citizens groups, formed in the 1980s, continued to operate and blended with other violence-prone antigovernment and White supremacist organizations. The so-called Patriot movement, in which disillusioned veterans of Vietnam and the more recent Gulf War were prominent, organized paramilitary units or rogue "militias" that openly trained for guerrilla warfare and espoused "White identity" racialist views. The Militia of Michigan, organized in response to Waco, became notorious when two men associated with it committed the single worst act of domestic terrorism in American history. In April 1995, Timothy McVeigh and Terry Nichols bombed the Alfred P. Murrah Federal Building in Oklahoma City, killing 168 men, women, and preschool children. Their motive was revenge for Ruby Ridge and Waco.[28]

The bombing generated outrage against militias and other antigovernment groups. But Republicans and conservatives were divided. The NRA condemned McVeigh but continued its post-Waco campaign against the "jack-booted thugs" of the ATF and FBI. Ex-president Bush, disgusted by that "vicious slander," resigned his life membership. But in the newly burgeoning field of right-wing talk radio, commentators—among them G. Gordon Liddy, former FBI agent and principal in the Watergate scandal—called for the shooting of federal agents, the "mercy killing" of environmentalists and gun control advocates, and the "cleansing" of the nation's capital by armed vigilantes. Paramilitaries gained an important symbolic point when news media began to refer to them as "militias." In fact, they had no legal entitlement to the term. State and federal statutes require that a militia be organized and called into service by a state government. The new organizations were at best paramilitary clubs, at worst conspiracies bent on sedition. By tacitly accepting the groups' self-identification, the press allowed them to associate themselves with the heroes of the Frontier Myth and the Founding.[29]

By the end of Clinton's administration, the NRA had made its interpretation of gun rights an integral part of the New Right "culture war" alliance. It portrayed NRA members and conservatives generally as targets of "the political Left," which was "waging a culture war that threatens conservative values." The stakes were existential. The enemy are "not stupid, they're evil." NRA members were "the real Americans, the patriots, the ones who know what's best for the country," better than the "liberal media elite." Dissenters from this catechism were marked as RINOs (Republicans in name only) and threatened by well-funded primary challenges from the right. In the 2000 election the NRA's opposition to Al Gore's candidacy was credited with causing the Democrat's narrow defeat by George W. Bush.[30]

Since 1994, gun rights advocacy has become more radical and more closely enmeshed in conservative ideology. The drift can be traced in Republican presidential platforms. The 1996, 2000, and 2004 platforms affirmed the "basic human right" of self-defense but called for enhanced background checks. In 2008 the platform dropped support of background checks, because "gun control only penalizes law-abiding citizens." In 2012 the platform demanded federal "reciprocity" legislation, compelling each state to recognize concealed-carry permits from any other state—effectively negating stricter state licensing laws. In 2016 the platform endorsed "constitutional carry," which holds that the 2nd Amendment guarantees an absolute right to bear arms that the government has no authority to restrict.[31]

Gun rights also became the arena in which the ideological limits of the push for "deregulation" could be tested. Thus the 2005 Protection of Lawful Commerce in Arms Act forbade individuals and civil jurisdictions from suing gun makers or sellers for promoting the misuse of their product. The conservative turn against scientific understanding of problems like global warming and the COVID-19 pandemic was foreshadowed by the Dickey Amendment, a law sponsored by the NRA forbidding the Centers for Disease Control from gathering statistics on the relation of firearms and public health.[32]

Attracted by Norquist's linking of economic libertarianism, the Koch brothers acted through the American Legislative Exchange Council to advocate the passage of "stand your ground" laws by state legislatures. The version passed by Florida in 2005 expanded the *existing* "no duty to retreat" principle to permit preemptive use of deadly force to protect oneself *or* another person, *or* to prevent a forcible felony. According to Adam Winkler, professor of constitutional law at UCLA, Florida's law authorizes civilians "to pursue and confront others" and thus "encourages vigilantism. It tells people . . . carrying concealed weapons, that they can [act as] police officers." Since 2005 twenty-six states have adopted similar statutes, while eight others accept its premises in practice. In most of these states, the "no duty to retreat" principle was *already* recognized. The laws' effect is to encourage the use of firearms. A RAND Corporation study found that stand-your-ground laws "result in higher overall rates of gun homicide . . . [and] that the additional deaths . . . far surpass the documented cases of defensive gun use in the United States."[33]

Such encouragement is especially dangerous when race enters the equation. The stand-your-ground principle allows a person to use deadly force when faced with a reasonable expectation of death, serious harm, or felonious assault, to him- or herself or another. "Expectation" involves imagination, and fear of non-White people has always been rife along our racial borderlines. In adjudicating police shootings, and applying the stand-your-ground rule, judges and juries have tended to see fear of Black youths and men as justifiable grounds for killing. An analysis of FBI data by the Urban Institute found that in stand-your-ground states, White defendants are exonerated 17 percent of the time when shooting a Black person, while Black people are exonerated only 1 percent of the time when the victim is White. Women are also less likely to be successful than White men when claiming self-defense in a shooting—a sign that the tradition persists that accords White men the privilege of using force for the social control of women and racial minorities.[34]

Measures like stand your ground and constitutional carry are part of a feedback loop that maximizes the likelihood of violence. The broader the license for carrying concealed weapons, the more reasonable it is to expect your opposite in an angry encounter to be armed. The broader the license to *use* a gun (stand your ground), the more likely your opponent will shoot—unless you shoot first. When combined with our limited ability to regulate gun sales and illegal gun trafficking, the results are high rates of gun homicide and the epidemic of gun violence we see in cities like Chicago and Baltimore. This is the "ordinary violence" of American life.

But gun rights affect political discourse on a higher level.

Guns against the Government: The Palladium Principle on Steroids

During the Clinton and George W. Bush administrations, the NRA and its more radical twin, Gun Owners of America, began to lay greater stress on the palladium doctrine. The NRA's magazine, *America's First Freedom,* proclaimed that the "Second Amendment is the foundation of freedom: if gun rights are lost, all other individual rights and freedoms will soon follow."[35] That message would be broadcast by movie star Charlton Heston, who became president of the NRA in 1998. At the 2000 convention, he raised a "Daniel Boone" rifle, declaring that the government would only confiscate it from his "cold, dead hands." The gesture indelibly identified the NRA as the modern vessel of values embodied in the Myth of the Frontier. The antique gun was also a link to the Myth of the Founding—a symbolism most appropriate to the assertion that the 2nd Amendment protected the right of resistance to government.[36]

Heston brought to his role the powerful symbolism of his movie career. In the 1950s he had starred as Moses in *The Ten Commandments* and played the title role in *Ben-Hur*, which made him a cinematic embodiment of biblical heroism. After 1960 Heston's major roles distinctly presented him as a *White* hero battling racially marked enemies on a world-historical scale. In *El Cid* (1961) he defends medieval Spain against an invasion by hordes of African Muslim fanatics. In *55 Days at Peking* (1963) he is an American marine defending the Legation Quarter against hordes of fanatical Chinese "Boxers." In *Major Dundee* (1965) he leads a ragtag battalion against Apaches. In *Khartoum* (1966) he plays British general Charles Gordon, who defends the city against hordes of Muslim fanatics. In *Planet of the Apes* (1968) and *Beneath the Planet of the Apes* (1970)—films that Eric Greene has shown are allegories of American race relations in the 1960s—he is the lone "advanced" human on an ape-ruled Earth. Finally, in the *Omega Man* (1971) he is the lone White man on an Earth that has been taken over by zombies. In short, he was the perfect choice to symbolize the existential struggle of "real Americans"—White, Christian, traditional—against the "evil" Left, with its affirmative action clients. As he wrote in his 2000 book, *Courage to Be Free*, "Heaven help the God-fearing, law-abiding, Caucasian, middle-class, Protestant (or even worse *evangelical*) Christian, the Midwestern or southern (or even worse *rural*), apparently straight or admitted heterosexual gun-owning . . . average working stiff, or even worse *male* working stiff, because not only do you not count, you're a downright obstacle to social progress."[37]

Guns had to be defended because they were both a symbolic focus of the Left's cultural aggression and a real instrument by which that aggression could be repelled. "Among the cultural revisionists and contemporary thought police," Heston candidly proclaimed, "guns are the symbol of evil most often invoked against old-fashioned traditional, constitutional American culture." That last turn of phrase conflates the Constitution—a framework of laws—with cultural tradition, a set of values that exists apart from those laws, such as self-reliance, individualism, and free enterprise. Other NRA spokespeople echoed that theme and linked it to Christian nationalism: "Our Constitution and Bill of Rights are based on God's law. We must therefore defend and regard them as we would . . . the holy name of our Lord Jesus Christ." It follows that the 2nd Amendment is the palladium not only of constitutional liberties but of Christianity.[38]

Starting in the 1990s, the NRA and its allies pressed litigation to convince the Supreme Court to recognize the 2nd Amendment as the basis of an *individual* right to bear arms. That would make gun rights nearly "absolute," comparable to the freedoms of speech and religion, which can only be regulated in extreme circumstances. Culturally, it would root gun rights in the Myth of the Founding, the moral core of American republicanism, as the guarantor of all other civil liberties. Conservative "originalists" on the Supreme Court shared this understanding. In a 1997 decision, Justice Clarence Thomas suggested the Court should determine "at some future date . . . whether Justice Story was correct . . . that the right to bear arms 'has justly been considered, as the palladium of the liberties of a republic.'"[39]

Until the *District of Columbia v. Heller* decision of 2008, federal courts had found the language of the amendment and the intention of the Founders ambiguous with respect to an individual right to bear arms, apart from the requirements of militia service. An existing Washington, DC, law required weapons stored in the home to be kept unloaded, disassembled, or trigger-locked. The Court opinion, written by Justice Antonin Scalia, broke with precedent and recognized a 2nd Amendment right to the individual possession of weapons for self-defense. Although he held that the district's regulations infringed that right, Scalia did declare that the right did not license any person to possess any kind of weapon anywhere for any purpose, thus granting some leeway for governments (state or federal) to regulate gun use. However, the decision put the burden on the state to prove the necessity of regulation and explicitly validated the gun rights view of the palladium doctrine. Scalia invoked the version put forward by St. George Tucker in 1803, that *all* civil rights are threatened when individual citizens are disarmed. Justice John Paul Stevens, in his dissent, cites Justice Story's more limited version of the doctrine to argue that the right inheres in state militias, not individual citizens.

Scalia framed the decision as a return to the original text of the Constitution; but the textual language makes no reference to individual rights, and one of the chief motives for the creation of the Constitution was to protect state governments from rogue or self-constituted militias, like those responsible for Shays's Rebellion. Hence the emphasis on a "well-regulated" militia. The majority's interpretation of the law was based not on text or history but, as Reva Siegel argues in *Harvard Law Review,* on "moral and political choices disguised as historical narrative"—based, in other words, on a Myth of the Founding.[40]

The Obama Effect

From the perspective of gun rights conservatives, the election of Barack Obama signaled the return to power of all those elements they feared and detested. As a liberal he would not only increase taxation and regulation—for Norquist the hallmarks of tyranny—he would regulate firearms. Starting with gun safety and background checks, he would put America on the slippery slope to confiscation, and he would do this while advancing the interests of his race fellows at the expense of White Americans.

The modern gun rights movement had always had an implicit racial bias, most obviously in its emphasis on "crime in the streets" as the reason for buying a gun. The NRA never supported Black self-defense movements (such as the Black Panthers) as it did White militias; nor did it rise to the defense of individual Black men like Philando Castile, who was shot by a policeman after declaring truthfully that he was licensed for concealed carry. But in a 1999 presidential speech to the NRA, Charlton Heston made the racial connection explicit: "The Constitution was handed down to guide us by a bunch of wise old dead white guys who invented our country! Now some flinch when I say that. Why! It's true—they were white guys! So were most of the guys that died in Lincoln's name opposing slavery in the 1860s. So why should I be ashamed of white guys? Why is 'Hispanic Pride' or 'Black Pride' a good thing, while 'White Pride' conjures shaven heads and white hoods? . . . I'll tell you why: Cultural warfare!"[41] The "freedom" that guns protect is not simply the civil liberty of the Bill of Rights; it is what Thomas Dixon Jr. in *The Clansman* called "Civilization"—the right of White, Christian, native-born Americans to set the moral standards and cultural norms for our national life.[42]

Obama's election was the signal for an increase in vigilante rhetoric and activity. In 2009 NRA-incited fear of regulation and confiscation caused sales to jump 25 percent. They reverted to previous levels, then spiked another 50 percent a month after Obama's reelection.[43] Calls for political violence, open or implied, became applause lines at Republican rallies. Gun owners in open-carry states made a point of appearing at or near the site of Obama's appearances with assault rifles defiantly displayed. Obama received a wave of death threats, far beyond the norm for a new president. The passage of the Affordable Care Act produced a wave of angry town hall meetings, at some of which protesters appeared armed with assault rifles or carried signs calling for "2nd Amendment remedies" to overturn the act. The Tea Party, which led the anti-Obama movement in the 2010 midterms, adopted as its banner the

Gadsden flag—a Revolutionary War banner with a coiled rattlesnake on a yellow ground and the slogan, "Don't tread on me." The flag invoked the Myth of the Founding and carried the threat of armed resistance.[44]

Sarah Palin, the 2008 GOP vice-presidential nominee, posted a list of lawmakers who supported Obamacare, followed by the slogan, "Don't retreat, instead RELOAD." In 2016, when the Arkansas legislature approved the Medicaid expansion that was part of Obamacare, an opposition newsletter wrote, "The 2nd amendment means nothing unless those in power believe you would have no problem simply walking up and shooting them if they got too far out of line." Or as John Trochmann of the Militia of Montana put it, "When the ballot box doesn't work we'll switch to the cartridge box." Senator Joni Ernst of Iowa implied her willingness to engage in armed resistance to the Affordable Care Act without specifically threatening it: her right to bear arms gave her the right to defend herself, "whether it's from an intruder, or whether it's from the government."[45]

By the start of Obama's second term, the palladium doctrine had become a canon of right-wing orthodoxy. A 2013 article in the *Washington Times* by Judge Andrew Napolitano, a retired jurist, author, and frequent guest on Fox News, developed the thesis and its implications. "Government," he said, "whether voted in peacefully or thrust upon us by force—is essentially the negation of freedom," and hence a form of tyranny. "The historical reality of the Second Amendment . . . is not that it protects the right to shoot deer. It protects the right to shoot tyrants." As if this were not clear enough, he added, "It protects the right to shoot at them effectively, with the same instruments they would use upon us." Napolitano was probably thinking of military assault rifles, but by his logic the self-constituted Militia of Michigan, or any vigilante organization, would be entitled any weapon in the arsenal of the federal government.[46]

While Napolitano may have exaggerated this license to kill for political effect, a small but still considerable minority of gun owners were taking the palladium theory to heart and arming themselves for confrontation with a hostile government. Daryl Johnson, an official in Obama's Homeland Security Department, wrote a report warning that "Rightwing extremists have capitalized on the election of the first African American president"; are ramping up recruitment and mobilization efforts, especially among military veterans; and are planning for violent attacks. When the report produced a backlash from conservatives, Obama fired him, in yet another futile attempt at bipartisanship. But Johnson's warning was prescient. These organizations continued to grow, and burgeoned under the benign gaze of Obama's successor.[47]

Most of the gun purchases made during the two Obama-election "spikes" were not by first-time buyers. A study by Harvard and Northeastern Universities found that a small group of super-owners—7 million, or about 3 percent of the population—now owned nearly half the country's guns. "Each own an average of 17 guns, and some reported owning more than 100 individual firearms." Other studies confirm the trend, with varying figures. A 2004 survey found that the top 3 percent of gun owners owned about twenty-five guns each.[48]

The weapons preferred by this new wave of purchasers were not the hunter's rifle and the shopkeeper's .38 but military weapons capable of killing large numbers of people very rapidly.

America's Gun and the Return of the Vigilante

The weapon that became the symbol of the new gun rights movement is the AR15, the standard-issue rifle of the US military, adapted and sold for civilian use under various names, of which Bushmaster is the best known. Its symbolic status was enhanced by the 1994 assault weapons ban, which made this type of weapon the focus of political debate. When the ban lapsed in 2004, AR15 sales grew rapidly. The civilian version can only be sold legally as a semiautomatic weapon, but its automatic-fire capability can be recovered by the installation of components purchased separately (legally or illegally), or by the installation of a "bump stock"—a plastic device that enables a rate of fire just short of fully automatic. The rifle is built to hold large-capacity magazines of up to one hundred rounds. Even in semiautomatic mode, with its rate of fire of forty-five rounds per minute, the AR15 enables a shooter to produce a high volume of fire without having to reload. As a military rifle, the gun has a very high muzzle velocity. When combined with hollow-point bullets, each hit does extraordinary damage to the body. When used with armor-piercing bullets (legally available), it enables the user to kill a law officer wearing conventional Kevlar protective armor.[49]

The fame of the weapon was enhanced by its use in the Sandy Hook Elementary School massacre in Newtown, Connecticut, in December 2012—just weeks after Obama's reelection. Adam Lanza, a psychiatrically disturbed twenty-year-old, killed his mother with the pistol she had bought him as a present. Her friends told interviewers that she "loved her guns" and thought shooting would help Adam's mental state. Lanza then armed himself with a Bushmaster from her collection and shot his way into the Sandy Hook school, where he went from classroom to classroom shooting six- and seven-year-old first graders and their teachers, twenty-six in all. When police arrived he killed himself. The murders were extremely shocking, not only because it was the largest school shooting in US history but because of the age of the children—"our poor little babies," as one witness cried. President Obama visited the parents of the victims and was overcome by grief. There was a powerful public response calling for new gun control legislation.[50]

Senators Joe Manchin (D-WV) and Pat Toomey (R-PA), who enjoyed "A" ratings from the NRA, offered a moderate revision of background-check law to close some loopholes and forestall the demand for a new assault weapons ban. After first helping Manchin and Toomey, the NRA abruptly reversed course. It organized the defeat of the bill and doubled down on its defense of broadened access to firearms in general, and the AR15 in particular. The decision signaled its full embrace of culture-war politics, making an absolutist interpretation of gun rights a canon of the GOP's conservative catechism.[51]

In marketing the AR15 to the general public, manufacturers emphasized its military and police uses, suggesting that owning one confers on the owner the moral privilege of the soldier or cop to "protect" and "defend"—the assumption that underlies vigilantism. One Bushmaster ad reads, "Forces of opposition bow down. You are single-handedly outnumbered." Another urges the reader to "control your destiny" by buying the weapon. A competing product was marketed in 2015 as the Wilson Urban Super Sniper—which seems to deliberately invite purchase by would-be mass shooters. The AR15 thus replaced the Colt revolver as the symbolic "equalizer" between "real Americans" and their enemies, the key to ultimate victory when the culture war turns hot. Sandy Hook made the AR15 "America's gun."[52]

Vigilantism uses violence, or the threat of violence, as a means of social control, to subjugate or silence dissidents who threaten established social and value structures. In a society where guns are plentiful and easy to obtain, the liberalization of laws regulating when, where, and how a weapon may be carried enables both political murder and a vigilantism of menace. The use and abuse of state-mandated open-carry laws are a case in point. Open carry of long guns makes sense in rural areas, where a rifle or shotgun may be a tool in frequent use. But in urban and suburban communities, such laws hamstring law enforcement in the prevention of mass shootings. In the 2019 mass shooting in El Paso, "the rifle used in the shooting was purchased legally and the gunman was allowed to carry it openly. . . . A normal individual seeing that type of weapon might be alarmed, but technically it was in the realm of the law." In contrast, in New Haven, Connecticut, in 2014, a man with rifles and handguns was observed approaching a college campus. Since the state strictly limits open carry except in rural areas, police arrested the man and prevented a campus shooting.[53]

But open carry *does* allow demonstrators displaying weapons to use the threat of violence (implicit or explicit) to control public meetings and assemblies. Such displays became common during the Obama administration, when gun rights activists displayed their Bushmasters at Obama's campaign appearances, and later in the anti-Obamacare town halls.[54] Intimidation of this kind is not merely symbolic. The antigovernment ideology of the gun rights movement enabled new forms of vigilantism, in which individuals and small groups usurp or resist the government's law-enforcement function. The "community" defended by these twenty-first-century vigilantes was not the traditional town or neighborhood but a "virtual" community of like-minded activists, known through online contact. The pattern for such virtual vigilantism was set in motion by the wave of attacks on abortion clinics and providers, which began with bombings in the late 1970s and turned to murder or attempted murder in the 1990s—a total of eleven killings, more than forty bombings or arson attacks, and more than a thousand acts of clinic invasion or deadly threat. A smaller group, the "incel" movement (2010–present), is an online "community" of "involuntarily celibate" men that has perpetrated mass shootings of women.[55]

The number of violent attacks on US soil inspired by Far Right ideology has spiked, rising from a yearly average of 70 attacks in the 1990s to an average of more than 300 per year since 2001. The National Crime Victimization Survey found that between 2010 and 2014, roughly 43,000 hate crimes were committed in the United States that involved the use or threat of a gun. Since the election of Barack Obama in 2008, the number of groups espousing antigovernment ideology and White nationalism has been expanding. In 2016 the Southern Poverty Law Center counted 623, of which 165 were militias training for armed conflict. Some were formed by law enforcement officers (active and retired), including the Oath Keepers, an avowedly White supremacist group, and the Constitutional Sheriffs movement, an ideological offshoot of the racist and antigovernment Posse Comitatus and Christian Patriots of the 1970s and 1980s. The Constitutional Sheriffs movement holds that the sheriff has supreme legal authority in his county and may override state or federal law at will in order to "take back America county by county, state by state."[56]

Gun Rights and the Lost Cause

The belief that Obama's election signaled an existential threat to conservative culture led Tea Party Republicans to threaten "2nd Amendment remedies." When these failed, palladium resistance escalated into threats of secession, as if "freedom" were now a "Lost Cause."

Shortly after Obama's 2009 inauguration, Tea Party organizations in several states sponsored petition drives and legislative resolutions calling for secession. In 2014 HuffPost reported that 25 percent of Americans were open to secession as a response to their dissatisfaction with government. One Texas official called for an "amicable divorce" from the "maggots" who elected Obama. A Georgia congressman declared, "I think our enemy stands on 1600 Pennsylvania Avenue," and described President Obama and his wife, Michelle, as "uppity"—the classic Jim Crow epithet for Black people who did not know and keep to their place. Texas congressman Ron Paul, the right-wing libertarian and sometime presidential candidate, applauded Texas for defending the rights of "the people" by responding to Obama's election with a threat to secede—ignoring the fact that the American people, as the electorate, twice chose Obama by large majorities. Here again is the vigilante principle, which asserts the right of a morally privileged minority to overturn a government elected by a morally unfit majority.[57]

Secessionism was not a serious political movement but a symbolic expression of White conservatives' resentment that they, the "real Americans," were being outvoted and "subjugated" by a majority whose claim to American identity is suspect or fraudulent. A more broadly acceptable way to express that resentment was through the display of Lost Cause symbols. The civil rights movement and its aftermath of cultural "diversity" had established a new standard for racial discourse (and manners). So many of those who deployed the Confederate battle flag claimed it symbolized "heritage, not hate," honoring the South's history of adherence to traditional culture, rather than slavery or Jim Crow. Yet the heritage celebrated as Southern was exclusively *White*. The very different culture and historical experience of Black Southerners was not acknowledged, let alone honored, by heritage organizations like the Sons of Confederate Veterans and United Daughters of the Confederacy. Neither the injustice and cruelty of slavery nor the hate-mongering and violence of the Jim Crow era are ever recognized as part of that heritage. As Euan Hague wrote in his study of the neo-Confederate movement in politics, "Displaying the Confederate flag in 2015 is an indicator of a complex and reactionary politics that . . . harks back to the South's proud stand in the Civil War as a way of rallying opinion against the federal government—and against the country's changing demographic, economic, and moral character, of which Washington is often seen as the malign author." The ground theme of neo-Confederate ideology is the Lost Cause belief that an older, better, and more authentic America has been (or is being) destroyed by "activist judges" and radical academics who favor affirmative action and non-European immigration. "It is a politics of victimization, a sentiment that political correctness and anti-discrimination laws constrain right-thinking and hard-working people, and that for 150 years America has strayed from its preordained and righteous path."[58]

Two months after Hague's article appeared, on June 17, 2015, Dylann Roof, a twenty-one-year-old White supremacist, murdered nine African American worshipers at the historic Mother Emanuel African Methodist Episcopal Church in Charleston, South Carolina. Roof was a "virtual vigilante," an alienated loner who found an online a community to identify with and defend—the Council of Conservative Citizens, an offshoot of the White Citizens' Councils of the 1950s and 1960s. Its extreme racist propaganda led to its designation as a hate group by the Southern Poverty Law Center, and to the Republican National Committee's call for candidates to disassociate themselves from the organization. A number of prominent Republicans (including Senator Trent Lott, by turns the majority and minority leader) had been associated with the council, and many Mississippi officeholders remained members.[59]

What Roof found on its website were "pages on pages" detailing brutal murders and rapes of Whites by Black people, coupled with diatribes against affirmative action for empowering Black people and thus encouraging their criminal propensities. These led Roof to believe "blacks were taking over the world," along with Jews, "Hispanics," and "East Asians." The tide could not be turned unless White people undertook a racial civil war. Since Charleston had "no skinheads [and] no real KKK, no one doing anything but talking on the internet," Roof felt he had to act alone: "Well someone has to have the bravery to take it to the real world, and I guess that has to be me." He chose a target measured to his limited means but of sufficient symbolic weight to start the war: "I chose Charleston because it is most historic city in my state, and at one time had the highest ratio of blacks to Whites in the country."[60]

Roof entered the church during evening Bible study, joined the session, then pulled a pistol from a fanny pack and began deliberately shooting people. He told one victim, "I have to do it. You rape our women and you're taking over our country. And you have to go." He went from person to person to finish off his victims (though some escaped by playing dead), reloading five times. He fled, was captured shortly afterward, and proudly confessed to the killings.[61]

The symbols Roof chose to characterize his act of war were primarily those of the Confederacy. His website showed him visiting sites devoted to Confederate history, posing with Confederate battle flags, Nazi symbols, and a flag of the last White government of Rhodesia.

Like Sandy Hook, the murders at Mother Emanuel produced a wave of shock and outrage, calls for better gun control laws, and attacks on the race bigotry that motivated the massacre. The gun control pleas were dismissed out of hand. But the relation of neo-Confederate symbols to Roof's murderous acts provoked a serious and surprising response from South Carolina governor Nikki Haley. As a Southern conservative, she supported the NRA on gun rights. But she responded with empathy to the public reaction against neo-Confederate symbolism and ordered the removal of the Confederate battle flag from its place of honor on the state capitol grounds. It had been placed there in 1961 to signal the legislature's resistance to desegregation, and its symbolism had been affirmed by GOP candidates as recently as the 2008 presidential primaries. Haley understood that for Black South Carolinians, that flag was a symbol of hate and rejection; and whatever it might mean to White people, it was wrong to display it "where people gather to implement policies about the state's future."[62]

Her move had symbolic force. Haley was an Indian American and governor of the state that started the secession movement in 1860. Her action was paralleled by New Orleans mayor Mitch Landrieu, who issued a long-prepared call for the removal of Confederate and White League statues from city parks and plazas. The Southern Baptist Convention would echo her reasoning in calling for churches to cease displaying the battle flag, because to Christians of color it was a denial of welcome—what was wanted was a "sign of solidarity of the whole Body of Christ."[63]

To some it seemed there was, at the end of Obama's presidency, a possibility that America was prepared to move beyond traditional views on race, guns, and government, and the national myths that sustain those traditions: the Myths of the Frontier and the Lost Cause. The response to the Mother Emanuel shooting, and Haley's courageous gesture, might have marked a turn away from the poisonous nostalgia of the Lost Cause. The massacre of little children at Sandy Hook might have roused enough empathy for the victims to turn the tide against unlimited gun rights. The election of Barack Obama might have signaled a turning point in American history, away from the racial contempt and hatred that had disfigured our culture.

But there was also a powerful reaction against these possibilities. Traditionalists of the "heritage, not hate" school decried Haley's erasure of a heroic history, her surrender to "eastern elites" and political correctness. Of the many death threats Landrieu received, the most resonant came from Karl Oliver, a Mississippi state senator, who said that those who took down the New Orleans statues ought to be "lynched."[64] If the Mother Emanuel shooting exposed the murderous potential of White racial resentment, the often violent street protests that followed the police killings of unarmed Black men—Michael Brown in Ferguson, Missouri, in 2014 and Freddie Gray in Baltimore in 2015—revealed the potential for violence from an aggrieved Black community. Public response was split among liberals who offered moral support and offers of police reform, conservatives who decried attacks on the authority and power of the police, and city dwellers afraid of crime.

A Pew Research Center poll in 2014 had found that 30 percent of voters in *both* national parties believed the opposition was a threat to the nation's well-being. In 2016, as the next presidential election approached, the figure rose to 40 percent. Moreover, in both parties 5–15 percent of those surveyed either endorsed the idea of political violence or did not care if harm was done to members of the opposition. This was the state of opinion in a nation where gun ownership was widespread; where the gun rights movement had created a well-armed minority of super-owners who believe the 2nd Amendment entitles them to overrule with bullets a verdict reached by ballots.[65]

At a campaign rally in August 2016, shortly after he became the Republican nominee for president, Donald Trump accused his opponent, Hillary Clinton, of wanting to abolish the right to bear arms. "If she gets to pick her judges, nothing you can do, folks," he said. Then he added, "Although the Second Amendment people—maybe there is, I don't know." A man who played to the mob, and toyed with the slogans of antigovernment extremists, would become the nation's next president.[66]

16

The Trump Redemption
Make America Great Again

THE 2016 campaigns of Hillary Clinton and Donald Trump were waged on the field of culture war, pitting against each other two opposing concepts of American nationality, two ways of understanding of American history.

For the Left, America's rise to power had always been complicated by injustice: racial injustice to Native Americans, African Americans, and Mexican Americans; gender injustice to women; class injustice to workers. But the Good War and the success of the civil rights movement had made America a force for liberation in the world and engaged the government in a difficult but promising project of economic and social justice. It envisioned a "platoon movie" nationality in which every ethnic and racial community was entitled to enjoy both its particularity and its equal membership in America.

For the Right, the course of American history—the frontier with its promise of perpetual growth, the Founding that created an exceptional nation—had been disrupted by the rise of liberalism. Liberal critiques of racism, sexism, and corporate greed had discredited Americans' sense of belonging to a nation that was the exemplar of democracy, a "light unto the nations." Liberal secularism had undermined the reverence for religious belief and respect for religious institutions that had been a norm of civil life. The virtues of self-reliance had been weakened by the social welfare programs and overprotective regulations of what some called the "nanny state." Red-state America was a paradise lost, a temple polluted, a Second Lost Cause requiring a Second Redemption. That was the version of America that carried the day in 2016.

But its victory was hairsbreadth. Although Trump won the Electoral College, he lost the popular vote by a substantial margin. The election turned on the Rust Belt states of Wisconsin, Michigan, and Pennsylvania, which he won with fewer than 80,000 votes out of 13.5 million cast. The difference between victory and defeat in such an election can be attributed to poor campaign strategies and purely local anomalies, rather than a significant cultural turn. Clinton's personal unpopularity was a problem. The symbolism of Barack Obama's presidency, as the culmination of the Myth of the Movement, did not carry over to Clinton; and his achievements did not match (perhaps could not have matched) the promise of that symbolism. The party relied too heavily on the demographic growth of its "identity" constituencies, whose participation it failed to fully organize.

But the way in which Trump won did expose the changing and intensified character of culture-war politics. Though Trump's popular support fell short of a national majority, it was broader and more passionate than the typical twenty-first-century Republican electorate. He brought new voters into the GOP, White workers aggrieved by the long-term decline of wages under both establishment Republicans and business-friendly Democrats, and by the supposed favoring of non-White people by liberals' affirmative action and social welfare policies. He also won greater support from evangelicals than George W. Bush, whose personal story and authentic faith should have given his "compassionate conservatism" far more credibility than it ever earned. But Trump, noted for scandalous divorces, womanizing, and sensual indulgence, brought to his culture-war polemic an angry and aggressive tone that spoke to evangelicals' grievance for lost cultural authority.[1]

Trump identified himself as a "conservative" and embraced canonical Republican policies like tax cuts, deregulation, and the appointment of conservative justices to federal courts. However, he also ran as an insurgent against the Republican establishment, favoring protectionism over free trade and denouncing the neoconservatives' internationalism, their aggressive and alliance-based foreign policy. His Make America Great Again (MAGA) campaign succeeded because it won the hearts and minds of a supermajority of the party rank and file, who saw in him the incarnation of their values, their desires, their resentments, their identity as Americans. His most impressive achievement was leveraging the support of his emotionally committed base to parlay narrow electoral victories in the primaries and national election into a hostile takeover of the Republican Party. During his presidency he maintained his hold on 40–46 percent of the national electorate and 70–85 percent of Republicans, despite his volatile and unstable personality, the incoherence of his governing style, his open displays of racism and xenophobia, the evident self-dealing by the Trump Foundation and his family, his violations of the norms and rules of constitutional government, and his ignorance of history and current events. That high level of support even survived the electoral defeats of his party in the 2018 and 2022 midterms, and his own loss in 2020. The number of his supporters and the intensity of their commitment are significant signs of strength for the cultural worldview Trump represents. More, they mark MAGA as a distinct cultural and political movement, working through the Republican Party but with its own myths, ideology, symbols, and slogans.

Trump's relation to American national myth is complicated. As a historical illiterate, he could not effectively associate himself with figures from the mythic past, as earlier presidents had done. Rather, he created a purely personal myth of himself as an economic colossus and culture warrior. These connect with the larger patterns of national myth in two ways. He is, of course, a product of American culture, and in crafting his public persona, he consciously or unconsciously draws on the structures of thought that have shaped that culture. And because he was adept at echoing the pet resentments of his followers, Trump became a screen onto which they could project their preferred myths of America—the Myth of the Frontier for antienvironmentalists, or the Founding for gun rights fundamentalists, or the Lost Cause for ethnonationalists and cultural conservatives repelled by secular liberalism.

Since the 1960s, the Republican Party has represented what CNN's Ronald Brownstein calls a "coalition of restoration." The cultural trends inaugurated by the upheavals of the 1960s indicated that traditional values were in decline, as popular culture embodied the values of sexual, gender, and racial "liberation," and younger generations became increasingly secular or religiously unaffiliated. Gender and racial hierarchies were undone as women and minorities assumed a greater share of power in the workplace and in political, educational, cultural, and corporate hierarchies. For religious conservatives, these cultural shifts challenged their belief that America had been, and should remain, a "Christian nation." Culturally conservative segments of the urban White working class, whose value system was based on Christian faith and the gender dynamics of the traditional family structure, also turned against liberal Democrats to support Ronald Reagan and the two Bushes.[2]

These groups were alarmed by demographic trends indicating that by 2040 a majority of Americans would be non-White, making this a "majority-minority" nation. When Bill Clinton was elected in 1992, White people represented 87 percent of the electorate; by 2020 it was 67 percent. The racial contempt endemic to American culture was politicized by recognition that the interests of non-White minorities were favored by liberals, an alliance that seemed to promise a permanent liberal majority in the future. The election of Barack Obama appeared to mark the arrival of that new majority.[3]

Trump's MAGA campaign crystallized conservatives' sense of disempowerment and gave it historical resonance by framing it as an updating of the Lost Cause Myth. America had fallen from greatness because it had been taken over by liberal elites, who ignored the economic concerns of businessmen; favored women, gay people, and racial minorities and immigrants; and disdained the cultural values of "real Americans." To restore our golden age, real Americans must "take our country back"—from Hillary Clinton, the first woman nominated for president by a major party, but also from Barack Obama, the Black president whose father was African, an intellectual of elegant mien and manners. Trump promised to rebuild American manufacturing, increasing employment for the Rust Belt working class; protect Social Security and Medicare; and oppose the free-trade agreements and "corporate welfare" that had enriched the few and impoverished the many. But he had a limited and largely performative set of ideas for making these populist policies operative. In office, he would allow the Republican establishment to pass another massive tax cut favoring the rich and evade his own call for a jobs-creating infrastructure program.

The central theme of his campaign was strident opposition to immigration, to social welfare programs (especially Obamacare), and to the ideology of "political correctness" through which liberals "controlled" the culture. For his followers this was proof of his sympathy with their plight. Political correctness was responsible for "affirmative action" and its concomitant of open immigration, which undermined America's traditional social hierarchies and depressed wages for the White working class. Above all, political correctness mocked and humiliated "real Americans" by sneering at their racial manners. As Ezra Klein observed, "The simplest way to activate someone's identity is to threaten it. . . . The experience of losing status—and being told your loss of status is part of society's march to justice—is itself radicalizing." Trump would voice their outrage in ways that liberated his followers to openly express racial and ethnic antipathies they had mostly been constrained to keep private or express in coded ways.[4]

The MAGA movement would draw its structuring narrative from deeply rooted historical sources, especially the Myth of the Lost Cause. Although Trump lacked the historical knowledge to deliberately invoke its symbolism, his campaign would follow its paradigm by calling for a political insurrection against a regime that subordinated "real" Americans to liberal elites and non-White people, linking that call for racial Redemption with a pseudo-populist program that in the end would favor capital over labor.

MAGA's roots go deep in conservative political culture, from the ethno-nationalism and isolationism of the "America First" movement to Pat Buchanan's culture-war populism. But it was Trump whose candidacy crystallized an ideological tendency into a coherent political movement, offering a pseudo-populist platform as a way of adapting conservatism to the breakdown of the neoliberal order. He would give MAGA's political mythology the most essential organizing principles: an identifiable (and familiar) set of enemies and a single dominant hero—Trump himself. The identification of the MAGA movement with Trump became so intense that it threatened to reduce the movement to a cult of personality. We therefore need to look first at how Trump transformed himself into the hero of a political mythology.

Trump: From Magnate to MAGA Hero

Donald Trump brought to public life a grandiose persona, a large appetite for prestige and power, and a relatively small set of strongly held beliefs about the decline of America's economy and international prestige. During his long career as real estate mogul and TV celebrity, the idea of running for political office occasionally attracted him; but it was the resentment he felt at the election of Obama that triggered his impulse to act.

Trump would create a political persona, and learn to read the passions of his potential constituents, through the call-and-response of engagement with conservative media personalities and audiences. He sought interviews and did call-in appearances on the major outlets in the growing universe of conservative media, becoming a favorite interviewee on Fox News, particularly with commentators Sean Hannity and Bill O'Reilly, and on right-wing radio broadcasts like *The Rush Limbaugh Show*.

The way his dialogue with these audiences developed is observable in his addresses to the Conservative Political Action Conference (CPAC) in 2011 and 2013. Trump began with a perfunctory sketch of his ideas: "Just very briefly, I'm pro-life. [*cheers, applause*] I'm against gun control. [*applause*] . . . I will fight to end Obamacare and replace it [*cheers, applause*]— . . . I will not be raising taxes."[5] But his real theme was the menace of foreign competition—and the unique powers that would enable him to turn the tide:

> Over the years, I've participated in many battles and have really almost come out very, very victorious every single time. . . . I have fairly but intelligently earned many billions of dollars which in a sense was both a scorecard and acknowledgment of my abilities.

The enthusiastic response to those words surprised Trump, because he broke into his next sentence with "a little different, right? A little different than what you've been hearing." Trump had shocked but also gratified his audience by a display of unapologetic strength. He pushed the point: "So I have a reputation for telling it like it is, I'm known for my candor." And the theme of his candor was his superiority as a businessman and a *warrior:*

> I've beaten many people and companies and I've won many wars. . . . I am also well acquainted with winning, and that's what this country needs now: winning. [*cheers, applause*] . . . I've had a lot of great victories, and I may be willing to put that to work [as president].[6]

He would apply to politics the methods he had used in business: rhetorical extravagance, unscrupulous manipulation, hard bargaining, unapologetic vindictiveness, the will to dominate or destroy competitors, and pretensions to grandeur. All presidential campaigns focus on the candidate's personality, but Trump's was unique in its unabashed grandiosity. American life had become "a disaster," he blared, and "only I can fix it." It was not simply that Trump knew how the country might learn to win again—he was the *only* man who could do it. "No one knows the system better than me. That's why only I can fix it. . . . I have made billions of dollars in business making deals—now I'm going to make our country rich again." If the people would invest their faith in him, they would profit like those who invested in his companies. He would enlarge that theme during his campaign: "We're going to win so much. We're going to win at trade, we're going to win at the border. We're going to win so much, you're going to be so sick and tired of winning, you're going to come to me and go . . . 'Please, Mr. President, we beg you sir, we don't want to win anymore. It's too much. It's not fair to everybody else.' And I'm going to say 'I'm sorry, but we're going to keep winning, winning, winning, We're going to make America great again.'"[7] Exactly what "we" will win is not specified. Workers aggrieved by decades of stagnant wages were free to assume he would fill their wallets, though he had no plan to do so. What CPAC's response taught Trump was that the vague idea of "making America great again" allowed conservatives to see him as their man, and that conservatives responded positively to his "warrior" persona.

Trump lacked the knowledge that would have enabled him to enlarge his warrior persona by historical association. When he did invoke history, the results were ludicrous. Abraham Lincoln, he said, was "a great president," but "most people don't even know he was a Republican. Right? Does anyone know? A lot of people don't know that. We have to build that up a little more." The only history that matters to him is his own, and he refers continually to his petty triumphs in real estate and reality TV, and even his sexual conquests, as if these were the triumphs of a "warrior."[8] In American popular culture, the only heroes who inhabit such a self-referential world frame are the superheroes of comic books and their associated film genres.

Trump's identification with such figures is suggested by his speech to CPAC in 2013, in which he criticized a $400 million Republican ad campaign that ridiculed Obama by portraying him as a superhero. "I said what a great ad Obama did, and then I said, oh, wow, that was done by the Republicans." The truth, he said, is that "people want a superhero" for president: someone with supreme wisdom and irresistible power who can (and must) fix everything himself. That was, and would be, Trump's preferred way of framing himself. It was a ground of resentment that Obama got the title before he did.[9]

No superhero has the historical resonance of the frontiersman, the cowboy, or the World War II soldier. Superman and Batman have been around since the late 1930s and 1940s, but the modern superhero pantheon came out of Marvel Comics in the 1970s and 1980s, and provided the characters for a movie genre and set of franchises developed in the 1990s. The genre offers a menu of radically different types: some pure of heart and clear of mind like Superman, others troubled by teenage angst like Spiderman, or by darker impulses like the Marvel-influenced Dark Knight version of Batman. They are lone geniuses, bizarre in origin, manners, or appearance. Originally all were White men whose wisdom and special powers are either unknown to or unappreciated by the masses, disbelieved and disapproved by officialdom and the cultural elite of journalism and the universities. Some are also fabulously rich (Batman, Iron Man, the Punisher).

They do not live in a real-world frame of reference, like the heroes of the Western, the war film, and the cop movie. Rather, they inhabit a pseudo- or "alt-history," a time and place artificially constructed to display their superiority. And that is precisely Trump's understanding of the proper use of history: as a stage for the display of his powers. In the superhero world, as in Trump's, *all* conflicts are existential; and such threats can only be met by extraordinary men wielding extraordinary powers. Moreover, the superheroes' enemies are usually some combination of perverse intellectual genius and a distortion of body that makes them, visually, freaks or monsters, an alien race—nice analogies for the liberal cultural elite and their clients.[10]

It is tempting to liken Trump to the Joker: a psychologically damaged entertainer whose hatreds lift him to supervillain status. But a closer analogy is Marvel Comics' Punisher, an urban vigilante who fights the city's plague of "crime in the streets" by killing muggers and rapists. These were the years that saw Trump achieve notoriety for his ads calling for the death penalty against the teenagers charged in the 1989 Central Park jogger case: "I . . . hate these muggers and murderers. . . . I am looking to punish them." The Punisher is revenge driven and sees no reason to be politically correct in his methods. He represents the dark side of superhero fantasy, where the hero's actions make him very much like a villain.[11]

By refusing to be constrained by conventional morality, dark heroes like the Punisher demonstrate a seemingly limitless power. The directors of Trump's re-election campaign built on that idea, deliberately associating Trump with su-pervillains like Darth Vader from *Star Wars* or Thanos and Dr. Evil from the Marvel Comics universe. As *Politico*'s Derek Robinson observed, "It's not so much that Trump, *et. al.* actively identify as 'villains,' but that the behavior that makes one a 'villain' in fiction—deceit, wanton rule-breaking, a willful disregard for collateral damage—is, in real life, more likely to get one branded a 'winner.' . . . Rule-bound critics across the ideological spectrum can cry and moan as much as they want; the Trump administration has the power, is win-ning and will do as it pleases." QAnon conspiracists would adopt the Punisher figure to symbolize Trump's role in their fantasy of apocalyptic retribution against the "Satanist" liberal elite.[12]

For CNN's Michael D'Antonio, "the dark charisma, which [Trump] displays so vividly at his rallies, is his superpower. It thrills rank-and-file Trump voters who listen intently for the signals that cue their chanting and cheers." The keys to that dark charisma are *resentment* and *egotism*. What most rouses his audi-ences' enthusiasm and glee are his displays of self-righteous rage, his vaunting boasts of superiority to all who oppose them, demonstrating a pride and self-assurance his hearers can only aspire to. His own rich store of resentments, both cultural and personal, puts him in harmony with their mood of grievance. And his egotism—really, his narcissism—gave him the self-belief that enabled him to work his will on the campaign and then the government, over the objections, criticisms, or opposition of so many of his advisers.

Narcissism as a Superpower

Narcissism is an enduring pattern of behavior marked by obsessive concentration on the self, an excessive demand for admiration, and a lack of compassion or empathy. When a narcissist's need for approbation is not met, he or she will typi-cally feel deeply aggrieved, even persecuted. Narcissists then seek power so they can control those around them, including family and colleagues. But no degree of domination ever completely satisfies their need, so the power drive becomes authoritarian and (in the absence of empathy) verges on the sociopathic.[13]

Trump exhibits all of these traits. His Twitter feeds and speeches are rife with variations on "only I can fix it": "I am the only one who can Make America Great Again. . . . Nobody else can do it." "Nobody will protect our Nation like Donald J. Trump." "5000 ISIS fighters have infiltrated Europe. . . . I TOLD YOU SO! I alone can fix this problem!" "I am going to save Social Security without any cuts. I know where to get the money from. Nobody else does." His followers read that self-assurance as a mark of authenticity—he truly believes even the most extravagant claims he makes about himself.[14]

Grandiosity has always been central to the Trump brand. As a real estate developer, he promoted the construction of large, ornate buildings for the luxury trade, with his name in gilded all-caps over the entryways. He represented even his bankruptcies as triumphant displays of his power to evade consequences that would bring down an ordinary man. Such distortions can be dismissed as the pretenses of a pitchman concealing the defects in his product. But with Trump they reflect an inability or refusal to see his actions in relation to reality, especially when moral judgment is called for. Questioned about his evasion of military service during the Vietnam War, Trump claimed he had "sacrificed" for his country by building a successful business, making billions and employing thousands. He added the still more outrageous claim that the sexual promiscuity for which he was notorious was also a form of heroism: avoiding STDs in his hyperactive sex life was "my personal Vietnam. . . . It's pretty dangerous out there. . . . It's like Vietnam. . . . I feel like a very great and brave soldier."[15]

Trump's thought pattern is a closed circle. Ideas, people, and events either connect to him personally or have no importance. The over-the-top exaggeration with which he asserts his superior intelligence, expertise, and power reflects a fear that that circle may be breached, and it is a transparent register of his insecurity. A series of postings on Twitter in 2018 demonstrate this: "My I.Q. is one of the highest—and you all know it!" "My two greatest assets have been mental stability and being, like, really smart." The fact that he won his presidential bid on his first try "would qualify as not smart, but genius . . . and a very stable genius at that!"[16]

The effectiveness of Trump's speaking style owes a good deal to his narcissism. In press interviews, rally speeches, and Twitter rants, he follows no logic but his own free associations. In 2019 Trump was asked about his failure to get funding for his "beautiful" border wall, and the separation of parents and children crossing the border. He begins with a statement contrary to fact (implying he has actually *built* his wall), tosses a word salad, and ends with a "definition" that reads like a joke: "Now until I got the wall built, I got Mexico because we're not allowed, very simply, we have loopholes and they're called loopholes for a reason, because they're loopholes." His speeches are full of banalities endlessly repeated—how great he is, how he'll increase jobs or destroy North Korea "like you've never seen before," he's going to fix it, fake news, Crooked Hillary—but his followers respond with enthusiasm.[17]

For his followers, his unstructured style is another demonstration of authenticity. His opponents and critics find this astonishing, given the demonstrable fact that he continually lies, distorts, and misrepresents himself and whatever the subject at hand may be. For Trump himself, his own beliefs and needs are the measure of truth. He simply ignores exposures and refutations—they have no meaning for him and carry no weight with his followers, for whom the deeper truth of what he symbolizes matters more than facts. Faced with photographic proof that his inaugural audience was much smaller than Obama's, Trump's spokesperson simply asserted as "alternative facts" that Trump's crowd was much larger.

That denial of reality was similar to the infamous assertion of George W. Bush's administration that America is "an empire now, and when we act, we create our own reality." Trump's falsification (in this case) was less consequential, because symbolism was at stake, not substantive policy. But that distinction defines a central characteristic of Trump's culture-war politics: that symbolism and performance are a viable substitute for policy. The idea, attributed to celebrity venture capitalist Peter Thiel, is that "his supporters take him seriously, but not literally." Yet when Trump speaks or tweets, his performance has a political purpose. Ultimately his followers *are* being asked to take him literally—to believe and act on his assertion that the deep state is conspiring against him, or that Democrats are destroying American civilization.[18]

While Trump could not check the exposure of his lies and misrepresentations, he was able to weaken or neuter its effect by identifying journalists as either the unwitting tools or the malevolent agents of the politically correct elite. As he told CBS reporter Lesley Stahl in a May 2018 interview, "I do it to discredit you all and demean you all so when you write negative stories about me, no one will believe you. . . . So, put that in your head for a minute." By declaring mainstream media "enemies of the people," he licensed his followers to disbelieve any stories that might undercut or refute his assertions, exaggerations, misrepresentations, and outright lies—an average of sixteen per day during the first three years of his administration according to Glenn Kessler, who kept a running count in the *Washington Post*. Without a commonly accepted source of disinterested information, it has been extraordinarily difficult for Trump's opponents, whether inside or outside his party, to escape the closed circle of his rhetoric in order to oppose him with rational arguments.[19]

Trump succeeded in making himself the mirror of his supporters because he himself is a man of numerous passionately held resentments, many of which they share. As candidate and president, he made Twitter his primary mode of public communication, a medium that requires brief statements, informal and unedited, made as if spontaneously in response to some event or communication. It allowed him to speak directly to tens of millions of followers who were pleased and flattered at having unmediated access to the president of the United States. The effect was to build a powerful personal identification between Trump and his followers, and draw them into the closed circle of his obsessions and resentments.[20]

He offers his followers the same compensation for elite disrespect that he claims for himself, returning contempt for disdain. "I hate it," he says. "These people. I look at them, I say, 'That's elite?'" Then "I" becomes "we," and the true elite becomes his own class of successful businesspeople: "We got more money, we got more brains, we got better houses, apartments, we got nicer boats, we're smarter than they are, and they say they're elite? We're the elite." And then he shifts from "we" to "you," so his middle-income audience will understand he includes them: "You're the elite. We're the elite." Culture-war politics is a battle over symbols. By speaking spitefully and contemptuously of liberal elites, immigrants, and non-White people, by effectively performing his disdain for their symbols, Trump was winning their war.[21]

Presidential candidates succeed by making themselves the personification of their supporters' idealized self-image. Trump's success on that score would last beyond the campaign, to make his presidency something very close to a cult of personality—a tendency supported by the way he extended his personal control over the personnel of his administration and the offices of government. He would come to expect a cultlike loyalty from his public, such that no matter what he might do—"even shooting someone on Fifth Avenue," as he said during his campaign—they would still adore him. The most extreme expression of this tendency can be found in the QAnon movement: an online conspiracy that claims that the deep state is controlled by a hidden ring of liberal Satanist pedophiles who drink the blood of sacrificed child victims and that Trump is masterminding a secret operation that will lead to their exposure and extermination. The conspiracy theory obviously mimics the anti-Semitic "blood libel" that has been leveled against Jews since the Middle Ages, with Trump in the role of Christian avenger. Cultists have discussed, and some have actually performed, acts of violence in support of their movement.[22]

But the Trump cult of personality is not restricted to the lunatic fringe. His projection of himself as hero of a new Lost Cause and Redemption had special potency for the Christian Right, especially White evangelical Protestants. His wrathful and unceasing attacks on liberal "political correctness" gave voice to their fear and resentment of the dominance of secular values in American culture, especially in popular culture and the educational system. He also promised them a real restoration of power by pledging to fill the courts with conservative judges opposed to abortion and friendly to demands for extending the concept of "religious liberty" to embrace exceptions to antidiscrimination and affirmative action laws, as well as to bans on religious displays in public venues. Not even the scandalous revelation of Trump's sexual behavior on the *Access Hollywood* tapes could shake that belief. As Michael Gerson (himself an evangelical Protestant) wrote in the *Washington Post:* "Forty-seven percent of WEPs [White evangelical Protestants] say that Trump's behavior makes no difference to their support. Thirty-one percent say there is almost nothing that Trump could do to forfeit their approval. This is preemptive permission for any violation of the moral law or the constitutional order. It is not support; it is obeisance. . . . The result has properly been called cultlike." When Trump claimed, "I am the chosen one," God's agent for realizing American greatness, it might seem he was guilty of pride, if not blasphemy. But evangelical Protestant and Secretary of Energy Rick Perry affirmed that yes, indeed, Trump is "the chosen one," as did a number of noted preachers. Their theological rationales differed. For some he was indeed a Christlike figure; for others he was a modern-day Cyrus, the Persian king who allowed the Jews to return to Israel after the Babylonian exile. The net effect was to make Trump a central figure in the evangelical eschatology and an emerging Christian nationalist movement.[23]

Strategy and Instinct: Bannon and Trump

Trump's success in making himself the incarnation of the MAGA movement makes it hard to separate the development of MAGA ideology from his own psychological predilections. Despite his disdain for intellectuals, Trump did seek out conservative ideologues for advice on how to frame the political content of his presidential campaign. He was first tutored in right-wing politics by Republican political consultant Sam Nunberg and Roger Stone, who had

been a political consultant, lobbyist, and "dirty tricks" specialist for conservative campaigns and causes since the Nixon presidency. Knowing Trump's dis-
taste for reading, they recommended he listen to Mark Levin, whose radio show
they considered the best guide to the grievances of grassroots conservatives.
Levin was a former Department of Justice lawyer who also had a show on
Fox News and edited the *Conservative Review*. He supported the Tea Party
insurgency against mainstream Republicans and promoted extremist conspiracy theories: that Obamacare created "death panels" to deny care to the
elderly; that Obama was working with the Muslim Brotherhood to destroy
Israel. Immigration was a pet issue—he opposed any policy opening "a path
to citizenship."[24]

Steve Bannon, then the Breitbart News editor, set these grievances in a larger
ideological structure. Trump met Bannon at CPAC in 2010, and they conferred
often thereafter. Bannon would become a major adviser during the campaign
and chief strategist when Trump took office. He had developed an ideological
program dubbed America First, echoing the isolationist and chauvinistic movement opposing US entry to World War II. Bannon's version combined a populist critique of corporate power and free trade with elements of the extreme
Right's antigovernment ideology—specifically the desire to "take down the administrative state" or "deep state," the permanent bureaucracy in charge of
regulation, social services, law enforcement, and foreign policy. America First
was also an ethnonationalist ideology that sought to restore the primacy of
"real Americans" and their conservative Christian culture, and opposed non-
European immigration.[25]

Whereas Trump had little knowledge of history, Bannon had read widely in
American and world history and political theory, and had developed his own
ethnonationalist approach to restructuring the nation-states of America and
Europe. Bannon's views were informed and supplemented by those of other
Far Right thinkers and opinion makers, all of whom either contributed to Breitbart or ran their own blogs. Curtis Yarvin seconded Bannon's obsession with
the administrative state. Michael Anton was a businessman and intellectual who
saw American diversity as a weakness and who had written speeches for Rupert Murdoch, Condoleezza Rice, and other notable conservatives. He would
gain national attention after publishing an editorial in September 2016, "The
Flight 93 Election," comparing Hillary Clinton to the terrorist hijackers of 9/11
and suggesting her victory would pose an existential threat to the nation unless
voters "rushed the cockpit" in a last-ditch effort to stop the hijacking. Stephen
Miller, a Breitbart contributor and press aide to Jeff Sessions, the first senator
to endorse Trump, was obsessed with the "Great Replacement": the idea that

liberals promoted immigration and affirmative action to "replace" native-born White people with non-White people and immigrants who would inevitably vote for Democrats. In 2015 Miller joined Trump's campaign as speechwriter and adviser, and he would play both roles in the administration.[26]

Trump is at pains to deny racist beliefs, grandly proclaiming, "I am the least racist person there is." Since he is not disposed to systematic theorization, it is not clear whether he consciously embraces the racialist thought of Bannon and Miller, or of the White supremacists whose messages he sometimes retweets.[27] It may make sense to think of Trump's racism as the thoughtless and tacit presumption of racial superiority, a generalized contempt for non-White people that admits of individual exceptions, and a formulaic advocacy of "fair play." These are attitudes so broadly shared as to seem normative in many if not most White communities. Trump was "business friends" with several African American celebrities, including Oprah Winfrey, boxing promoter Don King, and the hip-hop star Kanye West, who were part of the entertainment world in which he lived and who showed him proper respect. But in referring to ordinary African Americans, Latinos, and Jews, he typically invokes the racial and ethnic stereotypes common in American society: Black people and Latinos are "poor" and live in neighborhoods "unfit for human beings"; immigrants come from "shithole countries"; Jews are "the best negotiators." The normative quality of his racism reflects, and enables him to represent, the way most of his followers feel about race.[28]

Trump came of age politically in the 1970s and 1980s, when New York was plagued by blighted ghetto neighborhoods, rising crime rates, the flight of White residents and businesses, and the threat of bankruptcy due in part to high welfare costs. This was the period in which Charles Bronson's *Death Wish* movies celebrated the heroism of a White urban vigilante and Bernhard Goetz won fame as "the Subway Vigilante" for shooting four young Black men.

In April 1989 a young White woman jogging in Central Park was brutally assaulted and raped. Five young men between the ages of fourteen and sixteen, three African Americans and two Latinos, were arrested, charged, and convicted of the crime. It would later be proved that their confessions were coerced and the crime was actually committed by a single adult male. However, the five had earlier been arrested for harassing people in the park, which newspapers (following police suggestions) called "wilding" and described (falsely) as a quasi-tribal custom in their lawless communities.

Trump seized headlines by placing full-page ads in the *New York Times, New York Post, New York Daily News,* and *Newsday* demanding that New York reinstate the death penalty and apply it to the Central Park Five. Like the Gilded

Age apologists for Indian extermination, Trump blamed devotion to "civil liberties" and sympathy for the underdog for undermining "respect for authority, the fear of retribution by the courts, society and the police." The arc of his rhetoric follows the classic paradigm of the Jim Crow call to lynching: civilization is threatened by a race of savages whose signature crime is the atrocious rape of a White woman. Not only must the perpetrators be killed, their punishment must serve to cow their tribesmen into subjugation. "I want to hate these muggers and murderers. They should be forced to suffer and, when they kill, they should be executed for their crimes [to] serve as examples." This is not to say that Trump is consciously mimicking James K. Vardaman and Benjamin Tillman. Rather, his response follows the logic or habitual thought pattern of American hate speech. "I hate these people," he said, "and let's all hate these people because maybe hate is what we need if we're gonna get something done."[29]

Barack Obama was a different matter: a liberal intellectual, one of those who had always treated Trump with contempt. Trump would try to delegitimize Obama by promoting the "birther" theory, that Obama was born in Kenya (and therefore ineligible to serve as president) and espoused a "Kenyan socialism" that was also anti-White. Later, he would bring a more overtly violent animus to his campaign against former first lady and secretary of state Hillary Clinton, Obama's chosen successor. As a powerful woman she was, in Trump's terms, as much a violation of category as a Black man in the White House. His campaign deployed various forms of misogyny against her. Trump put his emphasis on delegitimizing her as "Crooked Hillary"—and the convention that nominated him chanted, "Lock her up!"[30]

The Call to Violence

Trump's campaign needed an enemy as a foil for his own projection of "heroism," to justify his anger and demand for strong, even extreme action. War or the threat of war is a president's surest reliance for mobilizing public support, but Trump had no interest in the Global War on Terror. What he wanted was a moral equivalent of war, capable of stirring the rage of his supporters without entailing military action. Immigration from Mexico and Central America across the southern border had been almost uncontrollable for a generation, and attempts at reform had foundered on the conflicting demands of business interests seeking cheap labor, immigrant communities seeking to reunite families, and restrictionists who feared the crime and cultural influence associated with these communities. In cities and towns with high concentrations of Latino immigrants—a category that included major cities like Los Angeles and small towns built around agricultural or food-processing businesses—the growing presence of non-English speakers was both a daily annoyance and a serious problem for public schooling. As Steven Simon and Jonathan Stevenson observed, "To the extent [Trump] needs a war to mobilize his base, he has one on the southern border, to which he has deployed military units, and where the enemy cannot shoot back."[31]

Trump weaponized popular anxieties over immigration by framing the issue as a form of "savage war," identifying the enemy as non-White and primitive. His 2016 campaign began with a headline-grabbing attack on Mexican immigrants, people not like "you": "When Mexico sends its people, they're not sending their best. They're not sending you. They're not sending you. They're sending people that have lots of problems. . . . They're bringing drugs. They're bringing crime. They're rapists. And some, I assume, are good people."[32] But in Trump's rhetoric the racial opposition intrinsic to the Frontier Myth is masked by fear of intrusion by cultural aliens. The enduring effects of the civil rights movement had made explicitly racist statements by public figures unacceptable, but racialized xenophobia had acquired a degree of respectability through the symbolism of the Global War on Terror and the best-selling books by Samuel Huntington and Peter Brimelow that warned of the dire effects of Latino and non-White immigration. Trump's promotion of birtherism concealed an essentially racist message behind the screen of xenophobia.[33]

He would link the immigrant onslaught to a supposed economic war being waged by the Mexican state: through its exploitation of NAFTA, that Brown nation was humiliating White America: "They're laughing at us, at our stupidity." He would characterize the arrival of economic migrants and refugees as an "invasion" riding in "caravans" supported by Mexico; by sinister liberal activists like the Jewish billionaire philanthropist George Soros, an iconic bogeyman of the Far Right; and of course by politically correct Democrats. In a tweet he echoed Stephen Miller's "replacement" theory: "Democrats . . . want illegal immigrants, no matter how bad they may be, to pour into and infest our Country, like MS-13. They can't win on their terrible policies, so they view them as potential voters!" Trump's racialist attacks on Mexican and Latin American immigrants were also linked with the traditional tropes of anti-Black racism. He continued the traditional litany of "crime in the streets," declaring that "the overwhelming amount of violent crime in our major cities is committed by blacks and hispanics" and that in 81 percent of homicides, Whites were killed by Black people—a fabrication promoted by White supremacist websites like the Conservative Citizens Council, the same one cited by mass murderer Dylann Roof. Trump would make the same linkage of race, economic warfare, and rape in diatribes against China: "We can't continue to allow China to rape our country. And that's what they're doing."[34]

His other enemy of choice was Islam, but he preferred to frame this conflict as a war against the domestic menace of Islamic immigrants rather than military conflict overseas. As with immigration, welfare, and crime, the Islamic threat to American institutions arose from political correctness. Democrats refused to properly name the problem. In his speech to the 2016 Republican National Convention, Trump enthusiast Rudy Giuliani screamed it: "ISLAMIC EXTREMIST TERRORISM!!! . . . The vast majority of Americans today do not feel safe. . . . They fear for their children. They fear for themselves."[35]

Giuliani was sounding the central theme of the Trump campaign and the MAGA movement—that politically correct Democrats were sponsoring the "Great Replacement," which would devour and destroy "real Americans" and "their country." Giuliani: "There's—there's—there's no next election! This is it! There's no more time for us left to revive our great country!" That was why Michael Anton had called this the "Flight 93 election." It was the apocalypse Trump himself invoked on the Christian Broadcasting Network: "I think this is the last election the Republicans have a chance of winning because you are going to have people flowing across the border. . . . If we don't win this election . . . you'll never see another Republican."[36]

The rhetoric and symbolism of the campaign went beyond the standard-issue demonization of immigrants, to imagine a larger scope for violence as the necessary means to regenerating American greatness. At his rallies Trump would urge the audience to "beat the crap out of" protesters. In these politically correct days, "we've become weak" because "nobody wants to hurt each other anymore." He told a Las Vegas rally, "In the good old days this [protest] doesn't happen because they used to treat them very, very rough . . . and when they protested once, they would not do it again so easily." They'd be "carried out on a stretcher." Although his immediate targets were demonstrators who had crashed his rally, his call resonated with an audience that had been frightened by the violence that had attended the protests in Ferguson, Missouri, and Baltimore, Maryland, in response to the police killings of Michael Brown and Freddie Gray. Just as the liberals were soft on Islam, they coddled those (such as supporters of the Black Lives Matter movement) who criticized police for using excessive force.

Trump not only praised his brawlers, he wanted to join them: "I'd like to punch him in the face," he said at one rally, and at another, "I don't know if I'll do the fighting myself or if other people will." A rallier who took Trump at his word and punched a protester in the face said afterward, "Next time we see him, we might have to kill him." The National Rifle Association transformed suggestion into advocacy, calling for MAGA people to "strike back against protests by the left 'with the clenched fist of truth.'" A March 2018 study in the *American Journal of Epidemiology* found that, in cities where Trump rallies were held, violent assaults increased 12 percent on the day of the rally.[37]

The passions aroused by these rallies are akin to those of a lynch mob—or rather, they are the "moral equivalent" of a lynch mob in the same way Trump's obsession with the border is his "moral equivalent" of war. He delighted when his supporters responded to his tag line "Crooked Hillary" with chants of, "Lock her up!" And then, at an August 2016 rally, he made the direct connection to the vigilante code of the gun rights movement: "If she gets to pick her judges, nothing you can do, folks. . . . Although the Second Amendment people— maybe there is, I don't know."[38]

That same call to violence—sometimes rhetorical or symbolic, sometimes literal—would carry over to his way of governing. The "Flight 93 election" demanded a Flight 93 administration.

17

Trump in the White House

The President as Insurgent

BEFORE IT was anything else, and beyond the particulars of its policies, Make America Great Again was a narrative, a modern version of the Lost Cause and Redemption Myth. The original myth justified and provided a scenario for undoing the Second Founding—the Reconstruction programs intended to establish civil equality in the post–Civil War South. Following that paradigm, MAGA seeks to overthrow the Second Reconstruction of the 1960s. The supposed purpose of the Second Reconstruction, which was enacted by a liberal elite ruling through the media, the universities, and the administrative state, was to make the state a social welfare agency. Its "militant secularism" turned state and culture against traditional Christian values. Its "political correctness" and critical revisions of American history devalued the institutions and traditions that had given "real Americans" (White, native-born Christians) their cultural authority and control of economic, cultural, and political hierarchies.

In the MAGA narrative, Donald Trump figures as the uniquely gifted hero who alone has the power to redeem "real Americans" from political correctness, economic stagnation, onerous government regulations, and the demographic effects of the Great Replacement. Trump and his party would control all three branches of government for the first two years of his administration; and though Republicans would lose the House in 2018, they increased their majorities in the Senate and on the Supreme Court. Nevertheless, Trump would represent himself as a beleaguered insurgent, fighting his own government bureaucracy (the "deep state") as well as his ideological enemies. The paradox is succinctly captured in a *New York Times* headline about his response to the coronavirus pandemic: "Trump, Head of Government, Leans into Anti-government Message."[1]

In embracing the role as Redeemer of a new Lost Cause, Trump adopted the pose of the insurgent or vigilante, the righteous warrior who usurps the functions of legal government. He would treat the conduct of office as a series of "wars," variously directed against foreign foes and longtime allies, against the legacy of Barack Obama, against environmentalists, against immigrants and civil rights demonstrators—but also against his own appointed cabinet officers, the military high command, the Department of Justice, the FBI and CIA, and ultimately his own vice president and the US Congress.

Foreign Policy: War by Other Means

The basis of Trump's strength as a candidate and party leader was his ability to combine a conservative culture-war agenda with the promise of a populist economic program to restore America's manufacturing industries and high-wage jobs. He had defeated his Republican challengers and Democrat Hillary Clinton by tying them to free-trade policies and pacts like NAFTA and the Trans-Pacific Partnership, but neither he nor his advisers had developed a genuine alternative to the trickle-down economics of neoliberalism. As a result he was unable to persuade a Republican Congress to pass his job-creating infrastructure bill, and the 2017 Tax Reform Act followed the neoliberal script. It radically lowered corporate taxes and gave long-term benefits to the investing class, but only temporary relief to middle-class taxpayers. The editors of *The Economist,* who favored the business-friendly aspects of the act, saw the latter feature as a "ticking time-bomb" promising future political strife.[2]

Trump had a better understanding of the role trade policy played in the decline of the American working class. Opposition to free-trade pacts like NAFTA and the Trans-Pacific Partnership enjoyed broad public support, and as president he had wide authority to use tariff policy to create more favorable conditions for American manufacturers. Professional economists differed in their analysis of the role played by free-trade pacts in the development of the American economy, and they regarded tariff policy as at best a blunt instrument for dealing with a complex problem. What Trump saw most clearly was how to frame tariff policy as an element in the culture wars. From the ideological perspective of "America First," every political or economic contest is a battle for national self-preservation. If trade is war by other means (to paraphrase Carl von Clausewitz), then trading "partners" are actually enemies to be defeated. Criticized for having been bluffed out of northern Syria by Turkish president Recep Tayyip Erdoğan, Trump responded with extravagant threats. "As I have stated strongly before," he wrote on Twitter, "if Turkey does anything that I, in my great and unmatched wisdom, consider to be off limits, I will totally destroy and obliterate the Economy of Turkey (I've done before!)." Whereas Obama criticized NATO allies for lagging defense spending, Trump treated them as enemies on trade and free-riders on defense, and suggested the United States might withdraw from NATO or refuse to honor its treaty obligations.[3]

Trump's foreign policy was not a radical departure from that in effect when he took office. Obama had broken with the interventionist agenda of neoconservative foreign policy and begun the drawdown of troops from Iraq and Afghanistan. What was radical in Trump's foreign policy was the violence of his rhetoric and his insistence on personal rule. His policy statements were often self-contradictory, swinging between rhetorical belligerence and operational confusion. His America First program called for withdrawing US forces from "endless wars" in Iraq, Afghanistan, and Syria, but his deep hostility to Iran, and determination to destroy ISIS, led at first to deepening military engagement in the region. His trade-war enmities, nationalist ideology, and evident desire for some kind of rapprochement with Russia made him aggressively hostile to NATO and the European Union; but he also wanted NATO to join him in checking Iranian influence in the Middle East. He wanted to pressure North Korea to abandon its nuclear weapons through sanctions supported by regional powers, but he antagonized Japan and South Korea by attacking them on trade and questioning mutual defense treaties.

At a now-notorious meeting on July 20, 2017, Secretary of State Rex Tillerson, Defense Secretary James Mattis, and National Economic Council chief Gary Cohn prepared a comprehensive briefing on the basics of the world political situation. As reported by the *New York Times,* Trump "went ballistic" and angrily insulted the diplomatic and military personnel present: "You're all losers," he said. "You don't know how to win anymore. . . . I wouldn't go to war with you people. . . . You're a bunch of dopes and babies." Anonymous informants from within the administration told reporters that "senior US officials— including his former secretaries of state and defense, two national security advisers and his longest-serving chief of staff"—became convinced that the president was "delusional" and "posed a danger to . . . national security."[4]

What he wanted from advisers was not just loyalty but subservience. In four years Trump ran through five chiefs of staff, several secretaries of defense, and six chiefs of Homeland Security. By the end of his administration, most of the major cabinet posts were held by acting secretaries and deputies who were never confirmed by the Senate. When Chief of Staff John Kelly—a distinguished professional soldier with long experience in the Middle East—criticized Trump's impulsive decision to pull out of northern Syria and abandon our Kurdish allies, Press Secretary Stephanie Grisham dismissed him as "totally unequipped to handle the genius of our great President."[5] These are the crude hero-worshiping terms typically used by and for leaders like North Korea's "Dear Leader" Kim Jung Un or Chairman Mao Zedong and Joseph Stalin in the heyday of their personality cults. When morning news host Joe Scarborough asked him who he talks to about foreign policy, Trump answered, "I'm speaking with myself, number one, because I have a very good brain and I've said a lot of things. . . . I know what I'm doing and I listen to a lot of people, I talk to a lot of people and at the appropriate time I'll tell you who the people are. . . . [But] my primary consultant is myself, and I have, you know, I have a good instinct for this stuff."[6]

Trump rejected or ignored the analyses and policy recommendations presented to him by the intelligence services and Defense Department whenever these disagreed with his personal beliefs, firing or forcing the retirement of several secretaries of defense, directors of national intelligence, and heads of the National Security Council (NSC), CIA, and FBI. Asked by a Fox News commentator whether he was concerned by the number of unfilled positions in the State Department, he answered, "Let me tell you, the one that matters is me. . . . I'm the only one that matters, because when it comes to it, that's what the policy is going to be. You've seen that, you've seen it strongly." He carried out Steve Bannon's program of deconstructing the administrative state by indulging his personal peeves.[7]

Trump was less concerned with a policy's real-world effect than with how it reflected on his public persona. Although he decried Obama's "weakness" in refusing to use force against terrorism, he avoided military intervention in the face of numerous provocations by Iran, Syria, and North Korea, and moved precipitously to draw down US forces in Syria. To avoid the imputation of softness, he turned marginal issues into symbolic wars, declaring immigrant "caravans" from Central America an invasion and threatening to treat Mexico and Guatemala as enemies if they weren't blocked.

Behind the nominal enemies in Trump's various "wars" was Trump's superhero nemesis, Barack Obama. According to Fernando Cutz, who was for a time senior adviser to NSC chairman H. R. McMaster, "President Trump has fixated on President Obama, and . . . views President Obama as the metric he has to beat." When he attacked the "Iran nuclear deal" or undid an EPA regulation, he saw himself retroactively defeating Obama. This not only gave Trump the personal revenge his vindictive nature requires, it fulfilled his followers' wish for the symbolic undoing of liberalism.[8]

Trump withdrew the United States from Obama's two most significant diplomatic agreements: the Paris Climate Agreement of 2015, in which the United States used its influence to create an international alliance to address climate change; and the "Iran nuclear deal" or joint plan signed by all the Great Powers in 2015, which barred Iran from developing nuclear weapons for fifteen years and established a highly intrusive inspection regime. Trump portrayed the Paris Agreement as Obama's surrender to the "Chinese hoax" of global warming, a stab in the back to American industries. The joint plan was simply "the Worst Deal Ever," the result of Obama's "weakness" and insufficient love of America. In abrogating these agreements, Trump broke with US allies and an international consensus. He also went against the emphatic advice of his chief national security advisers, including Secretary of State Tillerson, Defense Secretary Mattis, NSC director H. R. McMaster, and Chief of Staff John Kelly—all of whom eventually resigned or were fired.

The sudden abandonment in October 2019 of our Kurdish allies in the battle against the ISIS terrorist "caliphate" in Syria was seen by most analysts as a historic blunder that imperiled the campaign against ISIS and America's reputation as a reliable ally. Trump declared his decision a brilliant strategic move that proved he was far more expert in dealing with the Middle East than his predecessor:

> Because President Obama—it was a mess. And I was told and you were told, and everybody told it would be years before you ever did what I did in about a month and a half after I started. I went over to Iraq, I met with our generals, . . . and it was done within a month and a half.

The victory belonged to him personally:

> I'm the one that did the capturing. I'm the one that knows more about it than you people or the—or the fake pundits. . . . As you know, most of the ISIS fighters that we captured—"we." We. Not Obama. We. We captured them. Me.[9]

The War on the Environment

The most prolonged assault on Obama's legacy was the rollback of policies related to the environment. Trump had declared his intention to withdraw from the Paris Climate Agreement, and he kept his word as soon as he was legally able to do so. The withdrawal could not take effect until January 1, 2020, but Trump's declaration was enough to undo years of diplomatic effort, led by the United States, to convince the major economic powers to accept the accord in principle.

Trump systematically worked to undo Obama-era regulations related to global warming, air and water pollution, and environmental preservation and to replace administrative and professional personnel with climate change deniers and representatives of the fossil fuel and pollution-producing industries. The capstone of this policy was an effort to corrupt the National Climate Assessment, the scientific analysis produced by the EPA, our government's most important contribution to the international movement to deal with climate change. The attempt was thwarted by the professional staff of the US Global Change Research Program, which outsmarted Trump's political appointees. As one former member of the program said, "Thank God they didn't know how to run a government. . . . It could have been a lot worse."[10]

The rationale for Trump's antienvironmentalism is the classic appeal of the Frontier Myth: the secret to perpetual economic growth is the discovery and unregulated exploitation of natural resources. Speaking to shale oil producers in August 2019, Trump declared, "That's our gold. . . . That's gold underneath our feet"—a phrase reminiscent of George Armstrong Custer's 1874 claim to have found "gold among the roots of the grass" in the Black Hills.[11]

But there was no bonanza to be found in the energy sector. Fracking was dirty and expensive, and oil was in abundant supply, driving down prices so that fracking operations were shutting down even before the coronavirus pandemic caused a drop in demand. Trump pursued the expansion of fossil fuel exploitation as if that were an end in itself. In May 2020 the administration used the coronavirus crisis as an excuse to reduce the royalties paid for oil and gas drilling on federal lands, at the same time that it retroactively billed solar and wind energy companies for rents unpaid during the crisis.

Despite the nation's achievement of energy independence under George W. Bush and Obama, Trump favored an American military presence in the Middle East if its purpose was to "take the oil." The needs of allies were of no interest or value. "If you remember," he said, "I didn't want to go into Iraq. . . . But I always said, 'If you're going in, keep the oil.' Same thing here [in Syria]: Keep the oil. We want to keep the oil. . . . We're keeping the oil. We have the oil. The oil is secure. . . . We left troops behind, only for the oil." When asked about US involvement in the Libyan crisis following the fall of Muammar al-Qaddafi, he said, "I'm only interested in Libya if we take the oil. If we don't take the oil, I'm not interested."[12]

   To win his energy war, Trump had to defeat the classic enemies of the fron-tiersman, Indigenous peoples and the wilderness, on one hand, and an "elite" power structure, on the other. His drive to open government land to fossil fuel production, and generally repeal regulations limiting real estate development and industrial pollution, was opposed by Native American tribes as well as gov-ernment scientists. Trump pressed hard on the two great symbolic battles of the Bush and Obama administrations: opening the Arctic National Wildlife Refuge to oil drilling and completing the Keystone XL pipeline. Acting through the EPA or the Department of Energy, he moved to eliminate regulations to limit the leakage of methane, one of the most harmful greenhouse gases, from wellheads, pipelines, and processing plants. He proposed the repeal of Obama's Clean Power Plan, which required new power plants to capture carbon dioxide emissions and limited the discharge of poisonous heavy metals like arsenic, lead, and mercury from coal-fired plants into local streams and aquifers. Trump also opposed regulations controlling the disposal or emission of other toxic chemi-cals, including chlorpyrifos, an agricultural pesticide that causes significant neural damage, and hydrofluorocarbons, long recognized as causing depletion of earth's ozone layer—as if it were a matter of principle to maximize pollu-tion in order to defeat "leftist environmentalism."

   The ideological animus in this newly militant antienvironmentalism goes be-yond the canonical Republican opposition to regulations affecting corporate balance sheets. Trump pursued his "war" even when business interests favored the environmentalist position. When automobile manufacturers (for economic reasons) agreed to follow California's fuel economy standards, rather than the EPA's less stringent rule, Trump attacked the automakers as dupes of "political correctness" and threatened them with antitrust action. As William K. Reilly, EPA head in the George W. Bush administration, said, "I don't think there is any precedent for a major industry to say, 'We are prepared to have a stronger regulation,' and to have the White House say, 'No, we know better.'"[13]

   Trump's rhetoric steeled his followers to ignore whatever facts science or jour-nalistic inquiry might produce. The war against environmentalism was first of all a struggle against the politically correct elite; and since scientists belong to that elite, science must be denied or discredited. Trump's first line of attack was simply to denounce climate science as a hoax—in fact a "Chinese hoax," in which treacherous scientific elites were allied with a foreign enemy. But even among Republicans, the weight of scientific argument and the impact of ex-treme weather events was being felt. So his second and more effective approach was to set guidelines making it more difficult for government scientists to use, or even cite in reports, the full range of climate information produced by scientists in the United States and elsewhere, which would prevent the government from taking public health into account when setting environmental regulations. As a final measure, the administration adopted policies designed to drive scientists away from service with federal departments like the EPA, Agriculture, and the Bureau of Land Management. When a small "antigovernment" vigilante group organized by Ammon Bundy subjected Bureau of Land Management officials to a campaign of vilification and staged a six-week armed occupation of the offices of the Malheur National Wildlife Refuge, Trump pardoned the perpetrators, moved the bureau's offices out of Washington (to force resignations by its staff), and appointed as director a man hostile to its very existence. The net effect was to retard or reverse US efforts to resist global warming, dropping the nation from twenty-fourth place to forty-third in the Environmental Performance Index during the Trump presidency.[14]

For Trump, environmental policy is primarily a battlefield for his ideological war against liberal elites, government experts, and Obama's legacy. To the extent that it has an economic rationale, it privileges incremental improvements in profit margins over the demands of public health. Environmental pollution has the cruelest effects on those at the bottom of the social and economic scale; but these are the people whose demands for public aid MAGA dismisses with extreme prejudice. In fact, MAGA ideology approves of cruelty as a sign of strength and hard-headed realism.

Cruelty, Toughness, and Strength

Cruelty, as a rhetorical device and a deliberate policy, is essential to Trump's performance as culture warrior. As Adam Serwer observed in *The Atlantic*, "President Trump and his supporters find community by rejoicing in the suffering of those they hate and fear. . . . The cruelty of the Trump administration's policies, and the ritual rhetorical flaying of his targets before his supporters, are intimately connected. . . . It is not just that the perpetrators of this cruelty enjoy it; it is that they enjoy it with one another. Their shared laughter at the suffering of others is an adhesive that binds them to one another, and to Trump." Conservative Peter Wehner makes a similar point: "[In] their ferocious defense of the president, Trump supporters are signaling that decency is a form of weakness, that cruelty is a welcome and highly effective political weapon. . . . They see the dehumanization of others as a form of entertainment."[15] Public acceptance of rhetorical cruelty sets the frame in which cruel policies can be enacted, executed, and justified. The most striking example of this took place in the summer of 2018, when immigration officials began separating very young children from families who crossed the border illegally. The policy was instituted by Attorney General Jeff Sessions, who famously said, "We need to take away children." Hundreds of children, including infants, were separated and then lost in the bureaucratic system for weeks and months. In some cases, parents were deported to their country of origin while their children remained in US custody, making reunification difficult or impossible. Strong public protests called attention to the inhumanity of these and other, similar policies. But such cruelty has a point. By it the administration shows the strength of its determination to fight the border war and demonstrates that the enemy is not entitled to normal human sympathy.[16]

Examples can be multiplied. The administration adopted work-requirement rules that deprived hundreds of thousands of people of access to food stamps— on the eve of Christmas 2019. According to the Georgetown University Center for Children and Families, the number of children without health insurance rose by more than 400,000 in the first two years of the Trump administration, as a result of the administration's war on Obamacare. At the height of the coronavirus pandemic, Trump refused to extend the Affordable Care Act registration period for people who lacked or had lost health insurance and ordered the Justice Department to continue pressing a Supreme Court suit to declare the act unconstitutional—although all of his health advisers, and even Attorney General William Barr, advised against these measures.[17]

While cruelty is Trump's favored way of displaying dominance, his occasional displays of "kindness" are, in a way, even more disturbing—take his response to the catastrophic effects of Hurricane Maria on Puerto Rico, where he tossed rolls of paper towels out into the crowd like a Roman emperor tossing coins to the plebeians. There is a similar pairing of cruelty with mercy in the wave of pardons he issued during his last days in office. He pardoned people who committed crimes in support of his election, while at the same time accelerating the executions of federal prisoners. The authoritarian's signature is his absolute power to slay or to spare.

These displays of arbitrary cruelty and equally arbitrary mercy serve the MAGA narrative in several ways. They identify enemies and degrade them, either by demonstrating that they are undeserving of human sympathy or by treating them as abject supplicants for charity. These are expressions of that contempt which is the core of racism. Those who perpetrate these acts of cruelty and contemptuous charity affirm their belief that *they* are (in Trump's terms) the winners, the racial elite, a people entitled by heritage and licensed by the summons of their hero-president to subjugate the losers and the lesser breeds.

Race and Replacement: The Battle of Charlottesville

Trump's attraction to vigilante violence and the xenophobic racism that informed his thinking were exposed by his response to the Unite the Right rally in Charlottesville, Virginia, in August 2017. The event grew out of the ongoing struggle in Southern communities over the public display of symbols associated with the Confederacy, such as the Southern battle flag and statues of Confederate generals. To most White Southerners, these symbolized their cultural heritage and celebrated the defense of the Southern homeland. To most Black Southerners, and increasing numbers of White people with more liberal sympathies, the flags and statues were symbols of enslavement and especially of Jim Crow. Most Confederate monuments had in fact been installed during the Jim Crow era, to symbolize the reestablishment of White supremacy and affirm the Lost Cause Myth as the canonical understanding of Southern history. A study by the National Academy of Sciences in 2021 found that counties that had larger numbers of Confederate memorials had also had a higher than average number of lynchings.[18]

Mitch Landrieu, the Democratic mayor of New Orleans, was one of the first officials to make removal of Confederate statues a civic project, because they alienated and demeaned Black citizens. The gesture fed into a broader movement that had developed in response to the murder of Black worshipers at Charleston's Mother Emanuel Church in 2015 by White supremacist Dylann Roof, whose online presence was swathed in Confederate symbolism. Republican governor Nikki Haley removed the Confederate battle flag from the South Carolina capitol grounds, and other cities across the South began considering or undertaking the removal of statues and changing street and school names that honored Confederate generals and political leaders. These included Birmingham and Demopolis, Alabama; Little Rock, Arkansas; Hillsborough, North Carolina; Memphis, Tennessee; and Austin, Texas.[19]

These efforts were strenuously opposed by people and organizations devoted to glorifying Southern heritage. In most cases, opposition took the form of a rhetorical defense of the soldiers who fought and the families that suffered for the Confederacy. But opposition sometimes took a more virulent form, echoing the language of the Jim Crow era. Mississippi state legislator Karl Oliver called for New Orleans officials to be "lynched" for removing monuments to the Confederacy. Georgia legislator Jason Spencer told a Black colleague that if she persisted in demanding the removal of Confederate monuments, she and people like her "will go missing in the Okefenokee [Swamp]. . . . Don't say I didn't warn you."[20]

In March 2016 the Charlottesville City Council began public consideration of a proposal to remove the statue of Robert E. Lee from the city park named for the general. Charlottesville is home to the University of Virginia and several major Southern heritage sites, especially the estates of James Madison and Thomas Jefferson. Although removing the statue had majority support on the council and in town, there was also substantial opposition, led by a resident named Jason Kessler. The controversy drew the attention of neo-Confederate organizations outside Charlottesville, who staged demonstrations in Lee Park in the spring of 2017.

In May Richard Spencer, leader of the National Policy Institute and advocate of the formation of an exclusively White American "ethno-state," began organizing marches in Charlottesville, mobilizing his and other White supremacist groups. Spencer was focused on the idea that a Jewish-led conspiracy, masterminded by philanthropist George Soros, was promoting immigration to "replace" real Americans with non-White foreigners. "Replacement" theory had sympathetic hearers in the Trump White House, as Spencer knew. He and Stephen Miller had begun their activism while they were students at Duke University, and Miller was now an important speechwriter and adviser for President Trump. He and Steve Bannon also believed in the "replacement" conspiracy theory, although they blamed liberals in general rather than Jews in particular.[21]

Kessler and Spencer were encouraged by the support their demonstrations received from like-minded organizations on alt-right websites and from prominent spokesmen like former Ku Klux Klan Grand Wizard David Duke. Their initial marches were outnumbered by sometimes disorderly counterprotesters, but that was good news. One goal of the racist Right is to provoke civil violence, rising to a race war that would end in the establishment of a White government. Primed by these skirmishes, Kessler and Spencer called for a "Unite the Right" rally in Charlottesville.

The major demonstration, for which permits had been obtained, was scheduled for Saturday, August 12, 2017. However, on Friday night some 250 demonstrators staged an unpermitted torchlit march through the University of Virginia's campus, the presumptive center of "liberal elitism" in the city, chanting, "Jews will not replace us." Among the organizations participating were Spencer's National Policy Institute, the neo-Nazi Traditionalist Workers Party, Vanguard America and the National Socialist Movement, several chapters of the Ku Klux Klan, the neo-Confederate League of the South and Identity Dixie, and the White-identity groups Identity Evropa and Rise Above Movement. They were joined by armed men representing various unnamed "militias" or paramilitaries, for whom 2nd Amendment fundamentalism was linked with strong antigovernment and White identity politics.

The following day saw confrontations in Charlottesville's city center between Unite the Right marchers and counterdemonstrators. Some of the latter were identified with Antifa, an organization willing to use violence to promote an anarchist agenda, and legally carried concealed weapons. Yet the potential for violence was most clearly expressed by the marchers, who were heavily armed and openly displayed their weapons. There were a number of violent clashes and assaults on counterprotesters, some involving weapons. But the signature act of violence was the murder of one counterdemonstrator by a White supremacist who drove his car at speed into a crowd.[22]

Media coverage was substantial and included dramatic scenes of the torchlit march and the chanting of "Jews will not replace us," a Black man assaulted by six White ralliers, and the car ramming. The reaction from Democrats was predictably strong. Republican reaction was strangely mixed. Establishment Republicans like Senators John McCain and Marco Rubio and former presidential candidate Mitt Romney joined in condemning the ralliers' violence and racism. Moderates in Trump's inner circle (notably including his daughter Ivanka and her husband, Jared Kushner, who are Jewish) and the establishment "grown-ups" who hoped to channel Trump's impulses along more conventional lines (such as Chief of Staff John Kelly, NSC director H. R. McMaster, and economic adviser Gary Cohn) wanted Trump to quickly offer the expected condemnation. Coming out against Klansmen and neo-Nazis seemed an easy way of refuting accusations that Trump himself was a racist. But this approach was problematic for Bannon and Miller, and those like them who believed it was necessary to attach ethnonationalists and White supremacists to Trump's cause—albeit as junior partners. So while Trump decried the "violence," he said that they were "his people" at the rally and hesitated to offer a stronger response—a hesitation that began to seem significant, as some Unite the Right figures, notably former Klansman David Duke, claimed that the fighting in Charlottesville was a "turning point" for a White identity movement whose aim was to "fulfill the promises of Donald Trump."[23]

When Trump did speak the day after the rally, he struck an awkward balance between these competing claims. He began by saying, "We condemn in the strongest possible terms this egregious display of hatred, bigotry and violence on many sides." He paused for emphasis and then repeated, "On many sides." When reporters challenged him, Trump defended Unite the Right as a vindication of Southern heritage and equated General Lee with George Washington and Thomas Jefferson: "George Washington was a slave-owner. . . . Are we going to take down statues of George Washington? How 'bout Thomas Jefferson? What do you think of Thomas Jefferson? You like him? Ok, good. Are we going to take down the statue because he was a major slave-owner?"[24] Although the point is crudely made, Trump was right in seeing the taking down of statues as the logical consequence of the critical revisionism that had reshaped American history writing since the 1960s. Most revisionists draw distinctions between Lee, who led Confederate troops in rebellion against the United States, and the two Founders who established the national union. But the fact remains that drawing attention to the moral compromises made by the Founders to accommodate slaveholding does diminish their glory.

Conservative historians and public intellectuals had mounted periodic challenges to such revisionist historiography since the controversy over the National History Standards in the 1990s. Trump would give their critique a populist audience by connecting it to his base's resentment of political correctness. He would condemn "the neo-Nazis or the white nationalists," but he would defend those ("And the press has treated them absolutely unfairly") who sought to prevent liberal revisionists from "changing history . . . changing culture" by privileging discussion of the nation's wrongs and ignoring its glories. He dismissed the press's response to the rally as proof of conscious bias against him and his people: "I think there's blame on both sides. And I have no doubt about it. And you don't have any doubt about it either. And, and if you reported it accurately, you would say it."[25]

Trump's response to Charlottesville was widely criticized by the mainstream press, and by some conservative publications. Some thought that this criticism had been taken seriously when, on August 18, Steve Bannon was fired as chief strategist. Bannon declared that Trump's failure to wholeheartedly support Unite the Right had doomed his populist program: "The Trump presidency that we fought for, and won, is over. We still have a huge movement, and we will make something of this Trump presidency. But that presidency is over." In fact the move to fire Bannon began weeks earlier, driven by in-house resentment of his personal influence. Stephen Miller remained as the central figure shaping Trump's rhetoric and policy on race and immigration, and Miller's ethnonationalism was as strong as Bannon's.[26]

Bannon was mistaken in thinking Trump's "both sides" rhetoric would discourage his followers. Some faulted his response, but the movement in general was encouraged, especially the Proud Boys. Although some were openly White supremacist, the Proud Boys stressed "Western chauvinism." One of their early leaders was Enrique Tarrio, who is of Afro-Cuban descent, and the membership included some Latinos and Asians.[27]

After Charlottesville, White supremacist and ethnonationalist propaganda was circulated with greater frequency in communities experiencing racial and ethnic tension and on college campuses, through various online forums but also through leafleting campaigns. According to the FBI, the number of hate crimes reached a sixteen-year high in 2018. The change was most dramatic in communities that had recently hosted Trump rallies. Latinos and Jews were targeted with greater frequency than Muslims and Arab Americans, the preferred targets in the previous decade. A larger percentage of these crimes (61 percent) involved violence against people, as opposed to destruction or defacement of property. The three worst mass murders of Jews and Latinos occurred in 2018 and 2019: at Pittsburgh's Tree of Life synagogue in 2018, at the Poway synagogue in California in 2019, and at the El Paso marketplace in 2019. These were the groups specifically targeted by Unite the Right. The Tree of Life shooter declared that he hated Jews because they were promoting Latino immigration to "replace" White Americans.[28]

Minoritarian Populism and Authoritarianism

Intrinsic to the MAGA narrative is the belief that the rising numbers of Black and Brown people in the electorate will entrench a liberal Democratic Party in power. Trump made the racial issue overt and linked it to the replacement theory: because of "people flowing across the border," he warned, "if we don't win this election . . . you'll never see another Republican." But it was the association of demographic change with the triumph of secular liberalism that made 2016 a "Flight 93" election, especially for MAGA's evangelical constituency, which was constitutionally disposed to apocalyptic thinking.[29]

But race was only the most inflammatory element in the emergence of an explicitly antidemocratic ideology among cultural conservatives. As the anti-Trump conservative David Frum wrote in 2018, "If conservatives become convinced that they cannot win democratically, they will not abandon conservatism. They will reject democracy." The traditional devices of gerrymandering and voter suppression at the state level took on new importance, guided by operatives from the national party and advisers from the American Legislative Exchange Council. That most of those disenfranchised by these policies were people of color highlights the resemblance between the Republican repudiation of civil rights liberalism and the overthrow of Reconstruction by devotees of the original Lost Cause. Of equal importance was the Right's desire to halt the liberal drift of American culture—a concern that echoes the Old South's resistance to the liberal values of "free society" and its wish to defend and later to restore structures of gender, class, and racial subordination. The basis of this newly reformulated ideology is an exclusive definition of American nationality, buttressed (unlike the reactionary politics of the 1960s) by an all-powerful president.[30]

During the era defined by the Vietnam War, the excesses of Lyndon Johnson's and Richard Nixon's "imperial presidencies" (as historian Arthur Schlesinger Jr. called them) had led to the legislation of additional strictures on the president's war-making powers. Neoconservatives thought such reforms went too far, and worked to strengthen presidential authority, especially (but not exclusively) in foreign affairs. They espoused the "unitary executive" interpretation of Article II of the Constitution, which defines the powers of the president. The theory holds that the president possesses *all* executive power, which cannot be limited by Congress except by impeachment. George W. Bush invoked this principle in his extensive use of "signing statements," which asserted his Article II power to modify the execution of a law, and in his sanctioning of "extraordinary measures" in the Global War on Terror.

Trump's second attorney general, William Barr, was a distinguished conservative lawyer who became a leading advocate of the strong unitary executive during his service in the Reagan and George H. W. Bush administrations. As Bush's attorney general he had refused to forward prosecutions of officials involved in the illegalities of the Iran-Contra affair, because the president's "absolute" power of action in foreign policy could not be constrained by Congress. He would make the same case in defending the use of torture during the Global War on Terror. He brought himself to Trump's attention by denying the legitimacy of Special Counsel Robert Mueller's investigation of Russian interference in Trump's 2016 campaign. After the 2018 midterms, Trump appointed Barr to replace Jeff Sessions as attorney general.

In Barr, Trump had found an official who combined personal loyalty and ideological commitment with an understanding of institutional power. Where Bannon's approach to "deconstructing" the administrative state was chaotic, Barr's was strategic. He would, of course, support the deregulation that was a staple of every Republican administration and freeze or roll back enforcement of civil rights and antidiscrimination laws. But he would also work to permanently alter the balance of institutional power by using a newly created "Schedule F," which reclassified hundreds of civil service jobs as political appointments. Barr also set about abolishing, "hollowing out," or delegitimizing those agencies and departments whose powers were independent of presidential authority, including the Federal Reserve, Bureau of Land Management, National Labor Relations Board, and Consumer Financial Protection Bureau.[31]

His targets were agencies empowered to investigate members of the executive branch and use judicial proceedings to thwart executive decisions and policies—the Justice Department and the FBI, over which Barr had direct control. He used his position to discredit the findings of Mueller's investigation into misconduct by Trump's campaign, and the FBI's decision to open the investigation. He also intervened in cases of personal interest to Trump, blocking or weakening prosecution of campaign aides and supporters like Paul Manafort and Michael Flynn, and trying to block the parole of ex-Trump fixer Michael Cohen, who was writing a tell-all book.[32]

Barr's maximalist conception of the presidency was not just a legal theory. He saw that kind of presidency as a necessary weapon in the war against secularism and liberalism, which (he believed) were destroying America's Christian culture. In an article in the *Catholic Lawyer* in 1995 and a 2019 speech at Notre Dame University, Barr condemned liberal programs not on the usual conservative "small government" grounds but on religious principles. The belief that government should "play an ever greater role in addressing social problems in our society," he argued, is the fundamental problem. "We live in an increasingly militant, secular age," he explained, dominated by liberals who "marginalize or 'ghettoize' orthodox religion." In so doing they have undermined the only adequate basis for moral behavior and judgment. "Traditional Judeo-Christian doctrine maintains that there is a transcendent moral order with objective standards of right and wrong," Barr insisted, which flows from "the divine will by which the whole of creation is ordered."[33]

Liberals have fatally disrupted this order, he explained, by eliminating laws that enforce traditional moral and gender norms. "Decades ago, we saw the barriers to divorce eliminated. Twenty years ago, we saw the laws against abortion swept away. Today, we are seeing the constant chipping away at laws designed to restrain sexual immorality, obscenity, or euthanasia." Equally dangerous are laws "that seek to ratify, or put on an equal plane, conduct that previously was considered immoral." The District of Columbia's attempt to compel Georgetown University (a Jesuit institution) "to treat homosexual activist groups like any other student group" is the "kind of law [that] dissolves any form of moral consensus in society." Barr's views were widely shared among movement conservatives. Dennis Prager, writing in *National Review*, condemned the Supreme Court's legalization of gay marriage as "the end of America as the Founders envisioned it . . . rooted in the Bible and its God."[34]

The principles Barr articulated are shared by most proponents of Christian nationalism, though that ideology is more typically associated with evangelical

Protestantism. The movement seeks to establish America as a Christian nation, deriving its laws, morals, and concept of nationality from biblical sources. Christian nationalism forms a distinct ideological element within the larger body of religious conservatives, who are not necessarily engaged by its political mythology and doctrine.

The modern version of Christian nationalism arose in the 1960s in response to the desegregation of public schools and gained strength as a counter to the sexual revolution of the 1960s and 1970s. Scholars who have studied the current shape of the movement see it combining two different but overlapping strains of belief. One identifies Christian identity with racial Whiteness, a belief system continuous with that of Southern churches in the Jim Crow era. The other focuses more exclusively on religious values and countering the effects of cultural liberalism by opposing secular curricula, abortion, permissive sexual mores, gay and transgender rights, and the banning of school prayer. The Christian Right's strong conservative positions on the patriarchal family and on gender and sexuality attract some support from Latino and Black voters. Studies of the movement by Robert Jones, Philip Gorski and Samuel Perry, and Ruth Braunstein suggest that, taken as a whole, Christian nationalism is a faith-centered variant of ethnonationalism that reads its cultural preferences into scripture. Its proponents are convinced that most Americans are currently "lost" or hostile to their Christian beliefs.[35]

For Christian nationalists, the moral decadence of abortion and gay rights follows from modern society's abandonment of Christian faith in favor of Enlightenment values: scientific rationalism, pluralism, the expansion of individual rights, and the separation of church and state. The doctrinal basis of this view was stated with theological specificity by Senator Josh Hawley (R-MO), a graduate of Stanford University and Yale Law School and a formidable legal scholar who had clerked for Chief Justice John Roberts. He sees the evils of modern society, its discontent, demoralization, and inequality, as the result of devotion to a "Promethean" idea of individual freedom, rooted in the "Pelagian heresy"—the doctrine espoused by the fourth-century theologian Pelagius, which denies that humanity is subject to original sin and insists that it is capable of achieving perfection through the exercise of free will. In a speech at the 2019 American Principles Project Gala, he explained that to cure this evil, "we are called to . . . take the Lordship of Christ, that message, into the public realm, and to seek the obedience of the nations. Of our nation!" For Hawley it is more vital that Christian civilization be saved than that democratic principles of government be vindicated.[36]

Christian nationalists and MAGA followers reach, by different routes, the conclusion of Thomas Dixon Jr.'s *The Clansman* and John Commons's 1907 report *Races and Immigrants in America* that, to preserve American society from the effects of ethnic and racial diversity, it may be necessary, as Commons put it, to "despotiz[e]our institutions."[37]

Authoritarianism and Vigilantism

President Trump may not have understood the nuances of Barr's legal arguments, but he fully grasped their implications. As he told his cabinet, "I have an Article 2 where I have the right to do whatever I want as president. . . . [When] somebody is the president of the United States, the authority is total, and that's the way it's going to be." He would take this doctrine as a license to center all executive power in his person. [38]

Trump's personal domination of the Republican Party was affirmed by the 2020 nominating convention, which for the first time in its history declined to offer a new platform—it simply reissued the 2016 platform, as if to say that Trump himself was the embodiment of everything the party stood for. He would frame his presidency as an insurgency, a war against cultural liberalism and the professionals of the "deep state." As chief of the insurgency, he would be a vigilante president, asserting the power of a righteous minority against malefactors and elected officials alike.

For Trump, toughness implies a willingness to break the rules to defeat your enemy. He expresses that belief in matters large and small: strongly approving the use of torture "and much worse" in prosecuting the War on Terror; urging police officers "not to be too nice" when arresting criminals; telling supporters to grab protesters and "treat 'em rough." His response to accusations that he or his agents bribed and extorted foreign governments was to propose that laws forbidding American businesses from paying bribes be repealed. Frustrated by his inability to stop migrants and asylum seekers from pressing the southern border, he asked his aides to assess the price of digging a border moat and stocking it with alligators and snakes, electrifying the border fence, and topping it with antipersonnel spikes. When migrants demonstrating on the Mexican side of the border threw rocks at American troops, he suggested the soldiers shoot them. When told that this was illegal, he proposed they shoot them in the legs. When told that *that* was illegal, he vented his anger on the relevant cabinet officers. He later laughed when, during a rally in Florida, an audience member suggested that migrants be shot.[39]

Trump values the military as the instrument through which he can project his own toughness, *his* willingness to kill. He refers to military commanders as "my generals." When he overruled them to pardon three soldiers convicted of war crimes, that was because "I have to protect my warfighters." He would extend that accolade to mercenaries, pardoning fourteen Blackwater military contractors who had been convicted of murdering Iraqi civilians. For Trump, war is "killing," and if "we throw people in jail for going to war for us," we weaken their willingness to kill. When Brett Baier of Fox News suggested that officers would disobey his order to torture terrorist captives because it was against American and international law, Trump smiled and said, "They're not going to refuse me. . . . I'm a leader. I'm a leader. I've always been a leader. I've never had any problem leading people. If I say do it, they're going to do it. That's what leadership is all about."[40]

Trump deployed the "savage war" symbolism of the Frontier Myth to mark his Democratic opponents. In a September 2019 Twitter message, he described liberal members of Congress Jerrold Nadler, Adam Schiff, and Alexandria Ocasio-Cortez as "Do Nothing Democrat Savages." Later that year, with his reelection imperiled by the coronavirus pandemic, Trump retweeted a video in which a supporter (paraphrasing General Philip Sheridan on Indians) says, "The only good Democrat is a dead Democrat."[41]

Trump's pardoning the three soldiers convicted of war crimes in Iraq and Afghanistan was particularly disturbing. At a rally following the pardons, he boasted that he had acted in defiance of the "deep state," a category now including his own military commanders. Officers in high command expressed concern that the pardons, coupled with his "divisive rhetoric," were politicizing the military: "Half are ardent Trump supporters that believe the President is watching out for the troops." These are mainly in the lower officer and enlisted ranks, while more-senior officers "believe the military must remain independent of partisan political influence [but] don't see the President adhering to that."[42]

In a December 2019 interview with Breitbart News, Trump boasted, "I have the support of the police, the support of the military, the support of the bikers for Trump. I have the tough people," and if they were pushed to "a certain point, . . . it would be bad, very bad." It is significant that he puts bikers and "tough people" on a par with the police and military. General Mark Milley, head of the Joint Chiefs of Staff in January 2020, would recall this statement and compare it to the combination of forces that brought European Fascists to power in the 1920s and 1930s.[43]

In assuming the role of an insurgent or vigilante president, Trump implicitly embraced an authoritarian concept of presidential power. Such a ruler, convinced that civilization is at stake and persuaded that he is the incarnation of the will of "real Americans," feels morally entitled to override ordinary laws and even the constitutional order so that he may save the country. At the June 2019 rally launching his reelection campaign, Trump told his followers, "Our radical Democrat opponents are driven by hatred, prejudice and rage. They want to destroy you and they want to destroy our country as we know it. Not acceptable. It's not going to happen."[44]

18

Imagining Civil War

The 2020 Election

INTRINSIC TO the Make American Great Again (MAGA) narrative is the belief that the story reaches its climax in a moment of life-or-death choice between social redemption and civilizational collapse. In that narrative, Donald Trump figures as the Redeemer. For the evangelical Christians who were his most loyal supporters, Trump was literally God's chosen instrument for national salvation. For culture-war conservatives, he was the voice of their grievances, and for economic conservatives the guarantor of business-friendly policies. If Trump could maintain his power over the government, he would restore the moral authority and social control lost by "real Americans" and revive America's economic and civilizational "greatness." If he were to be defeated, America itself would be corrupted, polluted, and destroyed.

In imagining a crisis of such extremity, conservative opinion makers explicitly invoked the Civil War, whose Lost Cause narrative rests on a similar claim of civilizational crisis. There's a "civil war on America's horizon," William Smith of *American Conservative* wrote in 2018, "a sense that a terrible clash is about to occur. . . . All that's needed now is a spark." For Michael Vlahos, a professor at Johns Hopkins University and former head of the Center for the Study of Foreign Affairs at the State Department, "American kinship today is fissuring into two visions of the nation's future way of life . . . [each] insistent on absolute control. . . . [The] effect is to condition the whole of society to believe that an existential clash is coming, that all must choose, and that there are no realistic alternatives to a final test of wills." Former US district attorney Joseph diGenova, a frequent guest thinker on Fox News, takes this a step further. He told listeners to Laura Ingraham's Fox News podcast, "We are in a civil war. . . . The suggestion that there's ever going to be civil discourse in this country for the foreseeable future is over. . . . It's going to be total war."[1]

The Civil War and Reconstruction connection highlights MAGA's support of insurrectionary measures to forward its program. Framing the 2020 campaign as an existential conflict created an expectation of violence and put people in the gun rights community, the paramilitaries, and the ethnonationalist movement on high alert. Gun purchases rose to record levels. When violence came, MAGA partisans would see it not as an outrage but as a fulfillment of their expectations.

When the presidential campaign began in the last months of 2019, Trump's strongest case for reelection rested on the booming economy, low unemployment, tax cuts, deregulation, and his success in appointing three conservative justices to the Supreme Court. MAGA supporters and conservatives could cheerfully embrace his slogans, "Promises made, promises kept" and "*Keep America great again.*" But the campaign was transformed by a pair of crises. The outbreak of the COVID-19 pandemic in February 2020 forced the nation into an economic and social lockdown for all but the most essential businesses. The long bull market in stocks ended in a crash. Although stock prices would recover surprisingly quickly over the next three months, the real economy was profoundly weakened as businesses large and small locked down or went bankrupt. Unemployment went from a record low of 3.6 percent to 14.8 percent or more; and though total employment would slowly recover, many of the job losses threatened to be permanent. The effects of the pandemic were exacerbated by the endemic economic and racial inequalities that had characterized American society since the 1980s, which contributed to disproportionate rates of illness and death among the poor, the lower levels of the working class, and communities of color.[2]

Then, in the midst of the pandemic, the killing of George Floyd, an unarmed Black man arrested on suspicion of trying to pass a counterfeit twenty-dollar bill, by Minneapolis police provoked a nationwide uprising against racial injustice. Videos of the killing, taken and transmitted by eyewitnesses using cell phone cameras, went viral. They showed Floyd prone on the ground and Officer Derek Chauvin deliberately pressing his knee into Floyd's neck, ignoring the victim's pleas and the onlookers' protests, until Floyd ceased to breathe. A wave of demonstrations swept cities, towns, and communities in every part of the nation, marked by varying combinations of violence and nonviolence, culminating in massive demonstrations in front of the White House. Most were organized or supported by Black Lives Matter (BLM).

In past crises, like 9/11, the appeal to myth had fostered patriotic solidarity, which supported the use of governmental powers to resolve the crisis. But in 2020 the twin crises of COVID and the BLM protests brought to the surface, and put in conflict, two very different versions of national myth. The Trump administration would follow the mythic paradigms that had shaped Trump's rhetoric from the start, the Frontier Myth and the Lost Cause. Trump's response to COVID invoked the same anti-science ideologies he had deployed to deny climate change, and for the same reason: to justify policies that would restart the economy. He linked COVID restrictions to attacks on American freedom, encouraging anti-quarantine demonstrations led by armed vigilantes sporting Confederate flags and gun rights symbols. Trump also stoked racial xenophobia by insisting COVID be called "the Chinese flu" or "Wuhan virus," and he used the pandemic as an excuse to block all immigration and consideration of asylum cases.[3]

The crises had a different effect on the blue side of the spectrum. BLM protesters reached into the lexicon of national myths, invoking the Myth of the Movement but going beyond it to recall and reclaim the Liberation Myth of the Civil War. Protests that focused on the symbolism of Confederate statues gave historical and *national* grounding to the narrative paradigm of the civil rights movement—which had been in danger of fragmenting into a constellation of identity-group claimants. The ground for this outreach had been prepared by the 1619 Project, a series of historical articles organized by Nikole Hannah-Jones and published by the *New York Times Magazine* in the summer of 2019, which recast the history of America with enslavement and race as the center of the narrative. Ibram X. Kendi's *How to Be an Antiracist,* published that same year, became a best seller by offering an analysis of systemic racism and proposing a set of ideas and approaches for overcoming it. Both were criticized for historical inaccuracies, and Kendi's proposed methods for becoming antiracist were highly problematic, except for his emphasis on changing policy rather than working on hearts and minds. But both were also highly influential and won critical praise for drawing attention to the historical process that had formed the nation's racial categories and the attendant structures of segregation and discrimination.[4]

The economic collapse engendered by the pandemic also reminded people of the Great Depression, just as the crash of 2008 had done. Only now Democrats openly invoked the New Deal as a model for economic recovery. In so doing, they altered the status of the New Deal, from an exception to the pattern of American history to an active and explicit historical exemplum—a potential first step in the formation of a myth. Those who invoked it envisioned not only the restoration of the pre-COVID status quo but a social justice program that would address the economic and social injustices of the neoliberal economic order. Because the public health, economic, and racial crises overlapped, these different strains of myth and ideology were braided together to produce a new mythic configuration on the blue side of the spectrum, integrating the New Deal and Myth of the Movement in a single narrative—a clear alternative to MAGA's Lost Cause.[5]

Good War versus Culture War: Trump Responds to COVID

The first US cases of the COVID-19 virus appeared in January 2020. By the first week in February, President Trump had been informed by the Centers for Disease Control and National Institutes of Health that the virus was extraordinarily contagious and far deadlier than the seasonal flu. He was advised that strong measures were needed to check the pandemic, including bans on international travel and the curtailment of economic and social activities that would bring large numbers together in close quarters—a requirement that would entail shutting down large sectors of the economy for an indefinite period.

The situation demanded a spirit of national unity to reconcile people to the sacrifices economic lockdowns would require. The Good War Myth offered the readiest model and was soon invoked by media outlets and political leaders. The *Detroit Free Press* declared, "2020 America is gravitating to World War II as the go-to comparison for the current battle against a deadly germ." New York governor Andrew Cuomo said, "Ventilators are to this war what bombs were to World War Two." It was a metaphor that suited President Trump, who soon invoked the productive energy that brought victory in World War II—"To this day, nobody has ever seen anything like it"—and also the spirit of wartime solidarity: "Now it's our time. We must sacrifice together, because we are all in this together, and we will come through together." He declared himself a "wartime president" and reminded the public of his "absolute powers" under Article II to deal with the pandemic. He declared a national emergency and invoked the Defense Production Act, empowering him to force medical equipment manufacturers to produce the masks, protective clothing, and ventilators for which hospitals were clamoring. He signed the Coronavirus Preparedness and Response Supplemental Appropriations Act, which provided $8.3 billion in emergency funding for federal agencies to respond to the outbreak. Guided by the Centers for Disease Control and the National Institute of Allergy and Infectious Diseases, the administration also authorized Operation Warp Speed, an ambitious and successful program for developing, testing, and rapidly bringing to market an anti-COVID vaccine.[6]

Trump assembled a team of government scientists and medical experts, led by Anthony Fauci, Robert Redfield, and Deborah Birx, and began holding news conferences on the crisis. Although the experts were allowed to speak freely at first, Trump typically took the podium and held it for an hour or more, exalting his own "instincts" and "gut feelings" over their scientific knowledge, poo-pooing their calls for stronger safety measures, and touting his own random and irrational nostrums for curing the disease—such as ingesting bleach to cleanse the body of viruses. At the Centers for Disease Control in March 2020, he told a group of reporters and officials,

> And, by the way, NIH [National Institutes of Health], what they've done—I spent time over there—and I like this stuff. You know, my uncle was a great person. He was at MIT. He taught at MIT for, I think, like a record number of years. He was a great super genius. Dr. John Trump. I like this stuff. I really get it. People are surprised that I understand it. Every one of these doctors said, "How do you know so much about this?" Maybe I have a natural ability. Maybe I should have done that instead of running for President. . . . I understand that whole world. I love that world. I really do.[7]

Faced with criticism that these press conferences were actually harming his public standing, he responded that he had wonderful "numbers" and that his Nielsen ratings were higher than "Monday Night Football."[8]

It soon became clear that the restrictions required to check the spread of disease would derail the economic success that was Trump's pride and chief reliance for reelection. As he admitted in a March 2020 interview with investigative journalist Bob Woodward, he knew in early February that COVID-19 was "more deadly than even your strenuous flu." However, he had decided to "always play it down," to forestall a panic that would threaten his "numbers"— rising Dow Jones, low unemployment, high GDP. When stock prices mounted a speculative rally in response to relief and stimulus, Trump hailed it as the end of the pandemic. In fact, the mismatch between the returning vigor of the stock market and the widespread losses and business failures of the "real economy" was one of the pandemic's lingering effects. It exacerbated the already dangerous levels of economic inequality that plagued America. By blaming Democratic governors and mayors for curtailing business operations,

Trump hoped to shift working-class resentment away from Wall Street and the Republican donor class.[9]

Epidemiologists in government, the universities, and major medical centers all agreed that widespread testing for the coronavirus was essential to understand how COVID was spreading and develop ways of dealing with it. Trump told the *Wall Street Journal* he personally thought testing "overrated." For one thing, it confirmed the increase in cases—which "makes us look bad." He would later suggest that one way to stop the spread of the disease was to stop testing for it. He refused to see that no matter what he *said* about it, the virus would continue to spread, and that in the long run the economy could only regain full strength if the spread was substantially checked. A study by the British medical journal *Lancet* estimated that Trump's response to the pandemic caused the United States to suffer approximately 40 percent more deaths than comparable European countries.[10]

The pandemic challenged the credibility of Trump's performance as a heroic leader. His response to the shortage of medical and protective equipment is a case in point. Governors in states whose hospitals were failing for lack of such equipment asked for aid from the federal stockpile. Trump refused to provide it. His son-in-law and senior adviser Jared Kushner, tasked with coordinating the response to the pandemic, treated the stockpile as if it were Trump's personal property. "[The] federal stockpile [is] supposed to be *our* stockpile. It's not supposed to be states' stockpiles that they then use," he told the press on April 3. When reporters noted that the Department of Health and Human Services website actually said the stockpile was *intended* for state use, Kushner had the website language changed. What Trump demanded of the governors, in return for supplies, was personal obeisance: "If they don't treat you right . . . I don't call." In effect, he was using control of the stockpile to blackmail the governors, providing not only salve for his ego but sound bites for his 2020 campaign. Even as he asserted his "full authority" to control the government's response, he insisted, "I don't take responsibility at all" for shortages of equipment.[11]

After some initial gestures at unity, Trump reverted to his instinctive preference for divisive polemics. Instead of invoking "platoon movie" analogies, Trump would frame the response to COVID as another battle in the culture war. To transform a simple public health recommendation into a major political and ideological issue, Trump and his associates reached into the lexicon of national myth for symbolic analogies. The Frontier Myth, linking vigilantism, gun rights, and a "libertarian" suspicion of government, was primary. Trump praised and incited demonstrations by his supporters to overturn the business closures, masking, and social distancing measures mandated by Democratic governors—although his own administration and its scientific advisers had recommended those policies at press conferences over which he himself had presided. The wearing of masks—an elementary and effective way to check the spread of the virus—was transformed into an act of partisan symbolism. Public health officials who advocated masking were subjected to death threats, threats of rape, and anti-Semitic or racial insults delivered by social media or by demonstrations outside their homes. MAGA demonstrators verbally abused and physically assaulted reporters, law officers, and counterprotesters for wearing masks.[12]

Trump's quasi-authoritarian assertion of power was a perverse affirmation of the reconception of personal freedom that had become central to conservative ideology. This was most strongly expressed by the gun rights movement, but it could also be found in the antigovernment libertarian economics of Grover Norquist: the idea that freedom is the absolute individual right to do as you prefer, without regard to social consequences or the moral claims of society or one's fellow citizens. Taking their cue from the president, virtual vigilantes issued death threats and vandalized the offices of state and local health officials who issued mask mandates or guidelines, forcing some from office and requiring others to receive police protection. In Michigan demonstrators opposing the state's pandemic measures included men in fatigues armed with military-style weapons. Some displayed nooses tagged "Tyrants must hang," Confederate and Nazi emblems, and the Tea Party's "Don't tread on me" flag. Michigan's open-carry laws allowed these men (and most were men) to bring their weapons into the state house. The threat they represented caused the legislators to adjourn their session. Trump provocatively tweeted, "Liberate Michigan," "Liberate Minnesota," and "Liberate Virginia"—all states with Democratic governors. In Virginia's case, he linked resistance to virus-related closures to the fight to "save your great 2nd Amendment. It's under siege!" As conservative columnist Michael Gerson wrote, Trump effectively "equated essential health measures with gun confiscation. . . . It is unique in its recklessness."[13]

These demonstrations were not simply uprisings by fringe movements or expressions of grassroots sentiment. Many were organized or funded by individuals and groups tied to Trump's reelection campaign and—more significantly—a network of right-wing organizations and movements including the Heritage Foundation, the American Legislative Exchange Council and the Koch brothers' network, and the Convention of States organization, the last of which was founded in 2015 by Robert Mercer, a major supporter of Breitbart News and the alt-right, who was the largest contributor to Trump's 2016 campaign. Steve Schmidt, former campaign manager for John McCain, warned on Twitter of "the noxious blend of Confederate flags, semiautomatic weaponry, conspiracy theorists, political cultists, extremists and nut jobs coming to a state Capitol near you . . . stoked by Trump every step of the way as they help make the air fertile for his blame gaming, scapegoating, evasions of responsibility, populist fulminations and nationalist incitements."[14]

In September 2020 Attorney General William Barr said stay-at-home orders and business lockdowns were "other than slavery, . . . the greatest intrusion on civil liberties in American history." The absurdity of the comparison is striking, all the more so because it was made at a time when Barr was tasking the Department of Justice to consider whether BLM protesters and officials who supported them should be charged with sedition.[15]

Making Black Lives Matter: The Battle of Lafayette Square

The pandemic exposed the social and public health consequences of America's long-standing economic and racial inequality. Rates of infection and death were higher among Hispanic and Black people, whose relative poverty made them less healthy to begin with, as they were more likely to suffer from illness related to poor diet, bad housing, and exposure to environmental pollutants. They were also more likely to work in settings that required them to be physically present, increasing their exposure to the disease: health services, grocery stores, meat-processing plants, agriculture. These jobs were ill-paying and rarely carried health-care benefits, and options under Medicaid were limited in many states. The Trump administration declared them to be "essential workers" but at the same time rolled back government workplace protections. As two of these workers wrote, "We're feeding America, but we're sacrificing ourselves."[16]

On May 25, George Floyd, a part-time security guard at a Latin dance club, was arrested by Minneapolis police on suspicion of passing a counterfeit twenty-dollar bill. To some he appeared slightly drunk, and the autopsy would show traces of fentanyl and methamphetamine in his blood. Although he was generally compliant and allowed himself to be handcuffed, he balked at being put in a police car, complaining he was claustrophobic. Officer Derek Chauvin pushed Floyd face down in the street, knelt with one knee pressed into the back of his neck—and held it there for almost nine minutes while Floyd repeated, "I can't breathe," begged for his life, and finally called for "Mama." An autopsy would show that he suffered from heart disease and sickle-cell disease and was infected by COVID, which would have weakened his ability to breathe under such pressure. While Floyd was dying, Chauvin's appearance was nonchalant—hands in pockets, expression relaxed. Three officers assisting him stared blankly at the bystanders who repeatedly protested. All of this was caught on cell-camera video, which vividly records the callous suffocation of a helpless man suspected of a petty crime.

The video went viral on TV and social media, not only in communities of color but in White communities as well. It brought to mind the series of killings of unarmed Black people by police that began with Michael Brown in 2014 and included the recent killing of Breonna Taylor by police enforcing a no-knock warrant at the wrong address. It also brought to mind older cases including those of Philando Castile (shot in a routine traffic stop), Tamir Rice (a twelve-year-old shot for wielding a toy gun), Trayvon Martin, and Eric Garner. The memory stream, once tapped, began to flow. Emmett Till's 1955 lynching was recalled, and that brought forward the long history of lynching that began with Reconstruction, burgeoned through the Jim Crow era, and continued with the lynching of returning veterans in the 1940s and of civil rights workers in the 1960s.[17]

A wave of demonstrations began in which large numbers of Whites joined Black people and other people of color. In most of them, the marchers adopted the "Black Lives Matter" slogan, aligning themselves with a movement that had begun in 2014, following the police killing of Michael Brown in Ferguson, Missouri. Through its local chapters, BLM had assiduously organized and agitated for police reform, arguing that police violence toward people of color was a reflection of the "systemic racism" that had marred American national life from its origins. The protests spread to over 400 American cities and towns, in every state and section of the country—and then became an international phenomenon, as European and Japanese protesters marched not only to express solidarity with the Americans but to protest forms of racism and xenophobia that marred their own societies.[18]

CNN commentator Van Jones wrote, "As a black man, I have spent my entire life trying to convince relatively small numbers of white people to take racial injustice seriously. I have usually failed. . . . This sudden, mass realization—and the multi-racial demonstrations that give it weight, life and substance—feels like a miracle to me." Not all Black opinion leaders agreed. Writing in the *Wall Street Journal,* Shelby Steele, a Black sociologist, conservative intellectual, and fellow of Stanford's Hoover Institution, rejected BLM as "inauthentic" and "systemic racism" as an ideology of victimhood. However, even conservative opinion leaders were impressed with BLM's achievement in putting race relations on the political agenda. Correspondents for the *Wall Street Journal,* writing during the demonstrations, noted that BLM's "years of pressure paved [the] way for sudden police overhaul." An article written on the anniversary of Floyd's death, in May 2021, credited the demonstrations with starting a debate about race relations that now "reaches across American life." The editors of *The Economist,* a journal noted for its pragmatic conservatism, urged Americans not to waste "a rich chance for social reform." It seemed possible that the twin crises of COVID and the Black Lives Matter protests had produced a hinge moment, when structural constraints were in disarray and new possibilities for thought and action had become available.[19]

Most demonstrations were peaceful, at least at the start. In a number of cities and towns, police expressed sympathy with the protesters, marched with them, or "took a knee" in memory of George Floyd. Elsewhere, police responded with aggressive anti-riot tactics, deploying their military hardware in ways that provoked violence as often as they deterred or suppressed it. In Minneapolis, Seattle, and Portland, Oregon, demonstrations turned violent, requiring large-scale deployment of police and the National Guard. In Portland a strong local chapter of Antifa actively sought to confront the Proud Boys and MAGA demonstrators, and joined in the destruction of property and attacks on police. Violence racked the city for three months, the officers of the special squad trained to deal with protests resigned, and a year later violent outbreaks were still occurring.[20]

Violence of that kind was the exception. A survey by the *Washington Post,* based on analyses of demonstrations by political crowds from 2017 to the fall of 2020, found that the demonstrations were overwhelmingly nonviolent and that most of the violence associated with the demonstrations was perpetrated by ordinary criminals taking advantage of a civil disorder, by right-wing counterprotesters, or by law enforcement personnel. Nevertheless, it would be a mistake to discount the fear and expectation of violence that the protests aroused. While the vast majority of demonstrations may have been nonviolent, the images of violence shown by news programs, both broadcast and cable, made a stronger impression. The marchers challenged legal authority, both symbolically and by their taking control of the streets. The attacks on public buildings and the destruction or defacing of public monuments were perceived by some as part of a broad-based assault on sacred symbols. This was especially true of the assaults on statues of Confederate soldiers and political leaders, traditional symbols of Southern heritage. The disorder associated with the marches recalled the mythologized memory of the 1960s, when nonviolent civil rights protests had seemingly morphed into urban uprisings. Given all that, it is remarkable that through the fall of 2020 a preponderance of the public continued to support the protests and seemed tolerant or at least understanding of the rage that underlay the violence that did occur. Even in the cities most affected by violence, voters would stand by their Democratic officials and candidates in the November elections.[21]

Flags and symbols framed the opposition between the BLM protesters and their MAGA antagonists in the language of myth. BLM protesters were generally (not always) unarmed, were clad in civilian motley, and flew the national flag along with their own BLM banners; the black, red, and green banners identified with African cultural identity or with Black Power; the peace symbol used by antiwar demonstrators in the 1960s; and the rainbow flag of LGBTQ liberation. Demonstrators invoked the nonviolent protests of the civil rights movement in the 1960s, which had served as the model for a wave of other liberation movements affecting women, gay men and lesbians, Chicanos, and Native Americans. Their attacks on Confederate statues engaged the mythology of the Civil War and identified their cause with Abraham Lincoln, Liberation, and the Union—although iconoclastic zeal or historical ignorance led some to attack monuments to Union soldiers, such as the statue in Madison, Wisconsin, of Colonel Hans Heg, a Norwegian American soldier and abolitionist. The protesters also invoked the Myth of the Good War, pointing up the ways in which Black and Brown people have served a nation that discriminates against them. Although they were protesting the actions of the government, and the injustices it has failed to address, they looked to the government for redress of wrongs.

The MAGA counterprotesters were sometimes led by armed paramilitaries in camouflage and Kevlar, and the flags they flew were "Trump 2020"—displaying the enlarged head of their leader—and two banners associated with antigovernment movements: the yellow Gadsden flag, with its coiled rattlesnake and "Don't tread on me" motto, originally flown by American revolutionaries in 1775 and latterly by Tea Party, gun rights, and antitax organizations vaunting their right to defy or resist the American government; and the Stars and Bars of the Confederacy. Less prominent were the banners of the Christian Right and signs identifying the participants as "pro-life."

Trump's initial response reflected uncertainty about the intent of the demonstrators and the state of public opinion. On May 30 that confusion produced a major embarrassment. Demonstrators in front of the White House were defying and harassing police and Secret Service. Fearing demonstrators might breach the White House perimeter, aides sent Trump and his family into the subterranean bunker designed for protection against a terrorist attack.

Trump was infuriated when word of this leaked to the press—it made him look weak, and he initially denied it had happened. He followed with a tweet boasting that anyone breaching the fence would be met by the most vicious dogs and incredible weaponry, which reinforced the impression of his having been badly scared.

It was vital to his campaign messaging, and to his self-esteem, that Trump demonstrate his power to control the chaos and check the movement that appeared to be emerging from it. Although some MAGA supporters were shaken by the Floyd video, most remained resistant or actively hostile to BLM, and to the accusation that police departments, and American society in general, were guilty of systemic racism. Trump and his advisers decided to play to the racial animus of their base rather than engage BLM protesters in dialogue. Trump planned a Rose Garden address for Monday, June 1, in which he would express sympathy for the Floyd family but then condemn the violence and destruction of property the protests had caused, and affirm his power to restore law and order. Demonstrations in front of the White House on May 31 provided a pretext for that rhetorical turn. They were marked by sporadic violence, including the throwing of various objects at police, and (most shockingly) arson in the basement of St. John's Episcopal Church, the historic "Church of the Presidents" a block from the White House. The result was a series of events on June 1, which culminated in what has been called the Battle of Lafayette Square.[22]

On Monday morning Trump placed a conference call to several governors, during which he berated them for letting demonstrations get out of hand. According to a transcript of his call published by CNN, he told them, "If you don't dominate you'll look like a bunch of jerks. You have to dominate, and you have to arrest people, and you have to try people and they have to go to jail for long periods of time." Attorney General Barr was in the room, Trump said, "and we will activate Bill Barr and activate him very strongly." General Mark Milley, chairman of the Joint Chiefs of Staff, was there as well, "a fighter, a war hero, a lot of victories and no losses and he hates to see the way it's being handled in the various states and I just put him in charge." Barr supported Trump's threat, promising to "flood the zone" with law enforcement. Defense Secretary Mark Esper said his goal was to "dominate the battlespace." Esper would later deny that he had intended to use military force against the demonstrations, but his words on June 1 supported Trump's threat. Although Milley opposed using the military to quell a civil disturbance, he did not contradict Trump's implication that he was "in charge" of forces about to be activated.[23]

The schedule called for Trump to speak in the Rose Garden at 6:30 p.m., after which he would walk to St. John's for a photo op that would represent him as the defender of the Christian church against the destructive forces of rampant radicalism. Before the speech, Attorney General Barr conferred with the security detail in Lafayette Square. Barr later claimed he was merely checking to see whether an earlier order to extend the security perimeter through the square had been carried out, and had not given the "tactical order" to clear the square. Even the conservative *National Review* found Barr's explanation insufficient—the original order to extend the perimeter could not be executed without forcibly doing so.[24]

The organizers of the demonstration had also been shocked and disturbed by Sunday's violence and the arson at St. John's. They had rebuked those responsible and set terms for a nonviolent protest on June 1. Although it was raucous and profane, reporters at the demonstration described it as "peaceful." From 4:00 p.m. onward, chants of "No justice, no peace" mingled with the sounds of Kendrick Lamar and Childish Gambino blaring from smartphones. "A group of young African Americans stepped and swiveled to the deep bass of 'This is America.'"[25]

Just as Trump was beginning his performance in the Rose Garden, security forces moved to clear the square. The officers were a motley mix, drawn from several federal agencies: the Park Police, Secret Service, Homeland Security, Bureau of Corrections, and military police, as well as the Arlington County Police. They moved on protesters behind a wall of plastic shields, hurling flash-bang grenades and pepper-spray canisters, then broke into a charge, wielding batons on demonstrators who fled too slowly. Although acting Park Police chief Gregory Monahan later claimed that the protesters were "unusually aggressive," Adam D. DeMarco, an Iraq veteran and a major in the DC National Guard, told reporters that "demonstrators were behaving peacefully" and that tear gas was deployed in an "excessive use of force."[26]

As the assault went forward, Trump spoke in the Rose Garden. "I am your president of law and order," he said. He claimed he was "an ally of all peaceful protesters" but said the wave of demonstrations that had swept the nation in the past few days were the work of "professional anarchists, violent mobs, arsonists, looters, criminals, rioters, antifa, and others." He called the demonstrations "a crime against God," echoing the Christian nationalism of so many of his followers. If local and state government refused to "take necessary action to safeguard their residents," he said, "I will deploy the United States military and quickly solve the problem for them." Although he had not invoked the Insurrection Act, the sole legal authority for federal intervention, he declared that he was "mobilizing all available federal resources—civilian and military— to stop the rioting and looting, to end the destruction and arson, and to protect the rights of law-abiding Americans, including your Second Amendment rights." The last phrase signaled his support for the armed right-wing paramilitaries who had intervened in several demonstrations.[27]

After the speech, with the sounds of the police action still ringing in the streets, Trump and his entourage walked across the White House grounds and into the street for the photo op in front of St. John's. Imagery was all Trump cared about: the picture of himself standing in front of the vandalized church holding up a bible. "Is that your Bible?" a reporter asked. "It's a Bible," he answered.[28] General Milley and Secretary Esper walked with Trump, which observers saw as tacit confirmation that the military supported his threat to use the armed forces. Both stepped away from the photo op, belatedly recognizing that they were compromising the armed forces' obligation to stay out of partisan politics.

Public reaction to the violent repression of the Lafayette Square demonstration, and the cynicism of the photo op, was swift and critical. As in the aftermath of Charlottesville, Trump was identified with a violent assault on peaceful marchers protesting racial injustice. The most powerful rebukes came from retired military officers who had held major commands and served in presidential cabinets and the National Security Council. Admiral Michael Mullen, chairman of the Joint Chiefs of Staff under Presidents George H. W. Bush and Barack Obama, told the press, "It sickened me" because it "laid bare [Trump's] disdain for the rights of peaceful protest in this country, gave succor to the leaders of other countries who take comfort in our domestic strife." General John Allen, who had commanded US forces in Afghanistan, watched "with horror, frankly. . . . It wasn't enough that peaceful protesters had just been deprived of their first-amendment rights—this photo-op sought to legitimize that abuse with a layer of religion. . . . That is what happens in authoritarian regimes." If such a man were to be reelected, he added, it might "well signal the beginning of the end of the American experiment." Michael Hayden, retired four-star general and head of the CIA under George W. Bush, agreed: if Trump were to be reelected, it would mean "we're done. America [would] not be the same. Period."[29]

The strongest criticism came from General James Mattis, a highly regarded marine officer and Trump's former defense secretary, who had resigned as an act of moral protest against the president's decision to desert the Kurdish allies in the war against ISIS. He issued a public statement declaring, "Donald Trump is the first president in my lifetime who does not try to unite the American people—does not even pretend to try." He said he believed the demonstrators were standing up for fundamental democratic values and national unification: "The words 'Equal Justice Under Law' are carved in the pediment of the United States Supreme Court. This is precisely what protesters are rightly demanding. It is a wholesome and unifying demand—one that all of us should be able to get behind. We must not be distracted by a small number of lawbreakers. The protests are defined by tens of thousands of people of conscience who are insisting that we live up to our values—our values as people and our values as a nation."[30]

What is remarkable in these statements is not only the sharpness of the rebuke but the sympathy they express for the demonstrations. In this they were joined by George W. Bush, who endorsed the protesters' assertion that American institutions were suffused with "systemic racism," urged everyone to listen to them, and indirectly criticized Trump by suggesting that "empathy" offered a better way than confrontation to deal with the crisis.[31]

The Battle of Lafayette Square focused attention on the administration's racial animus and the reality of racially biased policing that BLM was protesting. In the month of June, police in more than a hundred US cities used tear gas to disperse peaceful demonstrators, just the sort of stern measures Trump was demanding. But when armed White vigilantes tried to intimidate state legislators and health officials to end lockdowns and mandatory masking in Michigan and Virginia, Trump egged them on.

Stuart Stevens, an anti-Trump Republican, registered the historical analogy that evoked the myth. "History picks these moments. It picked the march on Selma. It picked Bull Connor sending dogs against children"—images that sparked the agitation that led to the Voting Rights Act. Now history seemed to be picking the images of heavily armed riot police attacking Lafayette Square to frame a renewal of the Myth of the Movement. Further, because the "battle" occurred in the context of the COVID depression, it was also likened to President Herbert Hoover's use of the army in 1932 to drive the Bonus Army demonstrators out of Washington, an event credited with ensuring Hoover's defeat and the installation of the New Deal. The Navigator Research poll for June 2020 showed that 59 percent of Americans disapproved Trump's handling of the protests, while only 33 percent approved. Four months before the election, Trump's standing against Joe Biden in several of the critical toss-up states went from dead heat to double-digit deficit.[32]

Demonstrators returned to Lafayette Square every day for two weeks after they were dispersed, in larger numbers, with better organization and a clearer message. They policed themselves to ensure there would be no violence or vandalism. They were led in prayer and song by ministers and popular singers, forging a connection between the narrative of their struggle and the legendary civil rights movement of the 1960s. At the height of the agitation, in June 2020, between 15 million and 26 million people were engaged in BLM-related demonstrations, making this the largest wave of demonstrations in American history.[33]

A Monmouth University poll taken in June 2020 found that 76 percent of Americans now considered racism a "big problem," up 26 points from 2015. Seventy-eight percent of voters thought the anger behind the demonstrations was fully or somewhat justified, though the violence was not. Polls also showed that a majority of Americans believed police were more likely to use deadly force against African Americans than against White people. "Never before in the history of modern polling has the country expressed such widespread agreement on racism's pervasiveness in policing, and in society at large." Republicans responded by proposing their own police reform bill, developed by Senator Tim Scott (R-SC), their lone African American senator, who would abandon the bill after the election.[34]

A survey by social scientists from UCLA found that White people made up 61 percent of the demonstrators in New York City, 65 percent in Washington, and 53 percent in Los Angeles. Professional athletes and celebrities joined in the protests, and thousands joined a March on Washington in August that mirrored the iconic 1963 demonstration. Sales of books on the history and politics of racism boomed, as did the sales of self-help approaches to getting past one's own racism like Ibram X. Kendi's *How to Be an Antiracist,* which became a best seller—indications that White people were trying to engage seriously with the issues posed by the new movement.[35]

The groundwork for this radical shift in public opinion had been long in development. The demographic shift toward a "minority-majority" population had provoked a White identity reaction, but it also meant that (at least in and around large cities) people of different races were more and more likely to live near, work, and interact with one another. Popular culture had consistently projected liberal views on race and gender in the integrated casts of cop and hospital shows and in the fictive families and romances of sitcoms. Democrats, and educated White people in general, who tended to cluster in cities, had been growing more and more liberal on racial issues for twenty years, a trend accentuated by developments in higher education, especially in the humanities and social sciences. Above all, civil rights organizations and the BLM movement had forced the media to pay attention to the killing of unarmed Black people by the police.

Unlike the civil rights movement of the 1950s and 1960s, BLM was not directed by a consortium of national organizations. It was decentralized, as chapters arose in particular communities, first in response to local events, then in sympathy with other communities. Its work was augmented by a number of similarly decentralized racial-justice organizations, including the Black Visions Collective, the Sunrise Movement, and the Latino/a group Mijente. Although its diffuse structure allowed chapters to act in ways suited to their immediate communities, BLM did have a communications center, the Black Lives Matter Global Network, whose staff oversaw the range of its activities and set some general rules for conduct—specifically an insistence on nonviolence. Kailee Scales, speaking for the network, refuted the administration's accusations that it sponsored violence. "Only BLM chapters who adhere to BLM's principles and code of ethics are permitted to use the BLM name," she said. Vandals "are confusing to people who may wrongly associate the unsanctioned group and its views and actions with BLM."[36]

White enthusiasm for BLM demonstrations fell as outbreaks of violence continued through the summer, especially in Seattle, Minneapolis, and Portland, Oregon. BLM demonstrations were often rowdy and abusive toward police and city leaders, and there were acts of vandalism and violence by radicals and opportunists exploiting the situation to break into or vandalize businesses. The demonstrations attracted armed White paramilitaries and individuals roused to vigilantism by the spectacle of street violence. In Kenosha, Wisconsin, a teenager named Kyle Rittenhouse shot and killed two protesters who had taken to the streets after the police killing of Jacob Blake. President Trump blamed Antifa and Black hoodlums for the violence and expressed support for Rittenhouse and the paramilitaries. Attorney General Barr followed the president's line, warning communities protesting police measures that they risked losing police protection entirely.[37]

Barr's warning chimed with public dismay at the sharp increase in crime across the nation in 2020. A July 2022 study by the Brennan Center for Justice, based primarily on FBI statistics, found that crimes against property had surged 8 percent and violent crime was up 5.7 percent over the 2019 rate. Homicides increased by a stunning 75 percent. The statistics do not quite capture the fear produced among people living in the affected communities. While it may have been true that nine out of ten BLM demonstrations were nonviolent, the experience of that violence—whether in person or vicariously through television viewing—reinforced the sense of societal breakdown and contributed to a backlash against BLM and liberal social policies, which would be reflected in the 2020 elections. Yet many of the assumptions behind that backlash were erroneous. Crime in general, and violent crime in particular, rose in 2020. However, the Brennan Center study found that there was no correlation between the rise in crime and the adoption of liberal policies on criminal justice. Nor was there a significant difference in the homicide rate between cities with liberal or progressive government and those governed by Republicans. There was some evidence that a pullback by police reacting against criticism and pressure for reform reduced the number of arrests and closed cases in particular localities, but the actual effect on crime rates was hard to measure. Studies of the homicide rate showed a contrary effect, with red states and cities experiencing higher numbers, especially in killings with firearms. Studies by the RAND Corporation and the *Journal of the American Medical Association* showed a high correlation between increases in the homicide rate and the operation of stand-your-ground laws.[38]

Although by fall support for BLM had fallen from its high of 60 percent, a Politico / Morning Consult poll found that a majority of Americans (52 percent) still supported the movement. Attacks on Confederate statues were met with surprising sympathy even from some conservatives. Rich Lowry, editor of the *National Review,* considered the statues "an unnecessary affront to black citizens, who shouldn't have to see defenders of chattel slavery put on a pedestal, literally." More significantly, BLM had achieved its primary goal of getting a majority of White Americans to recognize the existence of enduring patterns of racism and open their minds to the content of Black protests.[39]

The Movement as Myth versus the Lost Cause

The effect of the demonstrations and associated polemics that followed the killing of George Floyd was to convince a substantial majority of Americans that the civil rights movement had *not* succeeded in ending systemic racism; that though Martin Luther King Jr. had been adopted as a national hero, his work had not been completed. A new Myth of the Movement now emerged, which was not a celebration of triumph but a reminder of unfinished business. At the end of August, the anniversary of the original March on Washington was memorialized with a new march, smaller in scale but bringing on the scene veterans of the original event as well as younger people from BLM.

Other patterns of association led demonstrators, activists, and journalists to reach back past the Myth of the Movement to the historical origins of America's racial injustice in slavery and Jim Crow. Police officers in Wilmington, North Carolina, were caught on body cameras threatening violence against Black protesters: "We are just going to go out and start slaughtering

them f——n——. . . . That'll put 'em back about four or five generations."
A follow-up report reminded readers that such a massacre had actually occurred in Wilmington in 1898, when White supremacists overthrew a biracial government.[40]

Even in the South, the new Myth of the Movement registered victories
against the Lost Cause. There was a remarkable display of White support for
BLM demonstrations in May and June, not only in relatively liberal cities like
Atlanta but also in Montgomery, Alabama, where police joined the demonstrators, and the small town of Petal, Mississippi, where an elderly White
woman's protest led to the opening of a community dialogue. Joanna Adams's
CNN opinion piece, "White Southerners, Our Souls Are at Stake," is one of
several acts of witness published as op-eds, describing the life experience of
growing up White in a determinedly racist society. It seemed possible that an
opportunity had opened for public forums to address not only the immediate
occasions of grievance but the deeper, historically ingrained social and cultural
patterns of race-based inequality. There were successful drives for the removal
of Confederate statues and monuments in Louisville, Kentucky; Birmingham
and Mobile, Alabama; Jacksonville, Florida; Raleigh, North Carolina; and
Decatur, Georgia—and the governors of Arizona and Kentucky began conversations with community leaders on what to do with their Confederate monuments. By year's end 160 statues and other Confederate memorials would be
removed, almost all in the South.[41]

Two of these movements were particularly significant. Richmond, Virginia,
had been the capital of the Confederacy, and Monument Avenue leading to
the state house was lined with large statues of Confederate generals and political
leaders—presenting them as objects of veneration in a use of statuary borrowed
from imperial Rome. The centerpiece was the colossal equestrian statue of
Robert E. Lee, the sainted hero of the Lost Cause. Agitation aimed at removing
some or all of the statues predated the advent of BLM, and the issue had been
under serious discussion by community leaders for several years. But the killing
of George Floyd sparked demonstrations that grew increasingly militant. In a
demonstration following Lafayette Square, protesters filled Monument Avenue
demanding removal of the monuments, defacing the Lee statue with graffiti
and assaulting the statue of Jefferson Davis. Governor Ralph Northam had
been supportive of monument removal since Charlottesville; he now led the
state legislature to adopt measures to remove all the Monument Avenue statuary. (The removal of the Lee statue was postponed pending a judicial review.)
Of similar significance was the action by the legislature of Mississippi. In 1894
the state had incorporated the Confederate Stars and Bars as the canton of its

flag. On June 28, 2020, the legislature voted to commission a new flag, without the Confederate symbolism. The Southern Baptist Conference, originally a staunch defender of slavery and Jim Crow, passed a resolution grieving the killing of George Floyd and abandoned the use of a ceremonial gavel bequeathed by a Confederate slaveholder.[42]

The complement to this rejection of Confederate symbolism was a reassertion of the Liberation version of the Civil War mythology. Reaction to the killing of George Floyd and Lafayette Square swung the balance of political support behind an initiative to ban displays of the Confederate flag on military bases or by personnel on active duty, and to rename military bases named for Confederate generals to honor Union soldiers or heroes of later wars. Trump told a meeting of the Joint Chiefs of Staff to oppose the changes, because "it's Southern pride and heritage." But Joint Chiefs chairman Milley advocated for the change, saying that rebel generals "were traitors at the time, they are traitors today, and they're traitors in death for all eternity." Congress adopted the name-change recommendation in the defense appropriations bill, overcoming Trump's threat of a veto.[43]

It would be a mistake to see these actions, gestures, and statements as a sign that Southern heritage had been utterly transformed and liberalized. All, in fact, provoked strong negative reactions. Beyond the extremists who defended racism in principle, there were many who rejected the idea that American society was pervaded by systemic racism and objected to the tendency to divide people into "racist" and "antiracist" camps. What these actions signify is something smaller, but of great potential significance: the opening of a long-standing system to the possibility of change.

The Floyd murder and BLM demonstrations created a cultural crisis, in which recognition and recall of the historical basis of American racism became widespread. As the movement spread to the West and Southwest, other aspects of that history were recognized and became the focus of protest. Protests directed against statues of Christopher Columbus and the conquistador Juan de Oñate registered the anger of Native Americans at their history of dispossession and genocide. The equestrian statue of Theodore Roosevelt in front of the Museum of Natural History was slated for removal, because it represented Africans and Native Americans as subordinate peoples. The wave of reaction against symbols of the Lost Cause spread to symbols of the racialism inherent in the Frontier Myth. Two conservative senators, James Lankford (R-OK) and Ron Johnson (R-WI), proposed that "Juneteenth" replace Columbus Day as a national holiday, linking the celebration of Black emancipation to recognition of Native Americans' protest against the glorification of the European colonialism that had dispossessed them. The idea provoked a backlash, especially among Italian Americans for whom Columbus was the symbol of their American identity, which had once been denied by American nativists—a sign of just how complex issues of identity and group justice are in a society as diverse as the United States.

The movement for racial reckoning provoked by George Floyd's death triggered a wave of mythological thinking that brought to expression in the public sphere those strains of national myth most favorable to a liberal or progressive understanding of American history. The Myth of the Movement was the most salient, but now many Americans connected it to the deeper historical fable of the Liberation Myth of the Civil War. And because these myths were recalled in the context of the COVID-19 pandemic and its attendant economic depression, there was also a dawning recognition that the New Deal provided a potential model for responding to the crisis. Previously that story had been subsumed to near invisibility in the Good War Myth and the Myth of the Movement. Now it seemed to emerge as a story in its own right.[44]

The Biden Campaign: National Myth for Blue America

During the Democratic primaries in the summer of 2020, Joe Biden defeated his more progressive opponents, Bernie Sanders and Elizabeth Warren, by emphasizing moderation and bipartisanship as an antidote to the hyperpartisanship and vitriol of the Trump era. Key to his victory was his endorsement by South Carolina congressman James Clyburn, head of the Congressional Black Caucus, who identified Biden as a candidate committed to racial justice and asserted that he was the most electable. Biden's campaign would draw its energy and much of its agenda from initiatives generated by the party's progressive wing, and by a range of grassroots movements that had become active in the waning years of Obama's presidency. These included BLM, the numerous organizations devoted to fighting global warming, and a gun control movement roused by the March for Our Lives campaign, led by the teenage survivors of the Parkland school shooting. New forms of activism focused attention on the rights and condition of labor as the movement to unionize workers in the fast-food, online shopping, and "gig" industries was energized by the pandemic's effect on service workers. These developments were supported by leaders of organized labor, a number of unions, and a variety of social action movements, some based in minority communities (such as Black Visions Collective, Mijente, and the Poor People's Campaign). Since 2016 there had also been a quiet groundswell of national support for the Affordable Care Act, a tendency solidified by the pandemic, and renewed agitation for a single-payer, government-financed health-care system.

Biden rejected the most radical slogans of these movements: "Defund the police," "The Green New Deal," "Medicare for all," "Ban assault weapons." But the policies he espoused, and those adopted in the party platform, embraced the progressives' main goals: a commitment to tackling systemic racism; combining green energy policies with job creation and community redevelopment; expanding the Affordable Care Act to achieve universal coverage; increasing the national minimum wage; supporting unionization; and tightening firearms background checks. The progressive inflection of the campaign was reflected in the way Biden, advised by presidential historian Jon Meacham, would link himself to Abraham Lincoln and Franklin Roosevelt, and through them to three versions of national myth: the well-established Liberation Myth of the Civil War; the story of the New Deal, which had not been openly embraced as national myth; and the Good War, with its focus on unity in diversity.[45]

The Lincoln connection was made in dramatic fashion when Biden went to Gettysburg on October 6 to deliver a speech on national reconciliation and racial justice. Like Lincoln, he described America as "a house divided" by its failure to live up to its promise of universal liberty. "For President Lincoln, the Civil War was about the greatest of causes," he said. "As we stand here today . . . we should consider again, what can happen when equal justice is denied, when anger and violence and division are left unchecked." Biden made the struggle against racism the centerpiece of this appeal. "I made the decision to run for president after Charlottesville," he said. "Close your eyes, and remember what you saw. Neo-Nazis, white supremacists, and the KKK . . . with torches alight, veins bulging, chanting the same anti-Semitic bile heard across Europe in the '30s. It was hate on the march, in the open, in America."[46]

Without mentioning Trump by name, Biden vowed to reject the politics of hate: "As president . . . I will send a clear unequivocal message to the entire nation, there is no place for hate in America. It will be given no license. It will be given no oxygen. It'll be given no safe harbor. We have no need for armed militias roaming America's streets, and we should have no tolerance for extremist white supremacy groups, menacing our communities." Biden condemned the violence that accompanied some demonstrations, and rejected the appeal to defund the police. "This is [a] nation strong enough to both honestly face systemic racism and . . . provide safe streets for our families and small businesses." Although the statement was interpreted by some as a politic hedge against radicalism, Biden was affirming the New Deal principle that active, responsive government agencies, directed by an overall commitment to democracy and justice, could be trusted to heal the nation's wounds.

Biden described a line of historical descent linking liberal presidents to each other and sketching the outline of a "blue" national myth. He reminded his hearers that a century after Lincoln spoke at Gettysburg, Lyndon Johnson had come there to announce his commitment to a war against racial discrimination. Biden cast his own campaign as a continuation of that struggle: "Today, we're engaged, once again, in the battle for the soul of the nation, the forces of darkness, the forces of division, the forces of yesterday are pulling us apart," he said, "holding us down and holding us back. We must free ourselves of all of them."

Although racial justice and the Civil War were his primary referents, Biden turned to Lincoln to advocate economic justice: "America . . . has to be the kind of country where an Abraham Lincoln, a child of the distant frontier, can rise to the highest office in the land. America has to be about . . . prosperity, not just for the privileged few, but for the many, for all of us. Working people and their kids deserve an opportunity. Lincoln knew this. He said that the country had to give people, and I quote, 'An open field and a fair chance.' An open field and a fair chance. That's what we're going to do in America." Associating the promise of mobility with the Frontier made sense in a speech centering on the preindustrial period of American development. But as his economic program developed, the association with the New Deal, and with a post-Frontier stewardship of the environment, would come to the fore.[47]

Biden's (Green) New Deal

Biden went to Gettysburg to channel Lincoln and appeal for racial justice. In late October he went to Warm Springs, Georgia, where FDR built his polio rehabilitation center, to channel Roosevelt and the New Deal. The Warm Springs speech, delivered on October 27, was about healing the wounds inflicted by the pandemic. Biden assumed the role of mourner in chief, speaking of the cruel suffering of those afflicted with COVID and the profound anguish of their loved ones, with which, as a survivor of multiple personal tragedies, he could credibly empathize. He insisted that this suffering be seen in context with the nation's other crises, "the economic anguish, the systematic discrimination." And these had to be seen not as a momentary glitch but as problems endemic to American society. "[If] we're honest with ourselves, the pain striking at the heart of our country goes back not months but years." We've failed to deal with them because "we've stopped seeing dignity in one another. We've stopped showing each other respect." To change the spirit of political discourse, he argued, America needed a president who would embody an ideal of humane behavior. Roosevelt had come to Warm Springs for his own physical ailments, but the experience had enabled him to learn how to heal the wounds of the Depression, and later of a world ravaged by war.[48]

Biden would eventually promise his own "100 Days" of active reform, invoking the symbolism of FDR's "Hundred Days." His program would call for a generous relief and stimulus package, a well-funded infrastructure program to create jobs as FDR's rural electrification and Works Progress Administration had done, and a national service program for young Americans modeled on the Civilian Conservation Corps and on Kennedy- and Johnson-era programs like VISTA and the Peace Corps. He promised to rebuild the nation's physical infrastructure and to integrate these long-deferred public investments with "social infrastructure" programs designed to restore and protect the health and economic viability of families. He promised that his economic development programs would contribute to the international struggle against climate change, and that they would address the problem of racial injustice neglected by the New Deal.[49]

The ground for this shift in mainstream Democratic ideology had been prepared by a range of progressive organizations, which had worked for decades to link climate change policy or "environmental justice" with demands for economic and social justice, under the rubric of the "Green New Deal." The phrase was coined in 2007 by Thomas Friedman, a columnist for the *New York Times* whose primary interest was the promotion of globalization through free-trade agreements. He accepted the scientific consensus on the necessity of slowing or reversing climate change; but he also saw the development of clean energy resources and technologies as an opportunity for economic growth and urged Americans to exploit it through government and corporate sponsorship of research and development.[50]

After the 2018 Democratic takeover of the House, a group of progressive senators and members of Congress had met to formulate a Green New Deal legislative program. They offered a resolution or statement of principles for adoption by the House and (a faint hope) the Republican-controlled Senate. It called for a ten-year "national mobilization" to achieve a complete transition to renewable and zero-emission energy sources through the development of solar, wind, and other new technologies; electric cars; and a substantially enlarged mass transit system. The shift would be financed in part by some variation on Obama-era proposals to tax producers for the social cost of carbon emissions. The program would address the costs to workers and consumers by developing a federal jobs program, along the lines of FDR's Works Progress Administration, to rebuild the nation's crumbling and energy-inefficient infrastructure. There would be aid programs for communities affected by the turn away from fossil fuels and an enhanced safety net for individuals through universal health insurance, caps on drug prices, and an increase of the minimum wage. The specific measures called for in the resolution were controversial, not only with conservatives but among liberal and progressive groups, and some environmentalists as well. What concerns us here is not the merit of specific provisions but the effect of the proposal, and the movements that support it, on the discourse of national myth.[51]

Proponents of the Green New Deal sought to reestablish the connections between the social justice agenda of the New Deal and Great Society, the civil rights movement, and the patriotic idealism of the Good War. When Rep. Alexandria Ocasio-Cortez and Senator Edward Markey (D-MA) introduced the resolution in February 2019, they called for "a new national, social, industrial and economic mobilization on a scale not seen since World War II and the New Deal era." The Good War analogy was often invoked by advocates of programs to remediate climate change. Al Gore, Senator Lamar Alexander (R-TN), and several environmentalist organizations called for a war-time like mobilization to reduce carbon emissions. In 2016 the environmentalist Bill McKibben called climate change the equivalent of "World War III" and demanded that we "mobilize" against it "as we did for the last world war."[52]

Although Biden was initially resistant to the radical implications of the program and concerned about negative reactions, his campaign eventually adopted many of its salient features, and in some ways extended them. In Philadelphia in June 2020 he offered a plan for "elimination of carbon pollution from the electric sector by 2035, rejoining the international Paris climate accord and spending $2 trillion over four years to boost renewables and create incentives for more energy-efficient cars, homes and commercial buildings." He linked this "greening" program with proposals for job-creating infrastructure programs like the Works Progress Administration.[53]

The pandemic had prepared the ground for this turn by compelling even fiscal conservatives in Congress to adopt the most massive relief program in American history, adding significantly to the national debt. During Trump's presidency, $3 trillion was appropriated for various forms of relief, including direct payments to individuals and businesses, forgiveness of loan and mortgage payments, moratoriums on evictions, and the financing of anti-pandemic operations. The benefits were not well or equally distributed. Large corporations and politically connected businesspeople gobbled up resources intended for small businesses: "Crumbs for the Hungry but Windfalls for the Rich," as a *New York Times* headline put it. Nevertheless, the measure signaled broad acceptance of the Keynesian economic theory that informed the New Deal: that massive outlays of government funds are essential to checking and reversing the effects of a severe recession or depression. The action was markedly different from the response to the Great Recession of 2008, when conservative Democrats joined Republicans in severely restricting the Obama administration's efforts to pump cash into the economy.[54]

Biden's campaign would win him the presidency, but the verdict on his platform was mixed: Republicans gained seats in the House and in state races. In the end, his legislative program would fall short of its ambitious goals, thwarted by partisan and intraparty divisions. Nevertheless, his campaign had made a significant contribution to the discourse of American political culture. It had drawn the outline of a "progressive Myth of America," a narrative of struggle for racial and social justice running from Lincoln to the New Deal to the civil rights movement.

But the emergence of this new "progressive" movement, the agitation of BLM, and the disruptions of the COVID pandemic also roused the MAGA movement to a sense of imminent existential peril, by displaying the power of the liberals and racial minorities who, as Trump averred, were bent on destroying "our country."

19

"The Last President of the Confederacy"

Trump's Lost Cause

AT THE START of his 2020 campaign, Donald Trump made a bid for Black support, hoping to peel off a share of that Democratic constituency. Before the pandemic he could claim, with justification, that Black unemployment was at a record low and (less persuasively) that he had therefore done more for "the Black people" than Abraham Lincoln. However, as he told Bob Woodward, he felt no obligation to "understand the anger and pain" of Black Americans. "You really drank the Kool-Aid, didn't you? Just listen to you," he said when Woodward expressed sympathy for their plight. "Wow. No, I don't feel that at all." For Trump the Black Lives Matter (BLM) demonstrations offered an obvious way to rouse the ire and enthusiasm of his base. By rejecting the movement's accusation of systemic racism, he validated the feelings of his White supporters, and by condemning the disorder, he reasserted the GOP's claim to be the party of law and order.[1]

The most striking and peculiar gesture of Trump's racial politics was his decision to become the chief defender of Confederate symbolism. Trump's knowledge of Civil War history is negligible, but events since Charlottesville had taught him to recognize Confederate symbols as the trademark of his most militant supporters. In the spring and summer of 2020, he stepped forward to defend those symbols against their criminal destruction or defacing by BLM demonstrators, White liberal "socialists," "extreme radicals," and Antifa. In fact, while many Americans saw the desecration of monuments as criminal vandalism, many other supported the underlying message, even in the South. The rejection of Confederate symbolism had been embraced by the senior leadership of the military services and by bipartisan majorities in Congress, who voted to bar displays of Confederate flags, badges, and logos on military bases and authorized the renaming of bases named for Confederate generals.

Trump would not be deterred by that defeat. The base-naming issue was another opportunity for dramatizing his role as defender of traditional Americanism against liberals and the deep state. "My Administration will not even consider" the name changes, he declared. "Anarchists and left-wing extremists have sought to advance a fringe ideology that paints the United States of America as fundamentally unjust," and with the aid of Democrats they are trying to "cancel the nation's glorious history."[2]

Trump thus made the content and meaning of America's national myths an explicit campaign issue, and a centerpiece of his program for restoring American greatness. He would follow the Lost Cause paradigm, emphasizing the need for extreme and violent means to redeem an imperiled civilization, and he chose this over the themes of economic prosperity and "toughness" on international trade that advisers like Larry Kudlow and Stephen Moore wanted to make the basis of the campaign.

MSNBC commentator Nicolle Wallace noted the prevalence of Civil War symbolism in the campaign, and the threat of violence it implied. She thought Trump had "greenlit a war in this country around race. And if you think about the most dangerous thing he's done, that might be it." On June 26 Trump issued an executive order calling for the most severe punishment of protesters who vandalized statues: "We're going to get ready to send in the military slash National Guard to some of these poor bastards that don't know what they're doing, these poor radical lefts." With the support of William Barr's Justice Department, he promoted the false story that Antifa terrorists were behind the protests. On August 31 he announced on Laura Ingraham's Fox News show that BLM demonstrations were directed by "people that are in the dark shadows," who had sent planeloads of "thugs wearing these dark uniforms, black uniforms, with gear" to sow "chaos" in the streets. In response he was "dispatching thousands and thousands of heavily armed soldiers, military personnel and law enforcement officers to stop the rioting, looting, vandalism, assaults and the wanton destruction of property." In fact, statute law bars the use of regular military forces for civil law enforcement. When he sent a contingent of US Marshals to Portland, Oregon, on July 22, they wore black uniforms to conceal their identity. But what Trump actually did or failed to do was less important than the display of rhetorical violence, which dramatized his "toughness."[3]

His approach was supported by the most conservative and populist elements of his party. In a *New York Times* op-ed piece on June 3, Senator Tom Cotton

(R-AR) demanded "an overwhelming show of force" to "detain and ultimately deter lawbreakers," especially "nihilist criminals" and "left-wing radicals." In a later Tweet he declared that Trump should send in "the 10th Mountain, 82nd Airborne, 1st Cav, 3rd Infantry [Divisions], whatever it takes to restore order." Then he added, "No quarter for insurrectionists, anarchists, rioters, and looters." In strict military parlance, "no quarter" goes beyond the "shoot on sight" orders sometimes given during urban riots and insurrections. It literally means take no prisoners, that even those who attempt to surrender will be killed. Cotton, a veteran of the US Army's 101st Airborne Division, was speaking metaphorically, but his call to violence was incendiary enough to trigger a widespread reaction in the newsroom, leading to the resignation of the op-ed page editor.[4]

Joe Biden had chosen to deliver his major campaign addresses at Gettysburg and Warm Springs, to symbolically associate himself with Lincoln and Franklin D. Roosevelt. Trump would use Tulsa, Oklahoma, and Mount Rushmore National Memorial as settings for speeches affirming his connection to the historical traditionalism of the Lost Cause and the Frontier.

Since Charlottesville, Trump had made it a practice to exploit racial resentments by holding rallies where tensions were already high. His first rally after Charlottesville was held in Phoenix, Arizona, whose Democratic mayor had implored him to stay away, because his blue city's large Hispanic population was in an uproar over Trump's immigration policies. Trump ignored the request and used the event to pardon Sheriff Joe Arpaio, who was hated for his open racism and abuse of Latino prisoners. After Lafayette Square he held a Fox News town hall in Madison, Wisconsin, the scene of violent protests: "Every night, we're going to get tougher and tougher," he warned. "And at some point, there's going to be retribution because there has to be. These people are vandals, but they're agitators, but they're really—they're terrorists."[5]

The same thinking went into his decision to hold a rally in Tulsa in June 2020. This time he had multiple provocations in mind: he would use the full repertoire of racialist symbolism, from dog whistles to trumpet calls, and he would show his contempt for the scientific consensus on how to handle the pandemic.

The original date for the rally was June 19, or Juneteenth, celebrated by Black people as the anniversary of their liberation from slavery. In private, Trump scoffed that "changing the day of the rally . . . to accommodate these people" was "a ridiculous thing." In public he and his advisers professed ignorance of the date's significance, then agreed to change the schedule in the face of vociferous protests. But Tulsa had its own significance. In 1921 it was the site of one of the worst racial pogroms in American history, when White mobs (aided by police and National Guard) destroyed the prosperous Black neighborhood of Greenwood, killing as many as 300 people and driving thousands from their homes. Officials and educators in Tulsa had been campaigning for years, against stubborn resistance, for public recognition of the massacre. BLM demonstrations in Tulsa therefore had a particularly powerful historical resonance.[6]

Instead of seeking to defuse the issue, Trump issued threats and insults, as if daring BLM protesters to invite police repression. He characterized the protesters as anarchists, agitators, looters, and lowlifes. He invoked the traditional trope of the Black rapist, describing a hypothetical scenario of a "very tough hombre" breaking into a young woman's home "while her husband is away." But Trump would put the thugs in their place: if Antifa and the rest "are going to Oklahoma please understand, you will not be treated like you have been in New York, Seattle, or Minneapolis. It will be a much different scene!" Protesters would be met by police and MAGA counterprotesters in red hats, taking advantage of the state's open-carry law.[7]

At the rally itself, and in the associated news conference, Trump ran through his litany of racial dog whistles: the coronavirus was the "kung flu," the Floyd protesters were "thugs" whose attacks on Confederate statues were an attempt to "demolish our heritage. . . . We have a great heritage. We're a great country." Just as he would protect "our heritage" from being trashed by non-White people and liberals, he would resist the mandates of the scientific elites. The Centers for Disease Control had been warning for months that large public gatherings were likely to spread COVID-19. Tulsa was a demonstration of Trump's defiance of their authority. He spoke of the pandemic as a "hoax" perpetrated by his political enemies and a hostile scientific community and embraced the absurd conclusion that the way to diminish the harm caused by the pandemic was to stop testing people for infection.[8]

The spread of COVID-19 accelerated in June as red states followed Trump's incitement to reopen. Nor was the public impressed. Even in MAGA-friendly Oklahoma, people were afraid of COVID and followed the advice of state health officials to stay away. Instead of filling his arena, Trump saw rows and rows of empty seats. He blamed the low turnout on fear of protesters, but there were none near the arena.[9]

As a campaign tactic, the emphasis on race and "crime in the streets" was successful among Republicans. Surveys taken in late June and October showed that Republican support for the demonstrators, which had been remarkably high at the end of May, was declining significantly. But those same surveys found Trump's approval plummeting in the suburbs, especially among White women. To counter the trend, Trump reverted to a venerable dog whistle, familiar from his father's promotion of segregated housing in Queens and the suburbs. "By the way," he told a Texas rally on June 29, "just so we can get this straight, 30 percent of the people in the suburbs are low-income people. Thirty percent of the people in the suburbs are minorities. And so we're ruining this American dream for everybody." In a tweet issued at the same time, he reassured "the Suburban Housewives of America . . . I am happy to inform all of the people living their Suburban Lifestyle Dream that you will no longer be bothered or financially hurt by having low income housing built in your neighborhood. . . . Biden will destroy your neighborhood and your American Dream. I will preserve it, and make it even better!" To drive the message home he added, "If I don't win, America's Suburbs will be OVERRUN with Low Income Projects, Anarchists, Agitators, Looters and, of course, 'Friendly Protesters.'"[10]

National Myth Becomes a Campaign Issue

In the aftermath of the Tulsa debacle, and in the face of the COVID crisis and ensuing economic recession, Trump focused on all-out prosecution of the culture war. At a Michigan rally in October, he cast the election as a battle not just for the future but for the redemption of the past: "This election will decide whether we preserve our magnificent heritage or whether we let far left radicals wipe it all away," Trump said. "They constantly smear America as a racist country. . . . America is the most magnificent, most virtuous nation that has ever existed."[11]

His speeches on the July 4th weekend, delivered first at the White House and later at Mount Rushmore, were crafted by Stephen Miller, the adviser most strongly committed to White ethnonationalism, and they set forth a series of ideological touchstones for the MAGA base. In these speeches Trump portrayed himself as commander in chief in a new civil war, defending Western civilization and Christian values against a ruthless and barbaric enemy. There are no peaceful demonstrators, only mobs led by "the radical left, the Marxists, the anarchists, the agitators and the plunderers." They are bent on "demolishing our statues" to further their ultimate goal of "erasing our history and indoctrinating our children."[12]

The symbolism of Mount Rushmore was well chosen for a major address. If statues represented "our great heritage," the four colossal presidential heads carved into the face of the mountain were symbols of this heritage on a Pharaonic scale, fit for worship and beyond the reach of defacement. Trump framed his fight against BLM as a defense of Western civilization against a savage enemy: "1776 represented the culmination of thousands of years of Western civilization and the triumph of not only spirit, but of wisdom, philosophy, and reason. And yet, as we meet here tonight. . . . our nation is witnessing a merciless campaign to wipe out our history, defame our heroes, erase our values, and indoctrinate our children. Angry mobs are trying to tear down statues of our founders, deface our most sacred memorials, and unleash a wave of violent crime in our cities." These are "the predictable result of years of extreme indoctrination and bias in education, journalism, and other cultural institutions," which he claimed were dominated by liberals who enforce the codes of "political correctness" and use "cancel culture" to punish conservatives for their exercise of free speech.

The *New York Times'* 1619 Project, which proposed an American history curriculum centered on slavery and race, was emblematic of this leftist educational project. It began as a series of articles in the *New York Times* in the summer of 2019, curated by Nikole Hannah-Jones, an investigative reporter and recipient of a prestigious MacArthur Fellowship. The project won the Pulitzer Prize and was later corrected and expanded into a book suitable for classroom use. But the most threatening tendency was the propagation of "critical race theory" (CRT), a complex and somewhat abstruse school of academic thought that asserts that racism in the United States is "systemic," the product of historically rooted institutions, customs, and values. In a September interview with Fox News, Christopher Rufo—a fellow of the Manhattan Institute, a conservative think tank—identified CRT as "the default ideology of the federal bureaucracy" and claimed it "is now being weaponized against the American people." In October 2020 he published a highly influential article in the *Wall Street Journal,* "The Truth about Critical Race Theory," decrying CRT's domination of higher education and the public education establishment. As Rufo later admitted, he saw CRT as the "Achilles heel" of the liberal establishment, because of its radicalism and theoretical rigidity, and because it was advocated by some in the BLM movement and therefore associated with the disorder and statue desecration of BLM demonstrations. Any attempt to consider the deeply troubling history of race in America could be discredited by simply identifying it with CRT.[13]

At Mount Rushmore Trump accused "radical leftists" of transforming the call for social justice "into an instrument of division and vengeance," saying that "it would turn our free and inclusive society into a place of a repression, domination, and exclusion." He claimed, "Angry mobs are trying to tear down statues of our Founders, deface our most sacred memorials, and unleash a wave of violent crime in our cities. Many of these people have no idea why they are doing this, but some know exactly what they are doing. They think the American people are weak and soft and submissive. But no, the American people are strong and proud, and they will not allow our country, and all of its values, history, and culture, to be taken from them."[14] He then spelled out the ideas that in his view defined real Americans, and declared his determination to punish those who rejected those ideas to the full extent of the law.

The first principle was exceptionalism. "We declare that the United States of America is the most just and exceptional nation ever to exist on earth." The second was that American democratic principles are based on religious truth, not secular history—the Christian nationalist principle that had become so important to conservative ideology. It is "the fact that our country was founded on Judeo-Christian principles" that has enabled us to advance "the cause of peace and justice throughout the world." We also "know that the American family is the bedrock of American life"—an echo of the GOP's perennial assertion of "family values" in opposition to feminism, abortion, and LGBTQ rights. As an afterthought, he added, "We believe in equal opportunity, equal justice, and equal treatment for citizens of every race, background, religion and creed." But the basis of equality is theological, not civil: "Every child of every color, born and unborn, is made in the holy image of God."[15]

He nodded to the concept of America's perfectibility as voiced by Lincoln and Martin Luther King Jr. but rejected the 1619 Project's assertion that racism was intrinsic to the Founding and led to the dispossession of Native Americans, the enslavement of Black people, and the long, bitter oppression of Jim Crow. Americans must not question, they must *affirm* their identity, and do so by identifying unequivocally with a past defined by the Myth of the Frontier in its most traditional form: "Above all, our children from every community must be taught that to be American is to inherit the spirit of the most adventurous and confident people ever to walk the face of the Earth. Americans are the people who pursued our Manifest Destiny across the ocean, into the uncharted wilderness, over the tallest mountains, and then into the skies, and even into the stars." Trump sees no inconsistency in identifying Martin Luther King and Manifest Destiny as representing compatible values.[16]

Those who question the moral perfection of the Founders, or the glorious exceptionalism of America, must be treated not just as dissidents but as outlaws: "Against every law of society and nature, our children are taught in school to hate their own country, and to believe that the men and women who built it were not heroes, but that they were villains. The radical view of American history is a web of lies—all perspective is removed, every virtue is obscured, every motive is twisted, every fact is distorted, and every flaw is magnified until the history is purged and the record is disfigured beyond all recognition." This insistence on rewriting history is, for Trump, an "attack on our liberty, our magnificent liberty. It must be stopped and it will be stopped very quickly. We will . . . protect our nation's children from this radical assault, and preserve our beloved American way of life. . . . That is why I am deploying federal law enforcement to protect our monuments, arrest the rioters, and prosecute offenders to the fullest extent of the law."[17]

Trump vowed to form a 1776 Commission, charged with developing a "pro-American" history curriculum to replace the "left-wing indoctrination" that he claimed was being promoted in our schools. He thus made the interpretation of American history—which is to say the meaning of our national myth—the explicit focus of the ideological conflict.[18]

The curriculum issue would prove significant in 2020 and set the terms for the contentious debates in state and local school boards that continue to the present day. Trump's polemic struck a chord with a significant body of public opinion that was repelled by the combination of BLM's disorderly demonstrations and militant demands for curricular change. This was a critical matter in the summer of 2020, when reforms pressed by the BLM movement were being considered by local school boards.[19]

"Diversity, equity, and inclusion" and "sensitivity training" programs were especially vulnerable to the charge of "indoctrination," since they were designed to "train" people to overcome racial biases. The methods used by such programs have been questioned by liberals and social justice activists as well as conservatives for being simplistic and coercive, and similar complaints are made about the "antiracism" programs developed in response to the work of Ibram X. Kendi. Although these programs have no real connection to history teaching, in the fall of 2020 they were associated with the push for curricular changes based on the 1619 Project, and in his Mount Rushmore speech Trump declared his intention to ban the use of such programs in federal agencies.[20]

There is no comprehensive listing of the history curricula being used in the nation's hundreds of school systems, and no way of quantifying the extent to which race-centered or race-sensitive programs were actually operating in the fall of 2020. CRT as such was too abstruse to be taught in public schools, although some educators were influenced by having studied it in college. The curricular demands made by BLM were under discussion at contentious school board meetings in the summer of 2020, and some changes went into effect in September. What is clear is that the restructuring of curriculum was a major bone of contention in local communities, as well as an element in a highly partisan presidential campaign. School boards had to deal not only with the demands of Black activists and liberal academics but with the militant and sometimes menacing demands of conservatives for a restoration of patriotic education. The intimidation of school boards by armed paramilitaries drew fire from the press, but public support for BLM was also diminishing. Over the next two years, resistance to BLM's educational initiatives would take the form of a "parental rights" movement asserting the entitlement of parents to control what their children studied or read in school. Its strength would become manifest in 2021 with Republican Glenn Youngkin's election as governor in the blue state of Virginia and would be seen in a wave of school board and local elections across the country. According to a 2022 Harris Poll, public approval of BLM fell from a high approaching 60 percent to 55 percent overall and 47 percent among White people—still a substantial level of support. The Pew Research Center found that a majority of White people (53 percent) accepted the existence of "systemic racism," and 76 percent agreed that racial discrimination was a serious issue. This suggests that, whatever its flaws, BLM had achieved its basic goal of putting racism on the public's agenda.[21]

The electoral effect of Trump's polemic is hard to measure. His rhetorical strategy worked well with the MAGA base and cultural conservatives in general, who were roused by his attack on the liberal establishment, on the perceived social deterioration of Democrat-governed cities reflected in the spreading tent cities sheltering the homeless, and on the toleration of crime in general and BLM criminality in particular. Their enthusiasm would give him a record-setting popular vote in November. Yet neither Trump's rhetoric nor the growing disenchantment with BLM's pressure campaigns would halt the drift of independent and suburban voters away from Trump.

Trump defined victory in culture-war terms. The purpose of his attack on liberal historiography was to amplify the campaign's major theme, the warfare of real Americans against the intellectual and moral corruptions of the liberal elite. Since the 1990s, conservatives had fought a series of defensive battles against the revisionist historiography that had emerged from the cultural revolutions of the 1960s. In the late 1990s the flash points were "political correctness" and multiculturalism in universities, and the curricular changes recommended by a commission on National History Standards. In 2014 it was the College Board's rewriting of its AP American history curriculum. By establishing the 1776 Commission, Trump transformed the outrage generated by BLM's attack on Confederate symbols into a broader agenda for reshaping the way American history should be taught in schools and represented in museums and monuments.[22]

Laying the Groundwork for Sedition

By the summer of 2020 the coming election had been framed as a critical, perhaps an existential test of democracy. *The Atlantic* went so far as to call it "the election that could break America." That sense of crisis was intensified by the understanding that "democracy" had radically different meanings for MAGA and the Left. For liberals, a Trump victory would mean environmental catastrophe and the triumph of racial bigotry and voter suppression. For MAGA, a Democratic victory meant "socialism" and an end to "freedom" and civilization—a freedom whose ultimate guarantor was the 2nd Amendment right to bear arms.[23]

Trump raised the stakes by insisting throughout the campaign that Democrats planned a massive election fraud, exploiting the expanded use of mail-in ballots made necessary by the pandemic. He also reprised the grievance that was part of his administration's myth of origin—that voting by illegals had cost him the popular vote in 2016. These accusations raised the anxiety of Republican voters, and their commitment to turning out on election day. They were also a hedge against the possibility that Trump might lose.

Trump had begun to imagine, and to suggest to his audience, scenarios in which "his" warfighters would take part in open confrontation with his enemies: the deep state, RINOs, liberal Democrats, the press. His 2016 campaign had been marked by frequent incitement to individual acts of violence against protesters and reporters. Charlottesville had shown his sympathy for the violent Right. His antimasking campaign and calls to armed demonstrators to "liberate Michigan" or "liberate Virginia" crossed the line into advocacy of antigovernment violence. In his September debate with Joe Biden, when challenged on his indulgent attitude toward White supremacists, Trump told the violent ethnonationalist Proud Boys to "stand back, and stand by!" The group took this as a summons and inscribed it on their banners. He also encouraged violence by the pleasure he took in imagining it. At one rally he described law enforcement moving against BLM protesters in Minneapolis and cooed, "I don't know, there's something about that—when you watch everybody getting pushed around—there's something very beautiful about it. . . . Not politically correct. . . . But you people get it."[24]

Trump linked every conceivable issue to gun rights and the 2nd Amendment, implicitly invoking the "insurrectionary" version of the palladium doctrine. Gun rights became the symbol of *everything* MAGA was trying to protect. Trump told an Ohio rally that Biden was "following the radical left agenda. Take away your guns, destroy your Second Amendment. No religion, no anything, hurt the Bible, hurt God. He's against God, he's against guns, he's against energy, our kind of energy [i.e., fossil fuels]." When the Supreme Court rejected (on procedural grounds) his executive order ending Deferred Action for Childhood Arrivals exemptions for undocumented immigrants brought to the United States as children, Trump turned on the Court and the two conservative justices who voted to overturn the order, one of whom was his own appointee. "These horrible & politically charged decisions coming out of the Supreme Court are shotgun blasts into the face of people that are proud to call themselves Republicans or Conservatives. We need more Justices or we will lose our 2nd. Amendment & everything else. Vote Trump 2020!"[25]

The anticipation of violence was heightened in *both* political parties. Opinion polls taken before the election showed that 36 percent of Republicans and 33 percent of Democrats believed there was *some* justification for using violence to achieve their party's political goals; 20 percent of Republicans and 19 percent of Democrats thought there would be "'a great deal' of justification" if their party were to lose the election. A month before the election, record numbers of Americans were buying firearms and stocking up on ammunition. Whereas the buying sprees of 2008–2009 and 2012–2014 were driven by fear of regulation, the motive here was fear of actual violence by either left-wing demonstrators or right-wing gunmen—in some cases by a desire for open conflict.[26]

The opposing partisans responded to the threat in terms dictated by their myths of choice. Liberal groups planned to respond to a MAGA "coup" with massive nonviolent demonstrations and strikes, the scenario demanded by the Myth of the Movement. The MAGA side reverted to its preferred versions of the Myths of the Frontier, the Lost Cause, and the Founding, as vigilantes and paramilitaries armed themselves for violent resistance. From the MAGA perspective, the only legitimate outcome of the election was a Trump victory. Anything else must be the result of massive fraud, requiring vigilante justice.[27]

Cues for violence came from Trump himself, and from Republican officeholders. Michael Caputo, a veteran Republican lobbyist and consultant then serving in the Health and Human Services Department, warned on Facebook that scientists charged with combating the pandemic were planning "sedition" against the president, and leftist hit teams were preparing a postelection rebellion. He urged his readers, "If you carry guns, buy ammunition, ladies and gentlemen, because it's going to be hard to get." Marjorie Taylor Greene (R-GA), a congresswoman and sometime QAnon follower, posted statements suggesting "a bullet to the head" as the quickest way to remove Nancy Pelosi as Speaker of the House and, referring to Hillary Clinton and Barack Obama, said, "Now do we get to hang them??" In a post directed at four progressive Democratic congresswomen known as "the Squad," she posed with a gun, identified herself as their "worst nightmare," and declared, "We need strong conservative Christians to go on the offense against these socialists who want to rip our country apart."[28]

Calls for armed resistance emerged in the social media of QAnon supporters, the Proud Boys, and paramilitaries like the Oath Keepers and Three Percenters, who framed their actions in the familiar terms of the palladium doctrine: "What is the heart of the Second Amendment, pro-militia, anti-government patriot movement? It's the insurrectionist theory of the Second Amendment," said Stewart Rhodes of the Oath Keepers. "It says people can rise up against a tyrannical government." J. J. MacNab, a fellow at the George Washington University's Program on Extremism, testified before the US House Homeland Security Subcommittee on Intelligence and Counterterrorism, "Between gun control issues, civil unrest, the stresses placed on the country by a deadly pandemic, conspiracy theories, anti-press sentiments, and a highly divisive election cycle, the nation is one large event away from violence."[29]

On election night, facing the likelihood of defeat, Trump declared the election stolen and took the first steps in an aggressive campaign to overturn the election by legal and extralegal means. It is still not clear whether Trump believed that the election had been stolen, or built his new campaign on a knowing lie. For months, press and television reporters had been warning that election-night results would be inconclusive, as the prevalence of mail-in voting in most states would mean a delay in counting; and that late-counted ballots would likely favor Democrats, because Trump had made in-person voting a test of fealty. Nevertheless, as the mail-in votes began to accumulate, especially in the swing state of Pennsylvania, Trump cried foul. "This is a fraud on the American public," he said on election night. "This is an embarrassment to our country. We were getting ready to win this election—frankly, we did win this election." He then went a radical step further: "We want all voting to stop. We don't want them to find any ballots at 4 o'clock in the morning and add them to the list." He would press that charge in the weeks that followed, telling his supporters on November 25, "[This] election has to be turned around, because we won Pennsylvania by a lot and we won all these swing states by a lot. . . . A lot of horrible things happened. . . . This was not the United States of America. . . . It's a disgrace that this is happening to our country. . . . They're bad people, they're horrible people, and they're people that don't love our country."[30]

Trump's refusal to accept the count may have owed something to the projections of his pollsters, who led him to believe his election-day margin would

be too large for the late counting of mail-ins to overcome. They also overesti-
mated the significance of his rallies, which in 2016 had been an indicator that
conventional polling was underestimating his appeal. And in fairness, the 74
million votes Trump did receive would have been enough to have won any
other election. But he was given enough accurate information, on election night
and over the ensuing weeks and months, to have convinced a rational man that
he had lost. On December 1 Trump was informed by Barr that the Department of Justice had found no evidence of voter fraud on a scale sufficient to
reverse the outcome. That was unacceptable. When he spoke from the White
House the following day, Trump made no mention of Barr's report. Instead,
he drew on the false "evidence" produced for him by a new set of advisers, led
by Rudy Giuliani, who endorsed his belief that he was the victim of systematic persecution by establishment forces. "You've been watching it now for four
years. These entrenched interests oppose our movement, because we put America first. They don't put America first, and we're returning power to you the
American people. . . . If we don't root out the fraud, the tremendous and horrible fraud that's taken place in our 2020 election, we don't have a country
anymore."[31]

His raging and obsessive insistence that the election was "rigged" and "stolen"
has been attributed to the defects of a narcissistic personality, unable to admit
defeat, and to the huckster's hazard of believing his own hype. His response is
consistent with his behavior as a businessman, when he consistently pursued
litigation on often outrageous pretexts to exhaust the resources and endurance
of creditors and unpaid contractors. It has also been seen as a cynical effort to
create a new "Lost Cause" centered on himself, on which to base a comeback.
All of these interpretations are plausible, and all, in different degrees and combinations and at different stages of the campaign, may have shaped his thoughts,
words, and actions. It is one of Trump's paradoxical strengths as a politician
that his public psychodrama distracts attention from the serious consequences
of his actions.

Whatever his motives, Trump made a deliberate decision to overturn the
results of the election. His campaign, and the public delusion that sustained
it, would be supported by most leaders of the Republican establishment. Some
did so cynically, believing that as reality sank in, the tantrum would end. But
in the meantime their words helped keep the anger of true believers at fever
pitch. Kevin McCarthy, the House Republican leader, told Laura Ingraham
on Fox, "Everyone who's listening, do not be quiet, do not be silent about this.
We cannot allow this to happen before our very eyes." Lindsey Graham said
Democrats "can all go to hell as far as I'm concerned—I've had it with these

people. Let's fight back. . . . We lose elections because they cheat us." When Christopher Krebs, head of election security at the Department of Homeland Security, declared that the election had been free of significant fraud or interference, he was fired—and Joseph diGenova, a former US attorney and political commentator, called for him to be "shot at dawn." A *Washington Post* survey showed that in December 2020, "of the 249 Republicans in the House and the Senate, only 27 acknowledged Joe Biden won the election," and only 32 said they would accept him as the "legitimate" winner even if the Electoral College ratified the outcome. An *Economist*/YouGov poll taken in early December showed that 80 percent of Republicans believed the election was unfair and that Trump should not concede. This meant that 60 million Republican voters refused to accept Biden's victory.[32]

Having cloaked himself and the MAGA movement in the Myth of the Lost Cause, Trump was summoning his supporters to follow that narrative to its conclusion in a violent rebellion against the result of a free and fair election. As Eugene Robinson put it, he was casting himself as "the last president of the Confederacy."[33]

Taking Our Country Back: The Assault on the Capitol

The response of MAGA Republicans followed the secessionists' script of 1860: if you block our movement, we will have no choice but to break the system. Texas Republican Party chair Allen West suggested, "Perhaps law-abiding states should band together and form a Union of states that will abide by the constitution." A state representative went so far as to propose a referendum on Texas independence. But secession talk was just a way of venting. Trump and his loyalists had more substantial plans.[34]

Retired lieutenant general Michael Flynn, Trump's disgraced former national security adviser, urged Trump to invoke the Insurrection Act, impose "martial law," and deploy the military to force a "rerun" of the election in key states. The idea was supported by members of the congressional Freedom Caucus and gained wider currency as it was floated on social media, in press interviews by Republican officials, and on pro-Trump media outlets like Fox News, One America News Network, and Newsmax.[35] The growing influence of such ideas, and Trump's evident attraction to them, raised alarms at the highest levels of the national security apparatus. Secretary of State Mike Pompeo, Secretary of Defense Mark Esper, CIA director Gina Haspel, and Joint Chiefs of Staff chairman General Mark Milley were concerned (in Pompeo's words) that "the crazies were taking over." Haspel told Milley she feared "we are on the way to a right-wing coup." Milley came to believe Trump was following "the gospel of the Fuhrer": that he might foment public disorder and use it as a "Reichstag moment," as Adolph Hitler used the arson attack on the German parliament building, to justify a coup, using his paramilitaries as Hitler used his Brown-shirts. Milley began planning with his colleagues to thwart any attempt to block the peaceful transfer of power.[36]

On December 14 the electoral slates chosen by the states were officially certified. For those Republicans who hoped for a rational response from the White House and a peaceful transfer of power, the validity of the election was now settled. Mitch McConnell and several Republican senators and governors acknowledged Joe Biden as president-elect of the United States. This was the view of what some called "Team Normal" in the White House—the Counsel's Office headed by Pat Cipollone, other members of the staff, and William Barr's Justice Department.

There was, however, a "Team Crazy," which fully shared Trump's commitment to preventing the transfer of power, fronted by the ad hoc legal team organized by Rudy Giuliani, whose members had no official standing but acted as Trump's personal agents. They included Sidney Powell and John Eastman, who promoted a series of lawsuits so ill-conceived that the lawyers who brought them were threatened with disbarment. The group was joined from time to time by wild-card fanatics like My Pillow executive Mike Lindell, who would arrive bearing folders of bogus "evidence." They were joined by a group of professional conspiracists called the "War Room," who anticipated the failure of Giuliani's legal strategy and were planning for "direct action." From a command center in DC's Willard Hotel, they would attempt to influence, perhaps direct, demonstrations supporting the efforts of Republican legislators to thwart the counting of electoral votes. Steve Bannon, back in Trump's good graces, was among them, pleased at this chance to take on the political order and "burn it down." Roger Stone, the foppish political "dirty trickster" and conspiracy hawker recently pardoned by Trump, had anticipated the call to arms even before the election. He offered to provide liaison between the War Room, the Proud Boys and Oath Keepers, and Chief of Staff Mark Meadows. (The paramilitaries were ostensibly in DC to provide Stone with personal protection.) Michael Flynn brought to their planning the predilections and skills of a seasoned military commander and intelligence officer. He too was in contact with the Oath Keepers.[37]

At a series of secret White House meetings on December 18, Trump's official advisory team and the White House counselors found themselves pitted against "Team Crazy," represented by General Flynn, Giuliani, and Sidney Powell.

When the advisers insisted that there was no further legal recourse, they were angrily dismissed by Trump for their lack of "toughness." Although Trump accepted the White House counsel's advice that he not seize voting machines (as Flynn had advocated), he openly shifted his allegiance to "Team Crazy" because, as he said, they offered the only way forward.[38]

After that meeting, Trump sent his legal team and the War Room conspirators into action, with January 6, the day Congress was scheduled to count the electoral votes, as their focus. Giuliani's team, aided by various members of Congress and states' attorneys general, would pursue increasingly desperate and illegal efforts to decertify swing-state electors or appoint false electors in their place. Trump would speak directly to officials in Michigan, Georgia, and Pennsylvania, pressing them to alter the official vote count. The calls to Georgia's governor and secretary of state Brad Raffensperger show Trump alternately wheedling and threatening: "So look. All I want to do is this. I just want to find 11,780 votes, which is one more than we have. Because we won the state. . . . So what are we going to do here, folks? I only need 11,000 votes. Fellas, I need 11,000 votes. Give me a break." When the Department of Justice refused to endorse Trump's claim of massive electoral fraud, Trump tried to "decapitate" the agency, firing Attorney General Barr and attempting to fire his replacement, Jeffrey Rosen, in order to appoint Jeffrey Clark, a sycophantic nonentity, as acting attorney general. Only the threat of mass resignations prevented him.[39]

The next day Trump initiated a direct action campaign with a tweet summoning his followers: "Big protest in D.C. on January 6th. Be there, will be wild!" He would repeat the summons at regular intervals over the next two weeks. A confederacy of MAGA-related organizations moved to organize demonstrations in Washington, DC, starting with the Million MAGA Marches on November 14 and December 12, and culminating with the March to Save America on January 6.[40]

Before the election, Donald Trump Jr. had called on "able-bodied" supporters to form an "army" to help his father. Amy Kremer, a Tea Party activist who had organized Women Vote Trump, now formed Women for America First to plan the Washington demonstrations. She reached out to QAnon "decoders"; the paramilitary Proud Boys, Oath Keepers, and Three Percenters; and members of the Gun Owners of America, the NRA's more radical rival. Virginia Thomas, wife of Supreme Court justice Clarence Thomas and a leader of the Christian nationalist Council for National Policy and the action-oriented Groundswell, worked behind the scenes to help the rally organizers. She was also a link between them and White House chief of staff Mark Meadows, who shared her apocalyptic understanding of the electoral crisis. "We are living through what feels like the end of America," she told Meadows. "You guys fold, the evil just moves fast down underneath you all." Meadows agreed: "This is a fight of good versus evil," he said. "Evil always looks like the victor until the King of Kings triumphs. Do not grow weary in well doing. The fight continues." Thomas advised him that the situation required a ruthless disregard for legal niceties: "The most important thing you can realize right now is that there are no rules in war. There are no rules."[41]

According to the *Washington Post*, an "enemies list" posted on the dark web identified and "falsely accused swing-state governors, voting systems executives and the former top U.S. cybersecurity officials responsible for securing November's presidential election of 'changing votes and working against the President' in a treasonous attempt to 'overthrow our democracy.'" One of the hashtags for the list was #NoQuarterForTraitors. William Calhoun, a Georgia defense lawyer, began posting comments on social media advocating "'slaughtering' or 'executing' communists, Democrats and Black Lives Matter activists." Steve Bannon called for putting "heads on pikes" as a warning to federal bureaucrats. Rep. Paul Gosar (R-AZ) told the head of the Arizona Oath Keepers that the country was already in a civil war, "we just haven't started shooting each other yet." QAnon activist Kenneth Grayson posted on December 23, "I'm there for the greatest celebration of all time after Pence leads the Senate flip!! OR IM THERE IF TRUMP TELLS US TO STORM THE FUKIN CAPITAL IMA DO THAT THEN!" On January 5 Alan Hostetter told a rally of Virginia Women for Trump, "Our voices tomorrow are going to put the fear of God in the cowards and the traitors, the Republicans in name only, the communists of the Democrat Party, they need to know we as a people, a hundred million strong, are coming for them. . . . I will see you all tomorrow at the frontlines. . . . We are taking our country back."[42]

This course of action was justified by reference to MAGA's favored myths: the Myth of the Founding, which sanctioned revolution against tyranny or usurpation; the Myth of the Frontier, which sanctioned vigilantism; and the Myth of the Lost Cause, which sanctioned violence to save the White race from rule by an elected but morally and racially illegitimate government. YouTube personality Tim Pool framed January 6 as "Trump's Last Stand"—militant action was required if he was not to meet George Armstrong Custer's fate and find himself destroyed by savages. On January 6 a member of the Red-State Secession organization posted: "If you are not prepared to use force to defend civilization, then be prepared to accept barbarism." According to the insurrectionist theory of the 2nd Amendment, which is central to the thinking of gun rights fundamentalists, Christian nationalists, and neo-Confederates, the

Constitution authorizes the violent overthrow of a government guilty of "usurpation." In this case, the agents of overthrow would be "militias"—not the official state militias envisioned by Justice Joseph Story's "palladium doctrine," but rogue paramilitaries of the radical Right.[43]

Trump's "will be wild" tweet was read by the Oath Keepers, Proud Boys, and Three Percenters as an explicit call to violence. CNN reported that Proud Boys membership had risen "exponentially" after Trump had told them to "stand back and stand by." If Trump was reading his followers' online responses (as he usually did), he would have heard their chatter. The Anti-defamation League and CNN collected many of the messages they posted from the Capitol demonstration. They declared, "Trump or war. Today. That simple." "If you don't know how to shoot: You need to learn. NOW." "Storm the government buildings, kill cops, kill security guards, kill federal employees and agents, and demand a recount." One militant website offered Congress the choice: "'Certify Trump' [or] 'Get Lynched By Patriots.'"[44]

The knowledge that General Flynn was advising the White House to use the Insurrection Act encouraged the paramilitaries to plan for armed action on or after January 6. Stewart Rhodes told the audience of Alex Jones's Infowars that if and when Trump used the Insurrection Act to block the electoral count and "stop the deep state," his Oath Keepers would be waiting just outside Washington to provide support. Enrique Tarrio, the leader of the Proud Boys, established a "Ministry of Self Defense" to provide command and control. Its plans called for blockading every entrance or tunnel to pen the congresspeople in, then using a mob of "normies" (ordinary attendees of the rally) to break police lines and storm the Capitol. "Bring guns," one member of the Proud Boys wrote. "It's now or never." Another said it was "time to stack those bodies in front of Capitol Hill." They had stored weapons for their "quick reaction force" in Arlington, Virginia, hotel rooms.[45]

It is hard to say exactly what Trump intended to do on January 6. He had been hectoring Mike Pence and urging him to invalidate the electoral count, in whole or in part. He certainly hoped the appearance of massive support at the Stop the Steal rally on the Ellipse would weaken Pence's resistance. But he seems to have intended to take that pressure to a higher level by personally leading the crowd at the rally to join the demonstrations at the Capitol. By the morning of January 6, he knew that many of the ralliers were armed. The Secret Service reported the presence of long guns and pistols, knives, and flagpoles sharpened to spearheads, and had deployed magnetometers to prevent armed people from entering the Ellipse. Trump told them to remove the "mags." "Let my people in," he said. "They're not here to hurt me."[46]

But they *were* there to hurt—or at least threaten—the vice president and the RINOs and Democrats who were about to make Joe Biden president of the United States. Stop the Steal had called for the use of force to "take our country back" and save civilization from barbarism. The threat of violence was reinforced at the rally itself, as speakers warming up for Trump framed the day's events as the start of a war. Amy Kremer, who had organized the event, told Trump, "We are here for you . . . and we are ready to take our country back." She then added, "Defiantly . . . I stand with the Proud Boys." Tennessee senator Marsha Blackburn greeted the crowd as "all of you happy warrior freedom fighters." Donald Trump Jr. gave an expletive-riddled rant and warned those in Congress who were reluctant to challenge the swing-state electors, "We're coming for you, and we're going to have a good time doing it." Mo Brooks (R-AL) told the rally, "Today is the day American patriots start taking down names and kicking ass." Rudy Giuliani summoned the crowd to a "trial by combat."[47]

Faced with a crowd of perhaps 5,000 or 6,000, Trump began by reprising his administration's first lie. "We have hundreds of thousands of people here," he declared, "and I just want them to be recognized by the fake news media." The usual suspects had stolen the election, he railed, "radical-left Democrats . . . the fake news media." He was saving our great American heritage from cancel culture: "You hurt our monuments, you hurt our heroes, you go to jail for 10 years." His people were the only real Americans, but "they try and demean everybody having to do with us. And you're the real people, you're the people that built this nation. You're not the people that tore down our nation." They needed to "get tougher": "The Constitution doesn't allow me to send [the electors] back to the States. Well, I say, yes it does. . . . When you catch somebody in a fraud, you're allowed to go by very different rules."[48]

The point of the demonstration was to encourage Republicans in Congress, and especially Vice President Mike Pence, to accept the challenge to state electors that would be made by Senators Josh Hawley and Ted Cruz and "throw out" the votes of those states. Pence had told Trump that morning that he had no such authority and would refuse to do so. Trump now told the crowd it was Pence who stood in his (and their) way:

> All Vice President Pence has to do is send it back to the states to recertify and we become president and you are the happiest people. And I actually, I just spoke to Mike. I said: "Mike, that doesn't take courage. What takes courage is to do nothing. That takes courage."

The implication was that Pence would need more courage if he failed Trump, because MAGA people would be coming after him. Trump then gave the crowd its action script:

> And after this, we're going to walk down, and I'll be there with you, we're going to walk down . . . to the Capitol. . . . Because you'll never take back our country with weakness. You have to show strength and you have to be strong. . . . I know that everyone here will soon be marching over to the Capitol building to peacefully and patriotically make your voices heard.

It was this passage that would be cited as the "incitement of insurrection" for which Trump would be impeached a second time. He would be prevented by the Secret Service from leading the march, but by promising to do so he implied that the marchers acted with his authority. Much of the crowd took his request to protest "peacefully and patriotically" as sarcasm, or a pretext for deniability. Videos shot in the crowd show people responding with shouts of "Take the Capitol right now!" and "Invade the Capitol!"[49]

When Trump called for the rally crowd to accompany him to the Capitol, he was proposing to lead a mob, whose members he knew to be armed, against the seat of government. What did he think would happen?

There were historical precedents, of which at least some in the War Room were aware. Oliver Cromwell and his musketeers had dispersed the House of Commons in 1653 saying, "I say you are no parliament!" In 1799 Napoleon and his grenadiers had dismissed the delegates to the National Convention with, "The Republic has no government." But the most proximate model was Benito Mussolini's March on Rome in 1922, when the mere threat of a Fascist demonstration had led the Italian government to resign, and the king to name Mussolini prime minister. Trump might have counted on such a bluff to carry the day. Perhaps he thought he would make a speech on the Capitol steps, and the roar of the crowd would shake Pence's resolve. Or perhaps he envisioned entering the Capitol, the barriers removed for him because he was the president, backed by his armed Secret Service detail and behind them the angry mob, led by his "Tough People"—Bikers for Trump, Oath Keepers, Proud Boys—and approaching or entering the chamber with a show of force so impressive that Pence and Congress would simply bow to his demands.

To his chagrin, Trump was prevented from joining "his people" by the adamant opposition of the Secret Service and his legal counsel. Instead of starring in the confrontation, he became what he had been for much of his time in office: a spectator watching the play of symbols on television screens. Those most seriously committed to Stop the Steal had not waited for Trump's speech. They were already at the Capitol, pressing police lines. Members of the Proud Boys and Oath Keepers joined them, scouting for possible points of entry. When the crowd arrived from the rally, it gave their drive enough physical weight to break through the police lines.

If you watched the scene on television, you could see mobs piling on-screen in waves: Halloween patriots dressed as Continental soldiers and the Statue of Liberty, neo-Nazis with swastika armbands, a bare-chested QAnon "shaman" in face paint, horns, and fur hat. But ahead of the mass, threading through it in military formation toward the points of attack, were more than a hundred militants in combat gear, who had come with the intent to seize the Capitol and stop the counting of electoral votes—and, whether opportunistically or by plan, to take hostages or assassinate key figures. The Proud Boys had a nine-page plan, "1776 Returns," detailing how their cadres would seize the six congressional office buildings. Jessica Watkins and her crew from the Ohio State Regular Militia had joined up with Thomas Caldwell of the Oath Keepers and communicated with her comrades via cell phone. One man advised the group, "You are executing citizen's arrest. Arrest this assembly; we have probable cause for acts of treason, election fraud." Watkins answered that she and her group were under the main dome of the Capitol. Her hearer encouraged her, saying "this was what they 'trained for.'"[50]

Although paramilitaries moved in formation among the demonstrators, the vast majority of those who would ultimately storm the Capitol were what the cadres called "normies," ordinary citizens who had been radicalized by engagement with the alt-right internet and Fox News. They were "virtual vigilantes," acting in the name of an online community.

The mob that breached the Capitol, assaulted its defenders, trashed its ceremonial spaces, and threatened to kill Pence, Speaker Pelosi, and Mitt Romney by name and other legislators and staffers by category, was overwhelmingly White and predominantly male, although several women held leadership roles in the paramilitaries and Enrique Tarrio, leader of the Proud Boys, was of Afro-Cuban descent. As in past demonstrations, their flags invoked the myths they lived by. Those displaying the face of their leader were largest and perhaps most prevalent, with various mottoes annexed—some just "TRUMP 2020" or "America First," others touting the 2nd Amendment or denying COVID. There were Gadsden and Betsy Ross flags invoking the Myth of the Founding—one of the Proud Boys texted, "1776—motherf—ers," and Oath Keeper Kellye SoRelle tweeted, "We are acting like the founding fathers. Can't stand down." Confederate flags were preferred by gun rights champions and by antigovernment paramilitaries. There were QAnon flags of various designs—acolytes of "Q" were there to start "the Storm," an apocalypse that would see the mass executions of leaders of the liberal cabal. Others followed the flags of neo-Nazi and White separatist groups whose banners recalled the design of Nazi and imperial German flags. Cropping up everywhere in the mob were the banners of the gun rights movement, the silhouette of the AR15 stamped across the national flag, on images of Sylvester Stallone's muscular Rambo character with Trump's head, on the Christian cross, and over the slogan "Jesus saves!"[51]

The emblems, flags, and slogans of Christian nationalism were especially prominent. Of all the ideologies on display, this one had a prominent spokesman in Congress itself. "The name of God was everywhere," reported Emma Green of *The Atlantic.* "The mob carried signs and flags declaring Jesus Saves! and God, Guns & Guts Made America, Let's Keep All Three. . . . 'Shout if you love Jesus!' someone yelled, and the crowd cheered. 'Shout if you love Trump!' The crowd cheered louder." For some the combat at the Capitol was Armageddon and their victory would realize their vision of national redemption and transformation. Conservative David French said the riot was "a violent *Christian* insurrection. . . . Because so very many of the protesters told us they were Christian, as loudly and clearly as they could." Philip Gorski, a scholar specializing in the study of American civil religion, noted the "jarring mixture of Christian, nationalist and racist symbolism amongst the insurrectionists: there were Christian crosses and Jesus Saves banners, Trump flags and American flags, fascist insignia and a 'Camp Auschwitz' hoodie." For Gorski, this "fruit cocktail" reflected the long-standing consonance of resentments and obsessions linking the religious Right to White ethnonationalism.[52]

The violence of the mob gave Trump a pretext to invoke the Insurrection Act, as the Proud Boys and Oath Keepers still expected him to do. Perhaps he was deterred by his knowledge of General Milley's opposition, or perhaps he had simply neglected to plan for that contingency. He would let events play out, to see if they would produce the result he hoped for. He resisted pleas from his staff, from his daughter Ivanka, and from Republican allies trapped in the Capitol to call off the mob. Instead, he continued calling senators, urging them to object to the count, perhaps hoping that the violence would overawe Pence and his colleagues or physically prevent them from certifying Biden's victory. Some of those around him later testified that Trump seemed to enjoy the spectacle of violence, the sight of a great mass of people screaming and fighting the police in a show of their love for him. When minority leader Kevin

McCarthy begged him to call off the mob, Trump responded, "Well, Kevin, I guess these people are more upset about the election than you are. They like Trump more than you do." Loyalty to his person overrode all other concerns. The rioters who filled the halls were chanting, "Hang Mike Pence!" But Chief of Staff Meadows told the White House counsel that Trump wouldn't call them off to save Pence because "he thinks Mike deserves it. He doesn't think they are doing anything wrong." Instead of seeking to pacify the crowd, Trump issued an angry tweet condemning Pence, saying he "didn't have the courage to do what should have been done to protect our Country and our Constitution."[53]

When President Trump finally asked the rioters to leave, more than three hours after the Capitol had been breached, he praised them for what they had done. "These are the things and events that happen when a sacred landslide election victory is so unceremoniously & viciously stripped away from great patriots who have been badly & unfairly treated for so long," he tweeted. "Go home with love & in peace. Remember this day forever!" Later, in a prepared TV spot, he thanked them—"We love you; you're very special"—for having desecrated the Capitol, sought to thwart a constitutional procedure, killed and maimed Capitol and metro police, and attempted to make hostages of the vice president, the Speaker of the House, and any other legislators or staffers they might have seized.[54]

If the mob had succeeded in preventing the meeting of the Electoral College, or if Pence's Secret Service detail had prevented him from returning to the Capitol (as Pence feared they would), at least a temporary overthrow of the electoral system would have been achieved. If some or all of the boxes containing the electoral votes had been taken, it might not have been legally possible to complete the count. If hostages had been taken, Trump would have had a pretext to invoke the Insurrection Act. If any of these ploys had succeeded, January 6 might well have become the "Reichstag fire" moment that General Milley feared.

"Remember this day forever!" What if that half-farcical coup is not the end of Trump's story, but—like Hitler's equally farcical 1923 Beer Hall Putsch—the start of a new and more serious movement? Trump has certainly mimicked Hitler's "stab-in-the-back" myth, with his updated and personalized version of the Lost Cause, in which his return to office would figure as the promised Redemption from liberal rule.[55]

Trump's ultimate defeat did not erase the effects of his presidency on our political culture; nor has it diminished the convictions of his base. The actions of Trump and his supporters are now part of our history, available as precedents for future actors. The idiom of racial contempt that had become anathema in public discourse since the 1970s has been normalized by a president who sees moral equivalence between those who condemn White nationalism and those who assert it. Among our possible images of heroic leadership we must now include Trump, triumphing through shameless demagogy, and when we think about future elections we must include the possibility of sedition or an authoritarian coup.

Conclusion

National Myth and the Crisis of Democracy

THE 2020 presidential election was framed as a civil war between two very different Americas, red and blue. A survey by the Pew Research Center found that 90 percent of voters in each party believed a victory by the other would cause "lasting harm" to the nation. This passionate partisanship produced the largest voter turnout in American history, with a higher percentage of voter participation (66 percent) than in any election since 1900. But the election did not resolve the conflict or fundamentally alter the close balance of power between the parties and the cultural constituencies they represent. Joe Biden's total of 81 million popular votes was the highest in history, but in defeat Donald Trump received 74 million, higher than any previous *victor*. As in 2016, the shift of a few thousand votes among a few key states would have changed the outcome.[1]

Nor did the first three years of the Biden administration produce the national reconciliation for which many had hoped. The Democrats' legislative agenda had some successes, but Biden's Build Back Better program, modeled on the New Deal, was blocked by Republicans and conservative Democrats. Commentators who were quick to hail Biden's promise of a new New Deal were equally quick to write its epitaph as a failure of leftist overreach.

The 2022 midterms did not substantially alter the partisan standoff or the close balance of power between red and blue. Rising inflation and President Biden's low approval ratings, and the historically predictable loss of congressional seats by the party in power, suggested a "red wave" election. Instead the Democrats came within a few seats of retaining their House majority, held their majority in the Senate, and won several key governors' races. But there was no mandate for revival of the ambitious agenda of Build Back Better.

Some analysts saw evidence of a turn against the extremism of culture-war politics. Voters in the battleground states generally rejected candidates identified as "extremist" in their espousal of Make America Great Again (MAGA) conspiracy theories, Trump's election denial, or radical abortion restrictions. As symbolic head of his party, Trump was blamed for its poor performance, and his prestige was somewhat diminished. But the underlying strength of MAGA showed in the landslide victories of Governors Ron DeSantis in Florida and Greg Abbott in Texas, and wins by Senators J. D. Vance in Ohio and Ron Johnson in Wisconsin. Even defeated MAGA candidates won a substantial number of votes, and Trump remained the front-runner for nomination in 2024.[2]

The division of government between a Democratic president and Senate and a Republican House ensures that neither party will be able to enact its policy agenda, at least until 2025. If the 2024 election follows the patterns set in 2018, 2020, and 2022, there may be as few as four genuine "swing" states (Wisconsin, Arizona, Nevada, and Pennsylvania), whose narrow majorities would decide the election. In the meantime, the war in Ukraine and China's newly aggressive nationalism may change the political calculus, pitting Biden's preference for diplomatic coalition building against MAGA's isolationism and attraction to Vladimir Putin's authoritarianism.[3]

For all these reasons, it would be a mistake to read the elections as a final verdict on the future of American political culture. I therefore want to focus on the long term, and the way our repertoire of national myths has been affected by the MAGA movement and the countervailing rise of a reenergized liberal or progressive movement. From that perspective, what the 2022 midterms indicate is a sharpening divide between red and blue states, and between counties within states—a pattern that suggests the opening of a culture war between the states that may shape the development of our political culture going forward.

The Roots of the Crisis

In 1970 Daniel Moynihan wrote, "The central conservative truth is that it is culture, not politics, that determines the success of a society. The central liberal truth is that politics can change a culture and save it from itself." He had in mind liberals' use of politics to reform the cultural predispositions (favored by conservatives) that fostered segregation, racial and gender discrimination, and the excesses of laissez-faire capitalism. But that distinction no longer applies. Conservatives and liberals now agree that a nation's culture—the structures of belief that govern our understandings of human nature, moral obligation, and freedom—informs and shapes all the operations of social life and the terms of American nationality. They also agree that politics can and must change the culture—which is why politics has become a theater for culture war.[4]

But culture-war politics prevents our society from dealing with the structural problems that have bedeviled the United States, and indeed all developed nations, for more than thirty years. The result is a deadly feedback loop: government failure to alleviate these problems leads to deep mistrust of democratic institutions, and the substitution of culture war for rational policy debate; culture-war hyperpartisanship then prevents government from acting effectively, which intensifies mistrust of institutions and ratchets up the intensity of culture war.

The political grievances driving the culture war predate the advent of Trump and are best understood as the local instance of an international phenomenon. For thirty years, populist movements built on ethnonationalism have been rising worldwide. They provided the majority that took Britain out of the European Union (EU), and they used democratic elections to establish one-party or quasi-authoritarian regimes in Hungary, Poland, Turkey, India, and Brazil. These movements reflect the hardening of national consciousness in response to increased immigration, and the reaction of the working and lower-middle classes to their governments' failure to address the economic and social problems of the globalized neoliberal corporate order.[5]

The spread of new technologies, of automation and artificial intelligence, and the aggrandizement of global corporations at the expense of workers have profoundly altered the conditions of working life in advanced economies and, by dismantling established manufacturing industries, disrupted and degraded the social structures of hitherto prosperous communities. Wages have stagnated since the 1980s, in part because of the massive shift in employment from manufacturing to service jobs, and to the "gig" economy of irregular and temporary employment. In the United States, the gap in wealth and income between the richest class and those in the middle and working classes is greater than it has been since the Gilded Age. The wealth and power concentrated in large corporations and the hands of hedge-fund tycoons, private equity managers, and corporate CEOs—and the permissiveness of our laws—allows them to bend political parties to their will, discrediting the idea that democratic governments are willing or able to reverse the degradation of community, work, and economic security. While the Great Recession of 2008–2009 and the COVID-19 pandemic impoverished wage earners and small businesses, according to the Institute on Taxation and Economic Policy the wealthiest CEOs—some 745 individuals—"saw their collective wealth soar by 70 percent, exceeding $5 trillion." Under a tax code engineered by their lobbyists, most paid little or no tax on their gains.[6]

In the United States, government policy helped create the new regime of inequality through tax policies favoring the investing class and the adoption of free-trade pacts like NAFTA, which led to the large-scale off-shoring of manufacturing jobs and wage reduction. The power of unions was diminished by the weakening of the National Labor Relations Board, antiunion legislation, and adverse decisions by conservative courts. Deregulation made treatment of workers and their communities subservient to market value. The basic elements of these policies were followed by conservative governments in the United States and much of Europe, but also by Bill Clinton's New Democrats and Tony Blair's New Labour. So nominal liberals, when in power, did little to ameliorate the destructive effects of the new economy.[7]

Instead there was a radical decline in US investment in public goods like schools, public health, infrastructure, and basic research. In a period marked by tax reduction, spending on the military and policing increased, while spending on social programs drastically shrank. Despite the existence of government-supported health insurance under Medicare and Medicaid, and their expansion under the Affordable Care Act, public health infrastructure and delivery systems were allowed to deteriorate, creating "health deserts" and patterns of racial and class segregation in the delivery of services. The result would be felt during the COVID pandemic, as these underserved communities displayed mistrust of and resistance to government-sponsored vaccination programs.[8]

At the same time, the ethnic and racial demographics of European nations and America were being transformed. Most states of the EU had been largely homogeneous in ethnicity, until the EU's open borders, and waves of immigration from Africa and the Middle East, produced an unwonted and (for many) unwelcome diversity. In the United States the increase in racial and ethnic diversity was exponential, driven by a natural increase among native-born minorities as well as by new immigration, both legal and illegal. In the 1990s White people represented 87 percent of the voting-age population. Since then the White share has fallen to 67 percent or less, giving rise to the fear of "replacement" and the resentment of lost cultural privilege that figures so prominently among MAGA supporters.[9]

In the Black community, and parts of the Latino community, the counterpart to White status anxiety is disappointment and a simmering anger over the fact that since the 1980s so little has been done to address the effects of racialism in American society. Antidiscrimination and affirmative action laws aided the growth of the Black middle and professional class but did not alter the conditions that produce endemic poverty in most communities of color; and the harsh criminal justice regime promoted by Ronald Reagan and Clinton has made mass incarceration, especially of African Americans, a national and international scandal.[10] Since 2013 a conservative Supreme Court has rolled back two of the civil rights movement's core achievements: the Voting Rights Act's provisions against racial discrimination in registering voters and conducting elections, and affirmative action programs in college admissions. An indicator of the lack of progress toward racial justice is the fact that Black Lives Matter (BLM) demonstrations and riots were triggered by precisely the same grievances as those that produced the urban riots of the 1960s and the Harlem Riot of 1935—the ghettoization of the community and the bigotry and brutality of police forces who see their task as social control.

Looming over all these issues are the dire effects of climate change. Disastrous droughts and fire seasons, and the increase of catastrophic storms, have already affected the global economy, increasing poverty and driving emigration from Africa and Central America. A majority of Americans have come to accept the fact of global warming and the immense damage it may inflict on human civilization, yet there is no political consensus or clear program for reversing carbon emissions or ameliorating the effects of climate change.[11]

These problems are of long duration and will affect our lives for generations. America's political leaders have not only failed to deal effectively with them, they have not even been able to agree on ways to define and explain them to the public. Conservative Republicans have blocked all Democratic efforts at reform without offering any policy alternatives beyond the neoliberal nostrums of tax cuts and deregulation. The MAGA movement has protested the economic order created by "the elites," but instead of proposing reforms, it has exacerbated culture-war issues—attacking the "wokeness" of corporate management rather than seeking to change their treatment of labor or tackle their monopolistic structures. The Democratic Party's proposals for reform under Barack Obama and Biden were either blocked by Republican legislators or buried under culture-war polemics. And its proposals have not been framed—for both the public and the politicians—by a clear explanation of the new economy and the inequalities it produces, and a positive vision of the social and economic order that ought to succeed it.[12]

American democracy is caught in a potential death spiral, in which our failure to find political solutions for these endemic problems produces an enraged and aggrieved hyperpartisanship, which in turn makes it impossible for government to make the kinds of regulatory change and public investment needed to address the problems. To break out of the spiral, we must develop a durable social consensus about what has gone wrong and what should be done about it—a consensus that sets parameters within which both parties can operate and compromise, and has the moral legitimacy conferred by a shared understanding of national myth. The latter is especially important at a time when disagreement over the nature of American nationality and cultural identity is at the root of political conflict.

Over the past hundred years, American history has been shaped by two political orders: the New Deal order, which fell apart in the 1970s, and the neoliberal order, which lost most of its authority after the economic implosion of 2008. No comparable order has taken their place. What Antonio Gramsci wrote during the 1930s, when liberal societies were collapsing and Fascism and Communism were on the rise, rings true today: "The crisis consists precisely in the fact that the old is dying and the new cannot be born; in this interregnum a great variety of morbid symptoms appear."[13]

Two alternatives are on offer. The Democratic Party offers to reform our national imaginary through ordinary political means: by adopting a comprehensive multi-trillion-dollar program of pandemic relief, infrastructure rebuilding and development, job creation, family support, carbon emissions control, and racial justice. It invokes the New Deal and the civil rights movement as its myth-historical models. Its understanding of nationality is pluralistic, embracing different races and ethnicities on terms of social equality, and committed to including marginalized groups of all kinds. It is opposed by a MAGA-dominated Republican Party determined to fight for its cultural Lost Cause, resistant to the Democrats' policies without offering an alternative program for reform. The prevalence of ethnonationalism in MAGA ideology threatens the solidarity of the nation as a community; its authoritarian and illiberal character threatens to override the rules and structures that have governed democratic politics.[14]

It is uncertain which of these two systems of thought will gain the power to shape the nation's future.

MAGA and the Threat of Authoritarian Populism

MAGA's strength as a movement is based on the effectiveness with which it expresses the cultural and economic grievances felt by a large share of the electorate. Its adherents' identity, and their sense of moral authority, is reinforced by their embrace of the most traditional forms of the Myths of the Founding, the Frontier, and the Lost Cause. These provide them with a comprehensive theory of the American past, which they use as a template for charting the national future.

MAGA's relation to the Good War Myth is ambivalent. While America's victory in World War II is part of the "greatness" MAGA wants to restore, its isolationist strain rejects the extrapolation of that victory into a mandate for leadership of the free world and an activist, sometimes interventionist, foreign policy. Its isolationism is also consonant with the movement's attraction to authoritarian leaders and has led its partisans to oppose American support of Ukraine in its resistance to Putin's unprovoked invasion—now the most significant test of the international order and threat to world peace.

The movement is also united by Donald Trump's cult of personality. Professions of loyalty to his person and signature beliefs are demanded of all members in good standing. Party leaders who "broke" with Trump over the attack on the Capitol have since made pilgrimage to Mar-a-Lago to kiss his ring. However, it is not at all clear that MAGA's endurance as a political and cultural movement depends entirely on Trump. His addiction to self-serving fantasy makes it impossible to predict how his electoral success or failure might affect the movement he now personifies. To understand the power of MAGA, and its potential effect on our political system, we first need to appreciate the popular forces that drive the movement, and then consider how conservative thought leaders are translating these "populist" energies into new ideological and policy programs.[15]

In the two years following the 2020 election, MAGA true believers—those who actively favor Trump for president in 2024 and embrace his stolen election mantra—varied from a high of 70 percent to a low of 40 percent of Republicans. Even the lower figure gives them leverage enough to control the party. Given the limits of the two-party system, and of a constitutional order that gives rural states disproportionate representation in the Senate and Electoral College, it is possible for a minority amounting to less than 30 percent of the national electorate to win control of the government.[16]

The culture-wars element gives MAGA its ideological élan and political power. Its precursor, the Tea Party movement of 2010–2015, was the angry response of a traditionally Republican constituency, dedicated to lowering taxes and shrinking government, to the Obama administration's proposals for relieving the distress caused by the Great Recession and regulating the financial industry that had caused it. MAGA expanded that traditionally conservative core by voicing the grievances of what has been called the White working class but is more accurately defined by its culture rather than its relation to industrial labor: a class defined by educational level (no more than two years of college), religion, and region (rural or urban/suburban), which is generally middle and lower-middle class in income and occupational terms. Communities that have recently experienced a rise in non-White or immigrant residents, and border communities hit by rising illegal immigration, are particularly strong in their commitment to MAGA. Its most committed elements are rural and Southern White people and culturally conservative religious groups, especially evangelical Protestants, conservative Roman Catholics, and Orthodox Jews. The extremist tendencies of MAGA's ethnonationalists are accommodated (with a sigh) by a Republican Party whose membership has been predominantly White for generations.[17]

These groups believe they are defending traditional Americanism against the "liberal elites" who control schools and the media and use their power to secularize culture and push their legislative agenda. Liberals sponsor laws that infringe the social and religious liberty of people and institutions that find homosexuality morally unacceptable. Affirmative action policies privilege Black and Hispanic people at the expense of White people; and permissive approaches to immigration threaten American wage earners with cheap-labor competition and dilute American culture with alien elements. The liberalization of culture and demographic change threaten to make these predominantly White and Christian Americans a minority in their country.

MAGA constituencies have therefore embraced extreme measures of voter suppression, gerrymandering, and legislative control of election certification. In this regard, MAGA is building on values and practices already rooted in the conservative movement. As political scientists Thomas Mann and Norman Ornstein have argued, since the 1990s the GOP has been "ideologically extreme; scornful of compromise; unmoved by conventional understanding of facts, evidence and science; and dismissive of the legitimacy of its political opposition." Its agenda has been formulated as a canon, most tenets of which predate Trump: Grover Norquist's No-Tax Pledge, the Kochs' No Climate Change Pledge, the NRA's absolute rejection of gun safety, Right to Life's rejection of abortion under any circumstances, the anti-immigration bloc's No Amnesty Pledge. Its "Southern Strategy" dealt in dog-whistle racism to rouse resistance to social welfare programs. It has generally opposed the extension of social welfare programs and voting rights.[18]

Trump exaggerated those tendencies by an order of magnitude, and his cult of personality gave them shape, color, and the aura of insurgent populist heroism. Government was not just a problem to be minimized, but an administrative state to be deconstructed. Dog-whistle racism became explicit in the defamation of Mexican and Black people, and in the display of sympathy for White Power vigilantes. Climate change was not just a hoax, but a "Chinese hoax." Faced with a global pandemic, inescapable evidence of dangerous climate change, a public outcry for racial and social justice, and defeat at the polls, Trump chose repression over recognition.[19]

But Trump also shifted the focus of conservative politics from the neoliberal economic policies of Reagan and the two Bushes to the culture-war politics of Pat Buchanan. Christopher Rufo, one of the more effective public voices for this ideology, put the case plainly in a speech at the National Conservatism Conference in 2021: "The Reagan-era playbook is not enough; reform around the edges is not enough; a corporate tax cut is not enough. We must take the conditions of cultural revolution as our baseline, as the current reality, and our response must be framed in terms of a counterrevolution that plays not primarily on the axis of economy, but on the axis of culture." In 2022 the Heritage Foundation, formerly the bastion of neoliberal economics, shifted focus to the tropes of Trumpism: fighting "pandemic restrictions, 'critical race theory' in schools, and 'teaching transgenderism to kindergartners.'" Florida governor Ron DeSantis has become the most forceful proponent of this approach, reducing all policy questions—immigration, education, the power of globalism—to the repudiation of "wokeness," the updated term for "political correctness": "We must fight the woke in our schools. . . . We must fight the woke in our businesses. We must fight the woke in government agencies. We can never ever surrender to woke ideology. And I'll tell you this, the state of Florida is where woke goes to die."[20]

The driving force behind MAGA is resentment of the diversion of government resources to immigrants, Black people, and Latinos by liberal officials. A 2021 study by the Pew Research Center found that 88 percent of Republicans believed that in the era of affirmative action, White people were more discriminated against than Black people. This bitter animus is rooted in the cultural tradition glorified by the Myth of the Lost Cause.[21]

Behind that grievance are two different ideologies: ethnonationalism and White nationalism. Each has spawned extremist organizations whose members have combined forces in demonstrations like Unite the Right in Charlottesville and the January 6 insurrection. But their differences are significant. White nationalists demand a racially exclusive nationality, from which non-White people are expelled, or within which they are segregated and disenfranchised. White identity extremists may call for genocide or seek to foment a race war by committing terrorist acts. Their doctrines repeat almost word for word the racial nationalism espoused by John R. Commons in 1907 that held that "differences in blood" render some races incapable of full "amalgamation" with true Americans and that admitting them to citizenship would degrade and destroy our democracy.[22]

Ethnonationalist organizations declare their openness to the idea of a multiracial society, but demand adherence to a single "Western" culture or civilizational model, structured by Christian moral values, traditional families, free enterprise, and belief in the exceptional virtues of American society. They also advocate a "melting pot" model of assimilation, in which the ethnic particularity of immigrants is absorbed in the national standard. That distinction, which recognizes successful assimilation, taken with MAGA's growth-oriented economic ideology and cultural conservatism, earned Trump a significant share of Black and Latino voters.

The ethnic animus at the heart of MAGA is transformed into political energy and sporadic violence by the movement's embrace of "conspiratorialism," defined as the belief that "big events like wars, recessions, and the outcomes of elections are controlled by small groups of people who are working in secret against the rest of us." This is the aspect of MAGA ideology that focuses hostility on the elites who control the media, the universities, and the "deep state," whose secularizing programs and sponsorship of racial and sexual "liberations" have destroyed traditional social hierarchy, morality, and family structure. This too has long been a recurring theme in conservative politics, expressed in the McCarthy Red Scare and John Birch movement in the 1950s and 1960s. In the 1990s Pat Robertson assailed George H. W. Bush's neoliberal "new world order" as the program of international financiers and a (nonexistent) secret society called the Illuminati. The most extreme case in the MAGA era is the QAnon conspiracy, which is steeped in psychosexual fantasy rather than obsession with Communists or international bankers. It holds that Democratic political leaders have created child sex-trafficking rings, which practice ritual cannibalism, and serve a secret set of people who control world affairs. According to an *Economist*/YouGov Poll in April 2022, 52–54 percent of Republicans believe such conspiracies are definitely or probably true.[23]

The most respectable of these conspiracy theories is the belief that Democrats, liberals, and Jews (singly or in combination) are fostering uncontrolled immigration and advancing Black people through affirmative action and permissive voting laws in order to "replace" the native-born American (White) electorate with their clients. Their "minority majority" would control future elections, allowing Democrats to impose a socialistic regime on the country. This "Great Replacement" theory is espoused by White nationalist organizations, but it has also been promoted by mainstream media, especially on Fox News by Tucker Carlson, the most popular of the network's opinionators before his firing in 2023. It has also become a standard trope in Republican political campaigns. The French novel *Camp of the Saints* is usually identified as the inspiration of this conspiracy theory. But the idea has been a recurrent American response to disruptions of social or racial hierarchies. Proslavery advocates in the 1850s argued that abolition would result in racial replacement in the Black Belt states. In 1864 the Democratic opposition accused Republicans of planning the forced "miscegenation" of Black people and the Irish to produce a client working class. John Commons in 1907, Madison Grant in the 1920s, and Mississippi senator Theodore Bilbo in 1947 saw immigration and integration ending in racial or cultural mongrelization and a ruinous disempowerment of "real Americans."[24]

Polls taken by UMass-Amherst and the Associated Press–NORC Center for Public Affairs Research found that 66 percent of Republicans believe that "a group of people are trying to replace native-born Americans with immigrants for electoral gains," and that increased immigration "will result in native-born Americans losing economic, political, and cultural influence." But that survey also showed that as much as 60 percent of the general public shared that belief, which suggests that the idea has a wide potential audience. A survey of "varieties of American popular nationalism," conducted by Bart Bonikowski and Paul DiMaggio, found that more than half of those surveyed believed in a national identity defined in "ethnically and culturally exclusionary terms"— that "someone was 'truly American' only if they were Christian, spoke English and had been born in the United States." By these measures a large majority of Americans share the concerns embodied in the Great Replacement theory and are open to ethnonationalist appeals.[25]

MAGA's signature conspiracy theory is the belief that the 2020 election was "stolen." Polls taken since the election indicate that three-quarters of those who voted for Trump continue in that belief long after Trump has exhausted his legal appeals and in spite of the certification of the election on January 6. A survey by the Chicago Project on Security and Threats conducted in June 2021 found that 47 million Americans believed the election had been stolen and that Biden's presidency was illegitimate. Of that number, 9 million—some 20 percent of all American adults, and a preponderant majority of Republicans—believed violence was justified to reinstate Trump.[26]

By repeatedly advocating for the physical violence of January 6, MAGA conspiracists prepared their public for the subtler violence of altering the laws that govern democratic politics, to prevent their opponents from winning elections. Battle lines were drawn in state legislatures across the country. At a December 2022 meeting of the New York Young Republican Club, the group's president declared, "We want to cross the Rubicon. We want total war. We must be prepared to do battle in every arena. In the media. In the courtroom. At the ballot box. And in the streets. . . . This is the only language the left understands. The language of pure and unadulterated power."[27]

MAGA as a Political Order: Theories and Models

Trump knows the themes that will fire up his followers—"the radical left agenda" will "hurt God" and is "against guns, . . . against energy, our kind of energy"—but not how to turn them into a system of ideas and policies. Conservative think tanks, and ideologically sophisticated political leaders, are translating these memes into an ideological program. These include established organizations like the Koch brothers' American Legislative Exchange Council (ALEC) and Americans for Progress, the Claremont Institute, the Heritage Foundation and American Enterprise Institute, and the Federalist Society; but also new groups that reflect the transformation of conservatism's ideas and political constituency by Trump and MAGA, such as the Edmund Burke Foundation and national conservatism. Their agenda includes rejecting regulations that curtail the power of corporations and opposition to most forms of social welfare (radical Left agenda), favoring Christian values in social policy and law (against God), denying climate change or the necessity of reducing our carbon footprint (our kind of energy), and sympathizing with and encouraging vigilante intimidation and violence (against guns). If Trump or a like-minded successor were to win the presidency, these organizations could provide the administration with well-vetted and trained loyalists to staff its offices, as the Federalist Society has vetted conservative judges. But even if MAGA were to lose, these organizations would continue to provide the movement and its candidates with a coherent ideology and political program.[28]

Their influence is evident in the campaigns Republicans have mounted to maintain control of electoral institutions through antidemocratic devices like voter suppression, gerrymandering, removal of Democrats from local election boards, and empowerment of state legislatures to override the certification of elections. In June 2021, a panel of distinguished political scientists and former officials published a "Statement of Concern" pointing to these measures as a threat to democracy, which "could entrench extended minority rule, violating the basic and longstanding democratic principle that parties that get the most votes should win elections." That is precisely their purpose. Although these initiatives were taken by local party organizations, the campaigns have been financed, advised, and supplied with model statutes by organizations like ALEC, FreedomWorks, the Heritage Foundation, the Claremont Institute, and the Susan B. Anthony List. The thought leaders speaking for these institutions justify repressive measures by redefining American nationality to exclude those who, by race, ethnicity, or ideology, do not conform to the ethnonationalist model of "real Americans."[29]

Writing in the *American Mind*, Glenn Ellmers, a senior fellow at the conservative Claremont Institute, proposes a political philosophy for MAGA, the first principle of which is recognition that, at 75 million (the number of Trump voters), "real Americans" are nonetheless a minority: "Most people living in the United States today—certainly more than half—are not Americans in any meaningful sense of the term. . . . I'm really referring to the many native-born people . . . who may technically be citizens of the United States but are no longer (if they ever were) *Americans*. They do not believe in, live by, or even like the principles, traditions, and ideals that until recently defined America as a nation and as a people." What makes Americans "authentic," by this logic, is adherence to the traditional cultural beliefs that made up "the American way of life" before the 1960s. By that standard, very little in our current culture is truly American. As Ellmers explains, "*Our norms are now hopelessly corrupt and need to be destroyed.* . . . The political practices, institutions, and even rhetoric governing the United States have become hostile to *both* liberty and virtue. . . . The mainline churches, universities, popular culture, and the corporate world are rotten to the core." A movement to reverse those cultural trends cannot succeed using democratic methods. "The U.S. Constitution no longer works. . . . Overturning the existing post-American order, and re-establishing America's ancient principles in practice, is a sort of counter-revolution, and the only road forward." Ellmers envisions disruptions and power seizures in the name of the authentic minority, to establish rule by a single party representing substantially less than a majority of citizens.[30]

Some of Ellmers's Claremont colleagues have criticized his article as too extreme in its abandonment of constitutional republicanism. But conservatives have often defended the principle of rule by a virtuous minority by reference to the Myth of the Founding and the idea (attributed to James Madison) that

"America is a republic, not a democracy." While it is certainly true that the Constitution was designed to provide strong protection to minorities and limit the power of popular majorities, the Founders were equally hostile to the idea of oligarchy or rule by even a virtuous minority. But the conservative movement openly espouses that kind of rule and rejects majority rule in principle. A 2020 Heritage Foundation report argues that contemporary movements aiming at increasing political equality (e.g., by expanding voting rights) "weaken our republican customs and institutions" and undermine "the social, familial, religious, and economic distinctions and inequalities that undergird our political liberty."[31]

One rationale for minority rule is offered by Christian nationalism, which represents an important strain in conservative politics. The various schools of Christian nationalism share a political agenda, which includes banning abortion, restoring school prayer and religiosity in civil affairs, and restricting divorce, contraception, gay sexuality, and gender nonconformity. However, they rise from very different theological traditions and have very different ways of justifying their movement and framing its mythic narrative. While some parts of the movement espouse ethnonationalism or White identity, some of the most prominent preachers in the movement preside over megachurches in which White, Black, Asian, and Latino people participate equally.[32]

The literature of Christian nationalism is rich in storytelling, using a form of typological analysis that interprets Old Testament stories as prefigurations of the New Testament, and biblical stories in general as prefigurations of modern-day crises or markers on the road to the apocalypse. But because the sects that form the movement differ so widely in their theology and concept of church governance, they have not produced either a unified ideology or a distinctive national myth. An obvious model would be the Puritan myth of America as the New Israel, but for evangelical Protestants the return of the Jews to a restored state of Israel has been embraced as a milepost on the road to the Second Coming of Christ. Church-based Christian nationalists also share the belief that Donald Trump's presidency was a God-given blessing, but they set his persona and achievement in different narrative frames. For some, Trump figures as King Cyrus, the pagan monarch who redeemed the Jews from their Babylonian exile. For others he is himself a Christlike figure, and his election—as the exponents of Seven Mountain Dominionism see it—is a sign that the Day of Judgment prophesied in the New Testament book of Revelation is approaching.[33]

The extent of popular support for Christian nationalism is uncertain. A 2023 survey by the Public Religion Research Institute found that 10 percent of

Americans identified as "adherents" of Christian nationalism, and an additional 19 percent were sympathetic to the idea. But a Pew poll taken in October 2022 indicated that only 14 percent of those surveyed had heard very much about Christian nationalism, and of that group only 5 percent had a favorable opinion of it, whereas 24 percent had an unfavorable opinion. Of the whole sample, 54 percent explicitly rejected the idea of a theocratic government and 51 percent had an unfavorable opinion of Christian nationalism. However, the same poll showed that 45 percent of Americans thought the United States should be a "Christian nation," which they understood to mean a country adopting values like honesty, tolerance, respect for law—and separation of church and state, a concept that is anathema to Christian nationalists.[34]

That generalized understanding of Christianity as an American norm is common ground for Christian nationalists and the relatively new movement called national conservatism, which was formed by a group of conservative intellectuals in response to Trump's successful assault on the premises of Reaganomics. Their aim was to develop a political program that would turn Trump's polemics into an ideologically coherent and politically effective program for checking the dire effects of globalism and empowering cultural conservatives to overthrow the power of liberal secularism and "woke" culture. National conservatives propose using the power of the state to achieve these goals, an approach that has been criticized by libertarian and neoliberal conservatives, and by antigovernment ideologues like Steve Bannon. Nevertheless, it offers a glimpse of the "Trumpism without Trump" that is a likely future of the MAGA movement.[35]

The movement was founded in 2019 at a conference organized by Yoram Hazony, Israeli-born philosopher and political scientist and author of *The Virtue of Nationalism*, which had just been chosen as Conservative Book of the Year. Invitees included anti-Trump conservatives Yuval Levin and Reihan Salam; Michael Anton, whose "Flight 93 Election" essay gave Trump a campaign theme; billionaire entrepreneur Peter Thiel, and MAGA enthusiast Tucker Carlson. The conference was funded by the newly established Edmund Burke Foundation, which would support the movement's work going forward. The foundation's name carries important symbolic weight. Burke's *Reflections on the Revolution in France* (1790) became part of the conservative canon by offering a powerful critique of the Enlightenment rationalism that destroyed the French monarchy and led to the revolutionary Terror. For Burke, the health of society rests on respect for tradition and "prejudice," by which he meant long-continued customs and habits of thought whose proven value outweighed the claims of rational analysis. Heritage Foundation Fellow Kevin Roberts, in his article "The

Future of Conservatism," reframes Burke's "prejudices" as "noble habits," and identifies the political and economic programs of national conservatism as ancillary products of a "culture that is built on noble habits, practices, and worthy leisure." He explains, "In my view, borrowing from generations of conservative thought, culture is the very essence of what it means to be conservative, because it forms our political behavior. It originates in our homes, our neighborhoods, our communities, our cities, our schools, and it should guide our national debates. To use today's parlance, politics is downstream from culture." To fight what Anton had called "the soul-sapping effects of paternalistic Big Government and its cannibalization of civil society and religious institutions," conservatives must reassert "the importance of virtue, morality, religious faith, stability, character and so on in the individual" and reassert "family values" against the regime of sexual liberation.[36]

National conservatives ground their ideology in what they see as a traditional system of values that has prevailed through the course of national history. They share with Christian nationalists the belief that the United States is essentially a Christian nation, and that Christianity should have a privileged place in the legal order. But they ground their authority not in biblical mythology but in a myth that sees the Founders as essentially (if sometimes eccentrically) Christian in their values and ideological presumptions. Equally critical to their program is the assertion that the culture of White Christians has been the basis of American moral and social norms through all of our history. That traditional order was, in their view, corrupted and disempowered by the liberalism that arose in the 1960s, and their program calls for the redemption of that culture through the establishment of a new political order.

The movement's "Statement of Principles" outlines a political agenda that combines its cultural program with economic policies responsive to the demands of a populist constituency. True to the idea that politics is "downstream" of culture, the cultural program has the greater clarity. National conservatism's current economic program calls for using the power of the state to reassert national sovereignty against the demands of globalization, to "aggressively pursue economic independence from hostile powers, nurture industries crucial for national defense, and restore and upgrade manufacturing capabilities critical to the public welfare." But the movement opposes the government-directed industrial policy advocated by liberal economists like Robert Reich, and excessive interference with "free enterprise," so it is not clear what antiglobalization tools it would add to Trump's tariff-based protectionism. It does not support a more progressive tax structure that would require the rich to pay more. Similarly, its call for policies to support and strengthen families eschews social welfare measures, such as the expanded Child Tax Credit or federally supported child care for working parents. It does not acknowledge climate change as an issue requiring action, let alone offer conservative approaches to addressing it.

The movement's theory of nationality assumes, perhaps rightly, that the "working class" is as committed to cultural conservatism as to economic reforms. It implicitly rejects the concept of a civil social contract embodied in the Declaration of Independence and conceives the nation-state as the "authentic" expression of the will and character of an ethnically particular "People." It explicitly rejects a racial definition of nationality and defines the authenticity of national character in Christian nationalist terms: "No nation can long endure without humility and gratitude before God and fear of his judgment that are found in authentic religious tradition. For millennia, the Bible has been our surest guide, nourishing a fitting orientation toward God, to the political traditions of the nation, to public morals, to the defense of the weak, and to the recognition of things rightly regarded as sacred. The Bible should be read as the first among the sources of a shared Western civilization in schools and universities, and as the rightful inheritance of believers and non-believers alike." While the rights of religious minorities should be respected, the statement avers that "where a Christian majority exists, public life should be rooted in Christianity and its moral vision, which should be honored by the state and other institutions both public and private." Since nominal Christians are a majority in every state, it is not clear whether any states would be exempt from Christian rule.[37]

The "Statement of Principles" aligns national conservatism with Trump's culture-war policies while avoiding racist polemics. It advocates "federalism" and the delegation of important powers to the states but reserves the right of the national government to "intervene energetically to restore order" in states and counties "in which lawlessness, immorality, and dissolution reign." Repression of "lawlessness" and the "dissolution" of authority was the justification cited by Trump, and by national conservatives like Tom Cotton, for suppressing the BLM demonstrations.[38]

But the most intriguing justification for intervention is "immorality." The state policies that national conservatives would find immoral may be guessed from other parts of their program. Refusing to make the Bible intrinsic to school curricula might qualify. But the most dangerous "immoralities" are those that affect "the traditional family . . . built around a lifelong bond between a man and a woman, and on a lifelong bond between parents and children," which is (along with the Bible?) "the foundation of all other achievements of our civilization." The disintegration of the traditional family, marked by increasing rates of divorce and decreasing rates of childbearing, "gravely threatens the wellbeing and sustainability of democratic nations." The causes of this disintegration include "an unconstrained individualism that regards children as a burden, while encouraging ever more radical forms of sexual license and experimentation as an alternative to the responsibilities of family and congregational life."[39]

Behind the abstract language are implied condemnations of abortion ("unconstrained individualism") and LGBTQ lifestyles ("sexual license and experimentation"). William Barr stated the principle openly when he blamed toleration of homosexuality, adultery, and divorce for the moral decay of the West. The national conservative program frames a possible legal regime for restoring the moral opprobrium once attached to such behaviors, whose effect can be seen in the banning of books in schools and libraries that offer information on sexuality and gender, and of public celebrations of gay pride and other forms of nontraditional sexual expression. In the late stages of the 2022 midterms, ads targeting gay and trans people and their supporters were more prominent than racial or ethnic stereotyping in Republican campaigns. A large number of these ads were aimed at Black and Latino voters, whose religious beliefs tend to be conservative on gender issues, in an effort to increase the party's growing share of these voters. Shifting focus from race to sex and gender issues also allows conservatives to evade accusations of racism or ethnonationalism and center "Christian" moral values.[40]

This Christian nationalist moral agenda is also reflected in recent Supreme Court decisions and opinions. Justice Clarence Thomas has suggested that the *Dobbs* decision, overruling *Roe v. Wade* and ending federal protection of abortion rights, be used as precedent for annulling the rights of same-sex marriage, the use of contraceptives, and unregulated sexual activity among consenting adults. Over the past decade, Court decisions have increasingly disfavored cases supporting the separation of church and state, most recently in the *Kennedy v. Bremerton* school prayer case, which concerned state funding of religious schools—a pattern that legal scholar Laurence Tribe sees as "a theocratic movement to advance religious based governance." These decisions are grounded in the legal theory of "originalism," which holds that judicial interpretation of the law should be governed by the "original intent" of the Founders. Like the national conservatives' assertion that the United States is "a republic, not a democracy," this invocation of the Myth of the Founding uses a suppositious reading of the Founders' intent to sanctify the enactment of a conservative political and cultural program.[41]

National conservatives understand that the cultural views they espouse are not shared by most Americans. They therefore embrace the logic of Ellmers's politics, which requires a virtuous minority to impose its will on the whole of society by gaining control of state power. At his August 3, 2022, speech celebrating his nomination as Republican candidate for the Senate from Arizona, Blake Masters, a former COO of Thiel Capital, told his supporters that "coercive state power [is] an indispensable tool for achieving conservative ends: mandating patriotic curriculums in schools, supporting the formation of 'native-born' families, banning abortion and pornography, and turning back the rights revolution for L.G.B.T.Q. Americans." Masters narrowly lost the election to the incumbent and former astronaut Mark Kelly.[42]

National conservatism has attracted several rising political stars whose authoritarianism takes more pragmatic forms. They include Senator Tom Cotton, who topped Trump's demand that state governors "dominate" the BLM demonstrators by calling for deployment of the Eighty-Second Airborne and giving the protesters "no quarter." Senator Josh Hawley, a devout and highly educated evangelical Presbyterian, told the audience at the American Principles Project Gala that American ideas of individual freedom are based on the "Pelagian heresy," which sees humans as free and perfectible agents, and that national salvation requires us to "take the Lordship of Christ . . . into the public realm, and to seek the obedience of the nations." Hawley gained national fame when he gave a clenched-fist salute to the gathering mob on January 6. Tucker Carlson became the most-watched Fox commentator by openly advocating for the authoritarian, ethnonationalist, and antigay politics of Hungary's Viktor Orbán. All three supported challenges to invalidate swing-state electoral votes in the 2020 election; only Cotton has condemned the January 6 mob.[43]

All the strains of the Republican coalition—Trumpian MAGA, national conservative, neoliberal, libertarian, antigovernment—agree that a minoritarian and even authoritarian political turn is necessary to save the core cultural values and economic interests that define "Real America." In 1968 the "madness" of the Vietnam War was expressed in the phrase, "We had to destroy Ben Tre in order to save it." That same logic informs the politics of the MAGA movement: that it is necessary to destroy American democracy in order to save the nation from itself.

The MAGA movement has thus become the vehicle for the development of an authentically American Fascism: more neo-Confederate than neo-Nazi, an amalgam of American exceptionalism and Christian nationalism. Its self-concept and belief system are historically rooted in traditional forms of American national mythology. Instead of Nazism's Wotan / Siegfried mythos, it roots its world concept in the Myths of the Frontier and the Lost Cause, and therefore sees itself fighting a Last Stand to save America from "replacement." As with Fascism, its pseudo-populist rhetoric masks a vision of political order blending autocracy and oligarchy. With one of the two major parties committed to such a program, the future of liberal democracy will be at risk in national elections for at least the next decade.[44]

The Democratic Alternative: American Reformation

MAGA's power as a political movement is based on its combination of political and cultural appeals. Its ideologists have succeeded in reconciling populist hostility toward governing elites with the Republican Party's traditional business-friendly policies, especially wholesale deregulation and support of fossil fuel industries. It has embedded these ideas in a narrative that connects its adherents to the major American national myths and gives them the exhilarating sense of riding a wave of historical destiny.

Its power is offset by a blue coalition of various and discordant elements whose ethnic, racial, and ideological diversity makes it more representative of the political and cultural spectrum, but harder to unify behind a single political program. The common ground of the blue coalition is interest in political, economic, and social reform. At a time when trust in government is at historic lows, most Democrats still trust its capacity for achieving public good—the ideological legacy of the New Deal and Great Society era.

On balance, red and blue partisans are of nearly equal electoral strength, and are contending for the support of a shrinking but still significant body of uncommitted or politically unengaged independents. Democratic candidates for president and Congress often win popular majorities, but because of the overrepresentation of rural states in the Senate and Electoral College, and partisan gerrymandering at state and national levels, Democrats must win popular supermajorities to gain simple majorities in these assemblies. When we consider the future of American political culture, one key question is whether the blue coalition can develop as a movement comparable to MAGA, with ideological coherence and a story that will give it the appeal and authority of myth.

The blue coalition is centered in the Democratic Party, which is divided into factions that include progressives seeking a radical restructuring of politics and economics, moderates who share the Clintons' pro-business ideology, and conservative Democrats from red states or districts. It has ranged into traditional Republican territory to include educated suburbanites and even some movement conservatives appalled by Trump and what he stands for. Democrats retain some residual support among unionized White workers, and Biden did better than Hillary Clinton with these voters. There is some evidence that the younger generation of voters, now between eighteen and twenty-nine years old, favor blue positions on cultural issues (abortion, gay rights, climate, guns) and positive government, which suggests that conservatives are right to see a cultural drift that disfavors their politics and values. But Republicans have won over most of the Rust Belt White working class and enjoy solid support among White Southern rural and exurban voters. The Democratic Party is firmly based in the nation's large, relatively prosperous, and growing cities.

The blue coalition also includes "identity" groups whose experience of discrimination and economic injustice has been severe. Demographic trends have shown a steep rise in their population share when compared with native-born White people, suggesting that these minorities will ultimately form a ruling majority of the electorate. However, these groups vary in their cultural commitments and political agendas. African American activists range from culturally conservative Christians to secular urban progressives. Many Latin and Mexican Americans, Asian Americans, Native Americans, LGBTQ people, and the disabled share a commitment to social justice and antiracism but have special economic interests and different concerns about immigration, medical care, affirmative action, and tribal sovereignty. While there is potential strength in the coalition's breadth of inclusion, the values and interests of its varied constituents are often in conflict and difficult to reconcile in the legislative and policy-formation process. A large minority of Latino voters, and a significant minority of Black people, have favored Republican positions on immigration, sexual mores, religion, and the economy. Thus the Democrats' reliance on the emerging "minority majority" has produced disappointing results.

These divisions affected support for Biden's ambitious reform agenda. The administration achieved some substantial successes, despite narrow majorities in House and Senate, but Biden's most Rooseveltian initiative, the Build Back Better program, failed because of resistance by Senators Joe Manchin (D-WV) and Kyrsten Sinema (D-AZ). Rep. Abigail Spanberger (D-VA) earned headlines with her complaint that "nobody elected [Biden] to be F.D.R., they elected him to be normal and stop the chaos."[45]

Spanberger has a point. Biden was popularly perceived as a moderate by primary voters who preferred him to progressive candidates like Bernie Sanders and Elizabeth Warren. His success reflected popular revulsion against Trumpian extremism rather than commitment to progressive policy, as indicated by the turn against Democratic candidates in the House and Senate. But Biden did make his connection to FDR a major campaign theme, so he had some reason to think voters supported his ambitions.

Slogans aside, Biden's administration has been guided by the understanding that unless climate change and the structural inequities of the economy are addressed and corrected, the social disorder and political dysfunction that threaten the survival of republican government will only get worse. Whatever their faction label, Democrats agree on the necessity of government-based action on climate change, economic reform, and extension of the social safety net, though they differ on priorities and levels of financing.[46]

Thus the task facing the blue coalition is not just to enact policies but to combine political action with cultural reframing to convince a skeptical public that the federal government can be a force for meaningful change. Since the 1970s the Left and center Left have failed to formulate a coherent vision of the American future, or a version of national myth that would root their program in historical tradition. Bill Clinton's New Democratic turn rejected the New Deal and Great Society tradition, and reduced the Movement to "identity politics." The political upheavals of 2020 brought the history of the New Deal and the civil rights movement back into focus and began a process of narrative formation that may give liberals and progressives what they have lacked—a myth that roots their program in a broadly accepted understanding of American national history.

Implicit in the use of New Deal symbolism is the belief that only systematic reform, sponsored and in large part directed by the government, can hope to overcome the socioeconomic crises facing the nation. Biden embraced that principle at the start of his administration by issuing ads that explicitly begged comparison with Roosevelt's legendary "Hundred Days." He also set out long-term plans for a broad range of infrastructure, social welfare, and social justice reforms analogous to FDR's Second New Deal. When he called for the adoption of stringent public health measures to combat COVID, or acceptance of critical regulation and taxation proposals, he invoked the Good War Myth. The adaptation of the iconic World War II poster of Rosie the Riveter, "We Can Do It," as a pro-vaccine poster is a case in point. But whereas the Good War Myth co-opted New Deal populism to serve a world-power mission, Biden shifted the balance of symbolic power, co-opting the mystique of war to serve a social justice program.[47]

The cue for this imaginative enterprise was given by the proponents of the Green New Deal. Although Biden rejected that label during his campaign, his infrastructure plans followed the Green New Deal by focusing on its environmental effects. Build Back Better also followed that formula by advocating investment incentives to grow "green" technologies, a form of "industrial policy" like that advocated by Robert Reich during the Clinton administration. These policies were framed as growth oriented by linking them to the Frontier Myth—an early version of the legislation called it the "Endless Frontier" bill.[48]

Biden's agenda had some notable successes. He used executive authority to organize the national response to the pandemic, restore the personnel and moral integrity of executive departments, and reverse many of Trump's most destructive environmental policies. The administration was able to pass its massive COVID relief and stimulus bills, which included the expansion of Medicaid and the Child Tax Credit—a measure that temporarily cut the child poverty rate in half. Biden was also able to negotiate bipartisan bills investing over a trillion dollars in traditional infrastructure, clean water, and expanded broadband access, and providing government support of domestic semiconductor production. The administration sponsored the first bipartisan gun safety legislation in nearly thirty years and the Inflation Reduction Act, which tackled climate change and corporate taxes and reduced costs for health insurance and prescription drugs.

The administration also supported traditional civil rights issues like voting rights and antidiscrimination rules, applied affirmative action to infrastructure contracting, tried to ensure that Black farmers would get the kind of support traditionally denied them, and addressed the causes of environmental discrimination that places people of color in areas especially subject to environmental hazards. In framing this aspect of the reform program, blue spokespeople and opinion journalists invoked the memory of Martin Luther King Jr., John Lewis, and the civil rights movement of 1950–1970. However, in their retelling, the Myth of the Movement now functions not as a free-standing fable of moral action but as an integral part of a larger movement for social justice.

The connection marks a critical turn in political culture. The great legislative gains of the civil rights movement, the Civil Rights Act of 1964 and the Voting Rights Act of 1965, had been won in partnership with Attorney General Robert Kennedy and President Lyndon Johnson, while the movement provided the moral élan for Johnson's Great Society programs and War on Poverty. But the Great Society was discredited by its association with Vietnam and the urban uprisings that followed King's assassination. King eventually earned a place in the American pantheon, but purged of his revolutionary thought and ambition, available for the pieties of conservatives and liberals alike. Yet before his break with Johnson, King had actually been moving to build a national, transracial social justice movement, one that would have been in productive and critical dialogue with Johnson's Great Society. His death and the racial backlash of the 1970s and 1980s cut that promise short. The radical aspects of the movement were dismissively associated with the failure of pseudo-revolutionary organizations like Black Power and the Black Panthers. Its ongoing initiatives were seen as compensatory, seeking benefits for the disadvantaged. The movement's radical offshoots—countercultural anticapitalism, the women's movement, and other "liberation" movements— became symbols of the identity politics and secular liberalism that conservatives would run against for the next fifty years.[49]

Images of the Unite the Right riot in Charlottesville, the killing of George Floyd, and the assault on BLM demonstrators in Lafayette Square recalled the vivid pictures of vigilante and police violence in 1963 in Selma and Birmingham, and suggested the possibility that BLM could replicate the success of the 1960s civil rights movement. That possibility has not been realized. Some cities did begin police reform and expanded antidiscrimination programs; others saw a reaction against increases in crime that were attributed in part to the demoralization of police by BLM protests. The curricular initiatives sponsored by BLM and its allies were met with a reaction directed against critical race theory and the 1619 Project, as well as the elections of Governors Glenn Youngkin of Virginia and DeSantis of Florida on platforms asserting "parental rights" to control what their children are taught in school. BLM has not yet developed as the 1960s civil rights movement did, from a struggle for well-defined reforms to a broadly conceived movement for social justice.

The most important achievement of BLM was to bring the narrative of the movement back into the mainstream of political discourse in the form of a myth, a major historical referent and model for social reform and political action. A poll taken by the Pew Research Center in 2021 showed that 53 percent of White respondents agreed with BLM's major contention, that American society was marred by systemic racism, with 47 percent disagreeing. But 76 percent agreed that racial discrimination was a serious issue, suggesting a broad consensus on the movement's primary contention.[50]

The civil rights movement as *myth* now incorporated all the civil rights struggles that developed out of that movement, among Latin and Mexican Americans, Native Americans, women, undocumented immigrants, and LGBTQ people. The long debate over climate change that produced the Green New Deal made the connection between environmental degradation and systemic racism, specifically in housing discrimination and public health. The engagement with police shootings dovetailed with the gun control activism of youth movements like the Parkland students' March for Our Lives and community violence-prevention organizations like Moms Against Violence. The civil rights movement thus became a myth of origin for a constellation of progressive grass-roots initiatives.[51]

The integration of the New Deal and Movement myths is critical to the blue agenda. Taken separately, they symbolize the ideological split that has divided liberal politics since the 1970s. New Deal symbolism highlights the centrality of labor to the Democratic coalition and makes reform of labor-capital relations the core of the political agenda. The cultural program implicit in New Deal symbolism is nationalistic, insisting that reform depends on the solidarity of Americans as patriots. In the 1970s the Movement became the myth of choice for identity-based advocacy, which emphasized minority rights and ethnic identity, as well as the achievement of greater "diversity" in all institutions. It was also associated with a radical critique of America's history of gender, racial, and ethnic exclusion. The era of neoliberalism saw these two seemingly irreconcilable constituencies draw apart, as Clinton and the New Democrats neglected the interests of labor and communities affected by the off-shoring of manufacturing, and the Left embraced identity politics.

The success of the blue reform program will depend on its ability to reconcile these two myths. A study sponsored by the Pentagon's Office of Net Assessment, *The Societal Foundations of National Competitiveness,* found that America's unprecedented "diversity and pluralism" have given the country immense advantages in economic competition with rival states. However, "they must be achieved in ways that allow for unified national identity, stability, and the activities of an effective, coherent and active state," or social cohesion and political stability will become problematic.[52] Research conducted by Democracy Corps, Equis Research, and HIT Strategies showed strong support by working-class voters of all races for the reforms and benefits embodied in the American Rescue Plan and Build Back Better, and for policies addressing the inequality of wealth and power between the great corporations and the workers and communities damaged by neoliberal economics. Studies by the Race-Class Narrative Project had similar results, showing that Americans are drawn to stories that characterize workers of all races as sharing a life of labor; as victims of powerful interests that use racial division to deprive them of their rights and benefits; and as a nation whose strength is "our ability to work together—to knit together a landscape of people from different places and of different races into one nation."[53]

However the Biden administration fares in the near term, its adoption of the New Deal and Movement mythos ratifies a change in the political culture of the Democratic Party. As Zachary Carter writes in *Politico,* "The center of gravity in the party has fundamentally shifted. The establishment, led by Biden—no one's idea of a left-winger—is shrugging off the market-friendly mindset of the Clinton and Obama eras. A new gospel for Democrats has arrived, centered on aggressive federal intervention to improve people's lives, and it's unlikely to fade no matter what happens to Biden's agenda."[54] Carter may overstate the extent of the party's leftward tilt. But he is correct in thinking that the critical events of 2020 have brought New Deal—and Movement-style liberalism back from the outer darkness to which Clinton's New Democrats consigned it. As Corey Robin wrote in the *New York Times*, Build Back Better offered a coherent program, rather than "a laundry list of gripes and grievances." "[It] featured the consistent items of an alternative ideology and ascendant set of social interests. It promised to replace a sclerotic order that threatens to bury us all with a new order of common life. This was that rare moment when the most partisan of claims can sound like a reasonable defense of the whole."[55]

Robin also noted that the gap between the expectations roused by the Build Back Better program and its limited success in Congress has led to disappointment among Democrats and with the wider public. But Biden and his advisers have proposed a new economic paradigm, opposed to the top-down neoliberalism of the Reagan and Clinton years, which seeks to stimulate growth through social investments that benefit the middle class and reduce inequality. It thus represents a distinct pivot in the ideology of the liberal establishment and a substantive expansion of the terms of American political discourse, in which the New Deal (class) and Movement (race, gender) strains of liberalism can work together.[56]

Reforming National Myth: The Problem of the "Dark Side"

While it is clear that the elements of a new liberal and progressive national myth are present, it is not certain that they will become an operative mythos. The Democratic Party is by no means united in support of an active program of economic and racial reform. It has yet to form a truly coherent theory of the modern economy comparable in plausibility and broad appeal to the crisis-dependent Keynesianism of the New Deal. MAGA has an advantage in the "story wars" because it invokes narratives already sanctified in traditional mythology—the Frontier, the Founding, the Lost Cause—and applies these to define the crisis of our time in culture-war terms: American carnage, the Great Replacement, denying our heritage, Satanic elites. The ideological and ethnic diversity of the blue coalition, and the technocratic character of its reform program, makes it difficult for its spokespeople to tell a compelling story that will form a conceptual bridge to a desirable future.[57]

There is also a contradiction between the critical ideology that drives the movement for reform and the function of national myth, which is to produce affirmative belief. The liberal critique of American capitalism and social injustice depends on the truth value of its historical analysis. As Richard Rorty has said, "I do not think there is a nonmythological, nonideological way of telling a nation's story," though there may be myths that hew more closely to historical truth.[58]

Conservatives have a point when they worry that a full confession of America's past failings might make patriotism unsustainable. Liberals have traditionally overcome this contradiction by identifying America with its aspirations, its idealized self-image as free, inclusive, egalitarian, a nation of immigrants, "with liberty and justice for all." Invoking that concept of national identity makes it possible to assert that the Proud Boys and Oath Keepers, Trump, and MAGA are "not who we are." But in fact they *are* part of who we are and who we have been, as are the Ku Klux Klan and the Confederacy. Trump is as American as Martin Luther King Jr. MAGA's exclusive concept of "real Americans" denies the reality of American diversity. To deny the authentic Americanism of the Right is to make the same error in reverse.[59]

A pluralist national myth would require a new framing of our origins, one that would correct the racial and settler-state bias of the Frontier Myth. It would begin by recognizing that America's population has always been multiracial and multiethnic. From the colonial period onward, Indigenous peoples shared the territory with European settlers, who were themselves of varied national and ethnic origins, and with Africans, enslaved and free. From the first the problem of American nationality has been whether it was possible—and *desirable*—to form a single nationality, one People, and a just republican government out of diverse religious, racial, and ethnic elements. In the first stage of national development, the United States limited political citizenship almost exclusively to White men. The settler-state ideology that shaped national development made racial warfare on the border a foundational symbol of national identity. The United States is also unique among the democratic nations in having had a slavery regime within its national borders, as opposed to overseas colonies, which made racism intrinsic to its culture and fostered the long-lived antidemocratic regime of Jim Crow.

But if the dark side of our nationality is its history of racial violence and injustice, the glory of our history is the struggle Americans have waged to realize an extraordinarily broad and inclusive concept of nationality. If the dark side is the exploitation of land and labor by a rampant capitalism, its counterpart is the struggle for workers' rights, environmental conservation, and our determined efforts to strike a just and constructive balance between individual rights, corporate power, and the public good. It is for that willingness to struggle, as much as for our achievements, that America has been the goal of immigrants from every country and culture on earth.

This is the history to which our myths connect us: a dark and bloody ground in which slavery shares space with freedom, dispossession with progress, hatred with heritage. Since it has been the hope of liberals to purge the nation of its racialism, it has been their role (and the role of revisionist historians) to expose and discredit those myths. That has made it difficult for liberal reform movements to tap the sense of historical destiny that a national myth provides. Although he supported the removal of Confederate statues, Issac Bailey of *Politico* warned against an indiscriminate iconoclasm. "Refusing to acknowledge anything but the bad in our shared historical narrative would make it harder, not easier, to learn from our past. We can't purge these figures [like Washington and Jefferson] from our history without also purging our memories of what made this country possible and unique." Their real contributions to the establishment of an independent United States and the formation of its government are too great to be ignored. Jefferson gave us the moral principle—"all men are created equal"—by which we judge his failure as a man and a leader. The significance of Abraham Lincoln's achievement in ending slavery, or of Lyndon Johnson's in passing the Voting Rights Act, is enhanced by our knowing that they struggled to overcome the racialist premises of the culture in which they had been reared. As the poet and feminist Adrienne Rich writes, "A patriot is one who wrestles for the soul of her country/ as she wrestles for her own being." Jamelle Bouie echoes Rich, positing a choice between "the comfort of myth" and a willingness to "wrestle with everything . . . that keeps us apart, with all the discord and estrangement within and between our parties, movements, cultures and regions."[60]

A myth can be made of such struggles, tracing a path from Lincoln's "new birth of freedom" and Reconstruction's Second Founding to the New Deal's grand but imperfect project of economic and social reform, the triumphs of the Good War, the Great Society, and the Movement, and the cruel strokes that cut them off. Such a myth would provide the Left and center Left with something it has lacked since the 1970s: a narrative that roots its ideology and political program in history. This narrative links the struggle for racial justice to the broader task of securing economic justice for the working and middle classes, reversing the policies that aggrandize the wealthy at the expense of the rest, and breaking the monopolistic control of economic and financial operations by a few colossal corporations.

That narrative has the hallmarks of myth: it turns history into symbols for actual use, and the symbols it chooses correspond to fundamental features of our national history, culture, and politics. It also has that essential feature of myth: an imperative moral vision shaping a concept of national destiny, and a formulation of *unfinished business* that the current generation is called to complete. It might be called "American Reformation," which the *Oxford English Dictionary* defines as "a radical change for the better in political, religious, or social matters."[61]

There is some basis for thinking the Democratic program can appeal to a constituency broad enough to reestablish a center-Left political consensus. Surveys of public opinion show high levels of public agreement on the "essential rights important to being an American today." These include "clean air and water" (93 percent), "a quality education" (92 percent), "affordable health care" (89 percent), and the "right to a job" (85 percent). The same high levels of support exist for economic and social rights, including civil rights and equal opportunity (92–93 percent). Even on the most highly contentious culture-war issues, a vast majority (90 percent) favors increased regulation of firearms, and a substantial majority (57 percent) favors abortion rights. In "Moderates," a 2022 study of the American electorate, Anthony Fowler and his associates found that "a large proportion of the American public is neither consistently liberal nor consistently conservative" but remains "highly responsive to the ideologies and qualities of political candidates."[62]

On the other hand, the experience of the past thirty years suggests that despite these shared values and beliefs, when these citizens become voters, they revert to partisan identities and become culture warriors. Biden and the blue coalition have wagered that by dealing effectively with the endemic problems of the modern global and corporate economy, they can break the hold of culture-war politics and return to an age when policy could be made through a rational balancing of competing interests. But a study by Lynn Vavreck and John Sides of half a million voters found that the basis of partisan political engagement in 2020 continued the long-term shift away from "New Deal sorts of issues," such as taxes, entitlements, and bureaucracy, to culture-war issues that challenge people's sense of identity and beliefs about the kind of world they want to live in; whether and how religion should affect education, politics, and law; and "who gets to call themselves an American, who is going to be allowed to gain citizenship, what people are going to be able to do with their bodies."[63]

President Biden appealed, as Lincoln did in his first inaugural address, to "the better angels of our nature" who sound the "mystic chords of memory" that bind Americans to their history of common struggle and achievement. But he has found, as Lincoln did, that the "better angels" are hardly to be heard. Far from providing a basis of unity, historical memory is one of the main grounds of contention between the parties.

A Culture War between the States

With national governance in deadlock, culture-war combatants are reshaping state politics as vessels for their empowerment. As in the pre–Civil War period, two constellations of ideologically opposed states are developing regimes with radically different laws on voting rights and the conduct and certification of elections; on abortion and public health; on gender and sexuality issues, especially those affecting LGBTQ people; on gun rights, the relation of church and state, and the way history is taught in public schools; and on the use of fossil fuels and support for renewable alternatives.

States under one-party Republican control have taken the lead in this process, assisted by conservative think tanks and action groups, notably the Koch brothers' ALEC and Americans for Progress, the Heritage Foundation, and the Claremont Institute. But these initiatives succeed because they build on popular support from regional cultures that are strongly conservative on two or more of the major issues.

In the spring and summer of 2021, the Texas legislature passed a series of laws that illustrate the way in which gun rights, antiabortion and anti-LGBTQ legislation, and voter suppression interlock in such a red-state regime. Rejecting the appeal of local law enforcement following the El Paso mass shooting, the legislature adopted "constitutional carry," allowing any person other than a convicted felon to carry any firearm in public without requiring training, registration, or vetting for restraining orders. It also adopted a highly restrictive set of election laws, which licensed partisan poll watchers to intervene in the conduct of voting—an invitation to intimidation. It adopted restrictive abortion laws, to be enforced not by state officials but by individuals, who were invited to sue any person involved in providing an abortion, with the promise of a $10,000 bounty if successful—an application of the vigilante principle. The state attorney general issued a directive (later blocked by the courts) requiring that medical treatment of transgender children be prosecuted as "child abuse." Taken with the platform adopted by the Texas GOP, which calls for teaching "prayer, the Bible, and the Ten Commandments" in public schools, Texas seems to be carrying out the program of Christian nationalism.[64]

Other states have followed Texas's lead by abolishing or drastically curtailing abortion rights in ways that endanger women's health care in general; and in legislation aimed at controlling elections, expanding gun rights, and undoing laws designed to protect LGBTQ rights. The last trend has become especially poisonous in Florida, where Governor Ron DeSantis models the elective authoritarianism favored by some conservatives. Through voter restriction measures and extreme gerrymandering, DeSantis has established something like one-party rule, with a supermajority in the legislature and control of state courts. He has advertised his hostility to immigration by busing and flying immigrants and asylum seekers to northern cities. He removed from office an elected district attorney who defied his orders on abortion and transgender care. He used his office to organize and fund partisan takeovers of local school boards, which then fired superintendents who had opposed the governor's anti-masking COVID policies. "Florida," he said, "is where 'woke' comes to die," and he has used his powers to punish the Disney corporation, one of the state's biggest businesses, for objecting to his policies on LGBTQ rights.

DeSantis's attack on gay and transgender rights has been especially vicious. As in Texas, in Florida medical treatment for children identifying as trans has been barred. His Parental Rights in Education Act, known as the "Don't Say Gay" law, prohibited teaching about sexuality in the early grades. Although professedly based on theories of child development and parental rights, the governor's press spokesperson characterized it as the "Anti-Grooming Bill," suggesting that anyone teaching tolerance of homosexuality or gender nonconformity was grooming children for sexual abuse. How sex education should be taught, especially in the primary grades, is a subject of legitimate concern, and it has been a focus of the "parents' rights" movement that has burgeoned in blue states like Virginia as well as red Texas and Florida. But MAGA conservatives have used the issue as an opportunity to wage campaigns against gay and especially trans rights, by exploiting the psychosexual anxieties already reflected in the spread of the QAnon "liberal pedophile" conspiracy. These campaigns tap the emotional basis of racism while avoiding its moral taint, enabling an appeal to culturally conservative Black and Latino voters. Their actions are consonant with similar campaigns against "homosexual propaganda" by quasi-authoritarian regimes in Hungary, Poland, and Russia, which sanctify the regime by identifying it with Christian orthodoxy and traditional family structure.[65]

In response, blue states have not only reaffirmed the legality of abortion and the stringency of their gun laws, they have adopted rules forbidding attorneys general to cooperate with law enforcement from red states when they seek to prosecute women or their doctors in abortion cases. California developed a series of gun control laws using a mechanism like Texas's privatized antiabortion enforcement, and it has taken other tit-for-tat measures on abortion law, assault weapons, automobile emissions, and fossil fuel use. Other blue states are considering ways of following California's example. This juridical war between states took a new form in the summer of 2022, when Texas and Florida began sending busloads of asylum seekers from their immigration detention centers to blue-state cities like New York, Chicago, and Washington, DC.[66]

The argument in the states over curriculum under the auspices of "parental rights" goes beyond sex and gender to focus on the teaching of history. This is critical, because it is here that MAGA directly assumes the power of enforcing its version of national myth. Revisionist and conservative historians have been contending over history curricula since the 1990s. Publishers of history textbooks have followed the revisionists in paying greater attention to the dispossession of Indigenous peoples, slavery and Jim Crow, gender roles, and ethnic diversity. But their treatment of these issues has been modulated to suit the preferences of conservative legislators in big-market states like Texas on matters such as the centrality of slavery as a cause of the Civil War.

The latest form of the conflict is the opposition to the supposed use in some school systems of "critical race theory" (CRT), the 1619 Project, and antiracism protocols based on the work of Ibram X. Kendi, and more generally to the promotion of "woke" or politically correct history that is critical of American culture and institutions. The 1619 Project is accused of distorting American history by centering it on race, and CRT's concept of "systemic racism" is faulted for seeing racism as intrinsic to American culture and institutions. Both projects are also accused of promoting "White guilt" as a way of weakening resistance to liberal proposals for social reform. Programs that make use of Kendi's recommendations for antiracist learning are blamed for causing psychological stress and racial hostility. The Koch brothers, ALEC, the 1776 Project political action committee, and the American Principles Project have aided the movement by pouring funding into local school board elections. In a number of communities, armed activists have made school boards the scene of menacing and openly violent demonstrations against CRT and sex education. Under the rubric of "parental rights," it has become a key element in successful Republican campaigns, most notably the election of Glenn Youngkin as governor of Virginia in 2021, although its significance for the history curriculum is complicated by its linkage to concerns about sex education.[67]

CRT and the 1619 Project are specialized studies, useful in particular contexts but not suitable as the basis for an entire secondary-school curriculum. The 1619 Project works as a thought experiment that asks what American history would look like if the narrative centered on race. It has value to those who are already familiar with the standard historical paradigm and can appreciate the differences that become visible with a change in point of view. CRT is a complex academic movement, not a single ideology, whose value is its focus on the way racism has become embedded in and is perpetuated through our social order. School systems accused of using these "woke" programs respond that they do not, in fact, base their curricula on the 1619 Project, and that CRT as such is only taught at the college level.

To resolve the controversy responsibly on the national scale would require a deep dive into the recent history curriculum development. There are hundreds of school districts to be looked at. One would need to know what curricula have actually been adopted in each of them, whether these were 1619 Project or CRT influenced or merely responsive to trends in history textbook writing, and what kinds of curriculum were being replaced. Instead of making such a study, MAGA activists and Republican state legislators have tended to file any teaching that seems critical of America's racial history under the "CRT" label and move to ban it. Texas Republicans voted to bar any teaching about America's history of race relations that is likely to make some students "uncomfortable"—a standard vague enough to deter serious teaching about the history of Native dispossession, slavery, and Jim Crow. Similar laws have been passed in other red states. Some require punishment of teachers for presentations of critical material, others sanction suits by private individuals who are personally offended by the material—another case of vigilante enforcement. While there are special concerns about how to teach troublesome aspects of history at the primary-school level, in Florida state-mandated curricular bans restrict the teaching of this history up through the university level, forbidding any curriculum "based on theories that systemic racism, sexism, oppression, and privilege are inherent in the institutions of the United States and were created to maintain social, political, and economic inequities." Here again MAGA builds on tendencies already present in the conservative movement, which since the 1990s has waged a campaign against attempts to revise the standards for teaching American history.[68]

Laws that censor what can be taught as history are one step removed from "memory laws," through which authoritarian and totalitarian regimes impose a version of national history that gives their ideology the sanction of precedent and tradition. The restriction of teaching and educational materials was a cornerstone of the slave-state system of social control, and curricula based on the principles of the "Confederate Catechism" sustained the Jim Crow system that followed it.[69]

There is no doubt that studying the history of race in America can be disturbing, especially when it is applied to an analysis of present conditions. On the other hand, if you are *not* discomfited by studying American history—or the history of any country—you are probably not getting the real story. Every nation, whatever its virtues, has to some extent been built on deeds of violence, injustice, and exploitation. Our history created the conditions under which we live today. If we refuse to see the reality of that history, we limit our power to correct the problems that history bequeathed us.

That problem is compounded if the red and blue sections of the country are being taught radically different versions of national history. The urge to fight fire with fire can also bring out an illiberalism of the Left, expressed in "cancel culture," which has been used to curtail speech, ban books and speakers, and punish political incorrectness on college campuses and in progressive organizations. Although the operations of cancel culture lack the legal force of red-state curriculum laws, they have a chilling effect on learning and public discourse and seem to be harder to challenge through litigation. They have damaged liberal and progressive causes by dividing communities and organizations in the name of ideological purity. But in a culture war between the states, there would be a strong temptation to respond in kind to red-state curriculum purges and mirror MAGA's enforcement of ideological conformity.

The growing division of states into rival red and blue regimes is in some respects the culmination of the "Big Sort" that has been under way for thirty years. Its effect will be to institutionalize culture-war differences, with potentially catastrophic effects on Americans' ability to imagine anything like the common good or to unite in response to the crises of climate, public health, and international conflict that are sure to arise. There is an obvious analogy with the Free State / Slave State division that ended in the Civil War. Then, as now, states committed to an illiberal cultural regime used authoritarian laws and restrictions of speech, press, and education to ensure social control of potential dissidence.[70]

But a more appropriate analogy for our two-regime America is the Jim Crow era, which saw the states divided into liberal and illiberal regimes, and endured for a hundred years. We live closer to Jim Crow than we like to think. Emmett Till was lynched in 1955; Michael Schwerner, Andrew Goodman, and

James Chaney in 1964. There are people alive today in Valdosta, Georgia, whose grandparents were in the mob that tortured, mutilated, and burned Mary Turner to death in May 1918. The laws that began dismantling the legal basis of segregation were passed only fifty years ago; their enforcement was slow and Jim Crow's physical death was attenuated. The cultural forces that sustained it are nearly identical to those that inform the MAGA order. Herbert Kitschelt, a Duke political scientist specializing in comparative studies of democratic party formation, sees the MAGA / red-state order as "a form of clerofascism" rooted in the "Christian white-supremacist ideology that evolved to justify slavery": "a geographical generalization of what prevailed in the American South until the 1960s Civil Rights movement: a white Evangelical oligarchy with repression—jailtime, physical violence and death—inflicted on those who will not succumb to this oligarchy."[71]

Yet there is a critical difference between the divided regimes of the Jim Crow era and the MAGA-driven culture war between the states. MAGA enthusiasts, and their conservative allies, are not content with preserving a separate illiberal cultural sphere through the traditional defense of "states' rights." They aim to achieve control of the national government, and to use the power of the courts and of the House and Senate to impose something like a Texas / Florida legal regime nationwide.

The local acts of violence and intimidation sanctioned by MAGA are not merely devices for local control. They have become a way of "grooming" the public to expect political violence, both the real violence of a January 6 and the symbolic violence of laws that break the institutions, understandings, and values that sustain democratic government. In February 2022 the Republican National Committee officially declared that the January 6 attack was not an insurrection or riot but "legitimate political discourse." Republican candidates routinely display their guns, and sometimes urge their aggressive use, in campaign ads. In interviews with Colby Itkowitz of the *Washington Post,* Republican strategists and campaign aides affirmed that "such placements convey a cultural and political solidarity with conservatives more powerfully than most anything else. . . . It is their calling card to tell Republican voters that they are conservative."[72]

The glorification of political intimidation energizes individuals to act out the deeper forms of cultural resentment. Death threats against federal and state public officials, and actual attempts at assassination and kidnapping, have markedly increased. The FBI has reported that hate crimes in 2020 were the highest since 2001. The widespread circulation of firearms, and the ease with which the most lethal weapons can be obtained, has already created a situation in which fear of gun violence poisons a public sphere that is already threatened by fear of COVID and the seduction of electronic media. A study by the *New York Times* found in 2022 a sharp rise in armed demonstrations opposing LGBTQ-related events at libraries, at school board curriculum debates, and at protests of supposed electoral fraud. According to the *Times,* "Deploying the Second Amendment in service of the First has become a way to buttress a policy argument, a sort of silent, if intimidating, bullhorn."[73]

Gun deaths have topped 40,000 per year and become the most frequent cause of death in children to age seventeen. Active shooter incidents, mass shootings, school shootings, and "massacres" in supermarkets and places of worship have occurred at persistently high levels for the past decade. The sanctification of gun rights as the "palladium of our liberties," and the symbol of libertarian and neoliberal economic "freedom," has made acceptance of this kind of violence a test of MAGA loyalty. Forty-four percent of Republicans believe that mass shootings and school massacres are "unfortunately something we have to accept as part of a free society." The Federalist Society, which advocates broadening 2nd Amendment rights, suggests greater use of "home schooling," an idea that chimes with conservative efforts to defund and reduce the role of public schools.[74]

If these trends continue, we will begin to approximate the conditions that pertained in what I have called the Age of Vigilantism, from 1870 to 1920, when armed mobs and rogue militias formed to intimidate public officials or legislators and execute their own law. In one respect, our situation would be worse. The widespread ownership of military rifles, capable of killing large numbers of people very quickly, has empowered individuals—psychologically distressed, angry at wives or girlfriends or employers, sadistic by nature or inflamed and radicalized in online communities—to commit massacres on a scale hitherto unknown in civil life.

Since the January 6 insurrection, violence has becoming more acceptable as an instrument of political action. Surveys completed in 2022 found that 40 percent of Americans, and more than half of Republicans, believe a civil war is likely in the next ten years; one in four Americans believe that violence against the government could be justified, and one in ten believed it was justified now. As a practical matter, we are not likely to experience a "war between the states" like that of 1861–1865. What the poll signals is an expectation of political violence, and on the part of some Americans a desire for open conflict. We are therefore likely to experience some combination of terrorism, urban uprisings, and intercommunal violence of the kind that has plagued Israel and Northern Ireland. It will come from White nationalists, whether frustrated by defeat or encouraged by a MAGA victory to assault civil rights and left-wing demonstrators. We have also seen the potential for spontaneous violence to erupt on the margins of nonviolent protests, and for anarchist cells to indulge in what the nineteenth-century anarchist Mikhail Bakunin called the "propaganda of the deed." In 2020 Joint Chiefs of Staff chairman Mark Milley blocked Trump's attempts to use the military against civilian demonstrators. There can be no certainty that a different general would similarly defy the next commander in chief. Confrontations between nonviolent demonstrators and police or the National Guard would test the limits of the regime's ability to use force, and the willingness of uniformed services to support it. These things will occur in a country whose people, on both sides of the political divide, are more heavily and lethally armed than they were in the 1960s.[75]

Where We Stand

In his poem "A Connoisseur of Chaos," Wallace Stevens wrote that "a violent order is disorder" and "a great disorder is an order." As things stand, we may well be entering the age of the Great Disorder.

The culture wars are not simply quarrels about issues like abortion and gun safety. They are disagreements about the fundamental character of American nationality and the purposes of the American nation-state. Even if Biden's policies were to cure the disorder of our cities and restore the health of the American economy, MAGA Republicans would not accept this as "success" or validation of the blue coalition's principles. For them, the only acceptable end of the political struggle would be victory in the culture war and restoration of the White republic. Trump's "Big Lie" has convinced a majority of Republicans that Democrats cannot win an election without "stealing" it. And Democrats would have good reason to believe that the victory of *any* Republican candidate would be "stolen" in light of the Republicans' use of state legislatures to suppress or delegitimize Democratic votes. Politics cannot save the culture from itself if the electoral process loses its legitimacy.

Whatever the result of the 2024 elections, given the closely divided balance of partisan support, it seems likely that in the near future a MAGA-controlled Republican Party will win the presidency or Congress. Authoritarian tendencies are already apparent in MAGA's political leadership, and these are being given an ideological rationale by national conservatism and think tanks like the Claremont Institute. Under these circumstances, Republican control of the government would put the institutions and values that sustain democratic government in grave danger. The struggle to slow and reverse global warming would suffer a decisive defeat. America's alliances would be compromised, weakening our ability to respond effectively to the violent revanchism of Putin's Russia and the economic and military challenge of Xi Jinping's China. If Trump himself were to win reelection, the damage to republican institutions and the national interest might well be irreparable. His contempt for constitutional restraint has been amply demonstrated, and he now has a better-trained group of loyalists he can call on, and a firmer grasp of how to bend government agencies to his will and overcome legal restraints.

MAGA's problem is that it can *rule,* but it cannot *govern:* it can use the instruments of law and government, the dictates of a conservative supermajority on the Supreme Court, and vigilante intimidation to impose a degree of obedience. But its theory of politics precludes the possibility of working with the opposition toward mutually acceptable policies. Thus it cannot create a stable political order, such as the New Deal and neoliberal orders were in their time.

It is certainly possible for a Democratic presidential candidate to win in 2024, control the Senate, and perhaps regain a majority in the House. However, it is unlikely that in the near future the blue coalition will be able to establish the broad public consensus required to establish a "political order" capable of the sustained and systematic effort required to address the endemic issues of the twenty-first century. Its effort to form a political movement is just beginning; its version of national myth is just taking shape. The coherence of its ideology and constituencies has been deranged by the exigencies of governing through multiple crises, yet it offers the best hope for a politics that could address the endemic problems of the new world economy and also save our culture from itself.

The blue coalition will need to vastly expand grassroots organizing, focusing on issues that go to the heart of reform: racial justice, voting rights, gun safety, workers' rights, the preservation of democracy, women's rights, and climate change. Given the hysterical pitch of national political discourse, such action must begin at the community level. Although such organizing would be vital for building political strength, it could also have a subtler but no less critical effect on the way communities affirm and negotiate cultural values. Organized efforts will have to be made to meet people where they are and reopen lines of communication within and between communities to address the most critical issues facing these communities in terms appropriate to their heritage and circumstances. Public meetings, like those held by towns and cities to consider Confederate monuments, or the regular meetings of school boards and election commissions, will be important venues for such conversations. But they must be prepared for by door-to-door, person-to-person contact—by civil invitations to a mutually considerate exchange of views. There are useful models already in the field: Everytown for Gun Safety, the Parkland students' March for Our Lives, and local violence-prevention groups like Moms Against Violence. The Rev. William Barber's North Carolina–based Poor People's Campaign has revived Dr. King's community-based organizing for economic and social justice, and Bryan Stevenson's Equal Justice Initiative, whose museums on the history of enslavement and Jim Crow have become a center for community discussion and played an important role in urban redevelopment.[76]

It would be wise to think of such organizing not only as a way to build electoral support but as a basis for nonviolent resistance if MAGA should gain control of the government.

The actions we take and the political choices we make in the coming decade will be critical in determining the future of democratic government and the planetary environment. Implicit in our elections is a choice between national myths—those fables that express our sense of belonging to a single society, continuous in time, rooted in a given past, and moving toward an imagined future. Following the action script of its chosen myths, MAGA has decided it must destroy America in order to save its "authentic" culture, which is Christian, Euro-American, and implicitly White. It cannot win, and believes it can dispense with the consent of a majority of the governed. Its understanding of American nationality, of the rightful constituents of political discourse, denies the reality of the nation's racial, ethnic, and ideological diversity. The alternative offered by the blue coalition, clear in outline though not fully formed, embraces the unprecedented racial, ethnic, religious, and ideological diversity of the American people as both a reality and a source of energy and strength, and reads our historical passage from settler state to metropolis as a long struggle against the dark side of our cultural heritage to establish a just and equitable society.

The making of national myths has proved to be essential to the creation of nation-states, and to the maintenance of that sense of historically continuous community that allows them to function. The danger of mythological thinking is that it tempts us to reify our nostalgia for a falsely idealized past, and to sacrifice our future to that illusion. But we are not bound to live the mythic scenarios bequeathed to us by tradition. The history of national myth shows that change is possible. No single creative act can produce a national myth. But the actions we take, the stories we tell about those actions, and the historical frames in which we set them can add up over time to the formation of a new or reformed national myth. We ourselves can agitate and organize, protest or strike, enlist or resign, speak, write, criticize old stories, and tell new ones. We can teach American history in all its true complexity and difficulty, so that the roots of present conditions and dilemmas can be understood by the rising generations. We can make mythic discourse, the telling of American stories, one of the many ways we have of imagining a more perfect union.

Notes

Abbreviations

NYRB: New York Review of Books
NYT: New York Times
WP: Washington Post
WSJ: Wall Street Journal
All citations from journals, magazines, newspapers, foundation reports, videos, and broadcasts are from online editions, unless otherwise noted.

Introduction

1. PRRI Staff, "Fractured Nation: Widening Partisan Polarization and Key Issues in 2020 Presidential Elections," Public Religion Research Institute, Oct. 20, 2019, https://www.prri.org/research/fractured-nation-widening-partisan-polarization-and -key-issues-in-2020-presidential-elections/; Steven Levitsky and Daniel Ziblatt, *How Democracies Die* (New York: Crown, 2018); Susan Rice, "Our Democracy's Near-Death Experience," *NYT,* Dec. 1, 2020.

2. Michael Gerson, "This Election Was a Reflection of Who We Are as a Country," *WP,* Nov. 5, 2020.

3. Michael Vlahos, "We Were Made for Civil War," *American Conservative,* Nov. 6, 2019; George Packer, *The Unwinding: An Inner History of the New America* (New York: Farrar, Straus and Giroux, 2012); PRRI Staff, "Fractured Nation"; Yoni Applebaum, "How America Ends," *The Atlantic,* Dec. 2019; Larry Diamond et al., "Americans Increasingly Believe Violence Is Justified If the Other Side Wins," *Politico,* Oct. 9, 2020; Barbara F. Walter, *How Civil Wars Start: And How to Stop Them: The Civil War on America's Horizon* (New York: Crown, 2022); David Remnick, "Is a Civil War Ahead?," *New Yorker,*

Jan. 5, 2022; William G. Gale and Darrell M. West, "Is the US Headed for Another Civil War?," Brookings Institution, Sept. 16, 2021, https://www.brookings.edu/blog /fixgov/2021/09/16/is-the-us-headed-for-another-civil-war/; William S. Smith, "The Civil War on America's Horizon," *American Conservative,* Sept. 11, 2018.

4. Benedict Anderson, *Imagined Communities: Reflections on the Origin and Spread of Nationalism* (London: Verso, 1983); Anthony D. Smith, *Ethnic Origins of Nations* (New York: Oxford, 1987); Etienne Balibar and Immanuel Wallerstein, *Race, Nation, Class: Ambiguous Identities,* trans. Chris Turner (London: Verso, 1991), esp. 49; Wilbur Zelinsky, *Nation into State: The Shifting Symbolic Foundations of American Nationalism* (Chapel Hill: University of North Carolina Press, 1988), chaps. 1–2; Richard Rorty, *Achieving Our Country: Leftist Thought in Twentieth-Century America* (Cambridge, MA: Harvard University Press, 1997), 11.

5. Robert N. Bellah, *The Broken Covenant: American Civil Religion in a Time of Trial* (Chicago: University of Chicago Press, 1992); Catherine L. Albanese, *Sons of the Fathers: The Civil Religion of the American Revolution* (Philadelphia: Temple University Press, 1977).

6. William H. McNeill, "The Care and Repair of Public Myth," *Foreign Affairs,* Fall 1982, 1–13; "On the American Narrative," special issue, *Daedalus* 141, no. 1 (Winter 2012), esp. Jay Parini, "The American Mythos," 52–53; see also David Levering Lewis, "Exceptionalism's Exceptions: The Changing American Narrative," 101–117.

7. David Brooks, "The Unifying American Story," *NYT,* Mar. 21, 2017; W. Smith, "Civil War." The idea is not exclusive to conservatives. See liberal columnist Charles Blow, "The Lost Cause Is Back," *NYT,* July 28, 2021.

8. For a fuller discussion of the theory of myth, see Richard Slotkin, *Gunfighter Nation: The Myth of the Frontier in Twentieth-Century America* (New York: Atheneum, 1992), 1–10; Richard Slotkin, *The Fatal Environment: The Myth of the Frontier in the Age of Industrialization, 1800–1890* (New York: Atheneum, 1985), chap. 2; Richard Slotkin, *Lost Battalions: The Great War and the Crisis of American Nationality* (New York: Holt, 2005), chap. 2; Clifford Geertz, *The Interpretation of Cultures: Selected Essays* (New York: Basic Books, 1973), 211, 214, 218, 220, 231; Marshall Sahlins, *Historical Metaphors and Mythical Realities: Structure in the Early History of the Sandwich Island Kingdom* (Ann Arbor: University of Michigan Press, 1981), 8, 64–66, 72, chap. 4; and David E. Apter, ed., *Ideology and Discontent* (New York: Free Press of Glencoe, 1964). For comparison, see Orlando Figes, *The Story of Russia* (New York: Metropolitan Books, 2022), introduction; and Michael Cherniavsky, *Tsar and People: Studies in Russian Myths* (New Haven, CT: Yale University Press, 1961).

9. Jerome Bruner, "The Narrative Construction of Reality," *Critical Inquiry* 18, no. 1 (Autumn 1991): 1–21.

10. Geertz, *Interpretation of Cultures,* 211, 214, 231; Sahlins, *Historical Metaphors,* 67, 72.

11. Gary Gerstle, *The Rise and Fall of the Neoliberal Order: America and the World in the Free Market Era* (New York: Oxford University Press, 2022), esp. chaps. 4–6.

12. Lee Drutman, "How Hatred Came to Dominate American Politics," FiveThirtyEight, Oct. 5, 2020, https://fivethirtyeight.com/features/how-hatred-negative -partisanship-came-to-dominate-american-politics/.

13. Rich Lowry, *The Case for Nationalism: How It Made Us Powerful, United, and Free* (New York: Broadside, 2019); Liah Greenfeld, *Nationalism: A Short History* (Washington, DC: Brookings Institution Press, 2019); Amitai Etzioni, *Reclaiming Patriotism* (Charlottesville: University of Virginia Press, 2019); Jill Lepore, *This America: The Case for the Nation* (New York: Liveright, 2019); Alan Ryan, "Whose Nationalism?," review of *Why Nationalism*, by Yael Tamir, *NYRB*, Mar. 26, 2020.

14. Richard T. Hughes, *Myths America Lives By: White Supremacy and the Stories That Give Us Meaning*, 2nd ed. (Urbana: University of Illinois Press, 2018).

1. The Myth of the Frontier

1. On the Frontier Myth, see Richard Slotkin, *Regeneration through Violence: The Mythology of the American Frontier, 1600–1860* (Middletown, CT: Wesleyan University Press, 1973); Richard Slotkin, *The Fatal Environment: The Myth of the Frontier in the Age of Industrialization, 1800–1890* (New York: Atheneum, 1985), esp. chaps. 1–5; and Greg Grandin, *The End of the Myth: From the Frontier to the Border War* (New York: Metropolitan, 2020). On the history of settlement and conquest, see Roxanne Dunbar-Ortiz, *An Indigenous Peoples' History of the United States* (Boston: Beacon, 2015); Ned Blackhawk, *Violence over the Land: Indians and Empires in the Early American West* (Cambridge, MA: Harvard University Press, 2008); Richard White, *The Middle Ground: Indians, Empires, and Republics in the Great Lakes Region, 1650–1815* (New York: Cambridge University Press, 1991); Thomas King, *The Truth about Stories: A Native Narrative* (Minneapolis: University of Minnesota Press, 2008); and Wilbur Zelinsky, *The Cultural Geography of the United States* (New York: Pearson, 1992), esp. 41–44.

2. Arthur Barlow, *The First Voyage Made to the Coasts of America, with Two Barks, wherein Were Captains M. Philip Amadas and M. Arthur Barlowe, Who Discovered Part of the Countery Now Called Virginia, anno 1584* (Boston: Directors of the Old South Work), 8.

3. A detailed account is Slotkin, *Regeneration through Violence*, 58–65.

4. Slotkin, chap. 2. For an antidote to the myth, see Ned Blackhawk, *The Rediscovery of America: Native Peoples and the Unmaking of American History* (New Haven, CT: Yale University Press, 2022); and Blackhawk, *Violence over the Land*.

5. Slotkin, *Regeneration through Violence*, chap. 3.

6. Slotkin, chap. 3; Lisa Brooks, *Our Beloved Kin: A New History of King Philip's War* (New Haven, CT: Yale University Press, 2019).

7. Slotkin, *Regeneration through Violence*, chaps. 4–5. For the full text, see Richard Slotkin and James K. Folsom, eds., *So Dreadfull a Judgment: Puritan Responses to King Philip's War, 1676–1677* (Middletown, CT: Wesleyan University Press, 1978), 301–369.

8. Slotkin, *Regeneration through Violence,* 171–173. For the full text, see Slotkin and Folsom, *So Dreadfull a Judgment,* 370–470.

9. Slotkin, *Regeneration through Violence,* chap. 9.

10. John Filson, *The Discovery, Settlement, and Present State of Kentucke* (Wilmington, DE: James Adams, 1784), 65.

11. Slotkin, *Regeneration through Violence,* chap. 10.

12. Slotkin, *Fatal Environment,* 68–76.

13. Bernard W. Sheehen, *Seeds of Extinction: Jeffersonian Philanthropy and the American Indian* (New York: W. W. Norton, 1974).

14. Bill Gilbert, *God Gave Us This Country: Tekamthi and the First American Civil War* (New York: Atheneum, 1989), chap. 10

15. Theda Perdue and Michael Green, *The Cherokee Nation and the Trail of Tears* (New York: Penguin Books, 2008), chaps. 2–6; Claudio Saunt, *Unworthy Republic: The Dispossession of Native Americans and the Road to Indian Territory* (New York: W. W. Norton, 2020).

16. J. Hector St. John de Crèvecoeur, *Letters from an American Farmer and Sketches of Eighteenth Century America,* ed. Albert E. Stone (New York: Penguin, 1981), 66–105, esp. p. 69; Saunt, *Unworthy Republic,* sec. 1; Alexander Saxton, *The Rise and Fall of the White Republic: Class Politics and Mass Culture in Nineteenth-Century America* (London: Verso, 1990), introduction, chaps. 1–3.

17. Thomas Jefferson, *Notes on Virginia,* in *The Life and Selected Writings of Thomas Jefferson,* ed. Adrienne Koch and William Peden (New York: Modern Library, 1944), 255–257.

18. Saxton, *Rise and Fall.*

19. On Cooper's work, see Slotkin, *Regeneration through Violence,* chap. 13; and Slotkin, *Fatal Environment,* chap. 8.

20. James Fenimore Cooper, *The Last of the Mohicans,* ed. Richard Slotkin (New York: Penguin Books, 1986), 347.

21. Slotkin, *Fatal Environment,* chap. 10.

22. Slotkin, chap. 11.

23. Frederick Merk, *Manifest Destiny and Mission in American History: A Reinterpretation* (New York: Vintage, 1963); Slotkin, *Fatal Environment,* 229–232.

2. The Myth of the Founding

1. Gordon S. Wood, *The Idea of America: Reflections on the Birth of the United States* (New York: Penguin Press, 2012), esp. introduction and conclusion; Gordon S. Wood, *The Creation of the American Republic, 1776–1787* (New York: W. W. Norton, 1969); Gordon S. Wood, *Power and Liberty: Constitutionalism in the American Revolution* (New York: Oxford University Press, 2021); Pauline Maier, *American Scripture: Making the Declaration of Independence* (New York: Knopf, 1997).

2. Catherine L. Albanese, *Sons of the Fathers: The Civil Religion of the American Revolution* (Philadelphia: Temple University Press, 1977); Mary Anne Franks, *The Cult of the Constitution* (Palo Alto, CA: Stanford University Press, 2019), introduction, chap. 1; Laurence H. Tribe, "America's Constitutional Narrative," *Daedalus* 141, no. 1 (Winter 2012): 18–42; Peter Brooks, "Narratives of the Constitutional Covenant," *Daedalus* 141, no. 1 (Winter 2012): 43–51; Ray Raphael, *Constitutional Myths: What We Get Wrong and How to Get It Right* (New York: New Press, 2013); Frederick Merk, *Manifest Destiny and Mission in American History: A Reinterpretation* (New York: Vintage, 1963), chap. 2; Ernest Lee Tuveson, *Redeemer Nation: The Idea of America's Millennial Role* (Chicago: University of Chicago Press, 1968), chaps. 4–5.

3. Michael D. Hattem, *Past and Prologue: Politics and Memory in the American Revolution* (New Haven, CT: Yale University Press, 2021), esp. chap. 6.

4. Dennis C. Rasmussen, *Fears of a Setting Sun: The Disillusionment of America's Founders* (Princeton, NJ: Princeton University Press, 2021), prologue.

5. Carl Becker, *The Declaration of Independence: A Study in the History of Political Ideas* (New York: Harcourt, 1922); Maier, *American Scripture,* introduction, chap. 4.

6. Alexander Saxton, *The Rise and Fall of the White Republic: Class Politics and Mass Culture in Nineteenth-Century America* (London: Verso, 1990), introduction, part 1; David R. Roediger, *The Wages of Whiteness: Race and the Making of the American Working Class* (London: Verso, 1991), chaps. 2–4; Sean Wilentz, *No Property in Man: Slavery and Antislavery at the Nation's Founding* (Cambridge, MA: Harvard University Press, 2019), chaps. 3–5; Cheryl I. Harris, "Whiteness as Property," *Harvard Law Review* 106, no. 8 (1993): 1707–1791; Douglas R. Egerton, *Gabriel's Rebellion: The Virginia Slave Conspiracies of 1800 and 1802* (Chapel Hill: University of North Carolina Press, 1993), 172–173.

7. Dred Scott v. Sandford, 60 U.S. 393, 403–407 (1857); David M. Potter, *The Impending Crisis, 1848–1861* (New York: Harper Perennial, 2011), chap. 11; Abraham Lincoln, *Speeches and Writings, 1832–1858* (New York: Library of America, 1989), 395–403.

8. Lincoln, *Speeches,* 426–434.

9. Frederick Douglass, *Selected Speeches and Writings,* ed. Philip S. Foner and Yuval Taylor (Chicago: Lawrence Hill, 1999), 189.

10. Douglass, *Selected Speeches,* 196–197.

11. Douglass, *196.*

12. Potter, *Impending Crisis,* chap. 13; Eric Foner, *The Fiery Trial: Abraham Lincoln and American Slavery* (New York: W. W. Norton, 2010), chaps. 3–4.

13. Lincoln, *Speeches,* 807 (emphasis added).

14. Lincoln, 426, 514, 524 (emphasis in the original).

15. Lincoln, 525, 527, 430, 806, 808 (emphasis in the original).

16. Lincoln, 396–397, 510.

17. Lincoln, 794.

18. Stephen A. Douglas quoted in Lincoln, 556, 505–506, 672–673, 698.

19. Lincoln, 303 (emphasis in the original).

20. Lincoln, 512 (emphasis added).

21. Lincoln, 510–512 (emphasis added).

22. Lincoln, 510–511.

23. Lincoln, 807–811.

24. See Chapter 4.

25. Alexander H. Stephens, "Cornerstone Address, March 21, 1861," in Frank Moore, ed., *The Rebellion Record: A Diary of American Events with Documents, Narratives, Incidents, Poetry, etc.* (New York: O.P. Putnam, 1862), 1: 44–46.

26. James M. McPherson, *Battle Cry of Freedom: The Civil War Era* (New York: Ballantine, 1988), chap. 9; Loewen and Sebesta, *Confederate and Neo-Confederate Reader,* chap. 2.

27. Joseph Story, *Commentaries on the Constitution of the United States* (Boston: Hilliard, Gray, 1833), 708; Saul Cornell, *A Well-Regulated Militia: The Founding Fathers and the Origins of Gun Control in America* (New York: Oxford University Press, 2006), chaps. 2–3, pp. 134–135; Adam Winkler, *Gunfight: The Battle over the Right to Bear Arms in America* (New York: W. W. Norton, 2013), chaps. 4–5.

28. Jefferson Davis, "Inaugural Address," Feb. 8, 1861, Papers of Jefferson Davis, Rice University; McPherson, *Battle Cry of Freedom,* 241–245.

29. Foner, *Fiery Trial,* chap. 5; Potter, *Impending Crisis,* chaps. 7–8; Abraham Lincoln, *Speeches and Writings, 1859–1865* (New York: Library of America, 1989), 260.

3. Lincoln and Liberation

1. Frederick Douglass, *Selected Speeches and Writings,* ed. Philip S. Foner and Yuval Taylor (Chicago: Lawrence Hill, 1999), 189; Abraham Lincoln, *Speeches and Writings, 1859–1865* (New York: Library of America, 1989), 415.

2. Douglass, *Selected Speeches,* 189.

3. Shelby Foote in Ken Burns, *The Civil War,* episode 5, "Universe of Battle: 1863," aired Sep. 25, 1990, on PBS; William Faulkner, *Intruder in the Dust* (New York: Random House, 1948), chap. 9.

4. Barbara Fields in Burns, *Civil War,* episode 9, "Better Angels of Our Nature: 1865," aired Sep. 27, 1990, on PBS; Ta-Nehisi Coates, "Why Do So Few Blacks Study the Civil War?," *Atlantic,* Nov. 30, 2011.

5. J. David Hacker, "Recounting the Dead," *NYT,* Sept. 25, 2011; Al Nofi, "Statistics on the War's Costs," Louisiana State University Civil War Center, July 11, 2007, https://web.archive.org/web/20070711050249/http://www.cwc.lsu.edu/other/stats/warcost.htm; Brent Nosworthy, *The Bloody Crucible of Courage: Fighting Methods and Combat Experience of the Civil War* (New York: Carroll and Graf, 2003), esp. chaps. 12–15, 27, 30.

6. David M. Potter, *The Impending Crisis, 1848–1861* (New York: Harper Perennial, 2011), chap. 1.

7. Eric Foner, *Free Soil, Free Labor, Free Men: The Ideology of the Republican Party before the Civil War* (New York: Oxford University Press, 1970); James M. McPherson, *Battle Cry of Freedom: The Civil War Era* (New York: Ballantine, 1988), chaps. 6–7. The Southern side of the culture war is described in Chapter 4.

8. This discussion is based on McPherson, *Battle Cry of Freedom,* esp. chaps. 6–8, 16; James M. McPherson, *Abraham Lincoln and the Second American Revolution* (New York: Oxford University Press, 1990), chaps. 1–2, 7; Eric Foner, *The Fiery Trial: Abraham Lincoln and American Slavery* (New York: W. W. Norton, 2010), esp. chaps. 7–9; Eric Foner, *Reconstruction: America's Unfinished Revolution, 1863–1877* (New York: Harper and Row, 1988), chaps. 1–2; David W. Blight, *Race and Reunion: The Civil War in American Memory* (Cambridge, MA: Harvard University Press, 2001), esp. chaps. 1–2; Merrill D. Peterson, *Lincoln in American Memory* (New York: Oxford University Press, 1994), chaps. 2, 4–5; and Karl Marx, "On Events in North America," in *Karl Marx on America and the Civil War,* ed. Saul K. Padove (New York: McGraw-Hill, 1972), 221–223.

9. Adrienne Rich, "One night on Monterey Bay the death-freeze of the century," in *An Atlas of the Difficult World: Poems 1988–1991* (New York: W. W. Norton, 1991), 23.

10. Lincoln, *Speeches,* "Address at Gettysburg, Pennsylvania," 536.

11. Robert W. Johannsen, *Stephen A. Douglas* (New York: Oxford University Press, 1973), chap. 30; Maury Klein, *Days of Defiance: Sumter, Secession, and the Coming of the Civil War* (New York: Vintage, 1997), chap. 12; Foner, *Fiery Trial,* chap. 6; McPherson, *Battle Cry of Freedom,* chaps. 8–9.

12. Foner, *Fiery Trial,* chap. 5; Potter, *Impending Crisis,* chaps. 7–8; Lincoln, *Speeches,* 260.

13. Quoted in Richard Slotkin, *No Quarter: The Battle of the Petersburg Crater, 1864* (New York: Random House, 2009), 107.

14. Lincoln, *Speeches,* 357, 388–389.

15. Lincoln, 292; Richard Slotkin, *The Long Road to Antietam: How the Civil War Became a Revolution* (New York: Liveright, 2012), 412.

16. George B. McClellan, *The Civil War Papers of George B. McClellan: Selected Correspondence, 1861–1865,* ed. Stephen W. Sears (New York: Ticknor and Fields, 1989), 390; Slotkin, *Long Road,* 99–100, 103–104, 119–120.

17. Lincoln, *Speeches,* 415 (emphasis in original).

18. Lincoln, 536; Garry Wills, *Lincoln at Gettysburg: The Words That Remade America* (New York: Simon and Schuster, 1992), chaps. 3–4.

19. Lincoln, *Speeches,* 686–687.

20. Lincoln, 499.

21. Garrett Epps, "Ideas: The Citizenship Clause Means What It Says," *The Atlantic,* October 30, 2018. For a full discussion of the amendments, see Eric Foner, *The*

Second Founding: How the Civil War and Reconstruction Remade the Constitution (New York: W. W. Norton, 2019).

22. Foner, *Reconstruction,* chaps. 5–6, pp. 444–459; Epps, "Ideas."

23. Foner, *Reconstruction,* chaps. 4, 8, 10–11, and epilogue.

4. Confederate Founding

1. On Southern culture and nationalism, see Paul Quigley, *Shifting Grounds: Nationalism and the American South, 1848–1865* (New York: Oxford University Press, 2012), chap. 2; Maury Klein, *Days of Defiance: Sumter, Secession, and the Coming of the Civil War* (New York: Vintage, 1997), chap. 4; Eugene Genovese, *The World the Slaveholders Made: Two Essays in Interpretation* (Middletown, CT: Wesleyan University Press, 1988); Drew Gilpin Faust, *The Creation of Confederate Nationalism: Ideology and Identity in the Civil War South* (Baton Rouge: Louisiana State University Press, 1988), chaps. 1–2, conclusion; William W. Freehling, *The Road to Disunion: Secessionists at Bay, 1776–1854* (New York: Oxford University Press, 1990), pt. 2; Gary Gallagher, *The Confederate War* (Cambridge, MA: Harvard University Press, 2012), introduction, chaps. 1–2; Paul D. Escott, *After Secession: Jefferson Davis and the Failure of Confederate Nationalism* (Baton Rouge: Louisiana State University Press, 1978), chaps. 2, 6–8; and William C. Davis, *Look Away: A History of the Confederate States of America* (New York: Free Press, 2002), esp. chaps. 2, 4, 5, 11–12.

2. Charles B. Dew, *Apostles of Disunion: Southern Secession Commissioners and the Causes of the Civil War* (Charlottesville: University of Virginia Press, 2001), 72; Fergus M. Bordewich, *America's Great Debate: Henry Clay, Stephen A. Douglas, and the Compromise That Preserved the Union* (New York: Simon and Schuster, 2012), 395.

3. *State v. Mann,* in *American Legal History: Cases and Materials,* by Kermit L. Hall, William M. Wiecek, and Paul Finkelman (New York: Oxford University Press, 1991), 193–194.

4. George Fitzhugh, "Sociology for the South," in *Slavery Defended: The Views of the Old South*, ed. Eric L. McKitrick (New York: Columbia University Press, 1963), 45–46.

5. Fitzhugh, "Sociology for the South," 46; see also Richard Slotkin, *The Fatal Environment: The Myth of the Frontier in the Age of Industrialization, 1800–1890* (New York: Atheneum, 1985), 236–237; Genovese, *World the Slaveholders Made,* pt. 2; Mary B. Chesnut, *Mary Chesnut's Civil War,* ed. C. Vann Woodward (New Haven, CT: Yale University Press, 1981), xlviii–xlix, 44, 198, 211–212, 218, 277.

6. Manisha Sintha, "The Problem of Abolition in the Age of Capitalism," *American Historical Review* 124, no. 1 (Feb. 2, 2019): 157–158.

7. Bordewich, *America's Great Debate,* 375; James M. McPherson, *Battle Cry of Freedom: The Civil War Era* (New York: Ballantine, 1988), 242–243; Richard Hofstadter, *The American Political Tradition and the Men Who Made It* (New York: Vintage, 1973), chap. 4.

8. Hofstader, *American Political Tradition*, 86.

9. McKitrick, *Slavery Defended*, 7–19, 121–125, 169–178.

10. Thomas Jefferson, "Notes on Virginia," in Adrienne Koch and William Peden, eds., *The Life and Selected Writings of Thomas Jefferson* (New York: Modern Library, 1944), 256.

11. Dew, *Apostles of Disunion*, 13, 78–79; Jefferson Davis, *The Essential Writings*, ed. William J. Cooper Jr. (New York: Modern Library, 2003), 290–291; Slotkin, *Fatal Environment*, 233.

12. Bordewich, *America's Great Debate*, 148–149, 310–311.

13. Jefferson Davis, *Essential Writings*, 197, 290–291.

14. David M. Potter, *The Impending Crisis, 1848–1861* (New York: Harper Perennial, 2011), chap. 1; William R. Taylor, *Cavalier and Yankee: The Old South and American National Character* (New York: Oxford University Press, 1963), chaps. 4–6; D. W. Meinig, *The Shaping of America: A Geographical Perspective on 500 Years of History* (New Haven, CT: Yale University Press, 1986), 1:397–398, 2:278, 292; Wilbur Zelinsky, *Nation into State: The Shifting Symbolic Foundations of American Nationalism* (Chapel Hill: University of North Carolina Press, 1988), 122; James H. Webb, *Born Fighting* (New York: Crown, 2005), pt. 5, chaps 3–4.

15. McPherson, *Battle Cry of Freedom*, 242–243; Dew, *Apostles of Disunion*, 11, 28–29, 72, 76–77; Alexander H. Stephens, "African Slavery: The Corner-Stone of the Southern Confederacy," in *The Confederate and Neo-Confederate Reader: The "Great Truth" about the "Lost Cause,"* ed. James W. Loewen and Edward H. Sebesta (Oxford: University of Mississippi Press, 2010), 188.

16. Bruce Levine, *Confederate Emancipation: Southern Plans to Free and Arm Slaves during the Civil War* (New York: Oxford University Press, 2006), 17, 25.

17. Robert F. Durden, *The Gray and the Black: The Confederate Debate on Emancipation* (Baton Rouge: Louisiana State University Press, 1972), 58–60, 102–103; Levine, *Confederate Emancipation*, 26.

18. McPherson, *Battle Cry of Freedom*, 835.

19. Jefferson Davis, *The Papers of Jefferson Davis*, vol. 10, *October 1863–August 1864*, ed. Lynda Lasswell Crist, Kenneth H. Williams, and Peggy L. Dillard (Baton Rouge: Louisiana State University Press, 1999), 365–366, 511, 515; see also David Williams, *Rich Man's War: Class, Caste, and Confederate Defeat in the Lower Chattahoochee Valley* (Athens: University of Georgia Press, 1998), esp. chaps. 1–3; McPherson, *Battle Cry of Freedom*, 439–442, 611–620; Gallagher, *Confederate War*, 22–23; Levine, *Confederate Emancipation*, 23–24; and Durden, *Gray and the Black*, 184–185.

20. McPherson, *Battle Cry of Freedom*, 566, 634; Bruce Catton, *Terrible Swift Sword (New York: Simon and Schuster, Pocket Books, (1971), 444–445.

21. George S. Burkhardt, *Confederate Rage, Yankee Wrath: No Quarter in the Civil War* (Carbondale: Southern Illinois University Press, 2007); Richard Slotkin, *No Quarter: The Battle of the Petersburg Crater, 1864* (New York: Random House, 2009), 114–119, 289–295, 336–341.

22. Slotkin, *No Quarter,* 114–119; Durden, *Gray and the Black,* 95–96; McPherson, *Battle Cry of Freedom,* 695–699.

23. Emory M. Thomas, *Robert E. Lee: A Biography* (New York: W. W. Norton, 1995); Alan T. Nolan, *Lee Considered: General Robert E. Lee and Civil War Memory* (Chapel Hill: University of North Carolina Press, 1991), esp. chaps. 1, 8.

24. Quoted in Nolan, *Lee Considered,* 13–14.

25. Nolan, 12–15.

26. Carol Leonnig and Philip Rucker, *I Alone Can Fix It: Donald J. Trump's Catastrophic Final Year* (New York: Penguin Press, 2021), 182–184.

27. Bertram Wyatt-Brown, *Southern Honor: Ethics and Behavior in the Old South* (New York: Oxford University Press, 1982), esp. chaps. 4, 14–16; Slotkin, *No Quarter,* 340.

28. John S. Wise, *The End of an Era: The Story of a New Market Cadet,* ed. Lucy Booker Roper (n.p.: CreateSpace, 2017), 344. Originally published in 1899.

29. Edward A. Pollard, *The Lost Cause: A New Southern History of the War of the Confederates* (Richmond, VA: Treat, 1866), 740.

5. The Lost Cause

1. This chapter is based on Richard Slotkin, *The Fatal Environment: The Myth of the Frontier in the Age of Industrialization, 1800–1890* (New York: Atheneum, 1985), chaps. 13–14; Richard Slotkin, *Gunfighter Nation: The Myth of the Frontier in Twentieth-Century America* (New York: Atheneum, 1992), pts. 1, 2; David W. Blight, *Race and Reunion: The Civil War in American Memory* (Cambridge, MA: Harvard University Press, 2001); Eric Foner, *Reconstruction: America's Unfinished Revolution, 1863–1877* (New York: Harper and Row, 1988); Leon F. Litwack, *Trouble in Mind: Black Southerners in the Age of Jim Crow* (New York: Vintage, 1998); James W. Loewen and Edward H. Sebesta, eds., *The Confederate and Neo-Confederate Reader: The "Great Truth" about the "Lost Cause"* (Oxford: University of Mississippi Press, 2010), chaps. 4–5; and Wyn Craig Wade, *The Fiery Cross: The Ku Klux Klan in America* (New York: Simon and Schuster, 1987), bks. 1–2.

2. Wade, *Fiery Cross,* chap. 2.

3. Foner, *Reconstruction,* 587–601.

4. Nicholas Lemann, *Redemption: The Last Battle of the Civil War* (New York: Farrar, Straus and Giroux, 2007); Slotkin, *Fatal Environment,* chap. 14 and pp. 463–468.

5. Foner, *Reconstruction,* 525–526.

6. Slotkin, *Fatal Environment,* 334–335, 353–354, 360–361, 367–368, 463–464; Foner, *Reconstruction,* 570–571; "Anarchy in Louisiana: A War between the Races," *New York World,* Aug. 8, 1874; "The Indians!," *New York World,* Aug. 20, 1874; "Our Indian Policy" and "The Prostrate State," *New York World,* Aug. 25, 1874.

7. Foner, *Reconstruction,* 294–295.

8. Abraham Lincoln, *Speeches and Writings, 1859–1865* (New York: Library of America, 1989), 589; Foner, *Reconstruction*, 292–295, 335; Slotkin, *Fatal Environment*, 463–465; Manisha Sintha, "The Problem of Abolition in the Age of Capitalism," *American Historical Review* 124, no. 1 (Feb. 2, 2019): 157–158; Andrew Van Dam, "What Southern Dynasties' Post-Civil War Resurgence Tell Us about How Wealth Is Really Handed Down," *WP*, Apr. 4, 2019.

9. Quoted in Slotkin, *Fatal Environment*, 298–299. Also see Slotkin, chaps. 13–14; Blight, *Race and Reunion*, 124–139; and Foner, *Reconstruction*, 587–601.

10. Slotkin, *Fatal Environment*, 340–342, 482–483, 493–495.

11. E. L. Godkin, "The Late Riots," *The Nation*, Aug. 2, 1877, 68–70; Slotkin, 490–498; Eric Foner, *The Second Founding: How the Civil War and Reconstruction Remade the Constitution* (New York: W. W. Norton, 2019), chaps. 2–4; David A. Bateman, Ira Katznelson, and John S. Lapinski, *Southern Nation: Congress and White Supremacy after Reconstruction* (Princeton, NJ: Princeton University Press, 2018).

12. Godkin quoted in David Goldfield, *America Aflame: How the Civil War Created a Nation* (New York: Bloomsbury, 2011), 526; Blight, *Race and Reunion*, 124–139.

13. Foner, *Reconstruction*, chap. 12.

14. Foner, *Reconstruction*, 593–598.

15. Litwack, *Trouble in Mind*, 301. Also see Norman Pollack, ed., *The Populist Mind* (New York: Bobbs-Merrill, 1967), 360–403; C. Vann Woodward, *Tom Watson: Agrarian Rebel* (Savannah: Beehive, 1973), chaps. 13, 18, 20; C. Vann Woodward, *The Strange Career of Jim Crow* (New York: Oxford University Press, 2001), chaps. 1–2; and I. A. Newby, *Jim Crow's Defense: Anti-Negro Thought in America* (Baton Rouge: Louisiana State University Press, 1965), chaps. 4–6.

16. See, for example, John M. Barry, *Rising Tide: The Great Mississippi Flood of 1927 and How It Changed America* (New York: Simon and Schuster, 1998), pt. 2.

17. Litwack, *Trouble in Mind*, esp. chaps. 4–6; Bateman, Katznelson, and Lapinski, *Southern Nation*, esp. chaps. 5, 8–9; J. Morgan Kousser, *The Shaping of Southern Politics: Suffrage Restriction and the Establishment of the One-Party South, 1880–1910* (New Haven, CT: Yale University Press, 1974).

18. Dorothy Overstreet Pratt, *Sowing the Wind: The Mississippi Constitutional Convention of 1890* (Oxford: University of Mississippi Press, 2017), 7.

19. For a general history of lynching, see Philip Dray, *At the Hands of Persons Unknown: The Lynching of Black America* (New York: Modern Library, 2007). Also see Herbert Shapiro, *White Violence and Black Response: From Reconstruction to Montgomery* (Boston: University of Massachusetts Press, 1988), pts. 1–2; W. Fitzhugh Brundage, *Lynching in the New South: Georgia and Virginia, 1880–1930* (Urbana-Champaign: University of Illinois Press, 1993), chaps. 1–2; and Michael S. Rosenwald, "At Least 2,000 More Black People Were Lynched by White Mobs Than Previously Reported, New Research Finds," *WP*, June 16, 2020.

20. Brundage, *Lynching*, 36–37, 58–59, 65; Litwack, *Trouble in Mind*, 280–283.

21. Litwack, *Trouble in Mind*, 306–307; Brundage, *Lynching*, 61–62.

22. Quoted in Stephen Kantrowitz, *Bene Tillman and the Construction of White Supremacy* (Chapel Hill: University of North Carolina Press, 2000), 259.

23. Richard Slotkin, *Lost Battalions: The Great War and the Crisis of American Nationality* (New York: Holt, 2005), 143–145; Brundage, *Lynching*, 49, 65.

24. Litwack, *Trouble in Mind*, chap. 5 and pp. 294–295, 301–303; Slotkin, *Gunfighter Nation*, 183–184; Vardaman quoted in Rebecca Edwards, *Angels in the Machinery: Gender in American Party Politics from the Civil War to the Progressive Era* (New York: Oxford University Press, 1997), 140.

25. Patrick Philips, *Blood at the Root: A Racial Cleansing in America* (New York: W. W. Norton, 2017), introduction; Elliot Jaspin, "Leave or Die: America's Hidden History of Racial Expulsions," *The Statesman,* July 9, 2006.

26. Alexander H. Stephens, "Cornerstone Address, March 21, 1861," in Frank Moore, ed., *The Rebellion Record: A Diary of American Events with Documents, Narratives, Incidents, Poetry, etc.* (New York: O.P. Putnam, 1862), 1:44–46; "White Supremacy for North Carolina A White Man's Government," *Wilmington Messenger,* Nov. 10, 1898.

27. David Zuccino, *Wilmington's Lie: The Murderous Coup of 1898 and the Rise of White Supremacy* (New York: Atlantic Monthly Press, 2020).

28. Litwack, *Trouble in Mind*, 316–317; Brundage, *Lynching*, 212–213; Zuccino, *Wilmington's Lie.*

29. Slotkin, *Lost Battalions*, 115–116; Brundage, *Lynching*, 52–53; Litwack, *Trouble in Mind*, 156–157.

30. Michael J. Goleman, *Your Heritage Will Still Remain: Racial Identity and Mississippi's Lost Cause* (Oxford: University Press of Mississippi, 2017); Karen L. Cox, *Dixie's Daughters: The United Daughters of the Confederacy and the Preservation of Confederate Culture* (Tallahassee: University Press of Florida, 2019), esp. chaps. 1, 4; Catherine Clinton, ed., *Confederate Statues and Memorialization* (Athens: University of Georgia Press, 2019); Gillian Brockell, "Counties with More Confederate Monuments Also Had More Lynchings, Study Finds," *WP,* Oct. 13, 2021.

31. Blight, *Race and Reunion*, 279–282; Lyon Gardiner Tyler, *A Confederate Catechism* (n.p.: L. G. Tyler, 1929), 2, 8; Foner, *Reconstruction*, 557–558, 590.

32. Slotkin, *Gunfighter Nation*, 183–186.

33. Blight, *Race and Reunion*, chaps. 5, 7; Daniel Joseph Singal, "Ulrich B. Phillips: The Old South as the New," *Journal of American History* 63, no. 4 (Mar. 1977): 871–891.

34. Thomas Dixon Jr., *The Leopard's Spots: A Romance of the White Man's Burden* (New York: Doubleday and Page, 1902), 412; Thomas Dixon Jr., *The Clansman: An Historical Romance of the Ku Klux Klan* (Lexington: University of Kentucky Press, 1972), 290–292; Slotkin, *Fatal Environment*, 183–189.

35. See Eric S. Yellin, *Racism in the Nation's Service: Government Workers and the Color Line in Woodrow Wilson's America* (Chapel Hill: University of North Carolina Press, 2022), chaps. 5–6.

36. Ulrich Bonnell Phillips, *The Slave Economy of the Old South : Selected Essays in Economic and Social History*, ed. Eugene D. Genovese (Baton Rouge: Louisiana State University Press, 1968), esp. introduction and part 1; John David Smith and J. Vincent Lowery, eds., *The Dunning School: Historians, Race, and the Meaning of Reconstruction* (Lexington: University Press of Kentucky, 2013).

37. Slotkin, *Lost Battalions*, 17–18, emphasis added; Daniel J. Tichenor, *Dividing Lines: The Politics of Immigration Control in America* (Princeton, NJ: Princeton University Press, 2002), 71, 120.

38. Tichenor, *Dividing Lines*, 121–122, 125, 128–13; Slotkin, *Gunfighter Nation*, 37–38, 159–160; Slotkin, *Lost Battalions*, 14–23.

39. John R. Commons, *Races and Immigrants in America*, 2nd ed. (New York: Macmillan, 1920), 1–5, 8–13. On the use of "Nordic," see Madison Grant, *The Passing of the Great Race, or The Racial Basis of European Civilization* (New York: Chas. Scribner's Sons, 1927).

40. Commons, *Races and Immigrants*, 6–7.

41. Slotkin, *Lost Battalions*, chap. 13 and p. 460.

6. Industrialization, Vigilantism, and the Imperial Frontier

1. For a fuller treatment of this period, see Richard Slotkin, *The Fatal Environment: The Myth of the Frontier in the Age of Industrialization, 1800–1890* (New York: Atheneum, 1985), chap. 10 and pts. 6–8; and Richard Slotkin, *Gunfighter Nation: The Myth of the Frontier in Twentieth-Century America* (New York: Atheneum, 1992), pts. 1, 2.

2. Slotkin, *Fatal Environment*, 220–223, emphasis in original.

3. Slotkin, chaps. 13–15, 18–20; Everett Dick, *Lure of the Land: A Social History of the Public Lands from the Articles of Confederation to the New Deal* (Lincoln: University of Nebraska Press, 1970), chaps. 10, 11, 13, 18, 19; Gilbert M. Fite, *The Farmer's Frontier, 1865–1900* (New York: Holt, Rinehart and Winston, 1966), chaps. 2–6 and 11.

4. Slotkin, *Fatal Environment*, chap. 15; David Gordon, Richard Edwards, and Michael Reich, *Segmented Work, Divided Workers: The Historical Transformation of Labor in the United States* (New York: Cambridge University Press, 1982), 50, 52.

5. Daniel J. Tichenor, *Dividing Lines: The Politics of Immigration Control in America* (Princeton, NJ: Princeton University Press, 2002), 71, 79, 115; Roger Daniels, *Coming to America: A History of Immigration and Ethnicity in American Life* (New York: HarperCollins, 1990), chaps. 7–9 and pp. 274–275.

6. Slotkin, *Fatal Environment*, chaps. 15, 18, 19.

7. Slotkin, *Fatal Environment*, 14–15; Don Russell, *Custer's Last* (Dallas: Amon Carter Museum, 1968); Brian W. Dippie, *Custer's Last Stand: Anatomy of an American Myth* (Lincoln, NB: Bison Books, 1994).

8. Slotkin, *Fatal Environment*, chap. 13; Reinhard Bendix, *Work and Authority in Industry: Ideologies of Management in the Course of Industrialization* (Berkeley: University

of California Press, 1956), 1–20, 99–116, 198–274; Alfred D. Chandler, *The Visible Hand: The Managerial Revolution in American Business* (Cambridge, MA: Belknap Press of Harvard University Press, 1993), chaps. 2–5. On the response of workers, see Melvyn Dubofsky, *Industrialism and the American Worker, 1865–1920* (New York: Thomas Y. Crowell, 1975); and David Montgomery, *The Fall of the House of Labor: The Workplace, the State, and American Labor Activism, 1865–1925* (Cambridge: Cambridge University Press, 1989), chaps. 1, 5, 7–9.

9. Chicago *Inter-Ocean*, Aug. 27, 1874, 1, Sep. 5, 1874, 1; Slotkin, *Fatal Environment*, 345–358.

10. Slotkin, *Fatal Environment*, 469.

11. E. L. Godkin, "Our Indian Wards," *The Nation*, July 13, 1876, 21–22.

12. E. L. Godkin, "The Late Riots," *The Nation*, Aug. 2, 1877, 68–70; Godkin, "Our Indian Wards," 21–22; Slotkin, *Fatal Environment*, chap. 19.

13. William Serrin, *Homestead: The Glory and Tragedy of an American Steel Town* (New York: Vintage, 1993), pt. 1; David P. Demarest Jr., ed., *"The River Ran Red": Homestead 1892* (Pittsburgh: University of Pittsburgh Press, 1992); Toni Gilpin, *The Long Deep Grudge: A Story of Big Capital, Radical Labor, and Class War in the American Heartland* (Chicago: Haymarket Books, 2020), 22–41.

14. Richard M. Brown, *Strain of Violence: Historical Studies in American Violence and Vigilantism* (New York: Oxford University Press, 1975), chaps. 3, 4, 6; Richard M. Brown, *No Duty to Retreat: Violence and Values in American History and Society* (New York: Oxford University Press, 1992), chaps. 2–3; Catherine McNicol Stock, *Rural Radicals: From Bacon's Rebellion to the Oklahoma City Bombing* (New York: Penguin, 1997), chap. 2; Lee Kennett and James Anderson, *The Gun in America: The Origins of a National Dilemma* (New York: Praeger, 1975), chap. 6; Slotkin, *Gunfighter Nation*, chap. 5.

15. Frederic Remington, "The Affair of the—th of July," "Chicago under the Mob," and "Chicago under the Law," in *The Collected Writings of Frederic Remington*, ed. Peggy Samuels and Harold Samuels (Garden City, NY: Doubleday, 1979), 152–159, 176–183.

16. Brown, *No Duty to Retreat*, chap. 3; Robert Shogan, *The Battle of Blair Mountain: The Story of America's Largest Labor Uprising* (New York: Basic Books, 2006).

17. Thomas Dixon Jr., *The Clansman: An Historical Romance of the Ku Klux Klan* (Lexington: University of Kentucky Press, 1972), 290–292; Slotkin, *Fatal Environment*, 183–189.

18. For Turner and Roosevelt, see Slotkin, *Gunfighter Nation*, chap. 1 and pp. 283–287; Frederick Jackson Turner, *The Frontier in American History* (New York: Holt, Reinhardt and Winston, 1962), chap. 1; and Theodore Roosevelt, *The Winning of the West*, 7 vols. (New York: G. P. Putnam's Sons, 1907), esp. vol. 1.

19. Turner, *Frontier in American History*, 2–3, 316; Ray Allen Billington, *Frederick Jackson Turner: Historian, Scholar, Teacher* (Albuquerque: University of New Mexico Press, 1973), 108–109, 171–173, 436.

20. Theodore Roosevelt, *The Winning of the West* (New York: G.P. Putnam's Sons, 1907), 1:147–148; Slotkin, *Gunfighter Nation*, 42–51.

21. Theodore Roosevelt, "Expansion and Peace," in *The Works of Theodore Roosevelt*, ed. Herman Hagedorn (New York: Chas. Scribner's Sons, 1926), 12:28–29, 35–36; 115–116; Melvyn Dubofsky, *We Shall Be All: A History of the International Workers of the World* (New York: Quadrangle, 1969), chap. 2.

22. Theodore Roosevelt, "The Strenuous Life," in *Works,* 12:3–6.

23. Slotkin, *Gunfighter Nation,* chaps. 1, 3; Richard Slotkin, *Lost Battalions: The Great War and the Crisis of American Nationality* (New York: Holt, 2005), chap. 2; Roosevelt, "The Strenuous Life," 3–8, 11, 19.

24. Slotkin, *Gunfighter Nation,* chap. 2.

25. Dixon, *Clansman,* 290–292.

26. Thomas Dixon Jr., *The Leopard's Spots: A Romance of the White Man's Burden* (New York: Doubleday and Page, 1902), 412.

27. Albert J. Beveridge, "In Support of an American Empire," *Congressional Record,* 56th Cong., 1st Sess. (Jan. 9, 1900), 705, 711.

28. Brooks Adams, *The New Empire* (n.p.: Frontier, 1967).

29. Darren Dochuk, *Anointed with Oil: How Christianity and Crude Made Modern America* (New York: Basic Books, 2019), 32–33.

30. Dochuk, chaps. 2–3 and pp. 212–213; David Grann, *Killers of the Flower Moon: The Osage Murders and the Birth of the FBI* (New York: Doubleday, 2017).

31. Daniel Yergin, *The Prize: The Epic Quest for Oil, Money and Power* (New York: Free Press, 2008), chaps. 1–4.

32. Slotkin, *Gunfighter Nation,* 283–285; Charles A. Beard and Mary Beard, *The Rise of American Civilization* (New York: Macmillan, 1939), 1:514–517, 534–535.

33. Charles A. Beard and George H. E. Smith, *The Idea of National Interest: An Analytical Study in American Foreign Policy* (New York: Greenwood, 1977), 85; Charles A. Beard and George H. E. Smith, *The Open Door at Home: A Trial Philosophy* (New York: Macmillan, 1935); John R. Commons, *Races and Immigrants in America,* 2nd ed. (New York: Macmillan, 1920), 6–7.

7. The Great Exception

1. Jefferson Cowie, *The Great Exception: The New Deal and the Limits of American Politics* (Princeton, NJ: Princeton University Press, 2017), 9.

2. The concept of a political "order" is developed by Gary Gerstle, *The Rise and Fall of the Neoliberal Order: America and the World in the Free Market Era* (New York: Oxford University Press, 2022), esp. 1–3; and Steve Fraser and Gary Gerstle, eds., *The Rise and Fall of the New Deal Order, 1930–1980* (Princeton, NJ: Princeton University Press, 1989), introduction and chaps. 5, 7, 9–10. On the New Deal, see Alan Dawley, *Struggles for Justice: Social Responsibility and the Liberal State* (Cambridge, MA: Belknap Press of Harvard University Press, 1991), pt. 3; T. H. Watkins, *The Hungry Years: A*

Narrative History of the Great Depression in America (New York: Henry Holt, 1999), pts. 1–2; Ronald Edsforth, *The New Deal: America's Response to the Great Depression* (London: Blackwell, 2000); and Alan Brinkley, *Liberalism and Its Discontents* (Cambridge, MA: Harvard University Press, 1998), chaps. 2–3.

3. For an alternative view, see Nicholas Cords and Patrick Gerster, *Myth and the American Experience* (New York: Glencoe, 1973), 2:258–282.

4. Gene Smiley, "A Note on New Estimates of the Distribution of Income in the 1920s," *Journal of Economic History* 60, no. 4 (Dec. 2000): 1120–1128; Gary Burtless, "Has Rising Inequality Brought Us Back to the 1920s? It Depends on How We Measure Income," Brookings Institution, May 20, 2014, https://www.brookings.edu /blog/up-front/2014/05/20/has-rising-inequality-brought-us-back-to-the-1920s-it -depends-on-how-we-measure-income/.

5. David Cannadine, *Mellon: An American Life* (New York: Knopf, 2006), 444–445.

6. Franklin D. Roosevelt, "Commonwealth Club Speech," Sept. 23, 1932, Franklin D. Roosevelt—"The Great Communicator," Master Speech Files, Series 1, No. 522, esp. pp. 10–11.

7. Quoted in Richard Slotkin, *Lost Battalions: The Great War and the Crisis of American Nationality* (New York: Holt, 2005), 39–41, and see chap. 13.

8. Ira Katznelson, *When Affirmative Action Was White: An Untold History of Racial Inequality in Twentieth-Century America* (New York: W. W. Norton, 2006), chaps. 2–3, 5.

9. Sharon Ann Musher, *Democratic Art: The New Deal's Influence on American Culture* (Chicago: University of Chicago Press, 2015); Nancy Rose, *Put to Work: The WPA and Public Employment in the Great Depression* (New York: Monthly Review Press, 2009); David A. Taylor, *Soul of a People: The WPA Writers' Project Uncovers Depression America* (New York: Wiley, 2009); Roger G. Kennedy and David Larkin, *When Art Worked: The New Deal, Art and Democracy* (New York: Rizzoli, 2009); Nancy Lorance, "New Deal Art during the Great Depression," WPA Murals, last updated Aug. 6, 2007, http://www.wpamurals.org/.

10. Franklin D. Roosevelt, "A Rendezvous with Destiny," speech before the 1936 Democratic Convention, June 27, 1936.

11. Nina Silber, *This War Ain't Over: Fighting the Civil War in New Deal America* (Chapel Hill: University of North Carolina Press, 2018), introduction, chaps. 2 and 4, and pp. 102–105, 138; Merrill D. Peterson, *Lincoln in American Memory* (New York: Oxford University Press, 1994), 314–319.

12. Abraham Lincoln, "Annual Message to Congress," *Speeches and Writings, 1859–1865,* vol. 2 (New York: Library of America, 1989), 296.

13. Silber, *This War Ain't Over,* 107–109; Peterson, *Lincoln in American Memory,* chap. 6.

14. Anthony J. Badger, *Why White Liberals Fail: Race and Southern Politics from FDR to Trump* (Cambridge, MA: Harvard University Press, 2022), pt. 1.

15. Louis D. Rubin Jr., introduction; John Crowe Ransom, "Reconstructed by Unregenerate"; Frank Lawrence Owsley, "The Irrepressible Conflict"; Lyle H. Lanier, "A Critique of the Philosophy of Progress"; Allen Tate, "Remarks on the Southern Religion"; Robert Penn Warren, "The Briar Patch"; and Stark Young, "Not in Memoriam, but in Defense," all in *I'll Take My Stand: The South and the Agrarian Tradition,* by Twelve Southerners [John Crowe Ransom et al.], biographical essays by Virginia Rock (Baton Rouge: Louisiana State University Press, 1977), xi–xxxv, 1–27, 61–91, 122–154, 155–175, 246–264, 328–359.

16. Silber, *This War Ain't Over,* chap. 5.

17. Howard Mumford Jones, "Patriotism—but How?," *Atlantic Monthly,* Nov. 1938, 585–592; Cécile Whiting, "American Heroes and Invading Barbarians: The Regionalist Response to Fascism," *Prospects* 13 (Oct. 1988): 295–324; Richard Slotkin, *Gunfighter Nation: The Myth of the Frontier in Twentieth-Century America* (New York: Atheneum, 1992), chap. 9.

8. The Myth of the Good War

1. Gary Gerstle, *American Crucible: Race and Nation in the Twentieth Century* (Princeton, NJ: Princeton University Press, 2001), 42. See also Richard Rorty, *Achieving Our Country: Leftist Thought in Twentieth-Century America* (Cambridge, MA: Harvard University Press, 1998), 100.

2. Lance Morrow, "A Nation Mourns," *Time,* Feb. 10, 1986, 32.

3. The best work on the genre is Jeanine Basinger, *The World War II Combat Film: Anatomy of a Genre* (New York: Columbia University Press, 1986). See also Clayton R. Koppes and Gregory D. Black, *Hollywood Goes to War: How Politics, Profits, and Propaganda Shaped World War II Movies* (Berkeley: University of California Press, 1990); Lewis A. Erenberg and Susan E. Hirsch, eds., *The War in American Culture: Society and Consciousness during World War II* (Chicago: University of Chicago Press, 1996), pts. 2, 5.

4. Nancy Gentile Ford, *Americans All! Foreign-Born Soldiers in World War I* (College Station: Texas A&M University Press, 2001), chaps. 1–2, 5; US War Department, *Home Reading Course for Citizen-Soldiers,* War Information Series, No. 9 (Washington, DC: Government Printing Office, 1917), 3, 6, 10, 12–14, 17–18, 22–24, 55, 57; Ronald Schaffer, *America in the Great War: The Rise of the War Welfare State* (New York: Oxford University Press, 1991), 177–178.

5. Richard Slotkin, *Lost Battalions: The Great War and the Crisis of American Nationality* (New York: Holt, 2005), chaps. 3–5; W. E. B. DuBois, "Close Ranks," *The Crisis,* July 1918.

6. Slotkin, *Lost Battalions,* chap. 13.

7. Slotkin, 452–457; Clayton R. Koppes and Gregory D. Black, "Blacks, Loyalty, and Motion-Picture Propaganda in World War II," *Journal of American History* 73, no. 2 (1986): 383–406, esp. 400–401, 405.

8. See John W. Dower, *War without Mercy: Race and Power in the Pacific War* (New York: Pantheon, 1987), esp. chaps. 1, 3, 7, 9.

9. Elizabeth D. Samet, *Looking for the Good War: American Amnesia and the Violent Pursuit of Happiness* (New York: Farrar, Straus and Giroux, 2021), esp. chaps. 1, 4; Marianna Torgovnick, *The War Complex: World War II in Our Time* (Chicago: University of Chicago Press, 2005), introduction.

10. Jennifer D. Keene, *Doughboys, the Great War, and the Remaking of America* (Baltimore: Johns Hopkins University Press, 2001); Marcia G. Synnott, *The Half-Opened Door: Discrimination and Admissions at Harvard, Yale, and Princeton, 1900–1970* (Westport, CT: Greenwood, 1979).

11. Ronald Takaki, *Double Victory: A Multicultural History of America in World War II* (Boston: Little, Brown, 2000); Paul Dickson and Thomas B. Allen, *The Bonus Army: An American Epic* (New York: Walker, 2004), 270–273; Mary Dudziak, *Cold War Civil Rights: Race and the Image of American Democracy* (Princeton, NJ: Princeton University Press, 2011).

12. Richard Slotkin, *Gunfighter Nation: The Myth of the Frontier in Twentieth-Century America* (New York: Atheneum, 1992), 353–365.

13. Richard Slotkin, "Unit Pride: Ethnic Platoons and the Myths of American Nationality," *American Literary History* 13, no. 3 (2001): 469–498; S. L. A. Marshall, *Pork Chop Hill* (New York: Berkley, 2000); Samet, *Looking,* chap. 4.

14. George McTurnan Kahin, *Intervention: How America Became Involved in Vietnam* (New York: Anchor Books, 1987), 357, 374–375; Slotkin, *Gunfighter Nation,* 613–618.

9. The New Frontier

1. Robert J. Samuelson, "We're Facing the 'Great American Slowdown.' Should We Celebrate?," *WP,* Feb. 9, 2020.

2. Henry Steele Commager, "The Nineteenth Century American," *The Atlantic,* Dec., 1946; Henry Luce, "The American Century," *Life,* Feb. 17, 1941; Bruce J. Schulman, *Making the American Century: Essays on the Political Culture of Twentieth Century America* (New York: Oxford University Press, 2014); David M. Potter, *People of Plenty: Economic Abundance and the American Character* (Chicago: University of Chicago Press, 1954).

3. "Liberal consensus" is Godfrey Hodgson's term. See his *America in Our Time: From World War II to Nixon, What Happened and Why* (New York: Vintage, 1978), esp. chap. 4; Richard Slotkin, *Gunfighter Nation: The Myth of the Frontier in Twentieth-Century America* (New York: Atheneum, 1992), chap. 15; and Alan Brinkley, *Liberalism and Its Discontents* (Cambridge, MA: Harvard University Press, 1998), chap. 11.

4. Hodgson, *America in Our Time,* 80–81, 469–471; Thomas G. Paterson, *Kennedy's Quest for Victory: American Foreign Policy, 1961–1963* (New York: Oxford University Press, 1989), 12–14, 233–238; Walt Whitman Rostow, *The Stages of Economic*

Growth: A Non-Communist Manifesto (Cambridge: Cambridge University Press, 1960); Slotkin, *Gunfighter Nation,* 491–497.

5. Samuel Eliot Morison, *Oxford History of the American People* (New York: Oxford University Press, 1965), 1090; Theodore Roosevelt, "The Strenuous Life," in *The Works of Theodore Roosevelt,* ed. Herman Hagedorn (New York: Chas. Scribner's Sons, 1926), 12:7–8, 19; Richard Drinnon, *Facing West: The Metaphysics of Indian-Hating and Empire-Building* (Minneapolis: University of Minnesota Press, 1981), 355; Slotkin, *Gunfighter Nation,* 492–493.

6. Drinnon, *Facing West,* chaps. 23–29, esp. pp. 369, 435; George McTurnan Kahin, *Intervention: How America Became Involved in Vietnam* (New York: Anchor Books, 1987), 140–141; Slotkin, *Gunfighter Nation,* 495–496, 545–547; Lyndon Johnson quoted in John Hellmann, *American Myth and the Legacy of Vietnam* (New York: Columbia University Press, 1986), 46–48; Marcus G. Raskin and Bernard B. Fall, eds., *The Viet-Nam Reader* (New York: Vintage, 1967), 152–153, 343–350, esp. 347–350; Hugh Sidey, "The Presidency," *Life,* Oct. 10, 1969, 4.

7. Phil Hardy, *The Western: The Film Encyclopedia* (New York: Wm. Morrow, 1983), 188–202, 211–221, 230–236, 245–252, and appendix 8; Thomas Schatz, *The Genius of the System: Hollywood Filmmaking in the Studio Era* (New York: Pantheon, 1988), pt. 5. TV figures compiled from Tim Brooks and Earle Marsh, *The Complete Directory of Prime Time Network TV Shows, 1946–Present* (New York: Ballantine, 1979), esp. appendix 1; and Slotkin, *Gunfighter Nation,* chaps. 9–10.

8. Slotkin, *Gunfighter Nation,* chaps. 12–13.

9. Slotkin, chaps. 14, 16; Stanley Karnow, *Vietnam: A History* (New York: Penguin, 1984), 582–583, 588–589, 591–597, 600–602, 608–609, 652–656.

10. Slotkin, *Gunfighter Nation,* chap. 17.

11. James W. Gibson, *The Perfect War: The War We Couldn't Lose and How We Did* (New York: Vintage Books, 1988), 83–87, 135–136, 186.

12. Samuel P. Huntington, "The Bases of Accommodation," *Foreign Affairs,* July 1968; Gibson, *Perfect War,* 227–228, 234–237; Slotkin, *Gunfighter Nation,* 538; Guenter Lewy, *America in Vietnam* (Oxford: Oxford University Press, 1978), 105–106.

13. Slotkin, *Gunfighter Nation,* chap. 16; Karnow, *Vietnam,* chaps. 12–13.

14. Hodgson, *America in Our Time,* chaps. 20, 22; Karnow, *Vietnam,* 581–582, 594.

15. Richard M. Nixon, "Speech on Cambodia," Apr. 30, 1970.

10. Cultural Revolution

1. Godfrey Hodgson, *America in Our Time: From World War II to Nixon, What Happened and Why* (New York: Vintage, 1978), chaps. 15–17; Maurice Isserman and Michael Kazin, *America Divided: The Civil War of the 1960s* (New York: Oxford University Press, 2000), esp. chaps. 1–2, 8–9.

2. Taylor Branch, *Parting the Waters: America in the King Years, 1954–1963* (New York: Simon and Schuster, 1988), chaps. 1, 5, 7, 10–13, and pp. 819–820.

3. Isserman and Kazin, *America Divided,* chap. 5.

4. John F. Kennedy, "Civil Rights Address," June 11, 1963.

5. David W. Blight, *American Oracle: The Civil War in the Civil Rights Era* (Cambridge, MA: Belknap Press of Harvard University Press, 2013), esp. chaps. 2–3.

6. Kennedy, "Civil Rights Address."

7. Branch, *Parting the Waters,* chaps. 21–22.

8. Martin Luther King Jr., *A Testament of Hope: The Essential Writings and Speeches,* ed. James M. Washington (New York: Harper, 2003), 208–216.

9. Robert F. Williams, *Negroes with Guns,* facsimile of 1962 edition (n.p.: Martino, 2013), 3, 9.

10. Berry quoted in Nicholas Andrew Bryant, *The Bystander: John F. Kennedy And the Struggle for Black Equality* (New York: Basic Books, 2006), 2; Walter Dean Myers, *Malcolm X: By Any Means Necessary* (New York: Scholastic Focus, 2019), 104; Les Payne and Tamara Payne, *The Dead Are Arising: The Life of Malcolm X* (New York: Liveright, 2020), chap. 14; Stokely Carmichael and Charles V. Hamilton, *Black Power: The Politics of Liberation* (New York: Vintage, 1967); Isserman and Kazin, *America Divided,* 174–178; Joshua Bloom and Waldo E. Martin Jr., *Black against Empire: The History and Politics of the Black Panther Party* (Berkeley: University of California Press, 2013), esp. chaps. 2–6.

11. James R. Gaines, *The Fifties: An Underground History* (New York: Simon and Schuster, 2022), 106.

12. Robert Caro, *The Years of Lyndon B. Johnson: The Path to Power* (New York: Knopf, 1991), chap. 14; William Leuchtenburg, "Lyndon Johnson in the Shadow of Franklin Roosevelt," in *The Great Society and the High Tide of Liberalism,* ed. Sidney M. Milkis and Jerome M. Mileur (Amherst: University of Massachusetts Press, 2005), 185–213.

13. Isserman and Kazin, *America Divided,* chap. 7; Taylor Branch, *Pillar of Fire: America in the King Years, 1963–1968* (New York: Simon and Schuster, 1998), chaps. 5–6.

14. Lyndon B. Johnson, "Speech to Congress on Voting Rights," Mar. 15, 1965.

15. Sidney M. Milkis, "Lyndon Johnson, the Great Society, and the 'Twilight' of the Modern Presidency," in Milkis and Mileur, *Great Society,* 1–50; Nelson Lichtenstein, "Pluralism, Postwar Intellectuals, and the Demise of the Union Idea," in Milkis and Mileur, *Great Society,* 83–114; Milkis and Mileur, *Great Society,* pt. 3.

16. Michael Eric Dyson, *I May Not Get There with You: The True Martin Luther King, Jr.* (New York: Simon and Schuster, 2000), chap. 4.

17. "Detroit: City at the Blazing Heart of a Nation in Disorder," *Life,* Aug. 4, 1967, 16–29; Richard Slotkin, *Gunfighter Nation: The Myth of the Frontier in Twentieth-Century America* (New York: Atheneum, 1992), 549–554; Allen J. Matusow, *The Unraveling of America: A History of Liberalism in the 1960s* (Athens: University of Georgia Press, 2009), 363–367.

18. William R. Corson, *The Betrayal* (New York: W. W. Norton, 1968), 289; "The Battle That Ruined Hue," *Life,* Mar. 8, 1968, 26; "A Special Section: The Cycle of Despair: The Negro and the City," *Life,* Mar. 8, 1968; Albert Rosenfeld, "The Psychology of Violence," *Life,* June 21, 1968, 67–71.

19. National Commission on the Causes and Prevention of Violence, *Violence in America,* ed. Leon Friedman, 8 vols. (New York: Chelsea House, 1983), esp. vol. 2; Slotkin, *Gunfighter Nation,* 555–560.

20. Isserman and Kazin, *America Divided,* chaps. 8–9, 13.

21. See Leo Marx, "Believing in America: An Intellectual Project and a National Ideal," *Boston Review,* Dec. 1, 2003; and Donald E. Pease and Robin Wiegman, eds., *The Futures of American Studies* (Durham, NC: Duke University Press, 2002), 1–42.

22. The following are a few examples of historians' work that began in this period: my own work and that of Francis Jennings on the Indian-war origins of American culture and politics; John Blassingame, Eric Foner, Eugene Genovese, Herbert Gutman, Nathan Huggins, and Willie Lee Rose on enslavement; Gutman and David Montgomery on labor history; Sara Evans and Alice Kessler-Harris on women's history; Lawrence Levine on culture and cultural history; Ronald Takaki and Gary Nash on the multicultural reading of US history. See Eric Foner, ed., *The New American History* (Philadelphia: Temple University Press, 1990).

23. For opposition to the movement, and the lingering effects of these controversies, see Edith Kurzweil and William Phillips, eds., *Our Country, Our Culture: The Politics of Political Correctness* (New York: Partisan Review Press, 1994), discussed in Chapter 11; and James R. Grossman, "The New History Wars," *NYT,* Sept. 1, 2014.

24. Carl Bridenbaugh, "The Great Mutation," *American Historical Review* 68, no. 2 (Jan. 1963): 322–323.

25. William H. McNeill, "The Care and Repair of Public Myth," *Foreign Affairs,* Fall 1982, 1, 2, 4.

11. Back in the Saddle

1. Stephen B. Shepard, "The End of the Cowboy Economy," *NYT,* Dec. 9, 1973; William McNeill, "The Care and Repair of Public Myth," *Foreign Affairs,* Fall 1982, 1–13.

2. Gary Gerstle, *The Rise and Fall of the Neoliberal Order: America and the World in the Free Market Era* (New York: Oxford University Press, 2022), 1–2.

3. On the era, see Gerstle, chaps. 3–5; Sean Wilentz, *The Age of Reagan: A History, 1974–2000* (New York: Harper, 2009), esp. chaps. 5, 9–11; Garry Wills, *Reagan's America* (New York: Penguin, 1988), pts. 6–7; and Sidney Blumenthal, *The Rise of the Counter-establishment: From Conservative Ideology to Political Power* (New York: Crown, 1986).

4. Randall Balmer, *Bad Faith: Race and the Rise of the Religious Right* (Grand Rapids, MI: Eerdmans, 2021); Thomas B. Edsall, "Abortion Has Never Been Just about Abortion," *NYT,* Sept. 15, 2021.

5. Ronald W. Reagan, "A Time for Choosing Speech," Oct. 27, 1964, Ronald Reagan Presidential Library and Museum, https://www.reaganlibrary.gov/reagans /ronald-reagan/time-choosing-speech-october-27-1964.

6. Michael P. Rogin, *"Ronald Reagan," the Movie: And Other Episodes of Political Demonology* (Berkeley: University of California Press, 1987), chap. 1; Paul D. Erickson, *Reagan Speaks: The Making of an American Myth* (New York: New York University Press, 1985); Wills, *Reagan's America,* chaps. 16–22.

7. Milton Friedman, "A Friedman Doctrine—the Social Responsibility of Business Is to Increase Its Profits," *NYT,* Sept. 13, 1970; Thomas Frank, *One Market under God: Extreme Capitalism, Market Populism, and the End of Economic Democracy* (New York: Anchor, 2000), chaps. 1–2; Wills, *Reagan's America,* chap. 39; Benjamin M. Friedman, *Day of Reckoning: The Consequences of American Economic Policy* (New York: Vintage, 1989); Leo E. Strine Jr. and Joey Zwillinger, "What Milton Friedman Missed about Social Inequality," *NYT,* Sept. 10, 2020.

8. Wills, *Reagan's America,* chap. 39; B. Friedman, *Day of Reckoning;* Robert J. Shiller, "Narrative Economics," *American Economic Review* 107, no. 4 (2017): 967–1004.

9. Steven Waldman and Rich Thomas, "How Did It Happen?," *Newsweek,* May 21, 1990, 27.

10. The following are some exemplary titles: Frank H. Tucker, *The Frontier Spirit and Progress* (Chicago: Nelson-Hall, 1980); Gerard O'Neill, *The High Frontier: Human Colonies in Space* (Garden City, NY: Anchor Books, 1982); Daniel Graham, *High Frontier: A Strategy for National Survival* (New York: Tor, 1983); Robert M. Reich, *The Next American Frontier* (New York: Crown, 1983); and National Research Council, Office of International Affairs, *The Race for the New Frontier: International Competition in Advanced Technology* (New York: National Academy Press, 1984).

11. Thomas Philippon and Ariell Reshef, "An International Look at the Growth of Modern Finance," *Journal of Economic Perspectives* 27, no. 2 (Spring 2013): 73–96; B. Friedman, *Day of Reckoning,* esp. chaps. 6, 9; Larry Martz et al., "The Bonfire of the S & Ls," *Newsweek,* May 21, 1990, 20–25; Paul Krugman, "Warren, Bloomberg and What Really Matters," *NYT,* Feb. 20, 2020; Garry Wills, "The Politics of Grievance," *NYRB,* July 19, 1990, 3–4; Devin Singh, "Covid-19 Is Exposing Market Fundamentalism's Many Moral and Practical Flaws," *WP,* Apr. 10, 2020; Robert Heilbroner, "Lifting the Silent Depression," *NYRB,* Oct. 24, 1991, 6–8; Jerry Adler, "Down in the Dumps," *Newsweek,* Jan. 13, 1992, 18–22; Michel Crozier, *The Trouble with America: Why the System Is Breaking Down,* trans. Peter Henegg (Berkeley: University of California Press, 1994); Kurt Andersen, *Evil Geniuses: The Unmaking of America* (New York: Random House, 2020), pt. 3.

12. M. Friedman, "Friedman Doctrine."

13. Heather Cox Richardson, *To Make Men Free: A History of the Republican Party* (New York: Basic Books, 2021), chaps. 1, 10–12; Heather Cox Richardson, *How the South Won the Civil War: Oligarchy, Democracy, and the Continuing Fight for the Soul of America* (New York: Oxford University Press, 2020), introduction, chaps. 6, 8; Edsall, "Abortion"; Randall Balmer, "The Religious Right and the Abortion Myth," *Politico,* May 10, 2022; Balmer, *Bad Faith,* chaps. 5–8.

14. Philip A. Klinkner, *The Unsteady March: The Rise and Decline of Racial Equality in America,* with Rogers M. Smith (Chicago: University of Chicago Press, 1999), chap. 9; John Blake, "A New Supreme Court Is Poised to Take a Chunk out of MLK's Legacy," CNN, Jan. 21, 2019, https://www.cnn.com/2019/01/20/us/mlk-legacy-supreme-court/index.html; Jefferson Cowie, "The 'Hard Hat Riot' Was a Preview of Today's Political Divisions," *NYT,* May 11, 2020; Michael Kazin, "America's Never-Ending Culture War," *NYT,* Aug. 24, 2018; Omar Wasow, "Agenda Seeding: How 1960s Black Protests Moved Elites, Public Opinion and Voting," *American Political Science Review* 114, no. 3 (Aug. 2020): 638–659.

15. Douglas Kneeland, "Reagan Campaigns at Mississippi Fair," *NYT,* Aug. 4, 1980; Bob Herbert, "Righting Reagan's Wrongs?," *NYT,* Nov. 13, 2007.

16. M. Clifford Harrison, "The Southern Confederacy—Dead or Alive?," in *The Confederate and Neo-Confederate Reader: The "Great Truth" about the "Lost Cause,"* ed. James W. Loewen and Edward H. Sebesta (Oxford: University of Mississippi Press, 2010), 336–337; Nicole Hemmer, *Partisans: The Conservative Revolutionaries Who Remade American Politics in the 1990s* (New York: Basic Books, 2022), chaps. 3, 6–9; Ian Ward, "Reagan Was an End, Not a Beginning," *Politico,* Aug. 26, 2022; Nancy Mac-Lean, *Democracy in Chains: The Deep History of the Radical Right's Stealth Plan for America* (New York: Penguin, 2017), xvi–xxiv.

17. William F. Buckley, "Why the South Must Prevail," *National Review,* Aug. 24, 1957; MacLean, *Democracy in Chains,* 51–52; Gabrielle Bellot, "The Famous Baldwin-Buckley Debate Still Matters Today," *Atlantic,* Dec. 2, 2019.

18. John M. Coski, *The Confederate Battle Flag: America's Most Embattled Emblem* (Cambridge, MA: Belknap Press of Harvard University Press, 2005), chap. 6 and pp. 102–103, 120, 128, 134; Daniel L. Fountain, "Why Young Southerners Still Get Indoctrinated in the Lost Cause," *WP,* May 16, 2019. See also the books by James R. Kennedy and Walter D. Kennedy, including *The South Was Right!,* 2nd ed. (1991; Columbia, SC: Shotwell, 1994), and *Was Jefferson Davis Right?* (Columbia, SC: Shotwell, 1998); and critique of the Kennedys by Loewen and Sebesta, *Confederate and Neo-Confederate Reader,* 368–369.

19. Lott quoted in *Hartford Courant,* Jan. 12, 2001, A1, A14; *Southern Partisan* 2, no. 4 (1982): 4; Loewen and Sebesta, 366–367; Curtis Wilkie, "A 'Grand Bargain' That Secured the South for the GOP," *WP,* Aug. 16, 2019; Angie Maxwell and Todd Shields, *The Long Southern Strategy: How Chasing White Voters in the South Changed American Politics* (New York: Oxford University Press, 2021), introduction, chaps. 1–4.

20. H. Bruce Franklin, *M.I.A., or Myth-Making in America* (New Brunswick, NJ: Rutgers University Press, 1993), chap. 4.

21. Theodore Draper, *A Very Thin Line: The Iran-Contra Affair* (New York: Simon and Schuster, 1991); Mark Danner, *The Massacre at El Mozote* (New York: Vintage, 1994); Leslie Cockburn, *Out of Control: The Story of the Reagan Administration's Secret War in Nicaragua, the Illegal Arms Pipeline, and the Contra Drug Connection* (New York: Bloomsbury, 1988).

22. James Mann, *Rise of the Vulcans: The History of Bush's War Cabinet* (New York: Penguin, 2004), xiii–xvii, 52–53, 77, and chaps. 12–13, 15; Marvin Kalb and Deborah Kalb, *Haunting Legacy: Vietnam and the American Presidency from Ford to Obama* (Washington, DC: Brookings Institution Press, 2011), 106.

23. Charles Lane, "The Newest War," *Newsweek,* Jan. 6, 1992, 18–23; Mann, *Rise of the Vulcans,* 179–181.

24. Elizabeth D. Samet, *Looking for the Good War: American Amnesia and the Violent Pursuit of Happiness* (New York: Farrar, Straus and Giroux, 2021), esp. chap. 4. On the Gulf War, see Theodore Draper, "The True History of the Gulf War," *NYRB,* Jan. 30, 1992, 38–45; and Micah L. Sifry and Christopher Cerf, *The Gulf War Reader: History, Documents, Opinions* (New York: Three Rivers, 1991), 134–136, 172–179, 199, 210–212, 228–229, 311–314, 334–336, 343–344, 355–393, 449–495. For Bush's use of movie mythology, see Evan Thomas, "The One True Hawk in the Administration," *Newsweek,* Jan. 7, 1991, 19; and Robert Reich, "Is Japan Really Out to Get Us?," *NYT Book Review,* Feb. 9, 1992, 1, 24–25; for "jobs," see Tom Mathews et al., "The Road to War," *Newsweek,* Jan. 28, 1991, 54–65, esp. 64.

25. Kalb and Kalb, *Haunting Legacy,* 148; and Draper, "True History," 38–45.

26. See, for example, Heilbroner, "Lifting the Silent Depression"; Adler, "Down in the Dumps"; and Crozier, *Trouble with America,* chaps. 3–4.

27. James D. Hunter, *The Culture Wars: The Struggle to Control the Family, Art, Education, Law, and Politics in America* (New York: Basic Books, 1991), esp. chap. 1.

28. Pat Robertson, *The New World Order* (Dallas: Word Publishing, 1992), 96.

29. Nicole Hemmer, "Pat Buchanan Didn't Plan on It, but He Paved the Way for Trump," *NYT,* Sept. 8, 2022.

30. Patrick Buchanan, "Republican National Convention Speech," Aug. 17, 1992, Patrick J. Buchanan—Official Website, https://buchanan.org/blog/1992-republican-national-convention-speech-148?doing_wp_cron=1687281081.3747549057006835937500.

31. Pat Buchanan quoted in "Pat Buchanan: In His Own Words," Anti-Defamation League, accessed June 20, 2023, https://www.adl.org/resources/profiles/pat-buchanan-his-own-words.

32. Patrick J. Buchanan, *State of Emergency: The Third World Invasion and Conquest of America* (New York: St. Martin's, 2006), 248; Patrick J. Buchanan, *Death of the West: How Dying Populations and Immigrant Invasions Imperil Our Country and Civilization* (Lewisville, NC: Gryphon, 2019), 125.

33. Buchanan, *State of Emergency,* 248.

34. Pat Buchanan quoted in "Pat Buchanan: In His Own Words."

35. Nicole Hemmer, *Partisans: The Conservative Revolutionaries Who Remade American Politics in the 1990s* (New York: Basic Books, 2022), chaps. 3, 6, 9, 12; Will Bunch, *The Backlash: Right-Wing Radicals, High-Def Hucksters, and Paranoid Politics in the Age of Obama* (New York: Harper, 2011), chaps. 2–3; Zev Chafets, *Rush Limbaugh: An Army of One* (New York: Penguin Sentinel, 2010), esp. chaps. 9–10, 12.

36. Andersen, *Evil Geniuses,* chaps. 17–19; Gerstle, *Rise and Fall,* 137–138, 152–164, 173–178.

37. Gerstle, *Rise and Fall,* 173–178, 210–222.

38. Gerstle, 151–162.

39. Andersen, *Evil Geniuses,* 233–234. Clinton's "work-fare" program, which required most welfare aid recipients to seek work, proved successful in reducing child poverty: Oren Cass, "The Successful Policy That Progressives Love to Hate," CNN, Sept. 15, 2022, https://www.cnn.com/2022/09/15/opinions/child-poverty-welfare-reform-success-cass/index.html.

40. James Kwak, "The American Ideology, on the Left and the Right, That Props Up Inequality," *WP,* May 22, 2020.

41. Newt Gingrich, "Language: A Key Mechanism of Control," Information Clearing House, 1996, https://connectionslab.org/wp-content/uploads/2017/05/information clearinghouse-info-a-key-mechanism-of-control.pdf; Adam B. Kushner, "The Permanent Insurgency," *National Journal,* Oct. 1, 2013; Thomas E. Mann and Norman J. Ornstein, *It's Even Worse Than It Looks: How the American Constitutional System Collided with the New Politics of Extremism* (New York: Basic Books, 2012), chap. 2; Nina J. Easton, *Gang of Five: Leaders at the Center of the Conservative Crusade* (New York: Simon and Schuster, 2000), 281–283, 288–302.

42. Samuel P. Huntington, *The Clash of Civilizations and the Remaking of World Order* (New York: Simon and Schuster, 1998), esp. 22–27, 205; T. L. Stoddard, *The Rising Tide of Color against White World Supremacy* (New York: Chas. Scribner's Sons, 1920), esp. xix. The computer war game *Call of Duty* (2003–present) has a similar roster of enemies.

43. Kevin P. Phillips, *The Emerging Republican Majority* (Princeton, NJ: Princeton University Press, 2014), esp. pts. 3, 6; Peter Brimelow, *Alien Nation: Common Sense about America's Immigration Disaster* (New York: Harper, 1995); Samuel P. Huntington, *Who Are We? The Challenges to America's National identity* (New York: Simon and Schuster, 2005); Russell Jacoby and Naomi Glauberman, eds., *The Bell Curve Debate: History, Documents, Opinions* (New York: Times Books, 1995). For an analysis of racism in Brimelow's work, see David C. Hendrickson, review of *Alien Nation: Common Sense about America's Immigration Disaster,* by Peter Brimelow, *Foreign Affairs,* July 7, 1995.

44. Robert D. Kaplan, "The Coming Anarchy," *The Atlantic,* Feb. 1994.

45. Joseph Moreau, *Schoolbook Nation: Conflicts over American History Textbooks from the Civil War to the Present* (Ann Arbor: University of Michigan Press, 2004), chaps. 1, 5, 7; Diane Ravitch, "The Controversy over National History Standards," *Bulletin of*

the American Academy of Arts and Sciences 51, no. 3 (Jan.–Feb. 1998): 14–28; Gary Nash, "Reflections on the National History Standards," *National Forum,* Summer 1997.

46. Arthur M. Schlesinger Jr., "Multiculturalism v. the Bill of Rights," in *Our Country, Our Culture: The Politics of Political Correctness,* ed. Edith Kurzweil and William Phillips (New York: Partisan Review Press, 1994), 218; in this volume, see also Brigitte Berger, "Multiculturalism and the Modern University," 15–24; Mary Lefkowitz, "Multiculturalism, Uniculturalism, or Anticulturalism," 104–110, and Diane Ravitch, "The War on Standards," 210–226.

47. James D. Hunter, *Before the Shooting Begins: Searching for Democracy in America's Culture Wars* (New York: Free Press, 1994), 4. Emphasis in original.

12. Rising Tide

1. James Mann, *Rise of the Vulcans: The History of Bush's War Cabinet* (New York: Penguin, 2004), chaps. 12–14, 17, and pp. 259–260.

2. Ron Suskind, "Faith, Certainty and the Presidency of George W. Bush," *NYT,* Oct. 17, 2004; Patrick T. Brown, "The Failure of 'Compassionate Conservatism' Offers Lessons for the Trumpian Right," *Politico,* June 14, 2022.

3. Brown, "Failure of 'Compassionate Conservatism.'"

4. Daniel Yergin, *The Prize: The Epic Quest for Oil, Money and Power* (New York: Free Press, 2008), chaps. 26–27 and pt. 5; Matthew T. Huber, *Lifeblood: Oil, Freedom, and the Forces of Capital* (Minneapolis: University of Minnesota Press, 2013), pp. xii–xiii and chaps. 1, 4–5.

5. Daniel Yergin, *The Quest: Energy, Security, and the Remaking of the Modern World* (New York: Penguin, 2012), chaps. 6–8, 11.

6. Darren Dochuk, *Anointed with Oil: How Christianity and Crude Made Modern America* (New York: Basic Books, 2019), chaps. 2–3 and pp. 212–213; David Grann, *Killers of the Flower Moon: The Osage Murders and the Birth of the FBI* (New York: Doubleday, 2017), chaps. 1–7, 26.

7. Dochuk, *Anointed with Oil,* chap. 7 and pp. 11, 295–300; Henry Luce, "The American Century," *Life,* Feb. 17, 1941.

8. Dochuk, *Anointed with Oil,* chap. 12 and pp. 12–13, 193, 235–236, 352–353, 373–375, 423–425; Sara Diamond, *Roads to Dominion: Right-Wing Movements and Political Power in the United States* (New York: Guilford, 1995), 52; Fred C. Koch, *A Businessman Looks at Communism,* 3rd ed. (Wichita: F. C. Koch, 1961), 12.

9. Leslie Gelb, "Why Did Mr. Kissinger Say That?," *NYT,* Jan. 19, 1975.

10. Dochuk, *Anointed with Oil,* chap. 12, esp. p. 534.

11. Philip Smith and Nicholas Howe, *Climate Change as Social Drama: Global Warming in the Public Sphere* (New York: Cambridge University Press, 2015), 54–59.

12. Dino Grandoni, "The Energy 202: ExxonMobil Goes on Trial over Accusations It Misled Investors about Climate Change Costs," *WP,* Oct. 22, 2019; John Schwartz, "Rex Tillerson Testifies in Exxon Climate Change Case," *NYT,* Oct. 30, 2019.

13. Jane Mayer, *Dark Money: The Hidden History of the Billionaires behind the Rise of the Radical Right* (New York: Anchor, 2017), xvii.

14. Mayer, 159–169.

15. Mayer, 46–47, 55–56, 106, 149–150, 180; Christopher Leonard, "Charles Koch's Big Bet on Barrett," *NYT,* Oct. 12, 2020.

16. Mayer, *Dark Money,* 50–53, 132–133, 183; Nancy MacLean, *Democracy in Chains: The Deep History of the Radical Right's Stealth Plan for America* (New York: Penguin, 2017), xvi–xvii, xxvii, xx–xxiv; M. Clifford Harrison, "The Southern Confederacy— Dead or Alive?," in *The Confederate and Neo-Confederate Reader: The "Great Truth" about the "Lost Cause,"* ed. James W. Loewen and Edward H. Sebesta (Oxford: University of Mississippi Press, 2010), 336–337.

17. Mayer, *Dark Money,* xix.

18. Mayer, 175–177, 197–200; MacLean, *Democracy in Chains,* xvii.

19. Mayer, *Dark Money,* 200.

20. Smith and Howe, *Climate Change,* chaps. 3–4, esp. pp. 61, 75–81, 85.

21. Eric Pooley, *The Climate War: True Believers, Power Brokers, and the Fight to Save the Earth* (New York: Hyperion, 2010), 46–47; Smith and Howe, *Climate Change,* 120, 137, 245; David M. Standlea, *Oil, Globalization, and the War for the Arctic Refuge* (Albany: State University of New York Press, 2006), 17.

22. "2004 Republican Party Platform: A Safer World and a More Hopeful America," Aug. 30, 2004, American Presidency Project, https://www.presidency.ucsb.edu /documents/2004-republican-party-platform.

23. Jerome Corsi, "Drilling in the ANWR Will Reduce America's Dependence on Foreign Oil," in *Should Drilling Be Permitted in the Arctic National Wildlife Refuge?,* ed. David M. Haugen (New York: Greenhaven, 2008), 11–14.

24. National Resources Defense Council, "Drilling in the ANWR Will Not Reduce America's Dependence on Foreign Oil," in Haugen, *Should Drilling Be Permitted?,* 17.

25. Standlea, *Oil, Globalization,* x–xi, 3–4, 6, 14–17. For a broader view, see Herman E. Daley and Joshua Farley, *Ecological Economics: Principles and Practices,* 2nd ed. (Washington, DC: Island Press, 2010).

26. Vanessa Romo, "Native American Tribes File Lawsuit Seeking to Invalidate Keystone XL Pipeline Permit," NPR, Sept. 10, 2018, https://www.npr.org/2018/09/10 /646523140/native-american-tribes-file-lawsuit-seeking-to-invalidate-keystone-xl -pipeline-p.

27. Pooley, *Climate War,* 130–132; Mayer, *Dark Money,* 260–261.

13. Cowboys and Aliens

1. Joanne Esch, "Legitimizing the 'War on Terror': Political Myth in Official-Level Rhetoric," *Political Psychology* 31 (2010): 357–391; James Fallows, "Councils of War: Matching Confusing New Realities to Historical Experience," *The Atlantic,* Dec. 2001.

2. James Mann, *Rise of the Vulcans: The History of Bush's War Cabinet* (New York: Penguin, 2004), chaps. 12–13.

3. Mann, chap. 15 and p. 212; Ron Suskind, "Faith, Certainty and the Presidency of George W. Bush," *NYT,* Oct. 17, 2004, 44–51; Lloyd C. Gardner, *The Long Road to Baghdad: A History of U.S. Foreign Policy from the 1970s to the Present* (New York: New Press, 2008), 92, 105.

4. Mann, *Rise of the Vulcans,* chap. 20; Thomas E. Ricks, *Fiasco: The American Military Adventure in Iraq* (New York: Penguin, 2007), pt. 1; Spencer Ackerman, *Reign of Terror: How the 9/11 Era Destabilized America and Produced Trump* (New York: Viking, 2021), esp. chap. 2; Sam Smith, "A History of the Iraq War Told Entirely in Lies," *Sam Smith's Essays* (blog), Oct. 9, 2007, https://samsmitharchives.wordpress.com/2007 /10/09/from-our-overstocked-archives-a-history-of-the-iraq-war-all-told-in-lies/.

5. Suskind, "Faith, Certainty."

6. Mann, *Rise of the Vulcans,* 321–331; Nicholas D. Kristof, "The Wrong Lessons of the Somalia Debacle," *NYT,* Feb. 5, 2002, A25; John Barry, Richard Wolffe, and Evan Thomas, "War of Nerves," *Newsweek,* July 4, 2005, 25; Elizabeth Bumiller, "White House Letter; After Dark: Dinner Is Early and Quick," *NYT,* Jan. 28, 2002, A12; Michael R. Gordon, "Rumsfeld's Burden: Stilling Echoes of the Grisly Raid in Somalia," *NYT,* Mar. 7, 2002, A14.

7. Richard Slotkin, *Gunfighter Nation: The Myth of the Frontier in Twentieth-Century America* (New York: Atheneum, 1992), 521–533 and chap. 16. See Linda Dittmar and Gene Michaud, "America's Vietnam War Films: Marching toward Denial"; Michael Klein, "Historical Memory, Film, and the Vietnam Era"; Leo Cawley, "The War about the War: Vietnam Films and American Myth"; Frank P. Tomasulo, "The Politics of Ambivalence: *Apocalypse Now* as Prowar and Antiwar Film"; and Leonard Quart, "*The Deer Hunter:* The Superman in Vietnam," all in *From Hanoi to Hollywood: The Vietnam War in American Film,* ed. Linda Dittmar and Gene Michaud (New Brunswick, NJ: Rutgers University Press, 2000), 1–18, 19–40, 69–80, 145–158, 159–168. See also Michael Lee Lanning, *Vietnam at the Movies* (New York: Ballantine, 1994), chap. 6.

8. H. Bruce Franklin, *M.I.A., or Myth-Making in America* (New Brunswick, NJ: Rutgers University Press, 1993), esp. chap. 4; Gaylyn Studlar and David Desser, "Never Having to Say You're Sorry: *Rambo's* Rewriting of the Vietnam War," in Dittmar and Michaud, *From Hanoi to Hollywood,* 101–112; Gregory A. Waller, "*Rambo:* Getting to Win This Time," in Dittmar and Michaud, 113–128; Tony Williams, "Missing in Action—the Vietnam Construction of the Movie Star," in Dittmar and Michaud, 129–144. On the connection to antigovernment, White identity, and paramilitary activity, see Kathleen Belew, *Bring the War Home: The White Power Movement and Paramilitary America* (Cambridge, MA: Harvard University Press, 2018), pt. 1.

9. Keith M. Johnston, *Science Fiction Film: A Critical Introduction* (Oxford, UK: Berg, 2011), chaps, 1, 6–7; Edward Gross and Mark A. Altman, *The Fifty-Year Mission: The Complete, Uncensored, Unauthorized Oral History of Star Trek: The First 25 Years*

(New York: Thomas Dunne, 2016); Ina Ray Hark, *Star Trek: BFI Classics* (London: British Film Institute, 2008).

10. Chris Salewicz, *Oliver Stone: The Making of His Movies* (New York: Thunder's Mouth, 1998), chap. 4.

11. See the discussion of Huntington's work in Chapter 11.

12. Andrew J. Bacevich, *The New American Militarism: How Americans Are Seduced by War* (New York: Oxford University Press, 2005), esp. chap. 4.

13. Marianna Torgovnick, *The War Complex: World War II in Our Time* (Chicago: University of Chicago Press, 2005), chap. 1; Elizabeth D. Samet, *Looking for the Good War: American Amnesia and the Violent Pursuit of Happiness* (New York: Farrar, Straus and Giroux, 2021), chap. 1.

14. Micah L. Sifry and Christopher Cerf, *The Gulf War Reader: History, Documents, Opinions* (New York: Three Rivers, 1991), 3–84; Bacevich, *New American Militarism,* 14; Gardner, *Long Road to Baghdad,* 92; Mann, *Rise of the Vulcans,* pp. xiv, 192, 329, and chap. 13, esp. 210–214.

15. Ricks, *Fiasco,* pt. 1; Gardner, *Long Road to Baghdad,* chaps. 3–5.

16. Mark Bowden, *Black Hawk Down: A Story of Modern War* (New York: Signet, 2000), 371; Mark Bowden, phone conversation with the author; S. L. A. Marshall, *Pork Chop Hill* (New York: Berkley, 2000), bk. 1.

17. Frank Rich, "The Jerry Bruckheimer White House," *NYT,* May 11, 2003, AR 1.

18. Thomas E. Ricks, *Fiasco: The American Adventure in Iraq* (New York: Penguin Press, 2006).

19. Ackerman, *Reign of Terror,* esp. chaps. 7–9.

14. The Obama Presidency

1. Bill Bishop, *The Big Sort: Why the Clustering of Like-Minded America Is Tearing Us Apart,* with Robert G. Cushing (New York: Houghton Mifflin, 2004); Michael Kruse, "Why Trump Isn't to Blame for the Nation's Toxic Political Tribalism," *Politico,* May 30, 2020.

2. Obama quoted in Liz Halloran, "Obama Humbled by Election 'Shellacking,'" NPR, Nov. 3, 2010.

3. David Remnick, *The Bridge: The Life and Rise of Barack Obama* (New York: Knopf, 2010), esp. chaps. 1–8; Michael Eric Dyson, *The Black Presidency: Barack Obama and the Politics of Race in America* (New York: Houghton Mifflin Harcourt, 2016), chaps 1, 3–4, 6; Barack Obama, "A More Perfect Union," Mar. 18, 2008, American Rhetoric, https://www.americanrhetoric.com/speeches/barackobamaperfectunion.htm; Barack Obama, "2004 Democratic National Convention Keynote Address," July 27, 2004, American Rhetoric, https://www.americanrhetoric.com/speeches/convention2004/barackobama2004dnc.htm.

4. Barack Obama, "Official Announcement of Candidacy for US President," Feb. 10, 2007, American Rhetoric, https://www.americanrhetoric.com/speeches/barac

kobamacandidacyforpresident.htm; Barack Obama, "Democratic National Convention Presidential Nomination Acceptance," Aug. 28, 2008, American Rhetoric, https://www.americanrhetoric.com/speeches/convention2008/barackobama2008dnc.htm; Barack Obama, "First Presidential Inaugural Address: 'What Is Required: The Price and the Promise of Citizenship,'" Jan. 20, 2009, American Rhetoric, https://www.americanrhetoric.com/speeches/barackobama/barackobamainauguraladdress.htm; Barack Obama, "Ebenezer Baptist Church Address," Jan. 20, 2008, American Rhetoric, https://www.americanrhetoric.com/speeches/barackobama/barackobamaebenezerbaptist.htm; Barack Obama, "President-Elect Victory Speech," Nov. 4, 2008, American Rhetoric, https://www.americanrhetoric.com/speeches/convention2008/barackobamavictoryspeech.htm.

5. See the cover image for "The New New Deal," *Time,* Nov. 24, 2008.

6. Julian Zelizer, ed., *The Presidency of Barack Obama: A First Historical Assessment* (Princeton, NJ: Princeton University Press, 2018), chaps. 1–3; Robert Kuttner, *A Presidency in Peril: The Inside Story of Obama's Promise, Wall Street's Power, and the Struggle to Control Our Economic Future* (New York: Chelsea Green, 2010), chaps. 1–3, 6.

7. Barack Obama, "Speech at Georgetown," *New Foundation,* Apr. 14, 2009.

8. Reed Hundt, *A Crisis Wasted: Barack Obama's Defining Decisions* (New York: RosettaBooks, 2019), chaps. 8, 11–13; John Judis quoted in Jane Mayer, *Dark Money: The Hidden History of the Billionaires behind the Rise of the Radical Right* (New York: Anchor, 2017), 225.

9. Theda Skocpol and Vanessa Williamson, *The Tea Party and the Remaking of Republican Conservatism* (New York: Oxford University Press, 2012), 7, 45–46, 451; Mayer, *Dark Money,* 204–205, 215.

10. Nina J. Easton, *Gang of Five: Leaders at the Center of the Conservative Crusade* (New York: Simon and Schuster, 2000), 72, 74–77, 276–277; Murray Rothbard, *The Ethics of Liberty* (Atlantic Highlands, NJ: Humanities Press, 1982).

11. David Cannadine, *Mellon: An American Life* (New York: Knopf, 2006), 444–445; David Corn, "SECRET VIDEO: Romney Tells Millionaire Donors What He REALLY Thinks of Obama Voters," *Mother Jones,* Sept. 17, 2012.

12. Skocpol and Williamson, *Tea Party,* 9, 11, 23, 35, 30–31; Mayer, *Dark Money,* 241; Lilliana Mason, *Uncivil Agreement: How Politics Became Our Identity* (Chicago: University of Chicago Press, 2018), chaps. 1, 3, 5–6; Lilliana Mason, "Transcript: Ezra Klein Interviews Lilliana Mason," *NYT,* Aug. 13, 2021.

13. Jonathan Zimmerman, *Whose America? Culture Wars in the Public Schools,* 2nd ed. (2002; Chicago: University of Chicago Press, 2022), esp. chaps. 5, 8; Stanley Kurtz, "How the College Board Politicized U.S. History," *National Review,* Aug. 25, 2014; Ben Carson quoted in Valerie Strauss, "Ben Carson: New AP U.S. History Course Will Make Kids Want to 'Sign Up for ISIS,'" *WP,* Sep. 29, 2014.

14. Skocpol and Williamson, *Tea Party,* 35–9; Katherine Stewart, *The Power Worshippers: Inside the Dangerous Rise of Religious Nationalism* (London: Bloomsbury, 2020), esp. chaps. 5–7, 10; Robert P. Jones, *White Too Long: The Legacy of White*

Supremacy in American Christianity (New York: Simon and Schuster, 2020), esp. chaps. 2, 4–5.

15. Quoted in Jill Lepore, *The Whites of Their Eyes: The Tea Party and the Battle over American History* (Princeton, NJ: Princeton University Press, 2010), 4–5, 157, and see also epilogue.

16. "Racial and Ethnic Diversity in the United States: 2010 Census and 2020 Census," US Census Bureau, Aug. 12, 2021, https://www.census.gov/library /visualizations/interactive/racial-and-ethnic-diversity-in-the-united-states-2010-and -2020-census.html; William H. Frey, "The Nation Is Diversifying Even Faster Than Predicted, According to New Census Data," Brookings Institution, July 1, 2020, https://www.brookings.edu/research/new-census-data-shows-the-nation-is -diversifying-even-faster-than-predicted/; Mason, *Uncivil Agreement,* chaps. 1, 3, 5–6; Jane Adamy and Paul Overberg, "Population of Nonwhites Grows," *WSJ,* June 23, 2016.

17. Skocpol and Williamson, *Tea Party,* 102, 126, and chap. 6; Mayer, *Dark Money,* xvi–xvii, xxvii, xx–xxiv, 25, 200, 209, 216–219, 231, 245, 327.

18. Mayer, *Dark Money,* 204–205, 207, 275; Eric Pooley, *The Climate War: True Believers, Power Brokers, and the Fight to Save the Earth* (New York: Hyperion, 2010), 46–47; Philip Smith and Nicholas Howe, *Climate Change as Social Drama: Global Warming in the Public Sphere* (New York: Cambridge University Press, 2015), 120–121, 137.

19. Henry Fountain and Steve Eder, "The White House Saw Riches in the Arctic Refuge, but Reality May Fall Short," *NYT,* Aug. 21, 2019; Catherine Hausman and Ryan Kellogg, "Welfare and Distributional Implications of Shale Gas," Brookings Papers on Economic Activity, Spring 2015.

20. Mark Overholt, "The Environmental Benefits of Fracking," Tiger General, July 19, 2016, https://www.tigergeneral.com/the-environmental-benefits-of-fracking/; Fred Dews, "The Economic Benefits of Fracking," *Brookings Now* (blog), Brookings Institution, Mar. 23, 2015, https://www.brookings.edu/blog/brookings-now/2015/03 /23/the-economic-benefits-of-fracking/; "Conservation and Tribal Groups Sue to Block Repeal of Federal Fracking Regulations," Earthjustice, Jan. 24, 2018, https://earthjustice .org/press/2018/conservation-and-tribal-groups-sue-to-block-repeal-of-federal -fracking-regulations; Dino Grandoni, "The Energy 202: The U.S. Just Hit a Major Milestone as a Petroleum Exporter," *NYT,* Dec. 3, 2019.

21. Ben Lefebvre, "Oil Execs to Trump: Whose Side Are You On?," *Politico,* Mar. 24, 2020.

22. Matt Egan, "Solar, Wind and Hydro Power Could Soon Surpass Coal," CNN Business, Nov. 26, 2019, https://www.cnn.com/2019/11/26/business/renewable-energy -coal/index.html.

23. Frontiers of Freedom homepage, accessed June 21, 2023, https://www.ff.org. Greenpeace lists Frontiers of Freedom as a climate-denial front organization: "Frontiers of Freedom: Koch Industries Climate Denial Front Group," Greenpeace, accessed

June 21, 2023, https://www.greenpeace.org/usa/fighting-climate-chaos/climate-deniers/front-groups/frontiers-of-freedom/. For images equating oil and freedom, search "oil freedom meme" on Google.

24. Jonathan Cohn, *The Ten Year War: Obamacare and the Unfinished Crusade for Universal Health Care* (New York: St. Martin's, 2021), esp. chaps. 4–7, 14.

25. Skocpol and Williamson, *Tea Party,* 69, 78–80.

26. Mayer, *Dark Money,* xx; Larry Keller, "Resurgent Right Wing Militias," *Utne Reader,* Jan.–Feb. 2010; Skocpol and Williamson, *Tea Party,* 69, 78–80; John Bolton, foreword to *The Post-American Presidency: The Obama Administration's War on America,* by Pamela Geller (New York: Threshold, 2010); Chris McGreal, "Ground Zero Mosque Plans 'Fuelling Anti-Muslim Protests across US,'" *The Guardian,* Aug. 12, 2010.

27. George Packer, "The Corruption of the Republican Party," *The Atlantic,* Dec. 14, 2018; Ronald Brownstein, "Republicans Represent Almost None of the Places Most Immigrants Live," CNN Politics, July 16, 2019, https://www.cnn.com/2019/07/16/politics/republicans-immigrants-2020-election/index.html.

28. Danny Hakim and Jo Becker, "The Long Crusade of Clarence and Ginni Thomas," *NYT,* Feb. 23, 2022.

29. Thomas E. Mann and Norman J. Ornstein, *It's Even Worse Than It Looks: How the American Constitutional System Collided with the New Politics of Extremism* (New York: Basic Books, 2012), xx.

30. Tom W. Smith and Jaesok Son, *General Social Survey Final Report: Trends in Gun Ownership in the United States, 1972–2014* (Chicago: NORC at the University of Chicago, Mar. 2015).

15. Equalizers

1. Richard Hofstadter, "America as a Gun Culture," *American Heritage,* Oct. 1970. Mark R. Joslyn, *The Gun Gap* (New York: Oxford University Press, 2020), chap. 1, attributes the term to Hofstadter.

2. "Standard Reports," Gun Violence Archive, accessed June 23, 2023, https://www.gunviolencearchive.org/reports; Kevin Enochs, "The Real Story about Gun Sales in America," Voice of America News, Dec. 1, 2016, https://www.voanews.com/a/gun-sales-in-the-us/3619243.html; Jiaquan Xu et al., "Deaths: Final Data for 2013," *National Vital Statistics Reports* 64, no. 2 (Feb. 16, 2016): p. 84, table 18; Dustin Jones, "Firearms Overtook Auto Accidents as the Leading Cause of Death in Children," NPR, Apr. 22, 2022, https://www.npr.org/2022/04/22/1094364930/firearms-leading-cause-of-death-in-children; Philip J. Cook and Jens Ludwig, *Guns in America: National Survey on Private Ownership and Use of Firearms* (Washington, DC: National Institute of Justice, May 1997); Katherine Schaeffer, "Key Facts about Americans and Guns," Pew Research Center, Sept. 13, 2021, https://www.pewresearch.org/short-reads/2021/09/13/key-facts-about-americans-and-guns/; Kim Parker et al., "America's Complex

Relationship with Guns," Pew Research Center, June 22, 2017, https://www.pewresearch .org/social-trends/2017/06/22/americas-complex-relationship-with-guns/.

3. Bonnie Berkowitz and Chris Alcantara, "The Terrible Numbers That Grow with Each Mass Shooting," *WP,* May 12, 2021; "Standard Reports," Gun Violence Archive; "List of US Mass Shootings," Voice of America News, May 18, 2018, https://www .voanews.com/a/list-of-us-mass-shootings/4255503.html.

4. Frederic Lemieux, "Effect of Gun Culture and Firearm Laws on Gun Violence and Mass Shootings in the United States: A Multi-level Quantitative Analysis," *International Journal of Criminal Justice Sciences* 9, no. 1 (Jan.–June 2014): 74–93; Lee Kennett and James L. Anderson, *The Gun in America: The Origins of a National Dilemma* (New York: Praeger, 1975), 249; Deborah Prothrow-Stith, *Deadly Consequences: How Violence Is Destroying Our Teenage Population and a Plan to Begin Solving the Problem,* with Michael Weissman (New York: HarperCollins, 1991), 15.

5. Pamela Haag, *The Gunning of America: Business and the Making of American Gun Culture* (New York: Basic Books, 2016), 390; Jennifer Tucker, Barton C. Hacker, and Margaret Vining, *A Right to Bear Arms? The Contested Role of History in Contemporary Debates on the Second Amendment* (Washington, DC: Smithsonian Scholarly Press, 2009), chap. 6; Jennifer Carlson, *Policing the Second Amendment: Guns, Law Enforcement, and the Politics of Race* (Princeton, NJ: Princeton University Press, 2020), esp. chap. 5.

6. Scott Melzer, *Gun Crusaders: The NRA's Culture War* (New York: New York University Press, 2009), 19, 32–33, and pt. 1; Hofstadter, "America as a Gun Culture."

7. Kennett and Anderson, *Gun in America,* chap. 6 and pp. 73–76; Lawrence Delbert Cress, "An Armed Community: The Origins and Meaning of the Right to Bear Arms," *Journal of American History* 71, no. 1 (1984): 22–42; Saul Cornell, *A Well-Regulated Militia: The Founding Fathers and the Origins of Gun Control in America* (New York: Oxford University Press, 2006), chaps. 2–4, 6. For a contrary view, see Joyce Lee Malcolm, *To Keep and Bear Arms: The Origins of an Anglo-American Right* (Cambridge, MA: Harvard University Press, 1994), esp. chaps. 1, 8; and Tucker, Hacker, and Vining, *Right to Bear Arms?,* chap. 3.

8. Kenneth S. Greenberg, *Honor and Slavery* (Princeton, NJ: Princeton University Press, 1996), esp. chap. 1; Bertram Wyatt-Brown, *Southern Honor: Ethics and Behavior in the Old South* (New York: Oxford University Press, 1982), esp. pt. 3; Saul Cornell and Eric M. Ruben, "The Slave-State Origins of Modern Gun Rights," *The Atlantic,* Sept. 30, 2015.

9. Richard M. Brown, *No Duty to Retreat: Violence and Values in American History and Society* (New York: Oxford University Press, 1992), esp. chaps. 1, 4; Tucker, Hacker, and Vining, *Right to Bear Arms?,* chap. 7.

10. Joseph Story, *Commentaries on the Constitution of the United States* (Boston: Hillyard, Gray, 1833), 708; James Madison, Nos. 45–46, in *The Federalist: A Commentary on the Constitution of the United States,* ed. Robert Scigliano (New York: Modern

Library, 2001); Cornell, *Well-Regulated Militia,* 2–3, 135; Michael Waldman, *The Second Amendment: A Biography* (New York: Simon and Schuster, 2014), esp. chaps. 1, 4, and pt. 2.

11. Abraham Lincoln, *Speeches and Writings, 1859–1865* (New York: Library of America, 1989), 250, 499.

12. Richard Slotkin, *Gunfighter Nation: The Myth of the Frontier in Twentieth-Century America* (New York: Atheneum, 1992), chap. 5.

13. Brown, *No Duty to Retreat,* chaps. 2–3.

14. Melzer, *Gun Crusaders,* 25.

15. James E. Serven, *Colt Firearms from 1836* (New York: Foundation Press, 1954), 4–5.

16. H—H—, *Hero-Martyr* (n.p., 1859), 149–150.

17. Walter Prescott Webb, *The Great Plains* (1931; New York: Grossett and Dunlap, 1957), 171–172, 176, 179, 214–215; [E. L. Godkin], "The Late Riots," *The Nation,* Aug. 2, 1877, 68–70; Richard Slotkin, *The Fatal Environment: The Myth of the Frontier in the Age of Industrialization, 1800–1890* (New York: Atheneum, 1985), chap. 19; Haag, *Gunning of America,* 9, 19.

18. John Ellis, *The Social History of the Machine Gun* (New York: Pantheon Books, 1975), 21–29, 42–45, and chap. 4; Phil Patton, *Made in USA: The Secret Histories of the Things That Made America* (New York: Penguin, 1991), chap. 3; Adam Winkler, *Gunfight: The Battle over the Right to Bear Arms in America* (New York: W. W. Norton, 2013), chaps. 4–6.

19. Winkler, *Gunfight,* chaps. 6–8; Bryan Stevenson, "A Presumption of Guilt," *NYRB,* July 13, 2017.

20. Brown, *No Duty to Retreat,* chap. 4, esp. pp. 129–130, 134–136.

21. Newt Gingrich et al., *Contract with America: The Bold Plan by Rep. Newt Gingrich, Rep. Dick Armey and the House Republicans to Change the Nation* (New York: Times Books, 1994); Thomas E. Mann and Norman J. Ornstein, *It's Even Worse Than It Looks: How the American Constitutional System Collided with the New Politics of Extremism* (New York: Basic Books, 2012), chap. 2; Nina J. Easton, *Gang of Five: Leaders at the Center of the Conservative Crusade* (New York: Simon and Schuster, 2000), 281–283, 288–302.

22. Easton, *Gang of Five,* 72, 74–77, 276–277.

23. Quoted in Easton, 77–78, 88. See also Grover G. Norquist, *Rock the House: History of the New American Revolution* (Fort Lauderdale, FL: Vytis, 1995). It is worth noting that John R. Lott Jr., the gun rights movement's favorite social scientist, followed the same path from extreme free-market theory, to equation of taxation with tyranny, to gun rights absolutism. See John R. Lott Jr., *More Guns, Less Crime: Understanding Crime and Gun Control Laws* (Chicago: University of Chicago Press, 2010); and John R. Lott Jr., ed., *Uncertainty and Economic Evolution: Essays in Honor of Armen A. Alchian* (London: Routledge, 1997), esp. chap. 9, Gertrud M. Fremling and

John R. Lott Jr., "Freedom, Wealth, and Coercion." For a critique of Lott's methods, see Albert Alschuler, "Two Guns, Four Guns, Six Guns, More Guns: Does Arming the Public Reduce Crime?," ResearchGate, Mar. 1997, https://www.researchgate.net /publication/228274139_Two_Guns_Four_Guns_Six_Guns_More_Guns_Does _Arming_the_Public_Reduce_Crime.

24. Grover Norquist, *Leave Us Alone: Getting the Government's Hands Off Our Money, Our Guns, and Our Lives* (New York: William Morrow, 2008), pts. 1–2 and chap. 21.

25. Sara Diamond, *Roads to Dominion: Right-Wing Movements and Political Power in the United States* (New York: Guilford, 1995), chaps. 11–12; Catherine McNicol Stock, *Rural Radicals: From Bacon's Rebellion to the Oklahoma City Bombing* (New York: Penguin, 1997), chap. 3; Kathleen Belew, *Bring the War Home: The White Power Movement and Paramilitary America* (Cambridge, MA: Harvard University Press, 2018), pts. 2, 3; Daniel Levitas, *The Terrorist Next Door: The Militia Movement and the Radical Right* (New York: Thomas Dunne, 2002), esp. chaps. 6, 8, 13, 16–21, 39.

26. Josh Sugarmann, *National Rifle Association: Money, Firepower, Fear* (Washington, DC: National Press Books, 1992), 14; Melzer, *Gun Crusaders,* 11, 37, 40, 67, 91, 114–115; Adam Hochschild, "Bang for the Buck," *NYRB,* Apr. 5, 2018.

27. Easton, *Gang of Five,* 75–78, 88, 276, 299–301; Belew, *Bring the War Home,* chaps. 8–9; David Rohde, *In Deep: The FBI, the CIA, and the Truth about America's "Deep State"* (New York: W. W. Norton, 2020), chaps. 6–7.

28. Lou Michael and Dan Herbeck, *American Terrorist: Timothy McVeigh and the Tragedy of Oklahoma City* (New York: Avon, 2002), esp. chap. 3 and pt. 2; Kenneth S. Stern, *A Force upon the Plain: The American Militia Movement and the Politics of Hate* (New York: Simon and Schuster, 1996), chaps. 1–5.

29. George H. W. Bush, "Letter of Resignation Sent by Bush to Rifle Association," *NYT,* May 11, 1995; Easton, *Gang of Five,* 286, 299–300; Melzer, *Gun Crusaders,* 17, 200; Levitas, *Terrorist Next Door,* chaps. 39–40.

30. Melzer, *Gun Crusaders,* 9, 92, 100, 153.

31. "Republican Party Platforms," 1996, 2000, 2004, 2008, 2012, 2016, American Presidency Project, https://www.presidency.ucsb.edu/people/other/republican-party -platforms.

32. Melzer, *Gun Crusaders,* 11, 19–20, 114–115, chaps. 3–5, pts. 2 and 3; Maggie Koerth, "Why Nonprofits Can't Research Gun Violence as Well as the Feds," FiveThirtyEight, Nov. 14, 2019, https://fivethirtyeight.com/features/why-nonprofits-cant-research -gun-violence-as-well-as-the-feds/.

33. For the Kochs' place in the deregulation movement, see Charlie Savage, "E.P.A. Ruling Is Milestone in Long Pushback to Regulation of Business," *NYT,* June 30, 2022. On "stand your ground" laws, see "What Science Tells Us about the Effects of Gun Policies," RAND Corporation, updated Jan. 10, 2023, https://www.rand.org /research/gun-policy/key-findings/what-science-tells-us-about-the-effects-of-gun

-policies.html; Gregory O'Meara, "Stand Your Ground Laws Are Unnecessary," *NYT,* Mar. 21, 2012; Adam Winkler, "What the Florida Law Says," *NYT,* Mar. 21, 2012; Melissa Block and David Ovalle, "A History of 'Stand Your Ground' Law in Florida," NPR, Mar. 20, 2012, https://www.npr.org/2012/03/20/149014228/a-history-of-stand-your-ground-law-in-florida; Michelle Degli Esposti et al., "Analysis of 'Stand Your Ground' Self-Defense Laws and Statewide Rates of Homicides and Firearm Homicides," *JAMA Network Open* 5, no. 2 (Feb. 21, 2022): e220077.

34. Brandon Tensley, "How Race Permeates the Politics of Gun Control," CNN, Sept. 17, 2021; Daniel Lathrop and Anna Flagg, "Killings of Blacks by Whites Are Far More Likely to Be Ruled 'Justifiable,'" *NYT,* Aug. 14, 2017; Ailsa Chang and Elizabeth Flock, "Women and the Legal Bounds of Self-Defense," NPR, Jan. 20, 2020, https://www.npr.org/2020/01/20/797981402/women-and-the-legal-bounds-of-self-defense.

35. Quoted in Melzer, *Gun Crusaders,* 20, 59, 100, 116.

36. Melzer, 13, 29–35, 42, 191.

37. Eric Greene, Planet of the Apes *as American Myth: Race, Politics, and Popular Culture* (Middletown: Wesleyan University Press, 1998), 49, 150; Slotkin, *Gunfighter Nation,* 504–512; Heston quoted in Melzer, 16, 45, 162.

38. Melzer, *Gun Crusaders,* 69, 121.

39. Mary Anne Franks, *The Cult of the Constitution* (Palo Alto, CA: Stanford University Press, 2019), chaps. 1–2; Clarence Thomas on Printz v. United States (95-1478), 521 U.S. 898 Cornell Law School, Legal Information Institute, June 27, 1997, https://www.law.cornell.edu/supct/html/95-1478.ZC1.html.

40. Reva B. Siegel, "Dead or Alive: Originalism as Popular Constitutionalism in *Heller,*" *Harvard Law Review* 122 (2008): 194; Melzer, *Gun Crusaders,* 19, 33, 57–59, 100–101, chaps. 2–3; Joshua Zeitz, "The Supreme Court's Faux 'Originalism,'" *Politico,* June 26, 2022; Mary B. McCord, "The Plot against Gretchen Whitmer Shows the Danger of Private Militias," *NYT,* Oct. 8, 2020; Kaleigh Rogers, "Why Militias Are So Hard to Stop," FiveThirtyEight, May 18, 2021, https://fivethirtyeight.com/features/militias-pose-a-serious-threat-so-why-is-it-so-hard-to-stop-them/. The dependence of "originalism" on historical mythology, especially the gun rights version, is argued in Saul Cornell, "Cherry-Picked History and Ideology-Driven Outcomes: *Bruen*'s Originalist Distortions," *SCOTUSblog,* June 27, 2022, https://www.scotusblog.com/2022/06/cherry-picked-history-and-ideology-driven-outcomes-bruens-originalist-distortions/; Jennifer Tucker, "How the NRA Hijacked History," *WP,* Sept. 9, 2019; Tucker, Hacker, and Vining, *Right to Bear Arms?,* chap. 11.

41. Melzer, *Gun Crusaders,* 80–81; Charlton Heston, "Winning the Culture War," speech to the National Rifle Association, Feb. 16, 1999.

42. Thomas Dixon Jr., *The Clansman: An Historical Romance of the Ku Klux Klan* (Lexington: University of Kentucky Press, 1972), 290–292.

43. Tom W. Smith and Jaesok Son, *General Social Survey Final Report: Trends in Gun Ownership in the United States, 1972–2014* (Chicago: NORC at the University of Chicago, Mar. 2015); Colleen L. Barry et al., "After Newtown—Public Opinion on

Gun Policy and Mental Illness," *New England Journal of Medicine* 368 (Mar. 21, 2013): 1077–1081.

44. Brett Lunceford, "On the Rhetoric of Second Amendment Remedies," *Journal of Contemporary Rhetoric* 1, no. 1 (2011): 31–39; Mark Thompson, "When Protesters Bear Arms against Health-Care Reform," *Time,* Aug. 19, 2009; Toby Harnden, "Barack Obama Faces 30 Death Threats a Day, Stretching US Secret Service," *Telegraph* (UK), Aug. 3, 2009; Ronald Kessler, *In the President's Secret Service: Behind the Scenes with Agents in the Line of Fire and the Presidents They Protect* (New York: Crown, 2010), 217–220.

45. Sam Stein, "Sharron Angle Floated '2nd Amendment Remedies' as 'Cure' for 'the Harry Reid Problems,'" HuffPost, June 16, 2010, https://www.huffpost.com/entry/sharron-angle-floated-2nd_n_614003; Kevin Drum, "Time to Cool It on '2nd Amendment Solutions,'" *Mother Jones,* Oct. 15, 2015; Tierney Sneed, "Trump Just the Latest on Hard Right to Call for '2nd Amendment Remedies,'" Talking Points Memo, Aug. 11, 2016, https://talkingpointsmemo.com/dc/trump-second-amendment-people-context; Nick Corasaniti and Maggie Haberman, "Donald Trump Suggests 'Second Amendment People' Could Act against Hillary Clinton," *NYT,* Aug. 9, 2016.

46. Andrew Napolitano, "The Right to Shoot Tyrants, Not Deer: The Second Amendment Is the Guarantee of Freedom," *Washington Times,* Jan. 10, 2013; Wayne LaPierre, *Guns, Crime, and Freedom* (Washington, DC: Regnery, 1994), chap. 17.

47. Department of Homeland Security, Office of Intelligence and Analysis, "Assessment: (U//FOUO) Rightwing Extremism: Current Economic and Political Climate Fueling Resurgence in Radicalization and Recruitment," Apr. 7, 2009; Daryl Johnson, "I Warned of Right-Wing Violence in 2009. Republicans Objected. I Was Right," *WP,* Aug. 21, 2017.

48. Melzer, *Gun Crusaders,* 111, 175; Greg St. Martin, "Study: 70M More Firearms Added to US Gun Stock over Past 20 Years," News @ Northeastern, Sept. 26, 2016, https://news.northeastern.edu/2016/09/26/study-70m-more-firearms-added-to-us-gun-stock-over-past-20-years/; Rick Jervis, "3% of Americans Own Half the Country's 265 Million Guns," *USA Today,* Sept. 22, 2016; Enochs, "Real Story"; Barry et al., "After Newtown."

49. Brian Sullivan, "America's Gun: The Rise of the AR-15," CNBC, aired May 7, 2013; Heath Druzin, "From Banned to Beloved: The Rise of the AR-15," NPR Northern Colorado, Feb. 27, 2019; Alain Stephens, "Why the AR-15 Is America's Rifle," NPR, Feb. 15, 2018, https://www.npr.org/2018/02/15/586172062/why-the-ar-15-is-americas-rifle; John Schuppe, "America's Rifle: Why So Many People Love the AR-15," NBC News, Dec. 27, 2017, https://www.nbcnews.com/news/us-news/america-s-rifle-why-so-many-people-love-ar-15-n831171; Chris Woodyard, "Macho AR-15 Ads Called Reckless," *USA Today,* Mar. 29, 2019.

50. Stephen J. Sedensky III, *Report of the State's Attorney for the Judicial District of Danbury on the Shootings at Sandy Hook Elementary School and 36 Yogananda Street, Newtown, Connecticut on December 14, 2012* (Office of the State's Attorney, Judicial

District of Danbury, CT, Nov. 25, 2013); Harley Peterson, "The Mother Who Taught 'Goth Loner' Son to Shoot . . . Then He Killed Her Using Own Gun," *Daily Mail* (UK), Dec. 15, 2012.

51. Tim Mak, "The Moment the NRA Decided to Embrace the Culture Wars," *Politico,* Nov. 8, 2021.

52. Woodyard, "Macho AR-15 Ads"; Erik Larson, "How Macho Ads for Assault Rifles Might Backfire," *Bloomberg,* June 13, 2016; Mark Murrmann, "'Papa Says It's Safe': 20 Astounding Gun Ads," *Mother Jones,* Sept. 15, 2012; "The Militarized Marketing of Bushmaster Assault Rifles," Violence Policy Center, Apr. 2018, https://vpc .org/wp-content/uploads/2018/04/Bushmaster2018.pdf; Richard Johnson, "Wilson Combat Urban Super-Sniper," *Firearm Blog,* Feb. 13, 2015, https://www.thefirearmblog .com/blog/2015/02/13/wilson-combat-urban-super-sniper/.

53. Erin Coulehan, Katie Benner, and Manny Fernandez, "Federal Hate Crime Charges Filed in El Paso Shooting That Targeted Latinos," *NYT,* Feb. 6, 2020; Corey Hutchins, "In Colorado Springs, Dispatcher Brushed Off Reports of a Man with a Gun, Witness Says," *WP,* Nov. 3, 2015; Alaine Griffin, "No Added Prison Time for Man Who Brought Guns to UNH Campus," *Hartford Courant,* Jan. 29, 2015.

54. Jason Cherkis and Sam Stein, "How Obamacare Town Halls Went from Chaotic to Downright Frightening," HuffPost, May 24, 2016, https://www.huffpost.com/entry /obamacare-tom-perriello-candidate-confessional_n_57448c55e4b045cc9a7215bd; Martha Shanahan, "5 Memorable Moments When Town Hall Meetings Turned to Rage," NPR, Aug. 7, 2013, https://www.npr.org/sections/itsallpolitics/2013/08/07 /209919206/5-memorable-moments-when-town-hall-meetings-turned-to-rage.

55. Liam Stack, "A Brief History of Deadly Attacks on Abortion Providers," *NYT,* Nov. 29, 2015; Philip Rucker, "Elliot Rodger's Killing Spree: What Happened," *WP,* May 24, 2014; Amanda Coletta, "Man Accused of Killing 10 in Toronto Van Attack Told Police His 'Mission' Was 'Accomplished,'" *WP,* Sept. 27, 2019.

56. Arie Perliger, *Challengers from the Sidelines: Understanding America's Violent Far-Right* (New York: Combating Terrorism Center at West Point, Nov. 2012); Arie Perliger, "Homegrown Terrorism and Why the Threat of Right-Wing Extremism Is Rising in America," *Newsweek,* June 4, 2017; Chelsea Parsons, Eugenio Weigend Vargas, and Jordan Jones, "Hate and Guns: A Terrifying Combination," Center for American Progress, Feb. 24, 2016, https://www.americanprogress.org/article/hate-and-guns-a -terrifying-combination/; Robert L. Tsai, "The Troubling Sheriffs' Movement That Joe Arpaio Supports," *Politico,* Sept. 1, 2017; Larry Keller, "Resurgent Right Wing Militias," *Utne Reader,* Jan.–Feb. 2010.

57. Rick Perry, "Interview: Texas Governor Addresses Secession Issue," HuffPost, Sept. 21, 2011, https://www.huffpost.com/entry/rick-perry-interview-secession_n _974969; Ron Paul (@RepRonPaul), "Secession: Are We Free to Go," Twitter post, Nov. 19, 2012, https://twitter.com/RepRonPaul/status/270632276277202944?cxt =HHwWgMCQxOKnvcEHAAAA; Kevin Cirilli, "Ron Paul: 'Secession Is a Deeply

American Principle,'" *Politico,* Nov. 19, 2012; Rebecca Nelson, "Ron Paul Thinks There Should Be More Secessionist Movements in the U.S.," *The Atlantic,* Sept. 30, 2014; Jim Gaines, "Nearly a Quarter of Americans Support Their States' Secession," Huff-Post, Sept. 22, 2014, https://www.huffpost.com/entry/america-secession_n_5860600; Nick Wing, "Texas GOP Official, Calls for 'Amicable Divorce' from 'Maggots' Who Voted for Obama," HuffPost, Nov. 9, 2012, https://www.huffpost.com/entry/peter -morrison-texas-divorce_n_2100165.

58. Euan Hague, "Why the Confederacy Lives," *Politico,* Apr. 8, 2015.

59. Michael Wines and Lizette Alvarez, "Council of Conservative Citizens Promotes White Primacy, and G.O.P. Ties," *NYT,* June 22, 2015.

60. Roof quoted in Rachel Kaadzi Ghansah, "A Most American Terrorist: The Making of Dylann Roof," *GQ,* Aug. 21, 2015. See also the similar pattern in the racial massacre in Buffalo in 2022: Steven Lee Myers and Stuart A. Thompson, "Racist and Violent Ideas Jump from Web's Fringes to Mainstream Sites," *NYT,* June 1, 2022.

61. Roof quoted in Ghansah, "Most American Terrorist."

62. Eugene Scott, "Nikki Haley: Confederate Flag 'Should Have Never Been There,'" CNN, July 10, 2015, https://www.cnn.com/2015/07/10/politics/nikki-haley -confederate-flag-removal/index.html.

63. Steve Gorman, "U.S. Southern Baptists Formally Repudiate Confederate Flag," HuffPost, June 15, 2016, https://www.huffpost.com/entry/southern-baptists -confederate-flag_n_57610aa5e4b0df4d586e9983.

64. Michael Barbaro and Jonathan Martin, "5 Days That Left a Confederate Flag Wavering, and Likely to Fall," *NYT,* June 28, 2015; Katie Rogers, "Charleston Shooting Reignites Debate about Confederate Flag," *NYT,* June 19, 2015; Eugene Scott, "On Confederate Flag, Southern White Christians Do Some Soul Searching," CNN, June 30, 2015, https://www.cnn.com/2015/06/20/politics/confederate-flag-christians -south/index.html; Campbell Robertson, Monica Davey, and Julie Bosman, "Calls to Drop Confederate Emblems Spread Nationwide," *NYT,* June 23, 2015; Campbell Robertson, "Flag Supporters React with a Mix of Compromise, Caution and Outright Defiance," *NYT,* June 23, 2015.

65. Laura Paisley, "Political Polarization at Its Worst since the Civil War," USC News, Nov. 8, 2016, https://news.usc.edu/110124/political-polarization-at-its-worst -since-the-civil-war-2/.

66. Corasanti and Haberman, "Donald Trump Suggests."

16. The Trump Redemption

1. In this and the following chapters on the Trump presidency, I have referred to Timothy L. O'Brien, *TrumpNation: The Art of Being the Donald* (New York: Business Plus, 2005); Michael D'Antonio, *The Truth about Trump* (New York: Griffin, 2016); Maggie Haberman, *Confidence Man: The Making of Donald Trump and the Breaking of*

America (New York: Penguin, 2022); Peter Baker and Susan Glasser, *The Divider: Trump in the White House, 2017–2021* (New York: Doubleday, 2022); Philip Rucker and Carol Leonnig, *A Very Stable Genius: Donald J. Trump's Testing of America* (New York: Penguin, 2022); Michael Wolff, *Fire and Fury: Inside the Trump White House* (New York: Henry Holt, 2018); and Julian Zelizer, *The Presidency of Donald J. Trump: A First Historical Assessment* (Princeton, NJ: Princeton University Press, 2022). I have cited the original newspaper and magazine articles to show how Trump's public narrative developed in something like real time, in context with other events and stories, to create the "myth" of MAGA and its hero.

2. Ronald Brownstein, "How Religion Widens the Partisan Divide," CNN, Oct. 22, 2019, https://www.cnn.com/2019/10/22/politics/religion-gap-republican -democratic-voters-polling/index.html; Thomas E. Mann and Norman J. Ornstein, *It's Even Worse Than It Looks: How the American Constitutional System Collided with the New Politics of Extremism* (New York: Basic Books, 2012), pt. 1; Matthew Continetti, *The Right: The Hundred-Year War for American Conservatism* (New York: Basic Books, 2022), chaps. 12–14; Anne Case and Angus Deaton, *Deaths of Despair and the Future of Capitalism* (Princeton, NJ: Princeton University Press, 2020); Jennifer M. Silva, *We're Still Here: Pain and Politics in the Heart of America* (New York: Oxford University Press, 2019); Michael Lind, *The New Class War: Saving Democracy from the Managerial Elite* (New York: Portfolio, 2020).

3. Francis Fukuyama, "Why Red and Blue America Can't Hear Each Other Anymore," *WP,* Jan. 24, 2020; Brian F. Schaffner, Matthew MacWilliams, and Tatishe Nteta, "Understanding White Polarization in the 2016 Vote for President: The Sobering Role of Racism and Sexism," *Political Science Quarterly* 133, no. 1 (2018): 9–34.

4. Ezra Klein quoted in Norman J. Ornstein, "Why America's Political Divisions Will Only Get Worse," *NYT,* Jan. 28, 2020; Nell Irvin Painter, "What Is White America?," *Foreign Affairs,* Nov. / Dec. 2019.

5. Donald Trump, "Addresses the CPAC Convention in Washington, DC," CPAC, Feb. 10, 2011, https://factba.se/transcript/donald-trump-speech-washington-dc -february-10-2011.

6. Donald Trump, "Addresses the CPAC Convention."

7. Donald Trump, speech at the 2013 Conservative Political Action Conference, Mar. 15, 2013, https://www.p2016.org/photos13/cpac13/trump031513spt.html; Mary Clare Jalonick and Matthew Daly, "Trump Says US Will Be Safer, Richer If He Is President," AP, July 22, 2016; "Trump: We're Going to Win So Much," CNN, 2016, https://www.cnn.com/videos/politics/2017/08/18/trump-albany-rally-winning-sot.cnn.

8. John Wagner, "Trump: Most People Don't Know President Lincoln Was a Republican," *WP,* Mar. 22, 2017.

9. Donald Trump, speech at the 2013 2013 Conservative Political Action Conference.

10. Robert Jewett and John Shelton Lawrence, *The American Monomyth* (Garden City, NY: Anchor, 1977); Robert Jewett and John Shelton Lawrence, *The Myth of the*

American Superhero (Grand Rapids, MI: Eerdmans, 2002); Alyssa Rosenberg, "9/11 Helped Superhero Movies Conquer the World. They Never Moved On," *WP*, Sept. 10, 2021; Allen W. Austin and Patrick L. Hamilton, *All New, All Different? A History of Race and the American Superhero* (Chicago: University of Chicago Press, 2019), esp. chaps. 6–7; Sean Howe, *Marvel Comics: The Untold Story* (New York: Harper, 2013).

11. Rebecca Morin, "'They Admitted Their Guilt': 30 Years of Trump's Comments about the Central Park Five," *USA Today*, June 19, 2019; "Trump 1989 Interview on the 'Central Park Five,'" CNNMoney, Oct. 7, 2016, https://www.cnn.com/videos/cnnmoney/2016/10/07/trump-1989-central-park-five-interview-cnnmoney.cnnmoney.

12. Kyung Lah and Kimberly Berryman, "Residents of Washington Town Wonder If QAnon Has Taken Hold of Their Mayor," CNN, Jan. 30, 2021, https://www.cnn.com/2021/01/30/us/sequim-washington-mayor-qanon/index.html; Derek Robertson, "What Liberals Don't Get about Trump Supporters and Pop Culture," *Politico*, May 16, 2020; Thomas B. Edsall, "Trump Is Staking Out His Own Universe of 'Alternative Facts,'" *NYT*, May 13, 2020.

13. American Psychiatric Association, *Diagnostic and Statistical Manual of Mental Disorders: DSM-5* (Arlington, VA: American Psychiatric Association, 2013), 646–649; Eve Caligor, Kenneth N. Levy, and Frank E. Yeomans, "Narcissistic Personality Disorder: Diagnostic and Clinical Challenges," *Journal of American Psychiatry* 172, no. 5, published ahead of print, Apr. 30, 2015, https://ajp.psychiatryonline.org/doi/10.1176/appi.ajp.2014.14060723.

14. Trump's original tweets are now archived by Trump Twitter Archive, https://www.thetrumparchive.com, and Factbase: "Donald Trump—Twitter," Factbase, accessed June 26, 2023, https://factba.se/biden/topic/twitter.

15. Aaron Blake, "Trump's Flippant Talk about the Vietnam War," *WP*, June 5, 2019; Steve Turnham, "Donald Trump to Father of Fallen Soldier: 'I've Made a Lot of Sacrifices,'" ABC News, July 30, 2016, https://abcnews.go.com/Politics/donald-trump-father-fallen-soldier-ive-made-lot/story?id=41015051.

16. Meghan Keneally, "Trump Has Called Himself Smart Six Times Before," ABC News, Jan. 8, 2018, https://abcnews.go.com/Politics/president-trump-called-smart-six-times-before/story?id=52209712; Trump Twitter Archive, https://www.thetrumparchive.com, and "Donald Trump—Twitter," Factbase.

17. "Donald Trump Fox and Friends Interview Transcript—Trump Interviewed after Impeachment Hearings," Transcript Library, https://www.rev.com/blog/transcripts/donald-trump-fox-and-friends-interview-transcript-trump-interviewed-after-impeachment-hearings.

18. Ron Suskind, "Faith, Certainty and the Presidency of George W. Bush," *NYT*, Oct. 17, 2004; Trump Twitter Archive, https://www.thetrumparchive.com, and "Donald Trump—Twitter," Factbase; M. Rosenblum, J. Schroeder, and F. Gino, "Tell It like It Is: When Politically Incorrect Language Promotes Authenticity," *Journal of Personality and Social Psychology* 119, no. 1, published ahead of print, Aug. 15, 2019, https://psycnet

.apa.org/doiLanding?doi=10.1037%2Fpspi0000206; Salena Zito, "Taking Trump Seriously, Not Literally," *The Atlantic,* Sep. 2019; Joanna Weiss, "Trump Pokes Fun at Himself. Why Do Only Some People See It?," *Politico,* Nov. 9, 2019.

19. "Lesley Stahl: Trump Admitted Mission to 'Discredit' Press," CBS News, May 23, 2018, https://www.cbsnews.com/news/lesley-stahl-donald-trump-said-attacking-press-to-discredit-negative-stories/; Glenn Kessler, Salvador Rizzo, and Meg Kelly, "President Trump Made 16,241 False or Misleading Claims in His First Three Years," *WP,* Jan. 20, 2020.

20. Derek Robertson, "How @realDonaldTrump Changed Politics—and America," *Politico,* Jan. 9, 2021.

21. Jacqueline Thomsen, "Trump: My Supporters Should Be Called the 'Super Elite,'" *The Hill,* June 27, 2018.

22. Mike Rothschild, *The Storm Is upon Us: How QAnon Became a Movement, Cult, and Conspiracy Theory of Everything* (New York: Melville House, 2021).

23. C-SPAN, "President Trump: 'I Am the Chosen One,'" YouTube video, 2:52, Aug. 21, 2019, https://www.youtube.com/watch?v=lzlxrPC_E_U; Michael Gerson, "White Evangelical Protestants Are Fully Disrobed. And It Is an Embarrassing Sight," *WP,* Oct. 28, 2019; Jeff Sharlet, "'He's the Chosen One to Run America': Inside the Cult of Trump, His Rallies Are Church and He Is the Gospel," *Vanity Fair,* June 18, 2020; Daniel Burke, "Rick Perry Says Trump (and Obama) Were 'Ordained by God' to Be President," CNN, Nov. 25, 2019, https://www.cnn.com/2019/11/25/politics/rick-perry-donald-trump-god/index.html; Thomas Lecaque, "The Apocalyptic Myth That Helps Explain Evangelical Support for Trump," *WP,* Nov. 26, 2019; Andrew L. Whitehead and Samuel L. Perry, *Taking America Back for God: Christian Nationalism in the United States* (New York: Oxford University Press, 2020); Katherine Stewart, *The Power Worshippers: Inside the Dangerous Rise of Religious Nationalism* (London: Bloomsbury, 2020), esp. chaps. 5–7, 10; Robert P. Jones, *White Too Long: The Legacy of White Supremacy in American Christianity* (New York: Simon and Schuster, 2020), esp. chaps. 2, 4–5. See also Helgard Müller, *President Donald J. Trump: The Son of Man—the Christ* (n.p.: Outskirts, 2022).

24. Michael Kruse, "Trump's Art of the Steal," *Politico,* Jan. 10, 2020.

25. Joshua Green, *Devil's Bargain: Steve Bannon, Donald Trump, and the Storming of the Presidency* (New York: Penguin, 2017), esp. chaps. 2, 6–7, 10; David Rohde, *In Deep: The FBI, the CIA, and the Truth about America's "Deep State"* (New York: W. W. Norton, 2020), pt. 2.

26. Jean Guerrero, *Hatemonger: Stephen Miller, Donald Trump, and the White Nationalist Agenda* (New York: Wm. Morrow, 2020); Meghan Keneally, "A Timeline of Trump and Bannon's Turbulent Relationship," ABC News, Jan. 5, 2018, https://abcnews.go.com/Politics/timeline-trump-bannons-turbulent-relationship/story?id=52137016; Publius Decius Mus [Michael Anton], "The Flight 93 Election," *Claremont Review of Books,* Sep. 5, 2016.

27. Trump Twitter Archive, https://www.thetrumparchive.com, and "Donald Trump—Twitter," Factbase; Meagan Flynn, "Trump Accused of 'Dipping into a Deep

Well of Anti-Semitic Tropes' during Speech to Jewish Voters," *WP,* Dec. 9, 2019; Michael M. Grynbaum, "Site That Ran Anti-Semitic Remarks Got Passes for Trump Trip," *NYT,* Jan. 26, 2020.

28. Greg Miller, "Allegations of Racism Have Marked Trump's Presidency and Become Key Issue as Election Nears," *WP,* Sep. 23, 2020.

29. Morin, "'They Admitted Their Guilt'"; "Trump 1989 Interview."

30. Jeremy W. Peters, *Insurgency: How Republicans Lost Their Party and Got Everything They Ever Wanted* (New York: Crown, 2022), 126–129.

31. Steven Simon and Jonathan Stevenson, "Iran: The Case against War," *NYRB,* Aug. 15, 2019.

32. "Donald Trump's Presidential Announcement Speech," *Time,* June 16, 2015; Simon and Stevenson, "Iran." On the southern border, see Greg Grandin, *The End of the Myth: From the Frontier to the Border War* (New York: Metropolitan, 2020).

33. For an analysis of racism in Brimelow's work, see David C. Hendrickson, review of *Alien Nation: Common Sense about America's Immigration Disaster,* by Peter Brimelow, *Foreign Affairs,* July 7, 1995.

34. Trump Twitter Archive, https://www.thetrumparchive.com, and "Donald Trump—Twitter," Factbase; Nick Gass, "Trump: 'We Can't Continue to Allow China to Rape Our Country,'" CNN, May 2, 2016, https://www.cnn.com/2016/05/01/politics /donald-trump-china-rape/index.html.

35. Eric Bradner, "Rudy Giuliani Hammers Clinton, Pumps Up Crowd at RNC," CNN, July 19, 2016, https://www.cnn.com/2016/07/18/politics/rudy-giuliani-rnc -speech/index.html.

36. David A. Graham, "Matt Bevin's Apocalyptic Warnings of Bloodshed," *The Atlantic,* Sep. 13, 2016.

37. Niraj Chokshi, "Assaults Increased When Cities Hosted Trump Rallies, Study Finds," *NYT,* Mar. 16, 2018; Jonah Engel Bromwich, "N.R.A. Ad Condemning Protests against Trump Raises Partisan Anger," *NYT,* June 29, 2017.

38. Nick Corasaniti and Maggie Haberman, "Donald Trump Suggests 'Second Amendment People' Could Act against Hillary Clinton," *NYT,* Aug. 9, 2016. Once again he was borrowing ideas already current on the radical Right: Brett Lunceford, "On the Rhetoric of Second Amendment Remedies," *Journal of Contemporary Rhetoric* 1, no. 1 (2011): 31–39.

17. Trump in the White House

1. Maggie Haberman, "Trump, Head of Government, Leans into Antigovernment Message," *NYT,* Apr. 20, 2020.

2. H. C., "Tax Reform Has Passed, What Now?," *The Economist,* Dec. 20, 2017; "Assessing Donald Trump's Plans for Tax Reform," *The Economist,* Apr. 27, 2017.

3. Donald Trump, Trump Twitter Archive, www.thetrumparchive.com, Oct. 7, 2019; Mairead McArdle, "Trump Promises to 'Obliterate' Turkey's Economy If It Does Anything Off Limits," *National Review,* Oct. 7, 2019; Tariff Man, "An Assessment of

Donald Trump's Record on Trade," *The Economist,* Oct. 24, 2020; M. S., "Donald Trump Fails to Endorse NATO's Mutual Defence Pledge," *The Economist,* May 26, 2017.

4. Carol D. Leonnig and Philip Rucker, "'You're a Bunch of Dopes and Babies': Inside Trump's Stunning Tirade against Generals," *WP,* Jan. 17, 2020; Jennifer Steinhauer and Zolan Kanno-Youngs, "Job Vacancies and Inexperience Mar Federal Response to Coronavirus," *NYT,* Mar. 26, 2020.

5. Caroline Kelly and Nikki Carvajal, "White House: John Kelly 'Was Totally Unequipped to Handle the Genius of Our Great President,'" CNN, Oct. 28, 2019, https://www.cnn.com/2019/10/26/politics/john-kelly-trump-yes-man/index.html.

6. Meghan Keneally, "President Trump Has Called Himself Smart Six Times Before," ABC News, Jan. 8, 2018, https://abcnews.go.com/Politics/president-trump -called-smart-six-times-before/story?id=52209712.

7. Bill Chappell, "'I'm the Only One That Matters,' Trump Says of State Dept. Job Vacancies," NPR, Nov. 3, 2017, https://www.npr.org/sections/thetwo-way/2017/11 /03/561797675/im-the-only-one-that-matters-trump-says-of-state-dept-job-vacancies; Caitlin Oprysko, "Trump Tells Intel Chiefs to 'Go Back to School' after They Break with Him," *Politico,* Jan. 30, 2019.

8. Quoted in David Nakamura, "In Confrontation with Iran, Trump Wrestles with the Shadow of Obama, 'the Metric He Has to Beat,'" *WP,* Jan. 4, 2020.

9. "Remarks by President Trump in Cabinet Meeting," White House Archives, Oct. 21, 2019, https://trumpwhitehouse.archives.gov/briefings-statements/remarks -president-trump-cabinet-meeting-15/.

10. Christopher Flavelle, "How Trump Tried, but Largely Failed, to Derail America's Top Climate Report," *NYT,* Jan. 1, 2021; Hannah Pitt, Kate Larsen, and Maggie Young, "The Undoing of US Climate Policy: The Emissions Impact of Trump-Era Rollbacks," Rhodium Group, Sept. 17, 2020, https://rhg.com/research/the-rollback-of-us -climate-policy/.

11. Ben Lefebvre, "Oil Execs to Trump: Whose Side Are You On?," *Politico,* Mar. 24, 2020.

12. Missy Ryan, Dan Lamothe, and Kareem Fahim, "Trump's Focus on Protecting Oil in Syria Highlights an Evolving U.S. Mission," *WP,* Oct. 24, 2019.

13. Juliet Eilperin and Brady Dennis, "EPA Staff Warned That Mileage Rollbacks Had Flaws. Trump Officials Ignored Them," *WP,* May 19, 2020.

14. Joe Davidson, "Federal Land Employees Were Threatened or Assaulted 360 Times in Recent Years, GAO Says," *WP,* Oct. 21, 2019; Naomi Oreskes and Erik M. Conway, "From Anti-government to Anti-science: Why Conservatives Have Turned against Science," *Daedalus* 151, no. 4 (Fall 2022): 98–123; Maggie Astor, "Trump Policies Sent U.S. Tumbling in a Climate Ranking," *NYT,* May 31, 2022.

15. Adam Serwer, "The Cruelty Is the Point," *The Atlantic,* Oct. 3, 2018. See also Adam Serwer, *The Cruelty Is the Point: The Past, Present, and Future of Trump's America* (New York: One World, 2021); Peter Wehner, "Trump Is Betting That Anger Can Still Be Power," *NYT,* June 19, 2019.

16. Caitlin Dickerson, "We Need to Take Away the Children," *The Atlantic,* Sept. 2022; Department of Justice, Evaluation and Inspection Division, *Review of the Department of Justice's Planning and Implementation of Its Zero Tolerance Policy and Its Coordination with the Departments of Homeland Security and Health and Human Services* (Washington, DC: Government Printing Office, Jan. 2021), i–ii.

17. Laura Reiley, "Trump Administration Tightens Work Requirements for SNAP, Which Could Cut Hundreds of Thousands from Food Stamps," *WP,* Dec. 4, 2019; Joan Aiker and Lauren Roygardner, "The Number of Uninsured Children Is on the Rise," Georgetown University Center for Children and Families, Oct. 2019, https://ccf.georgetown.edu/2019/10/29/the-number-of-uninsured-children-in-on-the -rise-acs/; Devlin Barrett, "Trump Vows Complete End of Obamacare Law Despite Pandemic," *WP,* May 6, 2020.

18. Catherine Clinton, ed., *Confederate Statues and Memorialization* (Athens: University of Georgia Press, 2019); Kyshia Henderson et al., "Confederate Monuments and the History of Lynching in the American South: An Empirical Examination," *Proceedings of the National Academy of Sciences* 118, no. 42, published ahead of print, Oct. 11, 2021, https://doi.org/10.1073/pnas.2103519118.

19. See list of removals at "Removal of Confederate Monuments and Memorials," Wikipedia, last updated June 9, 2023, https://en.wikipedia.org/wiki/Removal_of _Confederate_monuments_and_memorials.

20. Greg Bluestein, "Georgia Lawmaker: Talk of Ditching Confederate Statues Could Cause Democrat to 'Go Missing,'" *Atlanta Journal-Constitution,* Aug. 29, 2017.

21. Jean Guerrero, *Hatemonger: Stephen Miller, Donald Trump, and the White Nationalist Agenda* (New York: Wm. Morrow, 2020), esp. chap. 13; Michael Edison Hayden, "Stephen Miller's Affinity for White Nationalism Revealed in Leaked Emails," SPLC Hatewatch, Nov. 12, 2019, https://www.splcenter.org/hatewatch/2019/11/12 /stephen-millers-affinity-white-nationalism-revealed-leaked-emails.

22. Hawes Spencer and Sheryl Gay Stolberg, "White Nationalists March on University of Virginia," *NYT,* Aug. 11, 2017; Brennan Gilmore, "What I Saw in Charlottesville Could Be Just the Beginning," *Politico,* Aug. 14, 2017.

23. Z. Byron Wolf, "Trump's Defense of the 'Very Fine People' at Charlottesville White Nationalist March Has David Duke Gushing," CNN, Aug. 15, 2017, https://www .cnn.com/2017/08/15/politics/donald-trump-david-duke-charlottesville/index.html.

24. Donald Trump, Trump Twitter Archive, www.thetrumparchive.com, Aug. 15, 2017.

25. Farah Stockman, "Who Were the Counterprotesters in Charlottesville?," *NYT,* Aug. 14, 2017.

26. Rahul Kalvapalle, "Steve Bannon, Ousted from White House, Says Trump Presidency He Helped Build Is 'Over,'" Global News, Aug. 19, 2017, https://globalnews .ca/news/3681791/steve-bannon-trump-presidency/; Doug Mataconis, "Trump Undercuts Bannon in Internal White House Power Struggle," *Outside the Beltway,* Apr. 13, 2017, https://www.outsidethebeltway.com/trump-undercuts-bannon-in-internal-white -house-power-struggle/; Doug Mataconis, "The Knives Are Out for Steve Bannon,"

Outside the Beltway Apr. 14, 2017, https://www.outsidethebeltway.com/the-knives-are
-out-for-steve-bannon/.

27. Joe Lowndes, "How the Far Right Weaponized America's Democratic Roots,"
New Republic, Aug. 10, 2021; Greg Sargent, "A Shocker in the Proud Boys Indictment
Exposes the Right's Long Game," *WP,* June 7, 2022; Andy B. Campbell, *We Are Proud
Boys: How a Right-Wing Street Gang Ushered in a New Era of American Extremism* (New
York: Hachette, 2022), chaps. 5, 8, 11, 12.

28. Adeel Hassan, "Hate-Crime Violence Hits 16-Year High, F.B.I. Reports,"
NYT, Nov. 12, 2019.

29. Martin Pengelly, "Trump Predicts Demographics Make 2016 'Last Election
Republicans Can Win,'" *The Guardian,* Sept. 9, 2016.

30. David Frum, "An Exit from Trumpocracy," *The Atlantic,* Jan. 18, 2018;
E. J. Dionne Jr., "What Unites Trump's Apologists? Minority Rule," *WP,* Nov. 24, 2019.

31. Mattathias Schwartz, "William Barr's State of Emergency," *NYT,* June 1,
2020; David Rohde, *In Deep: The FBI, the CIA, and the Truth about America's "Deep
State"* (New York: W. W. Norton, 2020), chaps. 9–10, 16–17.

32. William Barr, "Attorney General William P. Barr Delivers the 19th Annual Barbara K. Olson Memorial Lecture at the Federalist Society's 2019 National Lawyers
Convention," Department of Justice, Nov. 15, 2019, https://www.justice.gov/opa/speech
/attorney-general-william-p-barr-delivers-19th-annual-barbara-k-olson-memorial
-lecture; Emily Bazelon, "Who Is Bill Barr?," *NYT,* Oct. 26, 2019; Charlie Savage,
"Trump Suggests He Can Gag Inspector General for Stimulus Bailout Program," *NYT,*
Mar. 27, 2020.

33. William Barr, "Attorney General William P. Barr Delivers Remarks to the Law
School and the de Nicola Center for Ethics and Culture at the University of Notre
Dame," Department of Justice, Oct. 11, 2019, https://www.justice.gov/opa/speech
/attorney-general-william-p-barr-delivers-remarks-law-school-and-de-nicola-center
-ethics; William Barr, "Legal Issues in a New Political Order," *Catholic Lawyer* 36, no. 1
(1995): esp. 1–6.

34. Barr, "Legal Issues," esp. 1–6; George Packer, "How to Destroy a Government,"
The Atlantic, Apr. 4, 2020, 54–74, esp. 67–70; Dennis Prager, "The Court Follows Its
Heart and Completes the Secularization of America," *National Review,* June 30, 2015.

35. Robert P. Jones, *White Too Long: The Legacy of White Supremacy in American
Christianity* (New York: Simon and Schuster, 2021); Katherine Stewart, *The Power Worshippers: Inside the Dangerous Rise of Religious Nationalism* (London: Bloomsbury,
2020); Philip S. Gorski and Samuel L. Perry, *The Flag and the Cross: White Christian
Nationalism and the Threat to American Democracy* (New York: Oxford University Press,
2022); Andrew L. Whitehead and Samuel L. Perry, *Taking America Back for God: Christian Nationalism in the United States* (New York: Oxford University Press, 2020); Ruth
Braunstein, "The 'Right' History: Religion, Race, and Nostalgic Stories of Christian
America," *Religions* 12, no. 2 (Jan. 2021): article 95.

36. Josh Hawley, "Senator Josh Hawley's Speech at the 6th Annual American Principles Project Gala," Nov. 20, 2019, https://www.hawley.senate.gov/senator-josh -hawleys-speech-6th-annual-american-principles-project-gala; Emma Green, "Josh Hawley's Mission to Remake the GOP," *The Atlantic*, Nov. 24, 2019.

37. Heather Cox Richardson, *How the South Won the Civil War: Oligarchy, Democracy, and the Continuing Fight for the Soul of America* (New York: Oxford University Press, 2022), esp. introduction, chaps. 6–8, and conclusion; Thomas Dixon Jr., *The Clansman: An Historical Romance of the Ku Klux Klan* (Lexington: University of Kentucky Press, 1972), 290–292; John R. Commons, *Races and Immigrants in America*, 2nd ed. (New York: Macmillan, 1920), 6–7.

38. Tim O'Donnell, "Trump: 'I Have an Article 2 Where I Have the Right to Do Whatever I Want as President,'" *The Week*, July 23, 2019; Tom Wheeler, "The 2020 Republican Party Platform: 'L'Etat, C'est Moi,'" Brookings Institution, Aug. 25, 2020, https://www.brookings.edu/blog/up-front/2020/08/25/the-2020-republican-party -platform-letat-cest-moi/.

39. Melanie Eversley, "Trump Tells Law Enforcement: 'Don't Be Too Nice' with Suspects," *USA Today*, July 28, 2017; Jenna Johnson, "Trump Says 'Torture Works,' Backs Waterboarding and 'Much Worse,'" *WP*, Feb. 17, 2016; Michael D. Shear and Julie Hirschfeld Davis, "Shoot Migrants' Legs, Build Alligator Moat: Behind Trump's Ideas for Border," *NYT*, Oct. 1, 2019; William Cummings, "'Only in the Panhandle': Trump Chuckles When Audience Member Suggests Shooting Migrants," *USA Today*, May 9, 2019; Bess Levin, "Not a Joke: Trump Is Looking into Making Bribery Legal," *Vanity Fair*, Jan. 17, 2020.

40. Dan Lamothe and Josh Dawsey, "'Insurgents' Lobbied Trump for War Crimes Pardons with Little Pentagon Involvement, Officials Say," *WP*, Nov. 21, 2019; Helene Cooper, Maggie Haberman, and Thomas Gibbons-Neff, "Trump Says He Intervened in War Crimes Cases to Protect 'Warriors,'" *NYT*, Nov. 25, 2019.

41. Donald Trump, Trump Twitter Archive, www.thetrumparchive.com, Sept. 28, 2019; Jason Silverstein, "Trump Shares Video of Supporter Saying 'the Only Good Democrat Is a Dead Democrat,'" CBS News, May 28, 2020, https://www.cbsnews.com /news/president-trump-shares-video-of-supporter-saying-the-only-good-democrat-is -a-dead-democrat/.

42. Barbara Starr and Nicole Gaouette, "Worry Rises in Military over Trump's Decision-Making," CNN, Nov. 28, 2019, https://www.cnn.com/2019/11/27/politics /pentagon-concern-trump-decision-making/index.html.

43. Justin Wise, "Trump Suggests That It Could Get 'Very Bad' If Military, Police, Biker Supporters Play 'Tough,'" *The Hill*, Mar. 14, 2019; Bob Woodward and Robert Costa, *Peril* (New York: Simon and Schuster, 2021), 151.

44. Donald J. Trump, "Campaign Launch Rally," transcript, P2020 Democracy in Action, June 18, 2019, https://www.democracyinaction.us/2020/trump/trump061819sp .html.

18. Imagining Civil War

1. William S. Smith, "The Civil War on America's Horizon," *American Conservative,* Sept. 11, 2018; Michael Vlahos, "We Were Made for Civil War," *American Conservative,* Nov. 6, 2019; Greg Jaffe and Jenna Johnson, "In America, Talk Turns to Something Not Spoken of for 150 Years: Civil War," *WP,* Mar. 2, 2019; Joseph diGenova on *The Laura Ingraham Show Podcast,* Feb. 21, 2019; Astead W. Herndon, "'Nothing Less Than a Civil War': These White Voters on the Far Right See Doom without Trump," *NYT,* Dec. 28, 2019.

2. Gene Falk et al., *Unemployment Rates during the COVID-19 Pandemic* (Washington, DC: Congressional Research Service, Aug. 20, 2021); Yasmeen Abutaleb and Damian Paletta, *Nightmare Scenario: Inside the Trump Administration's Response to the Pandemic That Changed History* (New York: Harper, 2021).

3. This account of Trump's 2020 campaign draws on Jeremy W. Peters, *Insurgency: How Republicans Lost Their Party and Got Everything They Ever Wanted* (New York: Crown, 2022), chap. 15; Jonathan Karl, *Betrayal: The Final Act of the Trump Show* (New York: Dutton, 2021); Bob Woodward and Robert Costa, *Peril* (New York: Simon and Schuster, 2021); and Jonathan Martin and Alexander Burns, *This Will Not Pass: Trump, Biden, and the Battle for America's Future* (New York: Simon and Schuster, 2022). I have referenced contemporary news accounts to show how events developed as a public narrative.

4. Nikole Hannah-Jones, "The 1619 Project," *NYT Magazine,* Aug. 14, 2019; Nikole Hannah-Jones and *New York Times Magazine, The 1619 Project: A New Origin Story* (New York: Random House, 2020); Ibram X. Kendi, *How to Be an Antiracist* (New York: One World, 2019).

5. E. J. Dionne, "Trump and the GOP Are Making a New New Deal Necessary," *WP,* Aug. 2, 2020; Anthony Leiserowitz et al., *Climate Change in the American Mind: April 2020* (New Haven, CT: Yale Program on Climate Change Communication, May 19, 2020).

6. David Bossie, "Americans Uniting to Fight Coronavirus Just as We United to Fight World War II," Fox News, Mar. 21, 2020, https://www.foxnews.com/opinion /david-bossie-americans-uniting-to-fight-coronavirus-just-as-we-united-to-fight -world-war-ii; Joe Concha, "Scarborough: Coronavirus Pandemic More like World War II Than 9/11," *The Hill,* Mar. 17, 2020; Danielle Allen, "America Needs to Be on a War Footing," *WP,* Mar. 20, 2020; Mark R. Wilson, "The 5 WWII Lessons That Could Help the Government Fight Coronavirus," *Politico,* Mar. 19, 2020.

7. User Clip: Trump Speaks about His Uncle," C-SPAN, 0:41, Mar. 6, 2020, https://www.c-span.org/video/?c4859693/user-clip-trump-speaks-uncle.

8. Sarah Evanega et al., "Coronavirus Misinformation: Quantifying Sources and Themes in the COVID-19 'Infodemic,'" Cornell Alliance for Science, July 23, 2020, https://allianceforscience.org/wp-content/uploads/2020/10/Evanega-et-al-Coronavirus -misinformation-submitted_07_23_20.pdf.

9. Robert Costa and Philip Rucker, "Woodward Book: Trump Says He Knew Coronavirus Was Deadly," *WP,* Sep. 9, 2020.

10. "Trump Calls Coronavirus Testing 'Overrated,' Says It 'Makes Us Look Bad,'" Axios, June 18, 2020, https://www.axios.com/2020/06/18/trump-coronavirus-testing -overrated; Elliot Hannon, "Lancet Study Finds 40 Percent of U.S. COVID-19 Deaths Could Have Been Avoided," *Slate,* Feb. 11, 2020.

11. Aaron Blake, "The Trump Administration Just Changed Its Description of the National Stockpile to Jibe with Jared Kushner's Controversial Claim," *WP,* Apr. 3, 2020; Quint Forgey, "'We're Not a Shipping Clerk': Trump Tells Governors to Step Up Efforts to Get Medical Supplies," *Politico,* Mar. 19, 2020; Caitlin Oprysko, "'I Don't Take Responsibility at All': Trump Deflects Blame for Coronavirus Testing Fumble," *Politico,* Mar. 13, 2020.

12. Sarah Mervosh, Manny Fernandez, and Campbell Robertson, "Mask Rules Expand across U.S. as Clashes over the Mandates Intensify," *NYT,* July 16, 2020.

13. Meagan Flynn, "After a Day of Armed Protesters and a GOP Lawsuit Threat, Michigan Gov. Gretchen Whitmer Extends State of Emergency," *WP,* May 1, 2020; Christina Maxouris, "Local Health Officials Were Doing Their Job. In the Pandemic, That Came with Death Threats and Harassment," CNN, Jan. 31, 2021, https://www .cnn.com/2021/01/31/us/us-local-health-officials-pandemic/index.html; Michael Gerson, "The Stage Is Being Set for the Repudiation of Donald Trump in November," *WP,* June 18, 2020.

14. Isaac Stanley-Becker and Tony Romm, "Pro-gun Activists Using Facebook Groups to Push Anti-Quarantine Protests," *WP,* Apr. 19, 2020; Jack Date and Alexander Mallin, "Trump Uses Pandemic to Attack Virginia on Gun Control, but He's Done It Before," ABC News, Apr. 21, 2020, https://abcnews.go.com/Politics/trump-pandemic -attack-virginia-gun-control/story?id=70264025; Steve Schmidt (@SteveSchmidtSES), Twitter thread, Apr. 17, 2020, https://twitter.com/steveschmidtses/status/12512655 72534390788.

15. Quoted in Isabel Togoh, "Barr Labels Stay-at-Home Orders 'the Greatest Intrusion' on Civil Liberties since Slavery," *Forbes,* Sept. 17, 2020.

16. Jerald Brooks and Lakesha Bailey, "We're Feeding America, but We're Sacrificing Ourselves," *NYT,* June 15, 2020.

17. Karen Attiah, "George Floyd Has Become the Emmett Till of This Moment," *WP,* June 9, 2020.

18. Ruth Bender and David Winning, "Antiracism Protests Erupt around the World in Wake of George Floyd Killing," *WSJ,* June 7, 2020.

19. Van Jones, "Welcome to the 'Great Awakening,'" CNN, June 14, 2020, https://www.cnn.com/2020/06/12/opinions/great-awakening-empathy-solidarity -george-floyd-jones/index.html; Shelby Steele, "The Inauthenticity behind Black Lives Matter," *WSJ,* Nov. 22, 2020; Arian Campo-Flores and Joshua Jamerson, "Black Lives Matter's Years of Pressure Paved Way for Sudden Police Overhaul," *WSJ,* June 18, 2020; Arian Campo-Flores, Joshua Jamerson, and Douglas Belkin, "On the Anniversary of

George Floyd's Killing, Debate about Race Reaches across American Life," *WSJ*, May 25, 2020; "The Power of Protest and the Legacy of George Floyd," *The Economist,* June 11, 2020; Peter Bergen, "How the 'Hinge Event' of Covid Will Change Everything," CNN, May 7, 2020, https://www.cnn.com/2020/05/07/opinions/the-future-normal-hinge-event-bergen-rothenberg/index.html.

20. Gillian Flaccus, "Portland's Grim Reality: 100 Days of Protests, Many Violent," AP, Sept. 4, 2020.

21. Erica Chenoweth and Jeremy Pressman, "This Summer's Black Lives Matter Protesters Were Overwhelmingly Peaceful, Our Research Finds," *WP,* Oct. 16, 2020; Juliana Menasce Horowitz, "Support for Black Lives Matter Declined after George Floyd Protests, but Has Remained Unchanged Since," Pew Research Center, Sept. 27, 2021, https://www.pewresearch.org/short-reads/2021/09/27/support-for-black-lives-matter-declined-after-george-floyd-protests-but-has-remained-unchanged-since/.

22. This account is based on Dan Zak et al., "'This Can't Be Happening': An Oral History of 48 Surreal, Violent, Biblical Minutes in Washington," *WP,* June 2, 2020; Ashley Parker, Josh Dawsey, and Rebecca Tan, "Inside the Push to Tear-Gas Protesters ahead of a Trump Photo Op," *WP,* June 1, 2020; and Rachel Levy, "Trump's 2020 St. John's Church Visit Wasn't Reason Park Police Cleared Lafayette Square, Inspector General Finds," *WSJ,* June 10, 2021.

23. "READ: President Trump's Call with US Governors over Protests," CNN, June 1, 2020, https://www.cnn.com/2020/06/01/politics/wh-governors-call-protests/index.html; Michael S. Schmidt and Maggie Haberman, "Trump Aides Prepared Insurrection Act Order during Debate over Protests," *NYT,* June 25, 2021.

24. Jason Leigh Steorts, "An Afterthought on Lafayette Square," *National Review,* June 11, 2020; Aaron C. Davis et al., "Officials Familiar with Lafayette Square Confrontation Challenge Trump Administration Claim of What Drove Aggressive Expulsion of Protesters," *WP,* June 14, 2020.

25. Rachel Weiner et al., "Voices, Lifted," *WP,* June 8, 2020.

26. Byron Tau, "National Guard Officer Says Excessive Force Used to Clear Lafayette Square in D.C.," *WSJ,* July 28, 2020.

27. Donald Trump, "Donald Trump Speech Transcript June 1: Trump May Deploy Military to Cities," Rev, June 1, 2020, https://www.rev.com/blog/transcripts/donald-trump-speech-transcript-june-1-trump-may-deploy-us-military-to-cities.

28. Trump, "It's a Bible," *The Independent* (video), YouTube, https://www.youtube.com/watch?v=LWEuY_15iVc.

29. Mike Mullen, "I Cannot Remain Silent," *The Atlantic,* June 2020; Paul LeBlanc, "Retired Marine Gen. John Allen: Trump's Threats of Military Force May Be 'the Beginning of the End of the American Experiment,'" CNN, June 4, 2020, https://www.cnn.com/2020/06/04/politics/john-allen-trump-protests-george-floyd/index.html.

30. James Mattis, "In Union There Is Strength," *WP,* June 3, 2020.

31. Colby Itkowitz, "George W. Bush Calls Out Racial Injustices and Celebrates Protesters Who 'March for a Better Future,'" *WP,* June 2, 2020.

32. Peter Baker et al., "How Trump's Idea for a Photo Op Led to Havoc in a Park," *NYT,* June 2, 2020; Global Strategy Group, GBAO Navigator, June 4–8, 2020, https://navigatorresearch.org/wp-content/uploads/2020/06/Navigating-Coronavirus -Full-Topline-F06.11.20.pdf.

33. Tim Craig, "'The United States Is in Crisis': Report Tracks Thousands of Summer Protests, Most Nonviolent," *WP,* Sept. 3, 2020; Larry Buchanan, Quoctrung Bui, and Jugal K. Patel, "Black Lives Matter May Be the Largest Movement in U.S. History," *NYT,* July 3, 2020.

34. Patrick Murray, "Protestors' Anger Justified Even If Actions May Not Be," Monmouth University Poll Reports, June 2, 2020, https://www.monmouth.edu/polling -institute/reports/monmouthpoll_us_060220/; Nate Cohn and Kevin Quealy, "How Public Opinion Has Moved on Black Lives Matter," *NYT,* June 10, 2020; Catie Edmondson and Nicholas Fandos, "G.O.P. Scrambles to Respond to Public Demands for Police Overhaul," *NYT,* June 18, 2020; Giovanni Russonello, "Why Most Americans Support the Protests," *NYT,* June 5, 2020.

35. Annie Harmon and Sabrina Tavernise, "One Big Difference about George Floyd Protests: Many White Faces," *NYT,* June 17, 2020.

36. Christopher J. Lebron, *Making of Black Lives Matter: A Brief History of an Idea* (New York: Oxford University Press, 2017); Anne Helen Petersen, "Why the Small Protests in Small Towns across America Matter," BuzzFeed News, June 3, 2020, https://www.buzzfeednews.com/article/annehelenpetersen/black-lives-matter-protests -near-me-small-towns; Kailee Scales, "For Immediate Release, Statement by Kailee Scales, Managing Director of BLM Global Network," Black Lives Matter, June 25, 2020, https://blacklivesmatter.com/for-immediate-release-statement-by-kailee-scales -managing-director-of-blm-global-network/.

37. Joshua Partlow and Isaac Stanley-Becker Elyse Samuels, "As Clashes between Armed Groups and Leftist Protesters Turn Deadly, Police Face Complaints of Tolerating Vigilantes," *WP,* Aug. 30, 2020; Tim Elfrink, "William Barr Says 'Communities' That Protest Cops Could Lose 'the Police Protection They Need,'" *WP,* Dec. 4, 2019.

38. Ames Grawert and Noah Kim, "Myths and Realities: Understanding Recent Trends in Violent Crime," Brennan Center for Justice, July 12, 2022, https://www .brennancenter.org/our-work/research-reports/myths-and-realities-understanding -recent-trends-violent-crime; Colin Woodard, "The Geography of U.S. Gun Violence," Nationhood Lab at Salve Regina University, Apr. 21, 2023, https://www.nationhoodlab .org/the-geography-of-u-s-gun-violence/; "The Effects of Stand-Your-Ground Laws," RAND Corporation, Jan. 10, 2023, https://www.rand.org/research/gun-policy/analysis /stand-your-ground.html; Michelle Degli Esposti et al., "Analysis of 'Stand Your Ground' Self-Defense Laws and Statewide Rates of Homicides and Firearm Homicides," *JAMA Network Open* 5, no. 2 (Feb. 21, 2022): e220077.

39. Laura Barrón-López, "Trump Attacks Take a Toll on Black Lives Matter Support," *Politico,* Sept. 2, 2020; Rich Lowry, "Conservatives Should Feel No Investment in Confederate Monuments," *Politico,* June 17, 2020.

40. Crystal R. Sanders, "Racist Violence in Wilmington's Past Echoes in Police Officer Recordings Today," *WP,* June 26, 2020.

41. Joanna Adams, "White Southerners, Our Souls Are at Stake. We Must Speak Up Now," CNN, June 23, 2020, https://www.cnn.com/2020/06/23/opinions/white -southerners-must-speak-about-racism-adams/index.html; Rick Rojas, "A Small Mississippi Town, 'Asking for a Breath' after Mayor's Remarks Unleash Protests," *NYT,* June 9, 2020; Adam Serwer, "The New Reconstruction," *The Atlantic,* Oct. 2020; George Packer, "America's Plastic Hour Is upon Us," *The Atlantic,* Oct. 2020; Neil Vigdor and Daniel Victor, "Over 160 Confederate Symbols Were Removed in 2020, Group Says," *NYT,* Feb. 23, 2021.

42. John F. Harris, "On Monument Avenue, Liberal Illusions about Race Come Tumbling Down," *Politico,* June 11, 2020; Gregory S. Schneider and Laura Vozzella, "Northam to Announce Plans to Remove Richmond's Iconic Statue of Robert E. Lee," *WP,* June 3, 2020; Mark Berman and Ben Guarino, "Mississippi Governor Signs Bill Changing State's Flag, Abandoning Confederate Symbol," *WP,* June 30, 2020; Sarah Pulliam Bailey, "Southern Baptist President Wants to Retire Famed Gavel Named for Slave Holder," *WP,* June 10, 2020.

43. Woodward and Costa, *Peril,* 107–108; Lara Seligman, "Army Reverses Course, Will Consider Renaming Bases Named for Confederate Leaders," *Politico,* June 8, 2020.

44. Marc Fisher, "Confederate Statues: In 2020, a Renewed Battle in America's Enduring Civil War," *WP,* June 11, 2020.

45. Martin and Burns, *This Will Not Pass,* 109.

46. Joe Biden, "Gettysburg Campaign Speech," Oct. 6, 2020.

47. Biden, "Gettysburg Campaign Speech"; Joe Biden, "Pittsburgh Speech," Oct. 31, 2020.

48. Joe Biden, "Speech in Warm Springs, GA," Oct. 27, 2020. See also "Read Joe Biden's President-Elect Acceptance Speech: Full Transcript," *NYT,* Nov. 9, 2020.

49. Katie Glueck and Lisa Friedman, "Biden Announces $2 Trillion Climate Plan," *NYT,* July 14, 2020; K. Sabeel Rahman, "Imagining a New New Deal," *Democracy,* June 30, 2020; Packer, "America's Plastic Hour."

50. Thomas Friedman, *Hot, Flat, and Crowded: Why We Need a Green Revolution—and How It Can Renew America* (New York: Picador, 2009).

51. Naomi Klein, *This Changes Everything: Capitalism vs. the Climate* (New York: Simon and Schuster, 2014); Kate Aronoff et al., *A Planet to Win: Why We Need a Green New Deal* (London: Verso, 2019).

52. Bill McKibben, "A World at War," *New Republic,* Aug. 15, 2016. But Roy Scranton, in "Climate Change Is Not World War," *NYT,* Sep. 18, 2019, rejects the analogy.

53. Brady Dennis and Dino Grandoni, "How Joe Biden's Surprisingly Ambitious Climate Plan Came Together," *WP,* Aug. 1, 2020; Brady Dennis, "Most Americans Believe the Government Should Do More to Combat Climate Change, Poll Finds," *WP,* June 23, 2020.

54. Jamelle Bouie, "If Biden Wants to Be like F.D.R., He Needs the Left," *NYT,* Nov. 20, 2020; Megan Cassella, "Unions Predict a Great Awakening during a Biden Presidency," *Politico,* Oct. 9, 2020; Jeffrey Sachs, "Keynes and the Good Life," *American Prospect,* May 18, 2020; Nicholas Kristof, "Crumbs for the Hungry But Windfalls for the Rich," *NYT,* May 23, 2020.

19. "The Last President of the Confederacy"

1. Video of Woodward's interview with Trump is in Scott Pelley, "Donald Trump's Conversations with Bob Woodward about Coronavirus, Black Lives Matter and Nuclear War," *60 Minutes,* Sept. 13, 2020, https://www.cbsnews.com/news/donald -trump-bob-woodward-rage-60-minutes-2020-09-13/; and "Trump Dismisses Question on White Privilege: 'You Really Drank the Kool-Aid,'" *60 Minutes Overtime,* Sept. 10, 2020, video, https://www.cbsnews.com/video/trump-dismisses-question-on-white -privilege-you-really-drank-the-kool-aid/.

2. Anne Gearan, Colby Itkowitz, and Missy Ryan, "Trump Rejects Calls to Rename Military Bases Honoring Confederate Generals," *WP,* June 10, 2020.

3. Donald J. Trump, "Executive Order 13933: Protecting American Monuments, Memorials, and Statues and Combating Recent Criminal Violence," June 26, 2020; Nicolle Wallace, *Deadline: White House,* MSNBC, aired Feb. 22, 2019; Donald Trump on *The Ingraham Angle,* Fox News, aired Aug. 31, 2020.

4. Tom Cotton, "Send in the Troops," *NYT,* June 3, 2020; Tom Cotton (@TomCottonAR), Twitter post, June 1, 2020, https://twitter.com/TomCottonAR/status /1267459561675468800.

5. Jordan Muller, "Trump Calls Protesters 'Terrorists,' Pledges 'Retribution' for Tearing Down Statues," *Politico,* June 26, 2020.

6. Jonathan Martin and Alexander Burns, *This Will Not Pass: Trump, Biden, and the Battle for America's Future* (New York: Simon and Schuster, 2022), 49.

7. Quint Forgey, "Trump Threatens Tulsa Protesters as Mayor Lifts Curfew," *Politico,* June 19, 2020.

8. Jose A. Del Real, "With 'Kung Flu,' 'Thugs,' and 'Our Heritage,' Trump Leans on Racial Grievance as He Reaches for a Campaign Reset," *WP,* June 21, 2020.

9. Michael D. Shear, Maggie Haberman, and Astead W. Herndon, "Trump Rally Fizzles as Attendance Falls Short of Campaign's Expectations," *NYT,* June 20, 2020.

10. Maya King and Laura Barrón-López, "Trump Blames Low-Income People, Minorities for 'Ruining' Suburbia," *Politico,* Oct. 1, 2020; Trump Twitter Archive, https://www.thetrumparchive.com, July 23, 2020; Jennifer Agiesta, "CNN Poll: Trump Losing Ground to Biden amid Chaotic Week," CNN, June 8, 2020, https://www.cnn .com/2020/06/08/politics/cnn-poll-trump-biden-chaotic-week/index.html; "Washington Post / ABC News Wisconsin and Michigan Polls," *WP,* Oct. 28, 2020.

11. Donald Trump, "Donald Trump Michigan Rally Speech Transcript October 17," Rev, Oct. 17, 2020, https://www.rev.com/blog/transcripts/donald-trump-michigan-rally-speech-transcript-october-17.

12. Donald Trump, "Donald Trump Mount Rushmore Speech Transcript at 4th of July Event," Rev, July 3, 2020, https://www.rev.com/blog/transcripts/donald-trump-speech-transcript-at-mount-rushmore-4th-of-july-event.

13. Richard Delgado and Jean Stefancic, *Critical Race Theory: An Introduction,* 3rd ed. (New York: New York University Press, 2017); Sam Dorman, "Chris Rufo Calls on Trump to End Critical Race Theory 'Cult Indoctrination' in Federal Government," Fox News, Sept. 2, 2020, https://www.foxnews.com/politics/chris-rufo-race-theory-cult-federal-government; Christopher Rufo on *Tucker Carlson Tonight,* Fox News, aired Sept. 1, 2020; Christopher Rufo, "The Truth about Critical Race Theory," *WSJ,* Oct. 4, 2020; Christopher Rufo, "Critical Race Theory and Its Enemies," National Conservativism Conference II, Nov. 1, 2021; Sumantra Maitra, "Chipping Away at Critical Theory's Dominance of Higher Ed," James G. Martin Center for Academic Renewal, Dec. 10, 2021, https://www.jamesgmartin.center/2021/12/chipping-away-at-critical-theorys-dominance-of-higher-ed/.

14. Trump, "Mount Rushmore Speech"; George Packer, "How to Destroy a Government," *The Atlantic,* Apr. 4, 2020, 67–70.

15. Trump, "Mount Rushmore."

16. Trump.

17. Trump.

18. Trump; Juan Perez Jr. and Nicole Gaudiano, "Trump Blasts 1619 Project as DeVos Praises Alternative Black History Curriculum," *Politico,* Sept. 17, 2020.

19. Robin Young and Serena McMahon, "A Tale of Two Districts: How Schools Are Implementing Anti-racism Curriculums," WBUR, July 22, 2020, https://www.wbur.org/hereandnow/2020/07/22/schools-anti-racism-curriculum, is an account of the controversy in Albemarle, Virginia.

20. Beth Blum, "The Radical History of Sensitivity Training," *New Yorker,* Sept. 24, 2020; George Packer, "When the Culture War Comes for the Kids," *The Atlantic,* Oct. 2019; George Packer, "The Grown-Ups Are Losing It," *The Atlantic,* Apr. 2022; Paul Rossi, "I Refuse to Stand by While My Students Are Indoctrinated," Free Press, Apr. 13, 2021, https://www.thefp.com/p/i-refuse-to-stand-by-while-my-students; Bari Weiss, "You Have to Read This Letter," Free Press, Apr. 16, 2021, https://www.thefp.com/p/you-have-to-read-this-letter; Nathan Heller, "What Happens When an Elite Public School Becomes Open to All," *New Yorker,* Mar. 14, 2022.

21. Steven Ross Johnson, "As America Aims for Equity, Many Believe Systemic Racism Doesn't Exist," *U.S. News,* Nov. 16, 2022; Juliana Menasce Horowitz, "Support for Black Lives Matter Declined after George Floyd Protests, but Has Remained Unchanged Since," Pew Research Center, Sept. 27, 2021, https://www.pewresearch.org/short-reads/2021/09/27/support-for-black-lives-matter-declined-after-george-floyd-protests-but-has-remained-unchanged-since/.

22. Joseph Moreau, *Schoolbook Nation: Conflicts over American History Textbooks from the Civil War to the Present* (Ann Arbor: University of Michigan Press, 2004), chaps. 1, 5, 7; Diane Ravitch, "The Controversy over National History Standards," *Bulletin of the American Academy of Arts and Sciences* 51, no. 3 (Jan.–Feb. 1998): 14–28; Gary Nash, "Reflections on the National History Standards," *National Forum,* Summer 1997.

23. Barton Gellman, "The Election That Could Break America," *The Atlantic,* Nov. 2020; Marc Fisher, "The End of Democracy? To Many Americans, the Future Looks Dark If the Other Side Wins," *WP,* Oct. 25, 2020; Melissa Quinn and Kathryn Watson, "Full Text: Pence Says 'the Choice in This Election Is Whether America Remains America' in RNC Speech," CBS News, Aug. 27, 2020, https://www.cbsnews.com /news/mike-pence-rnc-speech-america/.

24. Kathleen Belew, "Why 'Stand Back and Stand By' Should Set Off Alarm Bells," *NYT,* Oct. 2, 2020; Andy B. Campbell, *We Are Proud Boys: How a Right-Wing Street Gang Ushered in a New Era of American Extremism* (New York: Hachette, 2022), chaps. 5–8.

25. "US Election 2020: Trump Says Opponent Biden Will 'Hurt God,'" BBC, Aug. 7, 2020, https://www.bbc.com/news/election-us-2020-53688009; Robert Barnes, "Supreme Court Blocks Trump's Bid to End DACA, a Win for Undocumented 'Dreamers,'" *WP,* June 18, 2020.

26. Larry Diamond et al., "Americans Increasingly Believe Violence Is Justified If the Other Side Wins," *Politico,* Oct. 1, 2020; Dionne Searcey and Richard A. Oppel Jr., "A Divided Nation Agrees on One Thing: Many People Want a Gun," *NYT,* Oct. 27, 2020.

27. Hampton Stall, Roudabeh Kishi, and Clionadh Raleigh, *Standing By: Right-Wing Militia Groups and the US Election* (Armed Conflict Location and Event Data Project, Oct. 2020); Amelia Thomson-DeVeaux and Maggie Koerth, "How Trump and COVID-19 Have Reshaped the Modern Militia Movement," FiveThirtyEight, Sept. 4, 2020, https://fivethirtyeight.com/features/how-trump-and-covid-19-have-reshaped -the-modern-militia-movement/.

28. Sharon LaFraniere, "Trump Health Aide Pushes Bizarre Conspiracies and Warns of Armed Revolt," *NYT,* Sept. 14, 2020; Rachael Bade and John Wagner, "GOP Candidate Poses with Rifle, Says She's Targeting 'Socialist' Congresswomen," *WP,* Sept. 4, 2020.

29. Stall, Kishi, and Raleigh, *Standing By;* Tina Nguyen, "Election Day Becomes Doomsday Scenario for Militia Groups," *Politico,* Nov. 1, 2020; Nathan P. Kalmoe and Lilliana Mason, "Most Americans Reject Partisan Violence, but There Is Still Cause for Concern," Democracy Fund: Voter Study Group, May 7, 2020, https://www .voterstudygroup.org/blog/has-american-partisanship-gone-too-far; Thomas B. Edsall, "Whose America Is It?," *NYT,* Sept. 16, 2020, quotes violence threats from the left and right.

30. Glenn Kessler, "Fact-Checking Trump's Cellphone Rant of Election False-hoods," *WP,* Nov. 26, 2020; "President Trump Says Election Was Rigged and Must Be

Overturned," clip of Pennsylvania Republican hearing on 2020 election, 10:47, C-SPAN, Nov. 25, 2020, https://www.c-span.org/video/?c4925781/president-trump-election-rigged-overturned.

31. Donald Trump, "Speech on Election Fraud Claims Transcript December 2," Rev, Dec. 2, 2020, https://www.rev.com/blog/transcripts/donald-trump-speech-on-election-fraud-claims-transcript-december-2.

32. Martin Pengelly, "Trump Lawyer: Ex-Election Security Chief Krebs Should Be 'Taken Out and Shot,'" *The Guardian,* Dec. 1, 2020; Pippa Norris, "Can Our Democracy Survive If Most Republicans Think the Government Is Illegitimate?," *WP,* Dec. 11, 2020; *The Economist* / YouGov Poll, November 21–24, 2020, https://today.yougov.com/topics/politics/explore/topic/The_Economist_YouGov_polls, 61–63.

33. Eugene Robinson, "Trump Might Go Down in History as the Last President of the Confederacy," *WP,* June 11, 2020.

34. Casey Michel, "What All the Secession Talk Really Means," *Politico,* Dec. 21, 2020; RPT Staff, "Chairman Allen West's Response to SCOTUS Decision," Republican Party of Texas, Dec. 11, 2020, https://texasgop.org/chairman-allen-wests-response-to-scotus-decision/.

35. Sonam Sheth, "Trump's Former National Security Advisor Says the President Should Impose Martial Law to Force New Elections in Battleground States," Business Insider, Dec 18, 2020, https://www.businessinsider.com/michael-flynn-trump-military-martial-law-overturn-election-2020-12; Howard Altman et al., "Calls for Martial Law and US Military Oversight of New Presidential Election Draws Criticism," *Military Times,* Dec. 2, 2020.

36. Reis Thebault, "Joint Chiefs Chairman Feared Potential 'Reichstag Moment' Aimed at Keeping Trump in Power," *WP,* July 14, 2021; Bob Woodward and Robert Costa, *Peril* (New York: Simon and Schuster, 2021), 150–153.

37. This account is based on public testimony before the US House Select Committee to Investigate the January 6 Attack public hearings, esp. on June 21 and 28. Jacqueline Alemany et al., "Ahead of Jan. 6, Willard Hotel in Downtown D.C. Was a Trump Team 'Command Center' for Effort to Deny Biden the Presidency," *WP,* Oct. 23, 2021.

38. US House Select Committee to Investigate the January 6 Attack hearings, July 12, 2022.

39. Andrew Restuccia and Ted Mann, "Jan. 6, 2021: How It Unfolded," *WSJ,* Feb. 12, 2021; Philip Rucker et al., "20 Days of Fantasy and Failure: Inside Trump's Quest to Overturn the Election," *WP,* Nov. 28, 2020; "Transcript: President Trump's Phone Call with Georgia Election Officials," *NYT,* Jan. 3, 2020.

40. Donald Trump, Trump Twitter Archive, https://www.thetrumparchive.com, Dec. 19, 2020.

41. Donie O'Sullivan and Daniel Dale, "Fact Check: Trump Jr. Touts Baseless Rigged-Election Claims to Recruit 'Army' for His Dad," CNN, Sept. 23, 2020, https://www.cnn.com/2020/09/23/politics/donald-trump-jr-baseless-rigged-election

-fact-check/index.html; Danny Hakim and Jo Becker, "The Long Crusade of Clarence and Ginni Thomas," *NYT Magazine,* Feb. 22, 2022; Danny Hakim, Luke Broadwater, and Jo Becker, "Ginni Thomas Pressed Trump's Chief of Staff to Overturn 2020 Vote, Texts Show," *NYT,* Mar. 24, 2022; Sarah Posner, "How the Christian Right Helped Foment Insurrection," *Rolling Stone,* Jan. 31, 2021.

42. Tom Jackman, "Oath Keeper Details Pre-Jan. 6 Planning, Pleads to Seditious Conspiracy," *WP,* May 4, 2020.

43. Tim Pool quoted in Rosalind S. Helderman, "Trump's Choices Escalated Tensions and Set U.S. on Path to Jan. 6, Panel Finds," *WP,* July 20, 2022; US House Select Committee to Investigate the January 6 Attack hearings, July 12, 2022.

44. Rob Kuznia et al., "Extremists Intensify Calls for Violence ahead of Inauguration Day," CNN, Jan. 8, 2021, https://www.cnn.com/2021/01/08/us/online-extremism -inauguration-capitol-invs/index.html; Craig Timberg, "Gallows or Guillotines? The Chilling Debate on TheDonald.win before the Capitol Siege," *WP,* Apr. 15, 2021.

45. Rebecca Ballhaus, Joe Palazzolo, and Andrew Restuccia, "Trump and His Allies Set the Stage for Riot Well before January 6," *WSJ,* Jan. 8, 2021; Jennifer Valentino-DeVries, Denise Lu, and Alex Leeds Matthews, "A Small Group of Militants' Outsize Role in the Capitol Attack," *NYT,* Feb. 21, 2021.

46. Jonathan Allen, "'They're Not Here to Hurt Me': Former Aide Says Trump Knew Jan. 6 Crowd Was Armed," *NBCNews,* June 28, 2022.

47. Editorial board, "The President Who Stood Still on Jan. 6," *WSJ,* July 22, 2022; Andrew Restuccia and Ted Mann, "Jan. 6, 2021: How It Unfolded," *WSJ,* Feb. 12, 2021; Isaac Arnsdorf, Josh Dawsey, and Carol D. Leonnig, "'Take Me up to the Capitol Now': How Close Trump Came to Joining Rioters," *WP,* July 1, 2022.

48. Donald Trump, "Transcript of Trump's Speech at Rally before US Capitol Riot," AP, Jan. 13, 2021.

49. Rosalind S. Helderman, Rachel Weiner, and Spencer S. Hsu, "On Cusp of Impeachment Trial, Court Documents Point to How Trump's Rhetoric Fueled Rioters Who Attacked Capitol," *WP,* Feb. 7, 2021.

50. Select Committee to Investigate the January 6th Attack on the United States Capitol, *Final Report* (Washington, DC: Government Printing Office, Dec. 2022), chaps. 6–8; *"This Is Our House!": A Preliminary Assessment of the Capitol Hill Siege Participants* (Washington, DC: George Washington University Program on Extremism, 2021).

51. Mallory Simon and Sara Sidner, "Decoding the Extremist Symbols and Groups at the Capitol Hill Insurrection," CNN, Jan. 11, 2021, https://www.cnn.com /2021/01/09/us/capitol-hill-insurrection-extremist-flags-soh/index.html; Danielle Taana Smith, "Images of the Capitol Riot Reflect a National Crisis," History News Network, George Washington University, Jan. 10, 2021, https://historynewsnetwork.org/article /178704.

52. Emma Green, "A Christian Insurrection," *The Atlantic,* Jan. 8, 2021; Evan Berry, moderator, "Insurrection, White Supremacy, and Religion: How Religiosity

Influenced the Attempt to Overturn the Election," American Academy of Religion, webinar, 1:31:44, Jan. 29, 2021, https://aarweb.org/AARMBR/AARMBR/Resources-/Webinars-and-Podcasts-/AAR/Insurrection-White-Supremacy-Religion.aspx.

53. Jamie Gangel et al., "New Details about Trump-McCarthy Shouting Match Show Trump Refused to Call Off the Rioters," CNN, Feb. 12, 2021, https://www.cnn.com/2021/02/12/politics/trump-mccarthy-shouting-match-details/index.html; Peter Baker, "Trump Is Depicted as a Would-Be Autocrat Seeking to Hang onto Power at All Costs," *NYT,* June 9, 2022.

54. Eliza Relman, Oma Seddiq, and Jake Lahut, "Trump Tells His Violent Supporters Who Stormed the Capitol 'You're Very Special,' but Asks Them 'to Go Home,'" Business Insider, Jan. 6, 2021, https://www.businessinsider.com/trump-video-statement-capitol-rioters-we-love-you-very-special-2021-1.

55. Karen L. Cox, "What Trump Shares with the 'Lost Cause' of the Confederacy," *NYT,* Jan. 8, 2021; Bret Stephens, "Trump Contrives His Stab-in-the-Back Myth," *NYT,* Nov. 24, 2020; Jeffrey Herf, "Trump's Refusal to Acknowledge Defeat Mirrors the Lie That Fueled the Nazi Rise," *WP,* Nov. 23, 2020. Note that the last two were written before January 6.

Conclusion

1. University of Virginia Center for Politics, "New Initiative Explores Deep, Persistent Divides between Biden and Trump Voters," *UVA Today,* Sept. 30, 2021; John Sides, Chris Tausanovich, and Lynn Vavrek, "A Hard 2020 Lesson for the Midterms: Our Politics Are Calcified," *WP,* Sept. 16, 2022; Thomas E. Ricks, "What Are the Chances of a Second American Civil War (a Best Defense Update)," *Foreign Policy,* June 28, 2017.

2. Richard Galant, "The Voters Sent a Message to Trump and Biden," CNN, Nov. 13, 2022, https://www.cnn.com/2022/11/13/opinions/five-lessons-midterms-opinion-columns-galant/index.html.

3. Ronald Brownstein, "Why Fewer States Than Ever Could Pick the Next President," CNN, Nov. 22, 2022, https://www.cnn.com/2022/11/22/politics/2022-preview-2024-presidential-election/index.html.

4. Moynihan quoted in Joe Klein, "Daniel Patrick Moynihan Was Often Right. Joe Klein on Why It Still Matters," *NYT,* May 15, 2021; James D. Hunter, *Before the Shooting Begins: Searching for Democracy in America's Culture Wars* (New York: Free Press, 1994), chap. 8.

5. Michael Bang Petersen, Mathias Osmundsen, and Alexander Bor, "Beyond Populism: The Psychology of Status-Seeking and Extreme Political Discontent," in *The Psychology of Populism: The Tribal Challenge to Liberal Democracy,* ed. Joseph P. Forgas, Bill Crano, and Klaus Fiedler (London: Routledge, 2021), chap. 4; Pippa Norris and Ron Inglehart, *Cultural Backlash: Trump, Brexit and Authoritarian Populism* (Cambridge: Cambridge University Press, 2019), esp. chaps. 1, 2, 4, 5.

6. Jamie K. McCallum, *Essential: How the Pandemic Transformed the Long Fight for Worker Justice* (New York: Basic Books, 2022); Stephen Greenhouse, *Beaten Down, Worked Up: The Past, Present, and Future of American Labor* (New York: Alfred A. Knopf, 2019). On the neoliberal economy, see Gary Gerstle, *The Rise and Fall of the Neoliberal Order: America and the World in the Free Market Era* (New York: Oxford University Press, 2022), chap. 7; and Thomas Piketty, *Capital in the Twenty-First Century,* trans. Arthur Goldhammer (Cambridge, MA: Belknap Press of Harvard University Press, 2017), chaps. 3, 6, 7–9. On the degradation of work and workers' communities, see Anne Case and Angus Deaton, *Deaths of Despair and the Future of Capitalism* (Princeton, NJ: Princeton University Press, 2021); and Jennifer M. Silva, *We're Still Here: Pain and Politics in the Heart of America* (New York: Oxford University Press, 2019), chaps. 1, 4, 6. See also Martin Gilens and Benjamin I. Page, "Testing Theories of American Politics: Elites, Interest Groups, and Average Citizens," *Perspectives on Politics* 12, no. 3, published ahead of print, Sept. 18, 2014, https://doi.org/10.1017/S1537592714001595; Jesse Eisinger, Jeff Ernsthausen, and Paul Kiel, "The Secret IRS Files: Trove of Never-Before-Seen Records Reveal How the Wealthiest Avoid Income Tax," *ProPublica,* June 8, 2021; and Matthew Gardner and Steve Wamhoff, "55 Corporations Paid $0 in Federal Taxes on 2020 Profits," Institute on Taxation and Economic Policy, Apr. 2, 2021, https://itep.org/55-profitable-corporations-zero-corporate-tax/.

7. Richard Rorty, *Achieving Our Country: Leftist Thought in Twentieth-Century America* (Cambridge, MA: Harvard University Press, 1997), 89–91; Thomas Piketty, *A Brief History of Equality,* trans. Steven Rendall (Cambridge, MA: Belknap Press of Harvard University Press, 2022), pp. 10–15, chap. 6, and pp. 230–238.

8. Griff Witte, Abigail Hauslohner, and Emily Wax-Thibodeaux, "In the Shadow of Its Exceptionalism, America Fails to Invest in the Basics," *NYT,* Mar. 13, 2021; Anita Sreedhar and Anand Gopal, "Behind Low Vaccination Rates Lurks a More Profound Social Weakness," *NYT,* Dec. 3, 2021.

9. Yascha Mounk, *The Great Experiment: Why Diverse Democracies Fall Apart and How They Can Endure* (New York: Penguin, 2022), chap. 2; Taylor Orth, "Which Groups of Americans Are Most Likely to Believe Conspiracy Theories?," YouGov, Mar. 30, 2022, https://today.yougov.com/topics/politics/articles-reports/2022/03/30/which-groups-americans-believe-conspiracies.

10. "Highest to Lowest—Prison Population Total," World Prison Brief, accessed June 28, 2023, https://www.prisonstudies.org/highest-to-lowest/prison-population-total.

11. Intergovernmental Panel on Climate Change, *Climate Change 2022: Impacts, Adaptation and Vulnerability: Summary for Policymakers,* ed. Hans-Otto Pörtner et al. (Intergovernmental Panel on Climate Change, Feb. 27, 2022).

12. Rana Foroohar, "Globalism Failed to Deliver the Economy We Need," *NYT,* Oct. 17, 2022. See Thomas Piketty, *Capital and Ideology* (Cambridge, MA: Belknap Press of Harvard University Press, 2020); and Piketty, *Brief History of Equality,* pp. 10–15, chap. 6, and pp. 230–238.

13. Gramsci quoted in Robert Kuttner, "Free Markets, Besieged Citizens," *NYRB,* July 21, 2022.

14. PRRI Staff, "Challenges in Moving toward a More Inclusive Democracy: Findings from the 2022 American Values Survey," PRRI, Oct. 27, 2022, https://www .prri.org/research/challenges-in-moving-toward-a-more-inclusive-democracy-findings -from-the-2022-american-values-survey/#page-section-0; PRRI Staff, "A Christian Nation? Understanding the Threat of Christian Nationalism to American Democracy and Culture," PRRI, Feb. 8, 2023, https://www.prri.org/research/a-christian-nation -understanding-the-threat-of-christian-nationalism-to-american-democracy-and -culture/; Steven Levitsky and Daniel Ziblatt, *How Democracies Die* (New York: Crown, 2018), 219–230; Thomas Edsall, "The Fragile Republic: American Democracy Has Never Faced So Many Threats All at Once," *Foreign Affairs,* Sept. 2020; Brian Klaas, "America's Self-Obsession Is Killing Its Democracy," *The Atlantic,* July 21, 2022.

15. Sidney M. Milkis and Daniel J. Tichenor, *Rivalry and Reform: Presidents, Social Movements, and the Transformation of American Politics* (Chicago: University of Chicago Press, 2018), chaps. 1, 7.

16. *The Economist* / YouGov Poll, July 30–Aug. 2, 2022, 247–248, https://docs.cdn .yougov.com/d1ik3gw9iw/econTabReport.pdf.

17. Carroll Doherty et al., "Beyond Red vs. Blue: The Political Typology," Pew Research Center, Nov. 9, 2021, https://www.pewresearch.org/politics/2021/11/09 /beyond-red-vs-blue-the-political-typology-2/; Alex Samuels and Neil Lewis Jr., "How White Victimhood Fuels Republican Politics," FiveThirtyEight, Mar. 21, 2022, https:// fivethirtyeight.com/features/how-white-victimhood-fuels-republican-politics/; Ryan Burge, "Why 'Evangelical' Is Becoming Another Word for 'Republican,'" *NYT,* Oct. 26, 2021; Michael H. Keller and David D. Kirkpatrick, "Their America Is Vanishing. Like Trump, They Insist They Were Cheated," *NYT,* Oct. 24, 2022; PRRI Staff, "Challenges in Moving."

18. Thomas E. Mann and Norman J. Ornstein, *It's Even Worse Than It Looks: How the American Constitutional System Collided with the New Politics of Extremism* (New York: Basic Books, 2012), xxiv; Levitsky and Ziblatt, *How Democracies Die,* 219–230; Matthew Continetti, *The Right: The Hundred-Year War for American Conservatism* (New York: Basic Books, 2022), chaps. 12–14; Daniel Schlozman and Sam Rosenfeld, "The Long New Right and the World It Made," paper prepared for the American Political Science Association meetings, Boston, Aug. 31, 2018.

19. Benjamin Newman et al., "The Trump Effect: An Experimental Investigation of the Emboldening Effect of Racially Inflammatory Elite Communication," *British Journal of Political Science* 51, no. 3 (July 2021): 1138–1159; Robert Kagan, "Our Constitutional Crisis Is Already Here," *WP,* Sept. 23, 2021.

20. Christopher Rufo, "Critical Race Theory and Its Enemies," National Conservatism Conference II, Nov. 1, 2021; Sumantra Maitra, "Chipping Away at Critical Theory's Dominance of Higher Ed," James G. Martin Center for Academic Renewal, Dec. 10, 2021, https://www.jamesgmartin.center/2021/12/chipping-away-at-critical

-theorys-dominance-of-higher-ed/; Jeff Stein and Yeganeh Torbati, "Heritage Foundation, Former Powerhouse of GOP Policy, Adjusts in Face of New Competition from Trump Allies," *WP,* Feb. 7, 2022; Katherine Miller, "Kari Lake, Glenn Youngkin, and a Post-Trump Era," *NYT,* Oct. 27, 2022.

21. Steven Simon and Jonathan Stevenson, "These Disunited States," *NYRB,* Sept. 22, 2022; Thomas Edsall, "The Forces Tearing Us Apart Aren't Quite What They Seem," *NYT,* Feb. 22, 2023; Kyle Peyton and Gregory A. Huber, "Racial Resentment, Prejudice and Discrimination," *Journal of Politics* 83, no. 4 (Oct. 2021): 1829–1836.

22. Nicholas A. Valentino and Kirill Zhirkov, "Blue Is Black and Red Is White? Affective Polarization and the Racialized Schemas of U.S. Party Coalitions," paper presented at the Midwest Political Science Association conference, Apr. 2018; Brian F. Schaffner, Matthew MacWilliams, and Tatishe Nteta, "Understanding White Polarization in the 2016 Vote for President: The Sobering Role of Racism and Sexism," *Political Science Quarterly* 133, no. 1 (2018): 9–34; John R. Commons, *Races and Immigrants in America,* 2nd ed. (New York: Macmillan, 1920), 5–6.

23. AP-NORC Center for Public Affairs Research, *Immigration Attitudes and Conspiratorial Thinkers: A Study Issued on the 10th Anniversary of the Associated Press-NORC Center for Public Affairs Research* (AP-NORC Center for Public Affairs Research, May 2022); *The Economist / YouGov Poll,* April 22–26, 2022, https://today.yougov.com /(popup:search/Economist%E2%80%89%2F%E2%80%89YouGov%20Poll,%20 April%202022), 269–270, 273–275.

24. Philip Bump, "Nearly Half of Republicans Agree with 'Great Replacement Theory,'" *WP,* May 9, 2022; Dave Davies, "Has Tucker Carlson Created the Most Racist Show in the History of Cable News?," NPR, May 12, 2022, https://www.npr .org/2022/05/12/1098488908/has-tucker-carlson-created-the-most-racist-show-in -the-history-of-cable-news; Hakeem Jefferson, "Storming the U.S. Capitol Was about Maintaining White Power in America," FiveThirtyEight, Jan. 8, 2021, https://five thirtyeight.com/features/storming-the-u-s-capitol-was-about-maintaining-white -power-in-america/.

25. Bart Bonikowski and Paul DiMaggio, "Varieties of American Popular Nationalism," *American Sociological Review* 81, no. 5 (2016): 949–980; Eric D. Knowles, Linda R. Tropp, and Mao Mogami, "When White Americans See 'Non-Whites' as a Group: Belief in Minority Collusion and Support for White Identity Politics," *Group Processes and Intergroup Relations* 25, no. 3, published ahead of print, Aug. 6, 2021, https://doi.org/10.1177/13684302211030009.

26. *The Economist / YouGov Poll,* Apr. 22–26, 2022, 389; Kevin Arceneaux and Rory Truex, "Donald Trump and the Lie," PsyArXiv Preprints, Mar. 8, 2021, https:// psyarxiv.com/e89ym; Robert Pape et al., *Deep, Destructive, and Disturbing: What We Know about the [sic] Today's Insurrectionist Movement* (Chicago: Chicago Project on Security and Threats at the University of Chicago, Aug. 6, 2021).

27. Hannah Gris and Michael Edison Hayden, "White Nationalists, Other Republicans Brace for 'Total War,'" Southern Poverty Law Center, Dec. 11, 2022, https://www

.splcenter.org/hatewatch/2022/12/11/white-nationalists-other-republicans-brace
-total-war.

28. "US Election 2020: Trump Says Opponent Biden Will 'Hurt God,'" BBC, Aug. 7, 2020, https://www.bbc.com/news/election-us-2020-53688009. See also the discussion of the Heritage Foundation, the Claremont Institute, and national conservatism later in this chapter.

29. John Aldrich et al., "Statement of Concern: The Threats to American Democracy and the Need for National Voting and Election Administration Standards," New America, June 1, 2021, https://www.newamerica.org/political-reform/statements/statement-of -concern/; Nick Corasaniti and Reid J. Epstein, "G.O.P. and Allies Draft 'Best Practices' for Restricting Voting," *NYT,* Mar. 23, 2021.

30. Glenn Ellmers, "'Conservatism' Is No Longer Enough," *American Mind,* Mar. 24, 2021 (emphasis in original). A more systematic attack on conservatives' traditional constitutionalism (and "originalism") is Adrian Vermeule, "Beyond Originalism," *The Atlantic,* Mar. 21, 2020.

31. William Voegeli, "The Right Now," *Claremont Review of Books,* Spring 2022; Bernard Dobski, *America Is a Republic, Not a Democracy,* First Principles No. 80 (Heritage Foundation, June 2020).

32. Andrew L. Whitehead and Samuel L. Perry, *Taking America Back for God: Christian Nationalism in the United States* (New York: Oxford University Press, 2020); Robert P. Jones, *White Too Long: The Legacy of White Supremacy in American Christianity* (New York: Simon and Schuster, 2020); Philip S. Gorski and Samuel L. Perry, *The Flag and the Cross: White Christian Nationalism and the Threat to American Democracy* (New York: Oxford University Press, 2022); Ruth Braunstein, "The 'Right' History: Religion, Race, and Nostalgic Stories of Christian America," *Religions* 12, no. 2 (Jan. 2021): article 95; Katherine Stewart, "What's Missing from Popular Discussions of Today's Christian Nationalism?," *Religion Dispatches,* Aug. 9, 2021, https:// religiondispatches.org/important-developments-weve-been-missing-about-todays -christian-nationalism/.

33. Sara Diamond, *Roads to Dominion: Right-Wing Movements and Political Power in the United States* (New York: Guilford, 1995); Thomas LeCaque, "The Twisted, Trumpist Religion of Jan. 6th," The Bulwark, Jan. 6, 2022, https://www.thebulwark .com/the-twisted-trumpist-religion-of-jan-6th/; Hank Willenbrink, "Vessel, Messiah, Warrior: Donald Trump in Evangelical Christian Narratives," *Ecumenica* 14, no. 2 (Nov. 1, 2021): 221–247; Rebecca Barrett Fox, "A King Cyrus President: How Donald Trump's Presidency Reasserts Conservative Christians' Right to Hegemony," *Humanity and Society* 42, no. 4, published ahead of print, Oct. 4, 2018, https://doi.org/10.1177 /0160597618802644; Bill Johnson et al., *Invading Babylon: The Seven Mountain Mandate* (Shippensburg, PA: Destiny Image, 2013).

34. PRRI Staff, "Christian Nation?"; "In Their Own Words: How Americans Describe 'Christian Nationalism,'" Pew Research Center, Oct. 27, 2022, https://www

.pewresearch.org/religion/2022/10/27/in-their-own-words-how-americans-describe
-christian-nationalism/. "The Religious Typology," Pew Research Center, Aug. 29, 2018,
https://www.pewresearch.org/religion/2018/08/29/the-religious-typology/, classified
12 percent of Americans as "God-and-Country Believers," presumably the core constituency of Christian nationalism.

35. Richard Reinsch, "Jobs, Family, Loyalty: Identifying the Governing Vision of
National Conservatives," Heritage Foundation, Apr. 6, 2022, https://www.heritage
.org/conservatism/commentary/jobs-family-loyalty-identifying-the-governing-vision
-national-conservatives; Will Chamberlain et al., "National Conservatism: A Statement
of Principles," Edmund Burke Foundation, accessed June 28, 2023, https://national
conservatism.org/national-conservatism-a-statement-of-principles/; Iain Murray and
Kent Lassman, "Lassman & Murray: Is New Conservatism Really Progressivism?,"
Competitive Enterprise Institute, Dec. 2, 2019, https://cei.org/opeds_articles/lassman
-murray-is-new-conservatism-really-progressivism/.

36. Daniel Luban, "The Man behind National Conservatism," *New Republic,*
July 26, 2019; Yoram Hazoni, *The Virtue of Nationalism* (New York: Basic Books, 2018);
Kevin D. Roberts, "The Future of Conservatism: Community, the Common Good,
and State Power," Heritage Foundation, May 24, 2022, https://www.heritage.org
/conservatism/commentary/the-future-conservatism-community-the-common-good
-and-state-power; Publius Decius Mus [Michael Anton], "The Flight 93 Election," *Claremont Review of Books,* Sept. 5, 2016; Roger Kimball, "The Right Targets: Introducing
'Common-Good Conservatism: A Debate,'" *New Criterion,* May 2023, 1.

37. Chamberlain et al., "National Conservatism."

38. Chamberlain et al.

39. Chamberlain et al.

40. Human Rights Campaign Staff, "In Final Weeks of Election, Extremist Candidates, Anti-LGBTQ+ Orgs Funnel Tens of Millions of Dollars in Ads Attacking Trans
Youth, Targeting Black and Spanish-Speaking Voters," Human Rights Campaign,
Oct. 28, 2022, https://www.hrc.org/press-releases/breaking-in-final-weeks-of-election
-extremist-candidates-anti-lgbtq-orgs-funnel-tens-of-millions-of-dollars-in-ads
-attacking-trans-youth-targeting-black-and-spanish-speaking-voters.

41. Erwin Chemerinsky, *Worse Than Nothing: The Dangerous Fallacy of Origi-
nalism* (New Haven, CT: Yale University Press, 2022), preface, chaps. 1, 7, 9; *Dobbs v.
Jackson Women's Health Association,* No. 19-1392 (2022), at 3 (Thomas, J., concurring);
Laurence Tribe, "Deconstructing *Dobbs,*" *NYRB,* Sept. 22, 2022.

42. "Blake Masters Claims Victory for GOP Nomination for US Senate," 6 News
WOWT, Aug. 3, 2022, https://www.wowt.com/video/2022/08/03/blake-masters
-claims-victory-gop-nomination-us-senate/ (video of the entire speech).

43. James Pogue, "Inside the New Right, Where Peter Thiel Is Placing His Biggest
Bets," *Vanity Fair,* Apr. 20, 2022; Craig Unger, "Why Is CPAC Having a Conference Next Month in Budapest?," *New Republic,* Apr. 21, 2022; Emma Green, "Josh

Hawley's Mission to Remake the GOP," *The Atlantic*, Nov. 24, 2019; Josh Hawley, "Senator Josh Hawley's Speech at the 6th Annual American Principles Project Gala," Nov. 20, 2019.

44. Robert O. Paxton, *The Anatomy of Fascism* (New York: Vintage, 2007), chaps. 1, 8; David A. Graham, "The New Lost Cause," *The Atlantic*, Oct. 18, 2021; Robert Kagan, "This Is How Fascism Comes to America," *WP*, May 18, 2016; Heather Cox Richardson, *How the South Won the Civil War: Oligarchy, Democracy, and the Continuing Fight for the Soul of America* (New York: Oxford University Press, 2022), esp. introduction, chaps. 6–8, and conclusion; Kevin Matthews, "Will the Republicans Take the Fascist Option?," History News Network, George Washington University, Jan. 10, 2020, https://historynewsnetwork.org/article/178702; PRRI Staff, "Christian Nation?"

45. Spanberger quoted in Jonathan Martin and Alexander Burns, "Reeling from Surprise Losses, Democrats Sound the Alarm for 2022," *NYT*, Nov. 3, 2021.

46. Robert Kuttner, *Going Big: FDR's Legacy, Biden's New Deal, and the Struggle to Save Democracy* (New York: New Press, 2022); Jonathan Martin and Alexander Burns, *This Will Not Pass: Trump, Biden, and the Battle for America's Future* (New York: Simon and Schuster, 2022), epilogue; Gerstle, *Rise and Fall*, 281–285.

47. Nick Hanauer and Eric Beinhocker, "Is 'Middle-Out' Biden's New Deal?," *Democracy*, Mar. 8, 2022; Ezra Klein, "Four Ways of Looking at the Radicalism of Joe Biden," *NYT*, Apr. 8, 2021.

48. John F. Harris, "Biden Just Gave the Most Ideologically Ambitious Speech of Any Democratic President in Generations," *Politico*, Apr. 29, 2021; Christopher Cadelago, "Biden Wants to Cement a Governing Majority. His Build Back Better Bill Is His Plan to Do It," *Politico*, Apr. 7, 2021; Ruby Cramer, "The Unusual Group Trying to Turn Biden into FDR," *Politico*, Aug. 1, 2021.

49. Michael Eric Dyson, *I May Not Get There with You: The True Martin Luther King, Jr.* (New York: Simon and Schuster, 2000), chap. 4.

50. Steven Ross Johnson, "As America Aims for Equity, Many Believe Systemic Racism Doesn't Exist," *U.S. News*, Nov. 16, 2022; Juliana Menasce Horowitz, "Support for Black Lives Matter Declined after George Floyd Protests, but Has Remained Unchanged Since," Pew Research Center, Sept. 27, 2021, https://www.pewresearch.org/short-reads/2021/09/27/support-for-black-lives-matter-declined-after-george-floyd-protests-but-has-remained-unchanged-since/; Clay Risen, "A Premature Victory Lap for Black Lives Matter," *NYT*, Sept. 9, 2022.

51. Peniel E. Joseph, *The Third Reconstruction: America's Struggle for Racial Justice in the Twenty-First Century* (New York: Basic Books, 2022).

52. Michael J. Mazarr, *The Societal Foundations of National Competitiveness* (Santa Monica, CA: RAND Corporation, 2022), https://www.rand.org/pubs/research_reports/RRA499-1.html.

53. For survey results and activist recommendations, see "Race-Class Narrative Handout" in "Race-Class Narrative Messaging Sources," Demos Action, accessed June 28, 2023, https://demosaction.org/raceclass-narrative. For examples of how

these ideas can be operationalized, see Thomas Edsall, "Should Biden Emphasize Race or Class or Both or None of the Above?," *NYT,* Apr. 28, 2021; and Alec Mac-Gillis, "Tim Ryan Is Winning the War for the Soul of the Democratic Party," *NYT,* Oct. 21, 2022.

54. Zachary D. Carter, "The Revolution Joe Manchin (Probably) Can't Stop," *Politico,* Nov. 4, 2021.

55. Corey Robin, "Why the Biden Presidency Feels like Such a Disappointment," *NYT,* Dec. 9, 2021. See also Michael Tomasky, *The Middle Out: The Rise of Progressive Economics and the Return to a Shared Prosperity* (New York: Doubleday, 2022), pt. 2; Ian Ward, "The Unexpected Ways Joe Biden Is Ushering in a New Economic Paradigm," *Politico,* Sept. 9, 2022.

56. Jake Sullivan, "Remarks by National Security Advisor Jake Sullivan on Renewing American Economic Leadership at the Brookings Institution," White House Briefing Room, Apr. 27, 2023, https://www.whitehouse.gov/briefing-room/speeches -remarks/2023/04/27/; Peter Coy, "The Many Minds Behind Biden's Biggest Economic Idea," *NYT,* June 23, 2023.

57. Rana Foroohar, "Globalism Failed to Deliver the Economy We Need," *NYT,* Oct. 17, 2022; "Economic Issues Outweigh Concerns about Rights in Midterm Vote," Monmouth University Polling Institute, Oct. 3, 2022, https://www.monmouth.edu /polling-institute/reports/monmouthpoll_us_100322/; Anand Giridharadas, "The Uncomfortable Truths That Could Yet Defeat Fascism," *NYT,* Oct. 17, 2022.

58. Rorty, *Achieving Our Country,* 11.

59. John Marini, "Donald Trump and the American Crisis," *Claremont Review of Books* (July 22, 2016) argues that "post-modern intellectuals have pronounced their historical judgment on America's past, finding it to be morally indefensible." I think he errs in conflating the complexities of what I've been calling "revisionist" historiography with a set of postmodern theories that affect parts of the academic study of the humanities. See also Fintan O'Toole, "Night and Day," *NYRB,* Sept. 24, 2020.

60. Issac J. Bailey, "We Don't Need to Cancel George Washington. But We Should Be Honest about Who He Was," *Politico,* June 28, 2020; Rorty, *Achieving Our Country,* 3–4, 101; Adrienne Rich, "One night on Monterey Bay the death-freeze of the century," in *An Atlas of the Difficult World: Poems* (New York: W. W. Norton, 1991), 23; Jamelle Bouie, "Don't Fool Yourself. Trump Is Not an Aberration," *NYT,* Oct. 30, 2020.

61. *Oxford English Dictionary,* s.v. "reformation," last revised March 2023, https://www-oed-com.ezproxy.spl.org/view/Entry/160997.

62. Christopher Hare, "Constrained Citizens: Ideological Structure and Conflict in the US Electorate, 1980–2016," *British Journal of Political Science* 52, no. 4, published ahead of print, Dec. 16, 2021, https://doi.org/10.1017/S000712342100051X; Anthony Fowler et al., "Moderates," *American Political Science Review* 117, no. 2 (May 2023): 643–660.

63. Lynn Vavreck quoted in Ezra Klein, "Transcript: Ezra Klein Interviews Lynn Vavreck and John Sides," *NYT,* Oct. 28, 2022.

64. Jacob Grumbach, *Laboratories against Democracy: How National Parties Transformed State Politics* (Princeton, NJ: Princeton University Press, 2022); Robert Kagan, "Our Constitutional Crisis Is Already Here," *WP,* Sept. 23, 2021; Rick Hasen, "My New Draft Paper: 'Identifying and Minimizing the Risk of Election Subversion and Stolen Elections in the Contemporary United States,'" *Election Law Blog,* Sept. 20, 2021, https://electionlawblog.org/?p=124686; Dana Milbank, "Texas Shows Us What Post-democracy America Would Look Like," *WP,* Sept. 1, 2021; Matt Patrick et al., *Report of the Permanent 2022 Platform Committee Recommendations* (June 6, 2022), https://texasgop.org/wp-content/uploads/2022/06/6-Permanent-Platform-Committee -FINAL-REPORT-6-16-2022.pdf.

65. Kimberly Kindy, "GOP Lawmakers Push Historic Wave of Bills Targeting Rights of LGBTQ Teens, Children and Their Families," *WP,* Mar. 25, 2022; Declan Leary, "Florida's Anti-grooming Bill," American Conservative, Mar. 12, 2022, https://www .theamericanconservative.com/floridas-anti-grooming-bill/; Lindsey Dawson, Jennifer Kates, and MaryBeth Musumeci, "Youth Access to Gender Affirming Care: The Federal and State Policy Landscape," Kaiser Family Foundation, June 1, 2022, https://www.kff .org/other/issue-brief/youth-access-to-gender-affirming-care-the-federal-and-state -policy-landscape/.

66. Veronica Stracqualursi, "Newsom Signs California Gun Bill Modeled after Texas Abortion Law," CNN, July 22, 2022, https://www.cnn.com/2022/07/22/politics /california-newsom-gun-bill-texas-abortion-law/index.html; Brad Plumer, "California Approves a Wave of Aggressive New Climate Measures," *NYT,* Sept. 1, 2022; Ronald Brownstein, "DeSantis' Migrant Flights Point toward an Ominous Future of Red and Blue Conflict," *Politico,* Sept. 20, 2022; Emily Bazelon, "Risking Everything to Offer Abortion across State Lines," *NYT,* Oct. 4, 2022.

67. R. R. Reno, "A Simple First Step for Youngkin to Stop Leftist Tyranny," *WSJ,* Nov. 7, 2021; Brittany Shammas, "School Boards Are 'under an Immediate Threat,' Organization Says in Request for Federal Help," *WP,* Sept. 30, 2021; Andrew Atterbury, "National Conservative Groups Pour Money into Local School Board Races," *Politico,* Sept. 19, 2022; Stephen Sawchuck, "What Is Critical Race Theory and Why Is It under Attack?," *Education Week,* May 18, 2021; "Critical Race Theory Is Being Weaponised. What's the Fuss About?," *The Economist,* July 14, 2022; Bonnie Kerrigan Snyder, "Critical Race Theory Is Appropriate in Universities, but Not Schools, Says Bonnie Kerrigan Snyder," *The Economist,* July 14, 2022.

68. John Rogers and Joseph Kahne, *Educating for a Diverse Democracy: The Chilling Role of Political Conflict in Blue, Purple, and Red Communities,* with the Educating for a Diverse Democracy Research Team (Los Angeles: UCLA Institute for Democracy, Education and Access, Nov. 2022), executive summary; Jeffrey Sachs, "Steep Rise in Gag Orders, Many Sloppily Drafted," PEN America, Jan. 24, 2022, https://pen .org/steep-rise-gag-orders-many-sloppily-drafted/; Rashawn Ray and Alexandra Gibbons, "Why Are States Banning Critical Race Theory?," Brookings Institution, Nov. 2021, https://www.brookings.edu/articles/why-are-states-banning-critical-race

-theory/; Florida State Senate, CS for SB 266: An Act relating to Higher Education (2023).

69. See the essays in Michael Dreiling and Pedro García-Caro, eds., "Memory Laws or Gag Laws? Disinformation Meets Academic Freedom," special issue, *Journal of Academic Freedom* 13 (2022), esp. Michael Dreiling and Pedro García-Caro, "Editors' Introduction"; John R. Wood, "Authoritarian Big Chill: Critical Race Theory versus Nostalgia in a Deep Red State"; and Harvey Graff, "The Nondebate about Critical Race Theory and Our American Moment."

70. Shawn Hubler and Jill Cowan, "Flurry of New Laws Move Blue and Red States Further Apart," *NYT*, Apr. 3, 2022; Rich Lowry, "A Surprising Share of Americans Wants to Break Up the Country. Here's Why They're Wrong," *Politico*, Oct. 6, 2021.

71. Charles Reagan Wilson, *Baptized in Blood: The Religion of the Lost Cause* (Chapel Hill: University of North Carolina Press, 2009), chaps. 1, 2, 5; Kitschelt quoted in Thomas Edsall, "When It Comes to Eating Away at Democracy, Trump Is a Winner," *NYT*, Aug. 24, 2022.

72. Jonathan Weisman and Reid J. Epstein, "G.O.P. Declares Jan. 6 Attack 'Legitimate Political Discourse,'" *NYT*, Feb. 4, 2022; Daniel A. Cox, "After the Ballots Are Counted: Conspiracies, Political Violence, and American Exceptionalism," American Enterprise Institute, Feb. 11, 2021, https://www.aei.org/research-products/report/after -the-ballots-are-counted-conspiracies-political-violence-and-american-exceptionalism/; David Weigel, "On the Campaign Trail, Many Republicans Talk of Violence," *WP*, July 23, 2022; Colby Itkowitz, "Guns Are All Over GOP Ads and Social Media, Prompting Some Criticism," *WP*, May 31, 2022.

73. Mikie McIntire, "At Protests, Guns Are Doing the Talking," *NYT*, Nov. 26, 2022.

74. Rachel Kleinfeld, "How Political Violence Went Mainstream on the Right," *Politico*, Nov. 7, 2022; Mark Berman et al., "The Staggering Scope of U.S. Gun Deaths Goes Far beyond Mass Shootings," *WP*, July 8, 2022; Jordan Boyd, "Tragedies like the Texas Shooting Make a Somber Case for Homeschooling," *The Federalist*, May 25, 2022, https://thefederalist.com/2022/05/25/tragedies-like-the-texas-shooting-make-a -somber-case-for-homeschooling/.

75. Nathan P. Kalmoe and Lilliana Mason, "Most Americans Reject Partisan Violence, but There Is Still Cause for Concern," Democracy Fund: Voter Study Group, May 7, 2020, https://www.voterstudygroup.org/blog/has-american-partisanship-gone -too-far; Taylor Orth, "Two in Five Americans Say a Civil War Is at Least Somewhat Likely in the Next Decade," YouGov, Aug. 26, 2022, https://today.yougov.com/topics /politics/articles-reports/2022/08/26/two-in-five-americans-civil-war-somewhat -likely; Monica Duffy Toft, "How Civil Wars Start," *Foreign Policy*, Feb. 18, 2021.

76. Joseph, *Third Reconstruction;* Anand Giridharas, *The Persuaders: At the Front Lines of the Fight for Hearts, Minds, and Democracy* (New York: Knopf, 2022), esp. chap. 7; Ian Frazer, "Guns Down," *New Yorker*, Apr. 5, 2021; William Barber II and Jonathan

Wilson-Hartgrove, "A Cry of 'I Can't Breathe' United a Generation in a Gasp for Justice," *NYT,* May 21, 2021; Steven Greenhouse, "Young Workers Are Organizing. Can Their Fervor Save Unions?," *WP,* Sept. 4, 2022; Keith Schneider, "Revitalizing Montgomery as It Embraces Its Past," *NYT,* May 21, 2019; Teo Armus, "With Scoop by Scoop of Soil, Alexandria Remembers Lynched Black Teens," *WP,* Sept. 27, 2022.

Acknowledgments

I would not and could not have written this book without the encouragement and support of Iris Slotkin. I am grateful to my agent, Henry Thayer, for the advice that kept the project alive through some difficult times, and his hard work on my behalf; and to Joy de Menil for her rigorous editing and support of this book. Thanks also to Joel Slotkin and Caroline Egan for their readings and advice. I also want to acknowledge the careful editorial work of Ashley Moore.

Index

Abbott, Greg, 379

Abe Lincoln in Illinois (film), 141

abolitionism, 43–51, 57, 66–71, 74, 83, 388

abortion: Affordable Care Act and, 251, 255, 262; in blue America, 409; Christian nationalism on, 324; *Dobbs* decision, 395; libertarianism on, 223; *Roe* decision, 197, 395; vigilantism and, 407

ACA. *See* Affordable Care Act of 2010

Adams, Brooks, 130–131

Adams, Charles Francis, Jr., 100

Adams, Joanna, 346

Adams, John, 42

affirmative action: in college admissions, 382; in employment, 186; neo-Confederate ideology on, 223; opposition to, 198, 206, 212, 257, 287, 291; political correctness and, 293; re-placement theory on, 303

Affordable Care Act of 2010 (ACA): conspiracy theories and, 302; during COVID-19 pandemic, 316, 349; national support for, 348–349; opposition to, 255, 262, 264, 281–282, 293, 294, 316; requirements of, 251, 262

Afghanistan: nation-building efforts in, 231, 232, 242; terrorist organizations in, 230, 231; withdrawal of US troops from, 242, 310

African Americans: citizenship for, 68, 71; civil equality for, 13, 63, 96; Civil War as viewed by, 62–63; COVID-19 pandemic and, 335; education for, 76, 96, 177; Juneteenth and, 347–348, 356; lynching of, 103, 105–109,

149, 181, 183, 269, 304, 336; New Deal and, 138, 149; political culture of, 208; as share-croppers, 102, 103; stereotypes of, 139, 143, 151; unemployment among, 354; voting rights for, 73, 96, 97, 102–107; World War I service of, 105, 138, 148–149; World War II service of, 150. *See also* Black Lives Matter movement; civil rights movement; free Blacks; police violence; racism; segregation; slaves and slavery

agriculture: bonanza economics in, 119; farm workers' movement, 189; Indigenous peoples and, 31; industrialization of, 167; pesticide use in, 314; sharecroppers, 102, 103, 119, 271; tenant farmers, 103, 119, 125, 271. *See also* plantation system

Ailes, Roger, 207

ALEC. *See* American Legislative Exchange Council

Alexander, Lamar, 352

Aliens (film), 235–236, 238–241

Allen, John, 341

All Quiet on the Western Front (film), 144, 155

All the Young Men (film), 146, 157–158, 240

al-Qaeda, 230–231, 237

America First movement, 150, 207, 293, 302, 309–310, 369

American Dream, 7, 23, 163, 358

American Enterprise Institute, 225, 264, 389

American exceptionalism, 41, 117, 127–128, 164, 194, 360, 396

American Indians. *See* Indigenous peoples; *specific nations*